Arabic Administration in Norman Sicily
The Royal Dīwān

Jeremy Johns' book represents the first comprehensive account, in any language, of the Arabic administration of Norman Sicily. It argues that the Arabic bureau, established by Roger II and his successors, was closely modelled upon that of the Fāṭimid caliphs of Egypt, and was designed less as an efficient organ of administration, than as a medium for the projection of the royal image.

In the traditional literature, it has been assumed that the Norman rulers simply inherited the Arabic administration of the Kalbid emirs of the island. In fact, on the completion of the Norman conquest in 1092, Greek administrators were employed to adapt Arabic records and these formed the basis of the post-conquest distribution of the land and its population. With the passing of the first generation of administrators, however, new Arabic records ceased to be issued and Arabic disappeared as a language of central administration for the following twenty years. It was only after the coronation of Roger II in 1130, that a new and highly professional Arabic bureau – the royal *dīwān* – began to issue a series of Arabic and bilingual (Arabic-Greek and Arabic-Latin) documents. A close analysis of these, and of the *dīwān* that produced them, reveals that the main inspiration for the renaissance of the royal *dīwān* came from the contemporary Islamic Mediterranean and, in particular, from Fāṭimid Egypt. An examination of the competence and reach of the Norman *dīwān* suggests that its primary function was not administrative efficiency, but the projection of the Arabic facet of the Norman monarchy.

Jeremy Johns is University Lecturer in Islamic Archaeology in The Oriental Institute, University of Oxford, and Fellow of Wolfson College, Oxford.

Greek, Arab and Latin scribes in the royal *dīwān*. Petrus de Ebulo, *Liber ad honorem Augusti, c.*1194 A.D. Burgerbibliothek Bern. Codex 120 II, f.101 r (detail).

CAMBRIDGE STUDIES IN ISLAMIC CIVILIZATION

Published titles in the series are listed at the back of the book

DEDICATION

To Sarah, Emma, and Jacob

'… se io non avessi fatto altro se non che indovinare, non si poteva indovinare più giusto; e … l'inventore di una produzione così singolare sarebbe, mi si permetta il dirlo, di un ben tutt'altro merito che il traduttore modesto d'una raccolta di lettere arabe riunite nella Cancelleria, nel tempo che li Arabi dominarono in Sicilia.'

Giuseppe Vella, *c.*1811
(from Varvaro 1905, p.328)

Arabic Administration in Norman Sicily

The Royal Dīwān

JEREMY JOHNS
University of Oxford

CAMBRIDGE
UNIVERSITY PRESS

CAMBRIDGE UNIVERSITY PRESS
Cambridge, New York, Melbourne, Madrid, Cape Town, Singapore, São Paulo

Cambridge University Press
The Edinburgh Building, Cambridge CB2 8RU, UK

Published in the United States of America by Cambridge University Press, New York

www.cambridge.org
Information on this title: www.cambridge.org/9780521816922

First published 2002
This digitally printed version 2007

A catalogue record for this publication is available from the British Library

National Library of Australia Cataloguing in Publication data
Johns, Jeremy.
Arabic administration in Norman Sicily: the Royal Diwan.
Bibliography.
Includes index.
ISBN 0 521 81692 0.
1. Normans – Italy – Sicily – History. 2. Sicily (Italy) –
History – 1016–1194. 3. Sicily (Italy) – Politics and
government – To 1282. 4. Islamic Empire – 750–1258. I.
Title. (Series: Cambridge studies in Islamic civilization).
945.803

ISBN 978-0-521-81692-2 hardback
ISBN 978-0-521-03702-0 paperback

Contents

Preface *page* viii
Tables xii
Abbreviations xiv
Genealogical table of the De Hautevilles of Sicily xvi
Note on Measurements xviii

Introduction 1
1 'In the time of the Saracens …' 11
2 'When first the Normans crossed into Sicily …' 31
3 'Our lady, the Regent Adelaide, and our Lord, the Count Roger, her son', 1101–30 63
4 The earliest products of the royal *dīwān*, 1130–43 91
5 The *jarāʾid* renewed, 1144–5 115
6 The records of the royal *dīwān*. Part I: the *jarāʾid al-rijāl* 144
7 The records of the royal *dīwān*. Part II: the *dafātir al-ḥudūd* 170
8 The duties and organisation of the royal *dīwān*, 1141–94 193
9 'The people of his state'. The 'palace Saracens' and the royal *dīwān* 212
10 The Norman *dīwān* and Fāṭimid Egypt 257
11 Royal *dīwān* and royal image 284
Appendix 1. Catalogue of *dīwānī* documents 301
Appendix 2. Provisional catalogue of private documents 315
Appendix 3. Abū Tillīs – 'Old Wheat-sack' 326

List of References 329
Index 358

Preface

This book has taken a long time to reach its present form. It began as part of my doctoral thesis, 'The Muslims of Norman Sicily, *c.*1060–*c.*1194', in the Faculty of Modern History at Oxford in 1983. Six years later, while I was Lecturer in Early Islamic Archaeology in the University of Newcastle upon Tyne, I completed the first draft of what was then called '*Duana Regis*: Arabic administration and Norman kingship in Sicily'. A second, heavily revised draft, known as both *Duana Regis II* and *Duana Regia* – and referred to as 'forthcoming', 'imminent' and even 'in press', by myself and over-trusting friends and colleagues – was produced in 1989, circulated in typescript, and then shelved. In 1990, *Duana Regia* returned with me from Newcastle to Oxford. On three or four occasions thereafter, during long vacations or terms of sabbatical leave, individual chapters were revised, but the whole remained incomplete. In the end, only by persuading the University and Wolfson to grant me a full sabbatical year 'in anticipation of the allowance', and by 'mortgaging' myself to the University until well into what was then the next millennium, was I able to revise and to rewrite the whole book so swiftly that by the time I reached the end I was still content with the beginning. To all those who, for nearly twenty years, have kindly continued to express an interest in this tardy book, I offer sincere apologies, but no excuse except that it is better now than it would then have been.

Henry Mayr-Harting, then of St Peter's College, Oxford, was my first supervisor, and he gave me two terms of excellent advice and boundless enthusiasm, while energetically seeking his successor. I believe that it was Peter Holt who gave him the name of Michael Brett, then Lecturer in African History at the School of Oriental and African Studies, at the University of London. Michael was a model supervisor: intellectually uncompromising; meticulous about the detail of argument and apparatus, with a clear vision of shape and structure; enthusiastic, loyal, supportive, and endlessly patient with my struggle to repaint myself as a *trompe l'œil* Islamicist. I wish that I were half as good a supervisor as he. From 1976–9, I was a Postgraduate Scholar at Balliol College, and was supported by a Full Postgraduate Award from the Department of Education and Science. When that came to an end, I was lucky enough to be awarded a Study Abroad Scholarship by The Leverhulme Trust, which enabled me to spend more than two years in Palermo, under the benevolent wing of the late Monsignor Paolo Collura, Professor of Latin Paleography at the University of Palermo. I do not have words to express adequately my gratitude to The Leverhulme Trust for permitting me the luxury of the extended spell in the archives, libraries, and landscape of Sicily that was to be crucial not just to the formation of this book but also to my career and, indeed, much of my life. I am particularly grateful to Miss Joan Bennett, then Administrative Secretary to The Trust, for her wholly exceptional kindness and support. In 1982, I returned to Oxford as Junior Research Fellow in Medieval History at Wolfson College, Oxford. Wolfson gave me the opportunity to write up eight years of research in easy reach of one of the best libraries in the world, and within a true community of scholars.

I am keenly aware of how fortunate and privileged I was to be given eight years of funding, which not only covered all University and College fees, but also included more than generous allowances for living, research, and travel expenses. It is with dismay and foreboding that I compare my good fortune with the grim circumstances in which my own students must work: those without independent means must incur heavy debts in order to conduct research, and all are harried by the authorities to complete within three or at most four years. In the humanities, especially in inter-disciplinary fields and in those requiring competence in one or more languages that were not studied for a first degree, this short-sighted policy is already stifling intellectual curiosity and threatens to provoke a serious decline in academic standards.

I am deeply grateful to many other individuals and institutions, only some of whom I can name here. In addition to those mentioned elsewhere, I wish to thank the following for their intellectual and professional generosity: Henri Bresc, Diego Ciccarelli, Piero Corrao, Vincenzo D'Alessandro, Franco D'Angelo, Adalgisa De Simone, Gioacchino Falsone, Marisa Famà, Ernst Grube, Ernst Kitzinger, Donald Matthew, Ferdinando Maurici, Annliese Nef, Beatrice Pasciuta, Carlo Pastena, Donald Richards, Umberto Rizzitano, Benedetto Rocco, Emilie Savage-Smith, Marina Scarlatta, Lucia Travaini, Vincenzo Tusa, Roger Wilson, and Vladimir Zorič; the directors and staff of the Archivio Diocesano (Catania), the Archivio Diocesano (Palermo), the Archivio Diocesano (Patti), the Archivio di Stato (Palermo), the Biblioteca Centrale della Regione Siciliana (Palermo), the Biblioteca Civica (Catania), the Biblioteca Comunale (Palermo), the Biblioteca della Società Siciliana per Storia Patria (Palermo), the Bibliothèque Nationale (Paris), the Biblioteca Vaticana, the British Library, the Library of the Oriental Institute (Oxford), the Library of the School of Oriental and African Studies, the Library of the University of Newcastle upon Tyne, and the Oriental Library of the University of Durham. For almost thirty years, I have regularly abused the unfailing courtesy, good-humour, kindness and patience of the staff of The Bodleian Library, and especially of the Oriental Reading Room: the late Eliahu Ashtor once described them to the incredulous guests at a Palermitan dinner party as *gli angeli in un piccolo paradiso*, and he was right.

I am especially grateful to the late Albrecht Noth for his encouragement, generosity and kindness. It is a great loss to scholarship that he was unable to complete the projected edition of the Arabic documents of the Norman rulers of Sicily. His preliminary study of the Arabic documents of Roger II included a list of those in the Archivo General de la Fundación Casa Ducal de Medinaceli which, with one exception, remain unpublished. Despite Albrecht Noth's best efforts on my behalf, I have not been able to gain access to these. However, I am extremely grateful to Aldo Sparti of the Soprintendenza Archivistica per la Sicilia (Palermo) for providing me with photocopies of prints of microfilms of them, and with a copy of the catalogue of the 1994 Messina exhibition in which they are reproduced as much reduced colour plates. With these, I have made the least bad readings possible in the circumstances.

Many friends and colleagues have sent me their own publications which I have found indispensable while preparing this study, but I wish to celebrate especially one act of singular generosity. Soon after I moved to Newcastle from Oxford, and beyond easy reach of any library with good holdings on medieval Sicily, Denis Mack Smith invited me to take all books that might be of use from his own collection. And so I came to have at my elbow scores of books which were not held, if anywhere in Britain, by any library between Edinburgh and Cambridge. When I reminded him of this, many years later, he pretended to have forgotten; but I suspect that he was anxious to forget the two bottles of cheap wine which, at the low ebb of my fortunes, was all that I could offer in thanks. But I remember them, and blush, every time that he pulls another venerable bottle from his cellar.

David Abulafia, Michael Brett, Vera von Falkenhausen, Geert Jan van Gelder, Alex Metcalfe, Michael Prestwich, and John Wansbrough all read various drafts of this book, and made many valuable comments. I am grateful to Marigold Acland and Paul Watt of Cambridge University Press for overseeing the process of production, and especially to Valina and Tony Rainer, respectively my copyeditor and proofreader.

Because I have relied so heavily upon the mastery – especially the linguistic mastery – of others, and should otherwise have been Jack of all trades and master of none, I have mastered the art of sticking to my own mistakes against the best advice.

* * *

James and Lisa Fentress have been the best of friends, the most generous of hosts, and the most challenging and stimulating of colleagues and critics, in Oxford, Rome, Sicily, and Tuscany. Dr Filippo Cucinella made a generous gift of his professional services on the sole condition that I wrote 'good things about Sicily'. The late Maria Stella De Simone Wirz, her son Gustavo Wirz, and Sylvia Wirz, were the most gracious, kind, and hospitable landlords in the Villa De Simone at Partanna in 1980–82. For nearly twenty years, Paolo and Costanza Sallier de la Tour, their elder son Filiberto and his wife Domitilla, their daughter Ariane, and many other members of their family and household, have shown me and mine the sort of boundless and unconditional generosity, hospitality, and love that lesser mortals restrict to family. Renata Pucci dei Benisichi Zanca has been a fascinating, generous, and loyal friend, who introduced me not only to the Wirz and the Sallier de la Tour, but also to Sicily itself.

My research on Sicily could never have been undertaken without the love and support of Leslie and Violet Johns, Sarah Johns, and Doris and Fred Blau. I can repay my debt to none of them.

Nadia Jamil was always there to help throughout the writing of the final version of this book and has suggested innumerable clarifications, corrections, and improvements. Were it not for her faith in the book, and in me, it would never have been finished, but I might well have been.

Tables

2.1 The *neogamos*-system in theory 49
2.2 The *neogamos*-system in practice 50
2.3 The Catania *jarīda*s of 1095 and their renewals of 1145 53
2.4 The same line from the 1095 *jarīda* and the renewal of 1145 compared 55
2.5 A family reconstructed from the Triocala *jarīda* illustrating the *neogamos*-system 59
3.1 The family of Abū l-Ḍawʾ Sirāj 89
4.1 The different versions of the boundary-description of Mirto compared 95
4.2 The different versions of the names of the witnesses to the boundaries of Mirto compared 97
4.3 The different versions of the names of two witnesses to the boundaries of Mirto compared 98
5.1 ***Dīwānī* 23** reconstructed 122
5.2 The villeins of San Cosma di Cefalù and San Giovanni di Roccella 124
5.3 The occurrence of the principal *alqāb* of the Norman kings in *dīwānī* documents (1145–83) 135
6.1 Summary of the principal terms used for Muslim villeins in Norman Sicily 151
6.2 The organisation of the 1178 Monreale *jarīda* (***Dīwānī* 43**) 154
6.3 Example of records from ***Dīwānī* 43** 156
6.4 Pairs of parental and *mutazawwijūn* lists (***Dīwānī* 43**) 157
6.5 Examples of relationships between *mutazawwijūn* and their parental households from Sūq al-Mirʾāh (***Dīwānī* 43**) 157
6.6 The family of Subʿu Dīnār (***Dīwānī* 43**) 158
6.7 The *aribbāʾ* of Corleone and their *arbāb* (***Dīwānī* 43**) 160
6.8 The actual sequence of the *aribbāʾ* of Corleone (***Dīwānī* 43**) 161
6.9 The reconstructed sequence of the *aribbāʾ* of Corleone in the source from which ***Dīwānī* 43** was copied 161
6.10 The organisation of the 1183 Monreale *jarīda* (***Dīwānī* 45**) 168

7.1 The boundaries of the lands held by San Nicolò di Chùrchuro at Raḥl al-Wazzān (***Dīwānī*** **29** and **44**) 178
7.2 The boundaries of Raḥl Ibn Sahl (***Dīwānī*** **33** and **44**) 179
7.3 The boundaries of Ḥajar al-Zanātī (***Dīwānī*** **34** and **44**) 182
7.4 The organisation of the 1182 Monreale *jarīdat al-ḥudūd* (***Dīwānī*** **44**) 186
7.5 The organisation of the 1182 Monreale *jarīdat al-ḥudūd* (***Dīwānī*** **44**) showing the individual *ḥudūd* 188
8.1 The languages of *dīwānī* documents and of their recipients 208
9.1 The descent claimed by Ibn Qalāqis for Abū l-Qāsim ibn Ḥammūd 237

Abbreviations

AASLAP	*Atti della Accademia di Scienze, Lettere e Arti di Palermo*
ADM	Archivo General de la Fundación Casa Ducal de Medinaceli
AdS	Archivio di Stato
AG	Agrigento (Sicily)
Arch. Dioc.	Archivio Diocesano
ASCL	*Archivio Storico per la Calabria e la Lucania*
ASPN	*Archivio Storico per le Provincie Napoletane*
ASS	*Archivio Storico Siciliano*
ASSO	*Archivio Storico per la Sicilia Orientale*
BAS^1	*Biblioteca arabo-sicula, ossia raccolta di testi Arabici che toccano la geografia eccetera della Sicilia. Testi arabici*, ed. Michele Amari, 1 vol. and 2 appendices, Leipzig, 1857–87 (reprinted and extensively revised as *BAS*^{2})
BAS^1*(It.)*	*Biblioteca arabo-sicula, ossia raccolta di testi Arabici che toccano la geografia, la storia, le biografie e la bibliografia della Sicilia. Traduzione italiana*, ed. Michele Amari, 2 vols and 1 appendix, Turin, 1880–9 (reprinted and extensively revised as *BAS*^{2}*(It.)*)
BAS^2	*Biblioteca arabo-sicula, ossia raccolta di testi Arabici che toccano la geografia, la storia, la biografia e la bibliografia della Sicilia*, 2nd rev. edn, ed. Michele Amari and Umberto Rizzitano, 2 vols, Edizione nazionale delle opere di Michele Amari, Palermo, 1988
BAS^2*(It.)*	*Biblioteca arabo-sicula, ossia raccolta di testi Arabici che toccano la geografia, la storia, la biografia e la bibliografia della Sicilia. Raccolti e tradotti in Italiano*, 2nd rev. edn, ed. Michele Amari, Umberto Rizzitano, Andrea Borruso, Mirella Cassarino and Adalgisa De Simone, 3 vols, Edizione nazionale delle opere di Michele Amari, Palermo, 1997–8
BGA	Bibliotheca geographorum Arabicorum, ed. Michael Jan de Goeje *et al.*, Leiden
Bibl. Com.	Biblioteca Comunale

BSOAS	*Bulletin of the School of Oriental and African Studies (University of London)*
BZ	*Byzantinische Zeitschrift*
CL	Caltanissetta (Sicily)
CS	Cosenza (Calabria)
CT	Catania (Sicily)
CZ	Catanzaro (Calabria)
DPSASDS	*Documenti per Servire alla Storia di Sicilia* (Società Siciliana per la Storia Patria, Palermo)
EI^1	*The Encyclopaedia of Islam*, ed. Martijn Theodor Houtsma *et al.*, 1st edn, 4 vols and supplement, Leiden, 1913–38
EI^2	*The Encyclopaedia of Islam*, ed. Hamilton Alexander Rosskeen Gibb *et al.*, 2nd edn, 10 vols to date, Leiden and London, 1960–
EN	Enna (Sicily)
FG	Foggia (Apulia)
FSI	Fonti per la Storia d'Italia (Istituto Storico Italiano per il Medio Evo, Rome)
JA	*Journal Asiatique*
JESHO	*Journal of the Economic and Social History of the Orient*
ME	Messina (Sicily)
MT	Matera (Basilicata)
NA	Naples (Campania)
PA	Palermo (Sicily)
QFIAB	*Quellen und Forschungen aus italienischen Archiven und Bibliotheken*
RC	Reggio di Calabria (Calabria)
RG	Ragusa (Sicily)
RIS	Rerum Italicarum Scriptores; raccolta degli storici italiani dal cinquecento al millecinquecento ordinata da Ludovico Antonio Muratori, 2nd series, Bologna
SA	Salerno (Campania)
SR	Syracuse (Sicily)
TP	Trapani (Sicily)
VV	Vibo Valentia (Calabria)

THE HOUSE OF HAUTEVILLE (1)

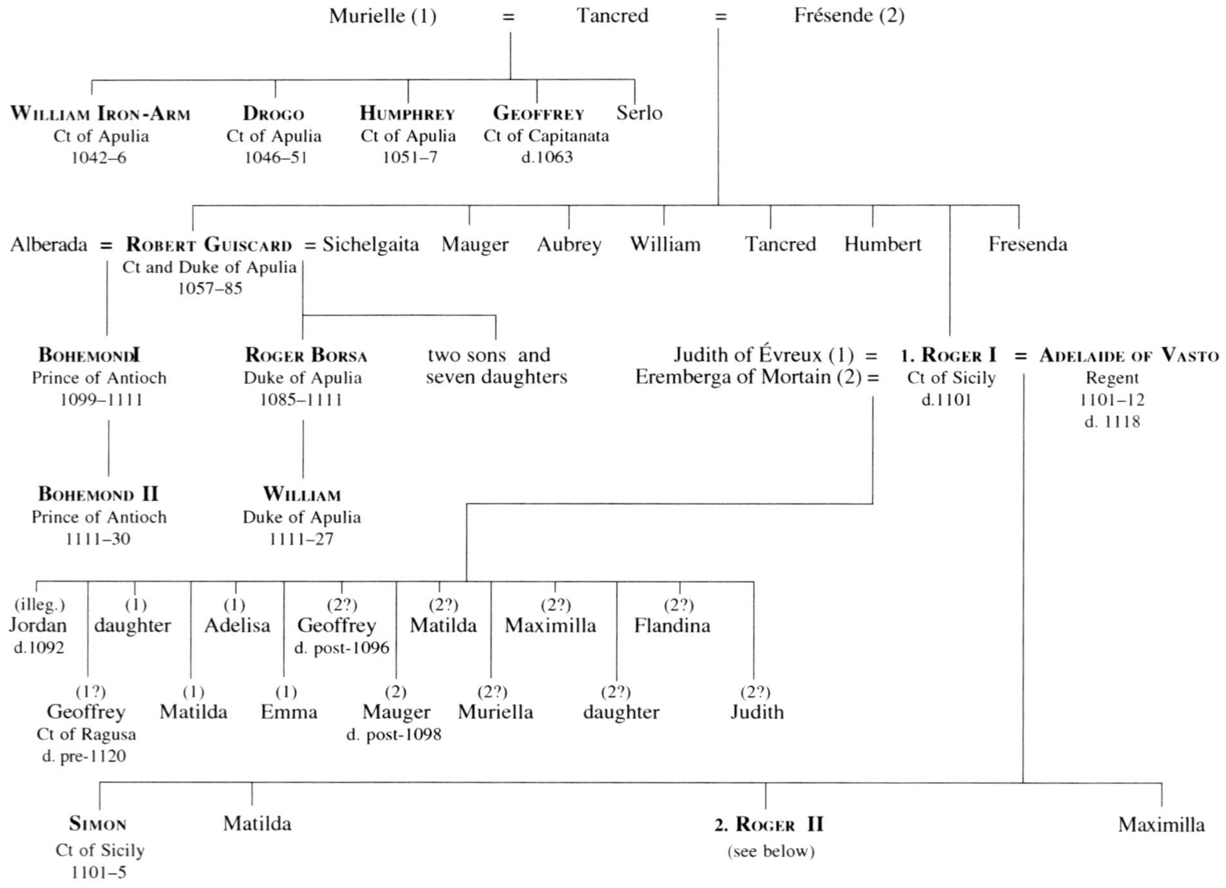

THE HOUSE OF HAUTEVILLE (2)

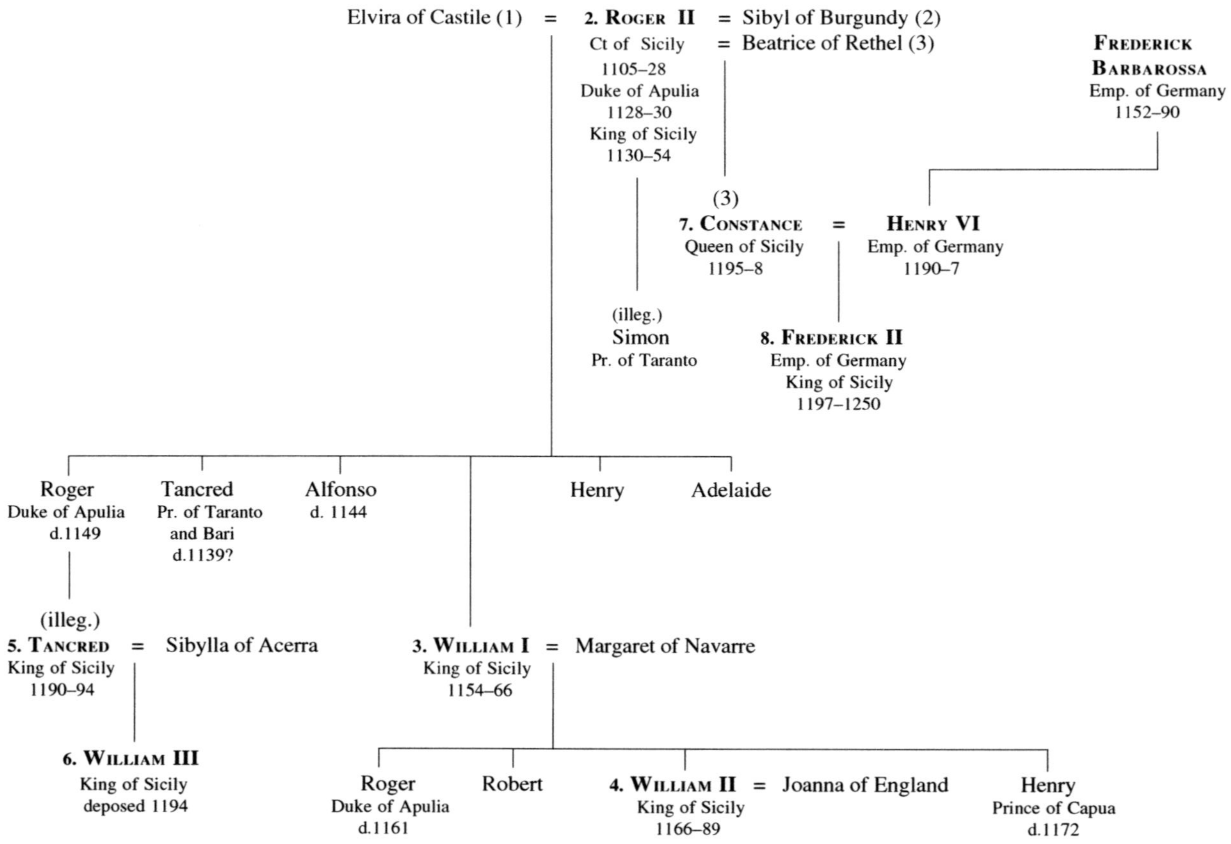

Note on measurements

In the Arabic-Latin estate register of Santa Maria di Monreale (***Dīwānī* 44**), the Arabic *mudd* is translated into Latin as *salma*, a measure of area equivalent to 1.75 hectares (4.3 acres). In the absence of evidence to the contrary, I have assumed that this was the area of the *mudd* throughout western Sicily in the Norman period, and that the Greek *modion*, whence the Arabic *mudd* (and the Latin *modius*) were derived, had the same area. The Arabic *zawja* (Greek *boidion* or *zeugarion*, Latin *pariclum*) comprised thirty *mudds* of land (52.5 hectares, 130 acres): in all three languages, the term refers to a yoke of oxen, and is here translated by the English 'plough-land'.

The terms *modion*, *modius*, *mudd* and *salma* were also used for dry measures, on the principle that one *mudd* of grain was required to seed one *mudd* of land. In medieval and early modern Sicily, there was considerable local variation in the dry *salma*, presumably because the sowing rate varied according to both the crop and the quality of the land. The *salma* used for wheat in the region of Palermo was therefore adopted as a general measure for the whole island, and was equivalent to 2.75 hectolitres (7.5 bushels). Again in the absence of evidence to the contrary, I have assumed this to be the size of the dry *modion*, *modius*, *mudd* and *salma* in western Sicily during the Norman period.

Introduction

This book is written with a particular audience in mind, and seeks to introduce western medievalists, who have been trained to observe Norman kingship through predominantly Latin eyes and in the environment of north-western Europe, to what may for many be a new and disturbingly unfamiliar perspective. I have therefore chosen to set out from a much frequented point of departure, and to progress at a leisurely pace towards the Mediterranean. But, should historians of medieval Islam happen to open this book, they will find the administrative culture that it describes so familiar that they may well wonder that anyone should think so peripheral a subject worthy of such detailed attention. The following paragraphs are therefore also intended to introduce them to one of the western medieval historiographical questions underlying this book: the nature – indeed, the very existence – of what, whether it is observed in Normandy, England, Sicily or Antioch, may be recognised as an administrative policy peculiar to Norman rule.

In 1969, David C. Douglas stated the case as follows:

> Before the twelfth century was far advanced, monarchies established by the Normans controlled the best organized kingdoms of Europe, and a Norman prince ruled the strongest of the Crusading states. This success was however not due merely to the facts of conquest or even to the establishment of notable rulers supported by strong feudal aristocracies. It derived also from a particular administrative policy which was everywhere adopted by the Normans. In all the states they governed, the Normans at this time were concerned to give fresh vitality to the administrative institutions which they found in the conquered lands, and to develop these constructively to their own advantage.[1]

The claims made by Douglas and his predecessors have since been challenged, most strongly for England. James Campbell and Wilfred Lewis Warren have suggested that the evidence for Anglo-Norman administration is open to a

[1] Douglas 1969, pp.181–2, writing very much in the tradition of Charles Homer Haskins who, more than a century earlier, had stressed that a 'genius for adaptation' had characterised Norman government in Normandy, England, Sicily and Antioch: Haskins 1911, especially pp.433–5; see also Haskins 1915.

fundamentally different interpretation.[2] Warren attacked 'the myth of Norman administrative efficiency' as follows:

> Until the end of the eleventh century Anglo-Norman England was largely managed by Englishmen. A crisis in continuity emerges not at the Conquest but as the generation personally familiar with pre-Conquest practice died off and the Normans had to cope for themselves. The critical questions are how far they were able to master the Anglo-Saxon inheritance, and how far they understood it. The innovations in administrative practices are ... at least in part a response to problems which the Normans themselves had inadvertently created, and an attempt not so much to improve upon the Anglo-Saxon system as to shore it up and stop it collapsing. And the lines of development in the government of England which the Normans helped to set were determined as much if not more by their administrative failures as by their successes.[3]

Warren concluded on a still more provocative note.

> I find myself unable to accept the view that the Normans were 'constructive builders on solid Anglo-Saxon achievements'.[4] Under the Normans the Anglo-Saxon system became ramshackle. Norman government was a matter of shifts and contrivances. Nor can I see Norman administrative methods as the precursor in an evolutionary sense, of effective royal government; they had to be rethought. Nevertheless, there *is* a break in continuity, not at the Conquest itself, not on the morrow of it, but within fifty years of it. The break occurred not because the Normans did not wish to preserve the Anglo-Saxon inheritance but because they did not know how to do so. It may have been an involuntary breach, but it was nonetheless fundamental because the consequence was transition from a sophisticated form of non-modern state managed through social mechanisms to a crude form of modern state organized through administrative institutions.[5]

Such re-evaluation of Anglo-Norman administration has provided a considerable stimulus to this study. Recent historians of Norman Sicily have been content to claim that there was 'no interruption of Moslem administrative practice' and that 'the Normans took from their Arab predecessors the centralized financial bureau of the *diwan*'. In Sicily, as in England, they have implied, the Norman rulers chose the best practices and institutions from the pre-conquest administration and incorporated them into the Norman system which their 'genius for adaptation' then developed into one that was more efficient and more successful than its predecessor.[6] And yet, there has been no re-examination of the sparse evidence for the administrative system of Muslim Sicily since Michele Amari wrote in the mid to late 19th century. Nor has a systematic study of the Arabic component of the Norman administration, throughout its history, ever been attempted by a historian familiar not just with the evidence from Sicily, but also with contemporary Islamic administrative practice.

[2] Campbell 1975; Warren 1984.
[3] Warren 1984, pp.115–16.
[4] Loyn 1983, p.197.
[5] Warren 1984, pp.131–2. See also the discussion of the implications of the 'break in continuity' in Clanchy 1993, pp.65–8.
[6] Douglas 1969, pp.185, 186, 189–91.

In part, this explains why extraordinary claims have been made that analogous instances of the Norman 'genius for adaptation' may found in England and Sicily: the De Hautevilles' use of the Muslim *iqlīm* or administrative district has been compared to Henry I's use of the English hundred;[7] the Sicilian *jarāʾid* or tax-registers have been compared to Domesday Book;[8] and scholars continue to debate the relationship between the Sicilian *dīwān* and the English exchequer.[9] But it is not overstating the case to object that such claims would not have been made had their authors been familiar with the history of Islamic administration outside Sicily, and with the detailed history of the Norman *dīwān*.

This book has not been written with one eye on the Anglo-Norman world; from my blinkered perspective, it seems that those analogies that may meaningfully be made between the administrative history of England and Sicily are of a different order. In Sicily, as in England, in the immediate post-conquest period, the Norman rulers sought to adapt indigenous administrative practices to their own needs. In Sicily, as in England, a generation after the conquest, there was a break in continuity caused by the failure of the conquerors to preserve the administrative system inherited from the previous rulers of the island. And in Sicily, as in England, Norman rulers subsequently introduced administrative innovations to repair the damage done to the pre-conquest system; innovations which underwent rigorous selection through a process of trial and error, and rapidly developed in new directions.

But, in the two islands, the Norman conquerors were heirs to indigenous administrative systems that were fundamentally different. The progress described by Warren – 'from a sophisticated form of non-modern state managed through social mechanisms to a crude form of modern state organized through administrative institutions' – is peculiar to England. Muslim Sicily, like most of the Islamic world, was governed through administrative institutions before the Norman conquest, and the De Hautevilles were to struggle hard, not least against themselves and their closest supporters, to prevent the erosion of administrative government by immigrant Latin society.

Again, the manner in which the Norman rulers of the two islands sought to adapt indigenous administrative practices to their own needs was fundamentally different. In England, the Norman kings sought to perpetuate the Anglo-Saxon inheritance by employing indigenous administrators.[10] Until 1071, a significant group of English earls and great thegns had retained power and status in the post-conquest settlement;[11] and thereafter, at the level of the shire, a small but vital community of Englishmen survived – 'by commending themselves to the incoming continental magnates, by undertaking ministerial duties, and by taking land at farm' – and ensured 'the continuance of English customs and traditions'.[12] After

[7] Douglas 1969, p.186, citing Chalandon 1907, vol.I, p.348.
[8] Genuardi 1910; Clementi 1961.
[9] Garufi 1901; Takayama 1993, pp.12–13, 169.
[10] Williams 1995, pp.98–125.
[11] Williams 1995, pp.24–70.
[12] Williams 1995, pp.71–97: quotes from p.96.

the conquest of Sicily was complete, there were no Muslim barons in Roger's *comitatus*, and no Muslim lords held land in fief. Although Sicilian Arabs must have been employed within the early Norman administration, we know the name of only one before 1130, while we can reconstruct the prosopography of an entire class of Greek Christian administrators who were imported from east Sicily and Calabria to manage and to adapt the Arabic and Islamic institutions through which the island had been administered. The immigrant Latin and indigenous Arab communities of Sicily were separated from each other by a cultural barrier which, if anything, grew less permeable with time; and the manner in which the Greek community acted as an intermediary between the Latin and the Arab may even have increased their distance from each other.

This is a convenient point to emphasise that the linguistic history of post-conquest England and Sicily was fundamentally different. Both islands have been called 'trilingual' as a result of Norman conquest. But it is as well to remember that such a concentration upon the big three languages oversimplifies the intricate linguistic puzzle that challenges the historian of both islands, and ignores, in particular, the linguistic diversity of north and west Britain, and the wide variation of Romance vernaculars in the Sicilian kingdom. It also neglects the Scandinavian communities of Britain, and the presence in southern Italy and Sicily of more than a handful of Normans who still bore Norse personal names.[13] Moreover, in both islands, Jews used Hebrew, Judaeo-Arabic, and occasional Aramaic words and phrases.[14] In Sicily, there are also traces of Berber. Nonetheless, it is to the big three that I must now return. In England, although English ('Standard Old English') was the administrative language before the conquest, Latin was already the dominant literary language, and soon after the conquest rapidly replaced English as the language of record, although English continued to be used as the unwritten language of local administration. French ('Anglo-Norman') was introduced at the conquest as the language of the victorious élite, but, except in the king's court, French-speakers were soon assimilated into English-speaking society; although French was soon established as a literary language, it was not until the mid-13th century that it was widely used as a language of record.[15] In pre-conquest Sicily, Arabic was the dominant language of administration at all levels, of literary culture, and of religion. Greek was confined to monastic communities and to the Greek urban societies of eastern Sicily. Even the non-Muslim minorities, Jews and Greek Christians, seem to have been predominantly Arabic-speaking. After the Norman conquest, Arabic continued to be used in some written documents for a generation, but was then dropped, and for more than fifteen years ceased to be used in documents issued by the central administration. Greek was established during the conquest as the language through which the Normans were to rule, and rapidly became the dominant language of administration throughout the whole island. By

[13] Ménager 1975, pp.267–96; Ménager 1981a, pp.6–10. This does not, of course, necessarily indicate that they or their fathers were Norse speakers.

[14] For Judaeo-Arabic in England, see Beit-Arié 1985, pp.33–56 and plates 6–7.

[15] Clanchy 1993, 198–223 *et passim*.

1110–15, the almost total replacement of Arabic by Greek, and of Arab Muslims by Greek Christians, in the central administration hastened the collapse of the pre-conquest administrative system, far more than did the as yet insignificant introduction of Latin. Although the new Greek structure incorporated spolia salvaged from pre-conquest Muslim administration, it was essentially foreign and new. At the local level, Latin lords and their Arab 'villeins' used, respectively, Latin (or a Romance vernacular) and Arabic, while Greek Christians acted as intermediaries between the two communities.[16] In post-conquest England, an educated person might read and write English, French, and Latin, but in Sicily such trilingualism was exceedingly rare and, I suspect, effectively confined to the Greek Christian community. In the long term, the language of the Norman conquerors enriched English but was replaced by it, as English became the dominant language, in all registers, not just in England but throughout Britain. In Sicily, the Romance vernaculars of the conquerors had almost completely ousted Arabic by the end of the 13th century, after which date it was used only by Jews and slaves of North African origin. Medieval Sicilian contains only some three hundred words of Arabic derivation.[17]

But, if the Anglo-Saxon and Muslim Sicilian inheritances were fundamentally different one from the other, and if the Norman conquerors of the two islands sought to adapt those diverse inheritances in strikingly different ways, the contrast is greater still between the manner in which Henry I and Roger II each sought to make good the damage done to the pre-conquest system in his respective island. Whereas in England, Henry I replaced Anglo-Saxon social mechanisms with a series of innovations amounting to the rapid expansion of the early state and the administrative machinery through which it was thenceforth to be governed, Roger II and his officers sought to preserve and to restore the ruined edifice inherited from Muslim Sicily by importing administrative practices, institutions, and personnel wholesale from the contemporary Islamic world, so that the Arabic administration of Sicily in the mid-12th century more closely approached the classical Islamic system, as exemplified in contemporary Fāṭimid Egypt, than had the administration of the Kalbid emirs before the Norman conquest. In England, the Normans had inherited the entire Anglo-Saxon system and when, a generation after the conquest, Norman rule had brought it close to collapse, Henry I had no choice but innovation. In Sicily, the De Hautevilles had conquered a province on the periphery of the Fāṭimid empire and when, a generation after their neglect had caused the collapse of the indigenous system, Roger II sought to repair it, he turned to the imperial centre for the men and machinery with which to do so. Roger thus gave a new lease of life to previously moribund Arabic and Islamic administrative institutions and practices, restoring them to such health that they outlasted his dynasty.

[16] The best (and yet unsatisfactory) summary of the language situation in Norman Sicily remains Varvaro 1981, pp.125–220. For Arabic in Norman Sicily, see Metcalfe 1999, soon to be published in revised form – Metcalfe 2002 (forthcoming).

[17] Caracausi 1983.

At the same time, however, Roger II and his successors also presided over a series of far-reaching innovations in the Greek and, especially, in the Latin branches of the administration. In this book, both because I am exclusively concerned with the island of Sicily and do not examine even Calabria let alone the other mainland provinces of the Norman kingdom, and because my main subject is the Arabic administration and the Arabic facet of Norman kingship, I have neglected such innovations in the Greek and Latin administration. They must not be forgotten, however, lest the overall effect of my argument be to exaggerate the importance of the reformed Arabic administration for the history of Norman Sicily as a whole.

I am especially conscious of this danger because I am so keenly aware that historians of Norman institutions remain almost completely uninformed about the nature of the Arabic administration of Norman Sicily. The brief review of King Roger's fiscal administration which Haskins gave in 1915 was still thought acceptable when Douglas returned to the theme in 1969 and when R.H.C. Davis began the work of deconstruction in 1976.[18] To this day, both the great pioneers – Erich Caspar, Ferdinand Chalandon, Haskins, and Evelyn Jamison – and such lesser figures as Carlo-Alberto Garufi, Karl Andreas Kehr, Ernst Mayer and Hans Niese, all of whom wrote before the First World War, still remain indispensable to the subject. Indeed, there are few topics for which one does not first open with profit the *Considerazioni* of Rosario Gregorio, published nearly two centuries ago. Theirs is the lead followed by the few modern scholars to have attempted original work, including Mario Caravale, Enrico Mazzarese Fardella and Hiroshi Takayama. And yet all of these scholars show themselves to be unfamiliar with the Islamic tradition to which the Arabic administration of Kalbid and Norman Sicily belonged. It is difficult to convey the consequences of this unfamiliarity, but a rough idea may be had by imagining what would be the result were four or five generations of Arab historians, with no knowledge of Latin, to have debated amongst themselves the nature of Anglo-Norman administration taking as their yardstick of contemporary administrative practice the *Aḥkām al-sulṭānīya* ('The ordinances of government') by the 11th-century Iraqi jurist al-Māwardī.

A few Arabists have struggled against the tide, and have sought to introduce their Latin medievalist colleagues to the essentially Islamic context in which alone the Arabic administration of Norman Sicily can be understood. Michele Amari had the misfortune to write with imperfect knowledge of the documentary evidence from Sicily, and at a date when knowledge of medieval Islamic institutions was still in its infancy, but his 1878 study was a model for its time. Amari's friend and correspondent, Otto Hartwig, had asked him a series of penetrating questions designed to lay bare what he clearly believed to be the close relationship between the English exchequer and the Sicilian *dīwān*.[19] Amari replied by comparing at some length Sicilian institutions with medieval Islamic administrations described by Arab authors, including al-Māwardī, Ibn Khaldūn, al-Yaᶜqūbī, al-Maqrīzī,

[18] Haskins 1915, pp.228–9; Douglas 1969, 181–2; Davis 1976.

[19] This was a matter of debate well before Haskins 1911: as early as the 18th century, the consensus in Sicily was that Norman administrative institutions had been imported wholesale to the island.

al-Nābulusī and others. His principal conclusion was that the Sicilian *dīwān* in the mid-12th century was essentially Arabic and Islamic in character, and more closely resembled the *dīwān* of Fāṭimid Egypt than the English exchequer. I am not aware of Hartwig's response, but the reaction of most of Amari's contemporaries was to reject his conclusion out of hand. For example, Carlo-Alberto Garufi, a figure of insular stature with none of Amari's breadth and depth of scholarship, pretended to disprove Amari's argument by means of a detailed philological discussion, regardless that he knew no Arabic.[20] And yet it is no exaggeration to claim that Garufi and his followers have been left in possession of the field to this day. With a handful of notable exceptions, the administration of Norman Sicily has continued to be studied from an Anglo-Norman perspective, and the essentially Arabic and Islamic character of the Norman *dīwān* is simply ignored. Why this should be so is in large part explained by the fate of the Arabic documents of Norman Sicily.

In the interval between the first publication of Amari's *Storia dei Musulmani di Sicilia* in 1854–72 and Nallino's revised second edition in 1933–9, Salvatore Cusa published *I Diplomi greci ed arabi di Sicilia*.[21] This transcription of most of the Arabic and bilingual (Arabic-Greek and Arabic-Latin) documents issued by the Norman rulers should have greatly facilitated the study of the Arabic administration, but the work was not without problems. In the first place, only Part One was published, in two volumes, and the second part, which was to contain critical apparatus and translations of the Greek and Arabic texts, never appeared. The Arabic documents thus remained inaccessible to those scholars most interested in the administrative history of Norman Sicily, none of whom were Arabists.[22] In the second place, it now seems clear that Cusa was not himself primarily responsible for the transcription of either the Arabic or the Greek documents, and that this was entrusted to his pupils, respectively Carlo Crispo Moncada and Isidoro Carini.[23] In fact, the detailed examination of the Arabic texts published under Cusa's name reveals so great a number of inconsistencies and such extreme linguistic unevenness as to suggest that at least two individuals were responsible for the edition. And yet, although Cusa's edition is incomplete, contains a substantial number of errors in all three languages, and lacks all critical apparatus, it is nonetheless an extraordinary achievement for its time, and no one should confront the original Arabic documents with Cusa's published texts without feeling admiration and gratitude towards whoever was actually responsible for the transcription.[24] The sad fact

[20] Garufi 1901, especially pp.234–8. See also below, pp.194–5.

[21] Vol.I bears the year 1868 but was not actually published until 1874; vol.II is dated 1882.

[22] Gaetano Trovato, self-styled 'Professor in Arabic Language and Literature', published an Italian translation of some of the Arabic documents edited by Cusa (Trovato 1949). His versions are based upon Cusa's imperfect texts, they abound with errors and unmarked lacunae, and they lack critical apparatus, philological rigour, and historical sensibility: see also De Simone 1999b, pp.95–6.

[23] De Simone 1984; De Simone 1999b, pp.77–81, 84–5.

[24] See Amari's review, now conveniently reprinted in Amari 1970, pp.207–10. ('Io, che de' codici e diplomi arabi n'ho pur maneggiati di molti e che ho visti gli originali pubblicati adesso dal professor Cusa, posso attestare che ve n'ha alcuno di quelli che a prima vista fanno gettare via lo scritto per disperazione. Ancorchè io non sia d'accordo circa qualche lezione qua e là, non posso non ammirare la somma perizia dello editore'.)

remains, however, that any serious study of the Norman *dīwān* must be based upon the original documents, and not on the texts published in Cusa's name.

In the year of the eight-hundredth anniversary of King Roger's death Paolo Collura first proposed a new and complete critical edition of the documents of the Norman rulers of Sicily in all three administrative languages: Arabic, Greek and Latin.[25] Work upon the *Codex diplomaticus regni Siciliae* (*CDRS*) did not actually get underway until the early 1970s, and only four volumes of edited documents have so far appeared – the Latin documents of Roger II, what purports to be all the documents of William I, the documents of Tancred and William III, and the documents of Constance.[26] Only two of the forty-five Arabic and bilingual documents issued by the Norman administration have yet been edited, both issued by William I. Unfortunately, the Greek text of the one original bilingual document was so badly mangled by the printers as to render it unusable, and the Arabic text contains several minor errors.[27] The second document is a Latin transumpt of a bilingual original, which was already published in a fuller version, and which also contains several minor errors.[28] One Arabic and one Greek-Arabic document, also issued by the Arabic administration of William I, were not included in the volume because of the rigidly Eurocentric definition of what does or does not constitute a public document: a definition adopted by the editors against the express advice of the late Albrecht Noth, who was responsible for the edition of the Arabic texts.[29] What was taken to be an Arabic *deperditum*, but is nothing of the kind, is also included amongst the documents of William I.[30]

Although this is not an auspicious start to the edition of the Arabic documents, the *CDRS* has made one important contribution to the study of the Arabic administration of Norman Sicily – the late Albrecht Noth's brief review of the Arabic documents of Roger II.[31] In this preliminary study, made prior to his projected edition of the documents themselves, Noth made almost the first attempt since Michele Amari to examine the Arabic documents of Norman Sicily within the context of contemporary Islamic administrative practice.[32] This important and perceptive study has been an inspiration to me.

The historiographical imbalance which this book seeks to redress is thus a particularly heavy one. If I am thought to have over-compensated, I have done my best to make this unfamiliar, and often troublesome, material as accessible as possible to readers who have no Arabic, Greek, and Latin, and no knowledge of medieval Islamic administration, so that they can retrace my steps and follow my

25 Collura 1955b.
26 Respectively: Brühl 1987; Enzensberger 1996; Zielinski 1982; Kölzer 1983.
27 See Appendix 1, ***Dīwānī* 36.**
28 See Appendix 1, ***Dīwānī* 34.**
29 See Appendix 1, ***Dīwānī* 33** and **35.**
30 Enzensberger 1996, *Deperditum* 3, p.102; see Appendix I, ***Dīwānī* 34.**
31 Noth 1978; critically reviewed by von Falkenhausen 1980b, and slightly revised for the Italian version (Noth 1983). See also Noth 1977 and Noth 1981–2.
32 See especially Noth 1983, pp.208–13, and compare with Amari 1878. See also Schack 1969, pp.54–87 and De Simone 1988.

argument at every stage. All words and phrases in Arabic have been transliterated and translated at their first occurrence, and often elsewhere in the text. Greek words and phrases are always given in transliteration when they occur in the text, and are translated on at least their first occurrence. There is no glossary, but the first occurrence in the index of an Arabic, Greek or Sicilian term will lead the reader to a definition or translation. Only in the notes and tables, and in specialist and technical discussion, have I occasionally left Arabic or Greek words in the original. Sicilian place-names are standardised as far as possible; where no standard exists, the reader is referred to an explanatory note. In the index, all place-names in Sicily and southern Italy are followed by the standard abbreviation for the modern province in which they are located (see *Abbreviations*), and are cross-referenced to any alternative place-names used in this book. Where dates are given according to the Islamic or Byzantine calendar, Julian equivalents are given.

Arabists may care to note that, so far as possible and with the exceptions given below, I have used a system of transliteration based on that now standard in the English-speaking world. Names and short phrases, titles, *etc.* are given without case endings (*iʿrāb*) – *e.g. ṣāḥib dīwān al-taḥqīq al-maʿmūr*, not *sāḥibu dīwāni l-taḥqīqi l-maʿmūri.*[33] But I have generally given as full as possible a vocalisation for longer passages of text in order to account in detail for the reading proposed. I have occasionally suspended this practice where the text quoted is too far removed from the grammatical and syntactical conventions standard in the written language – *e.g.* in quotations from the 1182 Monreale estate register (*jarīdat al-ḥudūd* – ***Dīwānī* 44**) given in the notes to Chapter 7.

Whereas I have always referred back to the original in quoting from Arabic documents, this has not always been possible for the far more numerous Greek and Latin documents. Greek quotations are transliterated by a rigid system of letter-for-letter equivalents, ignoring accents and breathings; this inevitably leads to such infelicities as *kapriliggas* for *kaprilingas* but, as with Arabic, I have preferred to reproduce orthography and not pronunciation. So far as possible, when quoting from the original, the orthography of quotations from Greek documents has been reproduced, and not made to correspond to a classical model, but abbreviations and contractions have been supplied. Quotations from edited Greek documents, however, are likely to reproduce the editor's classicising corrections.

Throughout the text, references to the catalogue of *dīwānī* documents, *i.e.* of the Arabic and bilingual documents issued by the Norman administration, presented as Appendix 1, are given in the form ***Dīwānī* 1**, ***Dīwānī* 2**, *etc.* A dagger symbol preceding a number – e.g. ***Dīwānī* †9** – indicates that the document is a forgery. A new and critical edition of all the Arabic and bilingual documents from Norman Sicily is now in preparation by myself, Nadia Jamil, and Alex Metcalfe. The first volume, publishing the private – *i.e.* the non-*dīwānī* documents – will appear in the

[33] Note, in particular: و – *w/ū* (*wāw mushaddada* – *ūw* not *ww*); ي – *y/ī* (*yāʾ mushaddada* – *īy* not *yy*); ء – ʾ (*hamzat al-waṣl* is elided as shown in the example cited in the text).

near future. (Appendix 2, below, is a provisional catalogue of the private Arabic documents: references to it are in the form **Private 1**, **Private 2**, *etc.*) The third volume, dedicated to the three great Monreale *jarāʾid* (***Dīwānī* 43–5**), will be largely the responsibility of Alex Metcalfe, whom the Arts and Humanities Research Board has granted a three-year Postdoctoral Research Fellowship at the University of Leeds to undertake the task. The second volume, in which the other *dīwānī* documents will be edited, will complete the series. An analytical study is also planned, which will compare the private and the *dīwānī* documents, not only to each other, but also to other corpora of medieval Arabic documents, in terms of diplomatic form, language, and script.

CHAPTER 1

'In the time of the Saracens ...'

'Privileges ... which, incidentally, have always been misinterpreted ...'

On 7 July 1674, the port of Messina, in the north-eastern corner of Sicily, rebelled against Spanish rule. The leaders of the revolt were the wealthy burghers of the city, members of the senatorial class, families whose names were inscribed in the exclusive register of nobility kept in the city archives, oligarchs proud of their right to wear hats in the presence of the viceroy. Their cause was essentially reactionary: to protect their ancient privileges against the perceived liberalism of the Spanish viceroy. They were encouraged and assisted by Louis XIV of France, who appointed the brother of his mistress to be governor of Sicily. To the rebels' dismay, the French governor was careless of their rights, and contemptuous of their petty provincialism. His officers seduced their wives, while his troops cut down the mulberry trees which fed the silk-worms from which the rebels had spun their wealth. The port remained closed, trade and commerce ceased, and the rebellion soon threatened to destroy the prosperity of its leaders. When Louis withdrew his support, the senatorial families fled the island with as much money and silk as they could carry, some to exile in Tunis and Constantinople. On 15 March 1678, Spanish troops entered the city, and the rebellion was over.[1]

The new Spanish viceroy, appointed in 1679, conceived a terrible revenge against the citizens of Messina. The town hall was razed to the ground, and its site ploughed and sowed with salt. In its place was set an equestrian statue, by Giacomo Serpotta, of King Carlo II trampling the hydra of rebellion. The metal from which it was cast came from the great bell in the cathedral tower which had summoned the citizens to rebellion. In the basement of that tower, the city archive was stored in great chests. On 9 January 1679 the viceroy ordered the entire archive to be seized:

> These privileges and their contents, which, incidentally, have always been misinterpreted, are the foundation upon which was raised the vast pile of excesses and irreverences which has done such damage to His Majesty, Our Lord King. So that the least of the said privileges may be wiped from the memory of the people [of Messina], I have decided that the originals shall be removed absolutely and completely from the archive.

[1] For a lively account of the rebellion, see Mack Smith 1968, pp.226–32.

With his own hands, the viceroy's agent opened the great chests and stuffed their contents into twenty-three sacks which were shipped to Spain. And there they remained until 1994, when they returned briefly to Messina for a lavish exhibition, entitled *Il Ritorno della Memoria*.[2]

The documents of the archive had indeed been used by the rebels to legitimise their claims to ancient rights and privileges. The great chests in the *campanile* had contained a document dated 483 *ab urbe condita* (270 B.C.), in which the consuls Appius Claudius and Quintus Fabius, on behalf of the senate and people of Rome, elevated Messina to the rank of capital of Sicily, granted Roman citizenship to its priests and citizens, and confirmed the boundary of its territory as stretching from Lentini to Patti. Another document, dated 620 *ab urbe condita* (133 B.C.), exempted Messina in perpetuity from all taxes and tribute. Privileges granted by the Byzantine emperor Arcadius, by the Norman kings, by Henry VI, Frederick II, and Manfred, and by Charles d'Anjou, confirmed and extended these ancient rights. All these were as authentic as the autograph letter of the Virgin, also preserved in the archive. They are the memorials, not to Messina's ancient glory, but to the boundless cheek of medieval forgers.[3]

The archive also contained two documents which sought to legitimise the claims of the churches of Catania and Messina to property which they had come to possess in the immediate aftermath of the Norman conquest, by invoking the memory of what had been done 'in the time of the Saracens'.[4] Their authenticity has always been in doubt but, now, thanks to the archive's brief return from obscurity, it is clear that they, unlike the crude Republican forgeries and their spurious confirmations, are contemporary – 12th-century – confections, and were very probably modelled upon genuine originals. The documents are false, but the memories that they preserve are authentic. Indeed, as will be seen in this chapter and the next, the fiscal administration of Norman Sicily developed in part from an adaptation to post-conquest circumstances of the Muslim institutions found by the Normans on their arrival on the island, and can only be understood in the wider context of Islamic administration. It is therefore necessary, by way of introduction, to dwell at some length 'in the time of the Saracens'; not only to discuss the fiscal administration of Muslim Sicily, but, first, to review briefly the evolution of Islamic fiscal administration, most especially in Egypt and the Maghrib. In particular, because it will later be argued that elements of administrative structure and practice were imported into Sicily during the reign of Roger II from Fāṭimid Egypt, the fiscal administration of medieval Egypt will here be treated in some detail, in order to serve both as an example of a sophisticated Arabic fiscal administration, and as a model to be tested in the course of this argument against the evidence from Norman Sicily. For, with the notable exception of the Egyptian papyri and the Cairo Geniza, the operation of medieval Islamic administrations is known not from the

2 *Messina* 1994, nos 131–2, 136, pp.208–9, 210.
3 Giardina 1937, pp.XXX–LI; Tricoli 1994, *passim* and bibliography.
4 *Messina* 1994, no.13, p.153 and no.15, p.154. Below, pp.39–42, 44.

documents that they produced but almost exclusively from chancery handbooks and scattered anecdotes. The Arabic documents of Norman Sicily, although produced on the periphery of the Islamic centre, can thus be used, rather like the letters of the Cairo Geniza, to establish or to confirm the Islamic original from which they ultimately derive.

The evolution of Islamic fiscal administration: a selective account

The history of administrative institutions under the first caliphs remains obscure, uncertain and controversial. The first Muslim rulers seem to have been content to adapt the fiscal systems of their conquests to their own needs. By the 10th century, at the latest, three principal taxes had come to characterise the fiscal administration of the Islamic world, and to constitute its main sources of revenue: *ᶜushr*, *kharāj* and *jizya*. Looking back upon the period of conquests, the historians and lawyers of the ᶜAbbāsid caliphate, and later, attempted to reconstruct the process through which the land and its inhabitants had been conquered, and to use that reconstruction as the theoretical basis that would account for the contemporary fiscal regime.[5] In practice, the system of taxation varied greatly from place to place within the Muslim conquests, and the rigid conceptualisation devised by ᶜAbbāsid lawyers was honoured more in the breach than in the observance. Thus, as we shall see below, even though Sicily was conquered well after the basic principles of the fiscal regime had been established in law, they were clearly not followed in practice, and this was to be a bone of contention throughout the Muslim period.

In theory, lands which had been abandoned to the Muslim armies, or which they had taken by force, and which were divided amongst the Muslims, were liable to the *ᶜushr*, or tithe of produce.[6] Lands which had been acquired by treaty, the so-called *ṣulḥ*-lands, were liable to the *kharāj*, which could be assessed at anything up to two-thirds of their produce.[7] Christians, Jews, and other subject communities, who surrendered themselves to the *dhimma*, or 'protection', of the Muslims, were known as *ahl al-dhimma* ('protected people') or *dhimmīyūn*, and they paid the *jizya*, a personal tax which, whatever its origins, came to be both a tribute levied upon the vanquished, and a tax paid by Christians and Jews for the privilege of maintaining their own religion.[8] The *kharāj* seems to have been originally a sort of tribute imposed upon *ṣulḥ*-lands, on payment of which the non-Muslim population was left in undisturbed possession. But, in time, as non-Muslim proprietors converted to Islam or sold their lands to Muslims, the lawyers came increasingly

[5] See, for example, al-Mawardī 1853, pp.245–6; al-Mawardī 1996, p.158. For reliable and relatively recent introductions to early Islamic taxation, see Morimoto 1981 and Simonsen 1988.
[6] Grohmann 1934.
[7] Cahen 1977a.
[8] Cahen 1963a; Cahen1963b.

to insist that the *kharāj* should be paid upon *kharāj*-land, regardless of the religion of its proprietors. The cultivators of *ᶜushr*-lands were effectively made serfs and paid heavy exactions, comparable to the *kharāj*. The *dhimmīyūn* were assessed for the *jizya* and, if they occupied productive land, they paid the *kharāj* as well. Converts to Islam were exempted from the *jizya* but continued to be liable for the *kharāj* upon their lands. In every province, local custom undermined the efforts of the lawyers to systematise the fiscal regime.

At an early date, the fiscal administration is called the *dīwān* (pl. *dawāwīn*, adj. *dīwānī*). *Dīwān* seems to be a loan-word into Arabic, and its origin is obscure. Most medieval authors derived it from the Persian *dīv*, meaning 'mad' or 'devil':[9] although the latter is a fair description of the tax-man, this etymology is not particularly helpful, and does not explain why, under the earliest caliphs, the first *dīwān* was a register of the Arab troops and their pay. Soon, the word *dīwān* acquired a wide range of meanings cognate with writing and, more particularly, with the collection of written matter. Thus its most common meanings are 'a collection of poems written by one author', and 'an administrative or governmental office'. It is in this last sense that the word is most frequently employed in this study, although it is also used for 'administration' in general.

Under the Umayyads, at the very the end of the 7th and in the 8th century, after the first great conquests were complete and the caliphs came to be increasingly preoccupied with taxing their new empire, the central and pre-eminent office of the fiscal administration seems to have been the *dīwān al-kharāj*. The Umayyad *dīwān al-kharāj*, which was situated in Damascus for at least part of the time, was fed revenue and fiscal data by the subsidiary *dawāwīn al-kharāj* of each province.[10] Each provincial *dīwān* is supposed to have kept records that listed, more or less efficiently and systematically, the extent and the boundaries of the lands taxed, the rates of taxation, the measurements used, and other relevant data. Revenue passed from the provinces, through the *dīwān al-kharāj*, into the *bayt al-māl* or central treasury.[11]

Under the ᶜAbbāsids, from the mid-8th to mid-9th centuries, an elaborate and sophisticated imperial bureaucracy seemed likely to overcome the provincial diversity which had characterised early Islamic institutions. At the same time, there was an unsteady move towards the centralised control of most administrative functions. The development of the office of *wazīr*, or vizier, is characteristic of this process of centralisation;[12] and we shall see how the Norman kings, like any

[9] For example, al-Maqrīzī 1853, vol.I, p.91; al-Maqrīzī 1911–27, vol.II, p.33; al-Maqrīzī, 1895–1920, vol.I, p.260: 'Sur l'origine du mot *divan* il y a deux versions: 1° Cosrou, regardant un jour les écrivains de son *divan*, les vit occupés à compter mentalement e s'écria "*dyouaneh* (les fous)" et ce nom fu donné au lieu où ces employés se réunissaient …; 2° *dyouan* est le nom persan des démons; et cette qualification fut donnée aux comptables parce qu'ils résolvent les affaires, qu'ils connaissent celles qui sont visibles et celles qui sont cachées, qu'ils peuvent rassembler les choses éparses et éloignées et qu'ils connaissent également celles qui sont près et celles qui sont éloignées'.

[10] Løkkegaard 1950, *passim*, esp. pp.143–63; Duri, Gottschalk and Colin 1962, pp.323–4.

[11] Duri, Gottschalk and Colin 1962, pp.324–6.

[12] Sourdel 1959–60; Goitein 1942 and Goitein, 1961 – both reprinted in Goitein 1966, pp.168–96.

contemporary Muslim ruler, also ruled through a vizier. At the same time, the number of separate *dawāwīn*, each with its own distinct responsibilities, tended to proliferate. Each of the principal *dawāwīn* came to have its own *zimām*, a sort of internal audit or controller's office which checked the accounts of the *dīwān*, supervised its business, and acted as an intermediary between the *dīwān* and the other *dawāwīn* and the *wazīr*. By the end of the 8th century, the *zimām al-azimma*, which tended to be under the direct control of the vizier or of his *kātib*, or secretary, had developed as 'the guardian of the rights of the treasury and the people', the office which supervised all the lesser *azimma* and thus the entire central financial administration.[13] We shall see a roughly analogous development in Norman Sicily with the creation of the *dīwān al-taḥqīq* to supervise the activities of the whole royal *dīwān*. After the dismemberment of the caliphate in the mid-9th century, when local administrative traditions tended to reassert themselves in the newly independent provinces, the pattern previously established in the ᶜAbbāsid centre dictated that administrative departments continued to proliferate, and that authority tended to be concentrated in the hands of a vizier or vizier-like official.

It is in Egypt, under the Fāṭimids, the Ayyūbids, and the early Mamlūks, that we can best observe a medieval Islamic fiscal administration at work. Most of our information is derived from administrative handbooks, but such descriptive and sometimes anecdotal accounts can be controlled against the harder evidence of the papyri or other documentary sources, such as the Cairo Geniza. For Fāṭimid Egypt, the chancery manuals composed by Ibn al-Ṣayrafī, under the vizier al-Afḍal Kutayfāt in 1130–1,[14] may be supplemented by references collected from late compilators, such as al-Qalqashandī (d.1418) and al-Maqrīzī (d.1442), who preserve much earlier material, including the important account of the Fāṭimid *dīwān* given by Ibn al-Ṭuwayr (d.1220).[15] In addition, the following Ayyūbid authorities are of particular value: al-Makhzūmī (*fl.*1169–85);[16] Ibn Mammāṭī (d.1209);[17] Ibn Shīth al-Qurashī (*fl. c.*1225);[18] and al-Nābulusī (*fl. c.*1245).[19]

According to the account of Ibn al-Ṭuwayr preserved in later sources, when the Fāṭimids first moved to Egypt, the whole administration was concentrated in a

[13] Løkkegaard 1950, pp.149–50; Duri, Gottschalk and Colin 1962, pp.324–6.

[14] Ibn al-Ṣayrafī 1905; Ibn al-Ṣayrafī 1914; Ibn al-Ṣayrafī 1924. For the period before 1074, the *Akhbār Miṣr* of al-Musabbiḥī (977–1029) must once have constituted a prime source. Only the Arabic text of vol.XL, covering the years 414–15/1023–24, has been published (al-Musabbiḥī 1978–84). The promised translation and annotated commentary has not yet appeared. Thierry Bianquis was kind enough to draw his edition to my attention in June 1986, when he suggested that it might throw light upon the origins of the Fāṭimid *dīwān al-taḥqīq* (see below, pp.195–7, 274). Although the passages relating to the *dīwān al-kharāj* (*ibid.*, vol.I, pp.12, 67, 71, 72) are of some general interest, I can find no reference to the *dīwān al-taḥqīq* in the edited volumes.

[15] al-Maqrīzī 1853, vol.I, pp.397–402. al-Qalqashandī 1913–20, vol.III, pp.490–6; Wüstenfeld 1879, pp.188–95; Björkman 1928, *passim*, esp. pp.17–36. For Ibn al-Ṭuawyr, see Cahen 1937–8, pp.10–14 and p.16, n.1. For a concise summary and instructive interpretation of the economy and fiscal administration of Fāṭimid Egypt in the 10th century, see Brett 2001, pp.275–92, 331–2, 339–44.

[16] Cahen 1962a; Cahen 1962b, pp.22–56; Frantz-Murphy 1986.

[17] Atiya 1968; Ibn Mammātī 1943; Ibn Mammātī 1986.

[18] Ibn Shīth al-Qurashī 1913, pp.23–32.

[19] Cahen 1956; al-Nābulusī 1958–60; Keenan 1999.

single office called the *dīwān al-majlis* ('bureau of the council').[20] Its chief, the *ṣāḥib* or 'lord of the *dīwān al-majlis*', was responsible for allocating *iqṭāᶜāt* ('estates')[21] in the post-conquest redistribution of the land of Egypt, and these grants were recorded in the *daftar al-majlis* or 'register of the council'. This essentially decision-making office worked in tandem with the chancery, known variously as the *dīwān al-inshāʾ*, *dīwān al-rasāʾil*, or *dīwān al-mukātabāt* – all titles which refer to its role as a writing office. The chancery issued decrees, diplomas, and letters-patent, and answered appeals and letters addressed to the caliph. It kept an elaborate archive of originals and copies, and its lesser officials included a *khāzin* (literally 'treasurer') who carefully preserved original documents,[22] a *nāsikh* ('copyist'), and a filing-clerk who kept copies and digests in *tadhākir* ('memoranda') and *dafātir* ('registers'), so that they could be available for consultation and as models for later documents.[23] Ibn al-Ṣayrafī explains that the head of the chancery (*dīwān al-rasāʾil*) was, in effect, the *wazīr* of the caliph. He argues at great length that its head and its chief-scribe should always be Muslims and never *dhimmī*s; but we know from other sources that the Fāṭimids often employed Christians and Jews to be the leading officers in their administration.[24] In time, the chancery came to have its own supervisor's office, known as the *dīwān al-naẓar* ('bureau of supervision'), and as the *ṣaḥāba* or 'lords of the *dīwān al-inshāʾ wa-l-mukātabāt*', headed by an official sometimes called the *ṣāḥib dīwān al-inshāʾ*. It is easy to see why Ibn Shīth al-Qurashī regarded the *dīwān al-inshāʾ* as the most important office of government even though, by the time he was writing, the number of lesser *dawāwīn*, each with its particular responsibilities, had grown enormously. Amongst these, for example, was the *dīwān al-juyūsh* ('bureau of the troops') which kept up-to-date *jarāʾid* ('registers') of the names and fiefs of all *iqṭāᶜ*-holders. As we shall see, many features of this structure and many of the terms employed for officials and records reappear, transformed, in Norman Sicily. Indeed, a strong case will be made that it was largely upon the model of the Fāṭimid administration that the Norman *dīwān* was reconstituted under Roger II.

The administrative system inherited by the Fāṭimids on their arrival in Egypt in 969–73 was essentially that of their predecessors, the ᶜAbbāsid, Ṭūlūnid and Ikhshīdid governors, but, by the end of the 11th century, the *dīwān al-amwāl*, or financial administration, had undergone considerable development and had expanded to contain a dozen or more subsidiary *dawāwīn*.[25] After 1074, when important changes were made to the Fāṭimid administration, the fiscal and military

[20] al-Maqrīzī 1853, vol.I, pp.397–400; Duri, Gottschalk and Colin 1962, pp.328–9.

[21] For the controversial subject of the *iqṭāᶜ*, see Cahen 1970, with bibliography up to 1969. For the Fāṭimid *iqṭāᶜ*, see Brett 1984, pp.44–56 – a review of Udovitch 1981 – and Frantz-Murphy 1999, pp.255–63. For Mamlūk Egypt, see Rabie 1972, pp.26–72 and Brett 1995. For the *rawk*, see Rabie 1972, pp.49–56 and Halm 1979–82, vol.I, pp.8–34.

[22] Ibn al-Ṣayrafī 1905, pp.142–4, 146–7; Ibn al-Ṣayrafī 1914, pp.108–10, 111–12.

[23] Ibn al-Ṣayrafī 1905, pp.137–41; Ibn al-Ṣayrafī 1914, pp.104–8.

[24] Ibn al-Ṣayrafī 1905, pp.94–7; Ibn al-Ṣayrafī 1914, pp.79–83.

[25] Duri, Gottschalk and Colin 1962, pp.326–7, 328–30; Rabie 1972, pp.144–9.

responsibilities of the provincial governors of Egypt were clearly separated. Fiscal administration, at the provincial level, came to be the responsibility of the *ᶜāmil* or *mushārif*, the district tax-official directly responsible to the *dīwān al-amwāl*.[26] This was also the case in Sicily under both Muslim and Norman rule.[27] Amongst their duties was the compilation of the *qawānīn* (sing. *qānūn*), or cadastral registers, used to levy the *kharāj*. These were supposed to be compiled twice a year, in the spring and autumn, by cadastral agents, updating the previous cadastral registers for their localities. The *qawānīn* were supposed to register all *kharāj*-lands, and to list for each its name, surface area, crop in the coming fiscal year, position with regard to the Nile flood, and tax-status, which was determined by an assessment of such variables as the nature and estimated yield of the crop to be grown. Estimates of production were made on the basis of known yields of the same land in previous years, and the situation of the land with regard to the flood.[28] Although no records as complex and elaborate as the Egyptian *qawānīn* survive from Norman Sicily, the *dafātir al-ḥudūd*, or registers of land-boundaries, compiled and maintained by the Norman *dīwān*, are broadly comparable and served, amongst other purposes, to collect the *qānūn* or land-tax from the royal demesne.

From at least the 8th century, the Muslim rulers of Egypt periodically undertook a *rawk*, a peculiarly Egyptian term for a general cadastral survey of all the land under cultivation, on the basis of which the levels of taxation were fixed and, from Fāṭimid times, the *iqṭāᶜāt* or tax-farms reassigned. Such general surveys of Egyptian cultivated land seem to have been sporadic and irregular.[29] This was especially the case before (but continued to be so after) the *rawk* of al-Afḍal ibn Badr al-Jamālī (501/1107–8), which appears to have been the first of what was intended to be a regular, approximately thirty-year cycle of *rawk*s, timed to coincide with the periodic adjustment of the fiscal calendar, necessitated by the discrepancy between the lunar financial year and the solar agricultural year.[30] The Afḍalī *rawk* was intended to revalue the *iqṭāᶜāt* according to their (average?) yield in 500/1106–7, which had obviously come to differ widely from the previous valuation (in *c.*1076?). There must always have existed something of a dual system in Egypt, with a degree of tension between the biannual valuations and the periodic valuations of the *iqṭāᶜāt*, which could be granted for periods as short as four years or for as long as the active life of the recipient. The institution of the *rawk* may have been intended to remove such anomalies from the system. Given the long intervals between *rawk*s, it comes as no surprise that al-Afḍal (*c.*1089–1121) and his successor al-Baṭāʾiḥī (1121–30) discovered that there had been extensive usurpation of the state demesne by private landlords. The Afḍalī *rawk*, the primary purpose of which was to redistribute the *iqṭāᶜāt* held by the troops, revealed that

[26] See Cahen 1972, pp.271–2.
[27] Below, pp.24–5, 29–30, 145, 170–1, 175, 184–5.
[28] Frantz-Murphy 1986, *passim*. See also: Rabie 1972, pp.73–9; Cooper 1974; Cooper 1976; Cahen 1962a, pp.258–75; Ibn Mammātī 1943, *passim*, esp. pp.258–70; Cahen 1956, pp.13–17.
[29] Rabie 1972, pp.50–51.
[30] Rabie 1972, pp.133–34; Brett 1984, p.51.

some large landholders already claimed as their own property the state lands which they were now to hold as *iqṭāʿāt*.[31] A little later, in the 1120s, al-Baṭāʾiḥī discovered that landholders, large and small, had been systematically usurping lands from the state demesne and adding them to their own estates.[32] The way in which such cadastral surveys and enquiries, instituted primarily for reasons of fiscal administration, also provided the means to control the integrity of the state demesne, is closely analogous, as we shall see, to the way in which King Roger's recall and reissue of privileges (1144–5) also served to reveal and to limit the usurpation of lands and villeins from the royal demesne.[33]

The *jizya*, too, was collected on the basis of annual registers, called *jarāʾid*, which were supposed to constitute a complete and accurate fiscal record of the *dhimmī* population during the last month of the (fiscal) year. The basic information for the *jarāʾid* was collected by *ḥushshār* ('gatherers'), aided by the *adillāʾ* (literally, 'guides'). They recorded a wide range of variables for each tax-payer, including his name, the year in which he attained his fiscal majority, and any distinguishing physical characteristics. At least three groups of non-tax-payers were listed separately from the majority: absentees, converts to Islam, and those who had died during the current fiscal year. The names of the tax-payers were arranged in alphabetical order and each register was made in two or more copies. In most areas, there were three levels of assessment according to the wealth of the tax-payer. Various categories of the *dhimmī* population were exempted from the *jizya*, including the aged, women, children, the insane, slaves and monks. The taxable population fell into three classes: *rātib* ('established'), who paid at the standard rate; *nashʾ* ('new generation'), first-time tax-payers who had attained their fiscal majority during the current year; and *ṭarīy* ('newcomer'), new arrivals to the region.[34] It is likely that the latter two classes received, for an introductory period, some form of reduction of the standard rate of tax.[35] As we shall see, similar practices governed the collection of the *jizya* from the Muslims and Jews of Norman Sicily.

The fiscal administration of Ifrīqiya

The sophisticated fiscal apparatus of Muslim Egypt reflects the peculiar circumstances of Nilotic agriculture and the rich heritage of indigenous fiscal techniques

31 al-Maqrīzī 1853, vol.I, p.83; Maqrīzī 1911–27, vol.II, pp.5–6; al-Maqrīzī 1895–20, vol.I, pp.238–9; Rabie 1972, pp.27–8, 51; Brett 1984, p.52.

32 al-Maqrīzī 1853, vol.I, p.85; al-Maqrīzī 1911–27, vol.II, pp.11–13; al-Maqrīzī 1895–20, vol.I, pp.243–4; Brett 1984, p.53.

33 Below, pp.115–43

34 Rabie 1972, pp.108–13, 134–6; Goitein, 1967–93, vol.II, pp.380–94; Cahen, 1962a, pp.248–52; Ibn Mammātī 1943, pp.304–6, 317–19; Cahen 1956, pp.21–2.

35 For similar classes in Norman Sicily, see below, pp.47–8, 55–7.

inherited by the Arab conquerors. Before moving towards Sicily, by way of Ifrīqiya, it will be as well to note John Hopkins' cautionary remarks. In the Maghrib, he says,

> administration was in general an *ad hoc* affair, subject to the whim of whoever happened at the moment to be capable of exercising his authority. There were few standard practices or methods of appointment, little specialization, no hierarchization, no well defined channels for the stream of government business. The officials were often hardly officials in the modern sense. Apart from the vagueness of their attributions, they had no special training or skill, might be appointed (or dismissed) for purely personal or political reasons [and so]
>
> ... definitions of government functions may only be formulated in general terms and accepted with reserve. Every case must be considered on its merits.[36]

In fact, we know very little of the fiscal administration of early Islamic Ifrīqiya and Hopkins' book, which is the only study devoted exclusively to the subject, concentrates upon Almohad administration and government. Before the late 12th century, it is possible to collect only scattered and predominantly anecdotal references to departments or officials.

The moment when this gloom lifts briefly coincides with the advent of the Fāṭimids. Hopkins notes confidently that, 'It is obvious that the Fāṭimids had an administration with a certain degree of departmentalization from the very beginning'.[37] He suggests that what appear to be Fāṭimid administrative innovations are the work of ᶜAbd Allāh al-Mahdī (909–34), who tried to introduce oriental practices in an attempt to rationalise the administration of his new state.[38] This is surely unlikely: al-Mahdī had no experience of office in the East, no expert knowledge of oriental administrative practices, and no retinue of professional administrators. While little is known of Aghlabid administration, Michael Brett has discerned the development of quite highly evolved fiscal techniques,[39] and Mohammed Talbi has attributed considerable administrative and financial ability to Ibrāhīm II (875–902).[40] Just as the Fāṭimids were to inherit, and then to adapt and reform, the Ikhshīdid administration of Egypt after the migration of 969–73, so, in Ifrīqiya, what appeared to Hopkins to be Fāṭimid innovation may in fact be nothing more than skilful reorganisation of the existing Aghlabid system. There is strong evidence that the Fāṭimids took over the Aghlabid administration complete with its officers, who had been Ḥanafīs, and now converted to Ismāᶜīlism.[41] The fact that we are better informed about Fāṭimid than about Aghlabid administration reflects a (temporary) improvement in the quantity and in the quality of the narrative sources, especially biography, rather than any major change in administrative practice.[42]

36 Hopkins 1958, pp.1–2.
37 Hopkins 1958, p.6.
38 Hopkins 1958, p.33.
39 Brett 1978, pp.594–9.
40 Talbi 1966, pp.250–6, 258–60, 265–73.
41 Nagel 1972, pp.38–44.
42 For Fāṭimid fiscal administration in Ifrīqiya, see now Brett 2001, 257–66.

Both the *dīwān al-kharāj* and the mint were initially left in the hands of their Aghlabid officials, although the *bayt al-māl* or treasury, the pre-eminent office of the financial administration, was entrusted to one of al-Mahdī's household slaves. Indeed, one of the characteristics of the Fāṭimid regime in Ifrīqiya was to be the near monopolisation of the great offices of the central administration by the personal slaves of the ruler: a similar development was later to characterise the Arabic administration of Norman Sicily. Similarly, loyal supporters were given charge of the two financial offices upon which the strength of al-Mahdī's state chiefly depended – the *dīwān al–ḍiyāᶜ*, which administered property abandoned by, or confiscated from, the Aghlabids and their clients; and the *dīwān al-ᶜaṭāʾ*, which disbursed salaries and pensions to al-Mahdī's followers.[43]

After the transfer of the central administration from Aghlabid Raqqāda to Fāṭimid al-Mahdīya, the financial offices were housed around the *dār al-muḥāsabāt* ('the Court of Accounts') in the palace. Al-Qāʾim (934–46) now appointed Jawdhar, one of his household slaves, to oversee the whole financial administration. Jawdhar's biography, written by another Fāṭimid slave and financial officer, constitutes the principal source for the organisation of Fāṭimid finances in Ifrīqiya. Jawdhar's title, on his appointment, was *nāẓir fī bayt al-māl* ('superintendent in the treasury'), and he was assisted by another of the caliph's household slaves, Nuṣayr, who held the office of *al-khāzin* ('treasurer'). Jawdhar's importance grew rapidly under al-Qāʾim and al-Manṣūr (946–53) so that he assumed the role of *safīr* or 'intermediary', both between the caliph and his officials, and between the two branches of the administration, civil and military.[44] According to his biographer, Jawdhar co-ordinated all the business of the administration, and submitted to the caliph written digests of only those matters which required the ruler's personal attention: Jawdhar 'left a blank space on the scroll of paper between each digest and in each of these the imam … would write in his own hand what was to be done'.[45] Soon after the accession of al-Muᶜizz (953–75), Jawdhar was transferred, together with the central administration, from al-Mahdīya to the new caliphal capital, al-Manṣūrīya. Here, the financial administration came to be known by the generic title of the *dīwān al-Manṣūrīya*, but three distinct departments can be dimly perceived: the *bayt al-māl* or 'public treasury'; the *dawāwīn al-jibāyāt* or 'offices of taxation'; and the *khāṣṣīyat bayt al-māl*, the caliph's private treasury.[46]

During the preparations for the migration to Egypt, al-Muᶜizz made various reorganisations to the financial administration in order to assure himself of the necessary funds. The general Jawhar (not to be confused with Jawdhar), who was to be the eventual commander of the expedition of 969, was given special responsibility for this task. In 967, he was dispatched to Tripolitania to raise troops and money, and Nuṣayr was temporarily installed at al-Manṣūrīya in his place. When

[43] Dachraoui 1981, pp.280–1, 323–4, 333.
[44] al-Manṣūr al-Jawdharī 1954, p.39; Canard 1957b, pp.51–3. See also Canard 1957a.
[45] al-Manṣūr al-Jawdharī 1954, p.86; Canard, 1957b, pp.125–6.
[46] Dachraoui 1981, pp.305–9, 325–6.

Jawhar returned, he resumed his old duties while Nuṣayr was sent east to organise the naval expedition. In the absence of Jawhar and Nuṣayr, the financial administration went into severe decline, suggesting that Jawdhar's own talents did not extend to the minutiae of fiscal administration, and that he had previously relied upon Jawhar, Nuṣayr, and their staff. Jawdhar remained in office, subject to stern caliphal censure, and the financial expert Yaᶜqūb ibn Killis, a defector from the Ikhshīdid regime in Egypt, was given charge of the fisc.[47]

The revenues administered by the financial apparatus were essentially two: the personal income of the caliph, which mostly derived from the Ismāᶜīlī community; and the *jibāyāt al-māl*, public taxes. It is only the latter which concern us here, but once again, our sources are far from perfect. Farhat Dachraoui writes of 'un régime complexe et obscur, sur lesquels les sources historiographiques, biographiques ou géographiques, à défaut de documents techniques, n'apportent qu'une clarté infime'.[48] Al-Mahdī seems to have concentrated upon the restoration and repair of the Aghlabid fiscal system, to which end the Aghlabid cadastral officer Ibn al-Qadīm was left in place and given the task of recreating the cadastral registers destroyed during the flight of the Aghlabid court.[49] Ibn al-Qadīm was replaced in 915–16 by another Aghlabid survivor, the Ḥanafī jurist ᶜImrūn ibn Aḥmad: under his influence, the cadaster was extended to include all cultivated lands upon which the *kharāj* was levied. The burden of the *kharāj* was distributed according to a rigid formula (*taqsīṭ*, literally 'payment in instalments'): the recorded maximum and minimum annual returns of the tithe (*ᶜushr*) were added together and then halved to give the target income from the *kharāj*, which was then gathered throughout the country in proportion to the size of the holdings recorded in the cadaster. In other words, it was the size of a holding, and not its productivity, that determined its taxable value. Extraordinary exactions were levied under the guise of arrears owing upon the *taqsīṭ* since the establishment of the regime. A wide range of other taxes, customs and duties were imposed, most of which were uncanonical, and provoked discontent, opposition, and active evasion.[50]

The overall picture, albeit dimly perceived, is one of considerable complexity, and reveals an active fiscal administration which sought to extend Fāṭimid control widely over the day-to-day business of agriculture, trade and commerce, in order to finance the imperial ambitions of the regime. Although both administrative structure and fiscal measures confirm that the Fāṭimids built upon Aghlabid foundations, they extended their control largely through *ad hoc* innovations, which originated in the caliphal household, and behind which can be discerned no guiding principle. The financial apparatus left by the Fāṭimids to their Zīrid successors was

[47] al-Manṣūr al-Jawdharī 1954, pp.118–19; Canard 1957b, pp.178–80 and n.402, p.214 n.469; Dachraoui 1981, pp.254–6, 326–7. See also: Monés 1975; Canard 1968; Brett 2001, pp.289, 298, 332, 338–40.

[48] For a more optimistic attitude and for more instructive conclusions, see Halm 1996, 149–54, 265–6, 355–65.

[49] This is curiously reminiscent of the task entrusted to Matthew of Salerno after the Norman registers were destroyed in the rebellion of 1160: see below, p.164, 177, 180.

[50] Dachraoui 1981, pp.331–40.

a far larger and more complicated edifice than that which they had themselves inherited from the Aghlabids, but the extent to which it survived the migration of the dynasty and its servants, and its influence upon the subsequent development of Zīrid finances, is far from clear.

For, after the move of the Fāṭimid court to Egypt, the fog descends again. Of the Zīrids, Hady Roger Idris states dejectedly, 'l'organisation administrative nous échappe complètement',[51] and one cannot but sympathise with this exaggeration. Although it appears to have been the intention of al-Muᶜizz to separate the financial from the civil administration of Ifrīqiya before he set out for Egypt, putting an end to the administrative co-ordination attained through Jawdhar and the office of *safīr*,[52] it was soon after his departure that these two sets of responsibilities were again combined in a single official.[53] From *c.*980 until the rule of Tamīm (1062–1108), a succession of powerful chief ministers, bearing a variety of official titles, were entrusted with the control of the whole administration.[54] With the accession of Tamīm, the financial and civil administrations were again separated and the power of the vizier was consequently limited. For a time, under Tamīm, the financial administration was apparently the responsibility of George of Antioch and his family, who was later to become the chief minister of Roger II of Sicily.[55]

The apparatus of financial administration, *al-ashghāl* or *al-amwāl*, is not to be traced in detail.[56] There was clearly some degree of centralisation for we find the *bayt al-māl* and other financial offices, known by the collective title of the *dīwān*, housed at al-Manṣūrīya until its destruction.[57] As one might expect, the *dīwān al-kharāj* appears to have been the principal financial office and there is mention, for example, of the *aṣḥāb* or 'lords of the *kharāj*' in 984–5,[58] and of the *ṣāḥib kharāj al-maghrib* or 'lord of the land-tax of the West' in the late 10th or early 11th century.[59] One has the distinct impression, however, that provincial tax officials, the *wulāt al-ashghāl*,[60] exercised a greater degree of independent authority within the fiscal system than had been the case under the Fāṭimids and than was the case in contemporary Egypt, and that the advance of centralisation which had characterised the years of Fāṭimid rule was considerably slowed, if not actually reversed.

The fiscal administration of Muslim Sicily

Paradoxically, we are rather better informed about Sicily, the fiscal administration of which one would expect to have been closely modelled upon that of Ifrīqiya. When the Arab invaders arrived in the mid-9th century, they found a working fiscal system throughout most of the island. Nonetheless, the extent to which

[51] Idris 1962a, vol.II, p.525.
[52] Idris 1962a, vol.I, pp.41–7, esp. p.45 and nn.19–20.
[53] Idris 1962a, vol.II, pp.514–15.
[54] Idris 1962a, vol.II, pp.515–18.
[55] Below, pp.74, 80–8, 282–3.
[56] Idris 1962a, vol.II, pp.543–8.
[57] Idris 1962a, vol.II, p.514.
[58] Idris 1962a, vol.II, p.545.
[59] Idris 1962a, vol.II, p.546.
[60] Idris 1962a, vol.II, p.544.

the Muslim fiscal administration of Sicily was derived from, or made use of, the Byzantine fiscal institutions existing on the island at the time of the conquest remains problematic because so little is yet known of the administration of Byzantine Sicily.

By the 6th century, when Belisarius annexed Sicily to the Eastern Empire, the golden days of the tithe or *decuma*, administered according to the *Lex Hieronica*, were long gone (if they had ever existed outside Cicero's oratory) and centuries of latifundism had succeeded. The steady accretion of land into *massae fundorum* owned by absentee landlords – patrician, imperial and, later, ecclesiastical and papal – led to the growth of a system of tenancy. By the 4th century, the typical landlord (*possessor*), away in the North, entrusted his affairs to an agent (*actor* or *rector*) who leased out parcels of land to entrepreneurs (*conductores*). Other landlords dealt directly with the *conductores*. These, in turn, sublet to the farmers who actually worked the land (*coloni*). In addition to the rents, fines and perquisites owed to the *possessor*, the *coloni* were also subject to imperial taxes. One suspects that the collection of these may have become less efficient after the confiscation of the vast papal estates by the iconoclast emperor Leo III in *c.*730. From the late 7th century, Sicily had been established as a theme, or military province, and, for the subsequent period, we have but a few scattered references to the fiscal officials of the theme. The civil administration was headed by the *prōtonotarios tou thematou*, the chief official of the central treasury in the theme. We have also the names of a few Sicilian *chartoularioi*, *prōtonotarioi*, and also *logothetai tou stratiotikou*, the officials responsible for financial accounts and for the provincial cadastral registers. It is worth noting that a roughly comparable administrative hierarchy persisted into Norman times on the mainland.[61]

While there is no hard evidence that the Muslims of Sicily did incorporate pre-existing Byzantine elements into their fiscal regime on the island, it is almost inconceivable that they did not base their administration, as much as possible, upon the existing fiscal apparatus. The Muslim laws of conquest, and the practices whereby *dhimmī* communities were incorporated into the Muslim state, are bound to have required the continuation of a large proportion of pre-conquest boundary divisions and fiscal arrangements. This alone is likely to have ensured the continuation of the apparatus of Byzantine land taxation. In particular, Christian communities in eastern Sicily were taken under Muslim rule according to the principle, itself ultimately derived from pre-Islamic east Mediterranean practice,[62] of autonomous communal organisation. Therefore, Byzantine fiscal institutions are likely to have survived at the local level. It should be remembered, however, that the Muslim conquerors of Sicily, unlike the Arab conquerors of the 1st century of the Hegira, were heirs to a developed Islamic fiscal regime; and this is likely to

[61] Holm 1870–98, vol.III, pp.282–337, 499–512; Borsari 1954, pp.149–51; Cracco Ruggini 1995, pp.296–321, 409–10, 412–15, 465–6; von Falkenhausen 1978, pp.111–29, 142–4; Guillou, 1975–6, pp.47–56, 67–9; Wilson 1990, pp.330–7. Below, pp.43–5, 60–1.

[62] For Byzantium, see Schacht 1957, pp.205–6; for Sassanian Iraq, Morony 1974, esp. p.119, and Morony 1984, pp.106–11.

have been of as great significance as any indigenous system, especially in those areas first conquered and most thoroughly Arabicised.

Turning to the evidence from the Muslim period, we possess no information whatsoever for the 9th-century fiscal administration. The existence of what should probably be interpreted as a central financial administration, based in Palermo, is first attested in the early 10th century, at the beginning of Fāṭimid rule. There is reference to the *ṣāḥib al-khums* ('lord of the fifth') at Palermo in 913:[63] this was probably an official responsible for the administration and collection of the *khums* according to Shīᶜī law, being the fifth part of all revenues, not just of the produce of land acquired by the Muslims through capture or unconditional surrender that was allowed by the Sunnīs.[64] A degree of proliferation and diversification within the financial administration is suggested by a reference from 947–8 to the *aṣḥāb al-dawāwīn* ('the lords of the *dīwāns*') at Palermo.[65] According to Ibn Ḥawqal, who visited the capital in 973, part of the papyrus grown in Palermo was reserved for the use of the sultan and used in the manufacture of the *ṭawāmīr* or scrolls of his administration. Ibn Ḥawqal also records that the *dīwān* – by which word he presumably meant the entire administration – was housed in al-Khāliṣa, the separate governmental quarter founded by the Fāṭimid governor in *c.*937.[66] It seems likely that, after the capture of Palermo in 831, the administrative centre of the Muslims in Sicily had previously been located in al-Qaṣr, on or near the site of what may well have been the Byzantine governor's palace, and was later to become the palace of the Norman kings, where their Arabic administration was housed.

Our most informative 10th-century source is a chapter of the *Kitāb al-amwāl* of al-Dāwudī, an Ifrīqiyan jurist who died in 1011. As Claude Cahen has pointed out, al-Dāwudī's work bears witness to the confusion of Maghribī jurists as to the precise interpretation of the *sharīᶜa* with regard to taxation:[67] it is therefore a source to be used with considerable care. The passage quoted below suggests that while a central fiscal administration, presumably based in Palermo, had authority over all the island under Muslim control, local centres maintained their own tax-registers, which were the responsibility of *amīns* or local tax-officials. The case is worth examining in some detail for it constitutes our sole account of the apparatus of the Muslim fiscal administration of the island.

Following a rebellion of the Muslim settlers of Agrigento against the sultan – no date is given, but the revolt intended may be that of 937–40 against the Fāṭimid governor, which Khalīl ibn Isḥāq al-Tamīmī was sent from Qayrawān to quell[68] – the town was depopulated and then resettled with colonists drawn from all over Sicily and from Ifrīqiya. Amongst them were some descendants of the original

[63] *BAS*², vol.I, p.167; *BAS*²*(It.)*, vol.I, pp.227–8: this passage is not found in the Greek version (Cozza-Luzi 1890a); Amari 1933–9, vol.II, pp.169, 171, 174, 179 n.1. For the *ṣāḥib al-khums*, see below, p.25. Alternatively, he may have been in charge of the collection of import duties from foreign merchants: see below, p.27. [64] Halm 1996, p.177.

[65] Ibn al-Athīr 1851–76, vol.VIII, p.355; *BAS*², vol.I, p.301; *BAS*²*(It.)*, vol.II, p.337.

[66] Ibn Ḥawqal 1938–9, p.122; Ibn Ḥawqal 1964, vol.I, p.121.

[67] Cahen 1977a, p.1032. [68] Halm 1996, 284–86.

settlers of Agrigento. Subsequently, a few of the latter and some of their descendants appealed to the sultan (one of the early Kalbids may be the ruler intended) to respect their prior rights and expel the newcomers. The sultan demanded that they substantiate their claims with documentary proof and, when they were unable to do so, he ruled that the town was *fay*ᵓ – or conquered booty belonging to the community of Muslims. He questioned some of the oldest *shaykh*s in Sicily as to the status of Agrigento:

> One of them replied, 'All the tax-registers (*dawāwīn*) were under the control of my father and he was lord of the fifth (*ṣāḥib al-khums*) of that town, and of its *kharāj*, and he was *amīn* over it. I was able to read [in the registers]: "This fortress [*i.e.* Agrigento] is confirmed in the register. Every year its population contributes a collective tax and every estate in it is taxable. It is the property of the treasury of the Muslims". However, the register was burnt in the days of Khalīl [ibn Isḥāq] ibn al-Ward'.[69]

As it stands, this story appears to be a literary device in which the verbal testimony of an individual witness, traditionally given more weight in Islamic law than a mere document, is reinforced by reference to a conveniently destroyed register. It is immaterial for our purposes whether or not the events described actually occurred, for the details of administrative practice, employed to give credence to the story, are likely to be authentic for the time at which al-Dāwudī was writing. The story may thus be taken as reliable evidence that, at the beginning of the 11th century (if not earlier), the provincial town of Agrigento had an *amīn* responsible for the fiscal administration of its territory. For tax purposes, its lands were divided into those upon which the *khums* was due, and those which were assessed for the *kharāj*: the distinction is the classic one between land conquered by force and land acquired by treaty.[70] The *amīn* maintained written tax-registers or *dawāwīn*. There is thus some reason to infer that all *khums*-lands and *kharāj*-lands in Sicily were administered by central fiscal offices at Palermo through local tax-offices, headed by *amīn*s who kept their own records.

The organisation for the celebration of the circumcision of the son of the Fāṭimid imam al-Muᶜizz during the month of Rabīᶜ I 351 (April 962) also indicates the existence in Sicily of sophisticated administrative structures. Edicts went out from al-Mahdīya to every corner of the Fāṭimid realm, from Barqa to Sijilmāsa, 'as far as the island of Sicily', commanding the entire population to have their sons circumcised during the month following the circumcision of the imam's own sons, and forbidding those who disobeyed from having their sons circumcised thereafter for a period of seven years. An elaborate festival was organised outside the Qaṣr al-Baḥr in al-Mahdīya, and substantial sums were dispatched to the provinces so that their governors could stage similar festivities and make lavish presents of money and clothing to the obedient fathers. In Sicily, the Kalbid governor was ordered to take a census of Muslim male infants, and fifteen thousand boys are said to have been circumcised; fifty coffers of cash were sent to the island, and one hundred thousand

[69] al-Dāwudī 1962, pp.416–18, 436–8.

[70] See above, pp.13–14. Dachraoui 1981, p.334.

dirhams were distributed in money, in addition to clothing and presents to the value of fifty thousand dirhams.[71] We need not accept the figures, but the account may nonetheless indicate the sophistication of Sicily's administrative apparatus.

For the 11th century, the narrative sources are rather less informative. Yāqūt quotes some verses collected by Ibn al-Qaṭṭāᶜ (a Sicilian poet born in 1041 who survived into the 12th century), and composed by a certain Abū l-Ḥasan ᶜAlī ibn Abī Isḥāq al-Waddānī to whom Ibn al-Qaṭṭāᶜ gives the title *ṣāḥib al-dīwān bi-Ṣiqillīya*.[72] It may be that here we see the administration of the island concentrated in the hands of a single, vizier-like official.

A second reference to the 11th century is rather more revealing, and suggests a similar development. Writing of the abdication of the emir Jaᶜfar ibn Yūsuf in 1019–20, Ibn al-Athīr explains that this was caused by Jaᶜfar's appointment of a tax-official who 'pressed hard upon them [the Sicilians] and took the tithe of their crops'.[73] Al-Nuwayrī, writing still longer after the event, but with some sources independent of Ibn al-Athīr, names the official as Jaᶜfar's secretary (*kātib*), al-Ḥasan ibn Muḥammad al-Bāghāʾī, and says that he had advised Jaᶜfar 'to take from Sicily the tithe of their crop and of their profits,' (or '... of their grain crop and of their fruit' – *min ṭaᶜāmi-him wa-thimāri-him*) 'according to the custom of other countries; for that custom had never been imposed upon them because, there, it was the custom to levy a fixed amount upon each plough-land, whatever happened to the crop'.[74]

According to this anecdote, it would seem that the practice in Sicily, as in 10th-century Ifrīqiya, had been to assess cultivated land at a fixed rate per ploughland, irrespective of the actual yield in any given year. Jaᶜfar, or rather al-Bāghāʾī, presumably estimated that the fixed rate system would yield less overall than a tithe of the crop, and tried accordingly to reform the system. If this were so, it would mark an attempt, albeit an unsuccessful one, to move away from a relatively primitive system of fixed rate assessment towards a more flexible and sophisticated apparatus – one paralleled in the Afḍalī *rawk* of 1107–8.[75]

As to the *jizya* and its collection, the matter is complicated. In practice, the *jizya* was of three sorts, according to whether it was levied upon individuals, or on the land, or was a collective tribute unrelated to any kind of census or cadastral assessment.[76] All three varieties are to be found in Sicily. The collective tribute occurred most frequently during the period of Muslim expansion into eastern Sicily, before *c.*902, and was then a tribute, a formal and material acknowledgement of Muslim military superiority, and a sort of protection money paid by Christian communities in return for temporary immunity from Muslim raids.[77] Al-Dāwudī constitutes our sole written source for the other two varieties of *jizya*. He suggests that Sicilian Christians who came to terms with the Muslims, even if they had previously offered resistance by force, might become *dhimmī*s under one of two kinds of treaty.

[71] al-Qāḍī l-Nuᶜmān 1978, pp.556–8; al-Maqrīzī, 1967–73, vol.I, 94–6; Halm 1996, 401–2; Pellitteri 1994, pp.138–40.

[72] Yāqūt 1866–73, p.381; *BAS*², vol.I, p.142; *BAS*²*(It.)*, vol.I, p.179.

[73] Ibn al-Athīr 1851–76, vol.X, p.130; *BAS*², vol.I, p.316; *BAS*²*(It.)*, vol.II, p.353.

[74] *BAS*², vol.II, p.496; *BAS*²*(It.)*, vol.II, pp.548–49.

[75] Above, pp.17–18.

[76] Cahen 1963b, p.559.

[77] For example, Ibn al-Athīr 1851–76, vol.V, p.141; vol.VI, p.236; vol.VII, p.197; vol. VIII, p.371; *BAS*², vol.I, pp.267, 270, 288, 304; *BAS*²*(It.)*, vol.II, pp.301, 304, 322, 340.

Under the first, *dhimmī*s agreed to pay a capitation tax (*ᶜalā jamājimi-him al-jizya*) and, in consequence, retained full property rights over their lands and could dispose of them as they wished. Under the second, *dhimmī*s agreed not merely to the capitation (*jizya ᶜalā l-jamājim*) but, also, to a regular tribute to be levied upon their lands (*jizya ᶜalā l-arḍ*), and thereby forfeited the right to dispose freely of their lands. If a *dhimmī*, under this second kind of treaty, converted to Islam, he was automatically exempted from both varieties of the *jizya*, and thus acquired the right freely to dispose of his lands.[78]

There may also be archaeological evidence for the poll-tax in Sicily. A 'hoard' of nine lead and copper seals, bearing the titles and dates of Aghlabid rulers for the years *c.*856–907, have been identified as seals that were attached to the necks of *dhimmī*s as receipts of payment of the *jizya*.[79] There is some reason to believe that the class of *dhimmī*s liable to wear such seals was not settled on the land, at least in Iraq.[80] This does not fit the evidence from Sicily where the seals were reported to have been found buried together in a single 'hoard', which would seem to suggest that, if they are indeed receipts of payment of the *jizya*, they belonged to a settled family unit, possibly one belonging to the class described by al-Dāwudī as paying *jizya* upon its lands.

The letters of Jewish merchants trading in Sicily preserved in the Cairo Geniza contain many complaints about taxation and, especially, about the duties on goods imported by non-Muslims: nearly all date from *c.*1020–68, from the last decades of Kalbid rule until shortly before the Norman capture of Palermo. One letter, written before 1020, provides some indication of the rate of the *jizya* under Kalbid rule. The writer complains about the 'penalties' (*ᶜoneshīm*) of four and one-third *tarì* per head imposed upon the Jews for several years, in addition to the ordinary *jizya* (*mas*) of thirteen *tarì* ('quarter-dinars'): 'a great burden of over seventeen *tarì*. They [the Jews] were sorry and preferred death to life. Most of them are poor and destitute. Through fear of the rulers, many went bankrupt, and unfortunately some fled overseas'. This may not be mere rhetoric – the total amounts to a little under four-and-a-half dinars, which, in contemporary Egypt, was the highest yearly rate.[81]

In these letters, import duty is often referred to by a generic term for 'tax', but was more specifically called a 'tithe' (*ᶜushr*) or a 'fifth' (*khums*). An official called the 'lord of the fifth' (*ṣāḥib al-khums*) administered the duty, assisted by a *ghulām* ('slave', or possibly 'clerk'), by customs officers known as *ᶜashshārūn* ('tithers'), and by 'raiders' (*ghuzāh*), as the rapacious collectors seem to have been called.[82] The *ᶜushr* was normally levied only upon foreign merchants, and it was clearly

[78] al-Dāwudī 1962, pp.411–12, 431–2. [79] Balog 1979.

[80] Løkkegaard 1950, pp.139–40. The intriguing matter of *jizya*-seals is currently being investigated by Chase Robinson, my colleague at The Oriental Institute, Oxford.

[81] Gil 1983, vol.II, no.45, pp.75–7, line 15; Simonsohn 1997, no.39, pp.39–40, line 15 ('sanctions'); Gil 1995, p.142. Egyptian rates: Goitein 1967–93, vol.II, pp.387–8.

[82] *Ghulām ṣāḥib al-khums*: Gil 1997, vol.II, no.201, pp.590–5, lines 24–5; Simonsohn 1997, no.32, pp.23–6, line 24 ('the clerk of the owner of the *khums*'); Gil 1995, p.142. *ᶜAshshārūn*: Gil 1997, vol.III, no.453, pp.515–19, right margin, line 6; Simonsohn 1997, no.155, pp.354–6, right margin ('customs men'); Gil 1995, pp.143–4. *Ghuzāh*: Gil 1997, vol.II, no.190, pp.555–60; Simonsohn 1997, no.33, pp.27–9, lines 10–11 ('guards').

common practice for Sicilian Jews to import under their own names cargoes belonging to Egyptian or Ifrīqiyan colleagues in order to evade duty.[83] The authorities attempted to stop this by demanding certificates proving ownership of imported cargoes, and by vigilance at the ports.[84] Evasion was a risky business that could end badly: leading Palermitan Jews were imprisoned for evading the duty, and there is a hint that a cantor may even have converted to Islam to escape liability.[85] In 1056, the authorities extended import duty to Sicilian Jews because they 'set up partnerships with foreigners and pass off the goods as their own'.[86] This was felt to be a real hardship and injustice, and Abū l-Ḥasan ibn Ḥayyīm (*i.e.* Eli ha-Kohen bar Yaḥyā or Yaᶜīsh-Ḥayyīm), the *parnās* ('welfare officer') of Fusṭāṭ, intervened, presumably with the Fāṭimid authorities, to have this innovation revoked in *c.*1058.[87]

What may be one of the earliest letters concerning Sicily in the Cairo Geniza, perhaps written in the 970s or '80s, seems to involve the evasion of tax or duty, and offers an interesting glimpse of how disputes between the Muslim authorities and their Jewish subjects were resolved. The letter reports the difficulties experienced in obtaining a legacy that the late Bundār [of Palermo], an emancipated slave, had left to the poor Jews of Palestine. Before his death, he, or possibly his agent, ran into trouble over some silk (the manuscript is lacunose and many details are missing); informers reported him to the authorities, and he was imprisoned 'in the dungeon of the fortress'. The case was resolved by the son of the late Moses al-Ghudāmisī, who may be identical with Rabbi Solomon –

> the saviour of our land, protector, champion and advocate of all those amongst us who appeal to the authorities, lords, deputies, the customs collectors, and tax men (*la-shilṭōnīm we-la-sarīm we-la-seganīm we-la-mōkesīm we-la-baᶜalē ha-mas)*, and he made a great effort, and paid bribes from his wealth and pleaded with all his might until he saved all he could for Bundār before his death. The rest was confiscated by the ruler (*shalīṭ*) and taken by force. He was unable to save it.[88]

[83] Gil 1983, vol.II, no.394, pp.721–23; Simonsohn 1997, no.123, pp.261–3; Gil 1995, pp.143, 144.

[84] Gil 1997, vol.IV, no.654, p.169, lines 21–2, p.170, line 6 – p.171, line 16; Simonsohn 1997, no.162, p.378, lines 21–2, p.379, line 6 – p.380, line 16.

[85] Gil 1997, vol.IV, no.651, pp.157–63; Simonsohn 1997, no.103, pp.202–6 (risks). Gil 1997, vol.III, no.561, p.863, lines 26–8; Simonsohn 1997, no.109, p.228, lines 26–7 (imprisonment). Gil 1997, vol.III, no.513, pp.710, line 18 – p.711, line 20; Simonsohn 1997, no.111, pp.232, lines 18–19 (conversion). See also Gil 1995, pp.143–4 and n.18.

[86] Gil 1997, vol.III, no.561, p.860, lines 3–5; Simonsohn 1997, no.109, p.227, lines 3–5; Gil 1995, p.143. See also Gil 1997, vol.IV, no.753, p.480, upper margin; Simonsohn 1997, no.108, p.222, upper margin; Gil 1995, p.144 (dating the letter to *c.*1068).

[87] Gil 1997, no.253, vol.II, pp.749–53; Simonsohn 1997, no.135, pp.287–9. For the date *c.*1058, see Gil 1983, vol.II, no.394, pp.721–3; Simonsohn 1997, no.123, pp.261–3. For the *parnās*, see Goitein 1967–93, vol.II, pp.77–82. Gil 1995, pp.142–3: his assertion that Ḥayyīm ibn ᶜAmmār – a representative of the Jewish merchants in Palermo, *c.*1040–60 (see references cited in Goitein 1967–93, vol.6, p.44) – claimed responsibility for the lifting of the *ᶜushr* from Sicilian Jews seems to be unjustified.

[88] Ben-Sasson 1991, no.32, pp.143–5; Simonsohn 1997, p.xxviii, and no.26, pp.17–18. Gil 1995, p.150. Sicily is not mentioned by name, but the sums mentioned are all reckoned in *tarì* (*ṭeriyyīm*), which would seem to indicate the island. The letter is dated to the 970s on both palaeographic and prosopographical grounds, so this may be the earliest attested use of Arabic *ṭarīy* meaning 'quarter-dinar': see Stern 1970, pp.180–1, 183.

A long letter written after 1035 by the Jewish community of Palermo to that of al-Mahdīya, in praise of Ḥayyīm, alias Khalaf ibn Yaᶜqūb the Spaniard, his son Nissīm, Moses ibn Yaḥyā the Perfumer, ᶜAmmār ibn Joshua al-Ḥalabī, and other of their leaders, gives a long and rambling account of many similar incidents; the manuscript is extremely lacunose and the precise details are exceedingly obscure. It opens with general praise of Ḥayyīm and his fellows for their intervention with the authorities over the (poll-?)tax:

> [...] their righteousness, in their hearts and their business; they did not require the assistance of their brethren to ask for money from them. Nothing from [...] many men, large sums of the tax (*mas*), with fear of God which is in their hearts, and with the favour which the Creator granted them with the tax man (*mekes*) [...] heavy. They exempted the poor from taxation (*mas*) and the tax collector (*mōkēs*) left them alone, and of the tax (*mas*) [...].

Next, Ḥayyīm is praised for recovering for some Jewish merchants part of the cargoes of wrecked ships that had been appropriated by the authorities (*shilēṭōn*). He and Nissīm also prevented the Muslim authorities in Palermo from confiscating part of the Jewish cemetery: the Jews had illegally extended its area, the authorities had 'measurements taken to confiscate from them about a third', but Ḥayyim and Nissīm 'had the measuring done away with ... [We did not g]ive a penny nor bribe anyone'. The Christians were less fortunate: 'The Uncircumcised were un[able to] save their property, [except] at great expense'. In another case, a renegade and excommunicant Jew, probably identical to Ḥākim 'the villain' (*ha-rashaᶜ*), appears to have denounced Nathan the cantor for tax-evasion to the lieutenant-governor (*shālīsh*); there is mention of informers, fabricated charges, oaths taken, a Muslim official (*pāqīd*) who searches the houses of Jews in vain; until, in the end, Ḥayyīm resolves all.[89]

* * *

Taken as a whole, the evidence for Muslim Sicily, slight as it is, suggests that from at least the early 10th century there existed in Palermo an evolved central administration, probably modelled upon that of Ifrīqiya. In particular, the simple hierarchical organisation of the fiscal administration can be discerned. In the capital, the central *dīwāns* of finance were supervised by a single official with responsibility for the whole island. A variety of different financial offices were under his control, but first amongst them was the *dīwān al-kharāj*. Provincial tax-offices, directed by local officials called *amīns*, maintained their own tax-records, which seem to have listed the types of lands taxed, their extent and boundaries, and the rates of taxation. Tax-registers should also be surmised for the *jizya*-taxes – as we shall see, there is strong circumstantial evidence that *jizya*-lists survived into the Norman period.[90]

[89] Gil 1997, vol.II, no.236, pp.689–94; Simonsohn 1997, no.57, pp.85–9. Goitein 1967–93, pp.60–1.
[90] Below, pp.57–8.

Although we do not possess a single anecdote which suggests that an individual landholder might be required to produce an official document to substantiate his claim to a particular piece of land, this should not be interpreted as meaning that the central or local tax-offices kept no record of the names of holders of taxable estates. Such records had been the rule in the East and in Egypt from the 8th century, and may be inferred for Byzantine South Italy: we should therefore assume their existence in Muslim Sicily. While it would probably be wrong to claim a high level of sophistication for 10th-century Sicilian tax-records, comparable to those of contemporary Egypt for example, Jaᶜfar's attempts at reform in 1019–20 do suggest that, by then, the fiscal administration was beginning to advance from relatively simple practices towards more complicated techniques.

The letters of the Cairo Geniza are a particularly valuable source for the last seventy years of Muslim rule. They reveal, although in an anecdotal and fragmentary manner, that the Muslim administration of Sicily had developed a large and energetic officialdom in order to supervise the affairs of resident non-Muslims and foreign merchants. Although they have nothing to say about the land-tax, the letters are full of incidental detail attesting to the extent and complexity of the administration of the *jizya* and, especially, of import taxes. They serve, therefore, as a useful corrective to the Arabic narrative sources, from which alone it would be tempting to conclude that the administration was smaller, less complex, and less active. Moreover, because most of the letters that have survived come from the mid-11th century, from the last years of Kalbid rule and, especially, from the period of civil war between the rival *qāʾid*s, which led directly to the Norman invasion, they demonstrate that the administration continued to function during these troubled years, right up until the Norman take-over. They thus confirm the impression to be had from the Arabic sources that, during the period of disintegration of central authority into a number of minor principalities, each local ruler attempted to establish his own independent administration, at times under the aegis of Fāṭimid authority. It is safe to assume that, when the Normans arrived on the island, they found the remnants of the centralised administration in Palermo and a number of local administrations serving the specific if limited needs of the petty rulers.[91]

[91] A close analogy may be seen in the history of the mint in these years: see Travaini 1995, pp.29–34, 37–8.

CHAPTER 2

'When first the Normans crossed into Sicily ...'

The military conquest and the terms of the settlement

The Norman conquest of Sicily lasted more than thirty years, from the first exploratory raid in the late summer of 1060,[1] to the surrender of Noto, the last Muslim stronghold, in February 1091.[2] Pitched battles and great sieges were comparatively rare. The difficulty of the terrain, Count Roger's shortage of manpower, and his determination to keep the conquest in his own hands and out of the grasp of potential rivals, combined to make surrender on terms the normal process through which military and political power was transferred from the Muslims to the Normans.[3]

From the first, the Normans were ready and able to treat with the Muslim communities of the island. During their advance through Calabria, the de Hautevilles had already come into contact with Muslim communities, and the Latin sources claim that they had succeeded in winning the co-operation of some of their new subjects: for example, after the autumn raid on Sicily in 1060, the inhabitants of Reggio 'wished to demonstrate their fidelity to the Duke [Robert Guiscard]. And, in order to avoid suspicion, both the Christians and the Saracens who lived there armed themselves against the Pagans of Sicily'.[4] Moreover, when the brothers

[1] Malaterra 1927–8, pp.29; Amari 1933–9, vol.III, p.63, n.1; Chalandon 1907, vol.I, p.192.

[2] Malaterra 1927–8, p.93; Amari 1933–9, vol.III, p.180; Chalandon 1907, vol.I, p.340.

[3] For a narrative account of the conquest, see Amari 1933–9, vol.III, pp.1–183; Chalandon, 1907, vol.I, pp.191–211, 327–40; Tramontana, 1986, pp.85–94. The date and course of events in the 1050s and '60s has recently been challenged by Gil 1995, pp.114–30, largely on the basis of letters of Jewish merchants from the Cairo Geniza. Although these do contribute important new evidence, Gil's claims that Ibn al-Thumna's appeal to the Normans and the main Norman invasion both occurred as early as 1056 (p.121) cannot be sustained, as I shall demonstrate in a forthcoming article (Johns forthcoming e): in the meantime, see Simonsohn 1997, pp.xviii–xxii, especially p.xix, n.20.

[4] *Et pour ce que en la cité de Rege habitoient Sarrazin et Chrestien, se volirent mostrer que estoient fidel à lo Duc. Et pour non faire soi suspect, tant li Chrestien quant li Sarrazin qui ilec habitoient, armerent soi contre li Pagan de Sycille*: Amatus of Monte Cassino 1935, p.234.

launched their invasion proper, in May 1061,[5] they did so at the invitation and in support of a Sicilian Muslim *qāʾid*, Muḥammad ibn Ibrāhīm ibn al-Thumna.

During the 1040s, Sicily had split into petty principalities, roughly analogous to the *ṭāʾifa*-kingdoms of 11th-century Spain. Gradually the *qāʾid* ʿAlī ibn Niʿma ibn al-Ḥawwās, ruler of central Sicily, emerged as the most powerful leader,[6] but, in *c.*1055, the *qāʾid* of Syracuse, Ibn al-Thumna, first attacked, defeated and killed the *qāʾid* of Catania, and then annexed the territory of Ibn Mankūd, ruler of the Val di Mazara. Ibn al-Thumna now seems to have laid claim to supreme authority in Sicily: he assumed the Fāṭimid title *al-qādir bi-llāh* ('the powerful through God'), and had the *khuṭba*, or Friday sermon, read in his own name – a clear sign that he laid claim to independent sovereignty. Soon, open conflict broke out between Ibn al-Thumna and Ibn al-Ḥawwās, and the former was defeated. In desperation, Ibn al-Thumna turned to the Normans on the mainland, and sought their aid against his rival.[7]

Norman interest in Sicily had long predated Ibn al-Thumna's plea for assistance,[8] but there can be little doubt that, until the *qāʾid*'s death in the summer of 1062, the role that the Norman leaders were content to play was that of mercenaries to Ibn al-Thumna.[9] On hearing of his assassination, the Normans were 'greatly disturbed'; they abandoned their outposts at Troina and Petralia, and withdrew to

[5] Malaterra 1927–8, p.30, dates Roger's second raid to the first week before Lent (18–25 February); Amari 1933–9, vol.III, pp.65–8; Chalandon 1907, vol.I, pp.193–4. The main invasion was launched after two months' preparation (March–April): Malaterra 1927–8, pp.31–2. Robert joined Roger at Reggio immediately before the invasion in the first days of May: Amatus of Monte Cassino 1935, pp.234–5 and notes; Amari 1933–9, vol.III, pp.68–9; Chalandon 1907, vol.I, pp.194–5.

[6] Amari 1933–9, vol.II, pp.614–20, vol.III, pp.68–77, 82, 84 n.2, 97, 111–13; Rizzitano 1968.

[7] Malaterra 1927–8, p.30; Amatus of Monte Cassino 1935, pp.229–32, 240 n.2; Amari 1933–9, vol.II, pp.616–20, vol.III, pp.63–89; Rizzitano 1969. Ibn al-Athīr 1851–76, vol.X, p.132 (*BAS*², vol.I, p.319; *BAS*²*(It.)*, vol.II, p.356), dates to Rajab 444 / November 1052 the joint invasion of Sicily by Ibn al-Thumna and Roger. He is followed by al-Nuwayrī (*BAS*², vol.II, p.499; *BAS*²*(It.)*, vol.II, p.552), and others, but the year 444 is clearly nothing but an error (for 454?). In 1052, Roger had not yet crossed the Alps and, in the rising anti-Norman tide that followed the assassination of Drogo in August 1051, Robert Guiscard – whose base was then Scribla (CS), not Mileto (VV) – would scarcely have appeared to Ibn al-Thumna as an attractive ally. (Such errors are not uncommon: in the middle of this passage in Ibn al-Athīr, the MSS confuse the year 472 for 371.)

[8] The title claimed by Robert Guiscard in August 1059 before Pope Nicholas II at the Council of Melfi was *Robertus Dei gratia et sancti Petri dux Apulie et Calabrie et utroque subveniente futurus Sicilie* ('By the grace of God and St Peter, duke of Calabria and Apulia, and – with the support of both – future duke of Sicily'): Fabre and Duschesne 1901–10, vol.I, pp.421–2. See also: Malaterra 1927–8, p.15. The Geniza letter written by a Jewish merchant in al-Mahdīya to his brother in Fusṭāṭ, which laments that 'People are worried this year because of the Franks, who are massing enormous forces against her', is dated only 12 Shvat (19 January), but is usually assigned to the year 1058: Ben-Sasson 1991, no.8, pp.36–47; Gil 1997, vol.IV, no.617, pp.36–45; Simonsohn 1997, no.122, pp.255–61. In January 1058, however, Robert Guiscard and Roger were in open conflict, and it is inconceivable that they would have allied to prepare for the invasion of Sicily: Malaterra 1927–8, pp.20–2. January 1061, when the Normans *were* at Reggio preparing for the invasion of the island, is a far more likely date for this letter: see Johns forthcoming e.

[9] The death of Ibn al-Thumna, reported by Malaterra 1927–8, p.36, is also mentioned in a letter from the Cairo Geniza, 'I went and asked them the news from Sicily. They said the news was good and everything was allright (*sic*), and that Ben al-Thumna was killed and the town [Mazara?] became quiet'. This letter is dated 4 Elul (= 12 August), but without the year: Gil 1997, vol.III, no.312, pp.29–34; Simonsohn 1997, no.147, pp.319–21.

Messina.[10] Only after Roger's major defensive victory over the Muslims of eastern Sicily, at Cerami in 1063, did his forces begin to act independently, and even then no major advance was made until as late as 1068. This early, close collaboration between the Normans and Ibn al-Thumna helps to explain both the readiness and the ability of the Norman leaders to treat with the Muslim communities of the island.

The Norman force included non-Muslim interpreters and experts upon Islamic law and custom. Amatus of Montecassino records that Robert Guiscard sent as ambassador to the emir of Palermo a certain Peter the Deacon, 'who could understand and speak very well, just like a Saracen'.[11] Geoffrey Malaterra recounts how one Philip, son of the patrician Gregory, was sent as captain of a ship to spy upon the Muslim fleet in Syracuse harbour. Philip and all of his companions are said to have been as fluent in Arabic as they were in Greek.[12] Peter and Philip both appear to have been South Italian or Sicilian Greeks who were well acquainted with the complexities of life on the frontier with Islam. Men such as these are likely to have served as interpreters and negotiators during the delicate business of surrender.

As early as the surrender of Rometta, the first fortified centre which the Normans encountered as they advanced west from Messina in May 1061, we can discern a fixed procedure for negotiating and accepting the surrender of Muslim communities – one which was based upon Islamic law and custom. The citizens of Rometta, warned by crowds of refugees about the fate of Messina, which had resisted the Norman assault, sent legates to Robert including their *qā'id*, 'who sued for peace ... and, surrendering the city and themselves, with the books of their superstitious law before them, they swore an oath of fealty'.[13]

A similar process of surrender can be observed at Palermo, but in greater detail.[14] The citizens were brought to terms when Robert Guiscard stormed al-Khāliṣa, the Fāṭimid foundation which lay within its own walls, below and to the north-east of the old city (al-Qaṣr). A massacre followed, and the assault upon al-Qaṣr began. According to Amatus, during the night of 7–8 January 1072, messages were exchanged laying out the terms of surrender. The following morning, a delegation of city elders, led by two *qā'id*s, met Count Roger and asked him to accept the surrender of the city.[15] Malaterra summarises the terms of the treaty conceded by

[10] Malaterra 1927–8, p.36.

[11] *Un qui se clamoit dyacone Pierre, liquel entendoit et parloit molt bien coment li Sarrazin*: Amatus of Monte Cassino 1935, p.244.

[12] *Nam et lingua eorum [Sarracenorum], sicut et graeca, ipse et naute omnes, qui cum ipso processerant, peritissimi erant*: Malaterra 1927–8, p.86.

[13] *Ramectentes ... legatos, qui pacem postulent, mittunt, urbemque et seipsos ditioni dedentes, libris superstitionis legis suae coram positis, juramento fidelitatem firmant*: Malaterra 1927–8, p.33; *Dont lo Caïte de celle cité, pour paour, lui ala à genoilz devant; et lui demanda paiz, et lui donna present pour tribut; et se obliga de estre à son [Robert's] comandement tout entierement*: Amatus of Monte Cassino 1935, p.238.

[14] For important new evidence on the last years of Muslim rule in Palermo, see Gil 1995, pp.125–30, and Johns forthcoming e.

[15] Amatus of Monte Cassino 1935, pp.278–82, claims that the Palermitans *prierent lo Conte que, sans nulle autre condition né covenance, doie recevoir la cité à son commandement*, and William of Apulia 1961, p.182, says that *Cuncta duci dedunt, se tantum vivere poscunt*, but the circumstantial and detailed account given by Malaterra is more convincing.

the two brothers to the Palermitans: they would neither abolish nor violate their law, nor introduce new and unjust laws; if the citizens remained Muslims, they were to pay the tribute.[16]

Similarly, when Roger landed on Malta in 1090, the *qāʾid* of the island led a delegation which sued for peace and, 'according to their own law, having given their oath, they became the *confoederati* of the count', in exchange for the release of all Christian captives on the island and for a tribute of horses, mules, arms, and vast amounts of money.[17]

The same process of surrender may be seen during the Norman conquest of the Ifrīqiyan coast in the 1140s, but here through the eyes of Arab writers. Tripoli fell by storm on 17 July 1147. After an initial massacre, looting and the enslavement of some of the population, an *amān*, or conditional truce, was proclaimed and a governor was appointed from amongst the dominant Arab faction in the city. In the same year, the *de facto* ruler of Gabès offered to submit to Roger, and to be his lieutenant (*nāʾib*), like the governor of Tripoli, in return for a robe of office and a diploma of investiture. When the Normans entered the abandoned the Zīrid capital, al-Mahdīya, on 22 June 1148, an *amān* was granted to the absent citizens who were permitted to return on the condition that they paid the *jizya*. *Amān*s were conceded to other cities as they fell or surrendered; and eventually, after the fall of Sfax in 1148, Roger wrote to the inhabitants of Ifrīqiya conceding a general *amān*.[18]

From these examples a clear picture begins to emerge of the process by which Muslim communities were incorporated under Norman rule. After negotiation, the leader or leaders of each Muslim community entered into a pact (*foedus* or *amān*) with the Normans whereby, in return for the tribute (*tributum, censum* or *jizya*), the Muslims became subjects (*confoederati* or *ahl al-dhimma*) and received the protection (*dhimma*) of the Normans, together with certain specified freedoms and privileges. Both the tribute exacted and the privileges awarded varied from community to community. For their part, the Muslims swore upon the *Qurʾān* to abide by the terms of the pact. Thus, the Muslims of Sicily became *ahl al-dhimma* in their own land, by means of an adaptation, to the needs of their Christian conquerors, of the Islamic law and practice governing the surrender of non-Muslim communities.[19]

As Claude Cahen has remarked, in the pacts or protection (*amān*s or *dhimmāt*) conceded by Muslim rulers to their non-Muslim subjects, 'the essential – and lasting – stipulation concerns the payment of the distinguishing tax or *djizya*'.[20]

[16] *Proximo mane primores, foedere interposito, utrisque fratribus locutum accedunt, legem suam nullatenus se violari vel relinquere velle dicentes, scilicet, si certi sint, quod non cogantur, vel injustis et novis legibus non atterantur. Quandoquidem fortuna praesenti sic hortabantur, urbis deditionem facere, se in famulando fideles persistere, tributa solvere: et hoc juramento legis suae firmare spopondunt*: Malaterra 1927–8, p.53.

[17] *Sicque more legis suae, sacramentis datis, comiti confoederati sunt*: Malaterra 1927–8, p.95.

[18] Ibn al-Athīr 1851–76, vol.XI, pp.66, 70–1, 79–85; *BAS*², vol.I, pp.329–36; *BAS*²*(It.)*, vol.II, pp.364–74. For the Normans in Ifrīqiya, see: Idris 1962a, vol.I, 319–24, 334–8, 345–7, 347–61, 374–6, 379–84, 390–4; Abulafia 1985; Brett 1986; Johns 1987; Brett 1999b. See also below, pp.290–1.

[19] See here the pertinent comments of Burns, 1984, pp.54–60.

[20] Cahen 1963a, p.227; also, Schacht 1957, pp.205–6.

But the *jizya* cannot be regarded as axiomatic when the pact or protection was conceded by Christian rulers to Muslim subjects. Indeed, Michele Amari, the great authority upon the Muslims of Sicily, insisted that it was only the Jews of Norman Sicily who were liable to the *jizya*.[21] Before proceeding, it is therefore important to review in greater detail the case for the imposition of the *jizya* on the Muslims of the island.

An Arabic document of *c.*1177 is the most important single piece of evidence which we must consider (**Private 16**).[22] It is the record of an agreement made between a household of 'men of the registers' (*rijāl al-jarāʾid*) adscripted to Manzil Yūsuf, modern Mezzoiuso (PA), and their lord, Donatus, abbot of the Palermitan abbey of San Giovanni degli Eremiti.[23] The three brothers who comprised the household had fled their lands, and now returned to renegotiate their terms of service with their lord. They undertook to pay 'collectively a *jizya* of thirty quarter-dinars annually, and a *qānūn* ('land-tax') of twenty *mudd*s of wheat and ten of barley'. They also requested the right to ask the whole chapter if they could dwell wherever they wished, presumably off the abbey's estates. There can be no doubt that they are Muslims: the brothers claimed to belong to the Arab tribe of Banū Laḥm (or possibly even to the ancient Banū Lakhm) and they swore fealty in the presence of *al-Muṣḥaf*, the *Qurʾān*; the witnesses to the agreement claimed descent from Quraysh, the tribe of the Prophet, and from Qays – both ancient Arab tribes.

Confirmation that the Muslims of Sicily did pay the *jizya* comes from an unexpected source, unknown to Michele Amari. In his Sicilian *roman à lettres*, *al-Zahr al-bāsim wa-l-ʿarf al-nāsim fī madīḥ al-ajall Abī l-Qāsim* (*Smiling flowers and redolent perfume in praise of the sublime Abū l-Qāsim*), the Alexandrian poet, Ibn Qalāqis visits Sicily, and enjoys the hospitality and patronage of the *qāʾid* Abū l-Qāsim ibn Ḥammūd, the hereditary leader of the Muslim community of the island, and at that time a senior official in the Norman *dīwān*.[24] During a hiccough in their relations, Ibn Qalāqis makes a long journey around the north and east of the island to Syracuse. There, in the winter of 1168–9, he is approached by the Muslim community of the city, and asked to intercede with the *qāʾid* Abū l-Qāsim 'to lift the *jizya* that diminishes their possessions and weighs down upon their hopes'.[25] Abū l-Qāsim replies, through a third person, expressing his esteem and goodwill, but pleading that pressure of work prevents him from immediately addressing the case. The final outcome is unknown, but Adalgisa De Simone is surely correct in doubting that such a petition could ever have been successful.[26]

[21] Amari 1933–9, vol.III, p.260–2, arguing against Gregorio 1972, vol.I, pp.103–4. See also Finocchiaro-Sartorio 1908, pp.247–55.

[22] Below, pp.145–6.

[23] Collura 1961, pp.250–7, 303.

[24] For Abū l-Qāsim ibn Ḥammūd, see below, pp.234–42.

[25] Ibn Qalāqis 1984a, pp.33–8: *fī rafʿi l-jizyati ʿani nkhifāḍi amwāli-him wa-ntiṣābi āmāli-him* (p.33); trans. De Simone 1996, pp.88–97.

[26] De Simone 1996, p.26. See also *ibid.*, p.88, n.155, where she suggests that the petition may have been ultimately aimed at Richard Palmer, bishop-elect of Syracuse, and one of the *familares regis*.

Late in 1184, when the Spanish pilgrim Ibn Jubayr visited Sicily, he noted that the Muslims paid an annual tax in two instalments, and linked it to the complaint that the Christians 'have come between them and the wealth of the land which they used to enjoy'.[27] The word that he uses for 'tax' – *itāwa* – is a generic term for tax or tribute; and it could be that he deliberately avoids using *jizya*, perhaps in order to contrast the inferior status of the Muslims of Sicily with those of the Kingdom of Jerusalem who, he specifies, did pay the *jizya* but did not suffer greatly thereby.[28] There can be little doubt, however, that the tax which Ibn Jubayr describes was the *jizya*. Clearly, the tax had been imposed upon the Muslims after the Christian conquest of Sicily. Moreover, payment in two annual instalments is characteristic of the money tribute paid by the Muslims of Sicily, and is attested as early as 1095.[29] More significant still, Ibn Jubayr thrice describes the status of the Muslims of the island in terms clearly implying that they lived as did *dhimmī*s under Islam: he writes of them being 'under the *dhimma* of the infidels', and 'under the contractual obligation of the *dhimma*'. He also reports that the Islamist minority amongst the Muslims of Palermo, who had cut themselves off from their fellow Muslims by rejecting the *dhimma*, had sacrificed security for their possessions and families.[30]

Much later, in the 13th century, the *jizya* was still paid by Muslim colonists of Lucera in Apulia, whither they had been transported from Sicily by Frederick II. In December 1239, for example, the emperor instructed his justiciar 'to collect on behalf of our *curia* from the *qā'id* and from all the Saracens of Lucera the *canon* (*i.e. qānūn*) and the *gesia* (*i.e. jizya*)'. A number of 13th-century privileges exempt certain Muslim *milites* of Lucera from specific taxes, including the *jizya*.[31] Similarly, Frederick II collected the *gisia* from the Muslims of Malta.[32]

Thus there can be no doubt that, from 1168–9 at least, the Christian rulers of Sicily did collect the *jizya* from the Muslims under their rule. But what of the earlier period? Working backwards, the *jizya* was imposed by the Normans upon the inhabitants of al-Mahdīya in Ifrīqiya in 1148, and the context strongly implies that the general *amān* subsequently granted by King Roger was equally conditional upon payment of the *jizya*.[33] It is highly probable that the Normans would have followed in Ifrīqiya the practice already current in Sicily.

[27] *Ḍarabū ʿalay-him itāwatan fī faṣlayni mina l-ʿāmi yuʾaddūna-hā wa-ḥālū bayna-hum wa-bayna saʿatin fī-l-arḍi kānū yajidūna-hā* ('They [the Christians] have imposed upon them [the Muslims] a tax which they pay in two instalments each year, and they have come between them and the wealth of the land which they used to enjoy'): Ibn Jubayr 1907, p.324; Ibn Jubayr 1949–65, vol.III, p.379; *BAS*², vol.I, p.85; *BAS*²*(It.)*, vol.I, pp.118–19.

[28] Ibn Jubayr 1907, p.301; Ibn Jubayr 1949–65, vol.III, p.353. He reports that Crusader taxes upon subject Muslims amounted to half the crop at harvest, a *jizya* of one dinar and five *qirāṭ* (5/24ths) a head, and a light tax on tree-fruits. See also Richards 1978.

[29] ***Dīwānī* 2**: see below, p.47.

[30] Ibn Jubayr 1907, p.332: *taḥta dhimmati l-kuffāri*, and p.340: *taḥta ʿuhdati l-dhimmati*; *BAS*², vol.I, pp.93, 101; *BAS*²*(It.)*, vol.I, pp.130, 141; Ibn Jubayr 1949–65, vol.III, pp.390, 399. See also below, p.297.

[31] Carcani 1992, p.307, col.b (Huillard-Bréholles 1852–61, vol.V, part 1, p.628); Egidi 1917, no.29, p.9; no.88, pp.28–9; no.190, p.71. See also Egidi 1911, pp.618–26. For the word *canon*, a back-formation from the Arabic *qānūn*, see below, p.145, note 3.

[32] Luttrell 1997, pp.20–1.

[33] Idris 1962a, vol.I, p.360. See also the sources and secondary bibliography cited in p.34, note 18.

Although this reference to the Ifrīqiyan *jizya* in 1148 is the earliest mention in Norman Sicily of the *jizya* by name, there exist clear references in Greek and Latin sources from the period of conquest and settlement to a 'tribute' which seems to be identical to the *jizya* in all but name. We have already encountered this *tributum* or *censum* (the two words appear to be interchangeable) as one of the standard conditions upon which the Norman *foedus* was granted to communities of subject Muslims, just as under Islamic law the *amān* was conditional upon the *jizya*. Malaterra describes the Sicilian Christians of the Valdemone, who had been *dhimmī*s under Muslim rule, as 'tributaries' (*tributarii*), and has them explain that they had submitted to the Muslims not out of love but because they feared for their lives, all the while remaining faithful Christians.[34] Other direct analogies between the Muslim *jizya* and the Norman *tributum* may be drawn, for example, from the following four passages from Malaterra. First, in his account of the treaty of Palermo, quoted above, Malaterra specifies that the citizens had to pay the tribute if they persisted in Islam: the Norman *tributum* or *censum*, like the Islamic *jizya*, was thus a penal, religious tax; a 'distinguishing tax', to use Cahen's happy phrase, which set apart the Muslims (and Jews) from the Christians just as, under Islam, the *jizya* distinguished Jews and Christians from their Muslim masters. Second, Malaterra reports that, in 1079, some of the Muslims of north-west Sicily rebelled and threw off their servile status and the tribute.[35] This linking of servile status with the tribute parallels what would have occurred under Islamic law: the transformation of the vanquished into an inferior *ahl al-dhimma*, whose protected status was dependent on their paying the *jizya*. Third, Malaterra records that when the Muslims of Noto finally surrendered, Roger I granted them two years' exemption from the *censum*.[36] In Islam, it was common practice for the victors to grant similar temporary exemptions from the *jizya*, either as a political expedient designed to sweeten the pill of conquest, or in order to encourage the economic recovery of districts and communities ravaged by war. In Valencia, James I made similar exemptions from the *besant* (in many ways the Valencian equivalent of the Norman *jizya*) a common ingredient of his *amān*s to the conquered Muslims.[37] Fourth, and finally, in his description of the treaty granted to the Muslims of Malta, quoted above, Malaterra specifies that it was drawn up *more legis suae*, 'according to their own law', *i.e.* according to the Muslim law of surrender.

There is thus no reason to doubt that the Normans did levy the *jizya* upon the Muslims of Sicily from the time of the conquest (we shall soon discuss the surviving fiscal registers from the 1090s on the basis of which the *jizya* was collected) until the final destruction of the Muslim community in the 13th century. That

[34] *Hic Christiani, in valle Deminae manentes, sub Sarracenis tributarii erant. De Christianorum adventu gavisi, illis occurrerunt, multaque exenia et donaria obtulerunt: hanc excusationem contra Sarracenos assumentes, quod, non causa amoris, sed ut seipsos et quae sua erant tuerentur, hoc facerunt, fidelitatem vero suam illis inviolabilem se servaturos*: Malaterra 1927–8, p.33.

[35] *Jatenses ... jugum nostrae gentis abhorrentes, statutum servitium et censum persolvere renuntiant*: Malaterra 1927–8, pp.69.

[36] *Comes itaque censum duorum annorum illis condonans ...* Malaterra 1927–8, p.93.

[37] Burns 1975, pp.79–85, especially p.81; Burns 1973, p.119.

the word *jizya* does not appear to have been used to describe this tribute until the middle of the 12th century is intriguing, but not particularly significant. It is not surprising that the Normans at first employed equivalent terms in Latin (*tributum, censum*) or Greek (δόμα, *doma*),[38] and only much later adopted the Sicilian *gesia* or *gisia*. It is easily understood why the Muslims might have been slow to give the name of *jizya* to a tribute forcibly exacted from them by Christian conquerors, when they regarded the *jizya* as a divinely sanctioned compensation to be extracted from the 'People of the Book' for their wilful refusal to accept Islam (*Qurʾān* 9.29).[39]

It is important to stress that, unlike the Islamic *jizya*, which was generally payable to and collected by the state, the tribute in Norman Sicily was paid to the lord of the community in which the tributary was registered, and was retained by him;[40] thus, the three brothers at Mezzoiuso owed their *jizya* to the abbot of San Giovanni degli Eremiti, not to the crown. The *jizya* of Jewish communities belonging to the royal demesne was occasionally granted to cathedral churches from as early as 1089, but this never seems to have occurred for Muslim communities.[41] Muslims belonging to the royal demesne, of course, owed their *jizya* directly to the crown as their immediate lord, as did the Muslim citizens of royal towns, such as those of Syracuse discussed above. Although there is no explicit evidence as to whom those 'free' (*i.e.* 'unregistered') Muslims who were not held by a feudal lord paid their *jizya*, the strong assumption must be that it went to the royal treasury.

While we have no explicit statement that the *amāns* which imposed the *jizya* upon the defeated Muslims took the form of written treaties, it would be strange if they had not done so. As we have already seen, during the conquest of the Ifrīqiyan littoral in the 1140s, diplomas and treaties were dispatched from Sicily to the new subject communities. Written treaties (*cartas pueblas*) were a standard part of the peace-making process in Aragon and Catalonia from the 12th century and in Valencia during the 13th.[42] In Spain, even minor war-lords such as the Cid made use of written pacts and accords as a matter of course.[43] And yet only one of the great written treaties, issued by James of Aragon to the Muslim communities of Valencia, has survived in the original. Others are preserved in Latin versions, and one bilingual treaty survives from shortly after James' death. In Valencia it seems that James and his successors preserved no copy of such treaties after the initial reason for their drafting had passed. They were preserved by the court 'only for its current files' and the 'originals of many surrender treaties … seem not to have

38 ***Dīwānī* 2**: below, pp.47, 146.

39 See, for example, al-Mawardī 1853, pp.245–7; al-Mawardī 1996, pp.158–9.

40 For a perceptive discussion of the possible relationship between Western feudalism and the *iqṭāʿ* in Syria and Palestine in the late 13th century, which stresses the complexity and variety of the *iqṭāʿ*, and argues against premature and ill-judged comparisons, see Irwin 1977.

41 For convenience, see now Simonsohn 1997, no.166, pp.387–8; no.170, p.391; no.206, pp.444–5. See also Houben 1992, p.16. In Byzantine south Italy, the secular authorities were already accustomed to grant the income of Jewish communities to the local bishop: von Falkenhausen 1996, pp.40–1.

42 Burns 1984, pp.52–79.

43 *The Cid* 1975, *e.g.* p.74, line 7 (*Moros en paz, ca escripta es la carta*); p.96, line 17 (*así lo an asmado e metudo en carta: / vendido les a Aloçer por tres mill marcos de plata*).

been registered by the crown or permanently preserved'.[44] It is no surprise that none have survived in Sicily.

We may assume, therefore, that the *amāns* conceded by the Normans to Muslim communities during the conquest of Sicily were written. If so, they would have been written in Arabic (this was the case in Ifrīqiya in the 1140s and in Spain), and possibly accompanied by Greek (or – unlikely, but just conceivable – even Latin) versions. Their composition would have been entrusted to the interpreters and negotiators attached to the de Hautevilles' staff. In this way, one root of the Arabic administration of Norman Sicily may have lain in the process of surrender and, specifically, in the need to draft and to conserve, at least in the short term, written peace treaties which determined the fiscal responsibilities accepted by vanquished Muslims as the price of their *dhimma*.

The division of the spoils: the land

With the completion of the military conquest, Count Roger turned his attention to the division of the spoils. The first beneficiary was the Latin church, and the foundation and endowment of the episcopal sees of Sicily appears to have begun as early as the 1080s.[45] Most of Roger's early donations, however, and almost all of the grants to his lay followers, seem to date from the 1090s. According to Malaterra, Roger summoned his supporters, and in recognition of the excellent service that they had done him, 'he repaid them for the sweat of their labours, some with lands and ample properties, some with various other prizes'.[46] In order to reward his followers with shares of the land and its inhabitants, it was first necessary to proceed with the division of the land itself and, even more urgently, to keep track of the inhabitants who made the land productive. The means adopted in the 1090s were those most readily available: wherever possible, existing land-boundaries and populations formed the basis of the post-conquest division of the spoils.

The two documents which are usually claimed to demonstrate that this was exactly what occurred are not originals, and may be neither authentic nor contemporary with Count Roger. First, in what purports to be a comital act of 1087, Roger granted to Robert, bishop of Messina, 'the *casale* of the Saracens which is called Butah, with all its tenements and appurtenances according to the ancient boundaries

[44] Burns 1973, pp.117–38, 155–83, especially 176–7; Burns 1985, pp.125, 133 n.6; Burns, Chevedden and De Epalza 1999.

[45] Starrabba 1893 is of little value; Caspar 1902, reproduced as appendix to Caspar 1904, pp.581–634, is more useful; Jordan 1922 and 1923 is the first critical study; Fonseca 1977, pp.47–56, contains a more recent, but not essentially different, review.

[46] Malaterra 1927–8, p.94.

of the Saracens'.[47] There are two glaring anachronisms in the text: Roger appears 'together with my wife Adelaide', whom he did not marry until 1089–1090;[48] and reference is made to the translation of the bishopric of Troina to Messina, although the latter see was not founded until early 1096,[49] and only on 9 June 1098 did Urban II recognise its independence.[50] The act of 1087 is written in Latin, but it seems probable that all of the genuine documents composed for the island at Count Roger's order were originally composed in Greek or Arabic.[51] It could be a Latin translation from the Greek, but the fact that it bears the plica and holes for attaching the seal suggests that it was intended to pass for an authentic original. The document is therefore best considered to be a forgery which, to judge from the script, dates from the early to mid-12th century.

Second, in what is supposed to be a copy of an original donation of December 1092, Roger granted to Ansgerius, abbot of Catania, 'the aforesaid city with all its appurtenances, just as the Saracens held the same city with all its appurtenances when first the Normans crossed into Sicily'. Roger also permitted the abbot to 'recover throughout the whole of Sicily all those Saracens who were then in the city of Catania at the time when the Normans first crossed into Sicily'. Finally, he granted 'to the aforesaid monastery the Saracens who were born, in whatsoever place in Sicily, of those Saracens who were then in the city of Catania and in Aci Castello at the time when first the Normans crossed into Sicily and, for fear of the Normans, fled thence to other parts'.[52] This document, too, pretends to be an authentic original: it bears what purport to be the signatures of Count Roger, his wife, his two sons, Geoffrey and Jordan, and other witnesses; and it is said to have borne the lead seal of Roger I until the beginning of the 20th century. The anachronisms and irregularities that it contains, however, reveal it to be a forgery:[53] the document is written in Latin not Greek; Adelaide is simply *uxor eius* without her

47 *Secundum antiquas divisiones Sarracenorum*: ADM, Messina no.1049. The original is not edited, but may be read from the photograph in *Messina* 1994, p.153, no.13. The 17th-century copy by Antonio Amico (= PA, Bibl. Com., MS Qq.H.4, ff.34r–v) is edited by Starrabba, 1876–90, no.2, pp.2–3. Casale Butah is probably to be identified with modern Regalbuto, Arabic *Raḥl ʿAbbūd*: Caracausi 1993, vol.II, p.1342.

48 Garufi 1905, pp.187–92 uses this document to argue that the marriage must have taken place in 1087, but see Pontieri 1955, pp.329–30, n.3; Houben 1991, 10–14; von Falkenhausen 1998, p.88.

49 Unedited original: ADM, Messina no.1347, *Messina* 1994, p.156, no.18. Cusa 1868–82, no.9, pp.289–91 reproduces an 18th-century copy.

50 Kehr, Holtzmann and Girgensohn 1906–75, vol.X, p.338, no.20. See also Fonseca 1994, p.36.

51 Enzensberger 1977, pp.16–18; Enzensberger 1995, pp.52–4; von Falkenhausen 1997, pp.253–6.

52 There exist two 12th-century copies: ADM, Messina no.1044, unedited but legible from the photograph in *Messina* 1994, p.154, no.15; and CT, Arch. Dioc., diploma latino no.4 (ex no.2, no.3 in register), ed. De Grossis 1654, pp.55–7 (with details of seal); Scalia 1961, no.3, pp.50–2.

53 Ménager 1956–7, pp.150–2, 164–5. In this careless and intemperate article, Ménager damned as forgeries all the early documents in the Archivio Diocesano di Catania. He was undoubtedly wrong thus to dismiss the Arabic and bilingual documents (see below, pp.52–3), but he was certainly correct to judge this document to be a forgery. Collura 1958–9, pp.134–5, substantially agreed with Ménager, whereas Scalia 1961, pp.34–45, insisted that it is 'an authentic copy of the molybdobul of the count, coeval and regular, without any interpretations and worthy of our trust' – this is mere *campanilismo*.

name; Jordan had died on 18 September 1092;[54] in the *datatio*, December Indiction XV corresponds to 1091, not 1092; and, finally, the phrase granting to the abbot those judicial rights 'which normally belong to kings and earthly princes' was clearly composed after the foundation of the monarchy in 1130.[55] However, although the donation to Catania may well be a forgery, Sant'Agata *did* lawfully hold the Muslim (and Jewish) populations of Catania and Aci Castello, as is proven by the *jarīda*s of 1095 (***Dīwānī* 3–4** – see pp.51–9, below).

Even if both documents are indeed forgeries, perhaps of the early to mid-12th century, it is highly suggestive that two apparently independent forgers, one working for Messina and the other for Catania, in order to impart an air of authenticity to their products, should have made the same claim that the earliest Norman boundaries were based upon those of the Muslims before the conquest, and should even have made use of similar formulae (*sicut Saraceni ... tenebant* and *secundum antiquas divisiones Sarracenorum*). Although it cannot now be proven, I believe it highly likely that both documents drew upon similar phrases in genuine, but lost, privileges granted by Count Roger.

Once again, the Spanish parallel is instructive: in Valencia, for example, post-conquest documents use repeatedly such formulae as 'boundaries...established and consigned before the Muslims left the land', or 'boundaries ... as ... were already decreed ... in the time of the Moors'; and, most commonly and simply, '... in the times of the Saracens'. In the Latin East, too, ancient Muslim territorial divisions are said to have been preserved and employed by the Crusaders.[56]

More significantly, many of the surviving donations of lands and populations granted by Count Roger in Sicily and Calabria confirm that, wherever possible, he made over to his followers existing estates complete with their resident population.[57] How these estates appeared to the Normans is less clear. Some of the earliest Norman documents from Sicily do trace the boundaries of the episcopal sees and, a little later, of estates granted by the count, but these may have been recorded specially for the donations in question and cannot be taken as proof of pre-existing written boundary records. There is no explicit reference from Muslim Sicily to written boundary records, although there seems to be little doubt that they did exist

[54] Malaterra 1927–8, pp.97–8 and notes, gives the year; the *Necrologia palermitana* (Winkelmann 1878, p.473) records Jordan's death on 18 September, but without the year.

[55] *Concessi ego Rogerius comes ... abbati prefati monasterii que solent pertinere ad reges et ad principes terrenos*: see Ménager, 1956–7, pp.150–1

[56] Burns 1984, pp.199–206. For the Latin East: Benvenisti 1970, pp.13–14; Riley-Smith 1977, pp.9–22; Prawer 1985, pp.106–13 *et pass.*; Richard 1985, pp.254–6 *et pass.*; Riley-Smith 1987, pp.64–9. But against the prevailing view of Crusader continuity with the Muslim past, see: Cahen 1957, pp.182–3; Mayer 1988, p.165. The evidence for continuity is strong, but the whole question of Islamic survivals in the administration and institutions of the Latin East needs thorough re-examination in the light of recent scholarship upon Muslim administration.

[57] In addition to the Sicilian *jarāʾid* discussed below, pp.46–59, see, for example, the following donations and polyptychs: Oct. 1086, ed. Ughelli 1717–21, vol.I, cols 943–52; 14 Nov., 6601 A.M., Ind. I [1093 A.D.], ed. Mongitore 1734, pp.8–10 (Latin transumpt of 1309 A.D. of Greek original); Sept. 1094, ed. Trinchera 1865, no.59, pp.76–7; Feb. 1097, *ibid.*, no.60, pp.77–8; and Feb. 1099, ed. *ibid.*, no.68, pp.85–6.

for state lands such as those to which al-Dāwudī's *Kitāb al-amwāl* refers.[58] It is also necessary to assume the existence in Muslim Sicily of some form of estate register, roughly analogous to the Egyptian *qawānīn*, for the administration of the *kharāj*.[59] It may well be, though, that land boundaries had not always been recorded in writing but had rather been preserved as part of the oral tradition of the resident community. Certainly, Norman boundary records were to rely heavily upon just such oral tradition.

In this context, a Latin translation of a Greek renewal issued by Roger II to Sant'Angelo di Brolo is particularly relevant. Sant'Angelo was one of the Greek monasteries which seems to have continued to function throughout the period of Muslim rule. In March 1145, during the great reorganisation of that year,[60] Theodosius, abbot of Sant'Angelo, brought to the royal court in Palermo a donation issued by Roger I in 1084 in order for it to be renewed. The comital donation confirmed the monastery in possession of everything that it had held 'in the time of the impious Hagarenes', and traced the boundaries of the monastery's lands. Although it is not stated explicitly, the strong implication is that these boundaries were reproduced from a pre-conquest record.[61]

From as early as 1095 in Sicily, and frequently thereafter, we encounter inquests held by comital and, later, by royal officials amongst the elders of a district in order to establish and to record estate boundaries.[62] This may indeed suggest that many estate boundaries were not written or, if once they had been, that the written record had not survived the years of conquest. More important is the fact that the jury of local elders consulted nearly always included a majority of indigenous inhabitants, Greeks or Saracens, and it was their expert knowledge of the pre-conquest boundaries that was required to record their course in writing. The most convincing argument that the Normans preserved and employed the same territorial divisions as their Muslim predecessors lies in the fact that they recorded them in Arabic and Greek and according to the testimony of the indigenous inhabitants.

The division of the spoils: the population

If estate boundaries could be established with relative ease by means of inquests held amongst the residents of an area, it was a very different matter to keep track of the residents themselves. But to do so was of crucial importance to the

58 Above, pp.24–5.
59 Above, p.17.
60 Below, pp.115–18.
61 Roger's grant of all lands *quae prius tenebat et possidebat tempore impiorum Agarenorum*, is contained within a Greek renewal of 1145 – Caspar 1904, p.560, reg.189 – which exists only in a Latin transumpt of 1478, ed. Pirri 1733, vol.II, pp.1021–2. The authenticity of the grant of 1084 cannot be established in the absence of the original, but – for what it is worth – it was questioned neither in 1145 nor in 1478.
62 An early Sicilian example is the inquest of Nov. 1095, ed. Cusa 1868–82, no.8, pp.367–8.

conquerors. It was not simply that members of the subject population were economically valuable as *jizya*-payers, and as tillers of the soil – they themselves might also constitute the definition of the estate to be bounded. Just as an estate might be granted *cum omnibus terris, villanis et pertinentiis suis*, 'with all its land, villeins, and appurtenances', so were men granted with the lands to which they were adscripted. Thus, instead of describing in detail the boundaries of lands granted, it was on occasion sufficient simply to name the men who were attached to them.[63] This common feature of the Sicilian rural regime, rare in Northern Europe, is frequently encountered in the Latin East. In both Sicily and Syria, the Christian lord inherited from his Muslim predecessor the status of rentier, rather than that of village squire with extensive demesne. Thus, as Joshua Prawer has remarked for Syria, 'it was simpler in making an economic donation ... to mention the villein and his family rather than describe his property'.[64] It was therefore doubly important for the conquerors to keep good track of their subject populations.

It will be useful, for comparative purposes, to consider first the case of Calabria, where polyptychs of the subject population began to be issued by Count Roger in the late 1080s to early 1090s. These were apparently based upon the pre-existing registers compiled by the tax-officials of the Byzantine catepanate for the collection of state taxes, and perhaps also upon the lists of the possessions (πρακτικά, *praktika*) of lay or ecclesiastical proprietors who were recipients of grants of lands and their inhabitants made by the state.[65] Although no example of either class of register is known to me from pre-Norman Calabria, their existence may be inferred from a variety of sources. For example, a confirmation of the rights of the monastery of Santa Maria del Rifugio,[66] issued in April 1023 by the catepan Basilios Boiōannēs, mentions that the abbot Kosmas had founded a new estate upon the monastery's lands and had assembled there settlers from two classes of peasants: πτωχοὶ (*ptōchoi*, literally 'beggars') and προσήλυτοι (*prosēlutoi*, 'new-arrivals').[67] Both are terms, like ἐλεύθεροι (*eleutheroi*, 'free') and ξένοι (*xenoi*, 'strangers'), used to describe the large and heterogeneous group of peasants who were not adscripted to the land, were 'unknown to the fisc', and were 'not registered in the polyptychs of the other proprietors'.[68] The appearance of this class in 1023 argues for the presence of their counterparts: villeins (πάροικοι, *paroikoi*),[69] who owed a variety of dues and services upon their own persons and upon the lands to which they were bound, and who were registered in the cadastral-lists of the state, or in the registers (πρακτικά, *praktika*) of other proprietors. A second document, issued in December 1046 by the catepan Eustathios to Buzantios, a judge of Bari, confirms

63 See, for example, the *jarāʾid* discussed below, pp.46–59.

64 Prawer 1985, pp.109–10.

65 For these see: Dölger 1927, pp.92–112; Ostrogorsky 1928, pp.88–91; Ostrogorsky 1954, pp.259–388. For the comprehensive study of a single cadastral register, see Svoronos 1959.

66 The monastery lay on the Basento, about 4–5km southeast of Tricarico (MT) itself.

67 Guillou and Holtzmann 1961, no.2, pp.20–8.

68 Ostrogorsky 1954, pp.330–47; Ostrogorsky 1956, *passim*, especially pp.34–40.

69 Note that πάροικος, too, originally meant 'stranger' or 'guest', and is occasionally used in this sense in Norman Sicily: see Cusa 1868–82, p.411.

the existence of registers compiled by fiscal officials of the catepanate for the collection of the personal tax (δουλεία, *douleia*) on behalf of the imperial treasury. In reward for his loyalty to the emperor, Buzantios was granted all the villeins (οἰκετωραι, *oiketōrai* – *sic*, for οἰκητωραι, *oikētōrai*) of the village of Fogliano with all the tribute that they used to pay to the fisc.[70] Such Byzantine tax-registers seem to have been imitated at a very early date by the Lombard rulers of the south. Thus, in documents from the mid and late 9th century issued by the princes Gisulf I of Salerno and Pandulf and Landulf of Benevento, the same distinction, already encountered in the confirmation of 1023, is made between free peasants (*homines liberi*), and *censiles* who owed dues and services to the Lombard state (*a parte reipublicae*).[71]

While there are good *a priori* reasons to expect the Normans to have rapidly adapted such tax-records as existed on their arrival in the south to their own needs, the document which is most frequently cited as evidence that this is what they actually did is – once again – a late forgery. This purports to be a confirmation issued to Santissima Trinità di Cava by Duke Roger Borsa in May 1087. It specifies that the abbey had been granted all of the inhabitants of *Castrum Sancti Adiutoris* with every due and service 'which they used to give and to pay to our *camera* ... just as is clearly stated in our tax-register (*in nostro fiscali quaterno*)'. Similarly, the inhabitants of Mitiliano were to give the abbot whatever 'they had been accustomed to give to our *camera* and [which] is listed in the tax-registers (*in quaternis fiscalibus*)'. But, as Charles Homer Haskins pointed out as long ago as 1911, and as Ménager has now confirmed in greater detail, this document is a forgery dating from the period of the Norman kingdom.[72]

Other, more trustworthy sources do attest to the early use made by the Normans in south Italy of fiscal records existing at the time of their arrival. For example, an act of November 1095 – issued by Henry, count of Monte San Michele, to the abbot and monks of San Giovanni di Lama – translated into Latin, and thereby confirmed, five Greek donations which had been issued to San Giovanni by the catepans of Italy between 1007 and 1052.[73] All five donations included detailed boundary-descriptions of the lands granted. Similarly, a confirmation of the foundation and endowment charter of Santa Maria di Matina, issued by Duke Robert Guiscard in March 1065, and later copied and amplified in the ducal chancery at some date before 1105, incorporates a pre-existing register of villeins.[74] That the division of the spoils after the conquest led to a proliferation of such registers and, thence, to a pressing need for some sort of central control and organisation of the

[70] Originally edited by Nitti Di Vito 1900–6, vol.I, no.32, pp.67–8 but, for a critical edition and full discussion, see now Lefort and Martin 1986. Buzantios' villeins appear to have been indigenous Lombards, for they were to be judged κατα τὸν νωμω(ν) (*sic*) τὸν Λ(ο)γγιβαρδ(ων).

[71] Gisulf I to bishop of Salerno: *Regii Neapolitani Archivii Monumenta* 1845–61, vol.I, no.45, pp.160–65. Pandulf and Landulf to Rodelpherius the priest: Ughelli 1717–21, vol.X, cols 479–80.

[72] Ménager 1981b, no.59, pp.203–12; Haskins 1911, p.656, n.196.

[73] Del Giudice 1863–9, vol.I, Appendix no.5, pp.xiii–xix: edited from a lost copy in the Naples archive.

[74] Ménager 1981b, no.16, pp.68–72.

cadastral regime, is highlighted by the case held before the Duchess Sichelgaita in October 1083, when no less than nine separate registers were presented in evidence.[75]

Thus, to return to the point at which this diversion began, it comes as no surprise to discover, within the earliest Calabrian polyptychs of Count Roger, the Byzantine originals upon which they are based. To cite but one example of many, the Greek and Latin donation and name-register (κατόνομα, *katonoma*) issued by Roger to the hermits of Stilo in February 1097 made a distinction between men already listed in the polyptych and unregistered newcomers (ξένοι, *xenoi*; Latin, *advenae*) who might later choose to commend themselves to the abbot.[76]

In Sicily, too, Count Roger incorporated into his earliest polyptychs existing tax-registers from the preceding period of Muslim rule. It has already been remarked that an essential element of the incorporation of Muslim communities under Norman rule was the imposition of an equivalent to the Islamic *jizya*, which Muslim communities 'agreed' to pay in return for the 'protection' granted them by the Normans. The very existence of the *jizya*, of course, implies that a mechanism existed for its assessment and collection. During the military conquest, the *jizya* was probably levied upon whole communities as a collective tribute unrelated to any kind of cadastral assessment. This was plainly the case on Malta in 1090.[77] But, once the fighting was over and the first polyptychs of the subject population were issued, it was these which enabled the count and his feudatories to levy the *jizya* upon individual households of Muslims. In west Sicily, which was pacified well before the fall of Noto, such tax-registers seem to have been employed as early as the late 1070s and certainly by the mid-1080s. In 1079, when the Muslims of west Sicily rebelled and withheld the *censum*, Malaterra remarks that they numbered 'up to thirteen thousand households': this could be taken as evidence that the tribute was already levied upon individual households on the basis of some form of cadastral survey, of which the chronicler had some knowledge.[78]

Our first clear evidence from Sicily for the registration of the subject population not only establishes the fact, but illustrates the two ways in which the division of the spoils could be achieved. It is the donation by Duke Roger Borsa to Palermo cathedral of the *casale* of Gallo and its villeins in 1086. The Latin original, written by the duke's Latin scribe but witnessed by his chief fiscal officer, Leo, who signs in Greek, grants both the *casale* of Gallo and four *rustici* (*i.e.* adscripted villeins with their lands) at Meselimi. Appended to the donation is the confirmation of Count Roger of Sicily, dated 7 November 1086, and in the same hand, the clarificatory note: 'There are 94 villeins at Gallo and 4 at Meselimi'.[79] We see very clearly

[75] Ménager 1981b, no.43, p.136–41.

[76] Trinchera 1865, no.60, p.78: στέργω δε συ καὶ μετα τοῦτον ολούς τούς ξενους τοῦς ερχομένους εἰς τὶν χοραν τὸν ερημιτων τοῦ εχην σάς αυτοῦς ακολιτως /*Concedo etiam eis advenas qui se voluerint eis commendare*. On commendation, see Antonucci, 1935.

[77] Above, pp.34, 37.

[78] Above, p.37.

[79] *Villani autem de Gallo sunt nonaginta iiij et de Meselimo iiii*: PA., Arch. Dioc., no.2, ed. Ménager 1981b, no.54, pp.185–6.

how, in the case of Gallo, it is an entire landed estate which is granted, together with its inhabitants; in that of Meselimi, on the other hand, it is the inhabitants who are granted, together with their lands. In both cases, the division depended upon the existing pattern of landholding and settlement; but in neither case, it would seem, did any full administrative record survive to be incorporated into the earliest Norman documents for these estates. However, the structure of the two surviving *jarīda*s of Count Roger not only provides further evidence of this two-fold classification, but also reveals how tax-registers from the period of Muslim rule in fact formed the basis for the earliest Norman polyptychs.

The Palermo *jarīda* of 1095 (*Dīwānī* 2)

The earliest surviving *jarīda* is contained within a Greek donation of villeins and lands made to Palermo cathedral. Before proceeding to an analysis of its structure and composition, we must first establish its date and briefly review its external features and content. In the dating clause (*datatio*), the month and day are given – 12 February – but neither the year nor the indiction. It is only specified that the document was given by Roger in Palermo. The donation was made 'for the remission of the sins of my [*i.e.* Roger's] son Jordan' and must, therefore, belong to the period between Jordan's death on 18 September 1092[80] and that of Roger himself on 22 June 1101. There survives a Latin transcript of uncertain diplomatic status of what purports to be a donation by Count Roger to Palermo cathedral and Archbishop Alcherius, also 'for the soul of Jordan my son', of the same area of land and the same number of villeins as are granted in the document under consideration.[81] The transcript bears the year 1095 but the indiction II.[82] Indiction II ran from 1 September 1093, but the donation cannot belong to that year for, in February 1094, Roger was not in Palermo but dealing with rebellious barons in Calabria.[83] On 20 February 1095, however, Roger was in Messina issuing similar *jarā'id* to various recipients.[84] It seems most likely, therefore, that the document was given on 12 February 1095. It was perhaps accompanied by the more detailed, more regular donation of which we now possess only a Latin transcript.

Having established the date of the *jarīda*, we may turn to its external features. The donation does not conform to the normal pattern (insofar as such existed) of

[80] Above, p.41, note 54.

[81] PA, Arch. Dioc., no.4: ed. Pirri 1733, vol.I, col.76. See also: Mongitore 1734, pp.12–13; Mortillaro 1843, pp.163, 375. The villeins are not named, but the boundaries of the land granted are here described in full: it seems to have lain on the right bank of the upper Belice Destro (*flumen de Magunuche*), in the modern *contrade* of Kaggio and Kaggiotto (PA), and to have been contained within the Monreale estate of al-Qumayṭ: see Cusa 1868–82, pp.193, 227; Nania 1995, pp.127–8.

[82] *Sic*: 1095 corresponds to Indiction III–IV.

[83] Chalandon 1907, vol.I, pp.299–300.

[84] The Catania *jarīda*s considered below, pp.51–8, were both issued in 1095; that for Aci Castello on 20 February.

Greek donations from the mainland or Sicily. The Greek protocol and text (lines 1–6) are much condensed and the document is dominated by the two lists of names of the villeins granted: the first written in Arabic, the second in Greek. After the second list, the document ends abruptly, with no conclusion, in Count Roger's impressive – but probably not autograph – Greek signature. There is no trace of a seal.

Turning now to the content, the principal gift is of seventy-five Hagarenes (Αγαρηνοί, *Agarēnoi*, *i.e.* Muslims) and their lands, amounting to eleven 'ox-lands' (βοίδια, *boidia*, literally 'oxen'). The lands are not described, and it was sufficient to list the names of the men adscripted to them. The Saracens were to give to the church a tribute (δόμα, *doma*) of seven hundred and fifty *tarì* twice a year, in August and during the winter. In addition, they were to give one hundred and fifty *modia* of wheat and the same amount of barley. This association of money tribute with tax in grain is directly comparable to the money *jizya* and grain *qānūn* levied upon the three runaway brothers from Mezzoiuso in *c.*1177, and to the '*canon* and *gesia*' to be extracted from the Saracens of Lucera; while the *doma*, paid in two instalments, recalls the *itāwa* mentioned by Ibn Jubayr.[85]

The Greek donation is followed by two name-lists: the Arabic *jarīda* of seventy-five names (which we shall call List C), and a Greek name-list of twenty names (List D).[86] The *jarīda* opens with one rubric in Greek – 'These are the names of the Hagarenes' – and another in Arabic – 'The names of the men whom the sultan (*i.e.* Roger) gave to the great church, the church of the Holy Virgin Blessed Mary in the capital of Sicily'. There follow seventy-five names, written in Arabic and arranged in eight lines, the first six of which are of ten columns while the seventh has eleven and the last has only four. The list ends with totals in both Arabic and Greek: seventy-five villeins.

The Greek name-list (List D) has the rubric in Greek only: 'And these are the νεόκαμοι (*neokamoi*, *i.e. neogamoi*, sing. *neogamos*, 'newlyweds') of the above-named [villeins]'.[87] There follow twenty names, written in Greek, arranged in five lines of four columns each. The list ends with a total in Greek only.[88] The term *neogamoi*, meaning 'newlyweds', is not used as the name of a category of villeins in any other source of which I am aware, but may be compared to the terms

[85] Above, pp.35–6, and below, p.146.

[86] The original structure of the *jarīda* has been obscured in Cusa's edition, where the names are published in two columns: the original order of the names can be retrieved by ignoring the columns and reading from right to left across the page.

[87] Mongitore 1734, pp.13–14, reads νεόγαμοι, and fantasises: *'Idest, Juvenes novi in fide, seu Neophyti: unde etiam Dominica prima post Pascha, Novella dicitur; in qua vestes albas, qui recens baptizati sunt Neophyti, deponunt. Cùm enim predictos 75. Agarenos, omnes Christianos esse dicat, & arabicis characteribus eosdem designet; juvenes novos inter eos, atque Neophytos in fide, graecè scriptis nominibus designavit, ac Novellos appellat'*. Cusa 1868–82, pp.3, 69 reads νεόκαμοι, and translates 'nuovi nati'. Caracausi 1990, p.401, also reads νεόκαμοι, but comments 'sta in luogo di greco antico νεόγαμοι "sposi novelli"'. On reviewing the MS, the reading νεόγαμοι does not seem wholly out of the question, but the doubtful character is written with an ambiguous flourish.

[88] Vera von Falkenhausen has suggested to me that the hand by which this list was written was not that of the scribe responsible for the Greek text. Note that, once again, Cusa's edition has obscured the order of the original list by printing the names in two columns: the names must be read from left to right across the page.

mutazawwijūn and ἐζευμένοι (*ezeumenoi*), both also meaning 'newlyweds', employed in the *jarāʾid* of King Roger and of William II, for households newly formed by marriage away from the parental household (***Dīwānī* 25 and 43**).[89] That this is exactly what the *neogamoi* are can be easily demonstrated by confronting List D with List C. Of the twenty names listed, seventeen can be shown to have family relationships with men registered in List C; twelve are sons, four are brothers, and one is a cousin.[90] Only for three *neogamoi* can no familial relationship with members of List C be reconstructed – perhaps they were not newlyweds but newcomers.[91] The *neogamoi* of List D are thus heads of households newly formed by marriage out of the established households of the community, most of which were listed in List C.

Why were the *neogamoi* distinguished and listed separately from the ordinary households? We have no direct evidence from Sicily, but the *neogamos* is in many respects comparable to the Egyptian *nashʾ* or 'youth'. The Egyptian *jizya*-lists record the *nashʾ* separately from the *rātib* or ordinary tax-payer. However, it was not marriage that categorised the class, but attaining the age of fiscal majority. The *nashʾ* qualified for tax relief from the ordinary rate for an introductory period, while he established his economic independence, which must normally have involved marriage and the formation of his own household.[92] A similar arrangement best explains why the *neogamoi* are listed separately from the ordinary heads of household: they too were presumably granted tax relief for an introductory period in order to keep them in their community and to discourage them from seeking better conditions elsewhere in which to start their independent lives.

Understanding how the list of *neogamoi* (List D) was compiled from the earlier *jarīda* (List C) helps us to see how List C was itself compiled from a still earlier *jarīda* (List B). Six names in List C are accompanied by the phrase 'his brother' (*akhū-hu*), which links each to the preceding name in the list; for example, *Ayyūb (C2)* and *Yūsuf akhū-hu (C3)*.[93] Here, too, we see what I shall henceforward call

[89] Cusa 1868–82, pp.146, 150, 152, 154, 158, 161, 177: *al-mutazawwijūn min awlād* = [οἱ] ἐζευμέν[οι] παιδ[ες] τῶν ἀνθρώπων.

[90] The numbers which follow each name correspond to the order of the original list: Ἴσεη ἀδελφὸς Ἰώβ (D1) is brother of Ayyūb (C2); Ἀβδεῤῥαχμὲν υἱός Ἄχμετ (D2) is probably son of Aḥmad (C25); Ὀθουμὲν ἔπιν Λίσκαρ (D3) is son of ʿAbd Allāh al-Ashqar (C38); Μβουσέμεξ ἔπιν Μαιμουν (D4) is son of Maymūn (C26); Ἄχμετ ἔπιν Μβουδίκηρ (D5) is son of Abū l-Dhikr (C63); Ὀθουμὲν ἔπιν Ὀθουμὲν (D7) is probably son of ʿUthmān (C13); Χαμμοὺτ ἔπιν Θουμέν (D8) is possibly the latter's brother; Βουλφὰδλ ἀδελφὸς αὐτοῦ (D9) is Chammout's brother; Μούσες ἀδελφὸς Ἰωσηφ (D10) is brother of Yūsuf (C3); Χάσεν ἐξάδελφος ἀυτοῦ (D11) is Mouses' cousin; Μουχάμμουτ ἔπιν (Ε)ννιγζιάρ (D12) is son of ʿAbd Allāh al-Najjār (C20); Βραχίμος ἔπιν Γεργέντι (D13) is son of ʿAlī al-Karkantī (C34); Ὀμουτ ἔπιν Βουαβδίλλα (D14) is probably son of ʿAbd Allāh (C1); Ὀθουμὲν ἀδελφὸς Μελλέκ (D15) is son of Mallāk (C47); Χάλεφ ἔπιν Ἰούσηφ (D16) is son of Yūsuf (C3); Χήλφε ἔπιν Σελλέμ (D17) is son of Salām (C54); Ὁ ἔπιν Σίακρα (D20) is probably the son of ʿAlī Siyakar(?) (C37).

[91] Ἀζοὺζ Ἐπιλούτιτ (D6), Μβουαβδίλλα (D18) and Ὁ Ἄγζιμος (D19).

[92] Rabie 1972, pp.108–13, 134–6; Goitein 1967–93, vol.II, pp.380–94; Cahen 1962a pp.248–52; Cahen 1956, pp.21–2. See also above, p.18.

[93] Ayyūb (C2) – his brother Yūsuf (C3); al-Tannūn(?) (C7) – his brother al-Jalāl (C8); Ḥusayn al-Baqqār (C12); – ʿUthmān his brother (C13); Aḥmad (C25) – his brother Maymūn (C26); Mujāhid (C43) – Wārith his brother (C44); ʿUmar and his brother (C75), the sons of al-S.y.rī.

the *neogamos*-system at work. This is crucially important for much of the discussion that follows concerning the dating of the *jarāʾid*, and so I shall labour the point.

Let us take the example of the following imaginary family as if it were registered in this *jarīda*. (In Arabic, *fulān* is the word used for an unnamed person, *i.e.* for 'so-and-so', *abū* means 'father', *ibn* 'son', and *akhū* 'brother'.) Abū Fulān was registered as a head of household in List A. He had two sons, Fulān and Akhū Fulān. By the time that his community was next registered in List B, Abū Fulān had died, and been succeeded as head of household by Fulān. Akhū Fulān had newly married, and was benefiting from the introductory reduction in taxes offered to newly formed households: in other words, he was a *neogamos*. When the community was next registered, in List C, the introductory period for Akhū Fulān had expired, so that both he and his brother were listed as ordinary tax-payers. Shortly before the next census for List D, Fulān's son, Ibn Fulān, married and moved away from his father's house to form a new – *neogamos* – household. This is expressed diagrammatically in Table 2.1.

Let us now look at a real family from the 1095 Palermo *jarīda*. In List B, Ayyūb (C2) was probably listed as an ordinary head of household, and his brother Yūsuf

Table 2.1 The *neogamos*-system in theory

Jarīda	**Ordinary household**	***Neogamos***
A	Abū Fulān	
B	Fulān	Akhū Fulān
C	Fulān Akhū Fulān	
D	Fulān Akhū Fulān	Ibn Fulān

(C3) as a *neogamos*. By the time that List C was compiled, the introductory period granted to Yūsuf had expired, and so he was listed after Ayyūb as an ordinary tax-payer. When the community was next registered, for the donation of 1095 (*i.e.* List D), their brother ᶜIsā (D1) had married and formed a *neogamos*-household. It follows that we can deduce a still earlier *jarīda* (List A), which would have registered the parental household of Abū Ayyūb from which all three brothers came. This is expressed diagrammatically in Table 2.2.

A second group of names also indicates how each new *jarīda* was based upon a predecessor, but is more problematic because the readings are uncertain: the names of two women are followed by a word which indicates that they have become widows;[94] and the name of one man is followed by a phrase which probably reads

Table 2.2 The *neogamos*-system in practice

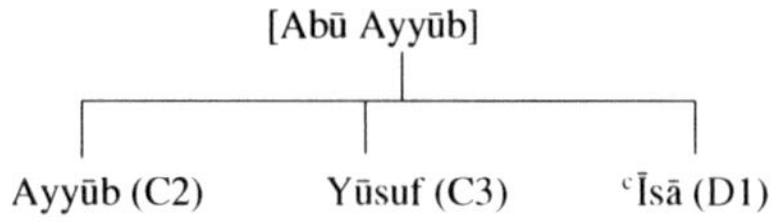

Jarīda	**Ordinary household**	***Neogamos***
A	[Abū Ayyūb]	
B	Ayyūb	Yūsuf
C	Ayyūb Yūsuf	
D	Ayyūb Yūsuf	ᶜĪsā

94 The names al-Saᶜda (C56) and Usba (C57) are both followed by *armal* which, although masculine, would here appear to stand for ‘a widow’ (*armala*). (The names could conceivably be masculine and refer to widowers, but this is unlikely because the death of a wife would not have affected the fiscal status of a male head of household.)

'he has left his wife'.[95] Like the names of the six pairs of brothers, these names also suggest that List C was compiled from an earlier *jarīda* (List B). This is most easily seen with the two widows: when List B was compiled, each still belonged to her husband's household, which was taxed at the full rate. But, in the interval before the compilation of List C, the two women lost their husbands and, in doing so, gained tax exemption. Again, the man who 'has left his wife' – if that *is* what he has done! – presumably did so in the interval between the compilation of Lists B and C, leaving his wife in charge of the household.

At long last, we now come to the point of the foregoing discussion: the list of *neogamoi* (List D) was in all probability at least a fourth-generation polyptych, compiled from the pre-existing Arabic *jarīda* (List C), which itself contains the traces of an earlier lost *jarīda* (List B), in which may be just discerned the ghostly image of a still earlier Arabic *jarīda* (List A). The donation dated 12 February 1095 gives an approximate date for the compilation of List D: Lists C, B, and A must all have been compiled before that date. Exactly how long before cannot be calculated from the evidence available, but the fact that List A would have registered the fathers and grandfathers of the adult men listed in List D suggests that one or two human generations separated the two registers. Allowing thirty-four years per generation gives a range of 34–68 years, which dates List A to 1027–61, to the period of Muslim rule, well before the capture of Palermo in 1072.

One final observation: unusually for a Sicilian *jarīda*, some evidence suggests that the Arabic name-list may have been used on at least two separate occasions after its issue to keep track of the registered population. One name is followed by a word which should probably be read as *rāḥil*, 'departed'; and after this name, into the intercolumnar space between it and the next, a new name has been interpolated in a different hand, followed by the word *ṭāliᶜ*, 'arrived'.[96] Second, above at least three names, a small cross has been added – whether as an *obiit*, or as an indication of conversion to Christianity, or as a symbol with some other significance.[97]

The Catania *jarīdas* of 1095 (*Dīwānī* 3–4)

The second surviving *jarīda* of Count Roger is appended to a Greek donation granting the indigenous population of Aci Castello to the bishop of Catania (***Dīwānī* 4**). The document is in the form of a long roll composed of three sheets of parchment sewn end-to-end with narrow parchment laces. The structure of the donation is again irregular. The protocol and text are restricted to just three and a half lines of Greek before the long Arabic name-list. The Greek conclusion of six

95 *Muḥammad rāḥilu l-marʾa (C49)*. Cusa 1868–82, p.2, reads *Muḥammad zāḥilu l-marʾa*.

96 Reading: *Aḥmad rāḥil* (C66) – *Bū Muḥammad ṭāliᶜ* (C67) – *al-S.ntāsī* (C68). Cusa 1868–82, p.2, reads *Aḥmad zāḥil* [?] and merges the last two names into one: *Bū Muḥammad ẓalaᶜ [?] al-Sh.nqāsī*.

97 For the use of *obiit*s and similar interlinear notes in Sicilian *jarāʾid*, see Johns and Metcalfe forthcoming.

lines fulfils many of the functions usually reserved for the opening protocol and text, as well as those proper to a conclusion. It seems likely that this document, like that of Palermo, was once accompanied by a fuller, more detailed and more regular donation which is now lost, although it is possible that the late forgery from Catania, discussed above, may be substantially based upon the missing original.[98]

Léon-Robert Ménager declared this *jarīda* to be a late copy and, although this judgement has not found general support, it demands detailed consideration.[99] He begins by arguing that all of the documents in the Archivio Diocesano of Catania cathedral must have been destroyed in the earthquake of 4 February 1168 (*sic!*), and by the fire of 1197 that destroyed the cathedral.[100] Next, he argues convincingly that all of the earlier Latin and Greek documents in the archive are either late copies or forgeries. But his treatment of the three surviving *jarā*ʾ*id* is cursory and careless:

> Deux mots suffiront en ce qui concerne les deux (*sic!*) ğarāʾid ou listes de serfs greco-arabes qui nous ont été conservées. Elles passent pour des originaux délivrés par Roger I, le 20 fevrier (*sic*) 6603/1095, et par Roger II, le 1er janvier 6653/1145. Or il convient d'être affirmatif tant pour l'une que pour l'autre: l'absence de toute trace de sigillation ne permet absolument pas de consentir à une telle vue. Nous n'avons là que des copies exécutées par le diwān al-maʾmūr (*sic*), à une date que nous ne saurions préciser, mais certainement pas antérieure à 1168.

He goes on argue that, unlike the *jarā*ʾ*id* of the comital period which are written in Arabic only and not furnished with a Greek interlinear transliteration of the names,[101] 'La "platea-ğarīda" de Roger I conservée à Catane, sans le moindre signe de validation, mais disposée selon la méthode commune aux platée de l'époque royale, n'a donc pu être rédigée qu'après l'élaboration parfaite des techniques domaniales du diwān al-maʾmūr (*sic*)'.[102]

In fact, the archive holds three, not two, *jarā*ʾ*id*: the *jarīda* of the inhabitants of Aci Castello, issued by Roger I on 20 February 1095 (***Dīwānī* 4**); its renewal, a roll originally composed of seven sheets sewn together, the first two of which are now missing (***Dīwānī* 22**); and a second renewal, issued by Roger II on 1 January 1145 (***Dīwānī* 21**), of a lost *jarīda* of the inhabitants of Catania issued by Count Roger in 1095 (***Dīwānī* 3**). To minimise confusion, it may help to illustrate their relationship diagrammatically (see Table 2.3).

Ménager appears to have mistaken the fragmentary renewal of the Aci Castello *jarīda* (***Dīwānī* 22**) for the original of 1095 (***Dīwānī* 4**). Only this can account for his puzzling insistence that the archive contains only two *jarīda*s, and that the one issued by Count Roger in 1095 bears all the external characteristics of a product

[98] Above, pp.40–1.
[99] Ménager 1956–7, pp.161–2 *et passim*.
[100] 'On devine, dans ces conditions, quel a pu être le sort du trésor où étaient enfermés les chartes … de l'abbaye … Nous pensons, pour notre part, qu'il y a tout lieu de le considérer comme perdu': Ménager 1956–7, p.147.
[101] See below, pp.92, 93, 101–2, 129.
[102] Ménager 1956–7, pp.161–2.

Table 2.3 The Catania *jarīda*s of 1095 and their renewals of 1145

1095	**1145**
Missing Catania *jarīda* (***Dīwānī* 3**) →	Renewal of Catania *jarīda* (***Dīwānī* 21**)
Aci Castello *jarīda* (***Dīwānī* 4**) →	Renewal of Aci Castello *jarīda* (***Dīwānī* 22**)

of the royal *dīwān al-ma^{c}mūr*. In fact, the name-lists in the 1095 *jarīda* are written in Arabic only, without Greek transliteration, and its unpolished script could never be mistaken for the elegant chancery hand employed by the royal *dīwān al-ma^{c}mūr* after 1132. In both respects, it differs clearly from the two renewals of 1145 (***Dīwānī* 21–22**) which are written in the distinctive royal *dīwānī* script, and have interlinear Greek transliteration of the Arabic names.

As to the Catania *jarāʾid* being 'sans le moindre signe de validation', all three have a plica and regular holes for the seal. The 1095 Aci Castello *jarīda* (***Dīwānī* 4**) is validated by the signature of the protonotary John of Troina, the official responsible for the cadaster.[103] The two renewals of 1145 (***Dīwānī* 21–2**) bear the regular Greek chancery signature of Roger II. In addition, their seams are 'sealed' on the verso with the regular *dīwānī* mottoes in Arabic and Greek.[104] Moreover, the two Catania renewals belong to a group of six issued in the first months of 1145, and share all of the features common to the group.[105]

In short, all three surviving Catania *jarāʾid* are genuine originals, and Ménager was absolutely wrong to dismiss them as late copies. He was probably right, however, to suggest that the archive had suffered a disaster, possibly in the earthquake of 4 February 1169:[106] the original *jarīda* of the population of Catania (***Dīwānī* 3**) is missing; the 1095 Aci Castello *jarīda* (***Dīwānī* 4**) is quite badly torn and damaged; and the first two sheets of its renewal (***Dīwānī* 22**) have been lost.

Now that it is established that, in ***Dīwānī* 4**, we are dealing with an authentic, original document of Roger I, issued on 20 February 1095, we can turn to its contents. It grants to the bishop of Catania 'that which is written in the polyptych (*plateia*) of the Hagarenes of Aci'. The name-list, *plateia* or *jarīda* proper, opens with one note in Greek – 'These are their names' – and another in Arabic – 'The *jarīda* of the people (*ahl*) of Aci. That was confirmed'.[107] There follow three hundred and ninety (*sic*) names written in Arabic only, in seventy-eight lines of

103 von Falkenhausen 1977, p.352 and n.147; von Falkenhausen 1979, p.147, n.68: ᾿Ιωάννης πρωτονοτάριος ὑπέγραψεν ἰδία χειρί. This may now be compared with his signature to ADM, Messina no.1347: *Messina* 1994, p.156, no.18 (above, p.40, note 49).

104 See below, p.129.

105 ***Dīwānī* 21–6**: below, pp.115–43.

106 Romuald of Salerno 1935, p.258; 'Hugo Falcandus' 1897, pp.164–5; 'Hugo Falcandus' 1998, pp.216–18.

107 *jarīdatu asmāʾi ahli liyāja ḍumina dhālika.*

five columns each. Line 73, which contains the rubric for the list of widows, has only four names: line 84 has but one. Some of the shorter names, which do not occupy a full column, are followed by two to seven vertical or oblique strokes which fill the vacant space and prevent the illicit addition of names.[108] At the foot of the text comes the autograph signature of the protonotary John of Troina, who was not the scribe but the official of the cadaster responsible for overseeing the compilation of the *jarīda*.[109] The document has a plica, with regular holes for the seal which is now missing.[110] The Greek conclusion is worth translating in full:

> This *plateia* was written at the order of me, Count Roger, being at Messina, in Indiction III of the year 6603 [1095 A.D.] and is based upon the *plateiai* of my own lands and of my barons, which were written at Mazarra (*sic*) in the year 6601 in Indiction I [1 January – 31 August 1093]. And therefore we command that any of the Hagarenes inscribed in this *plateia*, who is found in my *plateiai* or in the *plateiai* of my barons, shall be returned there [*i.e.* from Catania to his place of registration].[111]

The Arabic name-list is divided into two lists. The first (lines 5–73) is introduced by the bilingual heading given above, and lists the names of three hundred and thirty-seven male heads of household. The second (lines 73–84) is headed in Arabic only, 'The names of the widows (*al-arāmil*)', and gives the names of fifty-three female heads of household. The *jarīda* ends with a total in Greek only, which states that there are three hundred and ninety-seven (*sic*) Hagarenes named.

In 1145, the monks of Catania presented the 1095 Aci Castello polyptych for revalidation.[112] The renewal (***Dīwānī* 22**) was intended to contain an exact copy of the original *jarīda* of 1095, save only that the name of each male head of household was preceded by the word *awlād* ('the children of …'), and was transliterated into Greek. We shall return to the significance of this in Chapter 5, when we discuss the renewals of 1145. For the moment all that matters is that the 1145 renewal contained what was intended to be a precise copy of the 1095 original (see Table 2.4).

In order to understand what lies behind the organisation of the Aci Castello *jarīda*, it will be useful to consider it together with the Catania *jarīda*, also issued in 1095 (***Dīwānī* 3**). The original is missing, but its contents are preserved in the renewal issued in 1145 (***Dīwānī* 21**): the introduction tells how the monks of Catania came before King Roger at Palermo with 'the *jarīda* of the Great Count … which was issued to the episcopal church of Catania fifty years ago [*i.e.* in 1095]'.[113] Like the 1145 Aci Castello renewal illustrated above (***Dīwānī* 22**), the

[108] After one name – Hamdā[n] ibn Lijātī, line 54, col.4 – a compact ornamental ligature (*ḥayyā-hu llāh* [?], 'May God preserve his life') appears to serve, in part, the same purpose: Hamdān was perhaps a connection of the scribe, or even the scribe himself.

[109] Above, p.53, note 103.

[110] On the inside of the fold are two Latin notes which appear to be of the early 12th century or, possibly, contemporary with the document itself: *de Iacio* and, in a different hand, *p[ri]ma*. On the verso are the Latin notes *Carta villanorum Iacii* and *IACII*, also 12th-century.

[111] In the 1145 renewals (***Dīwānī* 21–2**) of the Catania and Aci Castello *jarīda*s originally issued in 1095 (***Dīwānī* 3–4**), the polyptychs compiled for Count Roger in 1093 (***Dīwānī* 1**) are referred to as 'the *jarāʾid* which were written at Mazara two years earlier': below, pp.119–21.

[112] For this series of renewals, see below, pp.115–43.

Table 2.4 The same line from the 1095 *jarīda* and the renewal of 1145 compared

***Dīwānī* 4: Aci Castello 1095, line 31**				
column 5	**column 4**	**column 3**	**column 2**	**column 1**
ولده	محمد بن عبد الحميد	ابرهيم بن المليلي	ايوب	خلف الله البشنكيلي
waladu-hu	*Muḥammad ibn* *ʿAbd al-Ḥamīd*	*Ibrāhīm ibn* *al-Malīlī (?)*	*Ayyūb*	*Khalaf Allāh* *al-Bashinkilī (?)*
***Dīwānī* 22: Aci Castello 1145, lines 1–2**				
line 2, col.2	**line 2, col.1**	**line 1, col.4**	**line 1, col.3**	**line 2, col.2**
اولاد ولده	اولاد محمد بن عبد الحميد	اولاد ابرهيم بن المليلي	اولاد ايوب	اولاد خلف الله البشنكيلي
οἱ παῖδες τοῦ υἱοῦ αὐτοῦ	οἱ παῖδες Μουχούμμουτ επιν ᾿Αβδελχαμήτ	οἱ παῖδες Βραχὶμ επιν ᾿Ηλμελέλι	οἱ παῖδες ᾿Ιώβ	οἱ παῖδες Χαλφάλλα ᾿Ελβεσήγγηλι
awlād *waladi-hi*	*awlād Muḥammad* *ibn ʿAbd al-Ḥamīd*	*awlād Ibrāhīm ibn* *al-Malīlī (?)*	*awlād Ayyūb*	*awlād Khalaf Allāh* *al-Bashinkīlī*

1145 Catania renewal contains what was intended to be an exact copy of the original of 1095, except for the addition of the word *awlād* (‘the children of …’) and of the Greek transliteration. In order to simplify matters, I shall now refer to the Aci Castello and Catania *jarīda*s, without mentioning their dates, as if the original 1095 versions of both were preserved.

The Catania *jarīda* is divided into five name-lists as follows:

1. Headed, ‘the people of Catania’ (*ahl Qaṭāniya*): five hundred and twenty-five names, all of the form *awlād Fulān, etc.*
2. Headed, ‘the names of the widows’ (*asmāʾ al-arāmil*): ninety-four names
3. Headed, ‘the slaves of the church’ (*ʿabīd al-kanīsa*): twenty-five names
4. Headed, ‘the Jews’ (*al-yahūd*): twenty-five names, all of the form *awlād Fulān, etc.*
5. Headed, ‘the names of the blind-men’ (*asmāʾ al-ʿumy*): eight names.

113 For these events, see below, pp.115–18.

In short, the Aci Castello and Catania *jarīda*s both list, first, the majority class of ordinary tax-payers, called simply *ahl*, being healthy, adult, male heads of household; and then up to four other classes that, from the fiscal point of view, were extraordinary: single women called 'widows' (Aci Castello and Catania); and slaves, Jews, and blind-men (Catania only). As in the Palermo *jarīda* discussed above, it is these extraordinary lists which reveal the way in which, and the purpose for which, the two polyptychs were compiled.

Amongst the *arāmil* listed in the Aci Castello polyptych are: twenty-four mothers with children, who may be defined as the wives, daughters, or sisters of absent men;[114] eight widows or abandoned wives;[115] four mothers;[116] four daughters;[117] three daughters-in-law;[118] two serving women;[119] a sister;[120] a pair of sisters;[121] and an old woman;[122] for five women we have only the personal name (*ism*) or the nick-name (*laqab*).[123] In other words, of the fifty-three *arāmil*, forty-seven are listed according to their household relationships with men who are absent – husbands, fathers, fathers-in-law, sons, brothers and masters.

Similarly, in the list of *arāmil* in the Catania polyptych, sixty-nine of the ninety-four 'widows' are recorded in terms of their household relationships with absent men: twenty-five mothers with children; fifteen daughters-in-law; twelve widows or abandoned wives; six sisters; four daughters; three serving women; one woman known only by a man's name; one blind woman, described as 'of the household (*dār*) of Ibn al-Hawwārī'; one woman who is both mother and sister; and 'the sweetheart (*ḥabība*) of ᶜUmar the muezzin'. Only the fifteen women who are known only by an *ism* or a *laqab* – the three old women, two washerwomen, the pair of sisters living together, the saleswoman, the jar-maker or jar-vendor, the midwife, and the hunchback – are listed without reference to an absent male household member.

It is clear that the *arāmil* are distinguished from the *ahl* because, in one way or another, they have 'lost' the male heads of the households to which they belonged. It follows that the lists of *arāmil* were compiled with reference to earlier lists of *ahl* which registered their men as heads of household. The earlier lists were compared against the results of a census, taken in or shortly before 1095, and the absent men,

[114] *e.g. ukht Ayyūb wa-bnatu-hā* (line 73, col.4), 'the sister of Ayyūb and her daughter'; *bint Maymūn al-Ḥarīrī wa-awlādu-hā* (line 74, col.1), 'the daughter of Maymūn al-Ḥarīrī and her children'.

[115] *e.g. zawjat Mūsā* (line 79, col.4), 'the wife of Mūsā'; *zawjat ᶜIyād* (line 79, col.5), 'the wife of ᶜIyād'.

[116] *e.g. Umm al-Ṣiqillī* (line 83, col.2), 'the mother of al-Ṣiqillī'; *Umm Ibn Madīnī* (line 83, col.3), 'the mother of Ibn Madīnī'.

[117] *e.g. Bint Niᶜma* (line 78, col.4), 'the daughter of Niᶜma'; *Bint Samrūn* (line 81, col.3), 'the daughter of Samrūn'.

[118] *e.g. khatanatu l-ᶜĀshiq* (line 79, col.3), 'the daughter-in-law of al-ᶜĀshiq'; *khatanat Maymūn* (line 81, col.2), 'the daughter-in-law of Maymūn'.

[119] *Khadīmat Ibn Wārith* (line 83, col.5), 'the serving-woman of Ibn Wārith'; *Fāṭima khādim al-Shabūtī* (line 84, col.1), 'Fāṭima the servant of al-Shabūtī'.

[120] *Ukht ᶜUmar Bū Ruqādī* (line 79, col.1), 'the sister of ᶜUmar Bū Ruqādī'.

[121] *Ṣaydāʾ(?) wa-ukhtu-hā* (line 78, col.3), 'Ṣaydāʾ(?) and her sister'.

[122] *al-ᶜAjūz al-Bayyāᶜa* (line 83, col.4), 'the old woman al-Bayyāᶜa [lit. 'the merchant', fem.].

[123] Samrīṭa (line 80, col.1), al-Muḥaqqaqa (line 81, col.1), al-Quwāliya (line 82, col.1), Qālī (line 83, col.1 – or possibly the Greek personal name Κάλλη?), al-Jāliṣīya (line 83, col.3).

who had died or disappeared since the compilation of the earlier register, were recorded in 1095 only through their relationships with the female members of the 'widowed' households which they left behind.

The lists of the ordinary heads of household also contain traces of the earlier registers from which those of 1095 were compiled according to the *neogamos*-system discussed above. In the Aci Castello *jarīda*, there are at least ten pairs of brothers of the type *ᶜUthmān ibn Ḥasan – Akhū-hu Nuᶜmān* which, we have already seen for the Palermo *jarīda*, indicate the existence of an earlier, missing register. There is also one father and son pair, and one father-in-law and son-in-law. In addition, there are fifteen clusters of two, three and even four successive names bearing the same patronymic;[124] these too seem to indicate the existence of an earlier register, updated according to the *neogamos*-system. Similarly, in the list of ordinary households in the Catania *jarīda*, there are over sixty pairs (or larger groups) of brothers of the type *Ḥasan ibn Badr – Ḥusayn akhū-hu*;[125] at least seven fathers and sons; several sons-in-law; three or four groups of successive names bearing the same patronymic; and a couple of 'foster-sons' (*aribbāʾ*).[126] In the much shorter list of Jews, there are three pairs of brothers, three sons-in-law, and two pairs of father and son. Neither the list of the slaves of the church, nor that of the blind-men contains such matches.

What was the nature of the earlier tax-registers and when were they compiled – before or after the Norman conquest? On the one hand, it could be argued that the form of the 1095 *jarīda*s suggests strongly that they were registers compiled for the collection of a capitation-tax comparable to the Islamic *jizya*. This might explain why single women, slaves, and blind-men were listed separately, for classical Islamic tax-law seems to have exempted, or assessed at a lower rate, women, children, slaves and invalids from the poll-tax.[127] On the other hand, while it is possible that the lists of Jews and slaves could have been compiled from pre-Norman *jizya*-lists, this can scarcely have been the case for the Muslim *ahl*, Muslim *arāmil* and Muslim blind-men – none of these categories would have been liable for the *jizya* under Islam. The possibilities, therefore, are two: either these lists were compiled after the conquest of Catania by the Normans and were designed, from the first, as poll-tax registers of the subject population; or they were drawn from some pre-conquest register, the precise nature and function of which cannot now be determined, but which was adapted to Norman needs. The fact that there

[124] *e.g.* line 16, col.4 – line 17, col.2: Sūdān ibn Khalaf, ᶜUthmān ibn Khalaf, Nuᶜmān ibn Khalaf, ᶜAlī ibn Khalaf.

[125] In the Catania renewal, but not the Aci Castello renewal, the scribe has frequently felt compelled to respect the grammatical consequences of the interpolated *awlād*, and to transform *Ḥusayn akhū-hu* into *awlād Ḥusayn akhī-hi*.

[126] See below, pp.159–62.

[127] Ibn Mammātī 1943, pp.317–18; Løkkegaard 1950, p.138; Rabie 1972, p.108. For problems surrounding the origins of classical Islamic practice, see Morimoto 1981, pp.176–81 (see also p.57, para.7, p.270, n.10, and p.58); Simonsen, 1988, pp.144–7, 148–50. For the late Fāṭimid period, Goitein 1967–93, vol.II, p.381, notes that 'The provisions of ancient Islamic law which exempted the indigent, the invalids and the old were no longer observed in the Geniza period and had also been discarded in theory by the Shāfiᶜī school of law that prevailed in Egypt' (but not in Sicily).

is strong internal evidence that the lists of *ahl* and *arāmil* were compiled from an earlier register, combines with the early date of the *jarīda*s, only fourteen years after the final subjugation of Catania in 1081, to argue strongly in favour of the second alternative.

Roger Forestal's *jarīda* (*Dīwānī* 5)

Some details survive of a fourth Arabic *jarīda* issued by Count Roger I. In March 1145, Walter Forestal brought to Palermo for renewal and confirmation a *jarīda* issued by Count Roger I to his father, Roger Forestal. The *jarīda* listed 'that which he [Count Roger] granted to him from the men of the *jarīda* of Jāliṣū, but excluding those inscribed in the *jarīda* of Corleone'.[128] If the words of the 1145 renewal (***Dīwānī* 25**) are to be taken literally, the register issued to Roger Forestal had been compiled with reference to two pre-existing polyptychs: those of Jāliṣū and Corleone. There is no hint as to whether these were records of the Muslim administration or registers newly compiled under Count Roger but if, as is probable, the donation to Roger Forestal dates from the period 1093–5, then it is more likely that they would have been pre-conquest.

The Triocala *jarīda* of 1097–8 (*Dīwānī* 6)

In 6606 A.M., Indiction VI (1097–8 A.D.), in memory of the Christians who had died in the wars of conquest, Count Roger founded the Greek monastery of San Giorgio di Triocala, near Sciacca,[129] and issued privileges (σιγίλλια, *sigillia*) endowing it with lands, and a register (πλατεῖα, *plateia*) listing its villeins. None of these documents have survived in the original, and they are only known through renewals issued in 1141 (***Dīwānī* 15–17**). The villeins themselves, however, are also mentioned in another, independent source. Until it became a *metochion* or dependence of the Greek archimandra of San Salvatore di Messina,[130] San Giorgio was under the jurisdiction of the bishop of Agrigento. The 13th-century *Libellus de successione pontificum Agrigenti* records that Roger founded San Giorgio and

[128] *mā aqṭaʿa-hu mina l-rijāli min jarīdati jāliṣū wa-laysa hum maktūbīna fī jarīdati qurlūna*: Cusa 1868–82, p.127, lines 7–9. Jāliṣū lay about 7km west of Prizzi (PA): the Arabic place-name survives in the modern form *Cangialeso*, possibly from *ʿAyn* ('the Spring of') *Jāliṣū*: Nania 1995, pp.152–3; Caracausi 1993, vol.I, pp.272–3.

[129] San Giorgio di Triocala lay at modern Sant'Anna (AG) (which occupies the site of ancient Triocala), about 1.5km south-east of Caltabellotta, and 12km north-east of Sciacca: the monastery is now destroyed, but a modern shrine to St George marks the site. For this monastery see Scaduto 1947, pp.125–6; Scaturro 1924–5, vol.I, pp.6, 226–8, vol.II, p.76.

[130] For San Salvatore, see Scaduto 1947, pp.165–244; von Falkenhausen 1994.

endowed it with 'many villeins' in memory of the one hundred Christian knights who died winning these lands from the Saracen.[131]

Although the original *plateia* is now lost, it is highly probable that the renewal issued to Triocala in November 1141 (***Dīwānī* 18**) was based upon it. Amongst the households that it lists are fifty at Triocala and another fifty at Raḥl al-Baṣal, a total of one hundred names. The names in these two lists suggest that they were compiled with reference to an earlier *jarīda* according to the *neogamos*-system, so that several families can be reconstructed, spanning up to three generations (*e.g.* see Table 2.5). In other words, the original upon which ***Dīwānī* 18** was based must have been compiled up to two generations before the generation registered in 1141, a sequence which fits comfortably with the date of ***Dīwānī* 6**, 1097–8 A.D.

The language of the original *plateia* is not specified but, if it is correct that ***Dīwānī* 18**, which is written entirely in Arabic, is based upon it and, indeed, is a renewal of it, then it follows that ***Dīwānī* 6** is most likely to have been an Arabic *jarīda*.

Table 2.5 A family reconstructed from the Triocala *jarīda* illustrating the *neogamos*-system

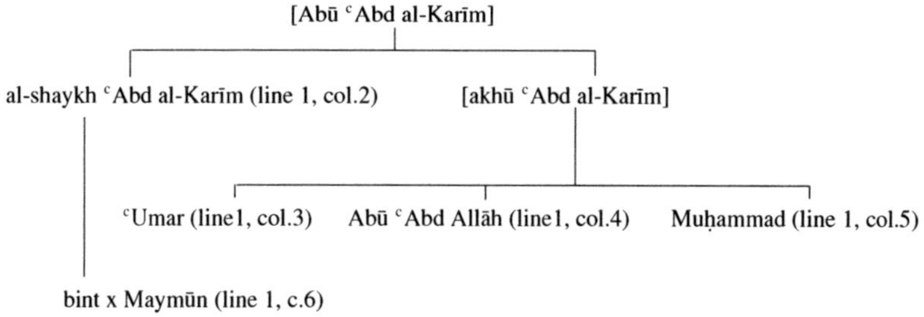

The functions of the earliest Norman *jarāʾid*

To sum up, there survive two original *jarīda*s of Count Roger (***Dīwānī* 2 and 4**), and there are details of three *deperdita* contained in renewals issued by King Roger (***Dīwānī* 3, 5 and 6**). In addition, the 1095 Aci Castello polyptych states that an unspecified number of polyptychs were drawn up and issued to Roger and his barons in 1093 (***Dīwānī* 1**). The polyptychs compiled at this time for Roger were apparently conserved until 1145 when they were referred to as *al-jarāʾid al-dīwānī*. There is

[131] It is probably this earlier *jarīda* to which the *Libellus de successione pontificum Agrigenti* refers: *Subt[us] Calatabellottam fuit institutum quoddam monasterium loco qui dicitur Trocculi, dotatum villanis multis pro honore sancti Georgii pro centum militibus ibi a Sarracenis occisis in acquisitione terrarum, quod Agrigentina Ecclesia tenuit fere per annos .LX. quod ex levi perdidit dum procurator suscipere noluit in hospicio nuncium regis et instinctu Grecorum magnatum datum fuit archimandrite Messane*: Collura 1961, p.305.

strong evidence that new *jarāʾid* issued to the churches of Catania and Palermo and to Roger Forestal were all compiled with reference to pre-existing registers. Those issued to Palermo and Catania did incorporate new data gathered by cadastral surveys held shortly before 1095, but this alone does not seem sufficient to demonstrate that, by 1093–5, Count Roger's officials had already conducted a general census of the subject population of the whole island, nor that the *jarāʾid* were wholly derived from such a survey .[132] On the contrary, an exceedingly strong case can be made that the origins of the Norman *jarāʾid* lay in the Muslim tax-registers of pre-conquest Sicily, and that these constituted both a model and the original source of information for the cadastral surveys and tax-registers of Count Roger.

The function of the earliest Norman *jarāʾid* was fourfold. First, they played an important role in the division of the spoils after the military conquest was complete. Together with descriptions of the boundaries of estates granted, the *jarāʾid* constituted the essential apparatus of the post-conquest partition of Sicily.

Second, the *jarāʾid* offered a partial solution to the problem of displaced and unregistered villeins. Once again, the point will be made more clearly by comparison with Calabria, where Roger had adopted the practice which his Byzantine predecessors had left to him and the other Norman rulers of the south. Thus, he granted proprietors not merely communities of unregistered villeins, but also what was later to be called *jus affidandi*, the right to commend unregistered and unlanded villeins into their own service.[133] A typical example of this practice can be seen in a grant made in 1114 by Count Roger II to Abbot Methodius of San Nicolò di Droso in Calabria. The count permitted the abbot to settle upon the lands of the monastery any prisoners (of war?), strangers and immigrants, so long as they were not already registered in the ἀκρόστιχα (*akrostikha*, 'polyptychs') of Duke Roger Borsa, nor in those of his barons, nor in the *plateiai* of Count Roger himself.[134] In Sicily, a similar, but significantly different stipulation – 'that any of the Hagarenes inscribed in this polyptych, who is found in my polyptychs or in the polyptychs of my barons, shall be returned there [*i.e.* to his place of registration]' – first appears in the Aci Castello *jarīda* of 1095 and, from 1141, occurs regularly in the royal *jarāʾid*:[135] no right is conceded with regard to the commendation of unregistered villeins, and it is clearly intended that a lord had legal right only to those villeins registered in his polyptychs. In contrast to the mainland, it would seem that the right of commendation was rarely granted with respect to the subject inhabitants of Sicily.[136]

The case of the colony of Focerò illustrates the Sicilian alternative in the time of Roger I. In *c.*1094, Roger held a special assembly at Troina to which all his

[132] Garufi 1928, p.13, believed Count Roger's polyptychs to be proof of a 'censimento generale di tutti gli arabi vinti sottoposti a servaggio'.

[133] Antonucci 1935, *passim*.

[134] von Falkenhausen 1980a, p.241, n.131, citing Rome, Bibl. Vat., Cod. Lat. Vat. 8201, f.124r. See also King Roger's renewal of a grant of villeins in Calabria made by Roger I to the church of Palermo in 1093: PA, Arch. Dioc., no.13; ed. Cusa 1868–82, no.81, pp.26–8; Caspar 1904, p.561, reg.192. Here, the stipulation runs: ὑπῆρχε ξησμένος καὶ εἰ μὲν εὑρεθῆ εἰς ἡμετέραν πλατείαν εἴτε τεῤῥερίων ἵνα ἀπόλλυτο αὐτόν.

[135] Above, p.54, and below, pp.107, 108, 139–40.

[136] Landholders on the island did, of course, commend villeins into service: for Muslim 'newcomers',

principal feudatories were summoned. On three consecutive days Roger's heralds proclaimed that anyone retaining a villein without legal right was to return him immediately to his place of origin, upon pain of public whipping and disgrace. Roger also gave notice that he had appointed three officials to ensure that this order was obeyed. They were also to collect all unregistered villeins and to settle them on the comital demesne at Focerò, near Patti. The three officials went to work and, in the zone between San Marco and Oliveri (only about 30km separates the two), they are said to have rounded up five hundred families of villeins. All were settled at Focerò, apportioned lands and exempted from all taxes and dues for an introductory period of five years.[137]

In Sicily, the count seems to have reserved to himself exclusively the right to commend villeins, and not to have permitted proprietors to commend villeins to themselves as was common practice on the mainland. King Roger and his successors were later to grant households of landless, 'unregistered' but named villeins,[138] but this is not to grant general, or even limited,[139] *jus affidandi*. As we shall see, the royal *dīwān* certainly kept registers of 'unregistered' villeins, and under William II, attempted to recall to the royal lands all its villeins, adscripted and not.[140]

The third, and principal function of the *jarāʾid* was fiscal. This is best illustrated in the Arabic document of *c.*1177, in which the three runaway villeins (*rijāl al-jarāʾid*, 'men of the registers) agreed to pay the *jizya* and the *qānūn,* or land-tax. The survival into Norman times of the traditional Muslim fiscal system, based upon the *jizya* and the *kharāj,* or land-tax, is here clearly apparent; as, indeed, it is in the Palermo *jarīda* of 1095 and in the 13th-century documents from Lucera and Malta.[141]

When the Normans adapted these taxes to their own needs, they were no longer paid to the state as had presumably been the case under Muslim rule. On the contrary, a Norman lord received as his own the *kharāj* from his land and the *jizya* from its inhabitants, so that only within the royal demesne did the revenue from these taxes pass to the fisc. It is striking that, in direct contrast to similar agreements between Latin lords and Greek villagers or Latin *coloni* in eastern Sicily,[142] there is no mention, in the *c.*1177 agreement, of labour services, customs, *banalités*, and other dues. While it must be acknowledged that the *jarāʾid* issued by the royal *dīwān*, which are rarely more than lists of names, are not the sources in which evidence for such services is likely to be found, references to Muslim villeins who owed anything but the *jizya* and the land-tax are extremely rare. In western Sicily,

i.e. muls and the *ghurabāʾ*, see below, pp.147–9; for an interesting case of a family of Greeks commending themselves into the service of a Greek convent as late as 1195, see Guillou 1963, no.18, pp.142–6.

137 The details are given in a letter of *c.*1142 addressed to King Roger by a group of petitioners, who chose as their spokesman at court Abbot John of San Bartolomeo di Lipari-Patti: Patti, Arch. Dioc. no.14; Girgensohn and Kamp 1965, p.18, reg.37; ed. Cusa 1868–82, no.41, pp.532–5; Caspar 1904, p.547, reg.149; with corrections by Collura 1955a, pp.612–13;

138 Above, pp.145–51.

139 For example, see the conditions imposed by Humphrey of Gravina in his grant of September 1092 to the bishop of Gravina in Del Giudice 1863–9, vol.I, App.no.15, pp.XXXII–XXXIV.

140 Above, pp.145–51, and ***Dīwānī* 45,** pp.165–9.

141 Above, pp.35–6, 47.

142 Greeks: *e.g.* Cusa 1868–82, no.35, pp.512–13; Girgensohn and Kamp 1965, p.14, reg.18. Latins: *e.g.* Garufi 1908, especially pp.19–20.

the lord tended to farm his estates indirectly, keeping no reserve for his own use and, therefore, required no agricultural services from his villeins. There is nonetheless some evidence that, on what appear to be the rare occasions when a lord did demand labour services, the *jarāʾid* provided him with the apparatus through which he could do so. This is the fourth and final function of the *jarāʾid*.

In *c.*1329–30, the bishop of Cefalù, Tommaso da Butera, had the documents and privileges of his church collected and transcribed into a single codex known as the *Rollus Rubeus*. Amongst them is an otherwise unknown Latin list of villeins.[143] The preamble to the list explained that these were villeins given to the church by King Roger and that, although not so much as the memory of the villeins remained, their names had been copied from ancient writings. There follow eighty-three names, each followed by the sum of *tarì* that its bearer owed the church.[144] The conclusion to the list is as follows:

> Each of the aforesaid villeins used to give 24 days labour and contributions (*dabat dietas viginti quatuor in angariis et collectis*) on the calends of August in the 2nd Indiction and every other indiction, in total 630 (*sic*) *tarì* from the 'external villeins' (*de villanis exteris*). The church used to receive the double from the 'urban villeins' (*de villanis civitatensibus*), who numbered 3,808.

I tentatively conclude that the distinction between *villani exteri* and *villani civitatenses* reflects a 13th-century Latin perspective upon the distinction between, respectively, unregistered and registered villeins that is standard in *dīwānī* documents of the 12th century. The term *villani exteri* most probably derives from the Greek οἱ ἐξώγραφοι (*oi exōgrafoi*) or may even translate the Arabic *al-ghurabāʾ* (literally, 'the strangers'), while *villani civitatenses* seems to be a close literal translation of the Arabic *rijāl al-maḥallāt*, 'the men of the settlements'.[145] The sense of the passage quoted above would seem to mean that the *villani exteri* owed twenty-four days and the *villani civitatenses* forty-eight days labour service, which they had commuted into money payment. It would, however, be possible to interpret the passage differently – as meaning that each villein owed *both* labour and money service. In either case, this list would seem to show a Latin lord using a *jarīda* to collect labour services (commuted or not) from his villeins. Such an exception to the general rule would only emphasise that the pattern of landholding pertaining in western Sicily after the conquest tended to work against the development of angariation.

143 *Rollus Rubeus. Privilegii ecclesie cephaleditane de diversis regibus et imperatoribus concessa* (PA, AdS, MS Miscellanea 2nda Bacheca no.5), ff.18v.–19v.; ed. *Rollus Rubeus* 1972, pp.39–41. The list is undated except for the indictional year mentioned in the conclusion (see below) but Carlo-Alberto Garufi, who published a poor edition of the list, argued that the indiction corresponded to 1244 A.D., and that this gave an approximate date for the list: Garufi 1928, pp.97–100. However, Metcalfe 1999, pp.151–2, has recently pointed out that several of the names in the Latin list also occur in the 1145 Cefalù *jarīda* (***Dīwānī* 24**): it follows that the indictional year must correspond to a date in the mid-12th century, probably to 1139 or 1153.

144 The rates were as follows: 1 villein owed 40 *tarì* (1:40), 1:16, 1:13, 3:12, 1:11, 3:10, 25:8, 5:7, 35:6, 8:4: a total of 623 *tarì*.

145 For further discussion of these categories of villeins, see below pp.147–51, and Johns forthcoming d.

CHAPTER 3

'Our Lady, the Regent Adelaide, and Our Lord, the Count Roger, Her Son', 1101–30

In the previous chapter, it was argued that the origins of the Arabic administration of Norman Sicily must be sought in the periods of conquest and of distribution of the spoils which followed the cessation of hostilities. During the conquest itself, a group of specialists attached to the de Hautevilles' staff was responsible for the negotiation and compilation of surrender treaties which recorded the terms of the post-conquest settlement. If, as is probable, these *amān*s were written, then they are likely to have constituted one root from which the Arabic administration grew. Again, during the period of conquest, it is likely that the same group of specialists, whenever possible, seized and preserved the tax-records of the Muslim administration. These were adapted to post-conquest needs, and used by Roger and his staff as the basis for the distribution of both lands and communities of the indigenous population. They are likely to have been the second root of the early Arabic administration of Norman Sicily. However, after an initial burst of activity, which seems to have been concentrated in *c.*1093–5, the Arabic administration becomes more difficult to observe. This is probably, in part, the result of a combination of factors, including political vicissitudes, the random distribution of surviving documents, and the high number of *deperdita*. Nonetheless, the issue of documents in Arabic does seem to have ceased after Roger II assumed sole rule in 1112 and, from then until his coronation in 1130, the comital administration was predominantly Greek, and its activities were concentrated in eastern Sicily and Calabria, rather than in the Arabic-speaking west of Sicily. It is thus extraordinary that, within two years of his coronation, King Roger's chancery was producing bilingual – Greek and Arabic – documents which attest to the existence of a professional and sophisticated Arabic *dīwān*. This chapter begins to investigate that apparent paradox by discussing the comital administration from the death of Roger I until his son's coronation on Christmas Day 1130.

The comital administration

After the surrender of Noto in 1091, the island was at peace, so long as Roger lived. The Zīrids of Ifrīqiya had ceased to intervene in Sicily in 1075,[1] and revolts

[1] Idris 1962a, vol.I, pp.285–6.

by Sicilian Muslims – such as at Iato in the hinterland of Palermo in 1079,[2] and at Pantalica near Syracuse in 1092[3] – were surprisingly rare. But, when Roger died, on 22 June 1101, he left no adult son. Simon, his eldest son and heir, was only seven years old and, therefore, the Countess Adelaide, who was Roger's widow and Simon's mother, assumed the position of regent. Simon died while still a minor, on 28 September 1105, and was succeeded as heir by his younger brother, Roger, who was then aged nine years. Roger assumed sole authority only in the second half of 1112, the year following his sixteenth birthday on 22 December 1111.[4]

The succession to Roger I did not go unchallenged, but the chroniclers of the dynasty are almost silent about the revolt which broke out on his death.[5] All that survive are a few isolated references to obscure events, which cannot be woven into a narrative and the significance of which is impossible to assess. In January 1123, witnesses in a case before Roger II's court made passing reference to 'the revolt of the barons', and the 'recapture of Ciminna'.[6] It may have been rebellion which caused the fortress of Qal^{c}at al-Ṣirāt to be razed to the ground, and moved to modern Collesano.[7] In the hinterland of Patti, rebellion rumbled on until at least the death of Adelaide in 1118, and was still a cause of grievance as late as 1142.[8] The Anglo-Norman historian, Orderic Vitalis, clearly knew something of Adelaide's difficulties, and claimed that she was unable to manage the regency alone, and so gave to Robert, the son of the duke of Burgundy, both her daughter in marriage and 'the whole principality of Sicily'. According to Orderic, Robert ruled and vigorously defended the county for ten years, while Adelaide concentrated upon raising her son; when Roger came of age, Adelaide had Robert poisoned.[9] The historicity of this report has been much discussed, and Hubert Houben has recently proposed that Robert should be identified with Robert Borrel, one of the leading barons of the *comitatus* under Roger I and Adelaide;[10] but most of the detail in Orderic's report is patently false. In part, Orderic is here indulging his ghoulish fascination

[2] Malaterra 1927–8, p.69.
[3] Malaterra 1927–8, p.98.
[4] Pontieri 1955, pp.356–7 and n.58, p.362 and n.69.
[5] There is one tantalising reference to a rebellion of 'Apulians' against Simon in *Anonymous Vaticanus* 1726, col.777: see Pontieri 1955, pp.363–4; Houben 1991, pp.23–4; von Falkenhausen 1998, p.88.
[6] 6631 A.M. [1123 A.D.], January, Ind.I. Original: PA, AdS, Cefalù, no.1: ed. Cusa 1868–82, no.38, pp.471–2. See also Caspar 1904, pp.26–8 and p.494, reg.42; Ménager 1960, Appendix 2, no.15, pp.190–1. For this reading of the phrase πρινὶ τοῦ μούρτου [*i.e.* μούλτου from Latin *tumultus*] τῶν τεῤῥερίων, see Caracausi 1990, p.393. See also von Falkenhausen 1980a, p.226, n.19; Houben 1991, p.29 and n.100; von Falkenhausen 1998, p.98. For a more detailed account of this fascinating document, see below, pp.73–4, 88, 89, 295.
[7] al-Idrīsī 1970–6, p.620; *BAS*², vol.I, p.66; *BAS*²*(It.)*, vol.I, p.94.
[8] See the following three documents (especially the second) from Patti, Arch. Dioc. (1) Girgensohn and Kamp 1965, p.18, no.37; Collura 1955a, p.612; ed. Cusa 1868–82, no.41, pp.532–5. (2) Girgensohn and Kamp 1965, p.18, no.38; Collura 1955a, p.584, no.58 and (ed.) pp.609–14. (3) Girgensohn and Kamp 1965, p.18, no.39; ed. Cusa 1868–82, no.67, pp.525–7; also Spata 1871, pp.30–9. They will be discussed in detail in Johns and Metcalfe forthcoming. I cannot agree with the brief account given by Houben 1991, p.29.
[9] Ordericus Vitalis 1969–80, vol.VI, pp.428, 432.
[10] See Houben 1991, pp.24–7, with references to earlier bibliography, and von Falkenhausen 1998, p.88 and p.96, n.55.

with women poisoners,[11] but there is more than monkish misogyny to his assumption that Adelaide could only have ruled through a doughty French knight. He was probably unaware, and in any case would have been unable to comprehend, that Adelaide, and after her, the young Roger II, relied above all upon a small staff of professional Greek bureaucrats.

Already before the conquest was complete, there begins to appear the small group of Greek administrators who were responsible for the post-conquest reorganisation and, in particular, for delimiting the boundaries, and registering the populations, of lands that were granted to feudatories out of the comital demesne. These administrators were often known collectively as 'the archons of the court' (οἱ ἄρχουντες τῆς κόρτης, *oi archontes tēs kortēs*). They also bore various individual titles – including chamberlain, emir, *hostiarius*, logothete, mystologue, notary, and protonotary – but these grandiloquent titles clearly did not yet correspond to precise duties and responsibilities. A few examples will serve to demonstrate that the members of Roger's staff were omnicompetent, and did whatever needed doing within the embryonic administration, without regard to the sort of demarcation and hierarchy that was later to characterise the royal bureaucracy.

We have already encountered the protonotary John of Troina, who compiled the Aci Castello *jarīda* of 1095 (***Dīwānī* 4**).[12] He may first appear in February 1091 as the scribe of a Greek privilege to the church of Mileto, known only in a Latin translation in which he is apparently given the titles of *notarius et magister rationalis comitis*.[13] In April 1096, he was responsible for a complex Greek privilege in which Roger effectively founded the see of Messina, delimited its boundaries, and listed its principal possessions.[14] In February 1097, with Nicholas de Mesa (see below), he oversaw the donation of villeins from the comital demesne at Arsafia (near Stilo) to Santa Maria di Turri.[15] From his appearances, it is clear that John was responsible for issuing donations of lands and villeins from the comital demesne, and for compiling and keeping records of their boundaries and populations.

Bonos, who also appears with the title protonotary (but is more usually styled notary), was a close relative of the famous Scholarios, the Greek chaplain of Roger I and founder of San Salvatore di Bordonaro,[16] and thus belonged to one of the leading Greek families of the county which held extensive lands on both shores of

[11] In addition to Adelaide see, for example, Ordericus Vitalis 1969–80, vol.II, p.122 and vol.IV, pp.28–30.

[12] Above, pp.53, 54.

[13] *Praesens sigillum ... scriptum fuit manu mei notarii et magistri rationalis comitis Ph.* (sic?) *Joannis domini S. Agathae de Gizofa*: February 6599 A.M., Ind.XIV (1091 A.D.): ed. Capialbi 1835, Appendix, no.11, pp.136–40. See also Kehr 1902, p.68; Takayama 1993, pp.34–5.

[14] Unpublished original: ADM, Messina no.1347: ed. (from late copy) Cusa 1868–82, no.9, pp.289–91. See also *Messina* 1994, p.156, no.18.

[15] Trinchera 1865, no.60, pp.77–8. See also von Falkenhausen 1977, p.352.

[16] For Bonos see: Ménager 1960, p.40, n.4, and, especially, von Falkenhausen 1998, pp.100, 101, and nn.80–3 and 86. For Scholarios and his family see: von Falkenhausen 1977, pp.355–6; von Falkenhausen 1979, p.146 and n.64. It is in the will of Scholarios, which exists only in a Latin translation, that Bonos appears as *Bonus protonoculus* (sic!?) *et suus germanus*: Pirri 1733, vol.II, p.1006, and Di Giovanni 1896, p.341; see von Falkenhausen 1998, p.101, n.86.

the Straits of Messina. Bonos first appears in February 1091 with the title of notary.[17] In April 1094, with the titles of notary and judge, he was sent by Roger I to settle an inheritance dispute in the comital court at Messina.[18] It was presumably both his illustrious family and his position in the Sicilian court that drew him to the attention of the Byzantine emperor, Alexius I Comnenus, who, sometime before January 1110, awarded him the title of *protonobilissimus*.[19] Like Nicholas the chamberlain and Leo the logothete (for both, see below), the protonotary Bonos may also have served as 'great judge of all Calabria'.[20] He last appears in 1117,[21] but his son, Roger, was in royal service in the 1140s,[22] as were Nicholas and Simon, the sons of Scholarios.[23]

There is no evidence whether the protonotary also had charge of the financial administration of the county, in the manner that the Byzantine official from whom his title was presumably derived (ὁ πρωτονοτάριος τοῦ θέματος, *o prōtonotarios tou thematos*) seems to have directed the financial administration of the theme.[24] Another protonotary on Roger's staff at this time, Nicholas de Mesa, was also styled chamberlain. In the duchy of Normandy, the *camera* had been the centre of financial administration, apparently since the days of Richard II (996–1026) and, under William II before 1066, the chamberlain grew into a figure of considerable importance.[25] The word *camera* was introduced into the administrative vocabulary of southern Italy by the Normans, and Robert Guiscard had a *camera* into which revenue was paid, although no ducal chamberlain is known.[26] It is therefore tempting to assume that, in Roger's Sicily, the chamberlain – ὁ καπριλίγγας (*o kapriliggas*), *camerarius* – had charge of the financial administration of the county, but no independent evidence corroborates such a conclusion. Nicholas bore the title of chamberlain under Roger I, Adelaide and the young Simon, from perhaps as early as 1090 until at least 1105. His career may be traced through an impressively large number of appearances from October 1086 until perhaps as late as November 1111, but the path is mined with many documents of dubious authenticity.[27] A few steps seem relatively safe. He was a Greek

[17] *Bonus noster notarius* in the document cited above, p.65, note 13. See also von Falkenhausen 1998, p.100.

[18] Unpublished original: ADM, Messina no.1419: *Messina* 1994, p.155, no.17; von Falkenhausen 1998, p.100.

[19] *Protonovellissimus noster compater* (sic!) *dominus Bonus*: Kehr 1902, doc.3, pp.413–15; Caspar 1904, p.485, reg.12; von Falkenhausen 1998, pp.108–9, no.13. The honour was shared by the chamberlain Nicholas and emir Christodoulos: below pp.67, 71.

[20] Schipa 1883, pp.159–60, no.17.

[21] Houben 1995, no.92, pp.327–8.

[22] Brühl 1987, no.59, pp.166–70, and Appendix 2, no.4, pp.267–8.

[23] Di Giovanni 1896, pp.334–5.

[24] Dölger 1927, p.68; Oikonomides 1972, pp.121, 315–16. However, the protonotary is not mentioned in Byzantine south Italy after the 10th century: von Falkenhausen 1978, pp.123–4.

[25] Bates 1982, pp.154–5.

[26] von Falkenhausen 1975, pp.130–1.

[27] The fullest account of Nicholas' career is Ménager 1960, pp.39–40, n.1. See also von Falkenhausen 1977, p.353; von Falkenhausen 1984, p.176 and n.12; von Falkenhausen 1998, pp.100, 106; von Falkenhausen 2000, pp.112–13. Both Garufi 1928, pp.32–6 and Takayama 1993, pp.28, 31–2, 34, 43, may also be consulted, but with some care.

Christian from Mesa (near Reggio) in Calabria, and held the offices of protonotary and chamberlain simultaneously under Roger I, but that of chamberlain alone under Adelaide and Simon. In June 1090, Nicholas of Mesa appears not just as protonotary and chamberlain, but also with the Byzantine palace dignity of *protospatharios.*[28] Like the protonotary John of Troina, Nicholas appears with what may be significant regularity when there are boundaries to be delimited and villeins to be granted or registered, but there is no clear evidence as to whether or not he was responsible for financial administration. Nicholas de Mesa is to be distinguished only with some difficulty from 'the archon of the great court, the *protonobilissimus* Nicholas, the protonotary, judge of all Calabria', who appears in August 1099. Like the *protospatharios* Nicholas de Mesa, and the *protonobilissimi* Bonos and the emir Christodoulos (as we shall see below), this Nicholas had apparently been awarded a Byzantine palace dignity by the Emperor Alexius.[29]

Another and, at least in his own opinion, highly important administrator was Leo the logothete. He is mentioned, alongside the chamberlain Nicholas, in the will of abbot Gregory, dated May 1105, as a benefactor of San Filippo di Fragalà.[30] Twenty years earlier, at Palermo in August 1086, he had witnessed three donations of Duke Roger Borsa with the self-important signature of 'Leo the chief president and logothete of the most splendid duke'.[31] Both Léon-Robert Ménager and Vera von Falkenhausen argued that he was in fact logothete to *Count* Roger, and that he here styles himself as the officer of *Duke* Roger as a polite fiction which acknowledges the latter's feudal lordship over the count of Sicily, but an unpublished document in the Archivo de Medinaceli now clearly establishes him as 'the servant of the duke'.[32] His son, Philip, appears in 1131 as 'great judge of all Calabria'.[33] Leo does not, however, appear with sufficient frequency to reconstruct his duties and responsibilities.

Vera von Falkenhausen has observed that, although Leo's title certainly derives from the Byzantine administrative repertoire, it is unlikely that his office was closely modelled upon any particular variety of Byzantine logothete: either Count

[28] Ed. Cusa 1868–82, no34, pp.383–5: the privilege is also witnessed by 'Nicholas, son of the *protospatharios* Garzēfa'.

[29] Kehr 1902, pp.68–9; Garufi 1899, p.9; Enzensberger 1971, p.47; Takayama 1993, p.34. For the document of August, 6607 A.M., Ind.VII (1099 A.D.), in which he appears as ὁ τε πρωτονοβελήσιμος καὶ πρωτοκριτὴς ἁπάσης Καλαβρίτιδος χώρας καὶ ὁ πρωτονοτάριος κυρὸς Νικόλαος (Jamison 1913, p.303, wrongly assumes that these titles refer to two individuals), see de Montfaucon 1708, pp.391–6; Guillou 1977, p.72, n.12.

[30] Ed. Cusa 1868–82, no.21, pp.396–400: ὁ ἐνδοξοτάτος Λέων ὁ λογοθέτης (p.400, line 1). See also Cozza-Luzi, 1890b, and von Falkenhausen 1984. For Nicholas and Leo, see also Ménager 1960, pp.39–40, and pp.26, 27, 167–8; and von Falkenhausen 1977, p.353.

[31] Λ(έων) πρωτοπρόεδρος καὶ λογοθέτ(ης) τοῦ πανὑπερλάμπρου δουκός ἰδιοχ(εί)ρ(ως) ὑπ(έγραψα). These three documents are edited and discussed by Ménager 1981b, nos 52–4, pp.181–6. See also von Falkenhausen 1977, p.352, n.146.

[32] ADM, Messina no.1231: *pace* Ménager 1960, pp.23–26; von Falkenhausen 1977, p.353. I am extremely grateful to Vera von Falkenhausen for this new information.

[33] de Montfaucon 1708, pp.401–2: reading Φιλίπος υἱός Λέοντου λογοθέτου καὶ μεγάλος κριτής πάσης καλαβρίας, 'Philip the great judge of all Calabria, son of Leo the logothete'. See also Jamison 1913, pp.303–4; Takayama 1993, p.32 and n.42.

Roger or, more probably, his Greek counsellors seem to have concluded that, in order to work properly, a state had to have a logothete.[34] This seems to me to be precisely the perspective from which all these official titles may best be understood. Roger and his staff seem to have believed that sonorous and splendid Byzantinising titles, such as *hostiarius*, logothete, mystologue, and protonotary, and even the Norman title of chamberlain, were somehow essential for the administration of a state; but the duties and responsibilities actually carried out in Sicily by the holders of those titles were not determined by any foreign model and, rather, developed *ad hoc* along original and, for several decades, extremely fluid lines.

This also holds good for the most prestigious of the titles held by Roger's staff – that of emir (*al-amīr*, ὁ ἀμηρᾶς, *ammiratus* and variants). In his classic study of the Sicilian emirate, Léon-Robert Ménager argued that the title of emir did not correspond to an office with fixed duties, but was rather an honorific title, 'une dignité palatine, ne conférant rien d'autre à son titulaire qu'un prestige particulier'.[35] Nonetheless, Ménager himself insisted that there was a clear difference between the first two emirs – Latin knights who were the military governors of Palermo[36] – and their successors – Greek Christians (at least until 1154), who all played greater or lesser rôles in central administration and government. Such a clear vision of the early history of the emirate was much improved by hindsight, for almost nothing is known of the careers of the Norman emirs before 1107, except that they were the officers of the duke of Apulia, not the the count of Sicily.

The first Norman emir is attested only in the following verses of William of Apulia, which refer to the actions of Robert Guiscard after the capture of Palermo in January 1072: 'After having taken some hostages and built the [aforesaid] castles, Robert the victor returned to the city of Reggio, leaving at Palermo a knight of his own name, who was given to the Sicilians to have as emir'.[37] Nothing more is known of this first emir, although Ménager speculates at some length as to his possible responsibilities.[38]

At Palermo, in August 1086, the second Norman emir witnessed two of the three donations by Duke Roger Borsa that were also signed by Leo the logothete.[39] In the list of witnesses – after the archbishops of Palermo and of Reggio; after Duke Roger Borsa, and his son Robert; after two barons, Peter of Alesna,[40] and Roger de Barneville;[41] and immediately before Leo, who is the last witness – comes 'Peter Bido (or Bidon?), emir of Palermo' (*Petro Bido, armeratus Palermi*). Thus, Peter Bido's only appearance is in the entourage of Duke Roger Borsa. After the conquest of Palermo, Robert Guiscard had retained half of the city, and it was only in 1122 that his grandson, Duke William, surrendered his share to the

[34] von Falkenhausen 1977, p.353. [35] Ménager 1960, p.87.

[36] Ménager 1960, pp.21–6. See also von Falkenhausen 1977, pp.351–2 and n.146.

[37] William of Apulia 1961, p.182, book 3, lines 340–3: *Obsidibus sumptis aliquot castrisque paratis / Reginam remeat Robertus victor ad urbem / Nominis eiusdem quodam remanente Panormi / Milite, qui Siculis datur amiratus haberi.*

[38] Ed. Ménager 1960, pp.21–3. [39] Above, p.67, note 31.

[40] Ménager 1981b, nos 52–3, pp.181–4.

[41] Ménager 1975, pp.353–4.

count of Sicily.[42] There is thus good reason to believe that the emir Peter was, in fact, the officer of Duke Roger Borsa, not of Count Roger of Sicily. This is again confirmed by the unpublished document ADM, Messina no.1231, which is signed by Πέτρος Βίδο στρατεγός Πανόρμου τοῦ ἠπερλαμπροῦ δοῦκας, 'Peter Bido, the strategos of Palermo of the most illustrious duke'.[43]

The title of emir does not reappear after 1086 until 1107, when it was held by a figure who was indisputably in charge of the administration of all Sicily and Calabria. To any one familiar with the accepted history of the comital administration, this may be a startling claim, because it seems to ignore Eugenios, the figure whom Ménager considered to be the first emir, or prime minister, of the Norman court of Sicily. In fact, Eugenios only appears with the title of emir long after his death and, during his lifetime, seems to have held no greater office than that of notary, the essential rank for holders of high administrative office.

The *notarius* Eugenios first appears in 1092, in the Latin translation of a Greek donation of Roger I, in which he was granted the ruined church of San Michele di Troina, so that he could restore it.[44] His only other live appearance is in the will of Gregory, the abbot of San Filippo di Fragalà, dated May 1105, where he is named amongst the benefactors of the monastery. In the will, all that identifies him as our Eugenios is the company that he keeps: after Nicholas the chamberlain, and Leo the logothete, he is listed as 'the most noble Eugenios of noble birth', but with no other title.[45] It is only in documents issued in the 1130s and later, long after his death, that Eugenios appears with the title of emir,[46] and it is difficult not to suspect that he may have been awarded the honour posthumously by his descendants who, as Vera von Falkenhausen has rightly remarked, constituted a whole 'dynasty of administrators',[47] and who certainly made the most of their ancestor. Be that as it may, Eugenios was indisputably a member of the comital staff, although apparently not its director. He was a Greek Christian, and probably came from the Valdemone, very possibly from Troina itself.[48]

In contrast to Eugenios, there can be no doubting the importance of the emir Christodoulos who, for at least twenty years from *c.*1107–*c.*1126, presided over the comital administration. Confusingly, he appears under four different names. Christodoulos of the Greek documents becomes Christoforus (and variants) in five Latin documents, but it is absolutely clear that both names refer to the same individual.[49] In the Arabic sources, he is ʿAbd al-Raḥmān al-Naṣrānī (literally,

[42] Amatus of Monte Cassino 1935, p.283 (*pace* Malaterra 1927–8 p.53); Falco of Benevento 1868, p.186. See also Ménager 1960, pp.23–4. [43] *Pace* Ménager 1960, pp.23–6.

[44] September 6601 A.M., Ind.I (1092 A.D.): ed. Pirri 1733, vol.II, p.1016. See von Falkenhausen 1977, p.354. Ménager 1960, pp.26–7 regards this as 'Un diplôme fort suspect'.

[45] Reading ὁ προγενέστατος [not προσηνέστατος] τῆς εὐγενείας εὐγένιος: above, p.67, note 30.

[46] He first appears with the title of emir in an unpublished document of 1131: ADM, Messina no.1384. See also Ménager 1960, p.26, nn.2–4, p.27, n.1 (above, p.68, note 44), and von Falkenhausen 1977, p.354 and n.161.

[47] von Falkenhausen 1977, p.354. [48] von Falkenhausen 1977, p.354.

[49] Below, p.72, note 70, nos (5), (7), (11), (12) and (19). Amari 1933–39, vol.III, pp.359–60, mistakenly, regarded Christodoulos and Christoforus as two individuals, but see Ménager 1960, p.29, and von Falkenhausen 1985, p.50, cols a–b.

'the slave of the Merciful [God], the Christian') and, once only, ᶜAbd Allāh ('the slave of God'): both names are translations of the one Greek name Christodoulos ('the slave of Christ').[50] We shall see below that it is possible that Christodoulos was also known as ᶜAbd al-Raḥmān ibn ᶜAbd al-ᶜAzīz ('... son of the slave of the Mighty [God]').[51] If so, the name ᶜAbd al-ᶜAzīz, like ᶜAbd al-Raḥmān, could be the Arabic version of a Greek theophoric name, and need not suggest that Christodoulos' father was an Arab or a Muslim.

Almost nothing is known about Christodoulos' origins. The one certainty is that he belonged to the Greek Christian community, for the only glimpses that we have of his private life is as the pious benefactor of Greek monasteries, including the great abbey overlooking Rossano dedicated to the Theotokos Odēgētria (now Santa Maria del Patire)[52] Santa Maria di Marsala,[53] and – perhaps – a Greek monastery in Palermo,[54] and the monastery of San Sebastiano near San Mauro in Calabria.[55] Ménager argued that Christodoulos' patronage of Rossano indicates that he was himself a native of that part of Calabria,[56] and it is quite true that his Calabrian land-transactions were concentrated in the valleys of the Coscile and the Crati near Rossano; and that it was at nearby San Mauro (near Corigliano Calabro) that he seems to have founded the monastery of San Sebastiano, which was perhaps governed by his children.[57] However, Vera von Falkenhausen has since pointed out that Christodoulos did not contribute from his own patrimony to the endowment of the monastery, but rather acquired all of the property that he donated to Rossano from Norman lords.[58] As she rightly observes, Christodoulos' personal property lay in Sicily – a house at Messina (see below),[59] lands at Giarratana near Ragusa,[60] and the property at Marsala with which he endowed Santa Maria. Moreover, the name Christodoulos, while exceedingly common in western Sicily, is almost unknown in Calabria. [61]

The year of Christodoulos' death is unknown but, given the frequency with which he appears between 1107 and 1125,[62] it must have occurred in, or soon after,

50 Ménager 1960, pp.29–30, and von Falkenhausen 1985, p.50, col.b. Amari 1933–9, vol.III, p.371, suggested that Christodoulos might have been 'one of the Sicilian Muslims of Greek or Italian race, [who had been] returned to Christianity after the conquest and employed by the rulers in public office'. 51 See below, p.86.

52 Zaccagni 1996, chap. 17, pp.216–17, 251–2. See also Ménager 1960, pp.30–1, p.32 n.11, and Appendix 2, no.8, pp.176–80, and no.9, pp.180–3; von Falkenhausen 1985, p.49, cols a–b.

53 Ménager 1960, pp.28, 30 and Appendix 2, no.3, pp.168–70; von Falkenhausen 1985, p.49, col.b.

54 1113, Ind.VI: ed. Garufi 1899, no.3, pp.9–11. Probably a 13th-century forgery, known in two versions: see Ménager 1960, Appendix 2, no.11, pp.185–7.

55 von Falkenhausen 1985, p.49, col.b. Vera von Falkenhausen tells me that she now questions whether our Christodoulos was necessarily the father of the monk Theodolos and nun Theodoloa who founded San Sebastiano – for whom, see below, pp.71–2, note 70, no. (13).

56 Ménager 1960, p.30 and n.5.

57 For this possibility, see von Falkenhausen 1985, p.49, col.b, who now questions whether it is necessarily the emir Christodoulos who was the father of the monk Theodolos and nun Theodoloa, the founders of San Sebastiano – for them, see below, pp.71–2, note 70, no. (13).

58 von Falkenhausen 1985, p.50, col.b. See also Amari 1933–9, vol.III, p.371.

59 Original: PA, Arch. Dioc., no.19: ed. Enzensberger 1996, no.27, pp.72–4.

60 Below, pp.71–2, note 70, no. (12): Ménager 1960, p.32, no.11; von Falkenhausen 1985, p.50, col.b.

61 von Falkenhausen 1985, p.50, col.b. 62 Below, pp.71–2, note 70.

1126. We shall see below that his fall from power was sudden and dramatic. After his death, Christodoulos' property seems to have reverted to the royal demesne, and as late as June 1159, William I granted to Archbishop Hugh of Messina 'the house of the late Christofalus, once emir'.[63] Despite his ignominious end, Christodoulos was warmly remembered after his death, not just by the monks of Santa Maria del Patire, who celebrated a mass in his honour on 30 September, presumably the anniversary of his death,[64] but also by Roger II in his privilege to that monastery dated May 1130.[65]

If little is known of Christodoulos' private life, what of his public career? Ménager speculates that, because Adelaide was too jealous of her authority as regent to have appointed Christodoulos emir, it must have been Roger I who elevated him to that rank before his death in June 1101; but there is no firm evidence that this was the case.[66] Christodoulos first appears in a Latin document of 1107 written by Adelaide's chaplain, John the Tuscan. The off-island origins of the scribe are sufficient to explain the document's eccentricities, without occasioning suspicion as to its authenticity. It grants Abbot Ambrose of San Bartolomeo di Lipari the tithe (*i.e.* the *jizya*?) of the Jews of Termini Imerese; and it was presumably in his capacity as one of the custodians of the comital demesne that Christodoulos heads the list of witnesses with his standard Latin name: *Chr[ist]oforus amiratus*.[67]

In April 1109, the Byzantine emperor, Alexius I Comnenus, issued a magnificent diploma, written in golden letters on purple parchment, in which he conferred the title of *protonobilissimus* upon the emir Christodoulos.[68] As we have already seen, Christodoulos was only one of three Sicilian administrators to receive this honour, including the judge and protonotary Nicholas and the protonotary Bonos, and it would seem that Alexius was systematically wooing the leading officers of the Norman court.[69] Although his precise motives in doing so remain obscure, their honours both emphasise the distinctly Greek environment in which Christodoulos, Bonos, Nicholas and their fellow bureaucrats must be seen, and demonstrate how important Byzantium perceived their influence to be in Norman Sicily.

Christodoulos appears in some fifteen authentic documents between 1107 and December 1125.[70] He is often flanked by other leading figures of the comital

[63] Above p.70, note 58.

[64] Cited by Mercati 1939, p.9: Εἰς τὰς λ [*i.e.* 30 September, the anniversary of his death?] ποιοῦμεν παραστάσιμον τοῦ κὺρ Χριστοδούλου τοῦ ἀμμηρᾶ.

[65] Below, pp.71–2, note 70, no. (20). [66] Ménager 1960, p.31.

[67] Original: Patti, Arch. Dioc., Fond.I, f.76: ed. Brühl 1987, no.1, pp.3–4. See also Ménager 1960, Appendix 2, no.4, pp.170–1; von Falkenhausen 1998, p.101 and p.107, no.9.

[68] Original: PA, Cappella Palatina, no.3: ed. Dölger 1929; repr. in Dölger 1956, pp.1–74. See also Ménager 1960, Appendix 2, no.5, pp.171–2; von Falkenhausen 1985, p.49, col.a.

[69] Ménager 1960, pp.39–41. The dignity of *protospatharios*, borne by Nicholas de Mesa and others, was also presumably granted by Constantinople: see above, p.67, note 29. For the Byzantine palatine dignity awarded to George of Antioch, see below, p.283, note 134.

[70] The list was originally given by Ménager 1960, pp.31–3, n.2, but that which follows is updated. **(1)** Above, p.67, note 30. **(2)** 6606 A.M. [corr. 6616 A.M. = 1107–8 A.D.] *Deperditum*. Caspar 1904, p.484, reg.6; Ménager 1960, Appendix 2, no.3, pp.168–70; von Falkenhausen 1998, p.107, reg.10. **(3)** Above, note 67. **(4)** 6618 A.M. [1109–10 A.D.]. Unedited original: ADM, Messina no.532. See von Falkenhausen 1998, p.110, reg.18; von Falkenhausen 1997, pp.283–4 and pl.5 (showing

administration, and clearly took precedence over all, including his fellow *protonobilissimi*, Bonos and Nicholas.[71] During the years of his emirate, several new figures and offices appear: Basil, who is apparently styled both treasurer (*thesaurarius*), and chamberlain (*camerarius*);[72] the chamberlain, and later protochamberlain, Paenos, whose name (presumably from Old French *Payen* or Latin *Paganus*) suggests that he was one of the few Latins at this time on Roger's staff;[73] his colleague and contemporary, the chamberlain Jordanus, another Latin;[74] Philip the logothete;[75] the emir John, son of Eugenios;[76] and George of Antioch, who makes his first appearance as emir in December 1125, in the same document in which Christodoulos last appears.[77] One receives the distinct impression that,

Christodoulos' autograph signature). **(5)** 1110 A.D., 17 February. Original: NA, AdS (destroyed 1943): ed. Brühl 1987, no.2, pp.4–6. Ménager 1960, Appendix 2, no.6, pp.172–5; von Falkenhausen 1998, p.109, reg.14. **(6)** 6620 A.M. [1111 A.D.], November, Ind.V. Original: Rome, San Basilio (now missing): ed. de Montfaucon 1708, pp.396–7. Ménager 1960, Appendix 2, no.7, pp.175–6. **(7)** 1112 [*sic* = 1111] A.D., November, Ind.V. Original: S. Maria del Patire (now missing): ed. Muratori 1738–42, vol.II, cols 785–7. Ménager 1960, Appendix 2, no.8, pp.176–80. **(8)** 6620 A.M. [1111 A.D.], 1 December, Ind.V. Original: Patti, Arch. Dioc., Girgensohn and Kamp 1965, p.13, reg.16: ed. Collura 1955a, pp.595–7. Ménager 1960, p.32, no.7; von Falkenhausen 1998, p.112, reg.24. **(9)** 1112 A.D., March, Ind.V. Original: Vatican, Cod. Chigi E.VI.182, perg. no.10: ed. Ménager 1960, Appendix 2, no.9, pp.180–3. **(10)** 1112 A.D., 12 June. *Deperditum*: 14th-century copy in PA, Arch. Dioc., *Registrum instrumentorum ecclesiae Panormitae*, ff.4–6: ed. Brühl 1987, no.3, pp.6–8. Ménager 1960, Appendix 2, no.10, pp.183–5; von Falkenhausen 1998, p.113, reg.28. **(11)** Above, p.70, note 54. **(12)** 6630 (*sic!* 6627) A.M. [1118 A.D.], September. Document of dubious authenticity, known only in late Latin translation, ed. Ughelli 1717–21, vol.IX, pp.291–2. Ménager 1957, pp.334–5, 343–8; Ménager 1960, p.32, no.11. **(13)** 1120: ed. Pirri 1733, vol.I, cols 457–8 (see also above, p.70, note 57). **(14)** [1121 A.D.?], August, Ind.XIV. Document exists only in an 18th-century copy: ed. Cusa 1868–82, no.52, pp.418–19. Ménager 1960, Appendix 2, no.13, pp.188–90, considers it a forgery. **(15)** 6630 A.M. [1122 A.D.], June, Ind.XV: ed. Ménager 1957, no.2, pp.335–9. See also Ménager 1958; Ménager 1960, p.33, no.13. **(16)** Above, p.64, note 6. **(17)** 1124 A.D., [September–December], Ind.III. Original: Rome, Archive Gencarelli (now missing): ed. Brühl 1987, no.6, pp.16–17. Ménager 1960, Appendix 2, no.17, pp.192–5. **(18)** 6634 A.M. [1125 A.D.], December. 12th-century chancery copy. CT, Arch. Dioc., no.6: ed. Ménager 1956–7, doc. no.5, pp.169–71. Ménager 1960, Appendix 2, no.18, pp.195–6; von Falkenhausen 1997, pp.279–80. **(19)** 1127, Ind.V. Forgery: ed. Brühl 1987, no.8, pp.20–1. Ménager 1960, Appendix 2, no.20, pp.198–9. **(20)** 6638 A.M. May, Ind.VIII [1130 A.D.]: Caspar 1904, p.510, reg.68; ed. Trinchera 1865, pp.138–41 (from late copy and de Montfaucon 1708, p.397–401). **(21)** Above, p.70, note 58.

71 Above, note 70, respectively, nos (5) and (8), and no. (13).

72 Brühl 1987, no.5, pp.13–15 (*thesaurarius*: October 1116), and Appendix 3, no.86, p.321 (*camerarius*: June 1117). Takayama 1993 seems to believe that the treasurer (pp.49 and 52) and chamberlain (pp.49, 55, and 68–9 n.117) were two individuals. Ménager 1960, p.189, identified Basil the chamberlain with 'the venerable lord Basil', who appears with the emir Christodoulos, and Paenos the chamberlain, in August 1121: above, note 70, no.(14). Garufi 1928, p.43, n.2, had already identified the latter Basil with the son of Trēcharēs, the archon of Demenna – see Cusa 1868–82, no.34, pp.382–5 (June 1117). Jamison 1957, pp.34 and 37, identified Basil the chamberlain with the emir Basil, who was in charge of the royal treasury in April 1140 – see Cusa 1868–82, no.58, pp.117–18 – and suggested that he belonged to the Graffeus family. This was hotly contested by Ménager 1960, p.64, n.1, who nonetheless agrees that the emir Basil was the uncle of William II's emir Eugenius (see also Appendix 2, no.13, pp.188–90, and no.27, p.207). The evidence is slight, and Basil is a very common name.

73 Above, note 70, nos (14) and (18). For his name, see Caracausi 1990, p.429.

74 Above, note 70 no. (14).

75 Above, note 70, no. (14).

76 Above, note 70, nos (14) and (18). For his subsequent career, see Ménager 1960, pp.59–61, 187, 195.

77 Above, note 70, no. (18).

during the early 1120s, the comital administration was becoming larger, more complex, and more hierarchical. The appearance of second-generation administrators, such as the emir John and, perhaps, Basil the chamberlain, contributes to the impression that the Norman civil service had come of age.

To judge from his appearances alone, Christodoulos kept an eye upon donations, and confirmations of donations, of lands and villeins out of the comital demesne. But this is surely a gross underestimation of his rôle. The only explanation for the regular appearance of this obscure Greek in the *comitatus*, alongside the great Latin churchmen and barons, is that his administrative duties and talents made him indispensable. Vera von Falkenhausen has recently proposed that Christodoulos may have been responsible for all the documents issued in the name of Adelaide and the young Roger II.[78] The Arabic sources which, as we shall see, are extremely well-informed and highly reliable, give him the title of *sulṭān*, and describe him as Roger's vizier and his *ṣāḥib al-ashghāl* ('director of financial administration'). The fullest account implies that he was effective ruler of the island during Roger's minority, and states that when Roger came of age, 'he shared absolute authority' with Christodoulos.[79]

Like the lesser members of Roger's staff, Christodoulos was omnicompetent. He appears as a judge in a fascinating document of January 1123, which shows how a dispute between Roger's own cousin and a family of Arabs, presumably Muslims, could be heard in the comital court and be decided, in part, upon the testimony of Arab witnesses and of an Arabic document interpreted by the *qāḍī* of Palermo.[80] It is thus a striking example of how important Arabic was as a language of administration and government at a time when there was no *dīwān* in the sense of a specialised bureau dedicated to Arabic administration.

Abū Maḍar ibn al-Biththirrānī[81] and his nephews came to court in Palermo to accuse Roger's cousin, Muriella of Petterrana, the daughter of Gosbert de Lucy,[82] of having usurped a mill on the Fiume San Leonardo which had belonged to their parents. Muriella sent her agents, John the priest, ᶜAbd al-Karīm, and the *qāʾid* ᶜAlī,[83] to testify that the mill had been built by the late Gosbert (d. before 1110), at a time before the reconquest of Ciminna and the rebellion of the barons, since when it had been held by the comital demesne.[84] Muriella's agents submitted as evidence an Arabic deed of sale in which Abū l-Dhikr ibn Sūdān[85] and his nephew, 'the men of the aforesaid Muriella', purchased the mill from Ibn Nāsikh[86] of

[78] von Falkenhausen 1997, pp.283–4. [79] Below, p.81. [80] Above, p.64, note 6.

[81] Βουμαδάρης ὁ υἱός Πεθθεῤῥάνου: from the Arabic place-name *Biththirrāna* (see al-Idrīsī, 1970–6, pp.604, 608, 616; al-Idrīsī 1883, pp.41–2): Latin *Petterrana*, modern Pizzo Pipitone 1km south of Sambuchi in the commune of Caccamo (PA): see Maurici 1998, p.94, no.167. For his *kunya* (which is apparently not Abū Muḍar), see Caracausi 1990, pp.116, 350, 366.

[82] Gosbert was married to Muriella (d. before 1119), Roger I's daughter, probably by his second wife Eremburga: Ménager 1975, pp.322–6.

[83] Ἀβδελκηρὶμ and Ἄλη κάΐτου. [84] Above, p.64. [85] Βουδίκερ ἔπεν Σεοτὲν.

[86] Ἔπεν Νάσαχ. In May 1143, amongst the gifts given by George of Antioch to his foundation of Santa Maria dell'Ammiraglio was a *funduq* in the Cassaro which he had bought from Ḥasan ibn Nāsikh: ***Dīwānī*** **20** and, below, p.110.

Palermo. The *qāḍī* of Palermo was summoned to read the document, which was found to uphold Muriella's rights. Finally, the elders of Ciminna and Muriella's neighbours testified that Ibn Biththirrānī and his nephews had no claim to the mill. The court, which found in Muriella's favour, was composed of Christodoulos and the judge Nicholas of Reggio, assisted by: John Zēkri; Chammetta; the *qāḍī* of Palermo; the *qāʾid* Boddaos;[87] and many others unnamed.

Christodoulos was a vizier not only of the pen, but also of the sword. In July 1123, with George of Antioch as his deputy, Christodoulos commanded the disastrous first attack upon the Zīrid capital al-Mahdīya.[88] Of the great fleet of three hundred ships, which had reportedly set sail with thirty thousand infantry and one thousand cavalry, only one hundred vessels and two horses are said to have returned to Palermo. Perhaps surprisingly, given the magnitude of this disaster, neither Christodoulos nor George of Antioch immediately fell from Roger's favour, and both appear side-by-side in his entourage until December 1125. However, this was Christodoulos' last living appearance. He was promptly succeeded as vizier by George of Antioch who, according to the fullest Arabic source, had engineered his downfall.

Like the other leading members of the comital administration, George of Antioch was a Greek but, unlike them, he was not a son of Magna Graecia.[89] George had received his training, first, in Antioch and elsewhere in the Byzantine East where he had learnt Arabic and the arts of financial administration,[90] and then in Zīrid Ifrīqiya, 1087–1108. When he arrived in Sicily, he was initially employed by Christodoulos as district governor of Iato in the hinterland of Palermo,[91] and it can only have been after his entry into the central administration, and especially after his elevation to the rank of prime minister on the fall of Christodoulos, probably in the course of 1126, that his unique experience and training began to have any significant influence. This is a convenient point, therefore, to break this account of the comital administration in general, and to retrace our steps in search of the Arabic element within it.

The Arabic documents of Adelaide and Roger II (*Dīwānī* 7–8), 1109 and 1111

From the period of Adelaide's regency and of the rule of Roger II before his coronation in 1130, there survive only two Arabic documents. The earlier (***Dīwānī* 7**) is a bilingual decree (*kitāb*, *entalma*), issued at Messina on 6 March 1109, in

[87] ᾿Ιωάννης Ζήκρι: probably the Arabic name Dhikrī or Zikrī, see Caracausi 1990, p.224. Χαμμέττα: presumably the Arabic name Ḥammād. Ὁ ἀλκαδί Πανόρμου: probably *al-shaykh al-faqīh al-qāḍī* Abū l-Qāsim ʿAbd al-Raḥmān ibn Rajāʾ, below, p.88. Ὁ κάϊτ Βοδδάος: almost certainly Abū l-Ḍawʾ Sirāj ibn Aḥmad ibn Rajāʾ: see below, p.88.

[88] Below pp.85–6. [89] For George, see below, pp.80–8 and index. [90] Below, p.80, note 124.

[91] Below, p.96, and note 13.

which Adelaide and Roger instruct their local officers,[92] in the district of Castrogiovanni, to protect the abbey of San Filippo di Fragalà at Demenna, in the valley of San Marco d'Alunzio. (The document is extremely lacunose, but there is reason to believe that the text also referred to the grant to San Filippo of the right to extract salt from the mines of Castrogiovanni.[93])

The Greek text opens with the *intitulatio* (line 1), and then moves briskly into the *dispositio* (lines 2–3: Διορίζωμεν ... *Diorizōmen* ...). A *sanctio* seems to follow, but the text is much damaged and cannot be fully reconstructed at this point. The eschatology (lines 11–12) explains that the writ was sealed with the 'usual' (συνήθης, *sunēthēs*) wax seal and gives the date and place of issue.[94] Finally, by way of *apprecatio*, comes the symbol of the cross.[95]

The Arabic opens with the *basmala* (line 13). In the *intitulatio* (line 14), Adelaide appears with a carefully articulated title, which occupies an important place in the development of the Arabic titulature of the Norman rulers of Sicily.[96] Next comes the *dispositio* (lines 15–16: *qad amarnā* ...). There follow two extremely lacunose lines (lines 17–18), and then the eschatology and the *datatio* (line 19). At the foot of the Arabic comes Adelaide's Greek signature (line 20), and the wax seal, now illegible. The document is written upon paper. Although it is the only *extant* paper document from the Norman chancery, others are known to have been issued by Roger I and Adelaide.[97]

So far as can be judged, although the Greek and the Arabic parts of this document deal with exactly the same matter, neither is a translation, nor even a close paraphrase of the other. Both parts are well-organised and regular in structure, and either could have served on its own. They are both the work of professional scribes who were clearly well-accustomed to drawing up decrees of this kind.

The second Arabic document of Adelaide and Roger II is completely different in character. It is an Arabic-Greek *jarīda* of May 1111 that lists eight Muslim villeins, who were apparently granted with their lands by the late Roger I to the knight

[92] Greek: ἐξουσιασταί, 'bailiffs'; βεσκόμιτες, 'viscounts'; and καΐτες, 'caids'. Arabic: *ʿummāl*, 'bailiffs', and *quwwād*, 'caids'.

[93] The recent restoration of the document (Prosperi 1996) brought to light 'una sorta di firma in caratteri presumibilmente greci' (*sic! – ibid.*, p.10 and fig.4). In fact, this is a Greek note reading της αλυκης, 'concerning the salt-mine'. Roger II's renewal of 1145 granted *ut Abbatia S. Philippi a salinis Castri Iohannis omni anno salmas sufficienter habeat*: Pirri 1733, vol.II, pp.1028–9; see also La Mantia 1908, pp.20–1. I am grateful to Vera von Falkenhausen for providing the reference to Pirri, and for confirming, and explaining, my reading of the Greek note.

[94] See von Falkenhausen 1997, p.287.

[95] For the Greek scribe, see von Falkenhausen 1997, p.276 and n.138.

[96] Johns 1986, pp.18–19, and below, pp.77 and 271. See also von Falkenhausen 1997, p.294.

[97] For example, in April 1110, Adelaide and Roger II renewed, for San Filippo di Fragalà, a donation of Roger I, dated 1097, and written ἐν βαμβακίνω χάρτω, 'on cotton paper': Spata 1862, no.9, pp.221–8; Cusa 1868–82, no.25, pp.405–7, 701; Caspar 1904, pp.485–6, reg.14. See also Brühl 1983, pp.47–9. If the use of paper was common at this time, it might help explain the large number of *deperdita*: see von Falkenhausen 1997, pp.275–6. Paper continued to be used, of course, throughout the 12th century, and the Arabic book-list discovered by Monsignor Benedetto Rocco wrapped around a saint's relics in the Cappella Palatina, and dated to soon after 1154, is also written on paper: *Età normanna* 1994, no.33, pp.220–1.

Julian: the Regent Adelaide and the young Count Roger II confirm the donation (***Dīwānī* 8**).[98] The Arabic *jarīda* opens with a concise introduction (lines 1–2):

> The *jarīda* of the names of the men who our lady the regent [Adelaide] and our lord the count Roger, her son, granted to the knight Julian on the date of the month of May of Indiction IV. And they are ... (*jarīdatu asmāʾi l-rijāli lladhīna aʿṭat mawlātu-nā l-sayyidatu wa-mawlā-nā l-qūmisu rujāru waladu-hā ilā l-fārisi juliyan wa-dhālika bi-taʾrīkhi shahri māyū l-indiqtusa l-rābiʿa wa-hum ...*)

There follows the list of 8 names, and a total (lines 3–5).[99] Next, comes the Greek text (lines 6–11):

> The abovenamed men with their lands are those whom the lord [*i.e.* the late Roger I?] granted at [or 'to'?] Labourzi.[100] The Countess Adelaide with her son, Roger, count of Calabria and Sicily, confirmed and granted these lands and men. She gave them to Julian in the month of May of the 4th indiction.

There was a seal, but no signature, although Adelaide's name is written in the body of the text in exactly the same form and script as her chancery signature.

This document was clearly composed *ad hoc* and not according to a formulary. It cannot, therefore, be regarded as significantly representative of the output of Adelaide's scribes, Arabic or Greek. Nonetheless, it provides an interesting indication that, as late as 1111, her administration was still engaged, albeit in a small way, in the issue of *jarāʾid* to the beneficiaries of the post-conquest distribution.[101]

The dating clauses of the Arabic texts of both documents require some comment. Each uses the Julian month, transliterated into Arabic (*marṭiyūs*, 'March'; and *māyū*, 'May'), and the Byzantine indictional year (*al-ḥawl*, and *al-indiqtus*). This sets the pattern for the documents issued by the royal *dīwān*, all of which, in one or more of the three administrative languages (Arabic, Greek, and Latin),

[98] Guillou misreads the name of the recipient in the Arabic: read *Juliyan* (جلين), not *Ḥalīq* (!), corresponding to the Greek Γιολλὲν.

[99] The following three names are misread by Guillou: *Muḥammad akhū* [not *abū*] *Nuʿmān al-musammā bi-l-rūmīyi Bātrū* [not *Banzūl*], 'Muḥammad, the brother of Nuʿmān, called Peter in Greek'; *Yūsuf al-Massīnī* [not *al-Masīlī*]; *ʿAlī ibn Taḥrīr* [not *Naḥrīr*]; *ʿAbd Allāh akhū-hu* [not *abū-hu*] *naṣrānī* 'ʿAbd Allāh, his brother [*i.e.* ʿAlī's], a Christian'.

[100] Guillou translates ὁ αὐθ(έν)τ(ης) τοῦ Λαβοῦρζι as 'le seigneur de Labourzi', whom he takes to be Julian, and assumes that, in the Greek text, he grants the villeins and their lands to Santa Maria di Messina. There is nothing in the text to justify this assumption, and the sense clearly demands that a De Hauteville, presumably the late Roger I, is the donor. It is unclear, however, whether Roger grants the lands *at* a place called Labourzi, or *to* an individual, perhaps identical with Julian, called Labourzi. If, as seems most likely, Labourzi is a place, it seems to have lain near Messina (see also Caracausi 1990, p.327). Guillou 1963, p.54, n.1, on the basis of a misreading of the Greek and the Latin notes on the verso, suggests that the villeins came from Agrigento: Ἀγρακάντ(ον) and [*Vi*]*llani d*(*e*) *Agrigen*[*to*]; but I tentatively propose, reading from Guillou pl.2b, ἀγ(α)ρ(ηνων) κατ(ό)ν(ομα) and *uillani ag*(*a*)*ren*(*i*). I am extremely grateful to Vera von Falkenhausen for her advice upon the Greek text.

[101] It is worth noting that Greek and Latin donations and polyptychs become more frequent from this time. See, for example: Cusa 1868–82, no.26, pp.511–12, 701; Garufi 1940, p.75, no.3; Girgensohn and Kamp 1965, p.13, reg.15.

employ the Julian month and the indictional year, together with at least one, and occasionally all of: the year of the Christian era; the year of the Hegira; and the year of the Creation. This is in complete contrast to the private Arabic documents which, when they are dated, and with only two exceptions, always employ the month and year according to the Islamic calendar.[102] The two exceptions are an Arabic bill of sale recording the purchase of a house by one Lady Margaret, which uses the Islamic and Julian months, the year of the Hegira, and the indiction;[103] and a Judaeo-Arabic document recording a grant of land for use as an extension to the cemetery of the Jewish community of Syracuse, which uses the Jewish year of creation [4]948, the feast of Christmas, and the Byzantine indiction.[104] Both of these use *al-ḥawl*, 'the year', for the indiction, as do the decree of 1109 and five other *dīwānī* documents.[105] But standard *dīwānī* practice, followed in no less than thirteen documents, was to use *al-indiqtus*.[106]

In short, the structure and, indeed, the script, and language of the decree of 1109 attests to the presence in Adelaide's chancery of at least one professional Arab scribe, who had been trained in an Islamic chancery. To him should also be attributed the Arabic title that Adelaide uses in this decree.[107] Immediately after the conquest of Palermo in 1072, Duke Robert Guiscard and Count Roger of Sicily began to mint Arabic coins on which they were styled by transliterations of their Latin feudal titles such as *al-dūqa* and *al-qūmis*. In about 1095, however, if not a little earlier, Roger adopted the style *al-sulṭān*, which was drawn from the Islamic repertoire of titles. Adelaide's title in the decree of 1109 – *al-sayyidatu l-jalīlatu malikatu ṣiqillīyata wa-qalāwriyata l-nāṣiratu li-dīni l-naṣrānīyati*, 'the great lady, sovereign of Sicily and Calabria, protector of the faith of Christianity' – is a much more elaborate protocol, which may even have been awarded to her by an Islamic chancery.[108] This inclines me to wonder whether the Arabic scribe of the decree of 1109 could not have come to Sicily with George of Antioch and his family in 1108, and have been trained in the Zīrid *dīwān*.[109] Be that as it may, a single document, written by a lone professional scribe, does not match the precocious development of the Greek chancery,[110] nor even the far more modest progress of the Latin.[111] There is still no trace of a real *dīwān*.

Although Roger I and Adelaide clearly could – and did – use pre-existing Islamic institutions, including the mint and the records of the fiscal administration, to present themselves in terms that would have been comprehensible to an Arabic-speaking audience, it is not clear whether this was the result of carefully considered policy, or the fortuitous result of having inherited mint-officials and scribes from the pre-conquest Islamic administration, or from Zīrid Ifrīqiya. I am inclined to favour the latter interpretation; not least because the practice seems to

[102] **Private 2, 5, 6, 9 and 29.** [103] **Private 19.** [104] **Private 25.**
[105] ***Dīwānī* 7, 31, 32, 35, 36, 45 and 46.**
[106] ***Dīwānī* 8, 13, 16, 17, 18, 21, 24, 25, 29, 33, 37, 38 and 39.**
[107] For the Arabic titles of the Norman rulers, see below, pp.268–74.
[108] Below, p.271. [109] George defected in 502 (11 August 1108 – 30 July 1109).
[110] von Falkenhausen 1997, pp.254–7. [111] Enzensberger 1975.

have been largely abandoned after Count Roger II assumed sole authority in 1112, more or less at the time that the generation of Arab officials inherited by the Normans might be expected to have passed away.

The problem of continuity under Roger II (1105–30)

Inasmuch as Roger I had a 'capital' or fixed residence, it had been Mileto in Calabria. Some time before 1110, Adelaide transferred her base to Messina.[112] Then, in early 1112, soon after Roger came of age, and only months before Adelaide ceased to appear at his side, they moved west to Palermo.[113] It would be difficult to overestimate the importance, in the long term, of their choice of Palermo. In Sicily, especially in western Sicily, feudal structures were weaker than on the mainland. From Palermo, the mainland was more distant than Africa, and the city, after just forty years of Norman rule, was still profoundly Arab and Muslim. This was the environment in which, after 1130, King Roger and his ministers were to attempt to create a centralised bureaucratic administration on Byzantine and Islamic models – what Mario Caravale has controversially described as 'un primo Stato unitario e nello stesso tempo feudale' and 'un primo embrionale apparato burocratico in uno Stato feudale'.[114] But the influence of Palermo upon the early development of Roger's administration was scarcely to be felt until after his coronation.

For most of his early career, Roger was at war on the mainland, and he spent only a small fraction of his time in Palermo and the Arabic-speaking west of Sicily. Vera von Falkenhausen has calculated, using the data in the registers of Erich Caspar and Paolo Collura, that, before his coronation, Roger II appeared only nine times in Palermo and western Sicily, against twenty-seven times in eastern Sicily and Calabria.[115] What is more, fifty-nine of his surviving authentic documents were addressed to recipients in eastern Sicily and in Calabria, and to only six in western Sicily and Palermo. Today, if the new documents discovered since Collura's time were added to those registers, the balance would be weighted still more heavily towards eastern Sicily and Calabria.

Not only did the young Roger spend most of his time in the old Byzantine provinces of his county, but also he had been educated by his parents' Greek ministers, the same men through whom, once he came of age, he continued to rule.[116] Vera von Falkenhausen, again, has perceptively stressed the significance of

[112] 17 February 1110 *in capella Messane*: Brühl 1987, no.2, pp.4–6. See Pontieri 1955, pp.384–6; Houben 1991, p.28.

[113] 12 June 1112 *ego Adelais comitissa et Rogerius, filius meus, Dei gratia iam miles, iam comes Sicilie et Calabrie, Panormi morantes et in thalamo superioris castri nostri*: Brühl 1987, no.3, pp.6–8. See Pontieri 1955, pp.386–90; Houben 1991, p.29.

[114] Caravale 1966, p.177. See the discussion in Tabacco 1985, pp.65–81.

[115] von Falkenhausen 1977, pp.356.

[116] Ménager 1959, p.313, wrote dismissively of 'les divagations byzantines' of the young Roger II, but I am not persuaded that Roger rejected his Greek education and upbringing after 1130. See, again, the discussion by Tabacco 1985, pp.67–81.

Roger's early training: 'il risultato di una educazione … nelle mani dei consiglieri greci di sua madre, specialmente del famoso Cristodulo, fu che Ruggero II diventò un burocrate'.[117] Alexander of Telese paints a vivid picture of this obsessive administrator which, despite its topical elements, is amply supported by the surviving documents of Roger's administration:

> He scarcely ever allowed himself rest or diversion, so much so that, when he happened to be free from other more useful occupations, he would look over public taxation, would remind himself about what was to be spent and what was to be collected, and would weary himself by checking whatever was to be reviewed, so that he always had written memoranda of how and where best to spend his treasure, and – that I may speak more fully – [so that] nothing that he had was stored away or paid out without a written record.[118]

We may doubt that Roger himself kept the accounts of his kingdom, and we may suspect that, rather, this was left to Christodoulos and his staff; but there can be little doubt that the accounts were kept in Greek.

There survive no Arabic documents issued by Roger after he assumed sole authority in 1112 and before his coronation in 1130. Moreover, the two documents which have occasionally been used to argue for the existence of an Arabic administration under Count Roger II cannot, in fact, be used for this purpose.

The first is a Greek act recording the sale, to the abbot of Santa Maria di Gala, of land from the royal demesne, which had previously been held illegally by his monastery (***Dīwānī* 19**). The original document is lost and, until recently, was widely known only through Carlo-Alberto Garufi's edition of Domenico Schiavo's copy of an anonymous, incomplete, and execrable translation into Latin. This copy gives the date of the act as March 1115, and states that the boundaries of the land sold were recorded in Arabic. Had the original document truly been issued in March 1115, then this would constitute hard evidence that a *dīwān* was active at that date. But Garufi himself realised that the date of 1115 did not match the *intitulatio* at the head of this copy – *Rogerius in Christo Deo pius fortis rex* – and so he tentatively suggested that it should be redated to 1131.[119] In fact, a vastly superior Latin translation of the Greek original was made in 1495 by Constantine Lascaris, and authenticated in 1516 by the notary Francesco de Silvestro of Messina. Lascaris' translation was later incorporated into the *Liber prelatarium* of Giovanni Luca Barberi; and two other, 17th-century, copies of the authenticated translation also survive.[120] The text preserved in the *Liber prelatarium* has recently been

[117] von Falkenhausen 1977, p.357.

[118] Alexander of Telese 1991, p.82 (book 4, chap.3): *Otio vel vagationi vix numquam subdebatur; in tantum, ut si quando a ceteris utilioribus occupationibus sibi vaccare contingeret, aut publicis exactionibus invigilaret, aut datorum sive dandorum seu eorum que accipienda erant reminisci, vel que recensenda erant recensere satageret; quatenus melius de suo tribuendum erario, vel ubi adeundum esset, sub chirographorum ratiociniis semper habebetur, et ut amplius dicam, nullum quid sibi erat, quod non sub scripti ratione servaretur aut erogaretur.*

[119] Ed. Garufi 1899, no.9, pp.19–20.

[120] Pirri 1733, vol.II, pp.1042–4 had already published an extract of the document with the correct date. See Caspar 1904, p.545, reg.144.

edited by Vera von Falkenhausen, and it establishes the true date of the document to be March 6650 A.M., Indiction 5 (1142 A.D.).[121] In other words, this document is a product of the royal *dīwān*, and has nothing to tell us of Roger's Arabic administration before he became king.

The second is an act issued in December 1188 by Geoffrey of Marturano, *magister justiciar* of William II, and Jordan of Calatahaly, which refers to 'the boundary-register of the royal *dīwān*, which was made by the protonotary of the court sixty-five years ago', *i.e.* in 1123 A.D.[122] This reference includes a glaring internal inconsistency in that the term *duana regie* obviously belongs to the period *after* 1130 and should not, therefore, be cited as evidence for the existence of a *dīwān* under *Count* Roger. There is no reason, however, to doubt that a protonotary of Count Roger did establish the boundaries of the district of Vicari in 1123: the document of 1188 is genuine enough, and it is only the reference to the *dīwān* that is anachronistic.

At first sight, therefore, it looks very much as if the young Roger II did not have an Arabic administration in the years 1112–30. And yet, only fifteen months after his coronation, his chancery began to issue a series of bilingual documents, in Greek and Arabic, which attest to the existence of a highly professional and sophisticated *dīwān*. The problem of continuity is thus how it was that, after a period of more than twenty years in which there is no trace of a *dīwān* in the sense of a specialised office dedicated to Arabic administration, in 1132, there suddenly emerges a highly developed and well-organised office which was to play a leading rôle in the administration of the Sicilian kingdom? The answer largely depends upon the careful examination of the products of the royal *dīwān*; but, before proceeding to that, we need first to consider an important Arabic source which was recently rediscovered by Adalgisa De Simone.[123]

Al-Maqrīzī's biography of George of Antioch

George, son of Michael, the Antiochene (*Jurjī ibn Mīkhāʾīl al-Anṭākī*), the vizier of Roger (*Rūjār*), king of the Franks in the island of Sicily, belonged to the Christian community. For some time, he and his family served the king of Constantinople,[124] but [a complaint] was lodged against him and his family,[125] and the king ordered them, women and children, to be brought before him. They were assembled in a boat, and set

[121] von Falkenhausen 2000, Appendix, no.1, pp.125–8.

[122] *Quatern[us] duane Regie, qui factus fuerat olim per manus protonotarii curie transactis annis sexaginta et quinque*: PA, AdS, Cefalù no.26, a 12th-century copy; ed. White 1938, Appendix no. 38, pp.280–2; Enzensberger 1971, p.135, reg.159.

[123] De Simone 1999a.

[124] The Emperor Alexius I Comnenus (1081–1118) seems to be intended. Antioch was governed by Byzantine dukes until 1084, when it fell to the Saljūqs. Al-Tījānī and Ibn Khaldūn report that George was trained 'in Syria, at Antioch and elsewhere' – below, pp.83, 84 – which might suggest that, after the fall of Antioch, George and his family moved to another Byzantine centre – but, if so, which? It is possible, of course, that they remained in Antioch to serve the Saljūqs or, perhaps, moved to serve one of the independent statelets in Cilician Armenia. See also below, p.264.

[125] *Wa-rufiʿa ʿalay-hi wa-ʿalā ahli-hi*: literally, 'was raised against him and his family'.

off in forty. But the fleet of the sultan Tamīm ibn al-Muᶜizz ibn Bādīs, the lord of the lands of the West, intercepted them. That was in about the year 480/1087–88, when [the fleet] was returning from a raid against the islands of Constantinople.[126]

They were taken and brought to al-Mahdīya in the land of Ifrīqīya. They requested an audience with Tamīm, and he ordered them to be brought to him. They stated that they were accountants (*ḥussāb*), and that the sultan would benefit from their service. Tamīm was good to them, and entrusted them with [his] affairs. Their good counsel prevailed, and he appointed this George governor (*ᶜāmil*) of the city of Sousse;[127] but he kept close to himself his brother, Simon (*Simᶜān*), who had not reached puberty. [The latter] set out to collect information about [the sultan's] brothers[128] and others,[129] and to report it to him. The prince Yaḥyā ibn Tamīm learnt that Simon had reported something that he had said, and this angered him; it weighed so heavily upon Yaḥyā ibn Tamīm that he gave order for [Simon] to be strangled by night.[130]

[When] the sultan Tamīm died,[131] and his son Yaḥyā ibn Tamīm succeeded him, George was frightened of him. So he wrote to the sultan ᶜAbd al-Raḥmān, the vizier of King Roger, son of Roger, king of the Franks, known as Abū Tillīs ('Old Wheat-sack'?),[132] lord of the island of Sicily, ordering him to send him a raiding-galley so that he could escape in it. The galley arrived at al-Mahdīya in the year 502/11 August 1108 – 30 July 1109, with an ambassador to the sultan Yaḥyā ibn Tamīm. It took [on board] George and all his relatives, and slipped away with them, without anyone realising it.

When they came before [ᶜAbd al-Raḥmān], he treated them well, and put them in charge of the *dawāwīn* of Sicily. They expounded good counsel, and acquired standing with him. [When] King Roger came of age, he shared absolute authority with the vizier ᶜAbd al-Raḥmān. Therefore, George insinuated himself with everything that was pleasing to him. Many times, he dispatched George as ambassador to Egypt. But George did not cease to calumniate the sultan ᶜAbd al-Raḥmān,[133] until Roger seized [the latter] and put him in an iron cage, and executed him.[134] [Roger] assigned [ᶜAbd al-Raḥmān's] vizierate to Abū l-Ḍawʾ, the *kātib al-inshāʾ*, but he was a man of letters and would not accept the authority. And so [Roger] appointed George to the vizierate.

126 I know of no other reference to this raid. It is intriguing that Romuald of Salerno 1935, p.47, records that George was *ab Antiochus abductus*. Note that the Pisan-Genoese raid on al-Mahdīya took place in August 1087: it is perhaps unlikely that the events described occurred in the same year.

127 Presumably after the attack on Sousse by Arabs headed by the *shaykh* of the Banū Ṣakhr, Mālik ibn ᶜAlawī, in 482/1089–90: see Idris 1962a, vol.I, p.293.

128 When al-Muᶜizz died in 1062, he seems to have left seven legitimate sons, of whom Tamīm was the eldest surviving and his heir apparent. Tamīm's brother, ᶜUmar ibn al-Muᶜizz rebelled in 489/1096: see Idris 1962a, vol.I, pp.240, 296–7.

129 Tamīm is reported to have fathered some 300 children: Idris 1962a, vol.I, p.302.

130 Yaḥyā seems to have rebelled against his father Tamīm in 488/1095: see Idris 1962a, vol.I, pp.250–1, 294–6, 297–8.

131 29 February 1108.

132 For a discussion of the meaning of this *kunya*, or nick-name, see Appendix 3, below.

133 *Wa-lam yazal jurjī yasᶜā bi-l-sulṭāni ᶜabdi l-raḥmāni*. For *saᶜā bi-* meaning 'to calumniate, slander, *etc.*', see Lane 1984, vol.I, p.1366, col.a; *cf. saᶜā fī* in the *Qurʾān* 2.114, 2.25, 22.51, *etc.* De Simone's translation – 'Non smise Giorgio di collaborare con il sultano' *etc.* – would properly require *saᶜā li-*, and it is clear from the context that the opposite sense is required.

134 George's unmanageably fiery character was proverbial amongst Arab authors – it was said of him *kāna lā yuṣṭalā la-hu bi-nār*, 'he was [a man] by means of whose fire one cannot warm oneself', *i.e.* 'he was unapproachable when inflamed with rage': see al-Ṣafadī 1931–, vol.XIII, p.304 (*BAS*², vol.II, p.797; *BAS*²*(It.)*, vol.III, p.858). And, further, al-Maydānī 1838–43, vol.II, p.588, no.8 (*mā yuṣṭalā bi-nāri-hi*), and Lane 1984, vol.II, p.1722a (where the satirical sense, perhaps inappropriate here, is also given: 'One will not seek his hospitality' [*i.e.* his hearth]').

> [George] amassed the revenues and organised the foundations of the kingdom (*fa-jammaʿa l-amwāla wa-rattaba qawāʿida l-mulki*). He veiled Roger from [his] subjects, and arranged for him to dress in clothes like the Muslims', and not to ride out, nor to show himself in public, except on holidays, when he would process, preceded by horses adorned with saddles of gold and silver, and with caparisons studded with gemstones, and by domed litters and gilded banners, with the parasol (*al-miẓalla*)[135] above him and the crown upon his head.
>
> George was entitled 'exalted master, pleasing [to God], glory of the victorious king, pride of majesty, rule of leadership, leader of armies, honour of ministers, emir of emirs'.[136] He acquainted Roger with the biographies of the kings, and ordered one of his secretaries, called al-Ḥanash ('the Snake'), to compile a biography of him.
>
> In the year 543/1148–49, at the capture of al-Mahdīya, [George's] warships (*shawānī-hi*) amounted to two hundred galleys (*shīnī*) and one hundred oared horse-carriers (*ṭarīda*),[137] not counting the transports (*al-ḥammāla*). George himself set out with the fleet, and captured the islands which are between al-Mahdīya and Sicily. Then the coast of Ifrīqīya came under his rule from the beginning of Tripolitania (*awwal ṭarābulus*) to al-Ḥammāmāt near Tunis and, inland, to near al-Qayrawān.
>
> Roger's state (*dawla*) grew under George's management. Thus, when high prices and civil disorders fell upon the Maghrib, there emigrated to him a vast galaxy of emirs, judges, lawyers, men of letters, and poets. Both George and Roger were lavish with their hospitality to them, and had them stay with them. Thus the island flourished in a most splendid way, and travellers from every land made for it with all sorts of goods and rare merchandise, until the year 546/ 20 April 1151 – 7 April 1152, [when] George the vizier died at the age of ninety.[138] And Roger confirmed his son Michael (*Mīkhāʾīl ibn Jurjī*) to the vizierate.[139]
>
> Roger died thereafter in the first decade of Dhū l-Ḥijja in the year 548 (17–26 February 1154).[140]

This extraordinary biography of George of Antioch occurs in a biographical dictionary compiled by the 15th-century Egyptian historian al-Maqrīzī, the original

135 For the parasol in Norman Sicily, see below, pp.265.

136 *Al-sayyidu l-ajallu l-murtaḍā [bi-llāhi] ʿizzu l-maliki l-muẓaffari fakhru l-jalāli niẓāmu l-riʾāsati zaʿīmu l-juyūshi sharafu l-wuzarāʾi amīru l-umarāʾi*. Compare the titles given to George in the letter addressed to Roger by the Fāṭimid caliph al-Ḥāfiẓ (below, pp.259–65): *[al-]wazīru l-amīru taʾyīdu l-dawlati wa-ʿaḍudu-hā ʿizzu l-mulki wa-fakhri-hi niẓāmu al-riʾāsati amīru l-umarāʾi*, 'the vizier, the emir, the support and strength of the state, the glory and the pride of the kingdom, rule of leadership, emir of emirs' (al-Qalqashandī 1913–72, vol.VI, p.459, lines 12–13).

137 The *ṭarīda* was one of several hybrid vessels combining sail- and oar-power. It was especially used for transporting horses. See Fahmy 1980, pp.136–7, and Pryor 1982, *passim*, especially pp.18–19, 113–20.

138 Ibn al-Athīr 1851–76, vol.XI, pp.123; *BAS*², vol.I, p.338; *BAS*²*(It.)*, vol.II, p.374) and al-Ṣafadī (*BAS*², vol.II, p.797; *BAS*²*(It.)*, vol.III, p.858), give the same year. According to the epitaph from his tomb, George died in the year 6659 A.M. (September 1150 – August 1151): Longo 1981, p.57, lines 24–6, and pp.39–40. He therefore seems to have died in April – August 1151. See Ménager 1960, p.54.

139 George had three sons: John, Simon, and Michael. The latter accompanied Roger to the mainland in 1143, and witnessed two charters as *Michael ammiratus*. Ménager 1960, pp.54, 64. Brühl 1987, no.59, p.169, line 29 and no.60, p.172, line 1b. George was succeeded as vizier by Maio of Bari (below, pp.197–8); and so it was, perhaps, in the rank of emir that Roger confirmed Michael upon his father's death. In May 1140, when Michael witnessed a royal charter with his father, he had no rank but that of his father's son – Ὁ τοῦ ἀρχ(όν)τ(ου) (*sic, pace* Brühl) τῶν ἀρχ(όν)τ(ων) υἱό(ς) Μιχα(ὴλ): Brühl 1987, no.48, p.138, lines 12–15a.

140 Roger died on 26 February 1154: below, p.198, note 25.

title of which seems to have been *Kitāb al-tārīkh al-kabīr al-muqaffā li-Miṣr* ('The great history limited to Egypt').[141] It is clearly a potentially important source, both for the careers of George of Antioch and the emir Christodoulos – the ᶜAbd al-Raḥmān of this account – and for the history of the *dīwān*. But how much trust should we place in this very literary story? It is well worth devoting some pages to a comprehensive answer to that question.

At first sight, the circumstantial evidence is strongly in favour of its authenticity. The basic events of the narrative – George's origins, his migration to Ifrīqiya, his employment under Tamīm, his defection to Sicily, the support of ᶜAbd al-Raḥmān-Christodoulos, his embassies to Egypt, and his glorious career as vizier to King Roger – are all confirmed by other sources. Those details that can be checked – such as the dates, the use of the *miẓalla* by the Norman kings, the titles ascribed to George – all prove to be accurate. In addition, Abū l-Ḍawʾ may be traced in wholly independent sources, in which he appears both as an officer of the court and precisely as a man of letters (see below); and George's son, Michael, did indeed follow his father in the office of emir, although not in that of emir of emirs or vizier.[142] What is more, some of the details which occur only in this biography seem to be impressively authentic: George's younger brother, Simon, was commemorated in the name which George gave to one of his own sons;[143] and the *kunya* that is given to King Roger – Abū Tillīs, 'Old Wheat-sack' – alludes to his jealous protection of the export of Sicilian wheat to Ifrīqiya,[144] a reference which would have been comprehensible only to his contemporaries, and which can have meant little or nothing to a 15th-century Egyptian audience. Even the greatest surprise that this new account contains – the disgrace and execution of Christodoulos – explains the emir's previously mysterious disappearance, and may account for the contemporary fall from favour at court of Christodoulos' most eminent protégé, St. Bartholomew of Simeri.[145]

I know of only one other version of this story, which appears in two slightly different redactions. The less complete, and the later, comes in Ibn Khaldūn's account of the reign of al-Ḥasan ibn ᶜAlī:

> This George (*Jurjī*) was a Christian, an emigrant from the East. He had learnt the [Arabic] tongue, and he excelled in accountancy. He had been trained in Syria, at Antioch and elsewhere,[146] and so Tamīm made use of him and gave him office. But Yaḥyā hated him, and so, when Tamīm died, George employed a trick to defect to Roger, and he defected to him. And he won favour with [Roger].[147]

A much fuller redaction occurs in the *Riḥla* of al-Tījānī, but is nevertheless clearly drawn from the same version of this account:[148]

141 al-Maqrīzī 1991, vol.III, pp.18–20.
142 Above, p.82, note 139.
143 Brühl 1987, Appendix 2, no.4, p.268, line 8.
144 Above, p.81, note 132.
145 Zaccagni 1996, chap. 29, pp.224–5, 269–70.
146 Above, p.80, note 124.
147 Ibn Khaldūn 1868, vol.VI, p.161; *BAS*², vol.II, p.539; *BAS*²*(It.)*, vol.II, p.593.
148 al-Tījānī 1958, p.333; *BAS*², vol.II, pp.448–9; *BAS*²*(It.)*, vol.II, p.500; Soudan 1990, pp.155–6. Compare, for example, the following passage in Ibn Khaldūn – *wa-qad taᶜallama l-lisāna wa-baraᶜa fī l-ḥisābi wa-tahadhdhaba fī l-shāmi bi-anṭākiyata wa-ghayri-hā* – with its equivalent in al-Tījānī – *wa-kāna qad ᶜarafa lisāna l-ᶜarabi wa-baraᶜa fī l-ḥisābi wa-tahadhdhaba bi-l-shāmi bi-anṭākīyata wa-ghayri-hā*.

> Amongst the events of [Tamīm's] reign, which was the cause leading to the Christians capturing al-Mahdīya for the second time, which [in turn] brought about the extinction of the dynasty of the Ṣanhāja [*i.e.* the Zīrids], was that a Christian, by name of George, son of So-and-so, the Antiochene (*Jirjīr ibn Fulān al-Anṭākī*)[149] migrated from the East to Tamīm. He had learned the Arabic language, he excelled in accountancy, and he had been trained in Syria, at Antioch and elsewhere, and so Tamīm put him in charge of his income and his outlay, and gave him oversight of the expenditure of the revenues, so all the revenues of the Muslims fell into his hands and into the hands of his relatives. And he grew rich from [their] revenues.[150]
>
> When Tamīm died, this Christian was frightened of Yaḥyā, and [he wrote][151] to Roger, the lord of Sicily, and told him that he wished to defect to him in a galley which would appear to be arriving with an embassy. And so this Christian and his relatives escaped, on a Friday while the people were gathered together for prayer. They were disguised as sailors and got aboard, so that their plan worked perfectly: no one knew what they had done till after they set sail.
>
> When they arrived in Sicily, ᶜAbd Allāh (*sic*) the Christian,[152] the chief of the [island's] financial administration (*ṣāḥibu ashghāli-hā*) put them in charge of the collection of taxes (*al-jibāyāt*). They gave good counsel and imparted [many things].[153] And so, [when] Roger needed to send an ambassador to Egypt, ᶜAbd al-Raḥman recommended this George, and [the king] dispatched him. He performed loyally, and returned with kingly treasures, for which he earned Roger's favour.

This is essentially the same story as that told in the second and third paragraphs of al-Maqrīzī's biography. What is more, each resounds with just sufficient echoes of the other's language to demonstrate that they share a source or sources in common.[154]

The structure of al-Tījānī's work is that of a *riḥla* – a journey. As he travels from town to town, he reports historical anecdotes and other titbits relevant to the

149 al-Tījānī has already named him as Jurjī ibn Mīkhāʾīl: al-Tījānī 1958, p.241; *BAS*², vol.II, p.444; *BAS²(It.)*, vol.II, p.496.

150 *Wa-kāna l-ittisāᶜu* [MS: *al-insāᶜu*] *fī-hi mina l-amwāli*: al-Tījānī 1958, p.333; *BAS*², vol.II, p.448: *mina l-amwāli-hi* (*sic!*). The phrase is ambiguous. Amari translates 'pure le entrate pubbliche crebbero per opera sua': *BAS¹(It.)*, vol.II, p.65; *BAS²(It.)*, vol.II, p.500. But, after the author's implied disapproval that the revenues of the Muslims should have fallen into the hands of a family of Christians, an unfavourable consequence is anticipated. Rousseau 1853, p.377, expands and confuses the sense of the Arabic ('Dès ce moment la fortune privée des musulmans se trouva livrée à la merci de Georgi et des ses familiers – Lorsque Temim mourut, Georgi, qui avait déjà amassé des grandes richesses et qui craignait que le nouveau prince, Yeh´ia, fils de Temim, ne sévit contre lui, se hâta de solliciter l'appui du roi Roger et un refuge dans ses états.'), while Soudan 1990, p.155, simply omits the phrase.

151 There is a lacuna in the MS. al-Tījānī 1958, p.333, supplies *fa-khāṭaba*.

152 ᶜAbd Allāh is presumably identical with ᶜAbd al-Raḥmān who appears below as Roger's chief advisor and, later in al-Tījānī's account, as joint commander, with George of Antioch, of the 1123 expedition against al-Mahdīya: al-Tījānī 1958, p.335; *BAS*², vol.II, p.452; *BAS²(It.)*, vol.II, p.502.

153 *Fa-naṣaḥū wa-aẓharū*. Amari translates: 'il quale ufizio esercitarono fedelmente e così acquistarono riputazione': *BAS¹(It.)*, vol.II, p.66; *BAS²(It.)*, vol.II, p.500. Rousseau 1853, p.378, 'il faut le dire, ils s'acquittèrent de ces fonctions avec capacité et intelligence'. Soudan 1990, p.156, 'fonction qu'ils s'appliquèrent à remplir avec loyauté et zèle'.

154 For example: M[aqrīzī]: *dhakarū anna-hum ḥussāb* – T[ījānī]: *baraᶜa fī l-ḥisābi*. M: *ẓahara naṣḥu-hum* and *aẓharū l-naṣḥu* – T: *naṣaḥū wa-aẓharū*. M: *khāfa-hu jurjī* – T: *khāfa hādhā l-naṣrānī*.

place in which he finds himself. The passage quoted above comes in his account of al-Mahdīya, which is dominated by his retelling of the struggle between the Zīrids and the Normans of Sicily for its possession.[155] Within this tale, al-Tījānī makes effective use of George as a villain, from his arrival as a fugitive at the court of Tamīm, to his conquest of al-Mahdīya for the Normans in 1148.

Al-Tījānī drew upon two main sources for George's career: the lost history of the Zīrids of al-Mahdīya by the celebrated polymath Abū l-Ṣalt Umayya ibn ^{c}Abd al-^{c}Azīz;[156] and one or more of the lost histories of the Zīrid prince, ^{c}Abd al-^{c}Azīz ibn Shaddād. Al-Tījānī begins his account of the Christian assault upon al-Mahdīya with the Genoese and Pisan raid of 1087, and closes this particular episode by quoting, from Abū l-Ṣalt, part of a *qaṣīda*, the last verse of which describes the Italian attackers as *ṣilāl* (sing. *ṣill*), 'deadly serpents'. Al-Tījānī then uses the passage quoted above to complete his account of the reigns of Tamīm and Yaḥyā. Next, he describes Roger of Sicily's intervention in support of Rāfi^{c} ibn Makkan, the Arab lord of Gabès, against ^{c}Alī ibn Yaḥyā (1117–18).[157] Al-Tījānī does not here give his source for the Gabès episode, but he had earlier relied upon Abū l-Ṣalt for a fuller account of the same events.[158] Moreover, he ends with verses containing the same vivid image comparing the Norman attackers, with their serpentine flame-throwers of Greek-fire, to *ṣilāl*, 'deadly serpents'. These verses are clearly quoted from the same passage in Abū l-Ṣalt from which the others were taken. There is thus good reason to assume that the meat of al-Tījānī's account of George's early career, which is sandwiched between the two pieces of verse, was also derived from Abū l-Ṣalt's history.

Al-Tījānī continues immediately with the disastrous first attack upon al-Mahdīya, for which his source was again Abū l-Ṣalt.[159] ^{c}Abd al-Raḥmān and George of Antioch were joint commanders of the Sicilian fleet that landed on the little islands of Le Sorelle (al-Aḥāsī), some 15km north of al-Mahdīya, at dusk on Saturday 21 July 1123. They spent Sunday cruising around the peninsula upon which al-Mahdīya is built, eyeing its strong walls lined with troops. They returned to find that an Arab raid had left their camp in ruins and many dead. On Monday, ^{c}Abd al-Raḥmān and George bribed the Arab garrison of the Qaṣr al-Dīmās, and a Sicilian force of one hundred men was installed.[160] On the following day, a fierce attack destroyed their camp on Le Sorelle, while a vast Muslim force besieged al-Dīmās before its garrison could be reinforced or supplied. For eight days, the two commanders watched helplessly from the sea, before turning back to Sicily. The

155 For a convenient, if not always reliable, French translation of the whole of this passage, see now Soudan 1990. 156 For Abū l-Ṣalt, see Idris 1962a, vol.I, pp.xvii–xviii.

157 al-Tījānī 1958, p.98–100; *BAS*^{2}, vol.II, p.437–40; *BAS*^{2}*(It.)*, vol.II, pp.500–1. See also Idris 1962a, vol.I, pp.319–24.

158 al-Tījānī 1958, p.98; *BAS*^{2}, vol.II, p.438; *BAS*^{2}*(It.)*, vol.II, p.491–3.

159 al-Tījānī 1958, pp.335–9; *BAS*^{2}, vol.II, pp.451–6; *BAS*^{2}*(It.)*, vol.II, pp.502–6. For this expedition see Idris 1962a, vol.I, pp.334–5 and n.183; and Brett 1997.

160 Al-Dīmās was apparently a *ribāṭ* built upon the site of ancient Thapsus, near to the modern village of Baqālṭa, on a promontory midway between al-Mahdīya and Monastīr. See Idris 1962a, vol.I, p.336 and n.194.

garrison in al-Dīmās held out for another eight days until, unable to negotiate their surrender, the Sicilians launched a desperate sortie, and were slaughtered to a man.

It is again Abū l-Ṣalt, but this time reported by Ibn ᶜIdhārī, who provides the following footnote to the Norman defeat at al-Dīmās.

> The annals of Abū l-Ṣalt relate: "ᶜAbd al-Raḥmān ibn ᶜAbd al-ᶜAzīz told me [the following]: "At the court of Roger in Sicily, I saw a man of the Franks with a long beard grasp the tip of his beard in his hand and swear on the gospel that he would not cut one hair of it until he had taken his vengeance upon the people of al-Mahdīya. I asked what had become of him, and I was told that, after the defeat [at al-Dīmās], he tore at it until it bled."' At this point, Abū l-Ṣalt ended [his] account of the history of al-Mahdīya and the emir al-Ḥasan ibn ᶜAlī ibn Yaḥyā ibn Tamīm, in the year 517[/1123].[161]

Although by no means certain, it is highly possible that the ᶜAbd al-Raḥmān ibn ᶜAbd al-ᶜAzīz in this passage is to be identified with ᶜAbd al-Raḥmān-Christodoulos. Ibn Khaldūn, in his account of the affair of al-Dīmās, which he too derives from Abū l-Ṣalt, has the Norman fleet commanded by ᶜAbd al-Raḥmān ibn ᶜAbd al-ᶜAzīz.[162] There is no evidence that Ibn Khaldūn was familiar with the story of the beard – the only other place where the Sicilian ᶜAbd al-Raḥmān ibn ᶜAbd al-ᶜAzīz appears – although he could, of course, have picked up the name from Ibn ᶜIdhārī without citing the story. Be that as it may, we shall see below that Abū l-Ṣalt is known to have corresponded and exchanged verses with Abū l-Ḍawʾ.[163] If Abū l-Ṣalt was a correspondent of the Sicilian *kātib al-inshāʾ*, then he could also have been in touch with the vizier himself, perhaps during one of the periods of *rapprochement* between the two courts.[164] Thus it is possible that Abū l-Ṣalt had information about George from two of the latter's closest colleagues – Christodoulos and Abū l-Ḍawʾ.

The passage just quoted demonstrates that al-Tījānī could not have used Abū l-Ṣalt as a source for events after 1123. On the one hand, this might explain why his account fails to mention the fall of ᶜAbd al-Raḥmān. On the other, al-Tījānī does pursue George until at least 1148, although he is interested exclusively in his activities in Ifrīqiya, and says nothing of his subsequent career in Sicily. His source for George's exploits after 1123 was clearly Ibn Shaddād. After the affair of al-Dīmās, al-Tījānī skips rapidly over the Almoravid raids against Sicily of 1127, and the Ḥammādid attack upon al-Mahdīya of 1135, in order to return to his main theme: the series of attacks upon al-Mahdīya commanded by George of Antioch.

161 Ibn ᶜIdhārī 1948–51, vol.I, p.309; Ibn ᶜIdhārī, 1901–4, vol.I, pp.463–4.

162 Ibn Khaldūn 1868, vol.VI, p.161; *BAS*², vol.II, p.539; *BAS²(It.)*, vol.II, p.593. Hady Roger Idris was initially unwilling to accept this identification, but later changed his mind: 'il semble bien que ᶜAbd al-Raḥmān ibn ᶜAbd al-ᶜAzīz qui tint à Abū l-Ṣalt le propos cité par l'auteur du *Bayān* soit le commandant de la flotte sicilienne appelé ᶜAbd al-Raḥmān b. ᶜAbd al-ᶜAzīz al-Naṣrānī par les sources arabes et Christodoulos par les chroniques chrétiennes; leur rencontre soit à Mahdia soit en Sicile n'a rien d'impossible': Idris 1962a, vol.I, p.335, n.188.

163 ᶜImād al-Dīn 1964–9, vol.I, p.345. ᶜImād al-Dīn 1966–72, vol.I, p.273; *BAS*², vol.II, pp.725–6; *BAS²(It.)*, vol.III, p.782–3.

164 De Simone 1999a, p.279 concludes, from the story of the beard, that Abū l-Ṣalt had an eyewitness at the Sicilian court.

He begins with George's raid on the port in 536/1140–1, after which, he says, Roger did not cease to send George repeatedly against al-Mahdīya until the final assault of 22 June 1148, when George commanded the fleet of three hundred ships which finally expelled al-Ḥasan and took the city for Roger. When he reports the pious words spoken by al-Ḥasan as he abandoned his capital, al-Tījānī explicitly names Ibn Shaddād as his source. Al-Tījānī then leaves al-Mahdīya for a couple of pages to follow al-Ḥasan westwards, but returns for ᶜAbd al-Muᵓmin's triumphal entry into the city on 30 July 1159, which he again has from Ibn Shaddād.

ᶜAbd al-ᶜAzīz ibn Shaddād was the grandson of the Zīrid sultan Tamīm, and the nephew of sultan Yaḥyā. He is known to have written a history of al-Qayrawān, which was much used by al-Tījānī, and a chronicle of Sicily, both now lost. It is not known when Ibn Shaddād was born, but he attended the court of al-Ḥasan until al-Mahdīya was captured by George in 1148. He may then have fled with al-Ḥasan to the court of ᶜAbd al-Muᵓmin. Ibn Shaddād was in Palermo in 551/1156–7,[165] possibly on his way to Damascus, where he was settled by 571/1175–6.[166] Ibn Shaddād is almost the *only* contemporary Arab source for the Zīrids after 517/1123, when Abū l-Ṣalt's history came to an end, and a passage cited by al-Tījānī reveals that he was still collecting information after 582/1186–7, the year concerning the events of which he interviewed a citizen of al-Mahdīya in Damascus.[167] He was thus the primary source of many of the reports about Zīrid Ifrīqiya and Norman Sicily recounted by Arab writers, including the Syrians Ibn al-Athīr (d.1232–3), Ibn Khallikān (d.1282), and Abū l-Fidāᵓ (d. 1331); the North Africans al-Tījānī (*fl.* 1307–1309), Ibn ᶜIdhārī (d. after 1312), and Ibn Khaldūn (d.1406); and the Egyptians al-Nuwayrī (d.1331–32) and al-Maqrīzī (d.1441).[168]

Michael Brett has demonstrated, by means of a meticulous analysis of the historiography of the battle of al-Ḥaydarān, that Ibn Shaddād's history circulated in two editions.[169] The first was used by the Maghribī historian, Ibn ᶜIdhārī, in *al-Bayān*; the second, which was substantially more detailed than the first, was used independently by Ibn al-Athīr and al-Nuwayrī. Brett suggests that the first edition was compiled before Ibn Shaddād's migration to the East, and was the only version available to later Maghribī authors; the second, fuller edition was compiled in Damascus, and was accessible only to Eastern scholars. If correct, this reconstruction might offer the solution to the problem of the sources for the rather different accounts of George of Antioch given by al-Tījānī and al-Maqrīzī. Al-Tījānī's account would be based upon Abū l-Ṣalt for George's career up to 1123, and thereafter upon the first edition of Ibn Shaddād's history. Al-Maqrīzī's biography would be based upon the

165 Nuwayrī 1923–92, vol.XXIV, p.319; Amari 1933–39, vol.III, p.486. It seems unlikely that Ibn Shaddād was in ᶜAbd al-Muᵓmin's camp at the naval battle of al-Mahdīya in 554/1159, as Amari believed: see Idris 1962a, vol.I, p.xviii, n.37.

166 ᶜImād al-Dīn 1964–9, vol.I, p.167; ᶜImād al-Dīn 1966–72, vol.I, p.142.

167 al-Tījānī 1958, p.14; Rousseau 1852, pp.81–2.

168 Talbi 1960; Idris 1962a, vol.I, pp.xviii–xix. For a detailed and perceptive analysis of the importance of Ibn Shaddād's works for the historiography of Zīrid Ifrīqiya, see Brett 1969, vol.I, pp.387–425, esp. 394–404; Brett 1999b, pp.6–7.

169 Brett 1969, vol.I, pp.387–425, esp. 394–404; Brett 1999b, pp.6–7.

second edition of Ibn Shaddād's history, which made use of Abū l-Ṣalt for George's early life, but which added much greater detail both for his career before 1123, and for later events. If this hypothesis is correct, then the primary sources upon which al-Tījānī and al-Maqrīzī drew were both eye-witnesses to the events which they described, and were personally acquainted with the main protagonists.

Having thus established a pedigree for al-Maqrīzī's biography of George, we can now return for a closer look at Abū l-Ḍawʾ. Abū l-Ḍawʾ Sirāj ibn Aḥmad ibn Rajāʾ came from the distinguished Palermitan family which provided the *qāḍī* of Palermo in three successive generations. The first, Abū l-Ḍawʾ's paternal uncle, *al-shaykh al-faqīh al-qāḍī* Abū l-Qāsim ʿAbd al-Raḥmān ibn Rajāʾ, presided over the sale of a house in Palermo in 1137–8.[170] He was also, presumably, the unnamed *qāḍī* who sat in judgement in the royal court beside Christodoulos and Abū l-Ḍawʾ in January 1123. The third, *al-shaykh al-faqīh al-qāḍī* Abū l-Faḍl Rajāʾ ibn *al-shaykh al-faqīh al-qāḍī* Abī l-Ḥasan ʿAlī, also presided over the sale of a house in Palermo, in September 1161.[171] His brother, Muḥammad, was one of the witnesses to the contract. Nothing is known of his father, Abū l-Ḥasan ʿAlī, except that he too was *qāḍī* of Palermo.

Abū l-Ḍawʾ Sirāj ibn Aḥmad ibn Rajāʾ *al-kātib* ('the secretary') appears as the recipient of verses by the Zīrid historian Abū l-Ṣalt Umayya in the vast anthology of verse, the *Kharīdat al-qaṣr*, compiled by ʿImād al-Dīn al-Iṣfahānī (d.1201).[172] ʿImād al-Dīn remarks that he had long sought examples of poetry by Abū l-Ḍawʾ himself when he came across a copy of *al-Mukhtār fī l-naẓm wa-l-nathr li-afāḍil ahl al-ʿaṣr* ('The anthology of poetry and of prose by the best men of the age') by the *kātib* Ibn Bashrūn al-Ṣiqillī.[173] This work, now lost, was compiled in Sicily, and published in 561/1165–6. From it, ʿImād al-Dīn quotes three extracts by Abū l-Ḍawʾ: an exchange of verses with the *faqīh* ʿĪsā ibn ʿAbd al-Munʿim al-Ṣiqillī, who had asked for the loan of a book;[174] five verses written upon the death of a friend;[175] and seventeen verses from a more than competent elegy composed on the death of 'the son of Roger the Frank, lord of Sicily'.[176] The son is not named but, as Amari pointed out, there are hints that he had recently come of age.[177] If so, this would indicate not, as Amari suggested, the first-born Roger (who was knighted in 1135, and who died in 1149, aged 31 years), nor the infant Henry (d. *c*.1145), but

170 **Private 6.** 171 **Private 9.**

172 ʿImād al-Dīn 1964–9, vol.I, p.345; ʿImād al-Dīn 1966–72, vol.I, p.273; *BAS*², vol.II, p.725; *BAS*²*(It.)*, vol.III, pp.782–3.

173 ʿImād al-Dīn 1964–9, vol.I, pp.348–9; ʿImād al-Dīn 1966–72, pp.275–6; *BAS*², vol.II, p.726; *BAS*²*(It.)*, vol.III, pp.782–3. For Ibn Bashrūn, see Amari 1933–9, vol.I, p.41, vol.III, pp.680–2, 781–3.

174 Amari 1933–9, vol.III, pp.707–8 and n.6, 768–70. The verses have recently been translated by De Simone 1999b, p.11. 175 De Simone 1999b, pp.11–12.

176 ʿImād al-Dīn 1964–9, vol.I, pp.350–2; ʿImād al-Dīn 1966–72, vol.I, pp.277–8; *BAS*², vol.II, pp.726–8; *BAS*²*(It.)*, vol.III, pp.784–5; Amari 1933–9, vol.III, pp.775–6, n.3.

177 Amari, *BAS*¹*(It.)*, vol.II, pp.470–1, n.2, suggested that the third verse quoted might imply that the son had died in the flower of his youth: *a-ḥīna stawā fī ḥusni-hi wa-jalāli-hi* … ('Just when he had come into his perfection and splendour …') – the use of the verb *istawā*, with an echo of *Qurʾān* 48.29 (and even 53.6) is particularly telling. Further on, verses 9–10, in which the tents, swords, spears, and horses of the deceased mourn him, could suggest that he was of martial age.

Table 3.1 The family of Abū l-Ḍawʾ Sirāj

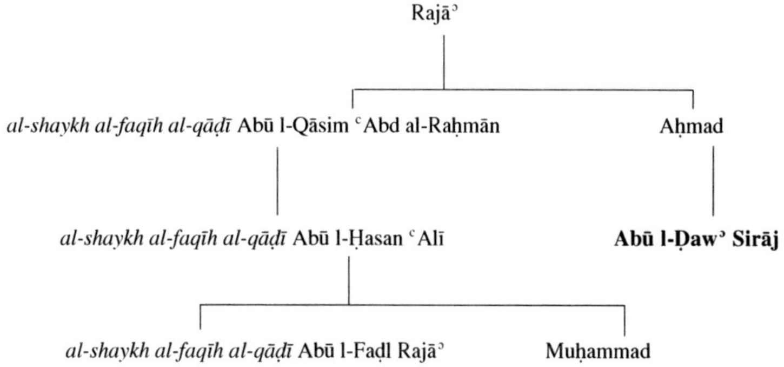

either Tancred (d.1138–42) or Alfonso (d.1144) who died in their mid to late teens or early twenties.[178] For whichever son Abū l-Ḍawʾ wrote the elegy, he was clearly still at the centre of things in the early 1140s.

Some twenty years earlier, in January 1123, as we saw above, Abū l-Ḍawʾ assisted the emir Christodoulos to decide the dispute between Muriella of Petterrana and Abū Maḍar ibn al-Biththirrānī. In this, his first recorded appearance, he bears the title *al-qāʾid* (ὁ καΐτος Βοδδάος, *o kaitos Boddaos*), the honorific which, later, was born by all the leading 'palace Saracens' and Arab officers of the royal *dīwān*. This seems to confirm that he was indeed a secretary in the comital administration, as is suggested by the titles given to him by ᶜImād al-Dīn – *al-kātib* – and in al-Maqrīzī's biography of George of Antioch – *kātib al-inshāʾ*. If Abū l-Ḍawʾ did indeed bear the latter title, then he may have been one of the most important members of Roger's staff. In Fāṭimid Egypt, the *dīwān al-inshāʾ* was by some regarded as the most important bureau in the central administration. There, the *kātib al-inshāʾ* was an official of the chief department of the *dīwān al-inshāʾ*, the *ṣaḥābat dīwān al-inshāʾ wa-l-mukātabāt*, also known as the *dīwān al-naẓar*. The director of this bureau, who is variously styled *raʾīs* ('head'), *mutawallī* ('superintendent'), *ṣāḥib* ('master'), *mushidd* ('inspector') and *kātib* ('secretary') was awarded the honorific title of *al-shaykh al-ajall* ('the sublime elder'). It was he who presented incoming paperwork to the caliph and advised how it should be answered; and it was he who submitted outgoing documents for the caliph's approval and, where appropriate, his signature. He not only worked, but also lived, in close proximity to the sovereign. With a salary of one hundred and twenty dinars a month, he was one of the most highly paid of all Fāṭimid civil servants.[179] It could well be misleading, however, to rely too heavily upon these Fāṭimid sources

[178] Houben 1999, p.48, n.10, pp.124–5.
[179] Ibn Khaldūn 1868, vol.I, p.402; Ibn al-Ṣayrafī, 1905, *passim*; Ibn al-Ṣayrafī 1924, pp.66, 68, 69, 71 *et pass.*; al-Qalqashandī 1913–72, vol.I, p.130, vol.III, p.490–2; Björkman 1928, pp.20–2.

for an assessment of the precise rôle played by Abū l-Ḍawʾ. We have no independent evidence that the Norman *dīwān* had a *kātib al-inshāʾ*, and still less do we know what duties such an officer might have performed in Sicily. The term could well be employed anachronistically or imprecisely by either al-Maqrīzī or his source, and it would be wrong to invest it with too great significance.

Al-Maqrīzī's biography of George of Antioch thus offers a new perspective upon the history of the *dīwān* under Roger II. On the one hand, the references to Christodoulos as Roger's *wazīr*, to the *dawāwīn* over which he appointed George of Antioch and his family, and to an official called the *kātib al-inshāʾ*, should probably not be used to argue for the existence of a true *dīwān* before 1130. The words *wazīr* and *dawāwīn* may here mean nothing more than 'chief minister' and 'bureaux', and need not imply that Christodoulos was an Islamic-style vizier who presided over an elaborate Arabic administration. On the other hand, there can be no doubt that Abū l-Ḍawʾ was an Arabic secretary (*kātib*) at the Sicilian court in the years *c.*1123–6. Indeed, if al-Maqrīzī's report that Abū l-Ḍawʾ was offered the vizierate on the fall of Christodoulos is correct, then either he must have been as competent in Greek as his predecessor, or the administration must have conducted much of its business in Arabic. However, as we shall see in the following chapters, the earliest surviving products of the royal *dīwān* yield no evidence for an active Arabic administration in the years 1112–30. On the contrary, they seem to indicate that it was only after 1130 that the royal *dīwān* was created, very largely through the importation of new elements from the wider Islamic world. I am thus inclined to conclude that the *kātib* Abū l-Ḍawʾ did not preside over a sophisticated Arabic administration. Such a conclusion does not, of course, rule out the likelihood of him having been responsible for any tasks that had to be done in Arabic. Indeed, his one live appearance as an administrator, in the court case of January 1123, involved an Arabic document and Arab witnesses. Moreover, the Sicilian court was in regular correspondence at this time with the Zīrids of al-Mahdīya.[180] It was also in touch with the Fāṭimids of Cairo,[181] and with other minor Muslim powers such as the rebel Arab lord of Gabès.[182] I suspect, but cannot prove, that Abū l-Ḍawʾ may have been responsible for Roger's foreign correspondence in Arabic, and that this may have represented the principal duty of his Arab scribes in the years 1112–30. It may not be, after all, pure coincidence that no Arabic administrative document is known to have been issued by Roger during these years, and that Abū l-Ḍawʾ is best known in the Arabic sources as the correspondent of Abū l-Ṣalt Umayya, the official historian of the Zīrid court.

[180] The two courts were clearly in almost constant contact at this time. They were bound by treaties and reciprocal agreements, and often exchanged ambassadors. Roger maintained *wukalāʾ* ('agents', sing. *wakīl*) in al-Mahdīya. See, for example, Idris 1962a, vol.I, pp.286, 290–1, 306, 308,323–4, 337–8.

[181] Below, pp.258–9.

[182] Idris 1962a, vol.I, pp.319–24.

CHAPTER 4

The earliest products of the royal *dīwān*, 1130–43

After the long interval during which no Arabic documents seem to have been issued to Sicilian recipients, in March 1132, little more than a year after Roger's coronation, Arabic documents suddenly began to be issued again. This is surprising. More than a generation had passed since the completion of the conquest and, in that time, Greek had become firmly established as the primary administrative language of the Norman regime. Greek was used to register Arab villeins, and to describe estate boundaries which proceeded from one Arabic boundary-mark to the next and which had been established on the testimony of Arab witnesses. Greek decrees were issued to royal officials who included Arabic-speakers amongst their number. There is no evidence that such Greek documents had failed to fulfil their administrative function. Latin, too, had gained a toe-hold, although it was only after 1130, and especially after the death of Roger II in 1154, that it was seriously to challenge the pre-eminence of Greek, and eventually to surpass it. What, then, dictated the return to Arabic? We must begin to seek the answer in the documents themselves.

The Cefalù *deperdita* (*Dīwānī* 10–11)

The earliest products known to have been issued by King Roger's *dīwān* were two bilingual documents in favour of the new royal foundation of San Salvatore di Cefalù. Neither survives in its original form.

The first was a register of the villeins of the estate of Mutata,[1] granted by King Roger to San Salvatore (***Dīwānī* 10**). It was accompanied by a Greek document, also issued in March 1132, which granted Mutata to San Salvatore, and recorded the findings of an inquest, held by George of Antioch in February of the same year, to establish the boundaries of the estate.[2] This Greek donation is now extremely

[1] Mutata appears to have lain to the west of the Fiume Torto, south of Monte San Calogero, about 17km south-west of Cefalù.

[2] PA, AdS, Cefalù no.5: ed. Spata 1862, 2nd ser., no.3, pp.423–8; Caspar 1904, p.513, reg.74.

fragmentary, but a Latin translation of it, apparently made *pro domo* at San Salvatore in the 12th century, does survive. It is this Greek donation that mentions the bilingual register of villeins now missing. King Roger states that 'I have given to the aforesaid episcopal church, together with other necessities, the men (τοῦς ἀνθρωπους, *tous anthrōpous*) whose personal names have been recorded in the register (ἐν τῇ πλατεῖα, *en tē plateia*) and, with them, I also give to it lands in the place called Mutata, the boundary-description of which lands is given in this document'. That boundary-description was 'fixed by George, emir of emirs, who presides over my whole kingdom (Greek missing: *qui preerat toti regno meo*), together with all those who were there present with him'; and there follow the names of more than thirty witnesses, roughly half Latin and half Arab. After the boundary is described, it is recorded that 'These boundaries were fixed by George, emir of emirs, in February, Indiction X [1132 A.D.], and the villeins given to the same church are in a register written in Greek and Saracen letters (Greek missing: *et villani dati ipsi ecclesie sunt in platia scripta litteris grecis et sarracenicis*)'. Apparently, the list of names was written in Arabic with interlinear Greek transliteration – the first appearance of a feature which characterises all but one of the royal *jarā'id*. It may be that the register was compiled on the basis of a survey of the population of Mutata, made at this time by George. This *jarīda* may be that renewed in the *jarīda* of January 1145 (***Dīwānī* 24**).

The second *deperditum*, also issued in March 1132, appears to have been a bilingual decree in favour of San Salvatore (***Dīwānī* 11**). According to an undated Latin translation, the original document was written 'in Greek and Saracen', and recorded King Roger's grant of the whole of the fishery of Cefalù, including the *tonnara*.[3] Also, San Salvatore's ships, especially those sailing between Cefalù and its mother house of Bagnara in Calabria, were to carry cargoes for the use of the church free of all customs and taxes, so long as they did not pass beyond Amalfi. Foodstuff and construction-timber for the use of the church, and carried by the citizens of Cefalù, were similarly exempted from duties in the port of Cefalù. But all merchandise transported by the church, by the citizens, or by foreign merchants was to be liable to the usual taxes. The bishop was to receive market and anchorage fees in Cefalù. Finally, the produce of the lands of Cefalù and Bagnara was exempted from all charges and taxes.

There is, however, a difficulty. What is apparently an authentic renewal of the original decree, made by the royal *dīwān* in January 1180,[4] bears little resemblance to what purports to be the Latin translation of the original of 1132, in that the renewal grants far fewer, and substantially different, rights and exemptions. Either King Roger issued two similar privileges to Cefalù: one parsimonious, which was renewed in 1180; and the other extravagantly munificent, which was translated at

[3] PA, AdS, Cefalù no.6: ed. Spata 1862, 2nd ser., no.4, pp.429–30; White 1938, p.190, n.4. Caspar 1904, p.513, reg.73, wrongly implies that the original Arabic-Greek privilege still survives complete with its lead seal, and wrongly dates the Latin translation to 1329, the year in which that Latin version was confirmed by Frederick II and Peter II of Aragon (*Rollus Rubeus* 1972, pp.61–3).

[4] Original: PA, AdS, Cefalù no.19: ed. Cusa 1868–82, no.136, pp.489–90.

an unknown date. Or the Latin 'translation' is in fact a spurious attempt to claim more extensive rights than San Salvatore had actually been granted.[5]

I am strongly inclined towards the second alternative, for two reasons. First and foremost, the undated Latin 'translation' is witnessed by John, bishop of Malta, and Roger, abbot of San Giovanni degli Eremiti, but at no time between 1132 and 1329 when a John was bishop of Malta was the abbot of San Giovanni called Roger. Between these dates, there seem to have been only three bishops of Malta called John: the first, a courtier and politician during the regency of Margaret, best known from the *History* of 'Hugo Falcandus', can be traced from 1167 to 1169, when Donatus was abbot of San Giovanni; the second flourished in the early reign of Frederick II, from 1211 to 1224, when the abbot of San Giovanni was Iucundus; and the third, *Iohannes normandus*, makes a brief appearance in 1268 when Advedutus was abbot of San Giovanni.[6] Second, the original which may be reconstructed from the renewal of 1180 would have been much closer in diplomatic form, and also in content, to the Greek text of the near contemporary Greek-Arabic decree issued to San Bartolomeo di Lipari-Patti in January 1134 (***Dīwānī* 13**).

If this suggestion is correct, then the original bilingual decree of March 1132 would have been addressed to the king's customs-officers and port-officials, and would have instructed them to allow San Salvatore to import and export, throughout Sicily, Calabria and the principality of Salerno, in its own vessels, free of all charges and duty, wheat, vegetables and other necessities for the use of the monks and other servants of the church. In addition, San Salvatore was to be allowed, without paying any duty or tax, to transport by land all necessities for the church, and to buy and sell in the interests of the church. The renewal implies that the original decree was actually carried by monks trading on behalf of the church, and that, by 1180, 'the great decree' of 1132 was no longer fit to travel, perhaps because of its antiquity, its unwieldy size, or – perhaps – because it was written in Greek and Arabic, for the renewal was made Latin and Greek.[7]

Although little can be deduced about the nature of the royal *dīwān* from the Cefalù *deperdita*, their importance is not simply that they attest to the re-emergence of an Arabic administration after a long silence. It is particularly striking that the earliest known product of the royal *dīwān* (***Dīwānī* 10**) should have been so closely associated with George of Antioch. Moreover, as we have already seen, this same document introduced name-lists written in Arabic with interlinear Greek transliteration, a feature which characterises the royal *jarāʾid*. Although, in the absence of the documents themselves, such clues cannot be regarded as conclusive proof, they strongly indicate that the re-emergence of the Arabic administration

[5] See Brühl 1987, doc.19, pp.52–4, for another privilege granted to San Salvatore also in March 1132.

[6] Kamp 1973–82, part 3, pp.1165–9, and Pirri 1733, vol.II, pp.1112–13. I am extremely grateful to Stanley Fiorini of the University of Malta for his most helpful comments upon the bishops of Malta called John.

[7] *Exemplar autem predicti privilegii ideo in presenti scripto fecimus declarari pro eo quod ipsum privilegium non potest eo deferri quo fuerit necessarium* / Διὰ τοῦτο ἐπιήθι αὐτοὺς τὼ παρὸν σιγίλλιον διά τε τὸ μέγαν σιγίλλιον τοῦ μακαριοτάτου ῥὴξ Ῥογερίου οὐ δίνονται αὐτὸι δίξε εἰς πάσαν τόπον ἀπερχομένους αὐτοὺς καὶ εἰσερχομένους.

was not haphazard, but rather the result of considered policy for which George of Antioch, who 'presided over the whole kingdom', seems to have been largely responsible.

Two Greek-Arabic documents for Lipari-Patti, 1133–4 (*Dīwānī* 12–13)

The bilingual act (τό σιγίλλιον, *to sigillion*; *sijill*) issued to John, bishop of Lipari-Patti, in February 1133, is the earliest surviving example of the new series of royal Arabic documents (***Dīwānī* 12**).[8] It appears to be an official chancery copy of a privilege,[9] which confirms the boundaries of the estate of Mirto, on the border between the districts of Iato and Partinico, in the hinterland of Palermo. This is essentially a Greek *sigillion*, into which has been inserted an Arabic boundary-description. The *sigillion* opens conventionally with the *arenga* (lines 1–5). In the *narratio* (lines 5–14), it is recorded how, in February, Indiction XI (1133 A.D.), Bishop John of Lipari came to Roger and asked him to issue him with a document (*sigillion*) that would clearly describe the boundaries of the estate of Mirto, which had been granted to the church of Lipari by the late Rainald Avenel, out of love for his wife Fresenda.[10] The boundaries had already been fixed: 'On our order, these were delimited, with our full authority,[11] by the archon of archons and emir of emirs, George, when he had command of Iato, and was strategos of all the pertaining district'. The worthies who assisted George to delimit the boundary are named: four Latins, and a dozen Saracens, plus more Saracens who are unnamed.[12] Next, in the *dispositio* (lines 14–16), Roger grants Bishop John's petition, and issues the boundary-description of Mirto 'in the present document ... written below in Greek and Saracen'. The Greek *periorismos* (lines 16–20) follows immediately, and then the Arabic *ḥudūd* (lines 21–24). The document ends with the Greek *corroboratio*, the *traditio* giving the year as 6641 A.M. (1133 A.D.), and Roger's chancery signature (lines 24–26). There is no trace of a seal.

The key to understanding the significance of this document lies in the relationship between the four surviving versions of the boundary-description (see Table 4.1):

[8] Original: Patti, Arch. Dioc. no.5; Girgensohn and Kamp 1965, p.16, reg.29; ed. Cusa 1868–82, no.45, pp.515–17. The original is now much damaged and has been extensively restored. Cusa was apparently able to read much that is now missing. In the extracts that follow, those passages which have been restored according to Cusa's often imperfect text are indicated by square brackets.

[9] This is one of the very rare surviving original documents of King Roger not to have borne a seal: Kehr 1902, p.186, n.2; Brühl 1983, p.64 and n.215.

[10] Below, p.96, note 13.

[11] Ménager 1960, p.201 translates ἐν πάντι τῶ κράτει ἡμῶν as 'dans tout notre domaine'.

[12] Note that Cusa misreads ἐρνοὺς ὁ κανονικός, πέτρος and thus creates a fifth Latin witness called Peter. The document is very worn and lacunose at this point, but there is little doubt that the correct name is ἐρνου(λφο)ς ὁ κανονικός (τῆς μητρόπολεως or possibly τοῦ πανόρμου or similar). The Latin versions are as follows: 1114, *Arnulfus, canonicus panormitanae ecclesiae* (Garufi 1912, p.350); February 1133, *Arnulf, Panormitane eccl(esi)e canonicus* (Brühl 1987, p.68).

Table 4.1 The different versions of the boundary-description of Mirto compared

Latin 1114	Greek 1133	Greek 1133 (trans.)	Arabic 1133	Arabic 1133 (trans.)	Latin 1133
A fonte qui Raclia nuncupatur quemadmodum uia ducit usque ad fluuium / Belliane. Inde reuersi ad supradictum fontem inchoauerunt aliam diuisionem, ab eo fonte per medium pantanum usque ad fonte[m] cognomento Bentellus (sic! read Bensellus) et usque ad coniunc- / tionem duorum fluuiorum, unius uidelicet Mirtae et alterius Partenici, et quodam riuulo qui descendit in fluuium preceps, ut idem riuulus ducit ab inferioribus ad inferiora / usque ad fontem Fici, qui est ad districtum Juniarii, et inde ut atque meatus ducet sursum, usque / ad fontem de Blato.	ἀρχεται ἐκ τῆς ὁδοῦ βιλλιὲνες μέχρι τοῦ αὐτου χωρί[ου βιλλιένες] εἰς τὸν μέγαν ποταμόν, / κακεῖθεν ὑποστρέφει [ἕως τὴν φαβάραν] τὴν ἐπονομαζομένην τοῦ ἡράκλη, κα[κ]εῖθεν διαμοιράζει ἐξ ἴσου τὸ [μάρτζον καὶ διασ]ώση εἰς τὸ ὄρος / καὶ ἐκβαΐνει εἰς τὸ πηγ[άδιον τὸ λεγόμενον] ἔπεν σέλου καὶ εἰς τὴν σμήξιν τῶν ὑδάτων, τοῦ ὕδατος τοῦ μύρτου [καὶ τοῦ ὕδατος τοῦ] στενοῦ τοῦ ἐπωνομασμένου / τζουνιέν, καὶ ἐκεῖθεν ἀνα[βαίνει ὡς] ἀναβαίνουσιν τὰ ὕδατα μέχρι τῆς φαβάρας τῆς διαγνωριζομ[ένης ἡβλάτου τῆς] οὔσης εἰς τὸν βουνόν, / πρὸς τούτοις δέ ἐστι κ[αὶ ὁ ......] ὀνομαζόμενος τοῦ μέχδεπ καὶ τὰ χωράφια τὰ ἐπωνομασμένα τ[οῦ σαφσάφ τὰ γν]ωριζόμενα τοῦ μύρτου.	It begins from the road of Villienes to this village of Villienes to the big river, and thence it turns back to the spring named the [Spring] of Heraklēs, and thence it cuts through the middle of the swamp and it arrives at the wooded mountain and it departs to the spring called Epen Selou and to the confluence of the waters of the water of Murton and the water of the pass called Tzounien, and thence it goes up like the rising of the water to the spring known as [Ēblatou] which is on the hill; in addition to [*or* near to] those are both the [… *lacuna* …] called the […] of Mechdep, and the fields named the [fields] of Safsaf, known as belonging to Murton.	وذلك من طريق بليانة [الى (الـ)ـرحل] الذى هو بليانة الى الوادى الكبير ثم الى ان يرجع [الحد/ الى فوارة رقلة] والنصف من المسرح الى ان ينتهى الشعرا فيخرج الى العين التى عر[ف عين] بن /سالوا الى ملقا المياه ما مارتو وما مضـ[ـيق جنيان] ويطلع مع مجرى الما الي فوارة إبلاطوا التى بالجبل ووطا عرف [بهـ]ـا بوطا مهدب ورباع عرف الى / الصفصاف [مارتو]	And that is: from the road of Billiyāna to the village which is Billiyāna to the big river, then until the boundary turns back to the Spring of Raqla and the middle of the pasture until it reaches the scrub(?). Then it departs to the spring which is known as the Spring of Ibn Sālū to the meeting of the waters, the water of Mārtū and the water of the Pass of Junyān. And it climbs with the flow of water to the Spring of Iblāṭū which is on the mountain, and a depression known by [the name of] the Depression of Mahdab, and the lands of al-Ṣafṣāf (the Willows), known to [belong to] Mārtū.	[A] via Billiana usq(ue) ad idem casale Villiane ad magnu(m) flumen, et inde re- / vertitur ad magnu(m) fonte(m) qui vocatur de Iracli, et inde dividit p(er) med[ium] Lumarge, quod Pantanu(m) vel terra Silvestris Latine nu(n)cupatur, usq(ue) dum / venit ad nem(us), et inde exit ad fonte(m) q(u)i vocatur Ebesselu, coniunctioni aquaru(m) de aqua Mirte et aqua Districti, que nomen habet Iunien, et inde / ascendit sicut aque ascendunt usq(ue) ad magnu(m) fonte(m) q(u)i vocatur Plato, q(u)i est ad monte(m) et campu(m) q(u)i vocatur Mehedep, et terras que vocantur de / Safsaf, que recognoscuntur de Mirta.

- Latin 1114 – a Latin document of uncertain date and diplomatic status, purporting to be an original record of a boundary-inquest held in 1114;[13]
- Greek 1133 – the Greek text of ***Dīwānī* 12**;
- Arabic 1133 – the Arabic text of ***Dīwānī* 12**;
- Latin 1133 – an original, authentic, and official Latin version of ***Dīwānī* 12**, issued on 26 February 1133.[14]

The *periorismos* of Greek 1133 claims to be based upon a boundary-description made in 1114. However, the *periorismos* of Greek 1133 contains so much that is not to be found in Latin 1114, and omits so much that it does contain, that the one cannot be based upon the other. (In Table 4.1, note in particular the beginnings and endings of the boundaries.) And yet, the very same jurors who are named in Latin 1114 as those who assisted George of Antioch, are also named in Greek 1133 and in Latin 1133, as is shown in Table 4.2. It follows that the three documents are in someway related. What is more, a comparison of the three lists of witnesses in Table 4.2 demonstrates that there is an especially close connection between Latin 1114 and Latin 1133, and that both differ significantly from Greek 1133. Compare the columns in Table 4.3: in the first line, both Latin versions make the same bizarre error, and inexplicably render the Arabic name *Ḥammūd* as *Peleu*; only the Greek gives the correct transliteration *Chammout*. In the second line, the two Latin versions fail to realise that *Muḥammad* is the name of the *qāʾid* of the *skaranoi* of Iato, and so they needlessly add *de Iato* after his name; only in the Greek is it clear that the title and name both refer to a single individual. There are also indications that the names of the Arab witnesses in Greek 1133 are more closely derived from their Arabic originals than the names in the two Latin versions: thus, for Arabic *ᶜAlī*, the Greek gives Ἀλλίους (*Allíous*), but the Latin *Alus* without the stressed - *í* -; and for Arabic *Isḥāq*, the Greek hash Ισχάκ (*Ischak*) with Arabic guttural *khāʾ* represented by Greek guttural *chi*, while the Latin falls back upon *Ysaac*, as in the Vulgate. The most likely explanation is that the scribe of Greek 1133 transcribed the list of witnesses directly from a Greek or Arabic original, perhaps an original record of the inquest of 1114; that Latin 1133 is carelessly based upon Greek 1133; and that Latin 1114 is a late, possibly 13th-century-confection, purporting to be an original document, but actually based upon Latin 1133.

Albrecht Noth concluded that Greek 1133 and Arabic 1133 were made independently or, at least, that the Arabic constituted the model for the Greek. He

[13] Patti, Arch. Dioc., ex MS Fond.I, f.43/82; Girgensohn and Kamp 1965, p.13, reg.17; ed. Garufi 1912, Appendix, no.II, pp.349–50; Ménager, 1960, p.46, n.2, comments that 'Sans aucune doute, nous avons là une traduction latine de l'original grec, effectué *pro domo* par un scribe de l'evêché de Patti à la fin du XIIe ou au début du XIIIe siècle', but Vera von Falkenhausen thinks it impossible that the Latin text could be based upon a Greek original. (Amongst its many anomalies, note, in particular: the use of the year *ab incarnatione domini*; the mention of the pope, Paschal II, but without his regnal year; and the eccentric style *regnante autem in Sicilia Rogerio consule filio Rogerii magni consulis*, again without a regnal year. These combine to suggest that the document may be a late Latin confection, not the translation of a Greek original.)

[14] Patti, Arch. Dioc., ex MS Fond.I, f.129; Girgensohn and Kamp 1965, pp.15–16, reg.28; ed. Brühl 1987, no.24, pp.66–8.

Table 4.2 The different versions of the names of the witnesses to the boundaries of Mirto compared

Latin 1114	Greek 1133	Latin 1133	Reconstruction of Arabic Names
Johannes miles de Parthenico interfuit ex iussu domini sui Roberti Auenelli	Ιωάννης καβαλλάριος τ(οῦ) Παρτηνίκου	Iohannes, miles de Partheniaco, iussu domini sui Roberti Avenelli interfuit	
Arnulfus canonicus panormitanae ecclesiae	᾿Ερνου(λφο)ς ὁ κανονικός (τῆς μητρόπολεως or τοῦ Πανόρμου?)	Arnulf, Panormitane ecclesie canonicus	
Guarnerius de Sartilleo	Γαρνέρης δε Σαρτελλή	Guarnerius de Sartilleo	
Robertus magister castelli Jatinensis	῾Ροπέρτος μαΐστορ τοῦ καστελλίου Γιάτου	Robertus, magister castelli Jatinensis	
Gaytus Micherez de Jatino	ὁ κα[ΐτης Μίχριζ] τοῦ Γιάτου	Gaytus Miheret de Iatino	al-qāʾid Muḥriz
Gaytus Bulcassin filius Alus de Jatino	ὁ καΐτης Βουλκάσιμος ἔπεν ᾿Αλλίους	Gaitus Bulcassin filius Alus de Iatino	al-qāʾid Abū l-Qāsim ibn ᶜAlī
Gaytus Othemen filius Peleu de Jatino	Οὐθμὲν ἔπεν Χαμμούτ	Gaytus Othemen, filius Peleu de Iatino	al-qāʾid ᶜUthmān ibn Ḥammūd
Boabdille filius Amor Jatinensis	Βουαβδίλλε ἔπεν ῎Ομουρ	Boabdille, filius Amor Iatinensis	Abū ᶜAbd Allāh ibn ᶜUmar
Gaytus Boabdille filius Alus de Jatino	Βουαβδίλλε ἔπεν ᾿Αλλίους	Gaytus Boabdille filius Alus de Iatino	al-qāʾid Abū ᶜAbd Allāh ibn ᶜAlī
gaytus de Scaranis Jatinae Maumet de Iato	ὁ κάΐτης τῶν σκαράνων [τοῦ Γιάτου] Μουχούμμουτ	Gaytus de […]nis Iatine Mahumet de Iato	al-qāʾid Muḥammad (commander of the *skaranoi – i.e.* ‘irregular troops’ – of Iato)
Bulcassin filius Miherez de Jato	Βουλκάσιμ	Bulcassin, filius Miheret de Iato	Abū l-Qāsim ibn Muḥriz
Bulhusseyn filius Ysaac de Jato	Βουλχούσεν ἔπεν ᾿Ισχάκ	Bulhussein, filius Ysaac de Iato	Abū l-Ḥusayn ibn Isḥāq
Bulhassin filius Maluf de Jato	Βου[...] ἔπεν Μαλούφ	Bulhassen, filius Maluf de Iato	Abū l-Ḥasan ibn Maᶜlūf
Fichi Abdelgasat de Jato	᾿Αβδελγαφὰρ ὁ φικής	[…]ichi Abdelgafar de Iato	ᶜAbd al-Ghaffār al-faqīh (‘the jurist’)
Gaytus Mirtae nominae Husseyn	ὁ κάΐτης τ(οῦ) Μύρτου Χουσεΐν	gaytus Myrte nomine Husseyn	al-qāʾid Ḥusayn (the qāʾid of Mirto)
Bulcassinus Myrtensis	Βουλκάσιμος	Bulcasinus Myrtensis	Abū l-Qāsim
Amut notarius Mirtensis	Χαμμοὺτ ὁ νοτ[...]	Hamut notarius Myrtensis	Ḥammūd al-kātib (‘the scribe’)

found it most improbable that the Greek was the original from which the Arabic was derived.[15] On the contrary, it is clear that the Arabic is substantially a translation of the Greek. In the first place, the Arabic opens with the following introductory sentence: 'The boundaries of this [estate] were established according to the description which is recorded in this document in Greek' (*thubita ḥudūdu hādhihi ʿalā l-sharḥi mā huwa mathbūtun fī hādhā l-sijilli bi-l-rūmī*). Second, the Arabic scribe clearly had difficulties over the translation of the final sentence of Greek 1133, which lists two pieces of land that apparently belonged to Mirto but were not included within its boundaries. The meaning of the Greek is clear enough: 'in addition to those (*i.e.* the lands delimited by the boundary), are both the [plain][17] called "of Mechdep", and the fields named "of Safsaf" known to belong to Murton'. But the Arab scribe, in struggling to adhere closely to the Greek, has sacrificed clarity: *wa-waṭāʾin ʿurifa bi-hā bi-waṭāʾi mahdab wa-ribāʿi l-ṣafṣāfi ʿurifa ilā mārtū [?]*, which seems to mean 'and a depression known by [the name of] the Depression of Mahdab, and the lands of al-Ṣafṣāf (the Willows), [which are] known to [belong to] Mārtū'; without the Greek, or, indeed, without Latin 1133,[18] this Arabic sentence would be extremely difficult to translate with confidence.

But the relationship between the Greek and Arabic is not quite so simple. In the first place, most of the place-names in the Greek either have Arabic roots or are transmitted through the medium of Arabic, so that it is necessary to hypothesise an Arabic original for the Greek *periorismos*. Second, there is at least one indication

Table 4.3 The different versions of the names of two witnesses to the boundaries of Mirto compared[16]

	Latin 1114	Greek 1133	Latin 1133	Reconstruction
1	Gaytus Othemen filius Peleu de Jatino	Οὐθμὲν ἔπεν Χαμμούτ	Gaytus Othemen, filius Peleu de Iatino	al-qāʾid ʿUthmān ibn Ḥammūd
2	gaytus de Scaranis Jatinae Maumet de Iato	ὁ κάϊτης τῶν σκαράνων [τοῦ Γιάτου] Μουχούμμουτ	Gaytus de [...]nis latine Mahumet de Iato	al-qāʾid Muḥammad (commander of the *skaranoi* – *i.e.* 'irregular troops' – of Iato)

[15] Noth 1983, pp.190–1.
[16] For σκαράνος, from Latin *scaranus*, see Caracausi 1990, p.529; but assimilation with ἀσκαράνος, from Arabic *ʿaskarī*, 'soldier', cannot be ruled out.
[17] We can fill the lacuna thanks to the Latin of 1133: *campu(m) q(ui) uocatur mehedep* (Brühl 1987, p.68). Clearly ὁμαλός or similar must be intended.
[18] Latin, 1133: *& campu(m) q(ui) uocatur mehedep, & terras que uocantur de safsaf, que recognoscuntur de mirta* (Brühl 1987, p.68).

that Arabic 1133, in addition to the Greek original upon which it was substantially based, may also have had an Arabic source. At one point, the Greek scribe uses the word τὸ μάρτζον (*to martzon*), a loan-word from Arabic meaning 'swampy ground' or 'water-meadow'. Had the Arab scribe merely translated the Greek text, he would surely have used *marj*, the Arabic original of μάρτζον (*martzon*), but instead he uses *masraḥ*, 'pasture'.[19] The hypothetical Arabic source need not have been written, and may have been nothing more than the oral testimony which was presumably given by local Arab witnesses in order to compile the new boundary-description.

The significance of this complicated history is considerable. First and foremost, it suggests that the royal *dīwān* in 1133 may have made use of a record of a boundary-description originally composed in 1114. There is no indication in either Greek 1133 or Latin 1133, however, as to whether the model was a document issued to Patti, or a copy filed in the royal chancery. In other words, this is not necessarily evidence that a boundary-description, whether Greek or bilingual Arabic-Greek, compiled in 1114 was still on file in the royal *dīwān* in 1133. Be that as it may, after the passage of twenty years, a new survey was made of the lands of Mirto, which produced the very different boundary-description confirmed in the documents of 1133. Second, therefore, the new royal *dīwān* was no mere writing-office, content to issue copies of outdated documents, but rather an active administrative department. Third, although its primary administrative language at this time was still Greek, and although the Arabic *ḥadd* was essentially translated from the Greek *periorismos*, both were ultimately based upon an Arabic original – presumably the oral account of the boundary given by witnesses – and at least one word from it somehow filtered through into the Arabic text, but not into the Greek.

The question of the relationship between the Greek and the Arabic texts also arises in a bilingual decree issued to Lipari-Patti on 22–31 January 1134 (***Dīwānī* 13**).[20] Albrecht Noth concluded that the Greek and the Arabic parts constitute, in effect, two separate documents: that the former was a privilege addressed to the bishop of Lipari-Patti, while the latter was a decree addressed to officials responsible for the collection of taxes.[21] Although the Greek and Arabic texts are, to a considerable extent, independent of each other, Noth's conclusion is overstated.

The Greek *sigillion* opens with a blessedly concise *arenga* (lines 1–2),[22] and then moves briskly into the *dispositio* (lines 2–14) which is explicitly directed at

[19] Interestingly, Latin 1133 seems to be affected by this confusion: the scribe translates τὸ μάρτζον with dialect *lumarge* (from Arabic *al-marj*, assimilating the definite article), but then continues 'which, in Latin, means *pantanum* or wooded land (*terra Silvestris*)'. *Pantanum* seems to be a relic of the pre-Greek substratum, and is attested in Apulia from the 10th century, and in Sicily from the 12th, as both a place-name and proper-noun, meaning 'a muddy or marshy place (Caracausi 1993, vol.II, p.1161). While *pantanum* is a precise translation of τὸ μάρτζον, *al-marj*, and *lumarge*, it certainly does not mean 'wooded land'. Note, however, that τὸ μάρτζον can no longer be read.

[20] Original: Patti, Arch. Dioc. no.6; Girgensohn and Kamp 1965, p.16, reg.31; ed. Cusa 1868–82, no.47, pp.517–19.

[21] 'La parte greca è un privilegio per il vescovo, quella araba un mandato ai funzionari competenti per la riscosione delle imposte': Noth 1983, p.191.

[22] von Falkenhausen 1997, p.300 and n.284.

the royal customs-officers: 'At the request of the ... bishop of Lipari, lord John of Pergana, Our Majesty ... commands, by means of this present document, that all our marine-officials,[23] and others in the land of Sicily', shall not to hinder the import or export to Lipari, in the bishop's own ships, of wheat, butter, or cheese, whether produced by the church's own monasteries, or donated for the love of God. So long as these commodities are for the church's own use, they may be imported and exported free of all customs and duty. But, if they are intended for commerce, then they are to be subject to the full weight of charges by the royal customs-officers and marine-officials, without any concession or remission. The Greek text ends with the *corroboratio* (lines 14–15) which gives the date as January, Indiction XII, 6642 A.M. (1134 A.D.)

Next comes the Arabic (lines 16–21). The published text is one of Cusa's least successful transcriptions, and it may therefore be helpful to give a literal translation made from the document itself:

> Whosoever amongst the strategoi, barons, district governors, and supervisors of the merchants [looks?] upon this our decree (*sijill*) shall not obstruct the monks of Patti / from loading into their boats (*i.e.* exporting) wheat, butter, and cheese for their personal use from all their places, and what is given to them as a gift for the formal business of the church. / Nor shall they be hindered from dispatching (*i.e.* importing) to Lipari and Patti, except for purchased wheat upon which they will pay whatever ship-clearance[24] is imposed according to the custom. / Let their business be conducted according to what is prescribed for them in this document; they have no leave to dispute what has been laid down herein. We have sealed it with the well-known seal in confirmation and as a proof of its authenticity. It was written on the date of the last decade of the month of January in the year 528, in Indiction XII [1134 A.D.] / God is sufficient for us. How excellent a representative is He![25]

At the foot of the Arabic comes Roger's chancery signature (line 22), and clear traces of the plica and seal.

The gist of the Greek and Arabic texts is essentially the same; they both bear the same date; and are both validated by the one signature and seal. Nonetheless, the Greek and Arabic parts are clearly independent: each contains details not to be found in the other; and neither is closely modelled upon the other. The diplomatic form of the Greek is concise – *arenga*, *dispositio*, *corroboratio*, signature, and seal – but by no means unique in its concision.[26] The diplomatic form of the Arabic is

[23] πράκτορισιν ἡμῶν παραθαλασσίταις τε καὶ λοιποῖς: see Caracausi 1990, p.438.

[24] For *sirāḥ*, 'ship-clearance': see Cahen 1972, pp.247, 262–3, 284, 299, and 301.

[25] *man* [lacuna] *ʿalā sijilli-nā hādhā mina l-sarādighati wa-l-tarrārīyati wa-l-ʿummāli wa-umanāʾi l-tujjāri fa-lā yaʿtariḍ ruhbāna baqṭisa / fī-mā yūsiqū-hu* [*sic*] *fī qawāribi-him mina al-qamḥi wa-l-samni wa-l-jubni lladhī huwa li-khaṣṣati-him min sāʾiri amākini-him wa-mā yuʿṭā la-hum hibatan bi-rasmi l-kanīsati / wa-lā yumnaʿū min tasfīri-hi ilā lībara wa-baqṭisa siwā mā kāna mina l-qamḥi l-mushtarī* [*sic – i.e.* with pointed *yāʾ*: read *mushtarā*?] *faʾinna-hum yuʾaddū* [*sic*] *mā yajibu ʿalay-hi mina l-sirāḥi ʿalā l-ʿādati / fa-l-yujra amru-hum ʿalā mā rusima la-hum fī hādhā l-sijilli wa-lā mukhrija maʿa-hum li-khilāfi mā thubita fī-hi wa-qad khatamnā-hu bi-l-ṭābaʿi l-mashhūri / taʾkīdan wa-dalīlan ʿalā ṣiḥḥat-hi wa-kutiba bi-l-taʾrīkhi l-ʿashri l-ākhiri min shahri yanāra min sanati thamānī* [*sic*] *wa-ʿishrīna wa-khamsimiʾatin bi-l-indiqtusi l-thāniya ʿashara / wa-ḥasbu-nā llāhu wa-niʿma l-wakīlu*

[26] See von Falkenhausen 1997.

exceptionally abbreviated, with only the *dispositio*, *corroboratio*, *datatio*, and *apprecatio* (*ḥasbala*),[27] and without the *invocatio* (*basmala*), *intitulatio*, and *arenga* which are more or less standard in the Arabic products of the royal *dīwān*. Nor does the Arabic adhere to the diplomatic form expected of decrees (*marāsīm*, sing. *marsūm*) issued in response to petitions (*qiṣaṣ*, sing. *qiṣṣa*).[28] While the Greek could have functioned on its own, it is debatable whether the Arabic, even equipped with the royal signature and seal, could have functioned without the Greek.

The bilingual donation to Adelina the wet-nurse, 1136 (*Dīwānī* 14)

In February 1290, Robert Coppula, son of Nicholas, a knight and citizen of Palermo, came before Ptolemy of Capua, the judge of the city of Palermo, and asked him for official translations of two ancient privileges: the Greek-Arabic privilege issued in April 1136 to Adelina, the wet-nurse of King Roger's son Henry (***Dīwānī* 14**); and the Arabic-Greek confirmation of it, dated 13 January 1145 (***Dīwānī* 23** – see below). The Greek texts were translated by Deodatus, a priest of the Greek rite; his son, Benedict; the notary Philip *de Ecclesiastico*; and the notary John of Naso. Three Jews were responsible for the translation of the Arabic: Magister David; Magister Moses; and his son, Magister Gaudius.[29] The Greek text of ***Dīwānī* 14** is also known

> From the Greek copy and Italian translation of Pasquale Baffi conserved in the Bibliotheca Maggiore in Naples, from which it is to be understood that the names of the villeins occur in the original, first, in Greek characters and, then, in Arabic; that six lines of Arabic characters precede the signature; and that there was a purple silk thread from which the seal used to hang.[30]

On the basis of Trinchera's edition of Baffi's copy of the Greek, and the 13th-century translation of the whole document, the structure of the original donation may be reconstructed with a fair degree of confidence.

The Greek *intitulatio* is followed by a highly unusual *arenga* which seems to be taken from a Byzantine formulary.[31] Next, in the Greek *dispositio*, which is also of an unusual character, Adelina is granted from the royal demesne an estate at Vicari,[32] measuring 5 ox-lands,[33] and five named Muslim villeins. Then, according to the

[27] For the *ḥasbala* – *wa-ḥasbu-nā llāhu wa-niʿma l-wakīlu*, 'God is sufficient for us. How excellent a representative is He!' – below, pp.279–80.

[28] Cahen 1978; Little 1984, pp.23, 24, 25, 36–7; Richards 1973; Richards 1977; and Stern 1962, Stern 1964b, Stern 1966 (all repr. in Stern 1986).

[29] Original: PA, AdS, Magione, no.208; ed. Garufi 1899, pp.27–33, nos 12 and 12bis.

[30] Trinchera 1865, no.117, p.157.

[31] von Falkenhausen 1997, pp.298–9.

[32] Variously, Ῥάχαλ Ἐξάμες (*Rachal Exames*), *Rahal Kerains* and *Rahal Binkyramis*: *i.e.* Raḥl Ibn [al]-Karrām? Caracausi 1990, p.493 proposes that Ῥάχαλ Ἐξάμες derives from Arabic *Raḥl al-Shāmis* but, in the light of the Latin, this seems improbable.

[33] μετὰ ζευγαρίων πέντε: von Falkenhausen 1980a, pp.242–3 & n.18.

description quoted above, the *jarīda* lists the names of the villeins in Arabic with Greek interlinear transliteration. It is followed by the Greek *periorismos*, and then by the Greek *corroboratio* and *traditio*. Next, the Arabic *ḥadd* is preceded by a short introduction: 'This is the inquiry into the boundaries of the lands which are known as *Binkyramis*, carried out by the caids summoned by the caid [or 'by the caid of caids'] *Bingelir*'.[34] The Arabic ends abruptly after the *ḥadd* with the *datatio* and the *ḥasbala*.[35]

Bingelir has not been identified, nor are his name and his Arabic title clear from the Latin translation. The most likely reconstruction of his name is *Ibn Jarīr*, assuming a very common dissimilation of Arabic *rāʾ* into Latin *l*. He may have been simply *qāʾid* or, reading ... *ex parte gayti gaytorum Bingelir*, he may have borne the grander title of *qāʾid al-quwwād*, 'caid of caids'. There is no indication of the date at which *Bingelir* held the inquest. It is certainly possible, but cannot be proven, that he is identical to the *protonotarius curie* who recorded the boundaries of Vicari in 1123 at the order of Count Roger II.[36]

The bilingual confirmation and *jarīda* to San Giorgio di Triocala, 1141 (*Dīwānī* 15–18)

In June 1141, King Roger reconfirmed the privileges granted by his father to the Greek monastery of San Giorgio di Triocala, a *metochion* of the Greek archimandra of San Salvatore di Messina. Uniquely, for a Greek-Arabic document, Roger's reconfirmation survives in three contemporary versions (***Dīwānī* 15–17**), all of which refer to the πλατέια (*plateia*) of San Giorgio's Muslim villeins. This triplication has, potentially, much to tell us about *dīwānī* procedures, and must therefore be investigated in some detail; but, first, a warning must be given. Until recently, these four documents, all in the Archivo Ducal de Medinaceli, were known only through late copies, summaries or translations. Only the *jarīda* (***Dīwānī* 18**) has yet been edited, albeit poorly and with many errors. Although a full and critical edition of all four is underway, it is at present delayed by bureaucratic and legal obstacles. The following discussion is based upon the reading made by Vera von Falkenhausen, who generously permitted me to make use of her transcription of the Greek text of ***Dīwānī* 16**, and upon my own reading of the documents. We have both worked not from the originals but from photocopies of prints taken from microfilm, and from the elegant but minuscule colour plates published in the catalogue of the 1994 Messina exhibition *Il ritorno della memoria*. Although we are confident that our readings are essentially accurate, they and any conclusions

34 Garufi 1899, p.30: *Hec est cognitio terrarum limitatarum per manus gaytorum statutorum ex parte gayti gayti* [*sic*] *Bingelir quod tenimentum cognoscitur Binkyramis*.

35 For the *ḥasbala* ('God is sufficient for us. How excellent a representative is He!'), the Latin gives *Et deus est spes nostra qui est optimus procreator*: below, pp.279–80.

36 Above, p.80 and note 122.

based upon them should be regarded as provisional, pending the final publication of the documents in a full and critical edition.[37]

The relationship between the three versions of the bilingual privilege to San Giorgio is complicated, but provides the key to their significance. It may, therefore, be helpful to anticipate the conclusion of this discussion: ***Dīwānī* 15** was the first of the three to be composed, and seems to have been, in effect but not in intention, the official working draft used to draw up ***Dīwānī* 16**, which is the only one of the three to be authenticated by the king's chancery signature and seal and thereby given legal force. ***Dīwānī* 17** is an official and contemporary copy of ***Dīwānī* 16**, and was presumably intended as a duplicate copy for the archives of whichever of San Giorgio and San Salvatore did not hold the authenticated original.

To begin with ***Dīwānī* 15**: after the Greek *intitulatio* (line 1), there is no *arenga*, and the text opens directly with the Greek *narratio* (lines 2–14). In June, Indiction IV, 6649 A.M. (1141 A.D.), King Roger was on a tour of Sicily. He stopped at Sciacca (on the south coast, midway between Mazara and Agrigento), where Luke, archimandrite of San Salvatore di Messina, presented for reconfirmation the privileges (τὰ σιγίλλια, *ta sigillia*) granted to San Giorgio di Triocala by Roger I in 6606 A.M., Indiction VI (1097–8 A.D.). Their tenor was that, having captured Sicily from the Muslims, in memory of the Christians who died in the wars of conquest, Roger I founded the monastery of San Giorgio near Sciacca, and endowed it with lands, the boundaries of which were described in the original documents. In the intervening four decades, however, certain barons had usurped some of the lands originally granted to San Giorgio, and the monastery had acquired other lands. Thus, in the Greek *dispositio* (lines 14–17), King Roger ordered the protonotary Philip,[38] the judge Stefanos Maleinos,[39] and the officers of the *dīwān* – the *qā'id* Perroun, John, and Abū ʿAlī[40] – to remake the boundary-description of the lands of San Giorgio di Triocala and of Raḥl al-Baṣal,[41] and to transcribe it in this document. There follows the Greek *periorismos* (***Dīwānī* 15**, lines 17–25). Next, the Greek *dispositio*

[37] I am extremely grateful to Dr Aldo Sparti of the Soprintendenza Archivistica per la Sicilia (Palermo) both for providing me with prints of the microfilms and for generously giving me a copy of the lavish catalogue of the 1994 Messina exhibition, and to Professor von Falkenhausen, with whom I am preparing an edition and study of these documents.

[38] A well-known figure. In March 1142, Philip the protonotary, by royal order, held an inquest to determine the boundaries between the lands of San Filippo d'Agira and Regalbuto. (Original: ADM, Messina, no.1319 (S 812); copy ed. Cusa 1868–82, no.63, pp.302–6.) In a royal privilege of May 1155, it is reported that the vineyard of Philip the protonotary at Palermo had been granted by Roger II to San Giovanni dei Lebbrosi: Enzensberger 1996, p.25, line 18. See also: Kehr 1902, p.51; von Falkenhausen 1979, p.151, n.92; Takayama 1993, p.71.

[39] The scion of an illustrious Calabrian-Greek family. In December 1142, he was one of a large group of notables ordered to determine the boundaries of the estate of Focerò for San Bartolomeo di Lipari-Patti. (Original: Patti, Arch. Dioc.; Girgensohn and Kamp 1965, p.18, reg.39; ed. Cusa 1868–82, no.67, pp.525–7. For his family, see von Falkenhausen 1977, p.355.

[40] ...καὶ τοὺς ἐπὶ τοῦ σεκρέτου τόν τε καΐτην Περροῦνι καὶ Ἰωάννην καὶ τὸν Βουάλην... Below, p.106 and note 46.

[41] Raḥl al-Baṣal, literally 'Estate of the Onions'. Unidentified. The lands in question seem to have lain to the south of Sant'Anna (AG), between the valley of the Tranchina to the west and that of Verdura to the east. None of the place-names in the boundary-description have yet been positively identified.

continues (lines 25–34) with the grant to San Giorgio of the right to graze one thousand sheep and two hundred cattle at Sciacca. Finally, the monks are confirmed in possession of the fifteen newly commended villeins whose names are added to the register (see below). The Greek text ends with the *sanctio* (lines 34–6), and with the *corroboratio* mentioning the gold seal and the *traditio* to the Archimandrite Luke (lines 36–7). Next, come four lines of Arabic (lines 38–41), which are nothing more than the Arabic text of the Greek *periorismos* (lines 17–25): the relationship between the Greek and Arabic boundary-descriptions will be discussed below. There is no signature and, although the foot of the parchment is folded as if to form a plica, there was no seal.

***Dīwānī* 16** differs from ***Dīwānī* 15** in three significant ways. First and foremost, at the foot of the parchment comes King Roger's authentic chancery signature (line 46), and the plica with the remains of the red silk tie through the regular holes, which once carried his gold seal. Second, although the text is essentially the same as that of ***Dīwānī* 15**, except for minor textual variants, orthography and punctuation, both the Greek *periorismos* (lines 24–9) and the Arabic *ḥadd* (lines 43–5) contain significant interpolations which relate to the settlement of a dispute over boundaries and water-rights between San Giorgio and William, son of Richard, the lord of Sciacca. Third, to the very end of the Arabic text (line 45) is added a *datatio* – June,[42] 535 A.H., Indiction IV (1141 A.D.) – and the *ḥasbala* by way of *apprecatio*, according to standard *dīwānī* practice.

The interpolations to the *periorismos* and *ḥadd* help to explain the existence of this document in multiple copies and, more important for our purposes, they reveal significant information about the development of the royal *dīwān*. It seems likely that ***Dīwānī* 15** was originally intended to be the final version for issue to the Archimandrite Luke but, before it could be authenticated, it somehow emerged that the Greek and Arabic boundary-descriptions transcribed therein failed to resolve the dispute between San Giorgio and one of the local barons referred to in the *narratio*. The *dīwān* therefore presided over a meeting between the two parties, and inserted into the text of the document a summary of the agreement reached, as follows:

> (*Greek*) After the aforesaid boundaries were determined, William, the son of Richard, of Sciacca, agreed with the monks of Triocala that, on account of the territorial dispute between them, the boundary will be as recorded below: *[boundary-description omitted]* William and the monks agreed between them that the monks could draw water from wherever they wished. Our Majesty has confirmed what they have agreed: [the boundaries] as delimited above [in the main *periorismos*], in addition to that which was agreed with William, son of Richard, of Sciacca.[43]

[42] Arabic *bruṭuyūn* from Greek Πρωτοϊούνης, literally 'first June': see Johns 2001.

[43] ***Dīwānī* 16**, lines 24–9: μετὰ δὲ τὸ γενέσθαι τοὺς ἀνωτέρω διαχωρισμοὺς συνεβιβάσθη ὁ Γουλιάλμος ὁ υἱός τοῦ Ῥικάρδου / τῆς Σιάκκας μετὰ τῶν μοναχῶν τῶν Τρόκλων ἵνα διὰ τὴν ἀμφιβολὴν τῶν χωραφίων τῶν μεταξὺ αὐτῶν ἔσται πάλιν διαχωρισμὸς ὡς κατωτέρω ῥηθήσεται *[boundary-description omitted]* καὶ συνεφώνησαν ὅτε Γουλιάλμος καὶ οἱ μοναχοὶ μεταξὺ αὐτῶν ἵνα οἱ μοναχοὶ ἐκβάλωσι τὸ ὕδωρ ὅθεν θελήσουσιν· / καὶ ταῦτα

(*Arabic*) Then, the monks and William, son of Richard, from Sciacca, agreed that the beginning of the boundary of the monastery is from al-Ukhtayn. *[boundary-description omitted]* And the royal *dīwān* (*al-dīwān al-maᶜmūr*) approved of this agreement, and authorised it, and passed it. There is to be no opposition to it, and no [further] dispute from this day forth. It was written on the date of the month of June in the year 535, Indiction IV (1141 A.D.). God is sufficient for us. How excellent a representative is He![44]

The Greek of ***Dīwānī* 17** adheres closely to ***Dīwānī* 16**, and includes the interpolations concerning the dispute with William of Sciacca. The Arabic, however, at the end of the description of the boundary between Triocala and the lands of William of Sciacca, the following clause is added: 'And they [*i.e.* the two parties] agreed that the monks could draw water from wherever they wished. And they came to terms on this. / And it is finished'.[45] It is impossible now to know precisely why this passage replaces those clauses in ***Dīwānī* 16** which confirm the *dīwān*'s approval of the settlement and forbid further dispute; but mere scribal oversight may be the explanation.

Turning to the relationship between the Greek *periorismos* and the Arabic *ḥadd*, a close comparison of the two reveals that the Greek is a faithful translation of the Arabic, and was amplified and clarified at a few points by additional information which probably came from an oral source. The Greek scribe repeatedly uses loan-words from Arabic which correspond precisely to the Arabic text, including κούδτϊε (*koudtie*) and variants for Arabic *kudya*, 'hill', and κοῦλλε (*koulle*) for Arabic *qulla*, 'summit'. He generally transliterates Arabic place-names, and, in doing so, he twice fails to recognise loan-words from Greek, and thereby obscures their meaning: Arabic *ghatshāna* ('chestnut', from Greek κάστανα, *kastana*) is rendered Γατσένε ('*Gatsene*'), and Arabic *Khandaq al-Munastīrā* becomes τὸν ῥύακα τὸν λεγόμενον Ἐλμοναστὴρ (*ton ruaka ton legomenon Elmonastēr*, 'the valley called *Elmonastēr*') instead of τὸν ῥύακα τοῦ μοναστήρι (*ton ruaka tou monastēri*, 'the valley of the monastery'). The Greek scribe frequently glosses his transliteration of Arabic place-names in order to make them easily comprehensible: Arabic *ilā ghadīri bni manṣūra* ('to the pool of Ibn Manṣūra') is clarified for non-Arabists as τῆς λίμνης τῆς λεγομένης Γαδΐρ ἐπὲν Μανσοὺρ (*tēs limnēs tēs legomenēs Gadir Epen Mansour*, 'to the pool called *Gadir Epen Mansour*'). Sometimes his glosses reveal that he had access to details not to be found in the

οὕτω καθὼς συνεβιβάσθησαν ἔστερξεν αὐτοῖς τὸ κράτος μου, «ταῦτα τοίνυν καθὼς εἴρηται ἀνωτέρω καὶ περιορίζεται» πλὴν ἐξ ὧν ὡς εἴρηται συνεβιβάσθήται μετὰ τοῦ Γουλιάλμου υἱοῦ Ῥικάρδου τῆς Σιάκκας. The phrase in line 29 enclosed within angular brackets also occurs in ***Dīwānī* 15**.

[44] ***Dīwānī* 16**, lines 43–5: *thumma ttafaqa l-ruhbānu wa-ghulyālimu bnu rijarḍa mina l-shāqqati ᶜalā anna badwa ḥaddi l-dayri mina l-ukhtayni [boundary-description omitted] wa-ttafaqū ᶜalā anna l-ruhbāna yukhrijū* [sic] *l-māʾa min ayna yurīdū* [sic] *wa-qad raḍiya / l-dīwānu l-maᶜmūru bi-hādhā l-ittifāqi wa-jawwaza-hu wa-amḍā-hu wa-lā qiyāma fī-hi wa-lā kalāma baᶜda l-yawmi wa-kutiba bi-taʾrīkhi shahri bruṭuyūna min sanati khamsin wa-thalāth[īna] wa-khamsimiʾatin bi-l-indiqtusi l-rābiᶜi wa-ḥasbu-nā llāhu wa-niᶜma l-wakīlu.*

[45] ***Dīwānī* 17**, lines 46–7: *wa-ttafaqū ᶜalā anna l-ruhbāna yukhrijū* [sic] *l-māʾa min ayna yurīdū* [sic] *wa-qad tarāḍaw bi-dhālika / wa-[nta]hā.*

Arabic *ḥadd*, as when he explains Arabic *mina l-Ukhtayn* (literally 'from the Two Sisters') as ἀπὸ τῶν δύο κιωνίων τῶν λεγομένων Ὀχτεὶν (*apo tōn duo kiōniōn tōn legomenōn Ochtein*, 'from the two columns called *Ochtein*): presumably he derived such additional details from an oral source.

We are now in a position to draw some conclusions as to the significance, for the history of the *dīwān*, of the bilingual privilege to San Giorgio di Triocala and its two versions. First and foremost, ***Dīwānī* 16**, line 45, contains the earliest reference to the royal *dīwān* by its Arabic title, *al-dīwān al-ma*ᶜ*mūr*. As we shall see in Chapter 5, this title – which means simply 'the busy ...', 'the [well-]served ...' or even, more loosely but perhaps more accurately, 'the royal *dīwān*' – was previously thought not to appear before 1145. Moreover, in the clauses concerning the agreement between San Giorgio and William of Sciacca quoted above, the Greek τὸ κράτος μου (*to kratos mou*, literally, 'my authority', 'Our Majesty'), a standard title used to refer impersonally to the sovereign, is rendered *al-dīwān al-ma*ᶜ*mūr* in the Arabic.

Second, these documents are the first in which the officers of the royal *dīwān* begin to emerge from the shadows. The Greek *dispositio* names those responsible for remaking the boundary-description of San Giorgio's lands. Of these, the protonotary Philip and the judge Stefanos Maleinos are royal officials appointed to resolve the disputes between the monks and their baronial neighbours. But it is specified that the *qā*ʾ*id* Perroun, John, and Abū ᶜAlī are 'those in charge of the *sekreton*' (οἱ ἐπὶ τοῦ σεκρέτου, *oi epi tou sekretou*). We shall see in Chapter 5 that τό σεκρέτον (*to sekreton*) is the standard Greek term for Arabic *al-dīwān*. These three officers were thus in charge of the royal *dīwān*. Neither Abū ᶜAlī nor John can be positively identified in any other document, but it seems highly probable that the *qā*ʾ*id* Perroun is identical with one of the most important officers of Roger II and William I, who next appears in December 1149 (***Dīwānī* 29**) with the titles *shaykh al-dīwān al-ma*ᶜ*mūr al-qā*ʾ*id Barrūn* ('the elder of the royal *dīwān*, the *qā*ʾ*id* Barrūn').[46] If this identification is correct, then this is the first appearance of a member of what we may call the dynasty of palace Saracens who were to control the *dīwān* until the fall of the Norman kings.

Third, although the bilingual privilege to San Giorgio is essentially a Greek *sigillion* into which has been inserted an Arabic boundary-description, there are indications that Arabic was attempting to reassert itself as an administrative language. We have already seen that the Greek *periorismos* was a faithful translation of the Arabic *ḥadd*. More than that, a rudimentary *ta*ʾ*kīd* (*sanctio*), and a *ta*ʾ*rīkh* (*datatio*) and *ḥasbala* (*apprecatio*) are all appended to the *ḥadd*, as if the scribe were seeking to give it all the diplomatic necessities that would enable it to stand in its own right.

[46] For Barrūn, see below pp.222–8. Vera von Falkenhausen has tentatively suggested to me that John could conceivably be the Ἰωάννης καπριλίγγας τοῦ μεγάλου ῥιγος ('John the chamberlain of the great king') who witnessed a donation to San Nicola di Chùrchuro in October 1133 (Cusa 1868–82, p.33), and the official of the *dīwān* who signs ***Dīwānī* 35 and 37** with his Greek signature (see below); but – as she so rightly notes – John is an extremely common name.

By July of the same year,[47] King Roger had reached Agrigento, and there he ordered that the *plateia* of San Giorgio's villeins, which is mentioned in the bilingual privilege of June 1141 (***Dīwānī* 15–17**), be renewed and updated. We have already seen (above, pp.58–9) that this *plateia* was probably an Arabic *jarīda* (***Dīwānī* 6**). The new *jarīda* (***Dīwānī* 18**) was written entirely in Arabic, except for the Greek chancery-signature of King Roger, which occupies the last line (line 26), above the plica and seal. The introductory text consists of two extremely terse lines: 'A *jarīda* attesting to the names of the men of Ṭ.r.q.l.sh [Triocala][48] / written on the date of the month of November 536 A.H., Indiction V [1141 A.D.]'. The name-list begins immediately on line 3, and lists fifty names, arranged in six columns (lines 3–11). After the fiftieth name, in large, bold characters across columns 3–5 of line 11, is written the rubric: 'The names of the men of Raḥl al-Baṣal'. There follow another fifty names, before the grand total for both estates: 'The total is one hundred men'.[49]

After the total for Triocala and Raḥl al-Baṣal, comes the following clause: 'Now, when it was the date of the month of July, Indiction IV [1141 A.D.], you petitioned us, when we were in Agrigento, may God protect it, concerning these names which are registered in this document / who were in your possession as newly commended villeins (*muls*).[50] And we granted them to you on the condition that if any of them is in our *jarā᾿id* or in the *jarā᾿id* of our landholders (*tarrārīyati-nā*), he shall be taken from you. / And these are their names' (lines 21–3).[51] There follow fifteen names, all but one with Ifrīqiyan *nisba*s (surnames), and the final note: 'The total is fifteen men – *muls*'. The *jarīda* once bore the royal seal.

This *jarīda* is remarkable for four reasons. First, it is the earliest of the surviving documents issued by the royal *dīwān* to be written purely in Arabic. Unlike all other surviving royal *jarā᾿id*, the name-list is written in Arabic only, without interlinear Greek transliteration of the names; why this should be so is unclear, but it suggests that the practices of the *duana regia* were not yet fixed. Be that as it may, this *jarīda* marks a significant advance in the reassertion of Arabic as an administrative language. Second, the extraordinarily terse introductory text of the document is much closer to the Arabic notes that accompany the *jarā᾿id* of the comital period (***Dīwānī* 2, 4 and 8**), than to the elaborate texts that introduce the *jarā᾿id* renewed in 1145 and those issued thereafter (***Dīwānī* 21, 24–5, 43 and 45**). This suggests that the diplomatic form of the Arabic documents issued by the *dīwān* was still at an embryonic stage. Third, as will be discussed in full in Chapter 6, this

47 Arabic *isṭiriyūn* from Greek Ὑστεροϊούνιος, literally 'second June': see Johns 2001.

48 The *ṭā᾿* carries a *ḍamma* and a *tashdīd*, possibly indicating a missing definite article – *[aṭ]-Ṭur.q.l.sh* - but *Ṭ.rruq.l.sh* may be intended: Gálvez 1995, p.173, line 1, reads *Ṭ.r.qul.sh* and translates Trioccala (*sic!*).

49 *Al-jumlatu mi᾿atu rajulin*: Gálvez 1995, p.175, line 20, reads *al-kalima* (*sic*) *mi᾿a rijāl* and translates 'En total cien nombres (*sic*)'.

50 For the *muls*, see below, pp.147-51.

51 The reading of this passage by Gálvez 1995, p.176, lines 21–23, must be corrected as follows:
ثم لما كان بتاريخ شهر اسطريون (أسطربير Gálvez) بالاندقتس الرابع (الربع Gálvez) سَالتنا ونحن بكركنت حماها الله فى هاولا
الا سما الذين يثبتوا فى هذا السجل / الذ ين وجدوا عندَك ملسا فسلمناهم لك على شريطة انه متى ما ظهر منهم فى
جرايدنا وجرايد ترار يتنا (قرابيننا Gálvez) احدا (؟) يو خد منك/ وهذه اسماهم

is the earliest appearance of the class of villeins called *muls*, and offers important clues as to their true identity. Fourth, although the order to compile this *jarīda* was given at Agrigento in July 1141, it was only issued in November 1141, which suggests that it must have been written in the royal *dīwān* in Palermo, after the king's return to the capital. Until the rediscovery of the original of this *jarīda*, it was known only through an 18th-century Latin translation. In his edition of the latter, the late Paolo Collura, building upon a hypothesis first proposed by Garufi and then resurrected by Caravale, suggested that it demonstrated that it was in the year 1141 that King Roger began the reforms that culminated in the renewals of 1145, and the foundation of the *dīwān al-taḥqīq al-maᶜmūr*.[52] This suggestion rests upon two foundations. First, the similarity of the stipulation employed in this *jarīda* to those used in the renewals of 1145: that there is a resemblance cannot be denied,[53] but it is no less close to the Greek stipulation employed in the conclusion to the Aci Castello *jarīda* of 1095 (***Dīwānī* 4**).[54] Second, that the Triocala *jarīda* is an updated renewal, like the *jarāʾid* of 1145: this is undeniable, but so too is the earliest surviving Sicilian *jarīda* – that issued to Palermo in 1095 (***Dīwānī* 2**). Indeed, the inevitable result of the *mutazawwij*-system was that each and every *jarīda* genuinely renewed was also updated. In fact, the Triocala *jarīda* displays none of the distinctive features of the *jarāʾid* reissued in 1145 (see below), and there is no good reason to see it as initiating that series.

The bilingual privilege to Santa Maria di Gala, 1142 (*Dīwānī* 19)

In March 6650, Indiction V (1142 A.D.), a bilingual Greek-Arabic privilege was issued to Santa Maria di Gala (***Dīwānī* 19**). The original is now lost, and it is known only through Latin translations of the Greek original.[55] The monastery had been founded at the beginning of the 12th century by Roger I's chamberlain, Nicholas de Mesa, and lay about 2km north-east of Castroreale, on the northern slope of the Monti Peloritani, 25km west of Messina. At an unspecified date, the monks had illegally occupied lands which properly belonged to the royal demesne, and which lay some 10km north of Mineo, near Santa Maria's distant dependence of San Nicola. The crime had clearly been discovered by the *dīwān* and, in the Greek *narratio*, the abbot humbly asked to purchase some of the land that his monastery had usurped. In the Greek *dispositio*, Roger II permitted the sale of twenty *paricla* or six hundred *modia* of land, 'of which the boundaries and records of the boundary-inquest are recorded below in Arabic'.[56] The price was two thousand *tarì*. The Greek text ended with the *sanctio* and *datatio*. Next, came the Arabic

[52] Garufi 1928 pp.66–7; Caravale 1966, pp.188–99; Collura 1969–70, pp.257–8.
[53] Noth 1983, pp.199, 207–8. [54] Above, p.54.
[55] Ed. von Falkenhausen 2000, Appendix, no.1, pp.125–8.
[56] *... quarum [terrarum] divise et cognitiones per arabicas litteras subnotantur.*

boundary-description, with no other Arabic text. The document ended with Roger's Greek chancery signature. Once again, this was a Greek *sigillion* into which an Arabic *ḥadd* was inserted, but, unlike ***Dīwānī* 12, 14 and 16**, this privilege apparently contained no Greek *periorismos*.

George of Antioch's bilingual endowment charter for Santa Maria dell'Ammiraglio, 1143 (*Dīwānī* 20)

One further document must be examined in this discussion of the earliest products of the royal *dīwān* – the endowment charter issued in May 1143 by George of Antioch to Santa Maria dell'Ammiraglio, in Palermo.[57] Santa Maria, which is frequently known as La Martorana, after the Benedictine convent founded, on land immediately adjacent to the church, by Geoffrey of Marturano in 1193–4, was George's personal foundation, and he and his wife were both buried within its walls.[58] Ernst Kitzinger has concluded that George 'built his church as an act of personal piety… [as] … a monument of his devotion to the Virgin Mary and his gratitude to her'.[59] This is undeniable but, at the same time, the church is the medium through which strongly political statements about the nature of Roger's kingdom and George of Antioch's rôle within it are made. Most important, the two famous dedicatory mosaics which were probably once located in the inner narthex of the church, represented, on the one hand, George presenting a petition to the Virgin, and, on the other, King Roger being crowned by Christ.[60] Indeed, the association of the king with his vizier's foundation was proclaimed in a substantial part of the mosaic decoration of the church, which Kitzinger has shown to be modelled after that of the sanctuary of the Cappella Palatina.[61] Moreover, two columns, which now support the vaulting of the lower storey in the west end of the church, but which may once have supported the arches of a forecourt lined with porticos, carry Arabic inscriptions which again refer, respectively, to the king and to his vizier.[62] This close involvement of the king in his vizier's private foundation is repeated in the endowment charter of 1143.

The document is headed with an Arabic motto written in an elaborately calligraphic style, in black ink which stands out against the light brown ink of the main text: *al-ḥamdu li-llāhi wa-shukrun li-an*ᶜ*umi-hi*, 'Praise be to God, and thanks for His blessings' (line 1). That this is King Roger's personal signature or ᶜ*alāma* is explained in the two lines of Arabic which come at the end of the Greek text (lines 27–8), immediately before George of Antioch's autograph:

[57] For the history, architecture, and decoration of the church, see Kitzinger 1990.
[58] Kitzinger 1990, pp.17–19. [59] Kitzinger 1990, p.264.
[60] See Kitzinger 1950 (repr. in Kitzinger 1976, pp.320–6) and Kitzinger 1990, p.126 and n.12, pp.189–211, and pls XXII–XXVI and 119–25, 164–71.
[61] Kitzinger 1990, p.261 and n.2.
[62] Below, p.279–80.

> When it was the month of May, in Indiction VI, we asked Our Majesty, the glorified and holy king – may God prolong his rule! – to place his noble signature (*ʿalāma*) upon this document (*sijill*) to let it be known that he, may God maintain his power, has approved that [gift] and signed it. He graciously gave his consent, and sanctioned it, and placed his exalted *ʿalāma* at the head of it. God is sufficient for us. How excellent a representative is He![63]

After Roger's *ʿalāma*, the Greek text lists the gifts with which George endowed his new foundation, the most important of which seem to have been the estate of Raḥl al-Shaʿrānī (τὸ Χωρίον Ἐσσιαράνη, *to Chōrion Essiaranē*), near Misilmeri, 12km south-east of Palermo, and ten Arab villeins (παροίκοι, *paroikoi*) from Misilmeri. Their names are listed in Greek and, beneath each Greek name, is written its original in Arabic (lines 6–8). At the end of the list come the totals in Greek and in Arabic.[64] Other gifts included: George's new *funduq* in Palermo near San Giacomo a Mare; another *funduq* in the Cassaro of Palermo that he had bought from Ḥasan ibn Nāsikh (Χάσεν υἱός Νάσαχ, *Chasen uios Nasach*);[65] an oven near the house of his daughter Mary; a garden that he had bought from the *qāḍī* of Palermo; a vineyard that he had bought from [*lacuna*];[66] vases of bronze and silver; lamps, oil, and wax for the illumination of the church; books (which were listed in a separate catalogue); and an annuity of thirty *tarì*, to last for the lifetime of the Abbess Marina, for her keep and that of the nuns. The document ends with George's Greek autograph – 'the archon of archons, George the emir' – and is sealed with his own lead seal, the reverse of which repeats the words used as his signature.[67]

Once again, this is a Greek document into which a little Arabic, which adds nothing to the essence of the Greek, has been inserted. The Greek text could have served on its own, without the Arabic; but the Arabic would have been meaningless without the Greek. And yet, these Arabic insertions at the same time attest to the growing sophistication of the *dīwān*. Two features have already been encountered in earlier documents of this series, and were to become standard *dīwānī* practice:

63 *lammā kāna fī shahri māyū l-indiqtusa l-sādisa saʾalnā mawlā-nā l-malika l-muʿaẓẓama l-qiddīsa khallada llāhu mulka-hu fī an yūqiʿa ʿalāmata-hu l-sharīfata bi-hādhā l-sijilli li-yuʿlima anna-hu thabbata llāhu ʿizza-hu ajāza dhālika wa-amḍā-hu fa-anʿama bi-l-ijābati wa-irtaḍā-hu wa-awqaʿa ʿalāmata-hu l-rafīʿata bi-aʿlā-hu wa-ḥasbu-nā llāhu wa-niʿma l-wakīl.* For the *ʿalāma* of the Norman kings, see below, pp.277–8.

64 Greek: 'ten names' (ὁμοῦ δέκα); Arabic: 'The total is ten names' (*al-jumlatu ʿasharatu asmāʾin*); a different hand has added in a darker ink *wa-Raḥl al-Shaʿranī*, 'and Raḥl [the estate of] al-Shaʿrānī.

65 In January 1123, the royal court heard a case involving the ownership of a mill which had been purchased from one Ibn Nāsikh: above, pp.73–74.

66 Strangely, the first half of line 16 was left blank, presumably so that the name of the vendor could be added at a later date. The line was never filled; nor was the open invitation to a medieval forger ever accepted. Note also that the name of the estate granted has been interpolated, after the total of names, by a different hand and in a different ink from the Arabic text: *wa-Raḥl al-Shaʿrānī*.

67 Autograph: † ὁ τῶν ἀρχόντων ἄρχων Γεώργιος ἀμηρας ††† The seal is now detached from the plica, but can be seen in place in a photograph taken by Garufi and now in the care of Prof. Monsignor Diego Ciccarelli in the Istituto di Paleografia, Università di Palermo. The obverse shows the Virgin and Child with the inscription MP.ΘΥ [Μήτηρ Θεοῦ, 'the Mother of God']. The reverse: † Ο Τ[Ω]Ν ΑΡΧΟΝΤ[Ω]Ν / ΑΡΧΩΝ ΓΕΩΡΓΙΟϹ / † ΑΜΗΡΑϹ † See Ménager 1960, p.209; Engel 1882, p.93, no.36, pl.3.8.

the registration of the names of villeins in Greek transliteration and the original Arabic (***Dīwānī* 10 and 14**); and the use of the *ḥasbala* as *apprecatio* (***Dīwānī* 12–14 and 16**). Other features appear for the first time, including the dynastic title *al-malik al-muʿaẓẓam* ('the glorified king').[68] Most important of all is the royal *ʿalāma*: the only surviving use by a Norman king, in an original document, of what Samuel Stern called 'the classical Islamic method of signature'.[69] The significance of the *ʿalāma* will be discussed in detail below.[70] Here, it is sufficient to observe that it is most unlikely to be Roger's autograph. There is no evidence that Roger could read, let alone write Arabic, but the royal *ʿalāma* is a polished and practised calligraphic flourish, written without once lifting the nib from the page, and ending with a fanciful trefoil ornament. It is the work of a professional pen-man, and, bearing in mind Vera von Falkenhausen's suggestion that Roger's Greek signature may have been signed by George of Antioch until his own death in 1151,[71] it is certainly possible that Roger's *ʿalāma* too was written by his vizier.

Conclusion

Of the documents examined in this chapter, only the Arabic *jarīda* to Triocala (***Dīwānī* 18**) was composed entirely in Arabic, and contained no Greek (except for the signature and seal). Only in the privilege to Santa Maria di Gala (***Dīwānī* 19**) did the Arabic text contain significant material which was not reproduced in the Greek, and without which the effectiveness of the document would have been fundamentally impaired. In every other case, the Greek text could have served on its own, without the Arabic, while (with the debatable exception of the decree for Lipari-Patti ***Dīwānī* 13**), the Arabic would have been useless without the Greek. Why, then, if Arabic was to be subordinate to Greek, which remained the principal administrative language of the new kingdom, did the administration begin again to issue documents in Arabic, after an interval of some twenty years?

The explanation that first occurs is that Arabic was used because it was the first language of either the recipient or of the functionaries who compiled any given document. Thus, for example, the Arab 'district governors, and supervisors of the merchants' (*al-ʿummāl wa-umanāʾ al-tujjār*) to whom, amongst others, the Arabic text of ***Dīwānī* 13** was addressed, would presumably have been more familiar with Arabic than with Greek. Similarly, because the villeins listed in the *jarāʾid* were Arabs, and the censuses of them must have been taken in Arabic, by Arab or Arabic-speaking functionaries of the *dīwān*, or because (as in the case of ***Dīwānī* 18**) a *jarīda* updated an earlier Arabic register, there were purely practical reasons

[68] Below, p.137 and note 82.
[69] Stern 1964a, p.123.
[70] Below, pp.277–8.
[71] von Falkenhausen 1997, pp.285–6.

for compiling the *jarāʾid* of villeins in Arabic. Again, because in areas where the local population was predominantly Arabic-speaking, the boundaries of a given estate would have been reported in Arabic, it made sense for them to be recorded in the same language. Although such an explanation may be partly correct, it cannot completely account for the use of Arabic in every case.

In the first place, with the probable exception of the Arab port-officials to whom, amongst others, the two decrees granting commercial privileges (***Dīwānī* 11 and 13**) were addressed, it is extremely doubtful that the recipients of any of these documents would have been able to read Arabic. Amongst the Augustinian canons of Cefalù, the Benedictine monks of Lipari-Patti, Adelina the royal wet-nurse, the Greek monks of Triocala, and the Greek nuns of Santa Maria dell' Ammiraglio, few, if any, would have been able to read Arabic. This is confirmed by the history of the documents themselves: the Greek-Arabic confirmation of the boundaries of Mirto (***Dīwānī* 12**) was accompanied by a simultaneous Latin version, and even the Greek-Arabic decree to Cefalù (***Dīwānī* 11**) was soon reissued in Greek and Latin.

Second, if the practical reasons for recording registers of villeins and boundary-descriptions in Arabic were sufficiently strong for Arabic to be reintroduced as an administrative language after an interval of twenty years, why were not all registers of Arab villeins, and all boundary-descriptions compiled on the testimony of Arab witnesses, thenceforth recorded in Arabic? This was certainly not the case. The same bilingual documents contained Greek *katonomata* and *periorismoi*: if only the Greek could be read by the recipients, why were they issued with Arabic versions; if Arabic was the only language in which Arab villeins could be registered and Arabic boundary-descriptions recorded, why was the Arabic nearly always accompanied by a Greek versions? Other contemporary documents, composed entirely in Greek, listed Arab villeins and described Arabic boundaries. The royal chancery, 1130–43, issued sufficient Greek registers of Arab villeins,[72] and Greek descriptions of boundaries delimited by Arab witnesses, or of estates in regions predominantly inhabited by Arabs,[73] to weaken severely the case that Arabic was reintroduced purely for practical reasons. Indeed, that case is further undermined by the boundary-description of Mirto confirmed for Lipari-Patti (***Dīwānī* 12**), in which the Arabic *ḥadd* was translated from the Greek *periorismos*, even though the Greek must have been ultimately derived from an Arabic original.

Something of the enigma surrounding the reintroduction of Arabic is encapsulated in George of Antioch's endowment charter to Santa Maria dell'Ammiraglio

[72] For example: April, 6640 A.M., Ind.X [1132 A.D.]; 30 Arab villeins at Ῥαχαλτζουχὰρ, near Cerami (Arabic *Raḥl Jawhar*?, see Caracausi 1990, p.493); Patti, Arch. Dioc.; Girgensohn and Kamp 1965, p.15, reg.26; ed. Cusa 1868–82, no.44, pp.513–15; Caspar 1904, p.513, reg.75.

[73] For example: 1132 A.D., the boundaries of *Rachaltzouchar*, cited in note 72 above. January, 6642 A.M., Ind.XII [1134 A.D.]; boundaries of lands at Misilmeri (near Palermo); copy in PA, Arch. Dioc.; ed. Cusa 1868–82, no.46, pp.13–15; Caspar 1904, p.521, reg.92. 30 March, 6650 A.M., Ind.V [1142 A.D.]; boundaries between lands of San Filippo d'Agira and Ῥαχαλβούτ (Arabic *Raḥl ʿAbbūd*), mod. Regalbuto; witnesses include at least 12 Arabs; ADM, Messina, no.1319 (S 812) – unedited original; copy ed. Cusa 1868–82, no.63, pp.302–6; Collura 1955a, pp.583–4, reg.57.

(***Dīwānī* 20**). On the one hand, it may be that the names of the ten Arab villeins were transcribed in Arabic in order to avoid any possible confusion that might have arisen had they been listed only in Greek. On the other, it is extremely difficult to regard the use of Arabic for King Roger's *ᶜalāma* as anything approaching an administrative or bureaucratic necessity. The established form by which the king gave his approval to donations made by his courtiers may be seen in the Greek *sigillion* issued by the king's godson, Roger-Aḥmad, a convert from Islam to Christianity, granting lands to Palermo cathedral. Like ***Dīwānī* 20**, this was a personal donation, made in Roger-Aḥmad's own name, and sealed with his seal, but written in the royal palace at Palermo, and issued with the explicit approval and support of the king himself.[74] But unlike ***Dīwānī* 20**, Roger-Aḥmad's *sigillion* was entirely in Greek, although the donor himself was an Arab, and the lands granted, complete with their *periorismos*, lay in the heavily Arabised region between Naro and Licata. The familiar, indeed standard, diplomatic form of this *sigillion* guaranteed the authenticity and security of the donation. In complete contrast, ***Dīwānī* 20** relied upon an Arabic *ᶜalāma* which, following Islamic practice, did not even mention the king's name, and which had to be explained by the Arabic note at the foot of the Greek text. This appears to have been the first and last time that the royal *ᶜalāma* was used on a privilege issued to a Sicilian recipient. No other surviving *dīwānī* document, not even one in which Arabic predominates, bears the royal *ᶜalāma*. On the other hand, Arab authors knew that the Norman kings employed *ᶜalāmāt*, just as if they had been Muslim rulers, and this familiarity suggests that the *ᶜalāma* was introduced more for correspondence with foreign Arab rulers than for use within Sicily. This hypothesis is supported by the fact that the only other surviving occurrence of a Norman *ᶜalāma* is on dinars struck at the mint of al-Mahdīya in the names of Roger II and William I.[75] Although Roger's *ᶜalāma* was undoubtedly added to the head of ***Dīwānī* 20** in order to proclaim royal approval of the endowment, the choice of this anomalous, foreign and outlandish method of signalling the king's consent, rather than the familiar and standard form employed in Roger-Aḥmad's Greek *sigillion*, appears to have been a deliberate experiment by George of Antioch. That the royal *ᶜalāma* was never again employed on any Sicilian document suggests that it was an experiment that failed.

In short, purely practical considerations alone did not determine the reappearance of Arabic as an administrative language in 1132. This is not, of course, to suggest that there was no connection between administrative practicalities and the language employed. On the contrary, Arabic was used for the *jarāʾid* and *ḥudūd* in these documents precisely because they listed Arab villeins and recorded boundary-descriptions which had originally been delimited in Arabic. But this was not the only reason for which Arabic was used. In these same documents, the Arab scribes of the *dīwān* began to experiment with elements of diplomatic form and titulature,

[74] February, 6649 A.M., Ind.IV [1141 A.D.] Original: PA, Arch. Dioc., no.10; ed. Cusa 1868–82, no.59, pp.16–19. Caspar 1904, p.543, reg.137. For Roger's seal, see below, p.238 note 107.

[75] Below, pp.277–8.

some of which, like Roger's *ʿalāma*, were soon abandoned on documents for Sicily, while others, such as the *ḥasbala*, the royal title *al-malik al-muʿaẓẓam*, and the *dīwān*'s own title *al-dīwān al-maʿmūr*, were to become standard in *dīwānī* documents. These were of a different order than the use of Arabic for *jarāʾid* and *ḥudūd*. In the first place, they had not been employed in Sicily before 1111, and were not reactivations of once established practices. In the second, their use was dictated neither by the content, nor by the administrative function of the documents in which they appeared, but by something which, at this stage of the argument, is still elusive.

CHAPTER 5

The *jarāʾid* renewed, 1144–5

De resignandis privilegiis

In the autumn of 1144, King Roger commanded his vassals in Calabria and Sicily to present, for scrutiny and renewal, all privileges previously granted by him and by his ancestors. The registers of Erich Caspar, Paolo Collura and Horst Enzensberger list thirty renewals issued between October 1144 and June 1145, and to these three more may be added from the archive of San Salvatore di Messina, giving a total of thirty-three known renewals.[1] Although most confirm between one and three ancient privileges, some feudatories would appear to have presented their entire archive: thirteen charters from San Filippo di Fragalà, and fifteen from Santa Maria di Turri, while Abbot Filadelfos of San Bartolomeo di Trigona submitted no less than nineteen privileges for renewal.[2] A rough calculation – and, given the poor editions in which most of these renewals are available, it is extremely rough – indicates that, in all, some one hundred and twenty earlier privileges were renewed, many of which are now lost, and thus known only through these renewals. The true number of both originals submitted for renewal and renewals issued must have been significantly higher, for it is clear that many renewals have been lost without trace, especially those issued to lay barons. The *jarāʾid* renewed in 1145 all refer to the registers of villeins renewed for the barons, but only one survives. In total, only two lay recipients are known to have had renewals in 1144–5, and that is because their lands happened later to pass to the church, so that the associated privileges were preserved in ecclesiastical archives.[3] Although it is now impossible to estimate how many of the series have been lost,[4] it is nonetheless absolutely clear that this was by far and away the busiest period

[1] Below, p.117, notes 11–13. This total includes at least three forgeries: Caspar 1904, no.170, Enzensberger 1971, no.17, and Collura 1955a, no.69.

[2] Respectively, Caspar 1904, nos.191, 177, and 175. For San Bartolomeo di Trigona, see von Falkenhausen 1999: where the nineteen privileges renewed are conveniently listed (pp.98–102).

[3] The notary Nicola Patrizio of Messina, whose renewal was preserved by San Salvatore di Messina (unedited original: ADM, Messina, no.1323; Caspar 1904, no.181); and Roger Forestal, whose *jarīda* went to Santa Maria di Monreale (see ***Dīwānī* 25**).

[4] See the discussion of survival in Brühl 1983, pp.11–17.

in the history of Roger's chancery, if not of the entire Norman kingdom. The late Carlrichard Brühl's summation – 'è quindi senz'altro presumibile ... l'impiego di un certo numero di aiuto notai' – is not just bathetic, but, in all probability, mistaken.[5] During a mere nine months, more than thirty documents were issued, over four times the annual average of approximately eight documents, calculated over the whole reign (1131–53).[6] The two years 1144–5 alone accounted for more than one-quarter of all the documents issued by King Roger. It would be difficult to overestimate how severely this administrative *tour de force* taxed the royal chancery, and how great an achievement it was for its officers and scribes. And yet, it has received astonishingly little attention from modern historians.[7] Thus, although the main focus of this chapter will be the bilingual *jarāʾid* renewed by the royal *dīwān*, a few paragraphs must first be dedicated to the series of renewals as a whole, in order to establish as clearly as possible the context in which the *jarāʾid* must be understood.

The process of revision began in the first half of October 1144 at Messina, and continued until at least 20 November. Early commentators took Roger's edict *de resignandis privilegiis* at its word, and assumed that it applied to the whole kingdom, but Brühl rightly observed that the recall was in effect restricted to Sicily and Calabria, and excluded the other mainland provinces. Geography seems to have determined the order of business: Calabrian recipients received their renewals first; then, in early November, it was the turn of north-eastern Sicily. After a break for the Christmas holidays, and a move to Palermo, work began again on Monday 1 January 1145, with the issue of the first of two large Arabic-Greek *jarāʾid* to the church of Catania (***Dīwānī* 21–2**); on 13 January, came the Greek-Arabic renewal to Adelina the royal wet-nurse (***Dīwānī* 23**); on 7 February (*sic*),[8] the Arabic-Greek *jarīda* to Cefalù (***Dīwānī* 24**); on 24 March, the Arabic-Greek *jarīda* to Walter Forestal (***Dīwānī* 25**); and, at an unknown date which probably lay between January and April, the fragmentary Greek-Arabic *jarīda* to Roger Fesca, archbishop-elect of Palermo (***Dīwānī* 26**).[9] Also in March, more Greek renewals were issued to Sicilian recipients; but also to the bishop of Squillace, in Calabria – an exception to the rule of geographical distribution. The court returned to Messina in May, where further Greek renewals were issued to Sicilian recipients.[10] The numerical weight of the renewals was heavily in favour of the Greek regions of the kingdom: twenty-five for recipients in Calabria and north-eastern Sicily, but only eight for

[5] Brühl 1983, p.45, and n.203 (which reveals that he principally had in mind *Latin* notaries!).
[6] Brühl 1983, p.14, gives much lower annual averages, calculated over the whole period of Roger II's government: 3.5 per annum over 48 years; 3.7 per annum over 41 years of sole rule.
[7] The best accounts, upon which I have drawn heavily, are those of von Falkenhausen 1997, pp.304–7, and Brühl 1983, pp.44–5. See also, but with care: Chalandon 1907, vol.II, pp.116–17; Niese 1910, pp.115–19; Caspar 1904, pp.320–4; Kehr 1902, pp.69–70, 111, 115–16, 348; Scheffer-Boichorst 1897, pp.245–6; Scheffer-Boichorst 1900, pp.133–4.
[8] Below, p.123, and p.126, note 28.
[9] Robert Fesca, *i.e.* of Fécamp, in Normandy: see Haskins 1924, p.187, n.148.
[10] Only if we accept the testimony of what is probably a forged document from San Michele di Mazara (***Dīwānī* †27**) need we believe that one further Greek-Arabic renewal was issued at Mazara in June 1145. For this forgery, see below, p.308.

recipients based in the rest of the island. Of the thirty-three known renewals, two-thirds (twenty-two, 66%) were written in Greek;[11] five (15%) were Latin,[12] and six (19%) were bilingual, including four Arabic-Greek and two Greek-Arabic (one of which is a forgery).[13]

More than half of the Greek renewals, after the standard *superscriptio* and *intitulatio*, open with the following *arenga*:[14]

> Since it is our duty to restore everything to a better condition and, especially, to protect zealously the rights of the holy churches, and to maintain them as far as possible in their present peaceful state, we have therefore ordered that the privileges of the churches and of the other subjects of my realm should be renewed and submitted for scrutiny, in order that they may be confirmed by the power of my sublime majesty.[15]

The *narratio* follows directly, and typically explains how, on such and such a date, at the royal palace in Messina or Palermo, in the presence of the counts and archons of the kingdom, the recipient had submitted the ancient privilege for renewal. This *arenga-narratio* of the majority of the Greek renewals clearly provided the model for the formula used in their Latin counterparts.[16] There follow the details of the privilege or privileges, which may be quoted *in extensio* or, when many privileges were to be renewed, concisely summarised. The *dispositio* then

[11] von Falkenhausen 1997, p.305. Twenty-two Greek renewals can be identified with confidence, and a further five may, or may not, belong to the same series: Caspar 1904, reg.172, 173, 174 (ADM, Messina no.533), 175, 178, 179, 180 (ADM, Messina nos 1352 and 1253), 181 (ADM, Messina no.1323), 182 (ADM, Messina no.1360), 183, 189, 190, 191, 192, 195, 196, and 197; Collura 1955a, reg.67; Enzensberger 1971, reg.17; Huillard-Bréholles 1852–61, vol.II.1, p.521; and the following, still inedited, documents in ADM, Messina nos 533 (Caspar 1904, reg.174), 1247, 1253 (Caspar 1904, reg.180, confused with ADM, Messina no.1352), 1323 (Caspar 1904, reg.181), 1352 (Caspar 1904, reg.180) and 1360 (Caspar 1904, reg.182). (See also the following possible additions to this series: Caspar 1904, reg.238, 250, 251; and Trinchera 1865, no.139, pp.182–5, and Appendix II, no.17, pp.559–60.) I am most grateful to Vera von Falkenhausen for her indispensable help in compiling this list.

[12] Brühl 1987, nos 63 (Caspar 1904, reg.170), 64 (Caspar 1904, reg.171), 65 (Collura 1955a, reg.65), 66 (Caspar 1904, reg.176) and 67 (Caspar 1904, reg.177).

[13] ***Dīwānī* 21** (Arabic-Greek: Caspar 1904, reg.185), ***Dīwānī* 22** (Arabic-Greek: Caspar 1904, reg.186), ***Dīwānī* 23** (Greek-Arabic: Caspar 1904, reg.187), ***Dīwānī* 24** (Arabic-Greek: Caspar 1904, reg.184), ***Dīwānī* 25** (Arabic-Greek: Caspar 1904, reg.193); ***Dīwānī* 26** (Greek-Arabic, Caspar 1904, reg.169); and ***Dīwānī* †27** (Greek-Arabic probable forgery: Collura 1955a, reg.69).

[14] At least three renewals, all issued at Messina in November 1144, employed a different form: see von Falkenhausen 1997, pp.306–7.

[15] Cusa 1868–82, p.26: Ἐπειδὴ ἐν τῇ ἡμετέρα ἐπιβλέψει διαφέρει πάσας τὰς ὑποθέσεις ἐπαναγαγεῖναι επὶ τὸ κρεῖττον καὶ τὸ δὴ πλεῖον τὰ τῶν θείων ναῶν διαφερόμενα μετὰ προθυμίας ἐπισφαλεῖσαι καὶ ἐπὶ τὸ πλεῖστον ἐνδυναμῶσαι ἐν ταύτη τῇ εἰρηνηκῇ καταστάσει, ἐνθέν τοι καὶ κελεύωμεν ἵνα ταῦτα τὰ σιγίλλια τῶν ἐκκλησίων καὶ τῶν λοιπῶν πιστῶν τοῦ κράτους μου ἀνανεῶσαι καὶ ἐπιδεῖξαι εἰς ἐμφάνειαν, καὶ ἵνα ἔσονται ἀσφαλεισμένα ὑπὸ τῆς δυνάμεως τοῦ ὑψιλωτάτου κράτους μου.

[16] von Falkenhausen 1997, p.307. The standard Latin *arenga-narratio* runs as follows: *Ad nostram spectat sollicitudinem cuncta in meliorem statum reducere et precipue, que ad liberalitatem ecclesiarum pertinent, libentius confirmare et serentitate nostri temporis validiora reddere. Iussimus itaque, ut omnia privilegia ecclesiarium et subiectorum regni nostri antiquitus composita a nostra clementia noviter essent elucidata et robore nostri culminis communita. Residentibus autem nobis in palatio Messanensis urbis cum comitibus et magnatibus nostris ...* See Brühl 1987, nos 63–7, pp.179–97.

confirmed the ancient privilege or privileges, often, where appropriate, repeating the names of the villeins or the boundaries of the lands granted. The renewal usually ended with the standard *corroboratio* and Roger's Greek chancery signature – all the Latin renewals, like the Greek and bilingual confirmations in this series, were signed with the king's Greek signature. The renewals of 1144–5 thus did nothing to undermine and, on the contrary, must have helped to prolong the dominance of Greek as the principal administrative language of the kingdom.

According to the *arengae* of the Greek and Latin renewals, the objective was to protect the rights of the churches of the kingdom. This is disingenuous, and there can be little doubt that the royal treasury and the royal demesne were the principal beneficiaries of the recall. The late Carlrichard Brühl insisted that the Sicilian measure differed fundamentally from Richard I of England's recall of privileges in order that they might be sealed with the new Great Seal – notoriously, Richard charged a heavy fee for the reissues, probably in order to finance his continental wars – which Brühl dismissed as 'a financial trick without legal foundation', implying that the Sicilian recall was no such thing.[17] I cannot agree. Although I know of no explicit testimony to this effect, it is inconceivable that feudatories were not charged for their renewals, and it is likely that the king was attempting to raise funds for his Ifrīqiyan campaign which, under the command of George of Antioch, was now approaching its climax. At the same time, Roger was making as strongly as possible the point that his subjects held their possessions not by right of inheritance but as privileges granted by the new king. Moreover, the recall of privileges from Calabria and Sicily, where the great bulk of the royal demesne was located, also permitted the king's officers to undertake a sort of stock-taking of royal possessions by limiting the privileges of his subjects – everything which could not be shown, by means of an authentic privilege, to be held by a vassal, must have belonged to the king. Brühl also took some pains to insist that Roger's recall was something absolutely new, but we shall see below that, on the contrary, there is reason to suspect that it may, in part, have been inspired by Fāṭimid practice.[18]

Having briefly described the recall of privileges of 1144–5, I shall now focus more closely upon the five *jarāʾid* renewed in January–March 1145 by *al-dīwān al-maʿmūr* at Palermo. Although all five share many characteristics, both external and internal, it will be most convenient to discuss these common features after the *jarāʾid* have first been described, one by one.

[17] Brühl 1983, p.45. For Richard I and the Great Seal, the main source is the so-called 'constitution' issued by King John on 7 June 1199, which purports to re-establish the fees for the application of the Great Seal charged by Henry II, and to abolish the ninefold increases introduced under Richard. The text of the constitution is given in Rymer, 1816–69, vol.I.1, pp.75–6. 'The correct fees to be charged henceforward were stated to be – For a charter making a new grant of lands, tenements or franchises, ten marks for the chancellor, one mark for the vice-chancellor, one mark for the prothonotary and five shillings for the wax (a total of twelve marks, five shillings): For a simple charter of confirmation, which added nothing to former grants, one mark for the chancellor, a besant for the vice-chancellor, a besant for the prothonotary and twelvepence for the wax (a total of eighteen shillings and fourpence)': Richardson 1943, pp.xxxv–xxxvii. See also: Round 1895, pp.539–55; Richardson and Sayles 1963, p.329 n.1, pp.374–5; Scheffer-Boichorst 1897, p.244, n.1.

[18] Below, pp.195–8.

Dīwānī 21: the renewal of the Catania *jarīda* of 1095 (*Dīwānī* 3)

A long *jarīda* in the form of a roll made of ten sheets of parchment sewn together with thread in large dog's-tooth stitches.[19] The seams are 'sealed' on the *verso* with notes written across the seams: on the right edge, the Arabic note *ṣaḥḥa bi-l-taʾrīkhi* ('It was authenticated on the date'); on the left, the Greek note ἐκυρώθη (*ekurōthē*, 'It has been authenticated').[20] The structure of the document may be summarised as follows:

- lines 1–7: *Narratio* (Arabic)
- lines 7–8: *Dispositio* (Arabic)
- lines 8–9: *Sharṭ* or stipulation (Arabic)
- lines 10–272: List headed in Arabic only *Ahl Qaṭāniya* ('People of Catania') – 525 names, all of the form *awlād Fulān*, written in four columns across the sheet from right to left, in Arabic with Greek transliteration above each name; the totals at the end of the list are given in both Arabic and Greek
- lines 273–321: List headed in Arabic only *Asmāʾ al-arāmil* ('The names of the widows') – 94 names, written in Arabic with Greek transliteration above each name; the totals at the end of the list are given in both Arabic and Greek
- lines 332–34: List headed in Arabic only *ʿAbīd al-kanīsa* ('The slaves of the church') – 23 names written as those of the *arāmil*
- lines 335–49: List headed in Arabic only *Al-Yahūd* ('The Jews') – 25 names, all of the form *awlād Fulān*, written as those of the *ahl*
- lines 350–55: List headed in Arabic only *Asmāʾ al-ʿumy* ('The names of the blind') – 8 names written as those of the *arāmil*
- line 356: Totals for all five lists in Arabic and Greek – 675 names
- line 357: *Sharṭ* or stipulation (Arabic): 'The names which are in this *jarīda* were written on the condition that the church is entitled to them'.[21]
- line 358: Arabic note that the *jarīda* was written upon ten sheets of parchment (*ruqūq*)
- line 359: Greek chancery signature of Roger II
- plica, pierced by regular holes for the seal

The *narratio*, *dispositio* and *sharṭ*, with which the *jarīda* opens, run as follows – note, in particular, that the crucial words 'at Mazara' (*bi-Mazāra*) in the *sharṭ* were misread by Cusa, so that the significance of the whole clause was obscured:

> [*Narratio*] When it was the date of Monday, the first of January, in Indiction VIII, in the year 539 [A.H.], and of the date of the world 6653 [1145 A.D.], there were present in

[19] The seam between sheets 9 and 10 has become largely, but not completely, unstitched, and has been crudely resewn.

[20] Below, p.129, note 39. Also on the *verso* of ***Dīwānī* 21** are two contemporary(?) Latin notes: *abdelmule* (*i.e.* ʿAbd al-Mawlā), which may conceivably be the name of the Arabic scribe; and *elgurab [et] elmukallat*, Latin transliterations of Arabic terms for categories of villeins (*i.e. al-ghurabāʾ wa-l-maḥallāt*), the significance of which will be discussed below, p.148.

[21] Cusa 1868–82, p.585: *l*[357] *wa-qad kutibati l-asmāʾu llatī fī hādhihi l-jarīdati ʿalā sharīṭati anna l-kanīsata mustaḥiqqatu-hum.*

> Palermo (may God protect it!) the archbishops, bishops, counts, barons, and others from all Sicily (may God preserve her!) in order to renew their *jarāʾid*, as a consequence of their having been scrutinised and repeatedly examined. And you, the monks of Catania were present, and you brought a *jarīda* – from the Great Sultan [*i.e.* Roger I] (may God sanctify his spirit and illuminate his tomb!), [who] had ordered it to be written for the episcopal church of Catania – which was dated fifty years ago, listing that which he had granted it of the men of Catania. Thus, the Most Exalted Seat (may God raise the roof of its glory!) was informed about the matter. [*Dispositio*] Then there went forth the high, the to-be-obeyed, the most royal, the most glorified, the most holy, the Rogerian order (may God increase its high standing and efficacy!) to renew it and to confirm the people who are in it, [*Sharṭ*] on the condition that if one of them should be found in the *jarāʾid* of the *dīwān al-maʿmūr*, or in the *jarāʾid* of the barons, or of anyone else, then the church must lose him, because the old *jarīda*, from which this *jarīda* was copied, was written after the *jarāʾid* which were written at Mazara [*sic* – Cusa reads *tamāmatan*, 'perfectly'] two years earlier.[22]

This *sharṭ* thus refers back to the Greek conclusion which must have come at the end of the *deperditum* ***Dīwānī* 3**, but which survives intact in ***Dīwānī* 4** (quoted below, ***Dīwānī* 22**).

Dīwānī 22: the renewal of the Aci Castello *jarīda* of 1095 (*Dīwānī* 4)

This was originally another long *jarīda* in the form of a roll made of seven sheets of parchment sewn together and 'sealed' on the *verso* in the same manner as ***Dīwānī* 21**. The first two sheets, which contained the *narratio-dispositio* and the first thirty-three lines of the register of names, are now missing.[23] The structure of the surviving parts of the renewal is as follows:

- lines 1–108: List which, in ***Dīwānī* 4**, was headed in Arabic only 'The *jarīda* of the people of Aci' – 337 names, of which 213 survive, all of the form *awlād Fulān*, written in four columns across the sheet from right to left, in Arabic with Greek transliteration above each name; the totals at the end of the list are given in both Arabic and Greek

[22] Cusa 1868–82, pp.563–4: /[1] *lammā kāna bi-taʾrīkhi yawmi l-ithnayni awwali yanāra l-indiqtusa l-thāmina* [Cusa: *li-thāmin*] *sanata tisʿin wa-thalāthīna wa-khamsimiʾatin wa-min taʾrīkhi l-ʿālami* /[2] *sittata ālāfin wa-sittamiʾatin wa-thalāthatan wa-khamsīna sanatan ḥaḍara bi-l-madīnati ḥamā-hā llāhu l-arākinatu wa-l-asāqifatu wa-l-qamāmisatu wa-l-tarrārīyatu* /[3] *wa-ghayru-hum min sāʾiri ṣiqillīyata ṣāna-hā llāhu li-tajdīdi jarāʾidi-him li-ajli tamḥīṣi-hā wa-ndirāsi-hā wa-ḥaḍartum antum ruhbānu qaṭāniyata* /[4] *wa-aḥḍartum jarīdatan min qibali l-sulṭāni l-kabīri qaddasa llāhu rūḥa-hu wa-nawwara ḍarīḥa-hu* /[5] *kāna amara bi-katbi-hā ilā kanīsati usqufīyati qaṭāniyata li-taʾrīkhi-hā khamsīna* [sic] *sanatan fī-hā dhikru mā kāna* /[6] *aqṭaʿa-hā mina l-rijāli bi-qaṭāniyata fa-ṭūliʿa l-majlisu l-sāmī rafaʿa llāhu samka majdi-hi* /[7] *bi-dhālika fa-kharaja l-amru l-ʿālī l-muṭāʿu l-malakīyu l-muʿaẓẓamīyu l-qiddīsīyu l-rujārīyu zāda-hu llāhu ʿalāʾan wa-maḍāʾan* /[8] *bi-tajdīdi-hā wa-ithbāti man bi-hā mina l-rijāli ʿalā sharīṭati anna-hu in kāna yūjadu aḥadun min-hum fī jarāʾidi l-dīwāni l-maʿmūri* /[9] *aw fī jarāʾidi l-tarrārīyati wa-ghayri-him fa-tutlifu-hu l-kanīsatu li-ajli anna l-jarīdata l-qadīmata llatī nusikhat min-hā hādhihi l-jarīdatu kutibat baʿda l-jarāʾidi llatī kutibat bi-Māzara* [Cusa misreads *tamāmatan*] *qadīman bi-sanatayni.*

[23] Above, p.53.

- lines 109–39: List headed in Arabic only *Asmāʾ al-arāmil* ('The names of the widows') – 53 names, written in Arabic with Greek transliteration above each name; the totals at the end of the list are given in both Arabic and Greek
- line 140: Totals for the two lists in Arabic and Greek – 390 names
- lines 141–3: *Sharṭ* or stipulation (Arabic)
- line 143: Arabic note that the *jarīda* was written upon seven sheets of parchment
- line 144: Greek chancery signature of Roger II
- plica, pierced by regular holes for the seal

The *sharṭ* (lines 141–2), which combines the two stipulations of ***Dīwānī* 21**, runs as follows:

> The names which are in this *jarīda* were written on the condition that the church is entitled to them, and that whenever one of them is found in the *jarāʾid* of the *dīwān al-maʿmūr*, or in the *jarāʾid* of the barons, or of anyone else, then the church must lose him, because the old *jarīda*, from which this *jarīda* was copied, was written after the *jarāʾid* [which were written] at Mazara two years earlier.[24]

Like the first *sharṭ* of ***Dīwānī* 21** (lines 8–9), this clause refers back to the Greek conclusion of the *jarīda*s issued to Catania in 1095, which, in ***Dīwānī* 4**, is as follows:

> This *plateia* was written at the order of me, Count Roger, being at Messina, in indiction III of the year 6603 [1095 A.D.] and is based upon the *plateiai* of my own lands and of my barons, which were written at Mazarra (*sic*) in the year 6601 in indiction I [1 January – 31 August 1093]. And therefore we command that any of the Hagarenes inscribed in this *plateia*, who is found in my *plateiai* or in the *plateiai* of my barons, shall be returned there [*i.e.* from Catania to his place of registration].[25]

Dīwānī 23: the renewal of the Greek-Arabic privilege to Adelina the royal wet-nurse (*Dīwānī* 14)

The original text of this Arabic renewal is lost, and it survives only in the official translation made, in February 1290, before Ptolemy of Capua, the judge of the city of Palermo, by three Jews: Magister David; Magister Moses; and his son, Magister Gaudius. The Arabic of much of the original can be confidently reconstructed from their Latin translation (see Table 5.1), largely because the format of the Arabic *narratio-dispositio* is so familiar from the other renewals in this series.

In the *narratio*, it is recorded that Adelina presented for renewal the privilege made nine years earlier which granted her lands and men at Fitalia, in the district of Vicari, the boundaries of which were listed in the original (***Dīwānī* 14**). The

[24] Cusa 1868–82, pp.594–5: /[141] *wa-qad kutibati l-asmāʾu llatī fī hādhihi l-jarīdati ʿalā l-sharīṭati anna l-kanīsata mustaḥiqqatu-hum wa-anna-hu matā wujida aḥadun min-hum fī jarāʾidi l-dīwāni l-maʿmūri* /[142] *aw fī jarāʾidi l-tarrārīyati wa-ghayri-him fa-tutlifu-hu l-kanīsatu li-ajli anna l-jarīdata l-qadīmata llatī nusikhat min-hā hādhihi l-jarīdatu kutibat baʿda l-jarāʾidi* [There is a lacuna: Cusa reads *al-dīwān* (*sic!*) but, on the model of ***Dīwānī* 21**, one would expect *llatī kutibat*] *bi-Māzara* [Cusa again misreads *tamāmatan*] *qadīman bi-sanatayni.*

[25] Above, p.54.

Table 5.1 *Dīwānī* 23 reconstructed

Latin translation 1290 A.D.	Reconstructed text of 1145 A.D.	Translation
Hoc fuit tricesimo mensis Januarij octave Indictionis. anno [arabico] quingentesimo tricesimo nono et anno mundi sexmillesimo. sexcentesimo. quinquagesimo tertio.	لما كانبتاريخ الثلث عشر من ينار الاندقتس الثامن سنة تسع وثلاثين وخمسماية ومن تاريخ العالم ستة الاف وستماية وثلثة وخمسين سنة	When it was the date of the 13th of January, in Indiction VIII, in the year 539 [A.H.], and of the date of the world 6653 [A.M.],
presentaverunt se in Midine [idest latine panormo.] quod defendat deus. Archiepiscopi. Episcopi. Comites. Barones et alij de tota Sicilia. custodit eam deus. ad renovandum privilegia eorum *pro eo quod erant quasi abolita incamulata et inveterata*	حضر بالمدينة حماها الله الاراكنة والاساقفة والقمامسة والترارية وغيرهم من ساير صقلية صانها الله لتجديد جريدها لاجل تمحيصها واندراسها	there were present at Palermo (may God protect it!) the archbishops, bishops, counts, barons, and others from all Sicily (may God preserve her!) in order to renew their *jarā'id*, as a consequence of their having been scrutinised and repeatedly examined.
et Tu Adelina lactatrix presentasti te.	وحضرت ...	And you [Adelaide the wet-nurse] were present …
et obtulisti privilegium quod fuerat scriptum de mandato expresso iam sunt annj novem elapsi in quo erat facta mencio de eo quod erat concessum et datum tibi videlicet de hominibus et terris sitis in contrata Biccari. in fitalia. et in dicto privilegio denotantur fines terrarum. que tibi fuerunt concesse in loco predicto		And you brought a *jarīda* – written by the legally valid order – which was dated nine years ago, in which were listed…
et sic constito exinde Curie excellenti. Cuius laudis altitudinem deus exaltet. Exijt factum mandatum excelsum magnificum Regium Rogerij. Cui deus altitudinem altitudinj augeat. de rescribenda et confermanda predicta.	فطولع المجلس السامى رفع الله سمك مجده بذلك فخرج الامر العالى المطاع الملكى المعظمى القديسى الرجارى زاده الله علا ومضا بتجديدها	Thus, the Most Exalted Seat (may God raise the roof of its glory!) was informed about the matter. Then there went forth the high, the to-be-obeyed, the most royal, the most glorified, the most holy, the Rogerian order (may God increase its high standing and efficacy!) to renew it and to confirm it.
Homines vero sunt hii.	وهم	And they are
Muse bin Suleyman	Μοῦσε ἔπιν Σουλειμάν موسى بن سليمان	Mūsā ibn Sulaymān
Nemes frater eius	Νεγήμε ὁ ἀδελφὸς αὐτοῦ نعمة اخوه	Niᶜma his brother
Hyse frater eius	῞Ισες ὁ ἀδελφὸς αὐτοῦ عيسى اخوه	ᶜĪsā his brother
Bulhasen frater eius	Βουλχάσεν ὁ ἀδελφὸς αὐτοῦ بو الحسن اخوه	Bū l-Ḥasan his brother
Muhammed Bin adderahmen buliste	Μουχούμμετ ἔπιν᾽ Αβδεῤῥαχμὲν... محمد بن عبد الرحمن ...	Muḥammad ibn ᶜAbd al-Raḥmān …
pro quo habitur Buabdille Munden	… Βουαβδέλλα ... بو عبد الله ...	… Bū ᶜAbd Allāh …
Summa nomina quinque	῾Ομοῦ ἄνδρες ζ´ الجملة خمسة اسما	The total is five names.
Rogerius in Christo deo pius potens et Christianorum adiutor	† ῾Ρογέριος ἐν Χριστῷ τῷ Θεῷ εὐσεβὴς κραταιὸς ῥὴξ καὶ τῶν Χριστιανῶν βοηθός †††	† Roger, through Christ the God, the pious, mighty king and defender of the Christians †††

dispositio was of standard form. The renewal did not repeat the estate boundaries from the old privilege, but did copy out the names of the five villeins, adding the note that, in the place of the fifth, Muḥammad ibn ᶜAbd al-Raḥmān *Buliste*, there was living a substitute, Abū ᶜAbd Allāh *Munden*. There does not seem to have been a *sharṭ*, and the document ended with Roger's Greek chancery signature immediately after the name-list.

The Latin translation of certain Arabic phrases raises interesting questions which will be discussed in full later in this chapter.

Dīwānī 24: the renewal of a *jarīda* issued to Cefalù twelve years earlier (*Dīwānī* 10)

A *jarīda* composed of three sheets, sewn together: sheets 1–2 are sown together with a wide strip of parchment, sheets 2–3 with a narrow lace, in both cases in a simple running stitch. The seams are 'sealed' on the *verso* in the same manner as ***Dīwānī* 21**. Also on the verso is a 12th-century Latin note, the first line of which reads *Platia de villanis Chephalude et Mutate*;[26] which indicates that this *jarīda* includes the renewal of the *plateia* of Mutata made by George of Antioch in 1132 (***Dīwānī* 10**). The structure of the renewal is as follows:

- lines 1–3: *Narratio*, part 1 (Arabic)
- lines 3–4: *Dispositio* (Arabic)
- lines 4–5: *Sharṭ* or stipulation (Arabic)
- lines 5–68: List headed, in Arabic only, 'And these are the names of the men' (*wa-hādhihi asmāʾu l-rijāli*) – 188 names, written in six columns across the sheet from right to left, in Arabic with Greek transliteration above each name; the totals at the end of the list in Arabic and Greek
- lines 69–70: *Narratio*, part 2 (Arabic)
- lines 71–84: List, with no heading except part 2 of the *narratio*, of the men of *Ṣant Quzimān* (San Cosimano), *Ṣakhrat al-Ḥarīr* (Roccella) and *Qalᶜat al-Ṣirāṭ* (Collesano) – 37 names, written in six columns across the sheet from right to left, in Arabic with Greek transliteration above each name; the totals at the end of the list in Arabic and Greek
- line 84: Arabic note that the *jarīda* was written upon three sheets of parchment
- line 85: Greek chancery signature of Roger II
- plica, pierced by regular holes for the seal

The *narratio* and *dispositio* are composed to the same model as was used for ***Dīwānī* 21**, but the *sharṭ* again differs in wording if not in effect:

> [*Narratio*] When it was the date of the 7th of February [*sic*], in Indiction VIII, in the year 539 [A.H.], and of the date of the world 6653 [A.M.], there were present in Palermo (may

[26] The note has been retraced in a darker, thicker ink which almost completely obscures the second line, which seems to refer to the exchange of villeins between Mileto and Cefalù.

Table 5.2 The Villeins of San Cosma di Cefalù and San Giovanni di Roccella

Latin 1136	Translation of Arabic 1145	Arabic 1145	Greek 1145
A. San Cosma (Christians)			
1. Nicholaus de lo mocheti	Niqūla Numūthātī	نقولة نموثاتي	Νικόλαος Νομοθέτης
2. Joseph filius ianuarii	Yūsuf son of Yanār	يوسف بن ينار	᾿Ιωσὴφ υἱός Γεννὰρ
3. Nicholaus filius leonis	Niqūla son of Lāw	نقولة بن لاو	Νικόλαος υἱός Λέοντος
4. Philippus filius buseit	Filīb son of Bū l-Sayyid	فليب بن بو السيد	Φίλιππος υἱός Βουσσίτ
5. Philippus filius calochuri frater Joseph	Filīb son of Qalūjurī	فليب بن قلوجرى	Φίλιππος υἱός Καλοκύρου
B. San Cosma (Saracens)			
6. Abdelcherin filius yse	ᶜAbd al-Karīm son of ᶜĪsā	عبد الكريم بن عيسى	Ἀβδελκερὴμ ἔπιν Ἴσε
7. Hamor filus Abdelcherin	ᶜUmar son of ᶜAbd al-Karīm	عمر بن عبد الكريم	Ὄμουρ ἔπιν Ἀβδελκερὴμ
8. Sidi filius ejusdem Abdelcherin	Sīduhum son of ᶜAbd al-Karīm	سيدهم بن عبد الكريم	Σήδουχουμ ἔπιν Ἀβδελκερὴμ
9. Mehib filius Abdelcherin	Muhīb son of ᶜAbd al-Karīm	مهيب بن عبد الكريم	Μουχὴπ ἔπιν Ἀβδελκερὴμ
10. Machalub filius Abdelcherin	Makhlūf son of ᶜAbd al-Karīm	مخلوف بن عبد الكريم	Μουχλοὺφ ἔπιν Ἀβδελκερὴμ
11. Samuehl filius yse frater Abdelcherin	Shamūʾal son of ᶜĪsā the brother of ᶜAbd al-Karīm	شموال بن عيسى اخو عبد الكريم	Σεμουὲλ ἔπιν Ἴσε ἀδελφὸς Ἀβδελκερὴμ
12. Moyses filius ali	Mūsā son of ᶜAlī	موسى بن علي	Μούσες ἀδελφὸς [*sic!*] Ἄλη
13. Hasen filius moysi	Ḥasan son of Mūsā	حسن بن موسى	Χάσεν ἔπιν Μούσε
14. hali filius moysi	ᶜAlī son of Mūsā	على بن موسى	Ἄλη ἔπιν Μούσε
15. hasen filius Amut et frater suus	Ḥasan son of Ḥammūd and his brother	حسن بن حمود واخوه	Χάσεν ἔπιν Χαμμοὺτ καὶ ὁ ἀδελφὸς αὐτοῦ
16. hali strambus filius ioseph	ᶜAlī al-Istranbū son of Yūsuf	على الاسطرنبو بن يوسف	Ἄλη Στράμβου υἱός Ιωσήφ
17. Hali loiel	ᶜAlī	على ...	Ἄλη
18. Abdella stultus	ᶜAbd Allāh al-Majnūn (lit. 'the Mad')	عبد الله المجنون	Ἀβδέλλα Ἐλμετζνούν
19. Bucher filius Rhooabdel	Abū Bakr son of Bū ᶜAbd Allāh	ابو بكر بن بو عبد الله	Βούγκερ ἔπιν Βουαβδέλλα

Latin 1136	Translation of Arabic 1145	Arabic 1145	Greek 1145
C. San Giovanni (Christians)			
20. Teodorus filius gafuri	Thawdir	ثودر ...	Θεόδωρος
21. Basilius filius leonis	Bāsīlī son of Lāw	باسيلي بن لاو	Βασίλιος υἱός Λέοντος
22. Basilius filius babe	Bāsīlī son of …	باسيلي بن ...	Βασίλιος
23. Iafar filius capre	Ja^cfar son of …	جعفر بن ...	Τζάφαρ
24. Robertus filius guarini	Rubart son of …	ربرت بن ...	ʽ Ρομβέρτος
D. San Giovanni (Saracens)			
25. Ali filius grisopoli	ʿAlī son of …	على بن ...	Ἄλη ...
26. Moyses frater eius	Mūsā his brother	موسى اخوه	Μούσες ἀδελφὸς αὐτοῦ
27. Abdesseit frater eius	ʿAbd al-Sayyid	عبد السيد ...	Αὐδεσσεΐτ
28. Othoman filius Busen	ʿUthmān son of …	عثمان بن ...	Ὀθμάν
29. Bucher frater eius	Abū Bakr his brother	ابو بكر اخوه	Βούγκερ ἀδελφὸς αὐτοῦ
30. hamor frater eius	ʿUmar, brother of both of them	عمر اخوهما	Ὄμουρ ἀδελφὸς αὐτοῦ
31. Taydon filius cafey	Zaytūn son of Qāsim	زيتون بن قاسم	Ζεϊδοὺν ἔπιν Κάσημ
32. hasen filius Boson	Ḥasan son of …	حسن بن ...	Χάσεν
33. hamuth frater eius	Ḥammūd his brother	حمود اخوه	Χαμμοὺτ ἀδελφὸς αὐτοῦ
34. Abdelchamith	ʿAbd al-Ḥamīd	عبد الحميد	Ἄβδελχαμήτ
35. Muchuluf	Makhlūf	مخلوف	Μαχλούφ
36. hamor et frater eius filii Marturine	ʿUmar and his brother	عمر واخوه ...	Ὄμουρ καὶ οἱ ἀδελφοὶ αὐτοῦ
37. …	Ḥusayn	حسين	Χουσέην

> God protect it!) the archbishops, bishops, counts, barons, and others from all Sicily (may God preserve her!) in order to renew their *jarāʾid*, as a consequence of their having been scrutinised and repeatedly examined. And Jocelm, the bishop-elect of Cefalù was present, with *S.kīn*[27] and Barnard, and you [*sic*] brought a *jarīda* – written by the legally valid order – which was dated twelve years ago, in which was listed what it granted to the great cathedral church at Cefalù. Thus, the Most Exalted Seat (may God raise the roof of its glory!) was informed about the matter. [*Dispositio*] Then there went forth the high, the to-be-obeyed, the most royal, the most glorified, the most holy, the Rogerian order (may God increase its high standing and efficacy!) to renew it and to confirm the men who are in it, [*Sharṭ*] on the condition set out in the aforementioned *jarīda*, namely: that, whenever one of these men is found in the *jarāʾid* of the barons or of others, you will send him back to his lord, and he will not compensate you for him with another one.[28]

After the register of the men granted to Cefalù, comes the following Arabic note, which should probably be regarded as a continuation of the *narratio*:

> They also presented a *jarīda* written in Latin from the abbot and monks possessed of the monastery of Sant'Angelo di Mileto.[29] In it was listed *Ṣant Quzimān* (San Cosimano) and the men who belonged to them there, and the men who belonged to them at *Ṣakhrat al-Ḥarīr* (Roccella) [and *Qalʿat al-Sirāṭ* (Collesano)].[30] And the royal *dīwān* exchanged them and granted to them [the abbot and monks of Mileto] substitutes for them in Calabria. And they granted the [following men] to the church of Cefalù with their lands and their cattle, as compensation for the church.[31]

27 The MS reads سكين (*s.kīn*). In this context, one expects a non-Arabic personal name. The closest matches that I can suggest are: Lombard(?) *Sighinus* (Brühl 1987, p.128, line 26); Lombard *Sichinolf etc.* (Caracausi 1990, pp.523, 524; Caracausi 1993, vol.II, p.1532); or, reading *sk[it]īn*, Greek Ἀσκεττίνος or Latin *Aschettinus*, and variants, from Norman *Ansketill* (Ménager 1975, pp.267–71; Caracausi 1990, p.77). None is wholly convincing.

28 Cusa 1868–82, pp.472–3: /[1] *lammā kāna bi-taʾrīkhi l-sābiʿi min iflābira* [Cusa misreads *aqalnār*: De Simone 1988, p.73, following a marginal note of Amari reads *iflibār*] *l-indiqtusa l-thāmina sanata tisʿin wa-thalāthīna wa-khamsimiʾatin wa-min taʾrīkhi l-ʿālami sittata ālāfin wa-sittamiʾatin wa-thalāthatan wa-khamsīna sanatan ḥaḍara bi-l-madīnati ḥamā-hā llāhu l-arākinatu wa-l-asāqifatu wa-l-qamāmisatu* /[2] *wa-l-tarrārīyatu wa-ghayru-hum min sāʾiri ṣiqillīyata ṣāna-hā llāhu li-tajdīdi jarāʾidi-him li-ajli tamḥīṣi-hā wa-ndirāsi-hā wa-ḥaḍara jutsālimu l-laththu* [transcription uncertain, from Latin *electus*] *bi-kanīsati jaflūdī wa-s.kīn* [above, note 27] *wa-barnārd* [Cusa reads *b.r.qār.d*] *wa-aḥḍartum jarīdatan kutibat bi-l-amri l-nāfidhi* /[3] *li-taʾrīkhi-hā ithnay ʿashara* [sic] *sanatan fī-hā dhikru mā aqṭaʿa-hu l-kanīsata l-kabīrata l-jāmiʿa* [sic] *bi-jaflūdī mina l-rijāli fa-ṭūliʿa l-majlisu l-sāmī rafaʿa llāhu samka majdi-hi bi-dhālika fa-kharaja l-amru l-ʿālī l-muṭāʿu* /[4] *l-malakīyu l-muʿaẓẓamīyu l-qiddīsīyu l-rujārīyu zāda-hu llāhu ʿalāʾan wa-maḍāʾan bi-tajdīdi-hā wa-ithbāti man bi-hā mina l-rijāli ʿalā l-sharṭi l-mathbūti bi-l-jarīdati l-mutaqaddimi dhikru-hā wa-huwa anna-hu matā wujida aḥadun min hāʾulāʾi l-rijāli fī* /[5] *jarāʾidi l-tarrārīyati aw ghayri-him radadtumū-hu li-ṣāḥibi-hi wa-lā yuʿawwiḍu la-kum ʿan-hu aḥadan.*

29 For the identification of Sant'Angelo with the Benedictine monastery of Santissima Trinità di Mileto, see Ménager 1958–9.

30 The words 'and Qalʿat al-Ṣirāt' are interpolated above the line: although they seem to have been written in the same hand and ink as the rest of the note, it remains possible that this was an attempt at fraud.

31 Cusa 1868–82, p.479: /[69] *wa-aḥḍarā ayḍan jarīdatan maktūbatan bi-l-lāṭīnī min qibali l-lighūni* [? from Greek ἡγούμενος, *ēgoumenos*, 'abbot': *cf. al-ghuman* in **Private 1**] *wa-l-ruhbāni matāʿa dayri ṣant anjalū bi-milīṭū fī-hā dhikru ṣant quzimāna wa-l-rijāli lladhīna kānū la-hum fī-hi wa-l-rijāli lladhīna kānū* /[70] *la-hum bi-ṣakhrati l-ḥarīri* [interpolated: *wa-qalʿati l-ṣirāṭi*] *wa-badala-hum min-humu l-dīwānu l-maʿmūru wa-aʿṭā la-hum ʿiwaḍan ʿan-hum bi-qalūrīyata wa-sallamū hāʾulāʾi li-kanīsati jaflūdī bi-ribāʿi-him wa-mawāshī-him wa-qarḍan li-l-kanīsati* [Cusa reads *wa-raḍiyā l-kanīsatu*].

The churches of San Cosimano (*i.e.* Cosma – on the outskirts of Cefalù) and San Giovanni di Roccella (12km west of the city) seem to have been granted to Santissima Trinità di Mileto by Roger I before 1098.[32] In January 1136, at Roger's request, and with his approval, Abbot David made over to San Salvatore the tithe of Cefalù, a mill, and the two churches with all their appurtenances, on the understanding that the king would compensate his monastery with lands and villeins in Calabria, closer to Mileto. With the two churches, came what the grant numbers as thirty-eight villeins, whose names are listed in Latin. All their names are recognisable in the 1145 *jarīda*, where they occur in the same order (see Table 5.2). This Latin grant was preserved in the tabulary of San Salvatore, and is therefore the Latin register mentioned in the Arabic clause quoted above.[33] The comparison of the three lists of villeins – the Latin of 1136, the Arabic of 1145, and the Greek of 1145 – shows clearly that the Arabic list was made from the Latin, and the Greek from the Arabic (see Table 5.2): the significance of this is discussed in the conclusion to this chapter.

Dīwānī 25: the renewal of the *jarīda* issued to Roger Forestal in 1093–5 (*Dīwānī* 5)

A *jarīda* composed of one full sheet of parchment, extended by the addition of a small piece. The two are sewn together with a narrow lace of parchment, in a simple running stitch, with the seams 'sealed' on the *verso* in the same manner as ***Dīwānī* 21**.[34] The structure of the renewal is as follows:

- lines 1–6: *Narratio* (Arabic)
- lines 6–7: *Dispositio* (Arabic)
- lines 8–21: List, headed in Arabic only 'And they are …' (*wa-hum* …) – 30 names, written in five columns across the sheet from right to left, in Arabic with Greek transliteration above each name; the totals at the end of the list are given in both Arabic and Greek
- lines 22: *Narratio* continued (Arabic)
- lines 22–5: List of the *mutazawwijūn*, headed in Arabic only by the explanatory note 'And there were found in the old *jarīda* from which this *jarīda* is copied the names of the *mutazawwijūn* amongst the children of the men confirmed in this register. And they are …'[35] – 5 names, written as in the main list
- lines 26–8: *Sharṭ* or stipulation (Arabic)

32 Ménager 1958–9, no.4, pp.20–4, no.15, pp.45–6, no.18, p.52, no.19, pp.52–3, and pp.63–4, 92, 93.

33 Original: PA, AdS, Cefalù, no.4; ed. Garufi 1899, pp.25–6, no.11; Ménager 1958–9, no.18, pp.52, 61. For the compensation given to Mileto, see Brühl 1987, no.42, pp.116–18, where the number of villeins granted to Cefalù is given as thirty-nine.

34 On the *verso* are two contemporary notes in Arabic – *ghartīl farastāl* and *jarīdatun li-ghartīli farastali* (both pointed) – and the 13th-century Latin note *D*°. † *MCC q(uo)d tenuit Adam Ferestal.*

35 Cusa 1868–82, p.129: /22 *wa-wujida fī l-jarīdati l-qadīmati llatī nusikhat min-hā hādhihi l-jarīdatu asmā'u l-mutazawwijīna min awlādi l-rijāli l-mathbūtīna fī hādhihi l-jarīdati wa-hum* …

- line 28: Arabic note 'Written on an extended parchment' (*kutibat fī raqqin rāʾiʿin*)[36]
- line 29: Greek chancery signature of Roger II
- plica, pierced by regular holes for the seal

The *narratio* and *dispositio* run as follows:

> [*Narratio*] When it was the date of 24 March, in Indiction VIII, in the year 539 [A.H.], and of the date of the world 6653 [A.M.], there were present in Palermo (may God protect it!) the archbishops, bishops, counts, barons, and others from all Sicily (may God preserve her!) in order to renew their *jarāʾid*, as a consequence of their having been scrutinised and repeatedly examined. And you, O Walter Forestal, were present, and you brought a *jarīda* from the Great Sultan [*i.e.* Roger I] (may God sanctify his spirit and illuminate his tomb!) to Roger Forestal, your father, in which was listed what he was granted of the men of the *jarīda* of Jāliṣū, but not those written in the *jarīda* of Corleone. Thus, the Most Exalted Seat (may God raise the roof of its glory!) was informed about the matter. [*Dispositio*] Then there went forth the high, the to-be-obeyed, the most royal, the most glorified, the most holy, the Rogerian order (may God increase its high standing and efficacy!) to renew it and to confirm the men who are in it.[37]

The *sharṭ* (lines 26–28) is based on the same model as the first part of the stipulation in ***Dīwānī* 22**, but with an additional clause inserted into the middle of it, covering the *mutazawwijūn*:

> The names which are in this *jarīda* were written on the condition[s] that you are legally entitled to them, and that the *mutazawwijūn* amongst the children are the children of those confirmed amongst the men in this *jarīda*, and [that], if any of them appears in the *jarāʾid* of the *dīwān al-maʿmūr* or in the *jarāʾid* of the barons, you will strike him out.[38]

[36] Cusa has *fī raqqin rātiʿin* (presumably thought to mean 'on an abundant parchment'). Metcalfe 1999, pp.85, 86 has *fī raqqin rābiʿin*, 'on a fourth sheet or ("on fine sheets")', but only two pieces of parchment are used. I read *rāʾiʿin* ('extended'), the active participle of *r.y.ʿ*. Although not particularly well-attested (but see Freytag 1830–7, vol.I, p.217, '*redundans* [overflowing]'), given the comparable notes on the other *jarāʾid* in this series, this seems to be the only possible sense. The only serious alternative – *rāʾiʿ*, from *r.w.ʿ*, meaning 'splendid' (see Metcalfe above) – does not seem appropriate here.

[37] Cusa 1868–82, p.127: /[1] *lammā kāna bi-taʾrīkhi l-rābiʿi wa-ʿishrīna* [sic] *min mārsū l-indiqtusa l-thāmina sanata tisʿin wa-thalāthīna wa-khamsimiʾatin wa-min taʾrīkhi l-ʿālami* /[2] *sittata ālāfin wa-sittamiʾatin wa-thalāthatan wa-khamsīna sanatan ḥaḍara bi-l-madīnati ḥamā-hā llāhu l-arākinatu wa-l-asāqifatu wa-l-qamāmisatu wa-l-tarrārīyatu* /[3] *wa-ghayru-hum min sāʾiri ṣiqillīyata ṣāna-hā llāhu li-tajdīdi jarāʾidi-him li-ajli tamḥīṣi-hā wa-ndirāsi-hā wa-ḥaḍarta anta* /[4] *yā ghartīl farastāl wa-aḥḍarta jarīdatan kāna kutibat* [sic] *bi-amri l-sulṭāni l-kabīri qaddasa llāhu rūḥa-hu wa-nawwara* [Cusa misreads *baʿatha*] *ḍarīḥa-hu* /[5] *ilā rujayr farastāl wālidi-ka fī-hā dhikru mā aqṭaʿa-hu mina l-rijāli min jarīdati jāliṣū wa-laysa hum maktūbīna fī* /[6] *jarīdati qurlūna fa-ṭūliʿa l-majlisu l-sāmī rafaʿa llāhu samka majdi-hi bi-dhālika fa-kharaja l-amru l-ʿālī l-muṭāʿu* /[7] *l-malakīyu l-muʿaẓẓamīyu l-qiddīsīyu l-rujārīyu zāda-hu llāhu ʿalāʾan wa-maḍāʾan bi-tajdīdi-hā wa-ithbāti man bi-hā mina l-rijāli.*

[38] Cusa 1868–82, p.129: /[26] *wa-qad kutibati l-asmāʾu llatī fī hādhihi l-jarīdati ʿalā sharīṭati anna-ka mustaḥiqqun bi-him wa-anna l-mutazawwijīna mina l-awlādi* /[27] *hum awlādu l-mathbūtīna fī hādhihi l-jarīdati mina l-rijāli wa-matā ẓahara aḥadun min-hum fī jarāʾidi l-dīwāni* /[28] *l-maʿmūri aw fī jarāʾidi l-tarrārīyati atlafta-hu.*

External features

The four *jarā'id* renewed in 1145 that survive as originals all share external features which immediately distinguish them as belonging to the same series. All are rolls composed of two or more rectangular sheets of parchment sewn together end-to-end. The sheets of the two *jarā'id* for Catania are sewn together with cotton or linen thread in large dog's-tooth stitches; those for Cefalù and Walter Forestal are sewn with strips or laces of parchment in a simple running stitch. The seams of all three are 'sealed' on the *verso* with Arabic and Greek notes written across the seams: on the right edge, *ṣaḥḥa bi-l-ta'rīkhi* ('It was authenticated on the date'); on the left, ἐκυρώθη (*ekurōthē*, 'It has been authenticated').[39]

In common with all the renewals of 1144–5, whatever the language in which they were written, the *jarā'id* are signed with King Roger's Greek chancery signature. Although none now bears its seal, it is evident from the plica and regular holes that each was originally sealed. That the seals were lead is confirmed by a note at the foot of ***Dīwānī* 25**, from the time of Archbishop Balsamo (1835), that it was then 'con sug[gel]lo di piombo attaccato, ed unito allo foglio'.

In all four originals, the text is written in Arabic, and Arabic only; while Greek is restricted to the interlinear transliteration of the names in the registers, to the bilingual rubrics and totals, to the notes across the seams on the *verso*, and to Roger's chancery signature: it is not clear from the Latin translation of ***Dīwānī* 23** whether or not it, too, conformed to this model. The detailed description of the Arabic scripts lies outside the scope of this study, but all four originals use the polished *dīwānī* introduced after 1130.[40] There can be no doubt that all were the work of highly-trained, professional scribes. At least two were at work, for the *narratio-dispositio* of ***Dīwānī* 21** is in a different hand from that used for ***Dīwānī* 24 and 25**.[41] As to the Greek scripts, my preliminary impression is that each of the four originals is written in a different hand. Vera von Falkenhausen has identified at least twelve Greek scribes under Roger II (1112–54), and she stresses that they, too, were all highly-trained professional scribes.[42] The competence, efficiency, and professionalism of all the scribes is abundantly manifest in these highly complex and strikingly elegant documents; all conforming to a common model, and all demanding the closest collaboration between the Arab and the Greek scribes, at every stage from planning to execution. Despite the heavy increase in work

[39] Noth 1983, p.203; von Falkenhausen 1980b, p.262. For an Islamic parallel for this practice of 'sealing' the seams of rolls made up of two or more sheets of parchment sewn together, see Wansbrough 1971, p.21. The use of *ṣaḥḥa* as a mark of registration and authentication is well attested in the Fāṭimid and other Islamic chanceries: Stern 1964a, pp.129, 139, 140–2; and Khan 1986, line 4 of doc. A Byzantine parallel may be found in the manner in which the seams of the *praktika*-rolls from Athos were 'sealed' with the date – *e.g.* † Ἐγεγόνει κατὰ μῆνα μάρτιον τῆς β ἁς ἰνδικτιῶνος ('Done in the month of March in the 2nd Indiction') : Pétit and Korablev 1911, pp.109, 111, 113; see also the same practice on privileges, pp.120, 125.

[40] Noth's R[oger]A[rabic]1: see Noth 1983, pp.204–5; and below, pp.275–7.

[41] Noth 1983, p.205.

[42] von Falkenhausen 1997, pp.276–8.

represented by the renewals of 1144–5, there is no trace – at least, not in these *jarāʾid* – of Brühl's *aiuto notai* – of temporary staff brought into the chancery to cope with the rush.[43]

The *narratio*

The *jarāʾid* of 1145 open with the *narratio*, which starts abruptly with the *taʾrīkh* or *datatio*: 'When it was the date of …' (*lammā kāna bi-taʾrīkhi* …).[44] In the four renewals in which the *narratio* is preserved, the order of the elements is the same: day, month, indiction (*al-indiqtus*), year of the Hegira, and year of the world according to the Byzantine calendar. Only ***Dīwānī* 21** gives the day of the week in addition to that of the month.[45] The use of the opening *datatio* is not restricted to the *jarāʾid* in this series,[46] but occurs in eleven other *dīwānī* documents, only four of which are *jarāʾid*;[47] it also appears in two of the private Arabic documents from Norman Sicily.[48] This usage is evidently inspired by the local Greek tradition which, in turn, follows the Byzantine.[49] The Latin documents, too, before 1127, generally exhibit an initial *datatio* joined to the *invocatio*, and, in them, only after 1140 does the *datatio* become a fixed element of the final eschatology; the initial *datatio* finally disappears from Latin documents in 1146.[50] The Fāṭimid, Ayyūbid, and Mamlūk *dīwān*s do not appear to have issued documents that opened with the *datatio*, although the phrase *lammā kāna* ... is standard opening of *narrationes*, with or without a following *datatio*.[51] The usage can be found, however, in Christian documents of the late 12th century from Sinai. The opening of an *iqrār* ('declaration') confirming the grant of a pious endowment in favour of St Catherine's by Mālik ibn Hubāra, the Christian *raʾīs* ('headman') of the western coastal region of Ṭūr in Sinai, in 1197 A.D. is particularly interesting in that it resembles so closely the opening employed by the *jarāʾid*: (after the *basmala* – always absent from the Sicilian *jarāʾid*!) *lammā kāna mustahallu dhī l-ḥijjati sanata thalāthin wa-tisʿīna wa-khamsimiʾatin ḥaḍara … Māliku bnu Ḥubārata* ('When it was the beginning of Dhū l-Ḥijja of the year 593, Mālik ibn Ḥubāra was present …').[52] Such Christian

[43] Brühl 1983, p.45: see also above, p.116.
[44] Noth 1983, p.206; Wansbrough 1984, p.15 and n.14.
[45] Caspar 1904, p.559, reg.185, and Noth 1983, 'F', p.193, both place this renewal after that issued to the church of Cefalù on 7 February (although they both followed Cusa's misreading of the month of the latter as 'January'), yet the *datatio* reads clearly *yawm al-ithnayn awwal yanār*, *i.e.* Monday 1 January.
[46] As might be misunderstood from the observations of Noth 1983, p.209.
[47] The Triocala *jarīda*, ***Dīwānī* 18**; ***Dīwānī* 31–2, 36–9 and 46**; and the three Monreale *jarāʾid*, ***Dīwānī* 43–5**.
[48] **Private 16** and **25**. Wansbrough 1984, p.15, is mistaken that this usage 'extends more or less consistently to private documents'.
[49] von Falkenhausen 1997, pp.273, 274, and 301 (*pace* Wansbrough 1984, p.15).
[50] Brühl 1987, pp.66, 69, 70.
[51] See, for example, the documents cited by al-Qalqashandī 1913–20, vol.XI, pp.41, 43, 46, 49, 51, 53, 54, 56, 57, 60, 61, 63, *etc.*
[52] Richards 1998, pp.163–4; Atiya 1955, no.185, p.35.

documents, like those of Norman Sicily, were presumably influenced directly by the Byzantine tradition.

All four *narrationes* describe, in the same words and in the third person (*ḥaḍara*), the constitution and the function of the court at Palermo. The four estates in attendance are called by Arabic words coined from Greek or Latin, respectively: archbishops, *arāk.na*, sing. *ar.k*, from the prefix in ἀρχι–επίσκοπος (*archi-episcopos*) or Latin *arci-episcopus*;[53] bishops, *asāqifa*, sing. *usquf*, coined by early Arabic from ἐπίσκοπος (*episcopos*); counts, *qamāmisa*, sing. *qūmis*, from Latin *comes*, possibly via κόμης (*komēs*); and *tarrārīya*,[54] sing. *tarrārī*, from Latin *terrarius*, possibly via τεῤῥέρης (*terrerēs*). They meet 'to renew their *jarā'id*' (*li-tajdīdi jarā'idi-him*). So far so good – but the following phrase (*li-ajli tamḥīṣi-hā wa-ndirāsi-hā*) is problematic.

Tamḥīṣ is the *maṣdar* or verbal noun of *maḥḥaṣa*, the primary meaning of which is 'to purify' or 'to purge', but also 'to separate' one thing from another. *Indirās* is the *maṣdar* of *indarasa*, which means originally 'to be passed over repeatedly', and thus 'to be worn out', 'to be effaced' and 'to be destroyed'; thence, 'to be read repeatedly' and 'to be studied', or 'to be trodden' or 'to be threshed' (as grain). Albrecht Noth translated *tamḥīṣ* as 'a careful examination', and *indirās* as 'cancellation', but hesitated over the precise meaning of the latter: either the old registers had become illegible with age; or, after a careful examination (*tamḥīṣ*), the old *jarā'id* were to be cancelled, and then renewed. There are several objections to this suggestion, not least that ***Dīwānī* 3** and ***Dīwānī* 14**, if none of the other originals, were *not* cancelled – the former still exists; the latter survived until the 18th century.[55] More seriously, one expects the pair of *maṣdar*s to be yoked together in a near-synonymous parallelism – a ubiquitous construction. This is in favour of John Wansbrough's suggestion that the phrase should be read 'as a consequence of them being examined and studied'.[56] However, the Palermitan Jews, who translated ***Dīwānī* 23** in 1290, understood that the churchmen and barons had met 'to renew their privileges because they were almost obliterated, worm-eaten, and worn out with age'.[57] Were this last, rather free, translation to be correct in essence, it

53 Noth 1983, p.192, and others, follow Cusa 1868–82, pp.715–17, in translating *arāk.na* as 'archons'. Archbishop Nicholas of Messina is referred to as *al-shaykh al-arāk Niqūla* (***Dīwānī* 37**); Archbishop Walter II of Palermo is *al-mawlā al-ajall al-ar.k al-qiddīs* (***Dīwānī* 39**); and Archbishop Henry of Messina is *al-shaykh al-ar.k h.r.z* [?] *bi-massīnā* (**Private 6**). See also Amari 1863, pp.1, 7 and 14, cited by Dozy 1881, vol.I, p.18, who regards the word as an abbreviation of *arkibishqufa*(?). The 13th-century Latin translation of ***Dīwānī* 23** made by Palermitan Jews gives *Archiepiscopi* for *al-arāk.na*.

54 Unless the plural should be vocalised *al-tarāriya* (*i.e. fa'ālilatun; cf. al-sarādighatu*, above, p.100, note 25). 55 Noth 1983, p.207.

56 Wansbrough 1984, p.15, where he notes *indarasa* meaning 'to be studied' in the 13th-century vocabulary attributed to Raymond Martin: Schiaparelli 1871, pp.308 (*conculcare*), 593 (*studere*), 607 (*terere*); for *tamḥīṣ*, the same list gives *temptare, titulare*.

57 Garufi 1899, p.31: *Ad renovandum privilegia eorum pro eo quod erant quasi abolita incamulata et inveterata*. For *incamulata*, a Sicilian dialect word from *camula*, 'worm, *etc*.' see Varvaro 1986, pp.136–8. (Varvaro rules out an Arabic derivation for *camula* on 'geographical and semantic grounds'[?], but see *qaml* or *quml* or *qummal*, pl. *qumūl*, 'grub, worm, weavil, maggot, louse', *etc*.: Freytag 1830–7, vol.II, p.500; Lane 1984, vol.I, p.1465; Dozy 1881, vol.II, p.415; Giarrizzo 1989, p.106.)

might contain an echo of the Latin *narrationes* of 1144 which refer to *privilegia ... antiquitus composita*. It must be admitted, however, that the Jewish translators of ***Dīwānī* 23** often fell rather short of the mark, as when they garble the list of titles and *adᶜiya* (sing. *duᶜāʾ*: 'invocations') in the *dispositio* (see Table 5.1). What is more, ***Dīwānī* 4** is still perfectly legible to this day; ***Dīwānī* 14** could still be read in the 18th century; and ***Dīwānī* 10 and 14** were, respectively, only twelve and nine years old in 1145, and are thus likely to have still been legible. While it is true that this phrase has all the ring of rhetoric – the true purpose of the renewals was to refill the royal treasury – there is no compelling reason to conclude that the rhetoric was completely empty. My own inclination, therefore is to take the phrase to mean that the *jarāʾid* were to be renewed after they had been *purged* (*i.e.* of villeins who were held illegally, in line with the *shurūṭ*), and *repeatedly examined*; and to translate 'as a consequence of their having been scrutinised and repeatedly examined'.

Next, the recipient is named, and the details given of the *jarīda* to be renewed. Typically, the recipient is addressed in the second person – in ***Dīwānī* 25**, Walter Forestal is even saluted in the vocative with the participle *yā*. This falters somewhat in ***Dīwānī* 24** where Jocelm and his two companions are first addressed in the third person (*ḥaḍara* instead of the expected *ḥaḍartum*): only subsequently does the scribe switch to the second person (*aḥḍartum*), but, in the second part of the *narratio*, he reverts to the third person (*aḥḍarū*).

Then, with a return to the impersonal third person, '*al-majlis al-sāmī* was informed ... about the matter' (*fa-ṭūliᶜa l-majlisu l-sāmīyu ... bi-dhālika*). *Majlis* means literally 'a place where one sits' but, when qualified by *sāmī*, meaning 'exalted' (and by other similar epithets), becomes a personal title: 'the exalted seat' is the standard translation.[58] According to al-Qalqashandī in the *Ṣubḥ al-aᶜshā fī kitābat al-inshāʾ* ('The dawn for those in the dark about the art of writing correspondence'), the title *al-majlis*, qualified by one of two near-synonyms *al-ᶜālī* and *al-sāmī*, was used by the Ayyūbid sultans of Egypt, in the late 12th – mid-13th century, as a *laqab* or 'personal title' for rulers and their equals. *Al-majlis al-ᶜālī* seems to have been the loftier style. As to *al-sāmī*, it could either be written either 'with the *yāʾ*' (السامىّ *al-sāmīy bi-l-yāʾ*) or 'without the *yāʾ*' (السامى *al-sāmī bi-ghayri yāʾ*). The former carried hyperbolic force (*mubālagha*), in exactly the same way as the relative adjectives employed in the *dispositio* (see below). It thus meant 'the most exalted', and was a more elevated style than *al-sāmī*.[59] In the Norman *jarāʾid*, the terminal *yāʾ* of *al-sāmī* does not bear a *tashdīd*, the sign that indicates 'strengthening' or 'doubling' of a letter. This is strong reason *a priori* to read the more modest of the two styles – *al-majlis al-sāmī*, 'the exalted seat'. However, the fact that the titles in the *dispositio* (see below) are strengthened by doubled *yāʾ* (*e.g. al-qiddīs*, 'the holy', becomes *al-qiddīsī*, 'the most holy') seems to require

[58] Stern 1962, p.182, line 6; Richards 1973, p.142, line 5;

[59] al-Qalqashandī 1913–72, vol.V, pp.496–7; vol.VI, pp.115–17. See also al-Bāshā 1957, pp.316, 455–9.

that *al-sāmī*, too, be strengthened, and that we should supply the missing *tashdīd* and read *al-sāmīy bi-l-yā'*. This is strongly supported by the invocation or *duʿā'* which follows the title (see below). For that reason, although I have strictly followed the orthography of the manuscript and transliterated *al-sāmī* throughout, I have availed myself of a translator's privilege to read 'the Most Exalted Seat'.

In the *jarā'id* renewed in 1145, *al-majlis al-sāmī* has generally been taken to refer to the whole court of archbishops, bishops, counts, barons, and others that is mentioned earlier in the *narratio*, and has thus been interpreted as the *curia regis*.[60] Albrecht Noth rightly observed that this could not be so. In the first place, the text of the *narratio* makes it quite clear that we are dealing with two separate bodies: the assembly of feudatories, who came to court as petitioners, bringing their *jarā'id* for scrutiny, cancellation and renewal; and *al-majlis al-sāmī* which, unlike the feudatories, had executive power. In the second, *al-majlis al-sāmī* (or *al-sāmīy*) is a *laqab* well-known in medieval Arabic diplomatics, and is always applied to individuals, never to institutions.[61] The index to al-Qalqashandī's *Ṣubḥ* lists one hundred and forty-four occurrences, and in every case it is a personal title.[62] Examples from the Fāṭimid chancery are less numerous, but sufficient to demonstrate its use. For example, *al-majlis al-sāmī* is used as one of the titles of the vizier in a late Fāṭimid petition from Sinai, while the more prestigious style *al-majlis al-ʿālī* is employed in exactly the same way in a petition of al-ʿĀḍid, perhaps of his vizier Ruzzīk (1161–2).[63]

Al-majlis al-sāmī and *al-majlis al-qā'idīy* are also used as personal titles by the Alexandrian poet Ibn Qalāqis, when writing of the Norman *dīwān* in 1168–9. In his Sicilian *roman à lettres*, the poet addresses a petition on behalf of the Muslims of Syracuse to his patron, the *qā'id* Abū l-Qāsim. Ibn Qalāqis encloses the petition in a letter to his friend, the poet al-Umāwī, and begs him to submit it 'to the lord *qā'id*'. Al-Umāwī replies describing how he had presented himself 'before *al-majlis al-sāmī* (may God grant happiness to his lands, and assist his supporters with good fortune!), and conveyed the letter as required'. From this, and from what follows, I understand *al-majlis al-sāmī* to be employed as an indirect address to Abū l-Qāsim. Indeed, just a few lines later, in his own voice, Ibn Qalāqis refers to Abū l-Qāsim as *al-majlis al-qā'idīy*.[64]

This is not to suggest that the title *al-majlis al-sāmī* as used in the *narrationes* of the renewals of 1145 was the personal style of the Sicilian vizier or of some other official. The Norman *jarā'id* were ostensibly royal documents, issued at the

60 Cusa 1868–82, p.716; Garufi 1901, p.258; Caspar 1904, pp.314–15.

61 Ernst 1960, index under *sāmī* (p.311) and *majlis* (p.315); Wansbrough 1963, pp.506–7.

62 al-Qalqashandī 1913–72, Index, p.422.

63 Richards 1973, p.141, line 5, and pp.148–9; Stern 1962, no.III, line 6, p.182. See also Wansbrough 1971, p.22, line 11.

64 Ibn Qalāqis 1984a, pp.37–8: *ḥaḍartu ilā l-majlisi l-sāmī ʿamara llāhu bi-l-saʿādati aqṭāra-hu wa-ʿaḍada bi-l-tawfīqi anṣāra-hu wa-addaytu l-risālata ʿalā muqtaḍā-hā*; trans. De Simone 1996, pp.95–7 (I cannot agree with n.172, that *al-majlis al-sāmī* was the Arabic title of the *curia*, a conclusion which seems to rest upon the ambiguous evidence of a late 13th-century Latin translation). For Abū l-Qāsim, see below, pp.234–42.

king's order, and authenticated by the royal signature and seal. Although the hand that actually wrote the royal signature may well have been George of Antioch's, that signature was nonetheless the king's.[65] In exactly the same way, although Roger is unlikely to have been personally informed about the details of every renewal, and to have individually ordered each to be issued, it was nonetheless his presence which occupied the *majlis al-sāmī*. The titles in the *dispositiones* of the 1145 *jarā'id* are also a calque upon those of Fāṭimid viziers (see below). The presence amongst them of the *nisba* 'the Rogerian' (*al-rujārīy*) need not indicate that the titles were exclusively for the use of the king himself, because a vizier would typically adopt the *nisba* which reflected his master's authority: for example, al-Ḥāfiẓ's vizier Bahrām was styled al-Ḥāfiẓī.[66] The vizier's authority belonged to (*mansūb ilā*) his master, and this was reflected in his title (*nisba*). The fact that, in the Sicilian documents, these same titles are also used of *al-ḥaḍra*, 'the [Royal] Presence' itself, makes it absolutely clear that the Norman *dīwān* fully appreciated the convention of Islamic diplomatics that such *nisab* related to the king himself (see Table 5.3). *Al-majlis al-sāmī* was a way of referring indirectly to the king, whether in person or as reflected in his vizier.

The *dispositio*

The *dispositio* consists of a single sentence: 'the order went forth ... to renew it [the *jarīda*] and to confirm those of the men who are in it' (*kharaja l-amru ... bi-tajdīdi-hā wa-ithbāti man bi-hā mina l-rijāli*).[67] Noth translates *bi ... ithbāti* as 'to register', but the men were, by definition and in fact, already registered; what was required was royal confirmation of the fact.[68] The formula *kharaja [l-]amr ...* is widely used in medieval Arabic diplomatics to introduce the *dispositio*.[69]

Separating the two parts of this sentence comes a long sequence of adjectives qualifying 'the order' (*al-amr*). Noth observed that the first two adjectives refer to the order itself, while the remainder are, in effect, royal titles.[70] Most of the latter are relative adjectives (*al-asmā' al-mansūbat* or *al-nisabāt*), formed by adding the suffix *-īy* to the words from which they are derived. Al-Qalqashandī insists that, in titles, such styles might have hyperbolic force (*li-l-mubālagha*), so that, for example, 'the holy' (*al-qiddīs*) became 'the most holy' (*al-qiddīs+īy*).[71] Such formulae in

[65] von Falkenhausen 1997, pp.285–6. [66] Stern 1964a, p.59, line 14.

[67] In six other documents, the same phrase marks the transition from the opening *ta'rīkh* to the *dispositio*: ***Dīwānī* 37–9 and 44–5**. In ***Dīwānī* 31–2**, it marks the passage from the short *narratio* to the *dispositio*. [68] Noth 1983, p.207.

[69] Fāṭimid: Stern 1964a, p.36, lines 16–17; p.48, line 23; p.59, line 12; p.71, lines 28–9; p.81, line 9; and pp.111–12. Richards 1973, p.142, lines 17–18. Ayyūbid: al-Qalqashandī 1913–72, vol.XI, pp.53 and 60. Stern 1964b, pp.29–31.

[70] Noth 1983, p.212; but with the slight reservation that, while *al-muṭā'* always qualifies *al-amr*, *al-'ālī* (feminine *al-'āliya*) can also be used of the king (*al-malik*) or of the royal presence (*al-ḥaḍra*).

[71] al-Qalqashandī 1913–72, vol.V, pp.503–4; Noth 1983, p.213.

Table 5.3 The occurence of the principal *alqāb* of the Norman Kings in *dīwānī* documents (1145–83)

***Dīwānī* No.**	**21**	**24**	**25**	**29**	**31**	**32**	**33**	**37**	**38**	**43**	**44**	**45a**	**45b**		
															1148 inscription*
al-amr (the order)	•	•	•	•	•	•	•	•	•			•			
al-ḥaḍra (the presence)										•	•		•		•
al-ʿālī / al-ʿāliya (the high)	•	•	•	•	•	•	•	•	•	•	•	•			•
al-ʿalīy / al-ʿalīya (the most high)										•	•				•
al-muṭāʿ (the to-be-obeyed)	•	•	•	•	•	•	•	•	•			•			
al-malakīy / al-malakīya (the most royal)	•	•	•					•	•	•	•		•		•
al-mālikīy / al-mālikīya (the ruling)										•	•		•		•
al-muʿaẓẓamīy / al-muʿaẓẓama (the glorified)	•	•	•					•	•	•	•		•		•
al-qiddīsīy / al-qiddīsīya (the holy)	•	•	•					•		•	•				•
al-rujārīy (the Rogerian)	•	•	•												
al-ghulyālimīy (the Williamian)								•	•	•	•		•		

* For the full formula in the 1149 inscription, see p.136, note 73.

Sicilian documents bear a marked similarity to the long lists of grandiose titles used by Fāṭimid viziers from the last quarter of the 11th century onwards.[72]

In the *jarāʾid* renewed in 1145, the following elements are present (see Table 5.3 for a comparison of their occurrence in other *dīwānī* documents, and in the famous quadrilingual inscription of 1149).[73]

- *Al-ᶜālī*, 'the high'. Among the Norman *alqāb*, both *al-ᶜālī*, and the near synonym *al-ᶜalīy*, 'the most high', are well-attested in two forms: 'the order' (*al-amr*) is always *al-ᶜālī*, never *al-ᶜalīy*; while 'the [royal] presence' (*al-ḥaḍra*) may be both *al-ᶜāliya* and *al-ᶜalīya* (see Table 5.1).[74] Elsewhere, the locution *al-amr al-ᶜālī* is amply attested in Fāṭimid, Ayyūbid, and Mamlūk documents.[75] *Al-ᶜālī* is also a much used adjective in Islamic titulature, most famously in *al-bāb al-ᶜālī*, 'the Sublime Porte', and we have already seen that *al-majlis al-ᶜālī* was one of the styles employed by the Fāṭimid vizier under al-ᶜĀḍid.[76]
- *Al-muṭāᶜ* is 'that which is obeyed' or 'that which is to be obeyed'. In the Sicilian formulae it is invariably used, as here, to qualify *al-amr*, 'the order' (see Table 5.1). The phrase *al-amr al-muṭāᶜ* was used in Fāṭimid and Ayyūbid petitions.[77] *Muṭāᶜ* can be used as a personal name (*ism*), but when definite with the article, as an individual title, I believe that *al-Muṭāᶜ* generally refers to the Prophet, presumably on the authority of the *Qurʾān* (81:19–21).
- *Al-malakīy*, 'the most royal', the *nisba* formed from *al-malik*, 'the king', is used in Sicily to qualify both *al-amr* ('the order') and *al-ḥaḍra* ('the [Royal] Presence'), while *al-mālikīya*, 'the ruling', is only to modify *al-ḥaḍra*. Note the parallel sonority of the pairs *al-mālikīya al-malakīya* and *al-ᶜāliya al-ᶜalīya*. *Al-malakīy* is, of course, extremely common in Islamic diplomatics, and tends to be used of rulers without caliphal authority, such as sultans and viziers.[78]

[72] For example, Stern 1964a, no.3, p.35, lines 1–5; no.5, p.53, lines 3–8; no.6, p.59, lines 12–14; no.7, p.65, lines 1–2; p.69; no.8, p.70, lines 2–10; pp.74–5; no.9, p.76, lines 1–5.

[73] 1149 inscription: Amari 1879, no.17, pp.80–94, pl.9.2; repr. Amari 1971, pp.201–12; with emendations by Lagumina, 1890; Johns 1987, p.91; and Johns 1995a, pp.139–41. See also Krönig 1989 and Zeitler, 1996 (both with care). The full title in the Arabic text reads, literally: 'The priest of the Presence, the ruling, the most royal, the high, the most high, the glorified, the splendid, the most holy, the magnificent, the strengthened by God, the made powerful by His power, the supported by His strength, the one who rules Italy, Lombardy, Calabria, Sicily, and Africa, the defender of the Pope of Rome, the protector of the Christian community, may God preserve its rule!' (*qissīsu l-ḥaḍrati l-mālikīyati l-malakīyati l-ᶜāliyati l-ᶜalīyati l-muᶜaẓẓamati l-sanīyati l-qiddīsīyati l-bahīyati l-muᶜtazzati bi-llāhi l-muqtadirati bi-qudrati-hi l-manṣūrati bi-qūwati-hi mālikati yinṭālīyata wa-nkabardhata wa-qalūrīyata wa-ṣiqillīyata wa-ifrīqīyata muᶜizzati imāmi rūmīyata l-nāṣirati li-l-millati l-naṣrānīyati ṣammada llāhu mamlakata-hā*).

[74] ***Dīwānī* 29, 31–2, 33** and **37**: *kharaja l-amru l-ᶜālī l-muṭāᶜu*

[75] Fāṭimid: Richards 1973, p.142, lines 17–18; Stern 1962, p.179, line 13 (*al-tawqīᶜ al-ᶜālī*). Ayyūbid: Stern 1964b, p.13, line 2; Stern 1965, p.26, line 2, and pp.30–3; Stern 1964a, p.154, n.1. Mamlūk: Wansbrough 1965a, p.52, line 9; Wansbrough 1965b, p.507, line 283; Wansbrough 1971, p.21, line 6; Richards 1999, p.32, line 2.

[76] See also: al-Qalqashandī 1913–72, vol.VI, p.20, and Index under *al-bāb al-ᶜālī*, *al-majlis al-ᶜālī*, *etc.*; al-Bāshā 1957, pp.390–2.

[77] Stern 1962, p.182, line 12; Stern 1964b, p.10, line 7.

[78] al-Qalqashandī 1913–72, vol.VI, p.30, where the vocalisation *malakīy* (with *fatḥa* not *kasra*) is discussed. See also al-Bāshā 1957, pp.260–4 (*ḥaḍra*), 444–6 (*mālik*), 496–506 (*malik*).

Similarly, according to Ibn Shīth, some held *al-ḥaḍrat* and *al-majlis* to be a titles appropriate to those holding the less than royal offices of *amīr* and *qāḍī*; but he seems to disapprove of this sort of inflationary titulature.[79] The standard formula in Ayyūbid and Mamlūk times seems to be *al-amr l-mawlawīy* ('the lordly order'), but *al-malakīy* does sometimes enter the repertoire.[80]

- *Al-muᶜaẓẓamīy*, 'the most glorified', the *nisba* formed from *al-muᶜaẓẓam*, literally 'he who is made great or revered or glorified'. Curiously, when it qualifies the feminine noun *al-ḥaḍra*, the suffix *-īya* is never applied – *i.e. al-ḥaḍrat al-muᶜaẓẓama*, not *al-muᶜaẓẓamīya*; perhaps on the model of *al-mawāqif al-muᶜaẓẓama*, 'the glorified presence', a form of address of the Fāṭimid caliph.[81] *Al-malik al-muᶜaẓẓam*, 'the glorified king', is the one title used by *all* the Norman kings (except the poor infant William III), and by Frederick II, on coins, *dīwānī* documents, and monumental inscriptions, and thus seems to have functioned almost as a dynastic title.[82] *Al-muᶜaẓẓam* seems to have entered the international vocabulary of royal titulature when it was adopted by the Samānids, Ghaznavids, and Great Saljūqs.[83] Significantly, al-Qalqashandī regarded *al-muᶜaẓẓam* as a particularly suitable title to award to non-Muslim rulers.[84]
- *Al-qiddīsīy*, 'the most holy', the *nisba* formed from *al-qiddīs*, 'the holy', was employed only occasionally in medieval Islamic diplomatics, presumably because of its strongly Christian associations. Al-Qalqashandī reports that *al-qiddīs* was employed for the pope and the patriarch,[85] and it is probable that the style was awarded to the Norman ruler by an Islamic chancery, together with other, more elaborate, Christian styles.[86] Alternatively, or simultaneously, this might reflect the influence of Christian Arabic documents, in which ecclesiastical dignitaries are often given the title *al-qiddīs*; in Sicily, however, this is only attested long after *al-qiddīs* was already established as a royal title.[87] There is no close parallel to this usage in the formal Greek and Latin titles of the Norman rulers: King Roger's Greek title was Ῥογέριος ἐν Χριστῷ τῷ Θεῷ

[79] Ibn Shīth al-Qurashī 1913, p.42; al-Bāshā 1957, pp.260–64; Bosworth 1972, p.73, n.2 (in fact, n.3).

[80] For example, Stern 1964a, p.154, note 1.

[81] Stern 1956, p.532. Cusa 1868–82, p.243, line 14, reads الماظمة – either the scribe has lazily dragged his pen from foot of the *ᶜayn* to the tip of the forward-sloping upright of the *ṭā'*, giving the impression of an *alif* that he did not intend, or he has been seduced by the heavy stress on the second syllable of *muᶜaẓẓam*, after the strong guttural *ᶜayn*, to give it a long vowel, thereby inventing a participle of the apparently unattested 3rd form.

[82] See Johns 1986, p.22 and Table 1. I note, but do not fully understand the comments by De Simone 1999a, n.38: my point was – and is – that *al-malik al-muᶜaẓẓam* was the only *laqab* to be used by *all* the Norman kings (amongst whom, in Sicily, I count Frederick II).

[83] Kramers and Bosworth 1997, p.850; Bosworth 1977, pp.55–6.

[84] al-Qalqashandī 1913–72, vol.VI, p.29. See also al-Bāshā 1957, pp.477–8.

[85] al-Qalqashandī 1913–72, vol.6, p.82. See also, Ernst 1960, p.144, line 8, p.192, line 16.

[86] Below, p.270–1.

[87] See, for example, the declaration (*iqrār*) made 'at the cathedra of the holy father, our father, Simeon, bishop of Mount Sinai the Blessed' in 1197 (*ilā majlisi l-abi l-qiddīsi abi-nā simᶜāna usqufi ṭūri sīnā l-maqdisi*): Richards 1998, p.163, lines 2–3. In Sicily, see the titles of Archbishop Walter II of Palermo: *al-mawlā al-ajall al-ar.k al-qiddīs* (***Dīwānī* 39**); and *al-mawlā al-ajall al-wazīr al-afḍal al-arshifisk(?) al-qiddīs ghaltīr* (**Private 18**).

εὐσεβὴς κραταιὸς ῥὴξ καὶ τῶν Χριστιανῶν βοηθός ('Roger, through Christ the God, the pious, mighty king and defender of the Christians'), and the style remained unchanged until the death of Tancred;[88] in Latin, Roger was *Dei gratia rex* or, after 1135, *divina favente clementia rex*.[89] However, the phrase ὁ ἁγίος ῥὴξ does occasionally appear, not as a formal style, but in the body of the text. The earliest case known to me occurs in an exchange of Arab villeins between the church of Patti and George of Antioch made, in May 1143, 'at the order of our mighty and holy king'.[90]

- *al-rujārīy*, 'the Rogerian', is a *nisba* formed from the personal name *Rujār*, and represents a typically Islamic convention, whereby the ruler is referred to indirectly and impersonally. Thus, for example, the Christian monks of St Catherine's in Sinai dwelt not under the rule of al-Ḥāfiẓ, King Roger's contemporary and correspondent, but 'in the shadow of the Ḥāfiẓian empire' (*fī ẓilli l-dawlati l-Ḥāfiẓīyati*).[91]

The *adᶜiya*

The *jarāʾid* renewed in 1145 employ five invocatory formulae known as *adᶜiya* (sing. *duᶜāʾ*).[92] This is not the first occasion that a *duᶜāʾ* is found in a *dīwānī* document (we have already encountered 'Agrigento – may God protect her!' in ***Dīwānī* 18**), but it is the first time in which a string of *adᶜiya* are systematically employed. *Adᶜiya* continue be a prominent feature in *dīwānī* documents until at least the reign of William II, becoming steadily longer and more grandiose. Such augural formulae, which typically call upon God to assist individuals, to protect places, and otherwise to intervene favourably in human affairs, are an important and ubiquitous feature of Islamic diplomatics.[93] Not just the practice, but also the wording of some of the Sicilian *adᶜiya* is closely paralleled in Islamic diplomatics: the examples cited below are by no means exhaustive, but serve to demonstrate the closeness of the calque.

- 'Palermo – may God protect it!' (*al-madīna ḥamā-hā llāhu*). Precisely the same formula is used of Alexandria in a Fāṭimid decree of al-Ḥāfiẓ.[94]
- 'Sicily – may God preserve her!' (*Ṣiqillīya ṣāna-hā llāhu*).
- 'The Great Sultan [Roger I] – may God sanctify his spirit and illuminate his tomb!' (*al-sulṭān al-kabīr qaddasa llāhu rūḥa-hu wa-nawwara ḍarīḥa-hu*). A

[88] von Falkenhausen 1997, p.278, 296. [89] Brühl 1983, p.68.

[90] Cusa 1868–82, no.71, pp.524–5 (τῇ προστάξει τοῦ κραταιοῦ καὶ ἁγίου ἡμῶν ῥηγὸς); Ménager 1960, Appendix 2, no.28, pp.207–8. See also, for example, ***Dīwānī* 37**, line 9 (παρὰ τοῦ κραταιοῦ καὶ ἁγίου ῥηγὸς); Cusa 1868–82, p.326 (ὄντως τοῦ κραταιοῦ καὶ ἁγίου ἡμῶν δεσπότου μεγάλου ῥηγὸς γουλιάλμου). [91] Stern 1964a, p.59, line 7.

[92] See Noth 1983, pp.210–11, upon which this discussion heavily relies.

[93] al-Qalqashandī 1913–72, vol.VI, pp.284–93; vol.VII, pp.140–53.

[94] Stern 1964a, p.48, line 29 (note also *madīnat miṣr ḥarasa-hā llāhu*); Khan 1986, p.441, line 12.

comparable formula is used of the late imams al-ᶜAzīz and al-Ḥākim in a decree of al-Ẓāhir: 'may God sanctify their spirits' (*qaddasa llāhu arwāḥa-hum*).[95]

- 'The Most Exalted Seat – may God raise the roof of its glory!' (*al-majlisu l-sāmī rafaᶜa llāhu samka majdi-hi*). The whole phrase, and not just the *duᶜā'*,[96] makes a precise reference to the *Qur'ān* 79:27–28, which dwell upon God's creation of the Heavens: 'Are you or Heaven the harder to create? He built it, / He raised its roof, and He put it in order' (*a-antum ashaddu khalqan ami l-samā'u banā-hā / rafaᶜa samka-hā fa-sawwā-hā*). The assonance of *samā'* ('Heaven') in the *Qur'ān*, and *sāmī* ('Most Exalted') in the *duᶜā'*, and the close etymological relationship between the two words, elevates the royal *majlis* to such a height that it almost becomes a heavenly one: indeed, I have been tempted to translate *al-majlis al-sāmī* as 'the Heavenly Throne', instead of the rather banal 'Exalted Seat'. The intrinsically Islamic character of this formula suggests that it was borrowed from Islamic diplomatics, but there can be little doubt that, at the same time, it contains a specific allusion to the Sicilian king and his audience hall.[97] Al-Qalqashandī reports that the *duᶜā'* most appropriate for *al-majlis al-sāmī* (and *al-sāmīy*) was *adāma llāhu taᶜālā rifᶜata-hu*, 'may God Most High perpetuate its height': the use of *rafaᶜa* in one and *rifᶜa* in the other seems to link the two *duᶜā'*s.[98]
- 'The order – may God increase its high standing and efficacy' (*al-amr zāda-hu llāhu ᶜalā'an wa-maḍā'an*). A near identical formula is used in a late Fāṭimid petition: 'the Exalted order – may God increase its penetration and efficacy' (*al-amr al-ᶜālī zāda-hā llāhu nafādhan wa-maḍā'an*).[99]

The *shurūṭ*

The previous sections have tended to demonstrate the extent to which features of the *jarā'id* renewed in 1145 were introduced upon the model of contemporary Islamic diplomatic practice. In contrast, all of the *shurūṭ* – to the effect that the men are registered on the condition that the recipient has a legal right to them and that if one is found in the royal polyptychs or in those of any other feudatory then the recipient will relinquish him – hark back to the Greek stipulation which

95 Stern 1964a, p.16, lines 16–17. 96 Noth 1983, p.212.

97 This is not the place to argue the point at length, but precisely the same association between God's throne and the king's is made visually in the west end of the Cappella Palatina, where the royal throne (*majlis*?) stood on a dais beneath a mosaic of Christ Enthroned. Directly above this, on the painted wooden ceiling, are representations of the Sun and Moon. The chapel ceiling is not only thought by art historians to represent the Heavenly sky, but was described as doing precisely that by the contemporary Philagathos of Cerami. The title *al-majlis al-sāmī* may thus contain a precise reference to this royal throne, while the phrase *rafaᶜa ... samka* may refer both to God's creation of Heaven, and to Roger 's construction of the ceiling.

98 al-Qalqashandī 1913–72, vol.XI, pp.78, 81, 83, *etc.*

99 Richards 1973, p.142, lines 17–18. See also Stern 1964a, p.59, line 14.

concludes ***Dīwānī* 4**, and which is closely paralleled, *mutatis mutandis*, in Greek documents from Norman Calabria.[100] Similarly, the *sharṭ* in ***Dīwānī* 25** – which confirms the Forestal in possession of the *mutazawwijūn* on the condition that the latter really are the offspring of the men registered – reflects the Greek part of ***Dīwānī* 2**, the Palermo *jarīda* of 1095 with its list of *neogamoi*. Moreover, if we believe the note that the list of *mutazawwijūn* was really copied from the original *jarīda* (of 1093–5?), then the stipulation itself must also be of that date. Unlike many of the other features of these *jarāʾid*, the Arabic *sharṭ* appears almost verbatim in Greek in the *plateiai* renewed in 1145.[101] I am aware of no prototype for the simple and common-sense conditions imposed by these clauses, and it is most likely that they were devised *ad hoc*, in 1093, by Count Roger's Greek administrators, to serve the particular needs of the post-conquest distribution of the conquered population. We shall see in the next section how well they had served their original purpose.

The utility of the name-lists

The format and content of the name-lists has already been described in detail for each renewal. Here, I wish to confine myself to a discussion of their utility. The surprising fact is that only two of the *jarāʾid* renewed in 1145 make what might conceivably have been useful alterations to the originals. Adelina's renewal (***Dīwānī* 23**) noted that one of the five villeins granted in 1136 had been replaced by another.[102] And the Cefalù renewal (***Dīwānī* 24**) added the names of the villeins given by Santissima Trinità di Mileto in 1136.

This last addition, however, was of dubious utility. In the first place, the 1145 renewal translated a Latin villein list back into Arabic, and then transliterated the Arabic into Greek, although Latin was, of course, the language with which the bishop and canons of Cefalù would have been most familiar. Second, the names of the villeins were translated from the 1136 register into the renewal of 1145, without making any attempt to record the significant demographic changes that must inevitably have occurred to the population during the intervening eighteen years. Third, details of place of registration and religion, which were included in the Latin register, were omitted from the renewal. And fourth, when ten of the names were translated from Latin into Arabic, they lost all details of their fathers' names: thus, for example, *Teodorus filius Gafuri*, became just *Thawdir*; *Ali filius Grisopoli*, just *ʿAlī ibn …*; and so on. In other words, what was once a detailed and – arguably – useful Latin register, was renewed in the form of an Arabic-Greek *jarīda* that was out of date, that omitted essential data, and that was composed in languages which

[100] See above, p.60.
[101] See above, p.60, note 134.
[102] After the last name there is added *pro quo habitur Buabdelle Munden*: Garufi 1899, p.32.

would have been more-or-less incomprehensible to its recipients. But even this idiocy is overshadowed by the immense monument to bureaucratic absurdity raised by the two renewals for the church of Catania and by that for Walter Forestal.

We have already seen that, if we are to take the Forestal renewal (***Dīwānī* 25**) at its word, the list of *mutazawwijūn* was copied from the original *jarīda* issued by Roger I, which probably dated to 1093–5, and cannot have been later than 1101. What is more, the *mutazawwijūn* were confirmed on the condition that they were the offspring of the households registered in the main name-list. Therefore that list too must have been copied from a *jarīda* written no less than forty-four years previously. However, because the original *jarīda* (***Dīwānī* 5**) no longer survives, it can not now be ascertained whether or not it really did register exactly the same names as appear in the renewal of 1145.

But, the original 1095 *jarīda* of Aci Castello (***Dīwānī* 4**) does survive, and may be compared with its renewal of 1145 (***Dīwānī* 22**). The latter lists exactly the same names as did the original, except that, to some of the names has been prefixed the word *awlād* (*awlād Fulān*, 'the sons of so-and-so'), while the other names are left unchanged. Given the close similarity of the 1145 *jarīda* of Aci Castello to that of Catania (***Dīwānī* 21**), there can be little doubt that it, too, was an exact copy of its original (***Dīwānī* 3**). There is, of course, no possibility whatsoever that the duplicate of a register first written in 1095 could give anything approaching an accurate account of the same population in 1145. All the male heads of household of 1095 appear in 1145 as the deceased fathers of an indeterminate number of children who had maintained every parental household. Not one new household has appeared, nor one old household disappeared. Women who were already 'widows' in 1095, some of whom were even then known as *al-ᶜAjūz*, 'the Old Woman', were still registered as heads of household fifty years later. In the *jarā'id* renewed in 1145, the *mutazawwij*-system was employed crazily, surreally, to 'update' the old registers. Of course, it did nothing of the kind. Instead of recording the demographic changes to the population listed in 1095, the renewals dwell in the past, amongst phantom communities of ghost-parents and their ghost-children. They were not *jarā'id al-rijāl*, registers of the living, but registers of the dead. The Arab scribes of the *dīwān* meticulously reproduced two huge registers, listing over a thousand names, and stretching over some six square metres of parchment; then, their Greek colleagues puzzled out and carefully added the interlinear transliteration for each name; when most, if not all of those named, were long dead.

It is not clear who was to blame: the *dīwān*, for insisting that the old *jarā'id* had to be renewed verbatim; or the recipients, for failing to keep their old registers up-to-date. In addition to the Latin list of the Sicilian villeins renewed in ***Dīwānī* 24**, at least two annotated Latin registers of Muslim villeins survive from the mid-12th century, and demonstrate that the churches of Cefalù, Mileto and Patti, at least, made some attempt to keep track of their Muslim villeins, by translating their *jarā'id* or *plateiai* into Latin, and by periodically updating the latter.[103] But I

[103] Cefalù: see above, p.62. Patti: Johns and Metcalfe forthcoming.

strongly suspect that it was beyond the means of most landlords to maintain a systematic written record of their servile populations.

If the renewals were of no use to their recipients, they served the interests of the royal *dīwān* in at least two ways. First, it is clear that Walter Forestal and the monks of Catania and, presumably, all of Roger's feudatories in Sicily, were compelled to have their *jarāʾid* renewed, whether or not the renewals were of any practical use to them. As was suggested at the beginning of this chapter, it is likely that they were required to pay heavily for this dubious privilege, and there can be little doubt that an important motive behind the renewals was the need of ready cash.

Second, the *dīwān* could have used the renewal of privileges as a means to ascertain, so far as was possible, that feudatories possessed only those lands and villeins to which they had legal right. The *shurūṭ*, which are a constant feature of this series, refer to the *jarāʾid* of the royal *dīwān*, some of which, according to ***Dīwānī* 21 and 22**, went back as far as 1093. There is no indication as to the completeness of the royal registers.[104] If, like the *jarāʾid* of the church of Catania and the Forestal, they were fifty years out of date, then the *dīwān* might have been attempting to define the royal possessions in 1145 by limiting feudatories to what they had held in 1095. If, on the other hand, and as is more likely,[105] the *dīwān* had kept the registers of royal villeins up-to-date, then its officers might have been seeking to regain for the royal demesne all fugitive villeins that had been usurped by the churches and barons. Whichever the case, it would not have mattered one bit to the *dīwān* that it confirmed *jarāʾid* which were long out of date, because the very process of renewal confined the recipients' claims to the villeins listed: all other villeins, by process of exclusion, must have belonged to the king. As we shall see in the next chapter, wherever possible upon royal lands, and especially for new grants of out of the royal demesne, the *dīwān* had already adopted the permanent system of registration of estate-boundaries or *ḥudūd*. The ephemeral *jarāʾid al-rijāl* were no longer widely employed by the monarchy for the registration of land, and, to the extent that they were maintained by the *dīwān*, they were primarily lists of tax-payers to the royal demesne, lists of the human resources without which *dīwānī* land was sterile.

104 It cannot be stated too strongly that Garufi 1928, p.67, was wholly mistaken in his assertion that, by 1144–5, the ancient *jarāʾid* had been 'entirely translated into Greek', and that the Arabic name-lists in the renewals of 1145 were 'translated [from Greek] into Arabic by Arab employees'. This extraordinary claim is, in part, the result of his mistaken belief that the royal *dīwān* held regular censuses of all the servile population of Sicily, and that it kept *jarāʾid* of all villeins, instead of just the villeins of the royal demesne. But more important is the fact that Garufi knew no Arabic, and was thus unable to make the crucial comparison of the Arabic and the Greek texts of these *jarāʾid* which would have immediately revealed to him that that the Greek names are transliterations, and occasionally translations, of Arabic originals.

105 Below, pp.144–5.

Conclusion

The proportion of the royal chancery's time and effort that was devoted to the *jarāʾid* within the recall of privileges of 1144–5 cannot now be measured. It appears that at least three months, January – March 1145, or most of the time between the great feasts of Christmas and Easter (15 April), were largely taken up by the *jarāʾid*, but at least four Greek privileges were also issued in March. The documents themselves, however, with their impressive size, elegant Arabic calligraphy, and careful organisation of columns of Arabic and Greek, proclaim that the greatest care was taken in their production. Had their recipients been able to judge, they might have consoled themselves that, although the renewals for which they had paid were of no practical use, they were at least beautiful. But the strong suspicion must be that any prestige emanating from these documents of power reflected on the royal *dīwān*, and not on their recipients.

At the beginning of this chapter, I stressed that the recall and renewals of 1144–5 did nothing to weaken, and may even have strengthened, the position of Greek as an administrative language. The role of Greek in the renewed *jarāʾid* is more ambiguous. On the one hand, that name-lists which had originally been written in Arabic alone, were now accompanied by a Greek transliteration, and confirmed by Roger's Greek signature, could indicate the advance of Greek. On the other, that Arabic replaced Greek as the language of the *narrationes*, *dispositiones*, and *shurūṭ*, clearly promoted it to the status of principal language in these bilingual documents. The Arab scribes of the *dīwān* rose to the occasion, and celebrated their victory with a bravura display of their craft: the refinement of indirect, impersonal reference to the ruler; the use of hyperbolic titles; the pious *adʿiya*; all in the polished *dīwānī* script which was the trade-mark of their high training and professionalism. Only now, more than fifty years after the conquest of Arab Sicily, and fifteen years after the foundation of the kingdom, did the royal *dīwān* begin to produce documents which, although still marred by the barbaric Greek signature of a Christian king, at least demonstrated that its scribes had been properly instructed in *adab al-kātib*, in the secretary's art as practised in an Islamic chancery.

CHAPTER 6

The records of the royal *dīwān*. Part I: the *jarāʾid al-rijāl*

The *jarāʾid al-rijāl*

None of the records used by the royal *dīwān* for the administration of Sicily have survived, and their very existence has to be inferred almost entirely from the few documents issued by the *dīwān* which are preserved in their original form. Most records, such as the accounts of income and expenditure, the registers of service owed by the barons and knights of the island, or the formularies used by scribes for composing documents, have disappeared practically without trace. Others, such as the *dafātir al-īṣāl al-dīwānīya*, the '*dīwānī* registers of receipt', are named but once (***Dīwānī* 35**). For only two sets of records does sufficient information survive to justify an attempt to reconstruct their coverage, format, and purpose. This chapter discusses the *jarāʾid al-rijāl*, or the registers of villeins on the royal demesne; the next is dedicated to the *dafātir al-ḥudūd*, or the registers of land boundaries.[1]

During the repartition of the lands and inhabitants of Sicily which took place immediately after the conquest was complete, the preferred method of redistribution was to grant the inhabitants with the lands to which they were bound, and to register their names in a *plateia* or *jarīda* – it was simpler and quicker to name the villeins than to describe their property. A large, but unknown, number of *plateiai* were compiled for Count Roger and for his barons at Mazara in 1093 (***Dīwānī* 1**). The stipulatory clauses, or *shurūṭ*, of the *jarāʾid* renewed in 1145 make repeated reference to 'the *jarāʾid* of the *dīwān al-maʿmūr*', and imply that they were the descendants of 'the *jarāʾid* which were written at Mazara'.[2] This is almost the only direct evidence, before the late 1170s, for what must have been one of the most important sets of records maintained by the royal *dīwān*; the registers of the villeins of the royal demesne. There is no firm evidence that the administration kept such registers up-to-date throughout the half century 1093–1145, but nor can it be proven that it did not. The assumption that it did is clearly a risky one, given the spectacular failure of feudal lords, such as the church of Catania, to maintain their *jarāʾid*.

[1] Only after this book was completed did Annliese Nef kindly send me her recent study of Muslim villeins in Norman Sicily (Nef 2000). Here, I have been able to do little more than refer to it, but I shall discuss fully some of the issues that it raises in Johns forthcoming d.

[2] Above, pp.120, 121.

Nor is it clear that the efficient collection of revenue from the villeins of the royal demesne necessarily depended upon their accurate registration. The Palermo *jarīda* of 1095 (***Dīwānī* 2**) implies that the land-tax and the *jizya* could be assessed collectively upon entire communities. So long as the communal leaders regularly paid to the king's bailiff the full sum due from their community at the half-yearly payment days, this steady income might, perhaps, have satisfied a *laissez-faire* administration in the short term, and discouraged it from conducting censuses and individually registering its villeins.

My own suspicion is that, in 1145, the *dīwān*'s registers were probably far more complete and up-to-date than the *jarāʾid* of most feudatories. Nonetheless, I also suspect that that they were far from perfect. One indication that this was so is the switch from *jarāʾid al-rijāl* to *dafātir al-ḥudūd* – from maintaining registers of villeins, to compiling registers of land-boundaries – as the primary tool for keeping track of land-holding; a change which began soon after the renewals of 1145, and which will be discussed in the next chapter. But, even if registers of villeins ceased to be important as records of land-holding, and were replaced by boundary-registers, after – say – the death of Roger II, their importance for the internal administration of the royal demesne, as records of population, may well have increased with time. There is ample evidence that, in addition to normal biological change, the villein population of Sicily was affected by both immigration and emigration, on a large scale. In order to understand this, and to prepare for an examination of the *jarāʾid al-rijāl* compiled by the royal *dīwān* for Santa Maria di Monreale in 1178 and 1183 (***Dīwānī* 43 and 45**), a brief introduction to the Muslim villeins of Norman Sicily is next required.

The Muslim villeins of Norman Sicily

In Chapter 2, we saw how, in the late 1170s, three brothers, all members of the same household, appeared before the Abbot Donatus of San Giovanni degli Eremiti in Palermo, and acknowledged that they and their ancestors were *rijāl al-jarāʾid*, 'men of the registers', on the abbey's estate of Manzil Yūsuf, modern Mezzoiuso, some 20km south-east of Palermo (**Private 16**). They had left the estate, and gone to live elsewhere, without obtaining the permission of their lord. Therefore, the abbot had seized their property, and constrained them to return. The brothers now swore upon the *Qurʾān* that they would henceforth obey their lord, and so he pardoned them, and returned their property to them. He imposed upon them a *jizya* of thirty *tarì*, and a land-tax (*qānūn*) of twenty *modii* of wheat and ten of barley.[3] The brothers asked the

[3] *Qānūn* is a loanword into Arabic from Greek *kanōn*, which had already come to mean 'assessment for taxation' or 'taxes' before the Islamic conquest of Egypt and Syria: Liddell and Scott 1940, p.875, col.b, (6). Very soon after the conquest, *qānūn al-kharāj* already meant both the registers and lists recording the land-taxes, and the cadastral survey on the basis of which the land-tax was assessed: Linant de Bellefonds, Cahen, and İnalcik 1975, pp.556–62. Here, by ellipsis, *qānūn* has apparently become the land-tax paid by those registered in what had once been called the *qānūn al-kharāj*.

abbot if they might dwell wherever they wished, and he seems to have consented to refer their request to his chapter, but the outcome is unknown. A record of their agreement was written in Arabic, and witnessed by a maternal uncle of the brothers, who bears the *nisba* al-Laḥmī (or possibly al-Lakhmī), by one witness from Qays, and by two from Quraysh – all venerable Arab tribes.

This contract shows a Christian abbot in the process of reconfirming the terms of service owed by a family of Muslim *rijāl al-jarāʾid*, after they had fled from his abbey's lands, and then returned. The family appears to have taken pride in tracing its ancestry back to the ancient tribes of early Arabia. The fact that the brothers sought permission to live elsewhere, suggests that they had other means of support than the lands which they held of the abbey, and that they were far from spending their lives in ceaseless agricultural toil: presumably, they employed labourers to work their lands, which seem to have been extensive.[4] And yet, the brothers were tied to the lands of a Christian monastery and had been forced to return to them by the confiscation of their goods. Although they did not owe labour service on the abbot's demesne, they did pay the *jizya* and a land-tax. But, at the same time, the Benedictine abbot drew up a contract with his villeins in Arabic, according to an approximation of Islamic legal forms, and permitted his villeins to swear their fealty to him upon the *Qurʾān*.

There is no indication that either the status of the three brothers from Manzil Yūsuf, or the services that they owed, was in any way exceptional. Indeed, the *jizya* and land-tax that they had to pay are directly comparable to the services imposed upon the Muslim villeins of the church of Palermo in the *jarīda* of 1095 (***Dīwānī* 2**), where the seventy-five households assessed at the full rate were to pay collectively seven hundred and fifty *tarì* twice a year as tribute (δόμα, *doma*), and one hundred and fifty *modii* of wheat and the same of barley, equivalent to an average annual service per household of twenty *tarì*, and twenty *modii* of wheat and the same amount of barley. It therefore seems probable that the service owed by the three brothers was more or less typical of that owed by Muslim *rijāl al-jarāʾid* of western Sicily.[5]

We have already seen that the *rijāl al-jarāʾid* were divided into those who paid full service, and those who were fully or partly exempted. The latter included both categories whose productive capacity was impaired, such as widows and blind-men, and households newly formed by marriage out of the parental household (νεόγαμοι,

[4] The total arable holding of the three brothers may be calculated to have been as great as 114 or 171 hectares (281 or 422 acres) – a large estate by any standards: see Johns forthcoming b.

[5] See also Nef 2000, pp.592–3. If so, of course, they were far from being 'villeins' in the sense in which the term is used of the most servile classes of villein in contemporary north-western Europe (see Noth 1983, p.221). And yet, in Sicily, in Latin and Greek documents, they *are* called *villani*, βελλᾶνοι (*bellanoi*), *servi glebae*, πάροικοι (*paroikoi*), *nativi*, ἐντόποι (*entopoi*), *etc.* This is not the place for a comparative study of villeinage in Norman Sicily and – say – the Anglo-Norman world (see Johns forthcoming d), but the argument that the *villani Saraceni* of Sicily were not 'villeins' because they were different from the *villani* of Domesday Book can clearly not be sustained. In Norman Sicily, the English question *utrum sit villanus necne* cannot be meaningfully asked of the Sicilian villein, whom all the sources call *villanus*.

neogamoi; *mutazawwijūn*), who were granted a honeymoon period which allowed them to establish their new household and their new lands.

Another group of villeins, *al-muls*, first appear in contraposition to the *rijāl al-jarāʾid* in the *jarīda* renewed for San Giorgio di Triocala in November 1141 (***Dīwānī* 18**).[6] After the lists of the *rijāl al-jarāʾid* of Triocala and Raḥl al-Baṣal comes a third list of the names of the *muls*. *Muls* is the plural of *amlas*, meaning 'smooth', 'soft', 'sleek', etcetera: 'a soft robe' is *thawb amlas*, 'a smooth wine', *khamr malsāʾ*, and an *amlas* is a sleek camel whose skin is free of mange. In the Sicilian documents, however, the word is always used in the plural, even in such a case as this, where a singular might be used.[7]

The *muls* appear in antithesis to the *ḥursh* in the two Chùrchuro documents of 1149 and 1154 (***Dīwānī* 29 and 33**).[8] Of the five households of Muslim *rijāl* granted to Chùrchuro, two are *ḥursh*, and three are *muls*. The word *ḥursh* is the plural of the adjectival form *aḥrash*, meaning 'rough', 'harsh', or 'coarse': an *aḥrash* is a camel with mange; a newly-minted dinar, with its edges still rough from the die, is *aḥrash*; a lizard or a snake with rough, coarse skin, is *ḍabb aḥrash* or *ḥayya ḥarshāʾ*. As with *muls*, only the plural form *ḥursh* is used for the Muslim villeins of Norman Sicily. The two terms clearly form a pair of contrasted opposites, the *ḥursh* and the *muls*, the 'rough' and the 'smooth'. Neither term, to the best of my knowledge, is employed in this sense anywhere in the Arabic-speaking world, except Sicily.

In the Triocala *jarīda* (***Dīwānī* 18**), all but one of the fifteen *muls* bore *nisba*s which indicate that they came from North Africa: six bore the *nisba* al-Ifrīqī, 'the (North) African'; two came from Sfax, and two from Tripoli; one each from Gabès, Tunis, and Qalānus; and one from the Berber tribe of Zuwāwa; the odd man out was known only by his personal name, Hilāl. This North African emphasis is in complete contrast to the *rijāl al-jarāʾid* of Triocala and Raḥl al-Baṣal, less than 10% of whom bore North African *nisba*s. The earliest appearance of the *muls* thus raises the strong suspicion that they were new immigrants to the lands upon which they were registered; in this case, immigrants from North Africa.

This supposition is supported by an Arabic-Greek privilege of July (*sic*) 1169,[9] in which the young king William II and his mother, the regent Margaret, grant the estate (*raḥl*) known as ᶜAyn al-Liyān near Termini Imerese,[10] and fourteen households of villeins to the new hospital in Khandaq al-Qayrūz (***Dīwānī* 38**). Of these fourteen, six are *mina l-rijāli l-ḥurshi*, 'of the rough men'; while the remaining

[6] For a different treatment of the *muls*, see Nef 2000, pp.600–2.

[7] The total at the end of the list reads *al-jumla khamsata ᶜashara rajulan mulsun* and not *al-jumla khamsata ᶜashara rajulan amlasa* (I am not inclined to read a non-standard use of the singular adjective *malis*, *i.e.* … *rajulan malisan*).

[8] Nef 2000, p.588 and *passim*, mistakenly refers to this category as *al-ḫurš*, *i.e. al-khursh* with an initial *khāʾ*.

[9] For the month, see Johns 2001.

[10] A Greek note at the head of the document begins: τὸ κατόνομα τῶν ἀνθρώπων τοῦ χωρίου ἀϊν λιαν τῶν δόθεντῶν εἰς τὸ σπιταλον τοῦ Κάμπο Γράσσου. Similarly, a Latin note names the casale as Ayn Lyen and locates the hospital at Campograsso in the district of Termini, presumably near Altavilla Milicia, 14km north-west of Termini, where there was the Greek monastery of Santa Maria di Campograsso, with which the hospital is perhaps identical (see Cusa 1868–82, no.46, pp.13–15). For the place-name ᶜAyn al-Liyān, see Caracausi 1993, vol.I, p.154, *s.v. Billiemi*.

eight are *mina l-rijāli l-ghurabāʾi wa-l-mulsi l-sākinīna bi-l-raḥli l-madhkūri*, 'of the strangers and the smooth men dwelling on the aforesaid estate'. The *ghurabāʾ* or 'strangers' are the Sicilian equivalents of the Egyptian *ṭāriyyūn*, newcomers to a village who, like the *mutazawwijūn*, were given an introductory tax-exemption as an incentive to settle down and form new households.[11] Their pairing with the *muls* in ***Dīwānī* 38** tends to confirm the hypothesis suggested by the North African *muls* in the Triocala *jarīda* (***Dīwānī* 18**) – that the *muls* were immigrants, newly commended to the estate upon which they were registered.

The *muls* also appear in the Arabic-Greek *jarīda* compiled for Santa Maria di Monreale in April 1183 (***Dīwānī* 45**; see below, pp.165–9). This *jarīda* mentions three categories of Muslim villeins: the *rijāl al-jarāʾid* and the *muls*, whom we have already encountered, and the *rijāl al-maḥallāt*.[12] *Al-maḥallāt* is the plural of the noun *maḥalla* meaning a 'stopping place', or 'encampment' and, thence, almost any kind of human settlement. The Arabic term means, literally, 'the men of the settlements'. Although the Greek text of this *jarīda* usually renders the Arabic *rijāl al-maḥallāt* with the less than helpful οἱ ἄνθρώποι μαχαλλὲτ (*oi anthrōpoi machallet*, 'the men [of the?] *maḥallāt*'), the term is occasionally translated as οἱ ἐντόποι or οἱ ἐντωπέοι (*oi entopoi* or *entōpeoi*) literally 'the natives' or 'those of the place'.[13] This term is used in Greek documents of the Norman period, from 1120 if not earlier, with the specific meaning of villeins who were tied to the lands upon which they were born by bonds of hereditary service.[14] In ***Dīwānī* 45**, therefore, the indigenous, native *rijāl al-maḥallāt* are distinguished from the newcomers or *muls*. A contemporary Latin note on the *verso* of the 1145 Catania renewal (***Dīwānī* 21**), implies precisely the same distinction between *elgurab [et] elmukallat* – that is, between *al-ghurabāʾ* or 'the strangers' and *[rijāl] al-maḥallāt* or '[the men of] the settlements', between the newcomers and the natives.[15]

The Arabic introduction to ***Dīwānī* 45**, however, clearly distinguishes between the *rijāl al-jarāʾid* or 'men of the registers' and the *rijāl al-maḥallāt* or 'men of the settlements'.[16] And yet, not only were both groups tied to the land in hereditary service, but, if the 1178 Monreale register of *rijāl al-jarāʾid* (***Dīwānī* 43**) is compared to that of 1183 (***Dīwānī* 45**), it would seem that any one estate had either *rijāl al-maḥallāt* or *rijāl al-jarāʾid*, but never both together.[17] It is tempting to suggest that the distinction between the two groups may therefore reflect the differing terms of the *dhimma* or 'protection' imposed by the Normans at the time of the conquest, and that the *rijāl al-jarāʾid* were the descendants of individuals who had agreed to pay the *jizya* and other services upon each household, while the *rijāl al-maḥallāt* belonged to communities which had agreed to pay their tribute and taxes collectively.[18]

[11] See above, p.18, note 34.
[12] This category is also discussed by Nef 2000, pp.602–4.
[13] ***Dīwānī* 45**, lines 83, 250, 256: Cusa 1868–82, pp.255, 276, 277.
[14] Caracausi 1990, p.196. [15] See above, p.119, note 20.
[16] See below, line 2 on p.166 and note 44.
[17] Below, pp.167. [18] See above, p.26 and note 76.

The Greek text of ***Dīwānī* 45**, however, offers a different, and perhaps more revealing, perspective upon the problem. The terms employed to translate *rijāl al-maḥallāt* (οἱ ἐντόποι, *oi entopoi*, 'the natives') and *rijāl al-muls* (οἱ ἐξώγραφοι, *oi exōgrafoi*, 'the not-registered') are both technical terms that ultimately derive from East Roman law. This suggests that the distinction between the *rijāl al-maḥallāt* and the *rijāl al-jarāʾid* may, similarly, derive from the East Roman distinction between *coloni originales* and *coloni adscriptitii*.[19] In which case, the *rijāl al-maḥallāt*, would be equivalent to the East Roman *originales*, the descendants of those villeins whom the Normans had found upon the land, and the *rijāl al-jarāʾid* would correspond to the *adscriptitii*, those villeins who were registered as belonging to the land, while the *muls* (and the *ghurabāʾ*) were previously unregistered 'strangers' whom the Normans had commended into service, settled on the land, and registered for the first time. Presumably, in due course, once they were well established, the *muls* became *rijāl al-jarāʾid*. In Norman Sicily, it would seem, as in the later East Roman Empire, these different terms reflected the various ways in which villeins had come to be tied to the land, but did not correspond to any significant variation in terms of service.

***Dīwānī* 45** thus provides us with the link between the Arabic terms for villeins, which have until now have seemed to be isolated in a tradition derived exclusively from Islamic law and practice, and two Graeco-Latin traditions: that of Roman Law, and that of feudal custom.

Turning first to Roman Law, the laws of Norman Sicily, first drawn up by Roger II, then extended by his son and grandson, and finally codified in Latin and Greek versions by Frederick II at Melfi in 1231, recognised essentially two categories of villeinage.[20] These categories, and the terms for them, were ultimately derived from Roman Law. On the one hand were villeins who owed service upon their own persons; this service was hereditable and was passed from one generation to another. On the other hand were villeins who owed service voluntarily because they held a fief or another benefit upon which service was due. This distinction is most clearly expressed in a law of William II concerning villeins who sought to become clerics (not a law, of course, which can often have applied to Muslim villeins):

> About those who enter the clerical order (King William).
>
> We correct by a generous interpretation the errors of those who say that certain villeins have been forbidden by royal constitution to enter the clergy. We order that it should be made known that the only villeins forbidden to become clerics are those *who are held to personal service, i.e. with respect to their own persons, like the registered, the serfs of the land, and others of that kind. But if any who owe service by reason of a holding or a benefice* desire to become clerics, they may do so even without the permission of their lords, after they have given up what they held from their lords into their hands.[21]

[19] See Jones 1964, vol.II, pp.799–803. I am grateful to Patrick Wormald, of Wolfson College, Oxford, for this most helpful suggestion.

[20] For a fuller discussion of the legal context, see Nef 2000, pp.582–6.

[21] Conrad, von der Lieck-Buyken and Wagner 1973, III.ii–iii, pp.248–50: … *qui personaliter, intuitu personae suae scilicet, servire tenentur, sicut sunt adscriptitii* [Greek οἱ ἐναπόγραφοι] *et servi glebae et huiusmodi alii. Qui vero respectu tenimenti vel alicuius beneficii servire tenentur* … ; von der Lieck-Buyken 1978, II.lii–liii, pp.102–3; Powell 1971, III.iii (53), p.106. See also Dilcher 1975, pp.563–7.

In law, according to this distinction, the difference should have been that the *rijāl al-jarāʾid*, the *rijāl al-maḥallāt*, and the *ḥursh* all owed hereditable service upon their own persons, and were tied to the land upon which they were registered, while the *ghurabāʾ* and the *muls* owed service voluntarily, and only by reason of the land which they freely held of their lord. All the indications are that this nice legal distinction can have meant very little in practice for the Muslim villeins of Norman Sicily. The Monreale *jarīda* of 1183 (***Dīwānī* 45**), for example, not only registered 569 households of villeins who are explicitly described as 'unregistered' (*al-muls*, οἱ ἐξώγραφοι, *oi exōgrafoi*, 'the not-registered'), and thereby effectively bound them to the lands upon which they were registered, but also refers to a general decree recalling all unregistered villeins back to the lands to which they were effectively tied. Moreover, if the *jizya* owed by Muslim villeins constituted part of their service, then they all owed at least this upon their own persons, as it were upon their own souls. Thus, Muslim *muls* and *ghurabāʾ* could be granted, with their families and possessions, together with the land upon which they were registered, just as if they owed hereditable service upon their own persons.

In fact, of course, the rights at law of the Muslims of Norman Sicily, villeins or not, depended entirely upon the ability and the will of the king to protect them. Even in times of civil peace, away from the royal lands and cities, Muslims were exposed to arbitrary acts of oppression by Latin lords and settlers who recognised no law. In times of civil disturbance, such as the rebellion against William I in 1160–2, and especially during the long period of civil war and disorder that followed the collapse of the Norman dynasty in 1189, in the absence of all protecting royal power, Muslims were driven from their lands, transported, enslaved, and massacred in great numbers. It would therefore be quite wrong to conclude that the legal distinction between service owed upon his own person and service owed by reason of his holding was of any great import to the Muslim villein. At the same time, the fact that the royal *dīwān* applied Greek technical terms, with more or less precise legal meanings, to Muslim villeins, reveals its concern somehow to squeeze them into the legal system, even though they patently did not fit.[22]

A similar concern may well account for the terms *ḥursh* and *muls*. We have already seen that, as Arabic terms for villeins, they are unique to Norman Sicily, and do not occur elsewhere in the Islamic world. In feudal Europe, however, the Latin terms *rusticus* and *glaber* are widespread, and mean precisely 'rough' and 'smooth'. I know of no evidence that they correspond to the Roman Law distinction between service owed on the person and by reason of a holding, but they are frequently employed as an antithetical pair in exactly the same way as *ḥursh* and *muls*, and often with the clear implication that the *rustici* had a rougher time of it than did the soft-living *glabri*. The Latin term *rusticus* – but not, to the best of my knowledge, *glaber* – occurs frequently in the Norman kingdom, more often on the

[22] Note that Arabs, and not just Latins and Greeks, could, and did, possess villeins – see, for example, the *rijāl al-jarāʾid* held by the *qāʾid* Yūsuf ibn Jabr, in ***Dīwānī* 43**, below Table 6.2, 3.A.c. But was Yūsuf a Christian or a Muslim?

mainland than on the island, but never as the precise equivalent of Arabic *ḥursh*. Nonetheless, although it cannot be proven, it seems to me highly probable that the Arabic terms *ḥursh* and *muls* were coined by officials of the royal *dīwān* as a calque of the Latin feudal terms *rusticus* and *glaber*, in much the same way that they also employed the Greek terms *enapografoi*, *exōgrafoi*, *entopoi*, *etcetera*.[23]

Table 6.1 Summary of the principal terms used for Muslim villeins in Norman Sicily

Registered	Unregistered
• *ahl* or *rijāl* (*iḍāfa* or preposition) *al-raḥl al-fulānī*, 'the people' or 'the men of such-and-such an estate'	
• *rijāl al-maḥallāt*, 'the men of the settlements'	• *al-ghurabāʾ*, 'the strangers'
• οἱ ἐντόποι (*oi entopoi*), 'the indigenes'	• οἱ ξένοι (*oi xenoi*), 'the strangers'
• *nativi*, 'indigenes'; *servi glebae*, 'serfs of the land'	• *advenae*, 'newcomers'; hospites, 'guests'
• *rijāl al-jarāʾid*, 'the men of the registers'	
• οἱ ἐναπόγραφοι (*oi enapografoi*), 'the registered'	• οἱ ἐξώγραφοι (*oi exōgrafoi*), 'the unregistered'
• *adscriptitii*, 'the registered'	• *inscriptitii*, 'the unregistered'
• *al-ḥursh*, *al-rijāl al-ḥursh*, 'the rough', 'the rough men'	• *al-muls, al-rijāl al-muls*, 'the smooth', 'the smooth men'
• *rustici*, 'rough'	• [*glabri*, 'smooth']
• *qui personaliter, intuitu personae suae scilicet, servire tenentur* 'those who are held to personal service, *i.e.* with respect to their own persons'	• *qui ... respectu tenimenti vel alicuius beneficii servire tenentur* 'those who … owe service by reason of a holding or other benefice'

The foundation and endowment of Santa Maria di Monreale

The Benedictine abbey of Santa Maria Nuova, overlooking Palermo from the slopes of the Conca d'Oro, 7km south-west of the city, was founded sometime before the

[23] Nef 2000, p.588, n.52, does not agree.

end of 1174.[24] But it was not until the feast of the Assumption of the Virgin in the year 1176 that King William II endowed his new foundation with much of its vast territory in the Val di Mazara. At the same time, the abbey acquired its first holdings in eastern Sicily and on the mainland, but these need not here concern us.

The greater part of Monreale's Sicilian territory was received from the royal demesne *en masse* in August 1176 – the *castella* of Iato, Corleone, and Calatrasi, with all their tenements and appurtenances, whether from the royal demesne or feudal land. The abbey was to hold the ex-royal land freely, but the king retained the service owed by the few remaining barons under Monreale's lordship, and the abbot was made responsible for ensuring that it was delivered. The fief of any baron who died without heir was to pass to the abbey. No taxes or services of any kind were to be exacted from the abbey, nor from its men, animals, and possessions, except only that, when the king or his heir should visit the abbey, he would receive food and wine as if he were one of the monks. The abbot was made justiciar, with authority *de personis et bonis*, throughout all the abbey's lands, present and future.[25] In 1178, again on the feast of the Assumption, William added all the lands and villeins of the late Godfrey of Battellaro, including the *castellum* of Battellaro, and – perhaps – the *casale* of Bisacquino.[26] In 1184–5, the estates of Rendicella, Juliana, Comicchi, Adragnum, Lachabuca, and Senure, all *casali* of the royal demesne, completed the royal gift.[27] Together, these territories made up a massive empire stretching unbroken over more than 1,200km^2 in the Val di Mazara.[28]

The gift of lands was followed by the issue of three massive bilingual *jarā᾿id* compiled from the records of the royal *dīwān*: in May 1178, a *jarīda* of the villeins of the *castella* of Corleone and Calatrasi (***Dīwānī* 43**); a second *jarīda* of villeins, issued in April 1183, listing the *rijāl al-maḥallāt* and the *rijāl al-muls* (***Dīwānī* 45**); and, third, the great Arabic-Latin estate roll, or *jarīdat al-ḥudūd*, of May 1182, listing the boundaries of Iato, Corleone, Battellaro, and Calatrasi (***Dīwānī* 44**), which will be discussed in the next chapter.

[24] Garufi 1902, nos 9–10, pp.7–8; White 1938, p.133, n.3.

[25] Garufi 1902, no.15, pp.10–11; Pirri 1733, vol.I, cols 453–5.

[26] Garufi 1902, no.24, p.16. Bisacquino is not mentioned by name, but was confirmed as belonging to Monreale by Lucius III in February 1183: Garufi 1902, no.41, pp.23–4. Bisacquino had once been held by Robert Malconvenant, and should have reverted to the crown on his death, but was retained illegally by his daughter, Maria, and her husband, Robert of Tarsia. In May 1183, they renounced all claim to Bisacquino in favour of Monreale. See also White 1938, p.143.

[27] Garufi 1902, nos 50 and 53, pp.27–9. Rendicella (unidentified, but presumably near other estates in this group); Juliana (mod. Giuliana, PA); Comicchi (unidentified, but between Sambuca di Sicilia and Caltabellotta, AG; see Bresc 1986, p.64); Adragnum (Monte Adranone, AG, north of Sambuca); Lachabuca (probably mod. Sambuca di Sicilia, AG); Senure (mod. Senore, PA, north of Sambuca). The donation dated March 1184, granting Terrusium (Ṭurrus; mod. Contrada Terrosa, PA, south-east of Sambuca), Fantasini (Faṭṭāsina; probably Cozzo Moli, PA, west of Campofiorito) – for both, see Nania 1995, pp.154–5 – and S. Maria Maddalena di Corleone (Garufi 1902, no.51, p.28), has been shown to be a early 14th-century forgery (Kehr 1902, pp.313–15): nonetheless, all three did belong to Monreale.

[28] For the Monreale lands, see: Di Giovanni 1892; La Corte 1902; White 1938, pp.132–45; D'Angelo 1973; Bercher, Courteaux and Mouton 1979; Johns 1983, vol.I, 186–230; Johns 1985; Johns 1988; Lima 1991, pp.61–70; Nania 1995; Bover Fonts 1996; Maurici 1998; D'Angelo 2001 (forthcoming).

The Monreale jarīda of 1178 (*Dīwānī* 43)

What follows is by no means a definitive and exhaustive analysis of this long and complex document; that must await the new critical edition of the text being prepared for *The Monreale Survey*. Instead, this section, and the next, concentrates upon what the Monreale *jarīdas* of villeins can tell us about the records of the royal *dīwān* from which it was drawn.

To begin with its external features, it is a long roll of six sheets of parchment sewn end-to-end with thin strips of parchment in a simple running stitch, to give a total length of 3.72m. The six sheets are of standard size, roughly 60cm–70cm square. At three of the seams, between sheets 1–2, 4–5, and 5–6, the text has been written across the seam on the *recto*. Between sheets 2–3 and 3–4, however, the seam falls conveniently between the end of one section and the beginning of the next, and there the text is not run across the join. On the *verso*, the seams are 'sealed' by signature of Eberardus, the same official who signs at the foot of the document, in order to prohibit the unauthorised addition of extra sheets.[29] In all but one of the name-lists (3.C.b), the names are written in Arabic with interlinear Greek transliteration. Rubrics and totals are normally given at the head and foot respectively of each name-list, in Arabic with Greek transliteration. At the foot of the document are the plica and regular holes for the lead seal, which was apparently that which is now loosely attached with a piece of modern string in place of the original silk tie.[30]

No accurate edition or translation of the introduction has yet been published, and so I quote it in full – the organisation of the whole *jarīda* is summarised in Table 6.2:

> (*Greek*) The name-list of the men of the registers of Corleone and Calatrasi written in the month of May, Indiction XI, /[2] of the year 6686 [A.M.].
>
> (*Arabic*) /[3] When it was of the date of the month of May, of the 11th [Indiction], and of the year of the world 6686 [A.M.], corresponding to the Arab date 573 [A.H. = 1178 A.D.], there went forth the order of the high presence, the most high, the ruling, the most royal, the glorified, the most holy, the Williamian, the powerful through God, the assisted by His omnipotence, the desirous of victory through His strength, the ruler of Italy, Langobardia, Calabria, and Sicily, /[4] the defender of the pope of Rome, the protector of the Christian community (may God perpetuate its days, and assist its standards, and fulfil its ordinances!), to write this *jarīda* containing the account of what was granted by it to the great holy monastery of Santa Maria. [The presence] (may God may prolong its rule!) granted to [the monastery] Corleone and Calatrasi, with all their lands, and their boundaries to their last extremities, and all their rights to /[5] their furthest extents, and everything which belongs to them, pertains to them, appertains to them, and is known [to belong] to them, and with all their men, [as] a perpetual grant, and an inalienable gift. [The presence's] to-be-obeyed order went forth (may God increase its efficacy!) to the lords of the royal *dīwān* of verification[31] to reveal [who were] the aforesaid men, and to extract them from the registers of the *dīwān al-maʿmūr* and from the old *jarāʾid*, and

[29] Eberardus also signs the 1182 *jarīdat al-ḥudūd* (***Dīwānī* 44**).
[30] Engel 1882, p.87, no.20, pl.1.16. [31] Below, pp.193–203.

Table 6.2 The organisation of the 1178 Monreale *jarīda* (*Dīwānī* 43)

Section No.	Description or Rubric	Lines	Cusa pp.
	INTRODUCTION		
1	***Greek introduction (see above, p.153)***	***1–2***	***134***
2	***Arabic introduction (see above, pp. 153, 156)***	***3–6***	***134–5***
	NAME-LISTS		
3	***Corleone District: the* jarīda *of the population of the district of Corleone, comprising 8 subsections and 23 parts. Total: 778 names.***	***6–180***	***135–64***
3.A	***Corleone town: the population of the town of Corleone, comprising 2 parts. Total: 345 names.***	***6–76***	***135–42***
3.A.a	The men of Corleone. Rubric: 'And they are from Corleone' (*wa-hum min Qurlūn*). Total: 251 names.	6–52	135–42
3.A.b	Rubric: 'The men of Roger' (*rijāl rujayr*; the Greek scribe mistranslates Χωρίον ῾Ρογέριου, *Chōrion Rogeriou*, 'the estate of Roger'). Total: 9 names.	51–4	143
3.A.c	The men of Yūsuf ibn Jabr. These men are not named, but are referred to in the following sub-section total: *i.e.* 'The total, including the four men who belong to the *qāʾid* Yūsuf ibn Jabr, is 259 men according to the commentary of the *jarīda* from which this *jarīda* was copied'.	53–4	143
3.A.d	The men of Bū Simāj. Rubric: 'And these are the names of the men of Bū Simāj, according to the commentary of the aforesaid *jarīda*'. Total: 4 names.	53–6	143
3.A.e	The *mutazawwijūn* of Corleone. Rubric: 'The children of the people of Corleone and their brothers'. Total: 24 names.	57–64	144
3.A.f	The Christians of Corleone. Rubric: 'The names of the Christians of Corleone'. Total: 47 names.	63–72	145–6
3.A.g	The *mutazawwijūn* of the Christians of Corleone. Rubric: 'The names of the *mutazawwijūn* amongst the children of the Christians and their brothers'. Total: 6 names.	73–6	146–7
3.B	***Jāliṣū with Rāya: the population of Jāliṣū with Rāya. Total: 92 names.***	***77–111***	***147–51***
3.B.a	The men of Jāliṣū with Rāya. Rubric: 'The names of the people of Jāliṣū, and amongst them the people of Rāya'. Total: 62 names.	77–90	147–9
3.B.b	Rubric: 'The names of the men of al-Ṭanābirī'. Total: 3 names.	91–4	149
3.B.c	Rubric: 'The names of the men who once belonged to Richard'. Total: 8 names.	93–4	150
3.B.d	The *mutazawwijūn* of [Jāliṣū with?] Rāya. Rubric: 'The names of the *mutazawwijūn* amongst the children of the men and their brothers at Rāya' (*asmāʾu l-mutazawwijīna min awlādi l-rijāli wa-ikhwati-him bi-rāyata*; the Greek scribe misreads the place-name as Βουρλιέ (*Bourlie*), and Cusa follows by misreading the Arabic برلية). Total: 19 names.	95–102	150–1

Section No.	Description or Rubric	Lines	Cusa pp.
3.C	***Qaṣṭana: the population of Qaṣṭana. Total: 20 names.***	***103–11***	***151–2***
3.C.a	The men of Qaṣṭana. Rubric: 'The names of the people of Qaṣṭana'. Total: 15 names.	103–8	151–2
3.C.b	The *mutazawwijūn* of Qaṣṭana (without interlinear Greek transliteration). Rubric: 'The names of the *mutazawwijūn* amongst the children and brothers of Qaṣṭana'. Total: 5 names.	109–11	152
3.D	***Sūq al-Mirʾāh: the population of Sūq al-Mirʾāh. Total 65 names.***	***112–34***	***152–5***
3.D.a	The men of Sūq al-Mirʾāh. Rubric: 'The names of the people of Sūq al-Mirʾāh'. Total: 34 names.	112–20	152–3
3.D.b	A list of five names, without rubric, separate from 3.D.a and 3.D.c, and followed by the note 'The total is 39 men' (*i.e.* the 34 names of 3.D.a plus the 5 names of 3.D.b = 39 names).	119–22	154
3.D.c	The *mutazawwijūn* of Sūq al-Mirʾāh. Rubric: 'And amongst the *mutazawwijūn* from their children and brothers'. Total: 4 names.	123–6	154
3.D.d	Then men from Qaṣṭana registered at Sūq al-Mirʾāh. Rubric: 'And amongst them from Sūq al-Mirʾāh'. Total: 22 names.	127–34	154–5
3.E	***Bū Kināna: the population of Bū Kināna. Total: 88 names.***	***133–50***	***155–8***
3.E.a	The men of Bū Kināna. Rubric: 'The names of the people of Bū Kināna'. Total: 69 names.	133–46	155–7
3.E.b	The *mutazawwijūn* of Bū Kināna. Rubric: 'And amongst the *mutazawwijūn* from their children and brothers'. Total: 19 names.	145–50	158
3.F	***Qabiyāna: the population of Qabiyāna. Total: 78 names.***	***151–66***	***159–61***
3.F.a	The men of Qabiyāna. Rubric: 'The names of the people of Qabiyāna'. Total: 73 names.	151–64	159–61
3.F.b	The *mutazawwijūn* of Qabiyāna. Rubric: 'And amongst the *mutazawwijūn* from their children and brothers'. Total: 5 names.	163–6	161
3.G.	***The aribbāʾ of Corleone. No rubric.***	***167–70***	***162***
3.H.	***A list without rubric, possibly of the population of Maghanūja (see below, p.162). Total: 70 names.***	***171–80***	***162–4***
4	***Calatrasi: the population of the ex-barony of Calatrasi, subdivided into 2 subsections. Total 424 names.***	***181–252***	***165–79***
4.a	The men of Calatrasi. Rubric: 'The names of the people of Calatrasi'. Total: 372 names.	181–240	165–76
4.b	The *mutazawwijūn* of Calatrasi. Rubric: 'The names of the *mutazawwijūn* amongst the children and the brothers at Calatrasi'. Total: 52 names.	241–52	177–9
5–6	***END MATTER***	**251–3**	**179**
5.	***Total of parchments***: 'And the total number of parchment sheets in this *jarīda* is six'.	***251–2***	***179***
6.	***Signature.*** †Eberardus	***253***	***179***

> to write /[6] [this new] *jarīda* of their names. This *jarīda* comprises the setting-out of their names, and includes the whole total of them all.[32]

Before proceeding to discuss the organisation of the register, a brief description of the method of analysis employed is required. The name-list consists of 247 lines of 11 to 14 columns each, written across the page from right to left. Beginning with the first name (line 7, col.1) and ending with the last (line 250, col.13), each name was assigned a progressive number from 0001 to 1202. Every name was then broken down into its constituent parts, and each part was entered as a separate record, together with the progressive number of the name, the subsection or part of the *jarīda* to which it belonged, and various other palaeographical, philological, and prosopographical data. Thus, in the following simplified example, three records were completed for the name Abū Bakr ibn Abī l-Ḥasan ibn al-Janaṭū.

Table 6.3 Example of records from *Dīwānī* 43

Name or name element	Part no.	Prog. no.
1. Abū Bakr ibn Abī l-Ḥasan ibn al-Janāṭū	3.E.b, lines 147–48, col.10	596
2. Abū l-Ḥasan ibn al-Janāṭū, Abū Bakr ibn	3.E.b, lines 147–48, col.10	596
3. al-Janāṭū, Abū Bakr ibn Abī l-Ḥasan ibn	3.E.b, lines 147–48, col.10	596

The records were then searched in a variety of ways to see if patterns emerged. For example, an alphabetical search was carried out to discover whether an individual had relatives listed elsewhere in the register. In this case, Abū l-Ḥasan ibn al-Janaṭū, Abū Bakr's father, was found to be registered in section 3.E.a. Such relationships may be obscured by Cusa's edition, which does not reproduce the lines and columns of the original. Almost fortuitously, these searches revealed

32 † Τὸ κατόνομα τῶν ἀν(θρ)ώ(π)ων τ(ῆ)ς πλατεί(ας) Κουρουλλού(νη) (καὶ) Καλατατράζη ἡ γραφῆσ(α) μ(ην)ὶ Μάϊ(ω) τ(ῆς) ἰνδ(ικτιῶνος) ια΄ /[2] τοῦ ἔτους ς΄χ΄π΄ς΄ † /[3] *Lammā kāna bi-taʾrīkhi shahri māyū l-ḥādiya ᶜashara wa-min sinī l-ᶜālami sittata ālāfin wa-sittamiʾatin wa-sittatan* [*sic*] *wa-thamānīna sanatan muwāfiq* [sic] *mina l-taʾrīkhi l-ᶜarabīyi ᶜāma khamsimiʾatin wa-thalāthatin wa-sabᶜīna sanatan kharaja amru l-ḥaḍrati l-ᶜāliyati l-ᶜalīyati l-mālikati l-malakīyati l-muᶜaẓẓamati l-qiddīsīyati l-ghulyālimīyati l-mustaᶜizzati bi-llāhi l-muᶜtaḍidati bi-qudrati-hi l-mustanṣirati bi-qūwati-hi mālikati īṭāliyata wa-nkabardhata wa-qalūrīyata wa-ṣiqillīyata* /[4] *muᶜizzati imāmi rūmīyata l-nāṣirati li-l-millati l-naṣrānīyati khallada llāhu ayyāma-hā wa-naṣara aᶜlāma-hā wa-naffadha aḥkāma-hā bi-katbi hādhihi l-jarīdati muḍamminatan dhikra mā anᶜamat bi-hi ᶜalā l-dayri l-kabīri l-muqaddasi ṣanta mārīya wa-dhālika anna-hā khallada llāhu mulka-hā anᶜamat ᶜalay-hi bi-qurlūna wa-qalᶜati l-ṭ.razī bi-kulli ribāᶜi-himā wa-ḥudūdi-himā ilā ākhiri nihāyāti-himā wa-jamīᶜi ḥuqūqi-himā ilā* /[5] *aqṣā ghāyāti-himā wa-bi-kulli mā huwa la-humā wa-min-humā wa-mansūbun ilay-himā wa-yuᶜrafu bi-himā wa-bi-jamīᶜi rijāli-himā inᶜāman muʾabbadan wa-ᶜaṭāʾan mukhalladan wa-kharaja amru-hā l-muṭāᶜu zāda-hu llāhu maḍāʾan ilā aṣḥābi dīwāni l-taḥqīqi l-maᶜmūri bi-l-kashfi ᶜani l-rijāli l-madhkūrīna wa-stikhrāji-him min dafātiri l-dīwāni l-maᶜmūri wa-mina l-jarāʾidi l-qudmi wa-katbi* /[6] *l-jarīdati bi-asmāʾi-him wa-qadi shtamalat hādhihi l-jarīdatu sharḥa asmāʾi-him wa-ḥawat jumlata jamīᶜi-him.*

how the register was compiled, and also uncovered some faint traces of the *dīwānī* records upon which it was based.

In Section 3, which registers the population of the district of Corleone, the lists of the *mutazawwijūn* households, *i.e.* those households formed by marriage away from the parental or fraternal household (which I shall call 'B Lists'), all contain the names of sons or brothers of heads of household recorded in the lists of the ordinary tax-payers and of the Christians of Corleone (the 'A Lists'). Thus, the following pairs of lists were readily identified:

Table 6.4 Pairs of parental and *mutazawwijūn* lists (*Dīwānī* 43)

Estate name	A Lists	B Lists (*mutazawwijūn*)
Corleone town	3.A.a	3.A.e
Christians of Corleone town	3.A.f	3.A.g
Jāliṣū with Rāya	3.B.a	3.B.d
Qaṣṭana	3.C.a	3.C.b
Sūq al-Mirʾāh	3.D.a	3.D.c
Bū Kināna	3.E.a	3.E.b
Qabiyāna	3.f.a	3.F.b

This organisation, of course, could have been deduced from the rubrics to the sections, but analysis of the names confirmed that the relationship between each pair was what it purported to be. It also revealed that the names in the B Lists occurred in exactly the same order as did those of their fathers and brothers in the A Lists. For example, in the A List of Sūq al-Mirʾāh (3.D.a), four of the thirty-four households listed produced *mutazawwijūn* households, as follows (note that the two sets of progressive numbers – indicated by arrows – are sequential):

Table 6.5 Examples of relationships between *mutazawwijūn* and their parental households from Sūq al-Mirʾāh (*Dīwānī* 43)

B List (*mutazawwijūn*)		relationship	A List (parental households)	
	↓			↓
Aḥmad	(492)	son of	ʿUmar ibn Zaydān(?)*	(457)
Abū Bakr	(493)	brother of	Muḥammad ibn Bū Shāma	(462)
Muḥammad	(494)	brother of	ʿAbd al-Qawīy	(478)
Muḥammad	(495)	brother of	Khalīl Bū Rijl and Bū l-Ḥusayn	(481) (482)

* The name here read as Zaydān is written at no.457 with neither points nor Greek transliteration, and at no.492 without points and transliterated as ρυδέν.

However, the 'generation gap' between the A and the B Lists is administrative, not biological. Thus, some fraternal households split away from the parental household before, and others after the A Lists were compiled. For example, at Sūq al-Mirʾāh, Bū l-Ḥusayn (482) left his parent household, which may already have been headed by his brother Khalīl (481), before the compilation of the A List, while Abū Bakr (493) and Muḥammad (495) both left their parental households after the A List was written, but before the B List was compiled. Similarly, some filial households were formed before the A Lists, so that their heads are registered as *rijāl* who were assessed at the full rate; while those who split away after the A Lists are registered in the B Lists as *mutazawwijūn*. For example, when the A List of Jāliṣū with Rāya (3.B.a) was compiled, the family of Subʿu Dīnār consisted of four sibling households, one of which had already sired a filial household.[33] But, by the time the B List was compiled, a further two filial (*mutazawwijūn*) households had been formed, as may be seen in the following genealogical table:

Table 6.6 The family of Subʿu Dīnār (*Dīwānī* 43)

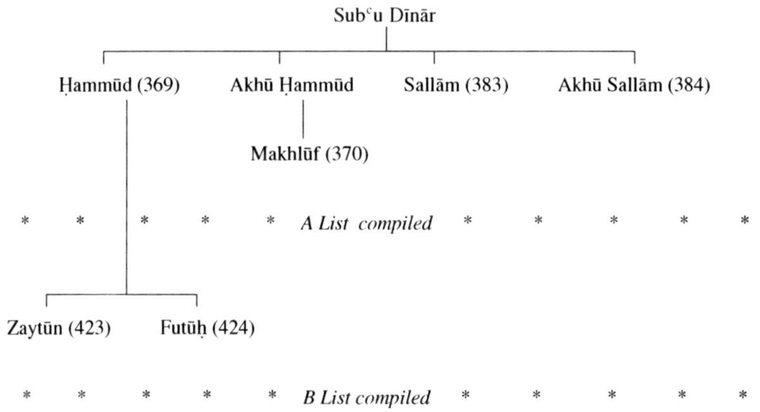

It can thus be seen that the B Lists were compiled from the A Lists in the simplest manner, using the *mutazawwij*-system already discussed in Chapters 2 and 5: the B Lists incorporate new material, but this was organised according to a structure determined by that of the A Lists. The compiler of the B Lists simply worked down each A List, and noted separately the names of the heads of the households formed by marriage away from the parental or fraternal household since its compilation. We shall return below to the significance of this observation.

33 Subʿu Dīnār (lit. 'One-seventh of a Dinar') seems an improbable nick-name but, if the Greek transliteration – σούπουγδινὰρ – is to be trusted, no other reading seems possible. Note that the correct reading of Nos 369–70 is Ḥammūd ibn Subʿu Dīnār; Ibn akhū-hu [*sic!*] Makhlūf: Cusa 1868–82, p.148, misreads 'Ibn akhū Makhlūf'.

First, however, we must consider the composition of the list of the *aribbāʾ* of Corleone (3.G), the explication of which reveals an intriguing scribal error that, in turn, throws light upon the mechanics of the production of the whole *jarīda*. The term *aribbāʾ* (singular *rabīb*; Greek ὁ πρόγονος, *o progonos*, 'step-son') means a boy who belongs to a household that is not his father's, and thus a 'foster-son', a 'step-son'and even a 'son-in-law'. It is possible that the *aribbāʾ* were simply immigrants who had married the daughters of men adscripted to estates in the district of Corleone. Alternatively, the term *rabīb* may be employed in a wider sense to mean a *mawlā* or 'client', in which case the *aribbāʾ* may have been immigrants who had somehow attached themselves to registered households in the district of Corleone. In any case, it seems highly probable that the *aribbāʾ* were newly adscripted to the district and, for this reason, were granted a temporary reduction or exemption of service.

In Table 6.7, Column 1 gives the names and numbers of the *aribbāʾ* in the order in which they occur in the register. Column 2 (headed '*Arbāb* 1') gives the progressive numbers of those *arbāb* (singular *rabb*, 'foster-father', *etc.*) who, because their names occur only once elsewhere in the register, can be instantly and securely identified. At first glance, there appears to be no correspondence between the order of the progressive numbers of the *aribbāʾ* and those of their *arbāb* in Column 2. But, a longer look reveals that the progressive numbers in *Arbāb 1* may belong to a single lacunose series beginning with 047 and ending with 537. That series has been broken into at least two parts which are no longer in sequence: 395–537 and 047–329. The two parts are separated by three names, the first and the last two in the list of *aribbāʾ*. In Table 6.7, these divisions are indicated by shaded lines. All this might, of course, be pure coincidence. But, if it were not, then it should be possible to fill the gaps in the column headed *Arbāb 1* by seeking the missing *arbāb* in the appropriate intervals – these are listed in column *Arbāb 2*. Thus, for example, the *rabb* of *rabīb* Ṣadiqa (686) should appear somewhere between nos 395–458: in fact, the name Ṣadiqa occurs only once in this interval, at no.448. In exactly the same way, ʿAṭīya is to be found at no.097, Abū l-Dhikr at no.108, Ibn al-Qaṣṣāṭī *primus* at no.50, and Ibn al-Qaṣṣāṭī *secundus* at no.313. These are entered in Column 3 (*Arbāb* 2). Emended in this way, the full list of the progressive numbers of the *arbāb* of the *aribbāʾ* is given in Column 4 (*Arbāb 3*). Column 5 gives the subsection and part numbers to which the *arbāb* belong. (This leaves two anomalies. First, the name Masʿūd (688) does not occur where one would expect to find it, between nos 458–537; but it occurs only once elsewhere in the register, at no.453, and so this must be he.[34] Second, of the three names separating the two parts of the sequence, only one has a *rabb* named elsewhere in the registers: Līya rabīb al-Bāz (702), from Yūsuf al-Bāz (293). The readings of the other two names are extremely uncertain, but neither is found elsewhere in the register of the district of Corleone.)

[34] It is not difficult to see how the scribe could have transposed the two names Masʿūd and al-Aswad: in this line there are three names in close proximity all with the letters *sīn*, *wāw*, and *dāl*, always in the same order.

Table 6.7 The *aribbāʾ* of Corleone and their *arbāb* (*Dīwānī* 43)

Aribbāʾ	Arbāb 1	Arbāb 2	Arbāb 3	Part no.
rabīb Mahdī (684)[a]	–	–	–	–
rabīb Abū Bakr ibn al-Muʿallim (685)	395	–	395	3.B.a
rabīb Ṣadiqa (686)	–	448	448	3.C.b
rabīb al-Aswad (687)	458	–	458	3.D.a
rabīb Masʿūd (688)	–	453	453	3.D.a
rabīb Bū l-Dhikr ibn al-Jinn (689)	537	–	537	3.E.a
rabīb Ibn Ḥulwa (690)	047	–	047	3.A.a
rabīb Ibn al-Qaṣṣāṭī (691)	–	050[b]	050	3.A.a
rabīb al-Sulṭān (692)	074	–	074	3.A.a
rabīb Naṣr (693)	092	–	092	3.A.a
rabīb ʿAṭīya (694)	–	097	097	3.A.a
rabīb Bū Dhikr (695)	–	108	108	3.A.a
rabīb al-Farṭās (696)	185	–	185	3.A.a
rabīb Khazrūn (697)	227	–	227	3.A.a
rabīb Abū l-Khayr (698)	–	300		3.A.f
rabīb al-Qaṣṣāṭī (699)	–	313	313	3.A.f
rabīb Ibn Misalla (700)	323	–	323	3.A.f
rabīb Quzmān (701)	329	–	329	3.A.f
rabīb al-Bāz (702)	293	–	293	3.A.f
rabīb Ibn L.?.ḥ (703)[c]	–	–	–	–

Notes:

a. The reading is uncertain: the scribe has employed an odd loop to attach the initial *mīm* to the *hāʾ*, which is written in its initial form. Greek: μουχεδή.

b. Written with a *sīn*, not a *ṣād*: 'Ibn Qassātī'.

c. Cusa, 1868–82, p.162 seems to read الح The Greek scribe does not attempt this part of the name.

The series displayed in Column 4, under *Arbāb 3*, reveals the scribal error; the manner in which it occurred can also be detected. Nearly all of the lists in this *jarīda* are arranged in 13 or 14 columns, written across the page, from right to left. The list of *aribbā'* (3.G) is arranged in only 11 columns. Thus (read, as indicated by the arrow, from right to left):

Table 6.8 The actual sequence of the *aribbā'* of Corleone (*Dīwānī* 43)

←

097	092	074	050	047	537	453	458	448	395	–	***line 168***
		–	293	329	323	313	300	227	185	108	***line 170***

If line 168 is divided where the break in the series occurs (shown by the two shaded cells) between nos 537 and 047, and if the series to the left of the break is added to the beginning (*i.e.* to the *right*) of line 170, this produces an unbroken sequence of twelve numbers, followed by the awkward three (shaded grey – the *aribbā* 684, 702 and 703, see Table 6.7 above), followed by the second sequence of five numbers, making a single (but interrupted) sequence 047–537. Thus:

Table 6.9 The reconstructed sequence of the *aribbā'* of Corleone in the source from which *Dīwānī* 43 was copied

←

–	293	329	323	313	300	227	185	108	097	092	074	050	047	***A***
								537	453	458	448	395	–	***B***

This cannot be coincidence. The scribe who compiled this *jarīda* (or he who was responsible for the source from which this register was taken) copied the list of *aribbā'* from an original arranged in 14 columns. In doing so, he mistakenly transposed the two lines of the list and, instead of beginning with the first name of Line A, no.047, he began with the first of Line B, which was presumably the first of the awkward three (Aḥmad rabīb Mahdī, no.684). When he arrived at no.537, the end of Line B, and of the whole list, he discovered his mistake and went back to the beginning of the Line A. The final result (see Table 6.8) had two lines, one of 11 columns and one of 9, in which the original order of the names is thoroughly muddled.

It is not the error itself which is significant here, but what it reveals about the compilation of the register, and about the sources from which it was drawn. It indicates that the list of *aribbā'* was drawn up in much the same way as the lists of *mutazawwijūn*: by taking a pre-existing list, checking it against the population, and adding the *aribbā'* households which had been formed since its compilation. There are, however, two important differences. First, the *aribbā'* are drawn from six different communities within the district of Corleone (see Table 6.7, Column 5), so that the list of their names was compiled from the following six pre-existing lists: the men of Corleone, the people of Jāliṣū with Rāya, the *mutazawwijūn* of Qaṣṭana, the people of Sūq al-Mirʾāh, the people of Bū Kināna, and the people of Qabiyāna. Second, because those six include both A Lists and a B List, the list of *aribbāʾ* must belong to the third generation (C List). This is why the *aribbāʾ* are listed at the end of Section 3, after the A Lists and B Lists for the whole district of Corleone. Again, the significance of this conclusion will be considered below.

First, before we move on, this is a convenient point to resolve a few outstanding questions concerning the registers of the district of Corleone, which also have implications for the *dīwānī* records from which they were drawn. In the middle of the list of the men of Corleone (3.A.a) comes a group of twelve *zawjāt* or 'wives' (lines 29–32, nos 151–62). Only the fact that they are grouped together distinguishes them from the rest of the list: the group is neither headed by a rubric, nor followed by a total. As in the Catania *jarīda*s discussed in Chapters 2 and 5, the *zawjāt* were female heads of household, who had somehow 'lost' their husbands and, presumably, bore a lightened fiscal burden.

Subsection 3.H bears no rubric. It lists 70 names, the bearers of which seem to have no family connections with households listed elsewhere in the register. This may be a list of immigrants into the district of Corleone, but it is also possible that these households were adscripted to a separate, unnamed estate. The position of Subsection 3.H, at the very end of the sections dealing with district of Corleone and before the start of Calatrasi, may possibly indicate that it belonged to neither district. In the boundary register issued to Monreale in 1182, the estate of Maghanūja in the district of Iato adjoins that of Sant'Agnese in the district of Corleone. The Latin version adds that *ubi sunt villani septuaginta*, exactly the number of households listed in 3.H.[35] This may – or may not – be coincidence.

Section 3.D.d is headed 'And with them (*i.e.* with the *mutazawwijūn* amongst the offspring and the brothers of the people of Sūq al-Mirʾāh) from Qaṣṭana'. It seems to be a list of households which had migrated to Sūq al-Mirʾāh from Qaṣṭana. Some families were split by the move. Abū Kawkab al-Ḥarīrī, for example, moved (or was moved) to Sūq al-Mirʾāh, while his son Abū Bakr chose (or was compelled) to remain in Qaṣṭana, where he formed his own household. This migration may have entitled them to an introductory reduction in service. That these households are described as being 'with' the *mutazawwijūn* of Sūq al-Mirʾāh, suggests that they had migrated after the compilation of the B Lists, and that this list, like that of the *aribbāʾ* of Corleone, is a C List.

There is some evidence in the *jarīda* of what may be the transfer to the royal demesne, and thence to Monreale, of men who had at one time been adscripted to minor feudal holdings. Four and possibly five lists from the district of Corleone seem to register households which had belonged to individuals: the men of Roger (3.A.b), the four unnamed men of the *qāʾid* Yūsuf ibn Jabr (3.A.c), the men of

[35] ***Dīwānī* 44**, line 26; Cusa 1868–82, p.182.

Bū Simāj (3.A.d), 'the men who once belonged to Richard' (3.B.c), and – possibly – the men of al-Ṭanābirī (3.B.b – this may be either a personal or a place-name). Finally, in the district of Corleone, I have no observations to offer about Section 3.D.b, which lists 5 names without rubric, but with a separate total.

Turning now from Corleone to Calatrasi, the first point to note is that the 424 households listed in sections 4.A and 4.B are not subdivided into various estates as are the 788 households of Corleone. It may be that we are here dealing with a single large settlement of some 2,000 individuals (assuming a multiplier of between four and five members per household). The site of Calatrasi has been located and intensively surveyed by both *The Monreale Survey* and Francesca Spatafora and other archaeologists from the Palermo Soprintendenza Archeologica: the surface spread of 12th-century material attests to a very large settlement indeed, beneath a small castle.[36] However, there is also reason to suspect that the register lists together the populations of both a central inhabited nucleus, and a number of satellite communities. In the Monreale *jarīda* of 1183 (***Dīwānī* 45**), the section which deals with Calatrasi is headed 'Calatrasi and its estates',[37] and archaeological survey carried out by *The Monreale Survey* has located a number of 12th-century settlements in the immediate vicinity of Calatrasi.

Section 4.B, which lists the *mutazawwijūn* of Calatrasi, was compiled in a manner quite different from that of the lists of *mutazawwijūn* of the district of Corleone: the names of the *mutazawwijūn* in 4.B do not occur in the order of the households listed in 4.A, and no scribal error can be found to account for this discrepancy – whatever did determine the order of the names in 4.B, it was not the order of the names in 4.A. Moreover, while most of the households listed in 4.B can be shown to have derived from parental or fraternal households listed in 4.A, for eleven households (21%) no connection whatsoever can be reconstructed.

It may be significant that Calatrasi, unlike Corleone, had been a feudal estate in the hands of the family of Malconvenant, until it reverted to the crown in 1162.[38] The fiscal records kept by the Malconvenant would seem to have been very different from those of the *duana regia*: we shall see below that the *ḥudūd* of Calatrasi also differed considerably from those of the domain districts of Iato and Corleone.[39] Indeed, we have already seen that the records of baronial and ecclesiastical lords were sometimes very different, and far less systematic and complete than those of the royal *dīwān*.

After this long review, we are now equipped to discuss how the *dīwān* compiled the ***Dīwānī* 43**, and what records it used to do so. In May 1178, William II or his ministers ordered the directors of the *dīwān al-taḥqīq al-maᶜmūr* – 'the royal *dīwān* of verification'[40] – to compile the new *jarīda* for issue to Monreale. According

[36] Calatrasi is modern Monte Maranfusa, approximately 34km south-west of Palermo, on the left bank of the Fiume Belice destro, 2km north-west of Roccamena (PA). See Spatafora and Fresina 1993; Spatafora 1995; Spatafora, Denaro and Brunazzi 1997; and bibliography cited therein.

[37] ***Dīwānī* 45**, line 134, *wa-mina l-mulsi bi-qalᶜati ṭirazī yi wa-raḥā'ili-hā*: Cusa 1868–82, p.261.

[38] Garufi 1902, no.7, pp.6–7 and Appendix, no.1, pp.161–3. See also below, p.185.

[39] Below, p.185. [40] Below, pp.193–203.

to the Arabic introduction, they, and presumably their scribes, had two sources at their disposal: the old *jarāʾid*, and the *dafātir dīwān al-maᶜmūr*. The latter were evidently *dafātir al-rijāl*, codices containing registers of villeins, and must not be confused with the *dafātir al-ḥudūd* or codices containing registers of land-boundaries.[41] That they really did draw upon the old *jarāʾid* is confirmed in subsection 3.A.c, which is, in effect, a subtotal carried over to the new *jarīda* from the old one (see Table 6.2): 'The total, including the four men belonging to the *qāʾid* Yūsuf ibn Jabr, is 259 men, according to the commentary of the *jarīda* from which this *jarīda* was copied'.[42] The old *jarīda* listed the population adscripted to the town of Corleone, including the men of Roger and of the *qāʾid* Yūsuf ibn Jabr.

We are not told when the old *jarāʾid* were compiled, but an approximate date can be estimated from demographic data. For example, families such as that of Subᶜu Dīnār (see Table 6.6) comprise at least two, and possibly three, generations of registered households. His sons, and one grandson, were registered in the list of *ahl* of Jāliṣū with Rāya (3.B.a, an A List). Assuming that all the members of his family who were registered as heads of household in 1178 were then still alive, it follows none of his sons is likely to have been born before *c.*1110 at the very earliest. Assuming that they formed their separate households, and sired their eldest sons, when in their twenties, then the *jarīda* in which they were registered, and upon which section 3.B.a was based, is unlikely to have been compiled before 1130–40. On this rather shaky basis, I am tempted to suggest that the old *jarāʾid* may have been based upon the registers renewed in 1145, and that they comprised at least the A Lists for Corleone, Jāliṣū with Rāya, Qaṣṭana, Sūq al-Mirʾāh, Bū Kināna, and Qabiyāna.

For four reasons, however, I suspect that the old *jarāʾid* had subsequently been updated to incorporate the lists of *mutazawwijūn* (*i.e.* the B Lists). First, because two of Subᶜu Dīnār's grandsons appear in the register of *mutazawwijūn* of Jāliṣū with Rāya (3.B.d), these A Lists are unlikely to have been compiled earlier than 1150–60. Second, the organisation of the register (see Table 6.2) suggests that the lists of *ahl* and of *mutazawwijūn* were both taken from a single source: that from which the lists of the *aribbāʾ* of Corleone (3.G) and of the men from Qaṣṭana at Sūq al-Mirʾāh (3.D.d) – both C Lists – were in turn compiled. Third, it seems probable that the registers of the *ahl* and *mutazawwijūn* of Calatrasi (4.a.b) came from the same source as those of the *ahl* and *mutazawwijūn* of the district of Corleone, but they are unlikely to have been compiled before that barony reverted to the royal demesne in 1162. And fourth, it is possible (although no more than possible) that the registers of villeins were amongst the records of the *dīwān* destroyed during the rebellion of 1161, and which had to be reconstituted thereafter by Matthew of Salerno.[43] I am therefore further tempted to suggest, that the old

[41] Below, pp.172–86.
[42] Line 54: *al-jumlatu bi-arbaᶜati rijālin li-l-qāʾidi yūsufa bni jabrin miʾatayni* [*sic*] *wa-tisᶜatun wa-khamsīna* [sic] *rajulan ᶜalā sharḥi l-jarīdati llatī nusikhat min-hā hādhihi l-jarīdatu*: Cusa 1868–82, p.143.
[43] Below, p.177 and note 34, p.180.

jarāʾid may have been compiled soon after 1162, on the basis of *jarāʾid* which dated back to *c.*1145, and that they contained both the lists of the men and of the *mutazawwijūn* of Corleone and Calatrasi. If so, then the C Lists of the *aribbāʾ* of Corleone (3.G) and of the men from Qaṣṭana at Sūq al-Mirʾāh (3.D.d), would have been compiled after the old *jarāʾid*, using them as a base, and entered into the *dafātir* of the *dīwān*, whence they were copied into the new *jarīda* of 1178.

If these speculations were to be accepted, the implication would be that, by combining the information about the adscripted population in the old *jarāʾid* with the data concerning *aribbāʾ* and internal migrants in the *dafātir*, the *dīwān* was able produce a composite register of the *rijāl al-jarāʾid* of Corleone and Calatrasi that was accurate and up-to-date. If this were correct, then it would demonstrate that cadastral information flowed regularly into the *dīwān*, and that the *dafātir* were maintained as current records.

The old *jarāʾid* were organised estate by estate. For each, they listed not just the villeins who owed full service, but also households headed by widows who were presumably exempted or assessed at a reduced rate. Similarly, they kept separate lists of the *mutazawwijūn*, who were presumably allowed an introductory exemption or reduction so that they could establish their new families and households; this, in itself, implies that they must have been updated at regular intervals, to permit the registration of new *mutazawwijūn*, and the reassessment of those who had exhausted their privileged status. Christians were registered separately, both as parental households and as *mutazawwijūn* – presumably, unlike the Muslims, they paid no *jizya*, but only the land-tax. The organisation of the *dafātir* seems to have been slightly different from that of the *jarāʾid*. The list of the *aribbāʾ* (3.G) grouped together households of this class drawn from all the different estates in the district of Corleone, while the list of the men from Qaṣṭana at Sūq al-Mirʾāh (3.D.d) recorded an internal migration from one estate to another. This may indicate that the *dafātir* were increasingly occupied with the problem of mobile villeins, the very concern which underlay the second *jarīdat al-rijāl* issued to Monreale in 1183.

The Monreale *jarīda* of 1183 (*Dīwānī* 45)

This register is a long roll of seven sheets of parchment, sewn end-to-end with narrow strips of parchment in a simple running stitch, to give a total length of 5.60m. The seven sheets are of a standard size, roughly 60cm–70cm square. At 4 of the seams, between sheets 2–3, 3–4, 4–5 and 6–7, the text of the *recto* has been carried across the seam. Unlike the *jarāʾid* of Roger II and ***Dīwānī* 43**, the seams on the *verso* are not 'sealed'. The names, rubrics and totals are written in Arabic with interlinear Greek transliteration. At the foot of the document is the plica and regular holes for the lead seal, which is now missing. There is no signature.

Again, no accurate edition or translation of the introduction has yet been published, and so I quote it in full:

/[1] When it was the date of the month of April, Indiction I, in the year 6691 according to the date of the world [= 1183 A.D.] – on the occasion of the issue of the high, the to-be-obeyed order (may God increase its exaltedness, efficacy, elevation, /[2] and duration!) to return all of the men of the *dīwān al-maʿmūr*, [whether] of the registers, of the settlements (*al-maḥallāt*), [or] of the smooth men (*al-muls*), who are dwelling on the lands of the holy churches and of the barons throughout Sicily (may God protect her!), and to transfer them /[3] from there to the lands of the *dīwān al-maʿmūr* – there went forth the order of the glorified presence, the ruling, the most royal, the Williamian, the magnificent, the powerful through God, /[4] the assisted by His omnipotence, the desirous of victory through His strength, the ruler of Italy, Langobardia, Calabria, and Sicily, the defender of the pope of Rome, the protector of the Christian community (may God perpetuate /[5] its reign and its days, make eternal its ages and its years, assist its armies and its standards, and support its swords and its pens!) to grant to the holy church of Santa Maria /[6] in the charge of the archbishop of Monreale that all those dwelling on his lands and on the estates of the churches and the land-holders /[7] within his boundaries, specifically the men of the settlements (*al-maḥallāt*) and the smooth men (*al-muls*), but excluding the men of the registers, should remain as they are now, and should be handed over to [the church], /[8] and be granted to it as a free, perpetual grant, and an inalienable, free donation, for which no service will be imposed upon them, nor will provisions, nor labour-service be incumbent upon them. /[9] [This] stands for as long as the days renew themselves, and is valid for as long as the months and years recur, for the sake of God (may He be praised!), and desirous of His mercy for [the presence] and for the souls of its ancestors, /[10] the glorified kings (may God sanctify their souls!). But, should it happen that any of these men, whose names are confirmed in this *jarīda*, is from similar *jarāʾid* /[11] from the *dīwānī* lands, or is one [of the men] of the land-holders, he is excluded from this grant, and is to return to his [rightful] place. /[12] The names of the men in this *plateia* were confirmed, and were sealed with the celebrated noble seal in confirmation of it and as proof of the validity /[13] of everything that it contains, on the aforesaid date.[44]

The name-list proper begins immediately after the introduction, and is divided into fifty-three sections, each corresponding to a separate estate within the Monreale lands. Each section is subdivided into two lists, one of the *rijāl al-maḥallāt* and one of the *rijāl al-muls*. A full summary of the organisation of the *jarīda* is given in Table 6.10. Much less can be said about what this register reveals about the *dīwānī* records from which it was compiled than for the 1178 *jarīda* (***Dīwānī* 43**).

[44] /[1] *Lammā kāna bi-taʾrīkhi shahri abrīla l-ḥawla l-awwala min sanati sittati ālāfin wa-sittimiʾatin wa-aḥadin wa-tisʿīna sanatan li-taʾrīkhi l-ʿālami ʿinda khurūji l-amri l-ʿālī l-muṭāʿi zāda-hu llāhu ʿulūwan wa-maḍāʾan* /[2] *wa-rtifāʿan wa-baqāʾan bi-rujūʿi jamīʿi man kāna sākinan min rijāli l-dīwāni l-maʿmūri mina l-jarāʾidi wa-l-maḥallāti wa-l-mulsi bi-bilādi l-kanāʾisi l-muqaddasati wa-l-bārūnīyati bi-sāʾiri ṣiqillīyata ḥamā-hā llāhu wa-ntiqāli-him* /[3] *min-hā ilā bilādi l-dīwāni l-maʿmūri kharaja amru l-ḥaḍrati l-muʿaẓẓamati l-mālikati l-malakīyati l-ghulyālimīyati l-bahīyati l-mustaʿizzati bi-llāhi* /[4] *l-muʿtaḍidati bi-qudrati-hi l-mustanṣirati bi-qūwati-hi mālikati īṭāliyata wa-nkabardata wa-qalūrīyata wa-ṣiqillīyata muʿizzati imāmi rūmīyata l-nāṣirati li-l-millati l-naṣrānīyati khallada llāhu* /[5] *mamlakata-hā wa-ayyāma-hā wa-abbada duhūra-hā wa-aʿwāma-hā wa-naṣara juyūsha-hā wa-aʿlāma-hā wa-ayyada suyūfa-hā wa-aqlāma-hā bi-l-inʿāmi ʿalā kanīsīyati ṣanta mārīya* /[6] *bi-arkanati munti riyāla l-muqaddasati bi-baqāʾi jamīʿi man kāna sākinan fī bilādi-hā wa-raḥāʾili l-kanāʾisi wa-l-tarrārīya l-dākhilati* /[7] *fī ḥudūdi-hā min rijāli l-maḥallāti wa-l-mulsi*

In particular, it is not possible to trace the ancestors of this register over three or more generations. This may perhaps indicate that it was based upon records compiled *ad hoc* for the recall of villeins to the royal demesne which is mentioned in the introduction.

The principle upon which this *jarīda* was organised is obscure. In Table 6.10, Column 2 shows, so far as is possible, the district to which each estate belonged. Although there does seem to have been some attempt to group together all the estates in a given district, this was neither systematic nor wholly successful. A comparison of the order in which estates appear in this register, and in the 1178 *jarīda* (***Dīwānī* 43**) and the 1182 boundary-register (***Dīwānī* 44**) reveals no common organising principle.

And yet, there was clearly a degree of co-ordination between this register and the 1178 *jarīda* (***Dīwānī* 43**). This *jarīda* is principally concerned with the district of Iato, while the 1178 *jarīda* listed the villeins of the districts of Corleone and Calatrasi. At least thirty-two of the fifty-one estates registered here lay in Iato, compared to nine in Corleone and two in Calatrasi; at least three hundred and eighty-six of the villeins registered dwelt in Iato, compared to one hundred and sixty-three in Corleone and twenty-one in Calatrasi. What is more, as was observed in the second section of this chapter, none of the estates on which *rijāl al-jarāʾid* were registered in the 1178 *jarīda*, had *rijāl al-maḥallāt* in 1183. Indeed, the vast majority of the *rijāl al-maḥallāt* dwelt in Iato: at least one hundred and nineteen, compared with twelve in Corleone, and none in Calatrasi. The precise significance of this for the villeins themselves is obscure, but it does demonstrate that the two *jarīda*s, and thus, presumably, the *dīwānī* records from which they were drawn, were carefully co-ordinated.

khāṣṣatan dūna rijāli l-jarāʾidi ʿalā ḥāli-him wa-taslīmi-him ilay-hā /[8] wa-l-inʿāmi bi-him ʿalay-hā inʿāman khāliṣan muʾabbadan wa-ʿaṭʾān sāliman mukhalladan lā talzamu-hā ʿan-hu khidmatun wa-lā talḥaqu-hā li-ajli-hi maʾūnatun wa-lā kulfatun /[9] bāqin mā tajaddadati l-ayyāmu thābitun mā takarrarati l-shuhūru wa-l-aʿwāmu li-wajhi llāhi subḥana[sic!]*-hu wa-btighāʾa raḥmati-hi la-hā wa-li-arwāḥi ābāʾi-hā l-mulūki /[10] l-muʿaẓẓamati qaddasa llāhu arwāḥa-hum wa-matā ẓahara anna aḥadan min hāʾulāʾi l-rijāli l-mathbūtīna asmāʾu-hum fī hādhihi l-jarīdati min jarāʾida sīyin mina /[11] l-bilādi l-dīwānīyati aw aḥadun mina l-tarrārīyati kāna khārijan ʿan hādhā l-inʿāmi wa-rājiʿan ilā makāni-hi wa-qad /[12] uthbitat asmāʾu hāʾulāʾi l-rijāli fī hādhihi l-iblāṭīyati wa-khutimat bi-l-ṭābaʿi l-sharīfi l-mashhūri taʾkīdan la-hā wa-dalīlan ʿalā ṣiḥḥati /[13] jamīʿi mā taḍammanat-hu bi-l-taʾrīkhi l-muqaddami dhikru-hu wa-hādhihi asmāʾu-hum.*

Table 6.10 The organisation of the 1183 Monreale *jarīda* (*Dīwānī 45*)

	District	*Maḥallāt*	*Muls*	*Lines*	*Cusa pp.*
INTRODUCTION				1–13	245–6
NAME-LISTS				13–307	246–86
1. Ghār al-Ṣ.r.fī	?	14	40	14–33	246–8
2. al-Darja	Iato	10	03	32–8	248–9
3. Jaṭīna	Iato	24	30	39–56	249–51
4. Manzil ʿAbd al-Raḥmān and al-Qumayṭ	Iato	03	25	57–68	252–3
5. Manzil ʿAbd Allāh	Iato	03	13	69–76	253–4
6. Manzil Zamūr	Iato	05	02	77–84	254–5
7. Manzil Krishtī	Iato	07	00	83–6	255
8. Raḥl ʿAbd al-Aʿlā	Iato	06	05	87–94	256
9. Raḥl al-Ghalīẓ	Iato	00	12	95–100	257
10. Dasīsa	Iato	23	32	101–17	257–9
11. Manzil Zarqūn	Iato	00	10	118–23	259–60
12. Laqamūqa	Iato	00	02	124–5	260
13. Raqla	Iato	00	08	124–7	260
14. al-Jurf and al-Khurāsānī	Iato?	00	07	128–31	261
15. ʿAyn al-Dāmūs	Iato?	03	00	132–5	261
16. Qalʿat al-Ṭ.razī and its estates	Calatrasi	00	20	134–41	261–2
17. Baṭallārū and its estates	Batallaro	00	16	140–5	262–3
18. Faṭṭāsina bi-Baṭallārū	Corleone?	00	01	146–7	263
19. Qurlūn	Corleone	00	26	146–55	263–4
20. Raḥl al-Mitāwī	Corleone	00	13	154–9	264–5
21. Qabiyāna	Corleone	00	24	160–7	265–6
22. Raḥl al-Balāṭ	Iato	00	04	168–71	266
23. Qaṣṭana	Corleone	00	10	172-7	266–7
24. Jimrīya	?	00	27	176–83	267–8
25. Abū Kināna	Corleone	00	29	184–93	268-9
26. al-Ghāmma	?	04	11	192–9	269

NAME-LISTS	*District*	*Maḥallāt*	*Muls*	*Lines*	*Cusa pp.*
27. Rāya	Corleone	11	36	200–17	270–2
28. al-Kanisīya and Shantaghnī	Corleone	01	06	216–19	272
29. al-Randa	Iato	06	00	220–3	273
30. al-Lūqa	?	07	00	224–7	273
31. al-Sikkāk	Iato	04	05	228–35	273–4
32. al-Andalūsīn	Iato	03	14	236–43	274–5
33. al-Maḍīq	Iato?	02	19	242–9	275–6
34. Manzil Nikhīṭa	?	02	02	250–3	276
35. Manzil Kharrāz	Iato	00	11	252–7	277
36. Rabanūsha	Calatrasi?	04	00	256–9	277
37. Raḥl Bū l-Luqum	Iato	00	06	258–61	278
38. Raḥl Ibn Ghurk	Calatrasi?	00	01	260–1	278
39. Malbīṭ	Iato	06	31	262–73	279–80
40. al-Qarīyānī	Iato?	00	10	272–5	280
41. Ghār Shuʿayb	Iato	00	13	276–9	280–1
42. Ḥajar al-Būqāl	Iato	00	02	278–81	281
43. Raḥl al-Maghāghī	Iato	00	07	280–3	281–2
44. Bijānū	Iato	00	10	282–5	282
45. Maghanūja	Iato	01	00	286–7	282
46. Manzil Handūn	Iato	01	00	286–7	283
47. al-Duqqī	Iato	01	00	288–9	283
48. Mārtū	Iato	07	00	288–91	284
49. Q.n.sh	Batallaro?	00	04	290–3	284
50. Qurūbnish al-Suflī	Iato	02	02	292–5	284
51. Ṭurrus	Corleone	00	17	296–301	285
52. Raḥl ʿAmmār	Iato	00	03	302–5	285
TOTALS		160 (sic)	569	304–5	286
GRAND TOTAL = 729 names				306–7	286

CHAPTER 7

The records of the royal *dīwān*. Part II: the *dafātir al-ḥudūd*

Gàrcia and Ottumarrano (*Dīwānī* 41)

By August 1175, the boundary-dispute between the peasants of Gàrcia and of Ottumarrano, deep in the very heart of the island, had erupted into open violence.[1] Gàrcia belonged to the church of Cefalù, but Ottumarrano was an estate of the royal demesne, and so Sanson, its bailiff, obtained an official record of its boundary from the royal *dīwān* in Palermo. When even this failed to settle the quarrel, one of the officers of the royal *dīwān* was dispatched in person. He was a Greek Christian, and seems to have come from just on the Greek side of the middle of the cultural scale that ran from Sicilian Arab to Sicilian Greek. His Greek name was Eugenios tou Kalou, a name which means literally 'he who is well-born of the good', while in Arabic he was Abū l-Ṭayyib, 'father of the good', a close equivalent of his Greek name.[2] In Greek he was 'the secretary Eugenios', while, in Arabic, with its more elaborate titulature, he was 'the elder, Abū l-Ṭayyib, lord of the royal *dīwān* of verification'.[3] He summoned the elders of all the surrounding royal estates to be witnesses before his inquiry into the disputed boundary: thirteen Christians, notaries, priests, and gentlemen, and fourteen Muslims, village head-men and elders, from Cammarata, Casaba, Cassaro, Ciminna, Cuscasino, Gurfa, Petralia, Polizzi, Regaleali, Vicari and Villalba.[4] They assembled on the southern boundary of Gàrcia, and Eugenios called upon them, in the name of the mighty and holy king, to relate everything that they knew about the boundary. Then, he took up the official

[1] The original, bilingual, Greek-Arabic, record of a boundary inquest is lost, and it survives only in the form of a Latin transumpt made in 1286. The two estates lay between Cammarata and Villalba: Gàrcia, possibly from Arabic *ḥarsh*, 'wood, forest' (Caracausi 1993, vol.I, p.681); Ottumarrano, modern Vallone Tumarrano, from Arabic *Wādī* + Sicilian *Marrano*, implausibly derived from Arabic *maḥram* (Caracausi 1993, vol.II, pp.969, 1663).

[2] See Ménager 1960, pp.222–34, and the bibliography there cited.

[3] Greek: *secretus*, *i.e.* ὁ σεκρετικός. Arabic: *senex Bittayb magister doane de secretis qui arabice dicitur duén tahkík elmama*, *i.e. al-shaykh Abū l-Ṭayyib ṣāḥib dīwān al-taḥqīq al-maʿmūr*. In Latin, he also appears as *Sehec* (*i.e.* Arabic [*al-*]*shaykh*, 'the elder') *Butahib Magister regie duane* (3 May, 1189, Ind.VII: original PA, AdS, Cefalù, no.27; ed. Garufi 1898, doc.3, pp.153–54; White 1938, Appendix no.39, pp.282–83, with wrong month).

[4] Cammarata, Ciminna, Petralia, Polizzi, Vicari, and Villalba (*Michiken*: Caracausi 1993, vol.II, p.1017) are all modern *comuni*, while Regaleali (*Casale Yhale*, *i.e. Raḥl ʿAlīy*) is justly famous for its

boundary-description of Ottumarrano that the bailiff Sanson had obtained from 'the God-protected *dīwān*', and read it out to the witnesses. They exclaimed, 'Yes, that's precisely right'.[5] Next, they examined, with their own eyes, the written account of that section of the boundary over which the inhabitants of Gàrcia and Ottumarrano had come to blows. They walked over the disputed boundary, examining and confirming each boundary-marker, 'and finally they stood reflecting ... about the aforesaid boundary and the names of the aforesaid places, and they confirmed their knowledge of them, one by one'.[6] Then, the witnesses of both religions swore upon their Holy Books that the boundary-description was true. And, finally, Eugenios-Abū l-Ṭayyib signed the bilingual record of their proceedings with his own signature in Greek, and with the standard Arabic *ḥasbala* used on *dīwānī* documents as the *apprecatio*.

This is the most elaborate record of a boundary inquest to survive amongst the documents issued by the royal *dīwān*. Its detail permits us to approach unusually close to the officials and the witnesses. More difficult to perceive, but no less interesting, are the concerns of the feuding peasants. If we can believe this *dīwānī* record, it was the peasants of Gàrcia, the villeins of the church of Cefalù, who were at fault, and who had unlawfully seized part of the land of the royal demesne, despite the protests of the royal bailiff. Nor were they willing to accept the testimony of an official record emanating from the royal *dīwān*, until it had been confirmed by local witnesses, and enforced by a powerful figure from the central administration. We are not told what lay behind the dispute: a later record of what seems to have been the continuing quarrel over the same boundary reveals that the rival communities were both 'Saracen', and that the land was arable.[7] The real victor was neither the bailiff, nor the peasants of Ottumarrano, but the royal *dīwān*, from which bailiff Sanson's official record had been drawn. By August 1175, both the office and its boundary-registers had been in existence for some thirty years, or a human generation, and Eugenios' success at Gàrcia shows what effective tools of administration – and even of government – they had become. But what were their beginnings, what form did they take, and what was their purpose?

wines. Casaba, Arabic *qaṣaba*, was perhaps a village near Enna (Caracausi 1993, vol.I, pp.321–2); Cassaro, Arabic *qaṣr*, near Valledolmo (Caracausi 1993, vol.I, p.330); Cuscasino, 6km north of Ália (Maurici 1998, p.79); Gurfa, from Arabic *ghurfa*, modern Grotte di Gulfa, south-east of Ália (Maurici 1998, p.84).

[5] The Latin translation of the Arabic appears to report what the witnesses actually said: '*ey da*' – perhaps Arabic *ī dhā*, as if reported speech, meaning 'Yes, [precisely] that', for the Latin glosses '*idest eamdem*' ('that is, [it is] the same').

[6] An obscure passage: ... *et confirmaverunt ea cognitione eorum eyéhe, hoc est particulariter*. The transliterated Arabic *eyéhe* would appear to be *īyā-hā*, here meaning something like 'of them [all]': I understand the Latin gloss *idest particulariter* to mean not so much 'particularly' as 'one by one' (*i.e. particulatim*).

[7] Document of 3 May 1189, Ind.VII, cited above, p.170, note 3.

The *dafātir al-ḥudūd*

Since the immediate aftermath of the conquest, lands and their inhabitants had been distributed amongst the conquerors in one of two ways: either a named estate was granted 'with all its lands, villeins, and appurtenances', in which case a description of its boundaries typically accompanied the donation; or it was the inhabitants who were granted with the lands on which they were registered, in which case it was sufficient to list the names of the heads of household in a *plateia* or *jarīda*. The latter seems to have been the preferred method in the post-conquest distribution, because it was simpler to name the villein than to describe his property.[8]

During the recall and renewal of *jarāʾid* of 1145, the *dīwān* would have had the opportunity to compare the effectiveness of these two types of grant over the half-century since the conquest. It could not have failed to notice that, while grants of estates with defined boundaries had left permanent marks upon the landscape, the *jarāʾid* had proved to be extremely ephemeral records which, because they had not been properly kept up-to-date, failed to provide an accurate account of landownership. At the moment of the grant, it had indeed been easier to name the villein than to describe his property. But, in the long run, it would have been far less trouble to record, once and forever, the unchanging boundary of an estate, than to keep track of the myriad demographic changes to its population. Even a few examples of the complete failure of the *jarāʾid* to work as records of landownership – such as the *jarāʾid* renewed for the church of Catania (***Dīwānī* 21–2**), which confirmed exactly the same villeins that had been granted in 1095 – would have convinced the officers of the *dīwān*, had they needed convincing, that boundary-records and not registers of population were the best means to achieve a permanent record both of the lands of the royal demesne, and of the fiefs granted to lay and ecclesiastical lords.

From as early as 1095 in Sicily, comital and, later, royal officials held inquests amongst the elders of a district in order to establish and record the boundaries of estates, either for inclusion in grants of land, or to settle territorial disputes between neighbours. Although most of the surviving boundary-descriptions date from the days of the kingdom, I was originally inclined to believe that they had been systematically preserved from earliest times, and thus constituted an unbroken link between the records used by Count Roger I in the post-conquest redistribution, and the *dafātir al-ḥudūd*, the famous boundary-registers maintained by the royal administration which, according to an imperial writ of 1229, listed 'the boundaries of every city, castle, *terra* and *casale* in Sicily'.[9] Only in redrafting this book, have I come to realise that I was almost certainly wrong. In the first

[8] Above, p.43.

[9] Note that, in this case, the registers did contain the boundary in question, and that it had belonged to the imperial demesne Genuardi 1909, doc.2, pp.238–43, esp. p.242: *dominus Soldanus de Gualdo, dominus Bulchalie ... nobis* [*i.e. Iohannes de Romania, imperialis dohane de secretis et questorum magister*] *humiliter supplicavit, ut inspectis quaternis imperialibus dohane de secretis, secundum*

place, the two pieces of evidence upon which I had rested the case for continuity proved, upon re-examination, to demonstrate nothing of the kind.[10] In the second, it is only from the late 1140s onwards that evidence for the collection of *ḥudūd* by the royal *dīwān* begins to accumulate. This does not, of course, exclude the possibility that the *dīwān* did keep a record of estate boundaries before that date, but it does indicate that it was not until the late 1140s that it began to do so systematically and with enthusiasm. What is more, it was only then that the *daftar al-ḥudūd*, 'the register of boundaries', kept by the royal *dīwān*, made its first appearance.

Daftar, plural *dafātir*, 'codex', ultimately derives from Greek διφθέρα (*difthera*), meaning 'a hide' and, thence, 'a hide prepared for writing'. The word *difthera* was frequently used in antiquity for papyrus, or for any other writing material, but seems to have gradually fallen out of use, so that medieval Greek δεφθέρι (*deftheri*) is said to be derived from Turkish *tefter*. *Daftar* seems to have entered Arabic from Greek via Pehlevi, probably under the early ᶜAbbāsids, when the codex first became widely used as a medium for keeping accounts and records in the central administration. The westward spread of the *daftar* from Iran and Iraq to Egypt is attested there by account-books composed of quires of papyrus. From Egypt, the *daftar* seems to have spread to the Maghrib, and parchment *dafātir* are attested in al-Andalus by the end of the 10th century.[11] The geographer al-Masᶜūdī, writing in the mid-10th century, noted that pumice from the Sicilian island of Vulcano 'is used to scrape away writing from *daftar*, from parchments and the like'.[12]

In Norman Sicily, the *dafātir* were clearly codices. 'Hugo Falcandus' refers to them as 'the books of records which they call *defetari*'.[13] In Latin documents, they are sometimes called *quaterni* or *quaterniones*, which, if taken literally, would indicate that they were codices formed of one or more quires of either four sheets folded in two, or one sheet folded thrice, so as to give eight folios, or sixteen pages.[14] This is upheld by the one Greek reference to the *dafātir*, which comes in a bilingual deed of February 1161 (***Dīwānī* 35**), where the Arabic *dafātir* is translated by the

quod in predictis quaternis imperialibus continetur, fines predicti casalis sui Buchallie sibi dare deberemus in scriptis et exinde sibi facere proprium instrumentum, cum presentibus annuentes, quare iusticiam continebant, vidimus et legimus sapienter et perlegimus predictos quaternos imperiales dohane de secretis, in quibus fines omnium civitatum, castrorum, villarum et casalium Sicilie scripte sunt. Vidimus et legimus fines predicti casalis Buchalbe [sic] *sic esse*: …'

10 These have already been discussed: above, p.80 (an anachronistic reference in 1188 to 'the boundary-register of the royal *dīwān*, which was made by the protonotary of the court sixty-five years ago'); and ***Dīwānī* 12,** see above pp.94–9.

11 Lewis 1954. See also Kriaras 1968–, vol.V, p.33.

12 *Huwa l-ḥajaru l-abyaḍu al-khafīfu lladhī yuḥakku bi-hi l-kitābatu mina l-dafātari wa-l-ruqūqi wa-ghayri-hā*: al-Masᶜūdī 1894, p.59 (*BAS*², vol.I, p.7; *BAS*²*(It.)*, vol.I, p.7).

13 'Hugo Falcandus' 1897, p.69 ('Hugo Falcandus' 1998, p.121): *libri consuetudinum quos defetarios appellant*.

14 Ed. Ménager 1981b, no.59, pp.203–12 (a forgery dating from the period of the kingdom): *in nostro fiscali quaterno*, and *in quaternibus fiscalibus*. Garofalo 1835, p.40: *sicut in … duanarum quaternionibus continetur*. White 1938, p.280: *quaternus duane regie*. Zielinski 1982, p.20, lines 6–7: *in quaternionibus doane baronum*; and p.44, lines 42–3: *in quaternionibus curie nostre*.

Greek τετράδιον (*tetradion*), the precise equivalent of the Latin *quaternion*.[15] But in at least one case, they are called *quinterni*, which indicates that the quires could also be of five sheets or twenty folios.[16]

This is a convenient moment correct a widespread misunderstanding, and to make it absolutely clear that the *dīwān* kept many different kinds of *dafātir*. Contemporary Islamic administrations kept large numbers of different *dafātir* divided into three broad groups – fiscal, military, and diplomatic – and it is probable that *dafātir* also proliferated in the Norman *dīwān*, although only a few varieties are mentioned in the surviving sources. As we saw in Chapter 6, the *dīwān* kept *dafātir* of villeins dwelling on the royal demesne.[17] The *dafātir al-īṣāl al-dīwānīya*, '*dīwānī* registers of receipt', in which income to the treasury from the sale of *dīwānī* land was recorded,[18] seem to have been different from the *dafātir* in which were recorded sales of property authorised by the *dīwān al-fawāʾid*.[19] The *quaterniones* of the *duana baronum* seem to have been registers of feudal holdings in the duchy of Apulia and the principality of Capua, and these are presumed to have been the records from which the *quaternus magne expeditionis* was compiled – the register of military service levied from those provinces in 1150–68, which forms the first and greater part of the so-called *Catalogus Baronum*.[20] The existence of similar registers of feudal holdings may be deduced for Calabria and the island.[21] Various taxes collected by the royal *dīwān*, for examples on mills, the marketing of foodstuffs and baths in Palermo, were also recorded *in ... duanarum quaternionibus*.[22] Under Frederick II, even district administrators kept *quaterniones* which they might be required to submit for scrutiny to the central administration.[23] In short, although I am principally concerned in this section with the *dafātir al-ḥudūd*, *daftar* means just 'register', not 'boundary-register', and not all *dafātir* were *dafātir al-ḥudūd*.[24]

[15] Cusa 1868–82, pp.622 (Greek) and 625 (Arabic): below, note 18. In Kehr 1902, pp.497–500, doc.53 (Caspar 1904, reg.168, pp.553–4), which exists only in a Latin translation, the reference to *quaterniones* would seem to be an late gloss – *servi qui non sunt in placia* [*i.e.* platea] *seu quaternionibus nostris*.

[16] Pirri 1733, vol.II, pp.1016–17: a boundary *transcripsit ex quinternis magni secreti, in quo continentur confines Siciliae*. But see Ménager 1960, pp.26-7, '*un diplôme fort suspect*'.

[17] Cusa 1868–82, p.134 (= ***Dīwānī* 43**, l.5: *kharaja amru l-ḥaḍrati ... ilā aṣḥābi l-dīwāni ... bi-l-kashfi ʿani l-rijāli al-madhkūrīna wa-stikhrāji-him min dafātiri l-dīwāni*, 'the order of the presence went forth ... to the lords of the *dīwān* ... to reveal [who were] the aforesaid men [*i.e.* the men of the districts of Iato and Corleone] and to extract them from the registers of the *dīwān al-maʿmūr*'). See also above, p.153 and p.156, note 32, line 5; and p.164.

[18] ***Dīwānī* 35**: see Cusa 1868–82, p.622 (Greek) and p.625 (Arabic): the proceeds of the sale of a piece of *dīwānī* land were recorded *min dafātiri l-īṣāli l-dīwānīyati*, 'in the *dīwānī* registers of receipt'; in the equivalent passage in the Greek text, the sum was 'paid into the royal treasury and written in the *tetradion*' (εἰσῆλθεν εἰς τὸ δεσποτικὸν συγκέλλιον καὶ ἐγράφησαν ἐν τῷ τετραδίῳ).

[19] Below, pp.204–6.

[20] Ed. Jamison, Cuozzo and Clementi 1972.

[21] Below, p.185.

[22] Garofalo 1835, p.40.

[23] Carcani 1992, p.243, col.b – p.244, col. a (Huillard-Bréholles 1852–61, vol.V.2, p.984).

[24] For example, Takayama 1993, p.87, fails to realise that the *dafātir* kept by the *dīwān al-taḥqīq* were boundary-registers, while those kept by the *dīwān al-maʿmūr* were registers of villeins. This misapprehension leads him to baseless criticism of Mario Caravale.

The first mention of the *daftar al-ḥudūd* comes in an Arabic donation of April 1149, which survives in the form of a copy made in the following December (***Dīwānī* 29**).[25] The *dīwān* ordered the *ᶜāmil* of Iato, Abū l-Ṭayyib, son of *shaykh* Stephen, to determine the boundaries of lands to be granted to the Greek monastery of San Nicolò di Chùrchuro out of Raḥl al-Wazzān. He was assisted by eleven witnesses: eight Christians, and three Muslims.[26] Before the lands were handed over to Chùrchuro, 'their boundaries were recorded in the *daftar al-ḥudūd* in the *dīwān al-taḥqīq al-maᶜmūr*,[27] according to what the strategos Abū l-Ṭayyib, son of Stephen, and the aforementioned Christian and Muslim elders defined' (lines 16–17). During the 1170s, King William II endowed his new foundation of Santa Maria di Monreale with massive estates in western Sicily, including the entire districts of Iato and Corleone, and, in May 1182, Monreale was granted a great register (***Dīwānī* 44**) listing the boundaries of these lands, which had been copied from 'the *dafātir* of the *dīwān al-taḥqīq al-maᶜmūr*'.[28] Amongst the *ḥudūd* registered in 1182 was one with the rubric: 'The boundary of the land which is in the hands of the monks of the church of Chùrchuro'.[29] The boundaries of this estate thus survive in two versions: that which was submitted to the *dīwān* in April 1149 for insertion into the *dafātir al-ḥudūd*, and that which was extracted from the *dafātir* for insertion into the Monreale boundary-register in May 1182.

The two versions are compared in Table 7.1. In addition to minor orthographic variations, there are more substantial divergences in vocabulary and style.[30] The

[25] This, and the second copy of 1154 (***Dīwānī* 33**), have recently been edited and studied by Johns and Metcalfe 1999. But I have since modified my views about these documents in two important ways. First, as will be apparent in what follows, I now understand that the original grant (*kitāb*) of April 1149 (***Dīwānī* 28** – a *deperditum*) must be more clearly distinguished from the copy (*nuskha*) of it made for the monks of Chùrchuro in December 1149 (***Dīwānī* 29** – extant). Second, the month in the copy of 1154 (***Dīwānī* 33**) should be read as June, not March: see Johns 2001.

[26] Johns and Metcalfe 1999, pp.244–5, lines 13–16: *wa-l-shuyūkhu l-ḥāḍirūna fī hādhā* /[14] *l-ḥaddi maᶜa l-s.r.dᶜūsa* [*sic* – here with unpointed *ᶜayn* not pointed *ghayn*] *abī l-ṭayyibi [ibni l-shaykhi iṣṭafana] l-madhkūri hum al-kātibu ursū wa-rijarẓu jāṭū wa-jāfarāy bnu yāna barṭinīq wa-martīn wa-niqūla* /[15] *akhū l-kātib ursū wa-rāw bnu yāna n.ẓ.r.d wa-tawdhir min dasīsa wa-lawranzu malisqālqū wa-min shuhūdi l-muslimīna ᶜumaru bnu ᶜabdi l-jabbāri wa-ᶜalīyu bnu ᶜabdi l-raḥmāni* /[16] *wa-bū l-futūḥi bnu ibrahīma,* 'and the elders present at this boundary with the aforesaid strategos [*i.e. ᶜāmil*] Abū l-Ṭayyib [son of shaykh Stephen] are: the scribe Urso; Richard of Iato; Geoffrey, son of John of Partinico; Martin, Nicholas, the brother of Urso the scribe; Ray, son of John *N.ẓ.r.d*; Theodore from Desisa; and Laurence Maliscalco. And amongst the Muslim witnesses are: ᶜUmar son of ᶜAbd al-Jabbār; ᶜAlī son of ᶜAbd al-Raḥmān; and Abū l-Futūḥ son of Ibrāhīm'.

[27] Literally 'the royal *dīwān* of verification', which also makes its first appearance here, will be discussed in the following chapter, pp.193–202.

[28] Cusa 1868–82, p.202: *al-jarīda … kutibat min dafātiri dīwāni l-taḥqīqi l-maᶜmūri* ('the *jarīda* … written from the registers of the *dīwān al-taḥqīq al-maᶜmūr*').

[29] Cusa 1868–82, pp.229–30.

[30] Johns and Metcalfe 1999, Appendix 3, pp.253–5. The following deserve particular notice:
- 1149, l.10: *wa-huwa an yabtadiʾa l-ḥaddu min raʾsi* vs 1182, l.313 *awwalu l-ḥaddi raʾsu*
- 1149, l.10: *maᶜa l-majrā mutamādiyan* vs 1182, l.313 *al-majrā l-majrā*
- 1149, l.12: *ilā an yantahiya ilā l-majrā l-thānī*; 1182 gives no equivalent for *an yantahiya ilā*
- 1149, l.12: *alladhī bi-l-qurbi min* has no equivalent in 1182
- 1149 prefers the imperfect indicative for verbs of motion; 1182 the active participle: respectively *yanzilu* vs *nāzilun*, *yaṭlaᶜu* vs *ṭāliᶜun*;
- 1149 uses the conjunction *thumma* where 1182 does not.

principal difference is that 1149 is more fluent and literary, 1182 more demotic and stilted. At the same time, 1149 and 1182 describe precisely the same boundaries and, although the text of 1149 is fuller, it contains no substantive information missing from 1182. Moreover, the language of the two versions is essentially the same. Both boundary descriptions are likely to derive from the same source. If this conclusion is correct, then it suggests either that the text of Abū l-Ṭayyib's boundary description was edited when it was inserted into the *dīwānī* register of boundaries, or that the description contained in the *dafātir al-ḥudūd* was edited when it was transcribed into the 1182 *jarīda*. The evidence of another document points towards the former alternative.

The copy issued to Chùrchuro in December 1149 (***Dīwānī* 29**) bore neither the king's signature nor the royal seal and, four years later, the monks requested a new copy 'because the first did not bear the noble seal which was used in this document in confirmation of it, and as a proof of its authenticity'.[31] Although the new copy of the donation issued in June 1154 claimed to be an exact duplicate of the old, and to have been carefully checked against it, it had in fact been compiled from the records of the *dīwān*. These included the *dafātir al-ḥudūd*, from which the estate-boundary was transcribed, and a summary (not a duplicate) of the original grant, which did not contain the boundary-description, but did include details of the donation, the names of the villeins, the boundary inquest, and the formulae used – each of which may have been recorded in a different file, perhaps in different *daftar*, as was suggested above. All this can be deduced from the fact that the scribe who issued the second copy to Chùrchuro in June 1154 (***Dīwānī* 33**) reproduced all of the details of the original grant, but transcribed the wrong boundary-description from the *dafātir al-ḥudūd* – that of Raḥl Ibn Sahl, not the estate at Raḥl al-Wazzān.

Raḥl Ibn Sahl also lay in the district of Iato, and was therefore amongst the lands granted to Monreale, so that its boundaries were also included in the great estate-register of 1182 (***Dīwānī* 44**). From the latter, it is clear that Raḥl Ibn Sahl was not held by Chùrchuro, but had remained within the royal demesne until it was granted to Monreale in 1176. In fact, there is no evidence that Chùrchuro ever laid claim to Raḥl Ibn Sahl, and it is tempting to conclude that the monks were never aware that the copy dated June 1154 erroneously stated that the estate had been granted to them. Be that as it may, the significance of the case here is that it resulted in two versions of the boundaries of Raḥl Ibn Sahl, both extracted from the *dafātir al-ḥudūd*: one in 1154, the other in 1182. They are compared in Table 7.2, and are almost identical, with only minor orthographical variations; both are obviously derived from a single source.

The two copies to Chùrchuro (***Dīwānī* 29 and 33**) disclose four important pieces of information about the *dafātir al-ḥudūd*. First, they reveal that the boundary-registers were kept in the *dīwān al-taḥqīq al-maʿmūr*, 'the *dīwān* of

[31] Johns and Metcalfe 1999, p.250, lines 15–17: *baʿda an qūbilat hādhihi l-nushkatu l-mujaddadatu bi-l-nuskhati l-ūlā l-maktūbati bi-l-taʾrīkhi l-mutaqaddimi fa-kānat muwāfiqatan naṣṣan sawāʾan wa-juddidat hādhihi l-nuskhatu li-kawni l-ūlā lā taḥmilu l-ṭābaʿa l-sharīfa lladhī ʿumila fī hādhā l-sijilli tāʾkīdan la-hu wa-dalīlan ʿalā ṣiḥḥati-hi.*

verification' – as already said, this office, which makes its first appearance hand-in-hand with the *daftar al-ḥudūd*, will be discussed in the following chapter.

Second, the fact that the 1154 and 1182 boundary-descriptions of Raḥl Ibn Sahl were both transcribed from the *dafātir al-ḥudūd*, and are identical, demonstrates that, at least in this case, the scribes who copied the 1182 estate-register from the *dafātir* adhered closely to the text of the register. This makes it highly likely that the 1182 boundary-description of the lands held by Chùrchuro at Raḥl al-Wazzān was also a near word-for-word transcription of the *ḥadd* in the *dafātir al-ḥudūd*. If so, then it must have been at the moment that it was entered into the *dafātir* that the boundary-description compiled by Abū l-Ṭayyib was edited.

Third, it may be possible to discern the development of the *dīwānī* boundary-registers over the four and a half years – December 1149 to June 1154 – between the two copies issued to Chùrchuro: that of 1149 refers to the *daftar al-ḥudūd*, to 'the register (singular) of boundaries';[32] that of 1154, to the *dafātir al-ḥudūd*, 'the registers (plural) of boundaries'. Before 1154, the only boundary-descriptions that we know were compiled at the order of the *dīwān* were of lands granted out of the royal demesne, or of boundaries at the heart of a territorial dispute between neighbours. But, while the boundary of the estate at Raḥl al-Wazzān was recorded for its donation to Chùrchuro, Raḥl Ibn Sahl remained within the royal demesne until it was granted to Monreale in 1174. It follows that, by 1154, the *dīwān* was already keeping three or more registers of boundary-descriptions, which included the *ḥudūd* of both lands belonging to the royal demesne, and fiefs granted to feudatories.

Fourth, the case of Raḥl Ibn Sahl, demonstrates that the *dafātir al-ḥudūd*, or at least some of them, remained intact in the *dīwān* from 1154 (or earlier) until 1182 (or later). This is significant, because it requires us to question the accuracy, or at least to modify the impact, of a report by 'Hugo Falcandus', of which much has been made by modern historians. Writing of the aftermath of the murder of Maio of Bari in November 1160, and the *coup d'état* attempted in the following March, 'Hugo Falcandus' describes how the new triumvirate of royal familiars – Richard Palmer, bishop-elect of Syracuse; Sylvester, count of Marsico; and Henry Aristippus – were completely ignorant of the administration of the kingdom, 'and were unable to find the books of records which are called *defetari*'. The notary Matthew of Salerno, who had been imprisoned in November 1160, allegedly for his involvement in Maio's theft of royal treasure,[33] was therefore released and recalled to office 'because he was considered to be capable of compiling new *defetari*, containing the same as the first'.[34] The two versions of the boundary-description of Raḥl Ibn Sahl compared in

[32] Unless, of course, the *-ā-* in *dafātir* is written defectively.

[33] 'Hugo Falcandus' 1897, p.45 ('Hugo Falcandus' 1998, p.99)

[34] 'Hugo Falcandus' 1897, p.69 ('Hugo Falcandus' 1998, p.121): *Cum autem eis terrarum feudorumque distinctiones, ususque et instituta curie prorsus essent incognita, neque libri consuetudinem, quos defetarios appellant, potuissent post captum palatium inveniri, placuit regi visumque est necesarium, ut Matheum notarium eductum de carcere in pristinum officium revocaret; qui cum in curia diutissime notarius extitisset, Maionisque semper adhesisset lateri, consuetudinum totius regni plenam sibi vindicabat peritiam, ut ad componendum novos defetarios, eadem prioribus continentes putaretur sufficere*. Matthew seems to have been out of prison and back in the *dīwān* by February 1161, when he appeared with the *qā'id* Martin as one of the directors of the *dīwān al-taḥqīq* (**Dīwānī 35**).

Table 7.1 The boundaries of the lands held by San Nicolò di Chùrchuro at Raḥl al-Wazzān (*Dīwānī* 29 and 44)

Arabic 1149 (*Dīwānī* 29)	Translation 1149 (*Dīwānī 29*)	Arabic 1182 (*Dīwānī* 44)	Translation 1182 (*Dīwānī* 44)
/10 ... وهو ان يبتدِي الحد من راس الكدية ينزل مع المجرا متمادياً الي دار البقر القديمة /11 المعروفة بوادي الفلو ينزل مع الوادي المذكور الي ان يلتقى مع وادى الوزان ثم يطلع الي تحت الخرب المعروفة /12 بالوزان القديم طالعاً الي مفرق الطرق ثم يطلع الى ان ينتهي الَي المجرا الثاني الذي بالقرب من المضيق ثم الى الصلب الثاني /13 الشرقي منه وقد غلق الحد يبذر هذا الربع المحدود ماية وعشرين مداً	/[10] ... That being: the boundary begins from the top of the hill; it goes down with the stream, keeping to it until the old cow-house /[11] known as Wādī l-Falūw; it goes down with the aforesaid wadi until it meets with the Wādī l-Wazzān; then it goes up beneath the ruins known as /[12] al-Wazzān al-Qadīm [Old al-Wazzān], going up to the cross-roads; then it goes up until eventually it reaches the other stream which is near the pass; from there to the other crest; /[13] to the east of it; thus closing the boundary. this defined land may be sown with 120 *mudd*s.	/313 حد الربع الذى بيد رهبان كنيسية الهرهر ه اول الحد راس الكدية مصب الما نازل المجرا المجرا الي دار البقر القديمة المعروفة بواد /314 الفلو نازل مع الوادي المذكور الى ان يلتقى مع وادى الوزا طالع الى تحت الخرب المعروفة بالوزان القديمة طالع الى مفرق الطرق طالع الى المجرا الثاني الى المضيق الى الصلب الثاني الشرقى غلق الحد وهو من رباع الوزان يبذر ماية وعشرين مد ه ه ه	/[313] The boundary of the land which is in the hands of the monks of the church of Chùrchuro – The beginning of the boundary is the top of the hill [at] the outlet of the water; going straight down the stream to the old cow-house known as Wādi /[314] al-Falūw; going down with the aforesaid wadi until it meets with the Wādī l-Wazzān; going up to beneath the ruins known as al-Wazzān al-Qadīm [Old al-Wazzān]; going up to the cross-roads; going up to the other stream, to the pass, to the other crest to the east of it. The boundary is closed. And it is from the lands of al-Wazzān [that which] may be sown with 120 *mudds finis, finis, finis*

Table 7.2 The boundaries of Raḥl Ibn Sahl (*Dīwānī* 33 and 44)

Arabic 1154 (*Dīwānī* 33)	**Translation 1154 (*Dīwānī* 44)**	**Arabic 1182 (*Dīwānī* 44)**	**Translation 1182 (*Dīwānī* 44)**
/9 الشرقي منه علي الجبل المُطلّ علي غار شُعيب الي الطَّرِيق الحاملِة الي غار شُعيب والحد الدَّبوري مع مجري الما الَّذِي ينزل القنطرة الى ان يجتمع /10 بوادي اشجار جُجواً ويرجع الحد الغربي مع الوادي المذكور الي أعلا الجبل المُطل عَلَي شلندة وهو الحد الغربي من الرحل ويرجع الحد القبلي /11 مع اعلا الجبل الي ان يجتمع باولِّ الحد الشرقي غبق الحد	/9 The eastern [boundary] of it is on the mountain overlooking Ghār Shuᶜayb; to the road leading to Ghār Shuᶜayb; and the northern boundary is with the stream of water which goes down the aqueduct(?) until it meets /10 with Wādī Ashjār Jujūw; and the western boundary turns back with the aforesaid wadi to the top of the mountain overlooking Shalanda; and it is the western boundary of the estate; and the southern boundary goes back /11 with the top of the mountain until it meets with the beginning of the eastern boundary. The boundary is closed.	/301 حد رحل ابن سهل ه الشرقي منه على الجبل المطل على غار شعيب الى الطريق الحاملة الى غار /302 شعيب والحد الدبوري مع مجري الما الذي ينزل القنطرة الى ان يجتمع بوادي اشجار ججواً ويرجع الحد الغربي مع الوادي المذكور الي اعلا الجبل المُطل على شلندة وهو الحد الغربي من الرحل ويرجع الحد القبلي مع اعلى الجبل الي ان يجتمع باول الحد الشرقي غبق الحد	/301 The boundary of Raḥl Ibn Sahl – The eastern [boundary] of it is on the mountain overlooking Ghār Shuᶜayb; to the road leading to Ghār /302 Shuᶜayb; and the northern boundary is with the stream of water which goes down the aqueduct(?) until it meets with Wādī Ashjār Jujūw; and the western boundary turns back with the aforesaid wadi to the top of the mountain overlooking Shalanda; and it is the western boundary of the estate; and the southern boundary goes back with the top of the mountain until it meets with the beginning of the eastern boundary. The boundary is closed.

Table 7.2 demonstrate that the *dafātir al-ḥudūd* contained the same text in 1154 and 1182: either these *dafātir* had survived intact, and had not been lost in 1161; or Matthew had managed to reconstitute perfect duplicates of the originals. The second alternative is *a priori* unlikely. In theory, Matthew could have transcribed the boundary-descriptions of estates that had been granted out of the royal demesne from the *ḥudūd* contained in the donations issued to recipients. But he would have had no written record of the boundaries of estates which belonged to the royal demesne – estates like Raḥl Ibn Sahl. The report that the *dafātir* were lost must therefore be modified: some, if not all, of the *dafātir al-ḥudūd* survived unscathed. There is further evidence to support this conclusion.

In December 1154, William I granted the estates of Margana and Ḥajar al-Zanātī to the monastery of San Giovanni dei Lebbrosi (***Dīwānī* 34**).[35] The original Arabic-Greek donation is lost, but it survives in two 13th-century Latin transumpts. Ḥajar al-Zanātī was one of the estates later granted to Monreale, and its boundaries were transcribed in the estate-register of 1182 (***Dīwānī* 44**). The latter was accompanied by a Latin translation of the Arabic. The three texts are compared in Table 7.3. The match between the 13th-century Latin translation of the lost Arabic boundary-description of December 1154 and the Arabic *ḥudūd* of 1182 is not as perfect as that between the two boundary-descriptions of Raḥl Ibn Sahl, but it is nonetheless sufficiently close to demonstrate that, in all probability, both boundary-descriptions were derived from the *dafātir al-ḥudūd*.

The boundary-description of Ḥajar al-Zanātī exhibits a common syntactic quirk of the *ḥudūd*, namely 'word-doubling', as in the phrases: *yatamādā l-ṭarīqa l-ṭarīq* ('it sticks to the road the road'), and *yarjiʿu qiblatan maʿa l-jabali l-jabal* ('it turns back southwards with the mountain the mountain'). In these cases, the subject of the verb is 'the boundary', and the doubled word appears to emphasise how it runs 'straight along the road' and 'straight along the mountain'. The origins of the usage are obscure: although it is extremely well-attested in Greek and Italian dialects in South Italy and Sicily, there is some evidence that it occurs in Egyptian Arabic as early as the 3rd century A.H. (9th century A.D.).[36] Alex Metcalfe has studied the occurrence of word-doubling in the Sicilian *ḥudūd*, and has analysed both the lexicon of doubled words, and the frequency of word-pairs, in the Monreale estate-register (***Dīwānī* 44**). On this basis, he has tentatively suggested, with all due caution, that the Monreale *ḥudūd* may be divided into three types, each of which might conceivably reflect the activities of a different scribe or group of scribes, who perhaps compiled the boundary-descriptions in the field. If correct, this hypothesis

[35] Margana, modern Castello della Margana, 9km south-west of Vicari: Maurici 1998, pp.87–8. Ḥajar al-Zanātī seems to have lain in the vicinity of modern Contrada Magione, 7km north-north-west of Corleone (Nania 1995, pp.150–1; Maurici 1998, p.84): in the 13th century, it was known as *Busamar*, *i.e.* Arabic (*Qalʿa*) *Bū Samrāʾ*, mod. Rocca Busambra (PA, AdS, Magione, nos 78 and 173, Latin notes on verso)

[36] Migliorini 1968; Caracausi 1977. For the comparable construction *al-sāʿa al-sāʿa*, meaning 'now', 'at once', in papyri of *c*.3rd century A.H., see Margoliouth 1933, §VIII, no.6, line 5, p.94, and §XV, no.2, line 4, p.151, cited by Hopkins 1984, §134, p.130.

might help to date the *ḥudūd*.[37] It so happens that each of the three of the boundary-descriptions which we know to have been registered in the *dīwānī dafātir al-ḥudūd* before 1155 belongs to a different type identified by Metcalfe: Type A, Raḥl al-Wazzān; Type B, Ḥajar al-Zanātī; and Type C, Raḥl Ibn Sahl. Of the three, Type A is too generic to be useful, and only Types B and C are diagnostic. Approximately half of the boundaries in the 1182 estate-register, covering a third of the district of Iato and most of that of Corleone, exhibit the characteristics of Types B and C. It could therefore be argued that they were compiled during a relatively short period of time in the mid-12th century. However, as Metcalfe himself is at pains to point out, such an analysis of word-pairs is 'a blunt linguistic tool'; its implications should be understood as working hypotheses that have yet to be tested by more extensive textual analysis.

This strict caveat can be somewhat relaxed, however, for an intriguing group of boundary-descriptions which are characterised by both a relatively extensive lexicon of doubled words, and a relatively frequent use of word-pairs. This is unlikely to be mere coincidence, because these *ḥudūd* all belong to estates in one particular area of the territory granted to Monreale: the district of Corleone, and its constituent estates, Ḥajar al-Zanātī, Faṭṭāsina, and Sant'Agnese.[38] The 1141 boundary-description of the lands of San Giorgio di Triocala (***Dīwānī* 15–17**), which lay close to the south of the district of Corleone, also exhibits the same features. A slightly stronger case could therefore be made that this set was compiled by the same scribe or group of scribes, active from no later than 1141 until at least 1154. The boundaries of Calatrasi and Battellaro exhibit a similar use of word-doubling to that found in this group, but they are separated from it by their distinctive vocabulary. They are unlikely to have been written before 1162, when Battellaro and Calatrasi reverted to the royal demesne.[39]

Be that as it may, it seems clear that, by the end of the reign of William I, the *dafātir al-ḥudūd* covered all fiefs granted since *c.*1140, and much of the royal demesne. In addition to the examples already discussed: in October 1168, the boundaries of the *casale* of Busenia[40] were said to have been reconstructed not from the original donation, but from 'the registers of the royal *dīwān*, in which the boundaries of Sicily are contained';[41] in October 1170, William II granted to Stephen, the venerable hermit of the monastery of Santa Maria la Virgine di Monte Gibello, near Paternò, the casale of Rahal Senec at Lentini, the boundaries of which were recorded *in deptariis Duane nostre de secretis*;[42] in February 1173, when the estate of Qurūbnish was granted by William II to Matthew of Salerno (***Dīwānī* 40**), its boundaries were listed 'according to what is recorded in the

[37] Metcalfe 1999, pp.35–50.

[38] This group almost corresponds to Metcalfe Type B; but with Faṭṭāsina, and without the district of Iato and the estate of Raḥl al-Jadīd.

[39] Garufi 1902, no.7, pp.6–7, and Appendix 1, no.1, pp.161–3.

[40] These may have been recorded as early as 1092 by the 'emir' Eugenios I, but Ménager 1960, pp.26–7, considers this *un diplôme fort suspect*.

[41] *ex quinternis magni secreti, in quo continentur confines Siciliae*: Pirri 1733, vol.II, pp.1016–17; Ménager 1960, p.27, n.1.

[42] Ed. Garufi 1899, no.54, pp.124–7.

Table 7.3 The boundaries of Ḥajar al-Zanātī (*Dīwānī* 34 and 44)

Latin 1154 (*Dīwānī* 34)	**Translation of Arabic 1182 (*Dīwānī* 44)**	**Arabic 1182 (*Dīwānī* 44)**	**Latin 1182 (*Dīwānī* 44)**
Hii sunt fines predicti casalis haiar zeneti. Incip[iunt in favara que exit de petra, que descendit i]nter occidentem et meridiem per flumen flumen usque ad molendinum andree, quod est in tenimento corilionis, et descendit ab occidente a petra magna nata que est prope molendinum Syelis, ascendens ad [petram magnam predictam et descendens per cursum] aque et ascendens per Caput rupie, et tendit per uiam usque ad aream que est super colle vinee, et tendit per uiam uiam usque ad aream que sunt subtus vinea predicta, et uadit per uiam uiam usque [ad vallem profundam, postea revertitur] ad septentrionem per cristam cristam, usque ad decursum aque, que descendit in ualle profunda predicta ad diuisam haiarzeneti pergens per cristam cristam usque ad fontem, qui cognoscitur aynes ker[afis, que vocatur fons] fetidus, et tendit directe usque ad aream que est prope uallem que descendit de petra longa, reuertens ad orientem per uallem antedictam petre longe que est intra divisam haiar zeneti,	/[324] The boundaries of Ḥajar al-Zanātī. The beginning of the boundary is from the spring (*al-fawwāra*) which issues from the rock; going down between the west and the south straight along the river al-wādī al-wādī to /[325] the mill of Andrea and the mill is in the boundary of Corleone; going down westwards to the big permanent rock which is near to the mill of al-Siyālī; going up to the big rock, likewise permanent; going down with the aqueduct to the head of the swamp; it sticks with the road to the threshing-floor which is above the neck of the aforesaid vineyard; it sticks straight along the road (*al-ṭarīq al-ṭarīq*) to the threshing-floor which is below the aforesaid vineyard; it sticks straight along the road (*al-ṭarīq al-ṭarīq*) to the sunken valley (*al-khandaq al-gharīq*). Then it turns southwards, straight along the ridge (*al-sharaf* /[326] *al-sharaf*) to the spring known as ᶜAyn al-Karāfs – and it is known as the stinking spring – and it continues straight on to the threshing-floor which is near the valley coming down from	/[324] حدود حجر الزناتى اول الحد من الفوارة التى تخرج من الحجر نازلا ما بين الغربى والقبلى الوادى الوادى الى /[325] مطحنة اندرية والمطحنة فى حد قرلون نازل غربيا الى الحجر الكبير الثابتة التى بالقرب من مطحنة السيالى طالع الى الحجر الكبيرة ايضا الثابتة نازل مع الساقية الى راس السواخ يتمادى مع الطريق الى الاندر الذى فوق رقبة الجنان المذكور يتمادى الطريق الطريق ‹الى الاندر التى تحت الجنان المذكور يتمادى الطريق الطريق›* الى الخندق الغريق ثم يرجع دبور الشرف /[326] الشرف مصب الما الى خندق الغريق فى حد حجر الزناتى ويتمادى الشرف الشرف الى العين المعروفة بعين الكرافس وتسمى بالعين المنتنة ويتمادى على الاستوا الى الاندر الذى بالقرب من الخندق النازل من الحجر الطويل ويرجع شرق من الخندق المذكور الى الحجر الطويل وهى داخلة فى حد /[327] حجر الزناتى ويشق بين زوج حجار ثابتة طالع شرق على الاستوا الى الجبل المعروف بالغرنزى الذى بالقرب من المرحلة والمرحلة فى حد المغاغى يرجع	/[156] Diuisa haiar zeneti, incipit a fauaria que exit de petra, descendendo uersus eam partem que est inter occidentalem et australem, et uadit per flumen flumen usque ad molendinum andree: Et molendinum est /[157] in tenimento corilionis. Descendit occidentaliter ad petram magnam plantatam que est prope molendinum syeli. Ascendit ad petram magnam postea plantatam. Descendit cum aqueductu usque ad caput diroitj. Uadit per uiam usque ad aream que est in capite uinee. Uadit per uiam uiam /[158] usque ad aream que est sub uinea. Uadit per uiam uiam usque ad uallonem Garik. Postea uertitur ad septemtrionem per serram serram. Effusio aque tendens ad uallonem elgarik, est infra diuisas haiar zeneti, Et uadit per cristam cristam, usque ad fontem apii. qui etiam uocatur fons fetidus /[159] et uadit directe usque ad aream que est prope uallonem descendentem a petra longa, et uertitur ad orientem cum uallone predicto, usque ad petram longam, et ipsa petra est infra diuisas haiar zenetj. Diuidit inter duas petras plantatas. Ascendit ad

Latin 1154 (*Dīwānī* 34) contd.	Translation of Arabic 1182 (*Dīwānī* 44) contd.	Arabic 1182 (*Dīwānī* 44) contd.	Latin 1182 (*Dīwānī* 44) contd.
et transit [inter duas lapides ibidem natos] ascendens ad orientem directe usque ad montem qui dicitur garnensis, qui est prope ouile, et hoc ouile est in diuisa magarum, deinde reuertitur ad meridiem per montem montem usque ad flumen haiarelzeneti, [et hec divisa est cum divisa] Iati. Postea ascendit per flumen salsum usque ad uiam Panormi quod custodiat deus. Deinde reuertitur occidentaliter per uiam predictam usque ad ecclesiam que est prope portam gructe filii b[inzeydun, et vadit per viam ad aream] textoris et reuertitur ad septentrionem ad uiam que tendit a bukeneni usque ad haiarzeneti, et ad caput balatii et ad primum montem qui dicitur haiarzeneti, et tendit per cristam cristam [usque ad locum, qui descendit ad favaram, et hec divisa] intrat in tenimento corilionis, et sic concluduntur fines casalis predicti haiarzeneti.	the tall rock. And it turns eastwards with the aforesaid valley to the tall rock. And it belongs to the boundary /[327] of Ḥajar al-Zanātī. And it passes between the pair of permanent rocks, going up eastwards straight to the mountain known as al-Gharīzī which is near the sheep-pen – and the sheep-pen is in the boundary of al-Maghāghī – it turns southwards straight along the mountain (*al-jabal al-jabal*) to the River Ḥajar al-Zanātī. And the whole of this boundary is within the boundary of Iato. Then it goes up east straight along the river (*al-wādī al-wādī*) to the road to Palermo. Then it turns /[328] west with the aforesaid road to the church which is near to the gate of the cave of Ibn Zaydūn; and it sticks with the road to the threshing-floor of the weaver. And it turns southwards with the road leading from Abū Kināna to Ḥajar al-Zanātī, to the top of the cliff (*al-balāṭ*) at the start of the mountain known as Ḥajar al-Zanātī. And it sticks straight along the ridge (*al-sharaf al-sharaf*) until it goes down to the spring (*al-fawwāra*). The boundary is closed.	قبلة مع الجبل الجبل الى وادى حجر الزناتى فجميع هذا الحد داخل حد جاطو ثم يطلع شرق الوادى الوادى الى طريق المدينة ثم يرجع /[328] غرب مع الطريق المذكورة الى الكنيسية التى بالقرب من باب غار ابن زيدون ويتمادى مع الطريق الى اندر الحريرى ويرجع دبورا مع الطريق الحاملة من ابى كنانة الى حجر الزناتى الى راس البلاط اول الجبل المسمى بحجر الزناتى ويتمادى الشرف الشرف الى ان ينزل الفوارة غلق الحد *Words enclosed in angular brackets are inserted in left margin.	orientem directe usque ad montem /[160] qui uocatur benaranzj. qui est prope mandram. et mandra est infra diuisas magagi. Uertitur ad austrum per montem montem usque ad flumen haiar zenetj. Et hec tota diuisa est infra diuisas iati. Postea ascendit uersus orientem per flumen flumen usque ad uiam panormi. Postea /[161] uertitur ad occidentem ad ecclesiam que est prope a porta Gar filii zedun: Uadit cum uia usque ad aream textoris. Uoluitur ad septemtrionem cum uia que ducit a bukcinene ad hayar zeneti, usque ad caput balate, ubi est principium montis, qui uocatur haiar zeneti. et uadit per cri- /[162] stam cristam quousque descendit ad fauariam et clauditur diuisa. Et hec diuisa iterum est inter diuisas corilionis.

registers of boundaries in the *dīwān*',[43] and, once again, what appears to be the identical boundary-description occurs in the Monreale register of 1182 (***Dīwānī* 43**);[44] in August 1175, an inquest held to settle a boundary-dispute consulted 'a document of the *dīwān al-maᶜmūr* – that is, the *doana secreti* – containing the description of the aforesaid boundary' (***Dīwānī* 41**);[45] and last, if anything but least, the massive *jarīdat al-ḥudūd* issued to Santa Maria di Monreale in May 1182 (***Dīwānī* 44**) was compiled from the *dafātir* of the royal *dīwān* of verification.

While all this amounts to undeniably impressive evidence for the wide extent of the *dafātir al-ḥudūd* from *c.*1140, it is clear that they did not yet constitute a complete record of the royal demesne, nor even of feudal holdings. In 1164, for example, when William I made a grant (***Dīwānī* 36**) from the royal demesne (literally 'from the *dīwānī* estates', *mina l-ribāᶜi l-dīwānīya*) to the monastery of Santa Maria la Gadera near Polizzi, the *dīwān* did not provide a boundary-description to accompany the grant, and simply instructed the abbot to help himself to two plough-lands near to the monastery. If, in the future, it was to be discovered that the monastery had taken more than it had been granted, then it was to forfeit even the two plough-lands of the original donation.[46] The clear implication is that, as late as 1164, the *duana regia* still possessed no detailed records of the boundaries of the royal demesne in the neighbourhood of Polizzi, which lay in the *iqlīm* of Petralia. Nor, of course, did the *dafātir* register the boundaries of the fief that had been so casually granted to Santa Maria la Gadera.

Indeed, although Frederick II's boundary-registers were said in 1229 to have constituted a complete cadastral record 'of every city, castle, estate (*villa*) and village (*casale*) in Sicily',[47] the fact that boundary inquests continued to be held demonstrates that this claim was not strictly true. For example, the only *dīwānī* document to survive from the reign of Frederick II records the findings of a boundary inquest (***Dīwānī* 46**). It is a Latin-Arabic writ, issued on 10 January 1242 to Geoffrey, a priest of the Cappella Palatina by Obert Fallamonaca, master of the imperial *dīwān*s and of the finances of all Sicily (*Obbertus Fallamonacha imperialis doane de secretis et questorum magister per totam Siciliam*; *ūbarta fallamūnaqa ṣāḥibu l-dawāwīni l-maᶜmūrati wa-l-fawāʾidi bi-jamīᶜi ṣiqillīya*).[48] Geoffrey, a cleric of the Cappella Palatina and the son of the notary Michael, a citizen of Palermo, had petitioned Obert to determine the boundaries of the Hospital of San Lorenzo in the territory of Cefalà [Diana], which Geoffrey held as a benefice from the church of Agrigento. Obert therefore wrote to the bailiff and judges of Vicari, in which district the estate seems to have lain, ordering them to

43 Collura 1975, pp.168. 44 Cusa 1868–82, pp.185–6, 212–13.

45 Ed. Spata 1862, 2nd ser., no.9, pp.451–6.

46 What should have been the definitive edition of this document (Enzensberger 1996, no.32, pp.85–7) is a typographical disaster, and cannot be used. A new edition will appear in Johns forthcoming a. Cusa 1868–82, p.650, misread the king's name as 'Roger' in the Greek *intitulatio*, and therefore proposed date of '1134(?)'. Noth, 1978, p.229, originally followed Cusa, but rectified the error in Noth 1983, p.198, 'L', after von Falkenhausen 1980b, pp.261–2. For S. Maria la Gadera, see Di Giovanni 1880, where he gives an Italian translation of the Greek text of this document, dated to September 6673 A.M. /1165 A.D. (*sic*), and correctly assigned to William I (pp.19–20).

47 Above, p.172–3, note 9. 48 For this reading of Obert's titles, see below, p.205.

summon a jury of the *boni homines* of the district to determine the boundaries. Their reply, naming the four Latin witnesses and describing the boundaries, is incorporated verbatim into the Latin text.

Very little evidence is available as to the internal structure of the *dafātir al-ḥudūd*. The Monreale estate register of 1182 (***Dīwānī* 44**) comprises, in effect, our only source (see below, in the next section). Just as Sicily was divided into districts (*magnae divisae*, *aqālim*) and each district was subdivided into numerous estates (*casalia, choria, raḥā'il*), so also was the register arranged (see Table 7.5). Thus, the first boundary (*magnae divisae* in Latin) in the 1182 register is that of the whole district of Iato, followed by the boundaries (*divisae*) of its forty-one constituent estates: the Latin terminology reflects the administrative structure. Similarly, the boundary of the district of Corleone is followed immediately by those of the estates within it. In the Monreale register, only the district boundaries of the ex-baronies Battellaro and Calatrasi are given, and not those of their constituent estates. Both of these districts had been held by the Malconvenant family and their retainers until as late as 1162, and it is possible that, unlike the crown, these feudal lords disturbed the dispersed pattern of settlement, and concentrated the population of their estates into large centres such as Calatrasi.[49]

In 1161, William I summoned John Malconvenant, the lord of Calatrasi, to Messina, where he was mustering his forces to put down the rebellion of the mainland barons. For the fee of the *castellum* of Calatrasi, John owed the service of eleven knights but, for whatever reason, he claimed that he could equip only three. After prolonged and clearly rather tense negotiations, he therefore renounced Calatrasi, which reverted to the royal demesne, and received instead the *casali* of Turrus and Cellaro, at the fee of, respectively, two knights and one.[50] The case suggests that *dafātir al-ḥudūd* included, or were cross-referenced to, registers of feudal holdings which listed the services owed to the king.[51] It is tempting, but almost certainly wrong, to assume that these resembled the *quaternus magne expeditionis*, the register of military service levied from the duchy of Apulia and principality of Capua in 1150–68, which survives in a 14th-century copy in the so-called *Catalogus Baronum*:[52] not only was that *quaternus* composed for the specific purpose of the *magna expeditio*, but also it was written in Latin, in all probability at the headquarters of the *duana baronum* in Salerno (see below, pp.206–7), far from the Arabic administration in Palermo.

In short, soon after the renewal of privileges of 1145, the *dīwān* systematically set about collecting estate-boundaries into the *dafātir al-ḥudūd*. These covered both the lands of the royal demesne, and fiefs granted to lay and ecclesiastical feudatories. The registers of fiefs recorded not just the boundaries of an estate granted to a feudatory, but also the service owed. The *dafātir al-ḥudūd* thus

49 Above, p.163.

50 Original: PA, Bibl. Reg., Monreale, no.7; ed. Garufi 1902, no.7, pp.6–7, and App, no.1, pp.161–3. See also Matthew 1992, pp.148–9.

51 Enzensberger 1981–2, p.32, nn.47–8, also points out that registers from Sicily, comparable to the *Catalogus Baronum*, did once exist, but have not survived.

52 Ed. Jamison, Cuozzo and Clementi 1972.

became the principal tool for the administration of both royal lands and fiefs. A new office, the *dīwān al-taḥqīq*, was introduced to manage them. But, before turning to discuss this innovation, it is first necessary to discuss in greater detail the most spectacular surviving product of the *dafātir al-ḥudūd*.

The Monreale estate-register of May 1182 (*Dīwānī* 44)

The register is written upon seven sheets of parchment sewn together end-to-end with a total length of 5.20m. The seven sheets are of a standard size, roughly 60cm–70cm square. Each seam was sealed with a crimson silk tie to which a lead seal was affixed. The seals are missing, but the ties can still to be seen at all the seams except that joining sheets 1–2, where clear stains of the red colour of the tie can be discerned. The first three sheets hold the Latin translation of the Arabic text, which occupies the last four sheets.

The organisation of the *jarīda* may be summarised as follows (see Table 7.5 for a detailed list of the boundary descriptions):

Table 7.4 The organisation of the 1182 Monreale *jarīdat al-ḥudūd* (*Dīwānī* 44)

Description	Lines	Cusa pp.
Latin *superscriptio*	1	179
Latin *arenga*	2–5	179–80
Latin translation of Arabic *jarīda*	5–213	180–202
Latin conclusion	213–16	202
Arabic introduction	217	202
Arabic *jarīda*	218–367	202–43
Boundary of district of Iato	218–30	202–5
Boundaries of estates within district of Iato	230–314	205–30
Boundary of district of Corleone	315–24	230–2
Boundaries of estates within district of Corleone	324–38	232–6
Boundary of ex-barony of Battallaro	339–58	236–41
Boundary of ex-barony of Calatrasi	358–67	241–43
Arabic conclusion	367–70	243–44
Signatures	371–3	244

The signatories to the register are those who were responsible for supervising its production. They fall into two groups. Pre-eminent, on the left of the page, come the signatures of the three *datarii*, the triumvirate of *familiares regis*, Walter II archbishop of Palermo, the vice-chancellor Matthew of Salerno, and Richard Palmer, bishop of Syracuse. On the right of the page come the elaborate notarial signatures of Gildeibertus *domini klericus*, Eberardus, and Riccardus. Eberardus was also responsible for supervising the *jarīdat al-rijāl* of 1178 (***Dīwānī* 43**).[53] Riccardus may be identical with the royal scribe who appears in 1170 and 1189, but both these documents are forgeries.[54] I am more strongly tempted to identify him with the *qāᵓid* Richard, who held the office of *magister regie duane de secretis* from 1168 until at least 1187, but this Latin signature has nothing in common with the *qāᵓid* Richard's only known autograph, his Arabic *ᶜalāma*.[55] Gildeibertus is not otherwise known to me. Yūsuf, the Arab scribe who actually copied the boundary descriptions from the *dafātir al-ḥudūd*, and Alexander, the Latin scribe who is said to have translated them into Latin, are mentioned in the Arabic conclusion: Yūsuf is not otherwise known,[56] but Alexander was the busiest of all the scribes of William II.[57]

I quote in full the Arabic introduction and conclusion:

> (*Introduction*) /[217] This *jarīda* contains the boundaries of [the district of] Iato and of the estates within its boundaries, of [the district of] Corleone and of the estates within its boundaries, of Battellaro, and of Calatrasi. They were written from the *dafātir* of the royal *dīwān* of verification …
>
> (*Conclusion*) /[367]… When it was the date of May, [Indiction] XV, in the year of the world 6690 [= 1182 A.D.], there went forth the order of the high presence, the most high, the ruling, the most royal, the glorified, the most holy, the powerful through God, the assisted /[368] by His omnipotence, the desirous of victory through His strength, the ruler of Italy, Langobardia, Calabria, and Sicily, the defender of the pope of Rome, the protector of the Christian community (may God perpetuate its days, and assist its standards, and fulfil its ordinances!), to write this *jarīda* containing the account of that which [the presence] granted to the great, holy monastery known /[369] as Santa Maria the Most Royal, of the lands of the towns and estates herein aforementioned; and that the aforesaid boundaries should be written in Latin by the hand of Alexander the Latin, and in Arabic by the hand of the scribe Yūsuf of the royal *dīwān* of verification, so that the high order (may God increase it in elevation and efficacy!) might be obeyed. /[370] It was translated from Arabic into Latin by the hand of the aforesaid scribe Alexander, and [copied] in Arabic by the hand of the aforesaid scribe Yūsuf from the *dafātir* of the royal *dīwān* of verification, on the aforementioned date. And God is sufficient for us. How excellent a representative is He![58]

[53] Above, p.153. [54] Enzensberger 1981–2, Table VII, nos 36 and 154.

[55] For Richard, see below, pp.228–34. For his *ᶜalāma*, see pp.251–2.

[56] Unless he is the Yūsuf ibn Yaᶜqūb of ***Dīwānī* 39**. I do not read 'Yūsuf' in the *ᶜalāma* at the foot of ***Dīwānī* 31**, *pace* Noth, 1983, 'P', pp.199–200. [57] Enzensberger 1981–2, pp.30–1.

[58] */[217] tashtamilu hādhihi l-jarīdatu ᶜalā ḥudūdi jāṭū wa-l-raḥāᵓili l-dākhilati fī ḥudūdi-hā wa-qurlūna wa-l-raḥāᵓili l-dākhilati fī ḥudūdi-hā wa-baṭṭallārū wa-qalᶜati l-ṭ.razī kutibat min dafātiri dīwāni l-taḥqīqi l-maᶜmūri … /[367] … lammā kāna bi-taᵓrīkhi māyū l-khāmisa ᶜashara wa-min sinī l-ᶜālami sittata ālāfin wa-sittamiᵓatin wa-tisᶜīna sanatan kharaja amru l-ḥaḍrati l-ᶜāliyati l-ᶜalīyati l-mālikati l-malakīyati l-muᶜaẓẓamati l-qiddīsīyati l-mustaᶜizzati bi-llāhi l-muᶜtaḍidati /[368] bi-qudrati-hi l-mustanṣirati bi-qūwati-hi mālikati īṭāliyata wa-nkabardata wa-qalūrīyata wa-ṣiqillīyata muᶜizzati imāmi rūmīyata l-nāṣirati li-l-millati l-naṣrānīyati khallada llāhu ayyāma-hā wa-naṣara aᶜlāma-hā wa-naffadha aḥkāma-hā bi-katbi hādhihi l-jarīdati muḍamminatan dhikra mā anᶜamat bi-hi ᶜalā l-dayri l-kabīri l-muqaddasi l-maᶜrūfi /[369] bi-ṣanta mārīya l-malakīyati min ḥudūdi ribāᶜi l-bilādi wa-l-raḥāᵓili l-madhkūrīna fī-hā wa-an tuktaba l-ḥudūdu l-madhkūratu bi-l-laṭīnīyi bi-khaṭṭi l-kātibi alaṣandara l-laṭīnīyi wa-bi-l-ᶜarabīyi bi-khaṭṭi l-kātibi yūsufa bi-dīwāni l-taḥqīqi l-maᶜmūri fa-mtuthila mā kharaja bi-hi l-amru l-ᶜālī zāda-hu llāhu ᶜalāᵓan wa-maḍāᵓan /[370] wa-shuriḥat mina l-ᶜarabīyi ilā l-laṭīnīyi bi-khaṭṭi l-kātibi alaṣandara l-madhkūri wa-bi-l-ᶜarabīyi bi-khaṭṭi l-kātibi yūsufa l-madhkūri min dafātiri dīwāni l-taḥqīqi l-maᶜmūri bi-l-taᵓrīkhi l-muqaddami dhikru-hu wa-ḥasbu-nā llāhu wa-niᶜma l-wakīlu.*

Table 7.5 The organisation of the 1182 Monreale *jarīdat al-ḥudūd* (*Dīwānī* 44) showing the individual *ḥudūd*

Name of Boundary	***Lines***	Cusa pp.
	Latin, Arabic	Latin, Arabic
1. District of Jāṭū	5–21, 218–30	180–1, 202–5
02. Maghanūja	21–6, 230–3	181–2, 205–6
03. al-Duqqī	26–31, 233–7	182, 206–7
04. al-Baluʾīn(?)	32–5, 237–9	182–3, 207
05. Raḥl Bū Furīra	35–9, 239–42	183, 208
06. Raḥl al-Miʾa = Jinān Ibn Kināna	40–3, 242–4	183–4, 208–9
07. al-Maghāghī	43–6, 245–6	184, 209
08. Sūmminī	46–53, 247–51	184–5, 210–11
09. Malbīṭ	53–61, 251–7	185, 211–12
10. Qurūbnish	62–5, 257–9	185–6, 212–13
11. Raḥl al-Kilāʿī	66–7, 260–1	186, 213
12. Qurūbnish al-Suflī	67–70, 261–3	186, 213–14
13. Raḥl al-Wuṭāʾ	70–2, 263–4	186–7, 214
14. al-Andalusīn	72–4, 264–6	187, 214–15
15. Manzil Zarqūn	74–6, 266–7	187, 215
16. Bū Nifāṭ	77–9, 267–9	187, 215–16
17. Raḥl Ibn Barka	79–82, 269–71	187–8, 216
18. Raḥl Laqamūqa	82–6, 272–4	188, 217
19. Raḥl al-Jadīd	86–7, 274–5	188, 217–18
20. Raḥl ʿAmrūn	87–90, 275–7	188, 218
21. Raḥl al-Būqāl	90–5, 281–3	189, 218–19
22. Raḥl al-Ghalīẓ	95–8, 281–3	189, 219–20
23. *bayna* Raḥl Marāʾus *wa-bayna* Bū Kināna	98–100, 283–5	189–90, 220
24. Mārtū	100–3, 285–7	190, 220–1
25. Raḥl al-Balāṭ	103–5, 287–9	190, 221

Name of Boundary	***Lines***	Cusa pp.
26. Raḥl al-Mudd	106–7, 289–90	190, 221–2
27. Raḥl al-Sikkāk	107–9, 291–2	190, 222
28. Dasīsa	109–13, 292–4	190–1, 222–3
29. Manzil Zamūr	113–14, 294–5	191, 223
30. Manzil Krishtī	123–4, 302–3	192, 225–6
31. Manzil ᶜAbd Allāh	125–7, 303–4	192, 226
32. Ghār Shuᶜayb	127–8, 305	192–3, 226
33. Raḥl Ibn Sahl	128–30, 305–7	193, 227
34. Jurf Bū Karīm	130–2, 307–8	193, 227
35. Raḥl Bijānū	132–4, 308–9	193, 228
36. Manzil ᶜAbd al-Raḥmān	134–5, 309–10	193, 228
37. al-Qumayṭ	136–8, 310–12	193–4, 228–9
38. Jaṭīna	138–40, 312–13	194, 229
39. al-Ghār	140–2, 313–14	194, 229–30
40. al-Randa	143–57, 315–24	194–6, 230–2
41. Raḥl al-Jawz	157–63, 324–8	196, 232–3
42. al-Aqbāṭ	163–6, 329–31	196–7, 234
43. Raḥl al-Wazzān	166–8, 331–2	197, 234–5
44. District of Qurlūn	168–75, 332–8	197–8, 233–4
45. Ḥajar al-Zanātī	175–200, 339–58	198–200, 236–41
46. Jāliṣū	201–13, 358–67	200–2, 241–3
47. Faṭṭāsina	166–8, 331–2	197, 234–5
48. Ribāᶜ Usbiṭāl Shantaghnī	168–75, 332–8	197, 235–6
49. Ex-barony of Battallārū	175–200, 339–58	198–200, 236–41
50. Ex-barony of Qalᶜat al-T.razī	200–13, 358–67	200–2, 241–43

From this, and from the Latin conclusion,[59] it is clear that the Arabic text was copied by the *kātib* Yūsuf from the *dafātir al-ḥudūd* maintained in the *dīwān*, while the Latin translation was made by Alexander specially for this *jarīda*. The process of translation does not seem to have been part of the day-to-day business of the royal *dīwān*.

The *ḥudūd* copied from the *dafātir* into the 1182 register had been determined in the usual manner, by inquests held by a royal official amongst the elders of the district.[60] It had not always been possible to reach agreement, and the *dafātir* also recorded ongoing disputes. For example, in the estate of Malbīṭ

> Five thousand *salme* are sown, of which six hundred *salme* are pasture, and an area of forty *salme* is disputed between the people of Corleone and the people of Malbīṭ. The men of the royal *dīwān* say that the lord of Malbīṭ usurped from them seed-land[61] of two hundred *salme*, and built a mill there; and this [seed-land] that he usurped is within the lands delimited for [Malbīṭ].[62] And there is also a boundary [*i.e.* an estate] between al-Aqbāṭ and the lands of the people of Manzil ʿAbd Allāh: the elders of Iato say that the boundary is from the base of Ibn al-Jarrāḥ, in the east to the meadow of al-Karank[?], to Proculus; it goes up with the foot of the mountain to ʿAyn al-Bārida. And the men of al-Aqbāṭ say that the *qāʾid* Yaḥyā traced the boundary for them from al-Maqtal to al-Inkirāt, [and] it goes straight to Ibn al-Jarrāḥ. The water-outlet belongs to al-Aqbāṭ. And that which is between [this] boundary is sown with twenty *salme*, of which ten *salme* are not worked.[63]

59 *Has aut[em] p[re]dictas divisas a deptariis n[os]tris de saracenico in latinu[m] transf[er]ri, ip[su]m q[ue] saracenicu[m], s[e]c[un]d[u]m q[uo]d in eisde[m] deptariis continet[ur], sub latino scribi p[re]cepim[us].*

60 Unlike the Arabic introduction, which largely adheres to the grammatical and syntactical conventions standard in the written language, the *ḥudūd* belong firmly to the spoken register and reflect the oral sources whence they derive. For this reason, in the passages quoted below (notes 63–71), I have suspended my usual practice of transliteration.

61 In this *jarīda*, *badhr*, literally 'seed' or 'sowing', is used in the specialised sense of an area of land. The Latin scribe translates it as *seminatura*. I have coined the compound noun 'seed-land' to remain as close as possible to both, and to distinguish *badhr* from *ḥarth*, 'arable-land'. *Badhr*, like *seminatura*, can also mean an area of any category of land, whether cultivated and sown or not (see below, notes 63–4, 68, 70).

62 Or, conceivably, 'for him [*i.e.* the lord of Malbīṭ]', but the Latin suggests not.

63 Lines 254–7 (Cusa 1868–82, pp.212): *yubdhar khamsat ālāf mudd min-hā masāriḥ sittmʾiat mudd wa-qadr arbaʿīn mudd /255 ikhtilāf bayna ahl qurlūn wa-ahl malbīṭ dhakar rijāl al-dīwān al-maʿmūr anna ṣāḥib malbīṭ taʿaddā la-hum ʿalā badhr miʾatayn mudd wa-ʿamila fī-hi maṭḥana wa-hādhā lladhī taʿaddā fī-hi min dākhil al-ribāʿ al-maḥdūda la-hu /256 wa-ḥadd ayḍan bayna l-aqbāṭ wa-ribāʿ ahl manzil ʿabd allāh dhakar shuyūkh jāṭū anna l-ḥadd min aṣl ibn al-jarrāḥ wa-l-sharqīy ilā marj al-karank[?] ilā bruqulūs yanzil maʿa rijl al-jabal ilā ʿayn al-bārida fa-dhakar ahl al-aqbāṭ anna l-qāʾid yaḥyā ḥadda la-hum min al-maqtal ilā l-inkirāt yamḍiy ʿalā l-istiwāʾ ilā bn al-jarrāḥ maṣabb al-māʾ li-l-aqbāṭ /257 wa-hādhā lladhī bayna l-ḥadd yubdhar ʿishrīn mudd min-hā lā yuʿmal ʿasharat amdād.* (Latin, lines 58–61, p.185: *Est seminat[ur]a qui[n]q[ue]milliu[m] salmar[um], de quib[us] s[un]t pascua /59 ad seminatura[m] sexcentar[um] salmar[um] [et] in quatraginta salmar[um] seminat[ur]a est discordia int[er] hom[ine]s Corilionis [et] h[o]m[in]es Malviti. Dixer[un]t h[o]m[in]es duane q[uo]d d[o]m[inu]s Malviti invasit eis t[er]ram ad seminatura[m] ducentar[um] salmar[um] [et] fecit ibidem molendin[um], que t[er]ra continet[ur] /60 infra sup[ra]dictas divisas. Et fuit divisum int[er] Lacbat [et] t[er]ras Miselabdella. Dixerunt vet[er]ani Iati q[uo]d divisa est a loco qui dicit[ur] radix bengerrak [et] oriental[is] pars ad pratu[m] karenc(?) vadit ad eu[m] loc[um] qui dicit[ur] p[ro]cul[us], descendit cu[m] pede montis ad fontem frigidum. /61 [Et] dixerunt h[o]m[in]es Lacbat q[uo]d gayt[us] Yhie constituit eis diuisas a loco qui dicit[ur] mactel usq[ue] ad hancarat, vadit*

Several of the boundaries enclosed lands which belonged to two or more different estates, and it was not uncommon for the men on one estate to farm land within another. It is difficult to discover precisely what lay behind such complexities, but they may have tended to encourage territorial disputes. For example, the estate of Raḥl al-Miʾa was also known as Jinān Ibn Kināna. More than half of its lands lay in the estate of Raḥl Bū Furīra, but an Arabic note, so confusing that the Latin translator and Cusa both ignored it, implies that Raḥl al-Miʾa lay entirely within Bū Furīra. Although it was registered under the district of Iato, some of Raḥl al-Miʾa's lands lay in the neighbouring districts of Corleone and Cefalà Diana.[64]

Notes upon area and land-use were appended to some boundary-descriptions. In the 1182 *jarīda*, such information is given for only twenty-three estates, all in the district of Iato. Such notes vary in detail and complexity. The simplest and most common are of the form 'X *salme* are sown'.[65] Confusingly, this indicates the total area of the estate, *not* the area sown, as can be seen from the next most common form, which express the total area, and the amount of pasture within it, as follows: 'X *salme* are sown, of which Y *salme* are pasture'.[66] Two notes give both the total area, and the area of the land within it which is not worth cultivating: 'X *salme* are sown, of which Y *salme* are not worth ploughing'.[67] One note distinguishes between 'worked' and 'idle' land.[68] Sometimes we learn how much of the total is worked,[69] sometimes how much is idle.[70] The note for the estate of Mārtū is exceptionally

directe usq[ue] ad beniarrak. Effusio aque p[er]tinet ad Lacbat [et] de hoc fuit alt[er]catio. Est seminatura viginti salmarum, de q[ui]b[us] dece[m] n[on] vale[n]t ad labora[n]d[um].)

64 Lines 242, 244 (Cusa 1868–82, pp.208, 209): 'And within [Raḥl Bū Furīra] is Raḥl al-Miʾa. And it is Jinān Ibn Kināna … /[244] The seed-land of the large boundary within which is the boundary of Raḥl al-Miʾa is five thousand and seven hundred *salme*, of which five hundred *salme* are in the lands of Corleone, two hundred *salme* are in the lands of Cefalà, three thousand *salme* in Raḥl al-Miʾa, and two thousand *salme* are in Bū Furīra.' (*wa-fī dākhili-h raḥl al-miʾa wa-huwa jinān ibn kināna … badhr al-ḥadd al-kabīr alladhī fī dākhili-h ḥadd raḥl al-mīʾa khamsat ālāf wa-sabʿmiʾat mudd min-hā fī ribāʿ qurlūn khamsmiʾat mudd wa-min-hā fī ribāʿ jafala miʾatayn mudd wa-min-hā fī raḥl al-miʾa thalāthat ālāf mudd wa-min-hā fī raḥl bū furīra alfayn mudd.* Latin, lines 42–3, pp.183–4: *Est seminat[ura] divisa magna, sub qua continet[ur] divisa Rahalmie, quinque milliu[m] [et] septi[n]gent[ar]u[m] salma[r]u[m]. de his sunt infra t[er]ras Corilionis quingente salme, [et] in t[er]ris Cefala ducente [et] intra Rahalmie tria millia salmar[um] /[43] [et] intra Bufurera duo millia salma[r]u[m].*)

65 *Yubdhar X mudd* (Latin: *Est seminatura X salmarum*). Nine occurrences: Qurūbnish, Qurūbnish al-Suflī, Raḥl al-Wuṭāʾ, al-Andalusīn, Manzil Zarqūn, Raḥl al-Balāṭ, Raḥl al-Mudd, Raḥl al-Sikkāk, Raḥl al-Wazzān.

66 *Yubdhar X mudd min-hā masāriḥ Y mudd* (Latin: *Est seminatura X salmarum, ex his Y salme sunt pascue*). Six occurrences: al-Maghāghī, Sūmminī, Malbīṭ, Raḥl al-Kilāʿī, Bū Nifāṭ, and Laqamūqa.

67 *Yubdhar X mudd min-hā Y mudd lā yaṣluḥ bi-ḥarth* or *li-l-ḥarth* (Latin: *Est seminatura X salmarum, de his non valent ad laborandum Y salme*). Two occurrences: Maghanūja and al-Balūʾīn.

68 Raḥl Ibn Barka: *badhru-h miʾa wa-ʿishrīn mudd ʿammālan wa-baṭṭālan min jumla hādhā l-ḥadd* (Latin: *Recipit p[re]dicta divisa seminatura[m] centu[m] viginti salmar[um] int[er] laborabiles [et] no[n] laborabiles*).

69 Raḥl al-Jadīd: 'One hundred and fifty *salme* are sown of which fifty *salme* are ploughed. And in it a small part remains as scrub' (*yubdhar miʾa wa-khamsīn mudd min-hā mā yuḥrath khamsīn mudd wa-fī-hi min al-shaʿrā juzʾ yasīr; Et est seminat[ur]a centu[m] quinquaginta salm[arum] [et] habet modica[m] parte[m] de silva*).

70 Raḥl ʿAmrūn: 'Fifty-two plough-lands are sown, of which that which is not ploughed is a seed-land of ten plough-lands' (*yubdharu thnayn wa-khamsīn zawjan min-hā mā lā yuḥrath badhr ʿasharat azwāj; Est seminat[ur]a ad pariccla bovu[m] quinquagi[n]taduo, ex iis sunt t[er]re que no[n] valent ad laborandum ad dece[m] pariccla*).

detailed: 'What is worth ploughing – eight hundred and ninety-seven *salme* – is sown; and what is not worth [ploughing] – mountains and pasture – is two hundred and seventy *salme*'.[71] These notes might represent a crude assessment of the productive capacity of the land. If so, and if we could be sure that they reproduced accurately and fully the data from the *dafātir*, then it would be tempting to conclude that the assessment made by the *dīwān* was neither sophisticated nor systematic. However, it is difficult to imagine that such sketchy notes could ever have served as the basis for a calculation of yield, and there can be little doubt that they were not the sole, nor even the principal data from which the *dīwān* assessed the revenue of its lands.

Conclusions

The three great Monreale *jarāʾid* (***Dīwānī* 43–5**) afford the fullest glimpse of the records of the *dīwān*. Even so, they reveal so extremely little of the way in which the registers of villeins and estate-boundaries were actually used to assess and collect revenue, that it seems legitimate to infer the existence of other, far more detailed records that have not survived. That said, there are a number of perplexing gaps in the coverage of the three Monreale registers which, because of the completeness of the Monreale tabulary, cannot be explained by the loss of documents which originally filled the lacunae. For example, the 1182 *jarīdat al-ḥudūd* gives no boundary-description for almost half of the estates listed in the 1183 register, and describes the boundaries of nineteen estates which do not appear in the two registers of villeins. This might indicate that, as late as the 1170s and '80s, only about half the territory was covered by records of both villeins and land-boundaries, and that the records of the *dīwān* were still far from complete.

We simply do not possess the evidence that would allow a sound judgement as to the quality of the records of the *dīwān*. What little survives is contradictory. On the one hand, the Arabic and bilingual documents issued by the *dīwān* itself for the island of Sicily, if taken at face value, could be interpreted to indicate that its records, even of the royal demesne, were crude and incomplete. On the other hand, the one record of the Norman administration that does survive in more or less its original form, the so-called *Catalogus Baronum*, demonstrates that it was capable of producing records of great detail and sophistication, which tempered bureaucratic rigour with the art of the possible. My own impression is that, in all probability, the *dīwān* did begin to develop records of considerable sophistication for the administration of the island from the 1140s, but that we must also take seriously the evidence which indicates that such records were still patchy and incomplete as late as the 1180s.

[71] *Yubdhar mā yaṣluḥ li-l-ḥarth thamānmiʾa wa-sabʿa wa-tisʿīn mudd wa-mā lā yaṣluḥ jibāl wa-masāriḥ miʾatayn wa-thalātha wa-sabʿīn mudd* (Latin: *Est seminat[ur]a de t[er]ris valentib[us] ad laborandu[m] octagentar[um] nonaginta septe[m] salmar[um]. Et de t[er]ris que no[n] valent ad laborandu[m] ducentar[um] septuaginta triu[m], s[cilic]et sunt montes [et] pascua*).

CHAPTER 8

The duties and organisation of the royal *dīwān*, 1141–94

Introduction

This review of the duties and the organisation of the royal *dīwān* is almost exclusively concerned with the Arabic administration, to the exclusion of the Greek and the Latin; with *al-dīwān*, not ἡ δουάνα (*ē douana*), nor the *duana*. As the very existence of these Greek and Latin terms indicates, this is a wholly artificial distinction, but a review of the entire administration of Norman Sicily lies beyond the scope of this work. It would, moreover, largely retrace the steps so recently taken by Hiroshi Takayama in his study of the administration of the Norman kingdom; and would do so without a significant corpus of new evidence yet being available. Although he and I may not always agree upon every twist and turn of that tortuous, and often still obscure path, our destination is essentially the same. Indeed, without Takayama's clear perception of the regional variations between the different provinces of the kingdom, it would have been impossible for me to focus so closely upon the Arabic administration of the island of Sicily, ignoring the mainland provinces of the duchy of Apulia, the principality of Capua, and – to a lesser extent – Calabria. Again, Takayama's vision of a flexible, omnicompetent administration, cuts the Gordian knot so tightly tied by generations of administrative and constitutional historians determined to identify a rigid organisational structure that might be compared to the English exchequer. It also makes room for a study such as this, which concentrates upon only one part of the loose and changeable whole.

The foundation of the *dīwān al-taḥqīq*

After Roger's coronation in 1130 there is, at first, no evidence that the Arabic administration possessed a clearly defined structure and organisation within the wider *curia regis*. Not until June 1141 (***Dīwānī* 16–17**) does it appear with a title – *al-dīwān al-maʿmūr* and, in Greek, τὸ σέκρετον (*to sekreton*). On that occasion, it authorised the settlement of a territorial dispute between San Giorgio di Triocala and William of Sciacca. Less than four years later, the *dīwān al-maᶜmūr* features regularly in the *jarāʾid* renewed in 1145 (***Dīwānī* 21–5**): the recipients are confirmed in possession of the villeins named, on the condition that they are not registered in the *jarāʾid* of the *dīwān al-maᶜmūr*. In the renewal to Cefalù (***Dīwānī* 24**), the *dīwān al-maᶜmūr* is said to have supervised the exchange of villeins from Mileto to Cefalù, and to have compensated Mileto with lands and villeins in Calabria out of the royal demesne. That exchange had taken place in 1136; therefore, if it is not an anachronism, this reference to *al-dīwān al-maᶜmūr* indicates that the title was in use at least five years before it occurs in a surviving document.

In April 1149 (***Dīwānī* 29**), an office called the *dīwān al-taḥqīq al-maᶜmūr* was ordered to grant to San Nicolò di Chùrchuro five households of villeins, and an estate at Raḥl al-Wazzān 'from the *dīwānī* lands'. In the same document, the *dīwān al-taḥqīq al-maᶜmūr* ordered the *ᶜāmil* of Jāṭū to determine the boundaries of the estate granted, which were then recorded in the *daftar al-ḥudūd* in the *dīwān al-taḥqīq al-maᶜmūr*. The copy of the original donation, dated December 1149, was issued by 'the elders of the *dīwān al-maᶜmūr*, the *qāʾid* Barrūn and the scribe ᶜUthmān'. Michele Amari, Dietlinde Schack, and Albrecht Noth all believed that, in this document, the titles *dīwān al-taḥqīq al-maᶜmūr* and *al-dīwān al-maᶜmūr* both referred to a single office, and they insisted that the *dīwān al-taḥqīq* and the *dīwān al-maᶜmūr* were one and the same.[1] Such an interpretation does not take account of the complicated transmission of the document. What has come down to us is a copy (*nuskha*) of the original privilege (*kitāb*). The order to issue the privilege was given to the *dīwān al-taḥqīq al-maᶜmūr* in April 1149, but the copy was made in the following December by the elders of the *dīwān al-maᶜmūr*. The original *kitāb* would have borne 'the noble seal', but the *nuskha* was signed merely with Barrūn's personal *ᶜalāma*.[2] This was insufficient for the monks of Chùrchuro, who duly requested a second copy of the *kitāb*. When what was supposed to be that second copy was issued in June 1154, it was not only sealed, but also signed by Maio of Bari, the emir of emirs (***Dīwānī* 33**). This second, legally authenticated and confirmed copy makes no mention of the *dīwān al-maᶜmūr*, and it appears to have been issued by the *dīwān al-taḥqīq*. On this basis, a strong *prima facie* case may be made that, from 1149 if not earlier, the *dīwān al-taḥqīq* was the executive department of the *dīwān* responsible for authenticating and confirming grants of lands and villeins out of the royal demesne; privileges, and even legally authenticated and confirmed copies, could only be issued by the *dīwān al-taḥqīq*, not by the ordinary officers and scribes of the *dīwān*.

Since the publication of Garufi's influential study of the *dīwān*, there has been considerable confusion about the significance of its titles, and this must be dispersed before proceeding further with this discussion of the *dīwān al-taḥqīq*.[3]

[1] Amari 1970, pp.86–7, 91; Schack 1969, pp.78–9; Noth 1983, pp.217–18 and n.200.
[2] Note that this is misread and misinterpreted in Johns and Metcalfe 1999, p.231: see below, p.222 note 39, and p.251.
[3] Garufi 1901.

Maᶜmūr is a passive participle of the verb *ᶜamara*, 'he inhabited', and has the primary meaning, in the classical language, of 'inhabited', 'frequented', 'peopled', 'flourishing', 'in good state of repair', *etcetera*. The word also carries strong Qurʾānic resonances. *Al-bayt al-maᶜmūr*, 'the much-frequented house', is generally understood to refer to the Kaᶜba (*Qurʾān* 52:4); and the verb *ᶜamara* is also used of mosques, perhaps most famously in the verse *innamā yaᶜmuru masājida llāhi man āmana bi-llāhi etc.*, 'Only he who believes in God shall attend the mosques of God *etc.*' (*Qurʾān* 9:18). *Maᶜmūr* has thereby acquired the secondary connotation of 'served' or 'worshipped'.[4] In medieval and later Islam, the epithet *al-maᶜmūr* is traditionally extended to royal institutions, and expresses the pious hope that the institution may always be 'inhabited', 'served', and 'busy'.[5] Thus, for example, a Fāṭimid decree of 1130 was issued by the office of correspondence, the *dīwān al-inshāʾ al-maᶜmūr*.[6] In Norman Sicily, we find *maᶜmūr* used of royal institutions which have nothing to do with the fiscal administration, such as the royal palace at Palermo,[7] and the royal *ṭirāz*.[8] It cannot be stressed too emphatically that *maᶜmūr* is in no way descriptive of the functions or activities of the *dīwān*.[9] Thus, the phrase *al-dīwān al-maᶜmūr* means simply 'the busy …', 'the [well-] served …' or, more loosely but more appropriately in Norman Sicily, 'the royal *dīwān*.[10]

The case of *taḥqīq* is rather different. It is a verbal noun from *ḥaqqaqa*, 'he verified [something]', and has the primary meaning of 'verification', and thence 'examination', 'investigation', 'control', *etc.* In the phrase *dīwān al-taḥqīq al-maᶜmūr*, the noun *al-taḥqīq* is attached to *dīwān al-maᶜmūr* by means of a genitive of possession (*iḍāfa*), and the whole title may be translated as 'the royal *dīwān* of verification'.[11]

Before the *dīwān al-taḥqīq* appears in Norman Sicily in 1149, it is known only in Fāṭimid Egypt. There, the *dīwān al-majlis* was the central bureau of the financial administration, with many subsidiary *dawāwīn*.[12] According to Ibn Ṭuwayr, its activities seem to have been co-ordinated and controlled by the *dīwān al-naẓar*, which had direct control over all the *dawāwīn* of finance (*amwāl*) and their officers, until 501/1107–8.[13] In that year, the *dīwān al-taḥqīq* was created by the vizier al-Afḍal ibn Badr al-Jamālī, the Armenian commander-in-chief and vizier, who governed Egypt almost unchecked under the caliphs al-Mustaᶜlī and al-Āmir, from 1094 until his assassination in 1121.[14] According to Ibn al-Ṭuwayr, as reported by

[4] Lane 1984, vol.II, p.2156.

[5] al-Qalqashandī 1913–72, vol.VI, pp.183–5 (see also Index, p.393, under *al-dīwān al-maᶜmūr*); al-Bāshā 1957, p.478; Amari 1933–9, vol.3, pp.327–8, n.2; Noth 1983, p.217.

[6] Stern 1964a, p.36, line 18.

[7] Cusa 1868–82, p.44.

[8] The best illustration of the inscription is to be found in the rare and unwieldy Bock 1864, vol.II, table VI, fig.8 (see also vol.I, pp.27–31).

[9] *Pace* Garufi 1901, pp.229, 236–8, and all those who have followed him.

[10] Amari 1933–9, p.327, n.2 (on p.328), urged that *maᶜmūr* 'torna a "regio, pubblico" e nulla più'. See also Noth 1983, p.215.

[11] For example, Stern 1964a, pp.166, 168.

[12] al-Maqrīzī 1853, vol.I, pp.397–402.

[13] al-Maqrīzī 1853, vol.I, pp.400–1; al-Qalqashandī 1913–72, vol.III, pp.493–4.

[14] For al-Afḍal, see: Dadoyan 1997, pp.127–39; Wiet 1955.

Ibn Muyassar and al-Maqrīzī, al-Afḍal's immediate objective in creating the *dīwān al-taḥqīq* was to secure absolute control of the fiscal administration in order to achieve his reform of the *iqṭāʿāt*. The *dīwān al-majlis* was then in the hands of one Ibn al-Usquf, who is said to have grown weak and feeble, and seems to have been more an immovable obstruction in the way of al-Afḍal's reforms than an active enemy. The *dīwān al-taḥqīq* was founded, and its first director, the Christian Yūḥannā ibn Abī l-Layth, assumed overall control of all the financial and administrative *dīwāns* (*fī l-dawāwīni l-amwāli wa-l-maṣāliḥi*). After Ibn al-Usquf finally died, Ibn Abī l-Layth supervised all the *dawāwīn*, from his position of director of the *dīwān al-taḥqīq*, until his own execution in 1124.[15]

What prompted the creation of the *dīwān al-taḥqīq* was the Afḍalī *rawk* of 501/1107–8. Al-Afḍal's father, Badr al-Jamālī had come to power during the social and economic crisis which followed the great famine of 1066–73. Lacking the cash to pay his troops, Badr had contented them with grants of tax-farms held as *iqṭāʿāt*. He could well afford to do so, because the famine seems to have resulted in sharp demographic decline and the consequent under-population of agricultural land. A generation later, by the turn of the century, as the rural population began to recover, there was extensive but unofficial re-occupation of abandoned lands, and large-scale, systematic usurpation of the state demesne. At the same time, the more powerful *iqṭāʿ*-holders increased their income and the size of their holdings at the expense of the state, while the smaller and more vulnerable tax-farmers came to bear an increasingly heavy burden. The Afḍalī *rawk* of 1107–8 cancelled the existing contracts by which *iqṭāʿāt* were held and, on the basis of a new cadastral survey of agricultural land, redistributed the tax-farms, eventually by means of auction on the open market. Al-Afḍal's reforms in no way settled the matter, however, and, over the next decades, there was both dissatisfaction with the redistribution amongst the tax-farmers, and further usurpation of the state domain.[16] The *dīwān al-taḥqīq* was thus created to provide al-Afḍal with the means to supervise and to control the *rawk* of 1107–8, and the subsequent reform of the system of *iqṭāʿāt*.

At this time, the *dīwān al-taḥqīq* seems to have been one of the most important of all the financial bureaux: al-Maqrīzī claims that it was 'directed by the supervisor (*nāẓir*) of the *dawāwīn*'; al-Qalqashandī, that 'it is directed by the most senior chief of the *dawāwīn*'.[17] However, the same sources elsewhere suggest that its director was an official of only middle rank, whose monthly salary of fifty dinars was significantly lower than other officers of the financial administration, including the director of the treasury, the *bayt al-māl*, and the head of the *dīwān al-naẓar*,

[15] Ibn Muyassar 1919, p.42; al-Maqrīzī 1967–73, vol.III, pp.39, 148. In an Arabic Geniza document dated to the last decade of Ramaḍān 504 (April 1111), Yuḥannā ibn Abī l-Layth responds to the endorsement of a petition that had been referred to *dīwāni l-taḥqīqi l-afḍalī l-saʿīdi*: Khan 1993, no.105, pp.415–16.

[16] al-Maqrīzī 1853, vol.I, pp.83–6; al-Maqrīzī 1911–27, vol.II, pp.5–14. See also Brett 1984, pp.52–5.

[17] al-Maqrīzī 1967–73, vol.III, p.338; al-Qalqashandī 1913–72, vol.III, p.493–4 (*yulḥaqu bi-raʾsi l-dawāwīni l-mutaqaddimi*).

whose monthly salaries were, respectively, one hundred and seventy dinars.[18] This would seem to indicate that, after the *dīwān al-taḥqīq* had served the immediate purpose for which it had been created, it became subsidiary to the *dīwān al-naẓar*, with the limited responsibility of checking the accounts of the other *dawāwīn* of finance.[19] After al-Afḍal's death, it may be that the office was often left vacant.[20] Under the Ayyūbids, the *dīwān al-taḥqīq* disappeared, when the duties of all the financial bureaux were assumed by a new office, the *dīwān bi-l-bāb*.[21] Some memory of the *dīwān al-taḥqīq*'s effectiveness under al-Afḍal must have survived, however, for both the Ayyūbid sultan, al-Kāmil, and the Mamlūk al-Muᶜizz Aybak are said to have contemplated its refoundation.[22]

The circumstances surrounding the first appearance of the *dīwān al-taḥqīq* in Norman Sicily bear a striking similarity to those which produced the office of the same name in Fāṭimid Egypt. In both cases, the office seems to be directly associated with major administrative reorganisation: in Egypt, the Afḍalī *rawk* of 1107–8, and the subsequent reform of the system of *iqṭāᶜāt*; in Sicily, the institution of the *dafātir al-ḥudūd*, after the renewals of 1145, as the primary tool for the administration of both the royal demesne and feudal lands in Sicily.

The foundation of the Sicilian *dīwān al-taḥqīq* may be associated with contemporary events in the royal palace. In the summer of 1151, George of Antioch, who had presided over the whole administration since 1126, died at the age of ninety. His successor was eventually to be Maio, the son of Leo de Rayza, a royal judge from Bari in Apulia. Maio had been archivist (*scriniarius*) in the royal chancery since 1144, and had acted as the *datarius* of documents in the absence of the chancellor, Robert of Selby. In 1149, Maio was appointed vice-chancellor, an office apparently created specially for him.[23] As both Romuald of Salerno and 'Hugo Falcandus' report, and as Maio's signature to ***Dīwānī* 31** now conclusively proves, he was made royal chancellor before May 1152, immediately upon the death of Robert of Selby.[24] By all accounts, Maio was not raised to the rank of emir of emirs until after the second catastrophe of these years, the death of King Roger himself on 26 or 27 February 1154. Both Arabic and Latin sources report that the last years of Roger's life were dogged by illness and premature senility, and it is tempting to

[18] For comparison, the monthly salary of some leading officials was as follows: the *wazīr* received 5,000 dinars; the *ṣāḥib bayt al-māl*, 100 dinars; the *mutawallī dīwān al-naẓar*, 70 dinars per month; the *mutawallī dīwān al-taḥqīq*, 50 dinars; the directors of the *dīwān al-majlis* and the *dīwān al-jaysh*, 40 dinars; the *ṣāḥib daftar al-majlis*, 35 dinars; and scribes from 30, 10, 7, or 5 dinars (al-Qalqashandī 1913–72, vol.III, pp.526–7). See also: al-Maqrīzī 1853, vol.I, p.402; al-Maqrīzī 1967–73, vol.III, pp.340–1.

[19] al-Qalqashandī 1913–72, vol.III, p.493.

[20] Duri, Gottschalk and Colin 1962, p.329 (citing Ibn al-Ṣayrafī 1914, p.82, n.1, where this is not, however, mentioned).

[21] al-Nābulusī 1958–60, p.٣٦, n.1, and p.٣٩; Duri, Gottschalk and Colin 1962, p.329.

[22] Ibn Muyassar 1919, p.42.

[23] Ménager 1960, p.55; ed. Brühl 1987, nos 64–5, 71 and 75, pp.183–9, 205–6, 214–16 (*scriniarius*); nos 78–9, pp.224–33 (*vicecancellarius*); Brühl 1983, pp.38–9.

[24] 'Hugo Falcandus' 1897, pp.7–8 ('Hugo Falcandus' 1998, p.60); Romuald of Salerno 1935, pp.234–5. He signs ***Dīwānī* 31**, dated May 1152, † *Maio d(omi)ni Regis Cancell(a)ri(us)*: see below, pp.198, 201. For the date of the death of Robert of Selby, see Brühl 1983, p.38 and n.125.

link Maio's rapid ascent with the deaths of George of Antioch and Robert of Selby, and with the king's decline.[25] Be that as it may, Romuald of Salerno's report that it was King Roger's son and heir, William I, who made Maio *magnus ammiratus*, is confirmed by his signature to ***Dīwānī* 33**.[26] One of the new king's first acts must have been to appoint Maio to the pre-eminent rank which had remained empty since the death of George of Antioch.

The recall of privileges of 1144–5 thus coincides with Maio's first appearance as *scriniarius*, or archivist, in the royal chancery. Maio was appointed to the specially created office of vice-chancellor in the year in which the *dīwān al-taḥqīq* and the *daftar al-ḥudūd* are first mentioned. In 1152, soon after he was promoted 'Chancellor of the Lord King', Maio signed an Arabic *dīwānī* document settling a boundary dispute (***Dīwānī* 31**). And in 1154, the year in which he assumed the rank of emir of emirs, Maio signed a legally authenticated and confirmed Arabic copy of a privilege issued by the *dīwān al-taḥqīq al-maᶜmūr* (***Dīwānī* 33**). This amounts to a strong circumstantial case that Maio of Bari was closely linked with the recall of 1144–5, the creation of the *dīwān al-taḥqīq*, and the institution of the *dafātir al-ḥudūd*. At the risk of stretching too far the analogy with the foundation of the Fāṭimid *dīwān al-taḥqīq*, the three main protagonists may be compared with their Sicilian counterparts: the reforming vizier al-Afḍal with George of Antioch; the loyal *kātib* Ibn Abī l-Layth with Maio of Bari; and – less appropriately, but just conceivably – the immovable obstacle, Ibn al-Usquf with Robert of Selby.

The duties and organisation of the *dīwān al-taḥqīq* and the *dīwān al-maᶜmūr*, 1154–94

Three factors combine to obscure a clear perception of the duties and organisation of the royal *dīwān*. First and foremost, none of its internal records survive, and nearly all the available evidence comes from documents issued to feudatories or royal officials. The evidence thus regards, almost exclusively, the donation and reconfirmation of grants of lands, villeins, and other privileges and rights out of the royal demesne, and the definition of estate boundaries. Moreover, the vast majority

[25] For the date, see Houben 1999, p.211, n.1. Romuald of Salerno 1935, p.236, has Roger die (in 1152!) of a fever. 'Hugo Falcandus' 1897, p.7 ('Hugo Falcandus' 1998, p.59), reports that 'not long after' William was consecrated and crowned as co-ruler on Easter Day 1151, Roger sank into 'premature senility', worn out by his immense labours, and by more sexual activity than was good for him (*tum immensis attritus laboribus, tum ultra qua bona corporis exigeret valetudo rebus assuetus veneris, immatura senectute consumptus, cessit in fata*). Ibn al-Athīr reports that, after the execution of Philip of Mahdīya in December 1153 (below, pp.216–17), God granted but little respite to Roger, who soon died of 'a blockage of the throat' (*al-khawānīq*): Ibn al-Athīr 1851–76, vol.XI, p.124 (*BAS*[2], vol.I, p.338; *BAS*[2]*(It.)*, vol.II, p.376, 'essendo morto il re di angina ...'). I am grateful to Dr Emilie Savage-Smith of the Oriental Institute, Oxford, for her comments on the probable meaning of the Arabic term.

[26] Romuald of Salerno 1935, p.237.

of surviving royal documents were issued to ecclesiastical beneficiaries, and were thus preserved in church archives. Comparatively few documents to lay feudatories have survived. This sample must represent only a tiny part of the work of the royal *dīwān*. Almost nothing is known about what must have been its principal task: the management of revenue and expenditure. Second, that the *dīwān* and its officers appear more frequently in Greek and Latin than in Arabic and bilingual documents, poses the problem of equivalent terminology across the three languages. Bilingual documents in Arabic and Greek or Latin occasionally give what appear to be standard equivalents for the Arabic terms. Thus, for example, after 1149, the *dīwān al-taḥqīq al-maᶜmūr* was generally τὸ σέκρετον (*to sekreton*) in Greek, and the *duana de secretis* in Latin; but it is not, alas, always quite so straightforward.[27] Third, only a small proportion of royal documents are yet available in modern critical editions, and many remain inedited. It is therefore unlikely that any review of the activities and organisation of the *dīwān* will consider all the relevant evidence, and the publication of a single hitherto unknown document could conceivably undermine the entire enterprise. This last factor should be no deterrent: the editors of the *Codex Diplomaticus Regni Siciliae* may be condemned to Sisyphean toil, but no one should therefore be obliged to suffer the pains of Tantalus.

It is, in part, because of such obstacles that the organisation of the royal *dīwān*, and the respective duties of its bureaux, has been hotly contested for two centuries, from Rosario Gregorio to Hiroshi Takayama. Fortunately, most scholars who have previously addressed this question have dutifully undertaken a more or less thorough review of the *status quo* before proceeding to new analysis, so that I can dispense with a detailed historiographical account, and concentrate upon the evidence itself.[28]

Towards the beginning of the previous section, I proposed, on the basis of ***Dīwānī* 29 and 33**, that the *dīwān al-taḥqīq* was created, in or before 1149, as the executive department of the *dīwān*. I shall now attempt to justify that claim, and to demonstrate that this remained the rôle of the *dīwān al-taḥqīq* throughout the period of Norman rule. Unlike some modern commentators, I do not believe that the two were separate offices. Indeed, I do not understand *al-dīwān al-maᶜmūr* to have been an office with clearly defined duties. It was rather an imprecise and flexible term, which could be used to cover the entire administration. For example, the phrase *al-dīwān al-maᶜmūr*, and the relative adjective *dīwānī*, are both used to qualify property as belonging to the royal demesne, as when royal lands are

[27] Note that, before 1149, the Greek term τὸ σέκρετον was used for the *dīwān al-maᶜmūr*: above, p.106. It is not clear to me that, thereafter, τὸ σέκρετον is used exclusively to mean the *dīwān al-taḥqīq*, and ὁ σεκρετικός exclusively for officers of the *dīwān al-taḥqīq*, as scholars from Garufi 1901 to Takayama 1993 have argued. I strongly suspect that, on the contrary, τὸ σέκρετον was equivalent to *al-dīwān*, and was not used exclusively for any one office within the *dīwān*.

[28] The question has already been the subject of two thorough reviews by Mario Caravale and Hiroshi Takayama permitting me to concentrate upon those aspects most relevant to my own interests. The following are the principal landmarks and are, perhaps, best read in antichronological order: Gregorio 1972, vol.I, pp.205–10; Amari 1878 (see also Amari 1933–9, p.327, n.2); Garufi 1901, pp.225–33; Garufi 1928, pp.1–6; Jamison 1957, pp.33–55; Caravale 1966, pp.169–77; Mazzarese Fardella 1966, pp.2–22; Takayama 1993, pp.1–24.

described as *al-ribāᶜ al-dīwānīya*,[29] or *bilād al-dīwān al-maᶜmūr*,[30] and royal villeins as *rijāl al-dīwān al-maᶜmūr*.[31] This should not be understood to mean that the royal demesne was the exclusive responsibility of the *dīwān al-maᶜmūr*, any more than a Latin phrase such as *demanium curie nostre* indicates that the royal demesne was the exclusive responsibility of the *curia regia*:[32] the administration of the royal demesne was amongst the many and varied tasks carried out by the central administration, whether it was called *al-dīwān al-maᶜmūr* or *curia regia*.

Much has been made of the fact that the *jarāʾid* and *dafātir* of royal villeins are always described as being 'of the *dīwān al-maᶜmūr*', and it has been suggested, on this basis, that it was specially responsible for maintaining registers of the inhabitants of both feudal and demesne lands, and for collecting taxes from the inhabitants of both.[33] The basis of such claims is extremely weak. First, although the *jarāʾid* renewed in 1145 do refer to 'the *jarāʾid* of the *dīwān al-maᶜmūr*', this was before the foundation of the *dīwān al-taḥqīq* and cannot, therefore, be used to argue for the differentiation of the two offices. Second, the only other reference to the *dafātir* and *jarāʾid* of villeins of the *dīwān al-maᶜmūr* demonstrates precisely the structure which I am proposing: the executive department of the *dīwān* (the *dīwān al-taḥqīq*) is ordered to supervise the composition of a *jarīda* of newly granted villeins from the registers of villeins and the old *jarāʾid* kept in the *dīwān*.[34] Third, if the *dīwān al-maᶜmūr* had been particularly responsible for the administration of the royal demesne, it should not have performed extraneous duties, nor should the *dīwān al-taḥqīq* have intervened in matters exclusively pertaining to the royal demesne. Amongst the extraneous duties performed by the *dīwān al-maᶜmūr* were: the issue of records of *dīwānī* documents (***Dīwānī* 29, 31–2**); the collection of revenue from the villeins of feudal lands (***Dīwānī* 34 and 38**); the keeping of registers of income to the treasury, and the scrutiny of sales of property out of the royal demesne through an officer known as 'the controller of the audit of the *dīwān al-maᶜmūr*' (*wakīl al-faḥṣ al-dīwānī l-maᶜmūr* – ***Dīwānī* 35**); the administration of vacant ecclesiastical jurisdictions (***Dīwānī* 37**); and the registration of sales of property authorised by the *dīwān al-fawāʾid*.[35] Amongst the interventions of the *dīwān al-taḥqīq* into the administration of the royal demesne are the inquiries that it held, or ordered to be held, into the usurpation of villeins and other royal property.[36] Again, much has been made of the fact that the *dafātir al-ḥudūd* are always described as being 'in' or 'of' the *dīwān al-taḥqīq*; and it has been suggested, on this basis, that the *dīwān al-taḥqīq* had exclusive responsibility for lands, while the *dīwān*

[29] ***Dīwānī* 29** and **33**: Johns and Metcalfe 1999, p.244, line 8 and p.249, line 7. ***Dīwānī* 36 and 43** (Latin, *terrae duane*): Cusa 1868–82, p.651 and p.215 (Latin, p.187).

[30] ***Dīwānī* 45**: Cusa, 1868–82, p.245.

[31] ***Dīwānī* 44** and **45**: Cusa 1868–82, pp.212 and 215 (Latin, *homines duane*, pp.185 and 188), p.245.

[32] Garufi, 1899, no.54, p.125. Indeed, from this case, it is clear that the royal *dīwān* was responsible for the demesne lands of the *curia regia*.

[33] Caravale 1966, pp.200–1; Takayama 1993, pp.87–8; see also Takayama 1985, pp.135–8.

[34] ***Dīwānī* 44**. See also above, p.153 and p.156, note 32, line 5; and pp.163–4.

[35] Below, p.204–6.

[36] Below, p.203, notes 52–3.

al-maᶜmūr was in charge of their inhabitants.[37] Again, this claim cannot be upheld. The *dafātir al-ḥudūd* were clearly not for the eyes only of the officers of the *dīwān al-taḥqīq*: they were consulted by scribes of the *dīwān al-maᶜmūr* to prepare records of *dīwānī* documents (***Dīwānī* 31–3**); and land-registers would, in any case, have been essential for the day-to-day administration of both royal and feudal lands. Moreover, as we have already seen, the *dīwān al-taḥqīq* was not exclusively concerned with lands and, in its capacity as the executive branch of the *dīwān*, it made grants of villeins, supervised the composition of *jarāʾid al-rijāl*, and investigated the usurpation of villeins from the royal demesne. Orders passed from the king or his ministers to the *dīwān al-taḥqīq*, which then supervised their performance within the omnicompetent administration, before confirming their execution to eventual beneficiaries of those orders. The *dīwān al-taḥqīq* thus acted as the interface between the administration and both the rulers and the ruled. In short, the title *al-dīwān al-maᶜmūr* was used of the whole Arabic administration, while the title *dīwān al-taḥqīq* was restricted to its executive department.

It seems likely that the *dīwān al-taḥqīq* was at first directed by Maio of Bari. The original privilege to Chùrchuro of April 1149 (***Dīwānī* 28**) does not survive, and so there is no record of the *datarius*, but the titles used in the *dispositio* are significantly different from those employed in the *jarāʾid* renewed in 1145. The latter were issued upon 'the high, the to-be-obeyed, the most royal, the most glorified, the most holy, the Rogerian order (may God increase its high standing and efficacy)', but the privilege to Chùrchuro was made on merely 'the high, the to-be-obeyed order (may God increase its high standing and efficacy)', without any reference to the king. Exactly the same short formula is found in the writ issued to the bailiff of Sciacca in May 1152 (***Dīwānī* 31**), which was issued and signed by the Chancellor Maio of Bari. With his new rank of emir of emirs, Maio also signed the 1154 copy for Chùrchuro, which has the same formula (***Dīwānī* 33**). It seems likely, therefore, that he was also the *datarius* of ***Dīwānī* 28**. The only other *dīwānī* document to survive as an original from Maio's time of is the Greek-Arabic *plateia* and Arabic *ḥadd*, issued at the request of Adelicia, abbess of Santa Maria Maddelena di Corleone (***Dīwānī* 30**). This bears Roger II's Greek chancery signature, but not in the usual form. Maio's is unlikely to be the hand responsible, because he always signs in Latin, even on Greek and Arabic documents.[38] After Maio's murder on 10 November 1160, the *dīwān al-taḥqīq* was directed by a small group of officers, known collectively as the *aṣḥāb dīwān al-taḥqīq al-maᶜmūr* ('the lords of the *dīwān al-taḥqīq al-maᶜmūr*') and οἱ … γέρωντες … ἐπὶ τοῦ σεκρέτου (*oi gerontes epi tou sekretou*, 'the elders who preside over the *sekreton*').[39] Foremost amongst these were the Arab *qāʾid*s Martin and Richard, whose careers will be examined in Chapter 9.

As will be seen below, a second executive bureau, called the *duana baronum* or τὸ σέκρετον τῶν ἀποκοπῶν (*to sekreton tōn apokopōn*, 'the bureau of the

[37] Above, p.200, note 33. [38] von Falkenhausen 1997, pp.285–6 and n.196.
[39] 1161 (***Dīwānī* 35**); 1166 (***Dīwānī* 37**).

fiefs'), was founded in 1167–8.[40] It seems that the creation of this new office caused the Greek title of the *dīwān* to be inflated into 'the great bureau' (τὸ μέγα σέκρετον, *to mega sekreton*), so that 'the secretary' became 'the great secretary (ὁ μέγας σεκρετικός, *o megas sekretikos*). The corresponding Latin title *magnum secretum* is occasionally found, but it usually remains the *duana de secretis*. There was no corresponding change to the Arabic titles of the *dīwān*.[41] At about the same time, or a little later, a small board of royal familiars was interposed between the ruler and the elders of the *dīwān al-taḥqīq*, occupying the executive space left vacant since the death of Maio. In October 1172, when it first appears, this group of directors comprised Archbishop Walter II of Palermo, the Vice-chancellor Matthew of Salerno, and Bartholomew, bishop-elect of Agrigento; the same triumvirate of royal familiars which comprised the king's closest council.[42] They are referred to collectively, in Greek, as 'the most illustrious and honoured-by-God archons of the mighty court' and, in Arabic, as 'the lord viziers'.[43]

The principal activity in which *dīwānī* documents show the *dīwān al-taḥqīq* was the confirmation of grants of lands and villeins out of the royal demesne. Under William II, for example, it was the *dīwān al-taḥqīq* that supervised the massive grant of lands and villeins to Santa Maria di Monreale, and compiled the register of villeins of May 1178 (***Dīwānī* 43**), and the Arabic text of the boundary-register of 1182 (***Dīwānī* 44**).[44] Again, it was the *dīwān al-taḥqīq* that confirmed the *jarīda* of the villeins of Baida, who were granted to Palermo cathedral as compensation for those which it had surrendered to Monreale (***Dīwānī* 42**).[45] Not just the granting of fiefs, but also the sale of royal property lay within the mandate of the *dīwān al-taḥqīq*: in February 1161, it sold an estate from the royal demesne to the Palermitan Jew, Yaᶜqūb ibn Faḍlūn (***Dīwānī* 35**).[46] It was also responsible for the transfer of other rights and privileges: in November 1166, it handed over the archdeaconry of Messina, which had previously been administered by the *dīwān*,

[40] Below, pp.206–7.

[41] Tὸ μέγα σέκρετον first appears in October 1170: see the document cited by Haskins 1911, p.650, n.160. See my comments above, p.199 note 27.

[42] ***Dīwānī* 39**, lines 1–3 (Greek) and lines 24–5 (Arabic): ed. Ménager 1960, Appendix 2, no.33, pp.214–24.

[43] οἱ μεγαλεπιφανεστάτοι καὶ θεοτιμήτων ἀρχόντες τῆς κραταίας κόρτης; *al-mawālī l-wuzarā*ʾ.

[44] The order to compile ***Dīwānī* 43** was issued 'to the lords of the *dīwān al-taḥqīq al-ma*ᶜ*mūr*' (*ilā aṣḥābi dīwāni l-taḥqīqi l-ma*ᶜ*mūri*: line 5 = Cusa 1868–82, p.135); the Arabic text of ***Dīwānī* 44** was written 'by the hand of the scribe Yūsuf belonging to the *dīwān al-taḥqīq al-ma*ᶜ*mūr* … from the *dafātir* of the *dīwān al-taḥqīq al-ma*ᶜ*mūr*' (*bi-khaṭṭi l-kātibi yūsufa bi-dīwāni l-taḥqīqi l-ma*ᶜ*mūri* … *min dafātiri dīwāni l-taḥqīqi l-ma*ᶜ*mūri*: lines 369–370 = *ibid.*, p.244).

[45] The original *jarīda* is lost but, in a Latin donation of March 1177, Ind.X, it is referred to as *platea facta inde a Doana nostra de secretis* (the Latin title of the *dīwān al-taḥqīq*), *quae est plumbeo sigillo nostro sigilata*: Pirri 1733, vol.I, cols 107–8.

[46] The vendors were 'the lords of the *dīwān al-taḥqīq al-ma*ᶜ*mūr*, the elder, the *qā*ʾ*id* Martin, and the elder, the *qā*ʾ*id* Matthew' (line 1: μαρτίνος καὶ ματθαῖος καὶ οἱ λοιποὶ γέρωντες οἱ καὶ ἐπὶ τοῦ σεκρέτου; l.26 *aṣḥābu dīwāni l-taḥqīqi l-ma*ᶜ*mūri l-shaykhu l-qā*ʾ*idu martīn wa-l-shaykhu l-qā*ʾ*idu māthāw* = Cusa 1868–82, pp.622, 624). For Martin, see below, pp.219–22 and index; for Matthew, see index.

to Archbishop Nicholas (***Dīwānī* 37**);[47] and in January 1180, it reconfirmed the commercial rights originally granted to Cefalù by the Greek-Arabic decree of 1132 (***Dīwānī* 11**).[48]

One of the duties of the *dīwān al-taḥqīq* was to supervise the maintenance of the *dafātir al-ḥudūd*. From 1149 until 1178, these are consistently said to be 'in' or 'of' the *dīwān al-taḥqīq*.[49] To this end, its officers were responsible for fixing estate-boundaries, either in order to make grants of land out of the royal demesne,[50] or to settle boundary-disputes:[51] they either performed such duties in person, or delegated them to local officials. Another responsibility which is explicitly mentioned by the sources (and the *dīwān al-taḥqīq* almost certainly had many other duties which are not reported) was to inquire into the losses from the royal demesne. For example, in December 1170, the *qāʾid* Richard was dispatched to the region of Messina to investigate the usurpation of the king's property and villeins.[52] Again, such duties could be delegated to local officials, as in January 1183, when the *qāʾid* Richard ordered royal justiciars in Calabria to inquire whether villeins and property, which had been established as belonging to the royal demesne 'at the time of the *qāʾid* Thomas, who was chamberlain of the *duana de secretis*', had subsequently been usurped.[53]

The authority of the *dīwān al-taḥqīq* seems to have been limited to Sicily and Calabria. Even before the foundation of the *duana baronum*, the *dīwān al-taḥqīq*, even in its Greek or Latin guise, does not appear in the duchy of Apulia or the principality of Capua. The Arabic administration does not seem to have been responsible for these mainland provinces before the reign of William II. Before turning, to the *duana baronum*, it remains to examine a third *dīwān*, which was based in Palermo.

[47] Original: ADM, Messina, no.1118 (S2004); ed. Cusa 1868–82, no.120, p.321 (Greek text only; from an 18th-century copy). The order was issued 'to the *dīwān al-taḥqīq al-maʿmūr* in the person of the elder, the *qāʾid* Martin, lord of the *dīwān*' (line 4: *li-dīwāni l-taḥqīqi l-maʿmūri ʿalā yadi l-shaykhi l-qāʾidi martīna ṣāḥibi l-dīwāni*; the Greek bears the *superscriptio* of 'the *qāʾid* Martin of the great palace and the other elders who are in charge of the *sekreton*' (line 8: Ὁ τοῦ μεγάλου παλατίου καϊτης Μαρτῆνος καὶ οἱ λοιποὶ γέροντες οἱ ἐπὶ τοῦ σεκρέτου †††).

[48] See above, p.92, and note 4; and below, p.206, note 63. The Latin-Greek reconfirmation was given *in regia duana de secretis* by Geoffrey de Modica, palatine chamberlain and master of the *duana de secretis* and *duana baronum* (*palatinus camerarius et magister regie duane de secretis et duane baronum* / Ὁ ἐπὶ τοῦ μεγάλου σεκρέτου καὶ ἐπὶ τοῦ σεκρέτου τῶν ἀποκοπῶν Ἰοσφρὲς τῆς Μοδὰκ ὁ παλατῖνος καπριλίγγας: Cusa 1868–82, no.136, pp.489–90).

[49] 1149: (***Dīwānī* 29**) *daftaru l-ḥudūdi bi-dīwāni l-taḥqīqi l-maʿmūri*. 1154: (***Dīwānī* 33**) *dafātiru l-ḥudūdi bi-dīwāni l-taḥqīqi l-maʿmūri*. 1170–1?: (Garufi 1899, p.125) *deptarii duane nostri de secretis*. 1173: (***Dīwānī* 40**) *quaterni finium seu divisarum in dohana constitit id est [ve]ractudinis abitabili*. 1175: (***Dīwānī* 41**) boundary-description described in Greek text as *scriptum ... quod detulit ... baiulus ... a deo custodito secreto doane* and in Arabic as *scriptum dohane mamur idest doane secreti*. 1182: (***Dīwānī* 44**) *dafātiru l-dīwāni l-taḥqīqi l-maʿmūri*.

[50] For example: 1149 (***Dīwānī* 29**); 1154 (***Dīwānī* 33**); 1172 (***Dīwānī* 39**); 1173 (***Dīwānī* 40**).

[51] For example: 1168 (Cusa 1868–82, no.108, pp.484–6); 1175 (***Dīwānī* 41**); 1183 (*ibid.*, no.142, pp.432–4); 1189 (Garufi 1898, doc. 3, pp.153–4).

[52] Haskins 1911, p.650 and n.160.

[53] Mattei-Cerasoli 1939, no.12, pp.292–4; Haskins 1911, p.654, n.191. It is intriguing to find, amongst the witnesses to this document, *Eleazar regie duane hostiarius*: his name might equally be Arabic or Hebrew.

The *dīwān al-fawāʾid*

In September 1190, Niqūla Ashqar, a servant of the royal palace, initiated the purchase of a house in the Old City of Palermo from Zaynab, the daughter of ᶜAbd Allāh al-Anṣārī, for the price of 500 *tarì*:

> /[18] ... The aforesaid house was offered for sale at the order of the Lord Protector (may God exalt him and give him good fortune!) /[19] and at the order of the lords of the *dīwān al-fawāʾid* (may God give them good fortune!) after they had established that Zaynab the vendor was a prisoner in the hands of foreign *Rūm*, and they had demanded from her a heavy /[20] ransom, and she had found no way to redeem herself. When they had established that, they therefore permitted the vendor to sell the aforesaid house to him whose name has been mentioned.[54]

The sale was completed after Zaynab's return from captivity, and was registered in the *dafātir al-dīwān al-maᶜmūr* on 10 October (?) 1190.

The document is not without ambiguities, and has no parallel; but it seems probable that the Lord Protector and the lords of the *dīwān al-fawāʾid* acted as brokers between the foreign Byzantines (or possibly Europeans) who had captured Zaynab, and the Muslim community of Palermo, possibly represented by the *qāḍī*. After ascertaining that she had indeed been captured and held for ransom, and that she possessed no other assets from which the sum demanded could be raised, they offered her house for sale. The purchaser was a servant of the royal palace, and seems to have been a Christian Arab; the contract makes it clear that he made the purchase on his own behalf, not as a representative of the palace or the *dīwān*. On initiation of the sale, the *dīwān* would seem to have paid Zaynab's ransom, and thereby secured her release. Only when both the vendor and the purchaser were present was the sale completed, under the supervision of a Muslim legal authority, presumably the *qāḍī* of Palermo. Upon its completion, the sale was entered into the *dafātir al-dīwān al-maᶜmūr*, a formality which presumably indicates that Zaynab had reimbursed the *dīwān* out of the proceeds of the sale. Alternatively, it is just possible that the close involvement of the *dīwān* indicates that Zaynab held her house from the royal demesne, and that what she sold to Niqūla Ashqar was not the property itself but her rights in it: an unpublished document (ADM, Messina no.1126) is concerned with such a case.[55]

The title of the *dīwān al-fawāʾid* has been variously translated 'l'ufizio dei proventi', 'l'Ufficio dei Profitti', 'the office of the profits'. On this basis, it has been proposed that this was the office responsible for recording incoming revenue

[54] **Private 26**: /[18]... *wa-ubīᶜati l-dāru l-madhkūratu bi-amri l-mawlā l-nāṣiri rafaᶜa-hu llāhu wa-asᶜada-hu* /[19] *wa-bi-amri aṣḥābi dīwāni l-fawāʾidi asᶜada-humu llāhu lammā thubita ᶜinda-hum anna zaynaba l-bāʾiᶜata kānat asīratan ᶜinda rūmin ghurabāʾa wa-ṭalabū min-hā thamanan* /[20] *kabīr* [*sic* – Cusa *kathīr*, but the word is unpointed] *wa-lam tajid min ayna tatakhallaṣu fa-lammā thubita dhālika ᶜinda-hum ṭallaqū yada* [Cusa misreads *bi-hi*] *l-bāʾiᶜata fī bayᶜi l-dāri l-madhkūrati li-man dhukira smu-hu.*

[55] The document is cited in von Falkenhausen (forthcoming).

into the royal treasury.[56] *Fā'ida*, plural *fawā'id*, does indeed mean 'profit', 'advantage', and 'benefit', spiritual and material, what is received and what is given. The word is used by 12th-century western Arab authors, including al-Idrīsī, who was writing at the Sicilian court, to mean 'revenue'.[57] Moreover, this may not be its sole occurrence in a *dīwānī* document. In a Latin-Arabic writ of 1242 (***Dīwānī* 46**), Frederick II's minister, Obert Fallamonaca, appears with the Latin title *dominus Obertus Fallamonacha imperialis doane de secretis et questorum magister per totam Siciliam* ('lord Obert Fallamonaca master of the imperial *duana de secretis* and of the quaestors for all Sicily'). His Arabic title was read by Cusa as follows: *al-mawlā ūbartu fallamūnaqa ṣāḥibu l-dawāwīni l-maᶜmūrati wa-l-qawā'iti bi-jamīᶜi ṣiqillīyata*.[58] Michele Amari, followed by Umberto Rizzitano, took the word here transcribed as *al-qawā'it* to be the plural of *qā'id*, deformed from the unusual but attested form *al-qawā'id*, through the influence of Greek κάϊτ (*kait*) and Latin *gaitus*. This seems forced. It has not yet been possible to consult the original, but, from the good photograph taken by Garufi, it seems that the word may well read *fawā'id*: if so, the *fā'* is unpointed, and the *dāl* so shallow and elongated as to resemble a *tā'*. The reading *fawā'id* both disposes of the implausible reading *al-qawā'it*, and offers a precise equivalent to the Latin, for the quaestors, in Frederick's Italy, as in ancient Rome, were officers of the fiscal administration, responsible for tax-collection: the *magister quaestorum* thus had charge of all revenues,[59] as is precisely expressed in the Arabic *ṣāḥib al-fawā'id*, 'lord of the revenues'. The full Arabic title would thus translate: 'the lord Obert Fallamonaca, lord of the royal *dīwāns* and of the revenues of all Sicily'. If this hypothesis is eventually supported by a close examination of the original, then *dīwān al-fawā'id* will be confirmed to mean 'the *dīwān* of the revenues'.

The precise rôle of the *dīwān al-fawā'id* in this affair is obscure, but the approval of its directors may have been required before Zaynab's ransom could be paid, and that the *dafātir* may have been registers of income. The title of the Lord Protector, *al-Mawlā al-Nāṣir*, perhaps indicates that he had some special responsibility for the welfare of those, like Zaynab, in need of protection.[60] He, the directors of the *dīwān al-fawā'id*, and the purchaser, are all likely to have been what the Latin sources call 'palace Saracens', and it is striking that Ibn Jubayr, writing of the winter of 1184–5, reports that

> they are Muslims; not one of them but fasts the [prescribed] months, voluntarily and in hope of [heavenly] reward, and gives alms in order to approach and to grow nearer to

[56] Amari 1970, p.88; Cusa 1868–82, p.737; Garufi 1928, pp.83–4; Caravale 1966, pp.200–1; Takayama 1993, pp.15–16. See also Amari 1933–9, vol.3, pp.330–1, n.1.

[57] Dozy 1881, vol.II, p.300, citing al-Idrīsī 1970–6, p.545, line 1 and Ibn Jubayr 1907, p.46, line 17, p.50, line 7, and p.112, lines 1–2 (Dozy's references have been updated).

[58] For Obert Fallamonaca, see below, pp.245–7.

[59] See, for example: Conrad, von der Lieck-Buyken and Wagner 1973, I.xxxvii, pp.94–6 (von der Lieck-Buyken 1978, I.xxxix, p.37; Powell 1971, I.lxi (39), pp.34–5); I.xxxvii, p.52 (von der Lieck-Buyken 1978, I.xl, pp.37–8; Powell, 1971, I.xxxvii (40), p.35); Kamp, 1974, pp.55.

[60] Trovato 1949, p.65, n.1, identifies al-Mawlā l-Nāṣir with King Tancred, but without argument or evidence. This is not amongst Tancred's Arabic titles: see Johns 1986, pp.48–9.

> God, and redeems prisoners, brings up those of them who are children, arranges their marriages, is charitable to them, and does what good he is able.[61]

Elsewhere, Ibn Jubayr reports that the *qāʾid* Abū l-Qāsim ibn Ḥammūd, the hereditary leader of the Muslim community of Sicily, also liberated prisoners. Given that Abū l-Qāsim had been a 'palace Saracen', and one of the lords of the *dīwān al-taḥqīq*, it is tempting to suggest that he may have been the Lord Protector.[62]

The *duana baronum*

In a Greek act of March 1168, another royal *dīwān* appears for the first time. The young William II, together with his mother, the regent Margaret, ordered the renewal of a privilege of Countess Adelaide to Abbot Hilarion of San Nicola a Monte Pellaro, in Calabria. The official responsible was 'the *qāʾid* Richard, my protochamberlain and familiar', who bears a new title ὁ ἐπὶ τοῦ σεκρέτου τῶν ἀποκοπῶν (*o epi tou sekretou tōn apokopōn*).[63] In a Latin-Greek privilege of January 1180, in the Greek text, the *datarius* is named as 'Geoffrey of Modica, the palatine chamberlain, who is in charge of the Great Bureau and in charge of τοῦ σεκρέτου τῶν ἀποκοπῶν (*tou sekretou tōn apokopōn*)'; in the Latin, he is *Goffridus de Moac palatinus camerarius et magister regie duane de secretis et duane baronum*.[64] The Greek office was thus equivalent to the Latin *duana baronum*.

The noun ἡ ἀποκοπή (*ē apokopē*) means 'something cut off', but seems to be used here in the specialised sense of a portion or fief granted to a feudatory.[65] Although no Arabic title for this office has survived, there is a distinct echo here, as Michele Amari observed, of the *dīwān al-iqṭāʿāt* ('bureau of fiefs'). Both *apokopē* and *iqṭāʿ* are derived from roots connoting 'division', 'partition', *etc.*, and it is possible that the Greek title translates a lost Arabic original.[66]

Hiroshi Takayama has recently re-examined in some detail the appearances of the *duana baronum*, and has concluded that this was the office, founded in 1167–8 and based at Salerno, that had responsibility for the entire administration of the

[61] Ibn Jubayr 1907, p.326: *wa-hum muslimūna mā min-hum illā man yaṣūmu l-ashhura taṭawwuʿan wa-taʾajjuran wa-yataṣaddaqu taqarruban ilā llāhi wa-tazallufan wa-yaftakku l-asrā wa-yurabbī l-aṣāghira min-hum wa-yuzawwiju-hum wa-yuḥsinu ilay-him wa-yafʿalu l-khayra mā staṭāʿa*. See also below, p.213.

[62] Ibn Jubayr 1907, p.341. Ibn Jubayr's report of Abū l-Qāsim's generosity to pilgrims is confirmed by his protégé Ibn Qalāqis. For Abū l-Qāsim, see below, pp.234–42.

[63] Kehr 1902, doc.19, pp.438–9: τῶ πρωτοκαμπ[ερ]έρι καὶ φαμελλιαρίω ἡμῶν τῶ ἐπὶ τοῦ σεκρέτου τῶν ἀποκοπῶν καίτη Ῥικάρδη (*tō prōtokampereri kai famelliariō ēmōn tō epi tou sekretou tōn apokopōn kaitē Rikardē*). For Richard, see below, pp.228–34.

[64] Original: PA, AdS, Cefalù, no.13: ed. Cusa 1868–82, no.136, pp.489–90. Only the indiction year XIII is given: Geoffrey of Modica appears with the relatively junior office of *magister iusticiarius* of the Val di Noto in a boundary-inquest of 1172 (Garufi 1899, no.62, pp.152–3). The customs exemption must surely be later than this and, therefore, 1180, indiction XIII, is the most likely year of issue.

[65] Caracausi 1990, p.57.

[66] Amari 1970, pp.87–8.

mainland provinces of the Norman kingdom, except only Calabria.[67] There is no evidence that this *dīwān* used Arabic although, as we shall see Chapter 9, 'palace Saracens' were amongst its staff. Its activities are therefore beyond the scope of this study. However, as Takayama points out, and as we have already seen, the creation of the *duana baronum* had at least one important consequence for the development of the Sicilian fiscal administration:[68] after 1168, the Greek title for the *dīwān*, τὸ σέκρετον (*to sekreton*), often becomes τὸ μέγα σέκρετον (*to mega sekreton*, 'the great *dīwān*'), presumably to distinguish it from *to sekreton tōn apokopōn*.[69]

The use of Arabic

By the 1140s, the trilingual Sicilian chancery was equipped to issue *sijillāt* to Arabs, *sigillia* to Greeks, and *privilegia* to Latins, each in the language of their recipients. And yet, of the thirty-six surviving royal documents containing Arabic, only one was issued to an Arabic-speaker, and a further two to groups of royal officials who may, perhaps, have included Arabic-speakers, while fifteen went to Greek-speakers, and eighteen to Latin-speakers. Clearly, the *dīwān* did not issue documents in Arabic in order to make them comprehensible to their recipients. But Arabic alone tells only part of the story, because just six *dīwānī* documents were composed solely in Arabic, while twenty-nine were written in Arabic and Greek, and one in Arabic and Latin. Table 8.1 gives a detailed break-down of how all three languages were used in *dīwānī* documents.

If we ignore for the moment the *jarāʾid* and the *ḥudūd*, and concentrate upon the main body of the texts of *dīwānī* documents, we see that half of them were written in Arabic alone, and that, of these, ten went to Greeks and eight to Latins. The texts of one-quarter of *dīwānī* documents were written in Greek only, and of these six went to Greeks and three to Latins. Only one-quarter of *dīwānī* documents had bilingual texts: of these, two Greek-Arabic texts went to Greeks, two to Latins, two to royal officials who may have spoken all three languages, and one to a Jew (whom I have counted as an Arabic-speaker); the lone Arabic-Greek text went to a Latin; as did the unique Latin translation of an Arabic text. This distribution confirms that the *dīwān* was not generally concerned to match the languages of its documents to those of their recipients.

A more significant pattern emerges when we consider the distribution of *dīwānī* languages over time. Until 1145, Greek was the dominant language in documents

[67] Takayama 1993, pp.140–2, 151–5; see also Takayama 1985, pp.152–4. If the *duana baronum* was indeed not responsible for Calabria, it is perplexing that its first appearance should have been concerned with a Calabrian monastery.

[68] Takayama 1993, p.147; see also Takayama 1985, pp.131–3.

[69] Τὸ μέγα σέκρετον first appears in October 1170: see the document cited by Haskins 1911, p.650, n.160.

Table 8.1 The languages of *dīwānī* documents and of their recipients

No.	Year	Subject	Text	*Jarīda*	*Ḥudūd*	Recipient
10	1132	Donation of villeins	Greek	Arabic-Greek	–	Latin
11	1132	Customs privilege	Greek-Arabic	–	–	Arabic, Greek & Latin
12	1133	Boundary record	Greek	–	Greek-Arabic	Latin
13	1134	Customs privilege	Greek-Arabic	–	–	Arabic, Greek & Latin
14	1136	Donation of land and villeins	Greek	Arabic-Greek	Arabic-Greek	Latin
15	1141	Donation and confirmation of grants of lands, villeins and other rights (working draft)	Greek	–	Arabic-Greek	Greek
16	1141	Donation and confirmation of grants of lands, villeins and other rights (original)	Greek	–	Arabic-Greek	Greek
17	1141	Donation and confirmation of grants of lands, villeins and other rights (copy)	Greek	–	Arabic-Greek	Greek
18	1141	Renewal of *jarīda*	Arabic	Arabic	–	Greek
19	1142	Sale of land	Greek-Arabic	–	Arabic-Greek	Greek
20	1143	Donation of lands, villeins, and other property	Greek	Arabic-Greek	–	Greek
21	1145	Renewal of *jarīda*	Arabic	Arabic-Greek	–	Latin
22	1145	Renewal of *jarīda*		Arabic	Arabic-Greek	Latin
23	1145	Renewal of *jarīda*		Arabic	Arabic-Greek	Latin
24	1145	Renewal of *jarīda*		Arabic	Arabic-Greek	Latin
25	1145	Renewal of *jarīda*		Arabic	Arabic-Greek	Latin
26	1145	Renewal of *jarīda*		Arabic	Arabic-Greek	Latin

No.	Year	Subject	Text	*Jarīda*	*Ḥudūd*	Recipient
†27	1145	Donation of lands and villeins	Greek	Arabic-Greek	Greek	Greek
28	1149	Donation of lands and villeins	Arabic	Arabic	Arabic	Greek
29	1149	Donation of lands and villeins (copy)	Arabic	Arabic	Arabic	Greek
30	1151	Confirmation of *jarīdas* and estate boundary	Greek	Arabic-Greek	Arabic	Greek
31	1152	Boundary record	Arabic	–	Arabic	Greek
32	1152	Boundary record (copy)	Arabic	–	Arabic	Greek
33	1154	Donation of lands and villeins (copy)	Arabic	Arabic	Arabic	Greek
34	1154	Donation of lands and villeins	Arabic	Arabic-Greek	Arabic	Greek
35	1161	Sale of land	Greek-Arabic	–	Arabic-Greek	Arabic
36	1164	Donation of land	Greek-Arabic	–	–	Latin
37	1166	Restoration of archdeaconry of Messina	Arabic-Greek	–	–	Latin
38	1169	Donation of land and villeins	Arabic	Arabic-Greek	–	Greek
39	1172	Boundary record	Greek-Arabic	–	Arabic-Greek	Greek
40	1173	Confirmation of donation of land and villeins	Arabic	Arabic-Greek	Arabic	Latin
41	1175	Boundary record	Greek-Arabic	–	Arabic-Greek	Latin
42	1177	Donation of villeins	Arabic	Arabic-Greek (?)	–	Latin
43	1178	Register of villeins	Arabic	Arabic-Greek	–	Latin
44	1182	Boundary register	Arabic-Latin	–	Arabic-Latin	Latin
45	1183	Register of villeins	Arabic	Arabic-Greek	–	Latin

issued by the *dīwān*. Before this date, the texts of most documents were composed in Greek, occasionally accompanied by versions in Arabic, while Arabic was usually restricted to *ḥudūd* and *jarāʾid*. But all the *jarāʾid* renewed by the *dīwān* in 1145 employed Arabic for the texts, as well as the name-lists, while Greek was confined to the transliterations of the names of villeins. Thereafter, Arabic was almost always used for the texts of documents, either on its own or with Greek versions, and was always used for *jarāʾid* and *ḥudūd*, usually (but not always) with Greek versions. Latin was only used once, to translate the Arabic text and *ḥudūd* of the 1182 Monreale boundary register.

It is no surprise that Greek was the dominant language in the earliest documents of the royal *dīwān*. When the *dīwān* was founded in *c.*1130, Greek was still the primary language of the Sicilian chancery, while no Arabic document had been issued for twenty years. But the way in which Arabic suddenly supplanted Greek in *dīwānī* documents in 1145, and thereafter remained the primary language within the *dīwān*, despite the meteoric rise of Latin to dominate the administration as a whole, is highly remarkable. So, too, is the fact that Greek continued to occupy second place in the *dīwān*, while Latin appears in only one document, and not until 1182. Two forces determined this unexpected pattern: tradition and innovation.

Tradition dictated that the royal demesne, at least in western Sicily, be administered in Arabic. The Norman conquerors of Sicily had adapted Arabic records left by the Muslim administration of the island to facilitate the distribution of the land and its inhabitants. Even after 1111, when Roger II ceased to issue documents written in Arabic, Arabic continued to be used for the internal administration of his demesne. The Monreale *jarāʾid* demonstrate that, as late as the 1170s and '80s, the registers of the lands and inhabitants of the royal demesne in western Sicily were still kept in Arabic. In large part, of course, this was because the inhabitants of these lands were predominantly Arabic-speaking, and because Arabic was the language most commonly used in the field to collect administrative data. That Arabic was the traditional language for the administration of the royal demesne is sufficient to explain why all the *jarāʾid* and *ḥudūd* in authentic *dīwānī* documents were composed in Arabic (with or without Greek or Latin versions). Again, that Greek had been used with Arabic in documents from 1095 until 1111, and had been the dominant language in the earliest documents issued by the royal *dīwān* between 1132 and 1143, accounts for its survival as the traditional second language in bilingual documents as late as 1183.

But administrative tradition cannot explain why, after an interval of more than twenty years, Arabic documents began to be issued again in 1132. The earliest Arabic products of the *dīwān* were wholly distinct from the Arabic documents that had been issued before 1111. Their script, format, and language demonstrate them to be the work of the new professional *dīwān*, founded in *c.*1130 on the model of a contemporary Islamic chancery. It was this innovation – the creation of the royal *dīwān* – that revived the fortunes of Arabic as an administrative language and, by 1145, established it as the dominant language, not merely for the internal administration of the royal demesne in Sicily, but also for documents issued by the royal *dīwān* to external recipients, irrespective of their linguistic culture.

The royal *dīwān*, as we shall see in the following chapters, came to play a rôle in the political life of the kingdom, in government, and in the formation of the monarchy itself, that transcended its administrative function. In much the same way, Arabic writing – on coins, documents, and monumental inscriptions – was to acquire a symbolic significance far greater than the literal meaning of the texts. In order to understand this, we must begin by examining the specialised and closed elite of crypto-Muslim eunuch slaves who controlled both the *dīwān*, and the use of Arabic for administration and government.

CHAPTER 9

'The people of his state'. The 'palace Saracens' and the royal *dīwān*

After the brief appearance of Abū l-Ḍawʾ in the 1120s, both the documentary and the literary sources fall more or less silent about the Arab staff of the royal *dīwān* until the 1140s. From then until the end of the kingdom, although almost no trace has survived of the internal records of the *dīwān*, and although its organisation and precise duties remain tantalisingly obscure, we are surprisingly well-informed about its Arab directors. This *embarras de richesse* should put us on our guard, and encourage us to ask why both Latin observers, such as 'Hugo Falcandus' and the interpolator of Romuald of Salerno, and Arab visitors to Sicily, such as Ibn Qalāqis and Ibn Jubayr, were so interested in, and so well-informed about, the Arab servants of the Norman kings. Such general questions must remain unanswered, until they are finally addressed in the conclusion of this chapter. It opens with the account of the palace servants in 1184–5 given by Ibn Jubayr, and then returns to the reign of King Roger for the first of six prosopographical sections on the Arab servants of the palace and the *dīwān*.

Ibn Jubayr and the eunuchs

During his enforced stay in Sicily, in the winter of 1184–5, the Spanish pilgrim Ibn Jubayr met leading Arab servants of King William II on several occasions in Messina and Palermo, and enjoyed the hospitality of Abū l-Qāsim ibn Ḥammūd in Palermo and Trapani. His account of the Arab servants provides a colourful and surprisingly detailed background to this chapter, and I shall return repeatedly to it. The following passages come from the beginning and middle of his stay, and are set first in Messina, then in Palermo.

> (*Messina*) The character of this king of theirs [William II] is astonishing for his good behaviour, for his employment of Muslims, and for his use of castrated youths (*al-fityān al-majābīb*), all or most of whom hide their faith but cling to the law of Islam. He is extremely trusting of Muslims, and reliant upon them in his affairs, and in the most important of his concerns, to the extent that the supervisor of his kitchen is a Muslim man. He has a troop of black Muslim slaves (*ʿabīd*), whose leader is one of them. His

ministers and his chamberlains are eunuchs (*wuzarāʾu-hu wa-ḥujjābu-hu l-fityānu*), of whom he has a great many. They are the people of his state, and are appointed as his familiars (*bi-khāṣṣati-hi*). The magnificence of his kingship radiates through them, because they abound with sumptuous robes and lively horses, and there is none of them but has his own entourage, personal servants (*khawal*), and followers.

This king has imposing palaces and elegant gardens, especially in the capital of his kingdom, the aforementioned al-Madīna [Palermo]. … He makes great use of eunuchs and slave-girls (*li-l-fityāni wa-l-jawārī*), and no Christian king rules in greater luxury, nor greater ease, nor greater refinement than he. He imitates the rulers of the Muslims in immersing himself in the luxury of his realm, in the provision of its laws, the invention of procedures, the allocation of degrees amongst his men, the elaboration of the ceremony of the realm, and the display of his finery. And his realm is extremely magnificent …

… As for the slave-girls and concubines (*jawārī-hi wa-ḥaẓāyā-hu*) in his palace, they are all Muslims. One of the most wonderful things that his aforesaid slave (*khadīmu-hu*) – one Yaḥyā ibn Fityān the Embroiderer, who embroiders in gold in the king's *ṭirāz* – told us about him was that the Frankish Christian women who enter his palace become Muslims, being converted to Islam by the aforesaid slave-girls. But they do all this in secret from their king. And they do wonderful good deeds.

We were told that there had been a powerful earthquake in this island which terrified this Christian (*mushrik*). He stared about his palace, and heard nothing but invocations to God and His Prophet from his women and his eunuchs (*min nisāʾi-hi wa-fityāni-hi*). Perhaps dismay overcame them at perceiving him, for he said, in order to calm them: 'Let every one of you invoke his own Deity, and the One in whom he believes'.

As to his eunuchs, who are the inspectors of his government, and the people of his administration in his realm (*wa-ammā fityānu-hu hum ᶜuyūnu dawlati-hi wa-ahlu ᶜamālati-hi fī mulki-hi*), they are Muslims; not one of them but fasts the [prescribed] months, voluntarily and in hope of [heavenly] reward, and gives alms in order to approach and to grow nearer to God, and redeems prisoners, brings up those of them who are children, arranges their marriages, is charitable to them, and does what good he is able. All this is the work of God, the Great and Mighty, for the Muslims of this island, and is one of the mysteries of the concern for them of God, the Great and Mighty.

In Messina, after he had expressed a wish to see us, we met one of the eunuchs (*min-hum … fatan*), called ᶜAbd al-Masīḥ [*i.e.* 'Servant of the Messiah'], who is one of their leaders, and one of the most prominent amongst them. He received us with honour and respect, and, after searching his sitting-room for his own protection and expelling all around him whom he suspected amongst his eunuchs (*min khuddāmi-hi*), he opened his heart to us. He asked us about Mecca (may God sanctify it!) and its glorified shrines, and about the shrines of Medina the blessed, and the shrines of Syria. We told him, and he was tormented with longing and pain. He begged us to give him some of the blessed relics that we had brought from Mecca and Medina (may God sanctify them!), and prayed us, if possible, not to be parsimonious. He said to us: 'You display Islam openly, are successful in your plans, and (God willing!) prosperous in your commercial dealings. But we hide our faith, fear for our lives, and cling to the worship of God and the performance of His precepts in secret, held in the possession of one who does not believe in God, and who has dropped the noose of slavery upon our necks. Our desire is to be blessed by meeting pilgrims such as you, to ask for their prayers, and to rejoice in whatever relics from those holy shrines we receive from them to use as instruments of faith, and as a treasure for our shrouds (*wa-dhakhīratan li-l-akfāni*)'. Our hearts were broken with compassion for him; we prayed that he might come to a good end, and presented him with some of what we had with us, as he had requested. He repaid and rewarded us generously, and asked us to respect the confidence of all his brother eunuchs (*sāʾira ikhwāni-hi mina l-fityāni*). Their good works are well known: by ransoming captives, they accomplish acts that deserve God's reward. All their servants (*jamīʿu khadamati-him*) are of their like.

One of the wonderful things about these eunuchs (*al-fityān*) is that when they are in attendance on their master, and the time for prayer draws near, they retire one by one to perform their prayers. Sometimes they are in a place where the eye of their king might catch them, but God, the Great and Mighty, conceals them. Thus, they cease not from their labours and their sincere intentions, nor from covertly inspiring the Muslims with endless holy endeavour (*fī jihādin dāʾimin*). May God assist them, and, through His grace, bring them to a good end.[1]

(*Palermo*) We were about to enter [the city from the south-east], when we were stopped, and led to the gate adjoining the palaces of the Frankish king (may God deliver the Muslims from his rule!). We were brought before the Procurator,[2] so that he could question us about our plans, for that is their practice with every stranger. We were led through open spaces, gates, and royal courtyards, as we gazed on towering palaces, orderly squares, gardens, and ante-chambers[3] occupied by the people in service, which startled our eyes and confused our thoughts, [until] we called to mind the words of God the Great and Powerful: 'But that mankind would have become one community [in its greed, so little do We value material things, that] We would have provided those who do not believe in the Merciful [God] with roofs of silver for their houses, and stairs by which to reach them' (*Qurʾān* 43:33). Amongst the things that we saw was an audience-chamber (*majlis*) in a spacious courtyard, surrounded by a garden, and with it sides occupied by colonnades (*balāṭāt*). The chamber occupied the whole length of the courtyard, so that we marvelled at its length, and at the height of its façades (*manāẓir*). We were told that it was where the king dined with his companions. Those colonnades and ante-chambers are where his judges (*ḥukkām*), and the servants and administrators (*ahlu l-khidmati wa-l-ʿamālati*), sit in his presence.

The Procurator came out to us, escorted by two slaves, who flanked him, and carried his train. We saw a noble old man, with a long white moustache, who questioned us about our plans, and our country, in polished Arabic (*bi-kalāmin arabīyin layyinin*). We answered him, and he showed sympathy with us and, with kindly salutations and good wishes, he gave us leave to depart. We were astonished at his behaviour. His first question to us was for news of great Constantinople, and what we knew about it, but we had nothing to tell him about it.[4] …

One of the stranger allurements that we experienced was that a Christian, who was sitting at the gate of the palace, said to us, as we were leaving the aforesaid palace: 'Protect what you have, O pilgrims, from the customs officials (*mina l-ʿummāli l-mumakkisīna*), lest they descend upon you!' (He thought that we had merchandise liable to duty.) Another Christian heard him, and said: 'How odd you are! Should these

[1] Ibn Jubayr 1907, pp.324–7 (*BAS*², vol.I, pp.86–8; *BAS*²*(It.)*, vol.I, pp.119–22. See also: Ibn Jubayr 1949–65, vol.III, pp.380–3; Ibn Jubayr 1952, pp.340–3.)

[2] Ibn Jubayr 1907, p.330: *mustakhlaf* (MS *mustaḥlaf*): see Dozy 1881, vol.I, pp.316 and 398.

[3] *Al-marātib*: see Dozy 1881, vol.I, p.508.

[4] Sicily launched an attack against Byzantium in June 1185.

men, entering the king's sanctum (*yadkhulūna ḥarama l-maliki*), have anything to fear? I expect nothing for them but thousands of *tarì*. Go in peace, you have nothing to fear'.

Overcome with amazement at what we had seen and heard, we departed to a caravanserai (*funduq*).[5]

Philip of al-Mahdīya

More than thirty years before Ibn Jubayr visited the royal palace in Palermo, it was the scene of the show-trial and execution of the first of the 'palace Saracens', after Abū l-Ḍawʾ, whose career can be traced in any detail.

It is just possible that the eunuch Philip, known to Arab authors as Fīlib al-Mahdawī – Philip of al-Mahdīya – may have been Abū l-Ḍawʾ's close contemporary. Amongst the witnesses to a Greek deed, dated 1 November 1129, in which Stephen of Carthage sells land at Mazara to his son Matthew, there appears the autograph of 'Philip the African' (Φίλιππος ὁ ἀπὸ Ἀφρικῆς, *Filippos o apo Afrikēs*) – *Africa* was the standard Latin name for the Ifrīqiyan capital, and his name could thus be translated Philip of al-Mahdīya.[6] If this is our Philip, then he had already learnt to write Greek well: perhaps he could have been a slave with whom George of Antioch fled to Sicily in 1108.[7]

Be that as it may, the following moral tale was inserted into the *Chronicon* of Romuald of Salerno, a contemporary record of the years 1127–77, which is largely devoted to relations between the Norman kings and the papacy.

> In order that the whole world may know plainly in what measure King Roger was orthodox in his whole purpose, and to what extent he was inflamed with fervour and zeal for the Christian faith, the testimony of the following deed will declare.
>
> King Roger had a certain eunuch (*quendam eunuchum*), by the name of Philip, who, on account of his honest service, became extremely dear and agreeable to him. The king put Philip in charge of the entire palace, and made him master of his whole household, because he seemed to be trustworthy in his affairs, and a capable manager of his business. With the passage of time, the king's affection and love for him grew. He made him admiral of his fleet (*stolii sui ammiratum*), and sent him with it to Bône, which he promptly took by the sword and looted, and returned in triumph and glory to Sicily.
>
> But, because Philip showed ingratitude towards the source of his many blessings, and repaid the Heavenly King with evil for good, he deservedly suffered the wrath and indignation of the earthly king. For, beneath the cloak of the name of a Christian, he behaved like a secret knight of the devil. Although he kept up the appearance of being a Christian, in mind and deed he was completely a Saracen. He hated Christians, but valued pagans most highly. He set foot in the churches of God unwillingly, but frequently attended the synagogues of the Evil One, and provided oil for filling their lamps, and whatever else they needed. Spitting out all Christian practices, he did not cease from

[5] Ibn Jubayr 1907, pp.330–1 (*BAS*[2], vol.I, pp.91–2; *BAS*[2]*(It.)*, vol.I, pp.126–8. See also: Ibn Jubayr 1949–65, vol.III, pp.387–8; Ibn Jubayr 1952, pp.346–8.)

[6] Grégoire 1932a, doc.3, pp.101–3 and plate C.

[7] Above, pp.81, 84.

eating meat on Fridays, nor in Lent. He sent his emissaries with offerings to the tomb of Muḥammad, and greatly commended himself to the priest of that place by his prayers.

When these and other wickednesses, which he had covered with the shade of the name of a Christian, reached the ears of King Roger, he, driven by the zeal of God, but according to his own wisdom, had him arraigned in his court for the aforementioned crimes. Philip, however, trusting in the grace and affection of the king, replied manfully to his accusers, and denied the charges which they brought against him, as if they were wholly false. But, through the operation of divine justice, his accusers proved that which they said to be true upon the testimony of trustworthy men. Then, Philip, believing himself to be convicted, and fearing the justice of the king, started to beg forgiveness, and to seek the king's pardon, promising that in future he would be an orthodox Christian.

Now, the king, fired by the flame of faith, burst into tears, and said: 'You should know, most distinguished sirs, that my soul has been pierced by the greatest grief, and roused to passion by severe torments, because this minister of mine, whom I raised from boyhood so that, having been purged of his sins, the Saracen might become Christian, is yet a Saracen and, under the name of faith, has done deeds of faithlessness. Had he only offended our majesty in other ways – had he carried off part of our treasure, even the greater part – he would certainly have been promised forgiveness by us, in recognition of his service, and have obtained mercy. But, because he has principally offended God by his action, and has furnished others with the opportunity and the precedent of sinning, and because I should not forgive an injury to our faith and a crime against the Christian religion by my own son, nor should I acquit anyone else. In this act, let the whole world learn that I love the Christian faith with absolute constancy, and do not refrain from avenging any injury to it, even by my own ministers. For this reason are laws set up, and our laws are armed with the sword of fairness; they wound the enemy of the faith with the sword of justice, and, thus, they set a terrible snare for the infidels'.

Then the counts, justiciars, barons, and judges, who were gathered there, paying mind to the just soul of the king, withdrew apart and, having deliberated in council for a long time, pronounced sentence, saying: 'We decree that Philip, a traitor to the name of Christian, and an agent of the works of faithlessness under the disguise of faith, shall be consumed by the vengeful flames, so that he who would not have the warmth of love, shall feel the fire that burns, and so that no trace shall remain of this worst of men, but that, having been turned to ashes by an earthly fire, he may proceed to perpetual torment in the eternal flames'.

Then, having been handed over to the justiciars, and tied to the hooves of unbroken horses, he was violently dragged to a lime-kiln, which lay in front of the palace. There, he was untied from the horses' hooves, thrown into the midst of the flames, and instantly consumed. The rest of his accomplices and fellows in evil suffered the death penalty.

Wherefore, in this action, it is manifestly apparent that King Roger was a most Christian and catholic king, who did not spare his own foster-son and chamberlain from punishment for an injury to the faith but, to his honour and glory, handed him over to be burned.[8]

A report by the Arab historian Ibn al-Athīr, which is wholly independent of the Latin, describes the same events, except that the pretext for Philip's arrest is said to be his leniency to the leading Muslims of Bône:

[8] Romuald of Salerno 1935, pp.234–6.

> In this year (548/1153–4), the fleet of Roger, the king of the Franks in Sicily, sailed to Bône. Its commander was his eunuch, Philip of al-Mahdīya. He blockaded it, recruited bedouin [to use] against it, and captured it in [the month of] Rajab (22 September – 21 October). He took captive its inhabitants, and seized what was within it, except that he spared a group of religious scholars and pious men, so that they fled with their families and possessions into the villages. He stayed there for ten days, then returned to al-Mahdīya, taking some of the captives with him, and went back to Sicily. Roger arrested him for the leniency that he had shown to the Muslims of Bône. Philip, and all his eunuchs, were accused of being Muslims, and of having concealed it. Witnesses were brought against him that he did not fast with the king, and that he was a Muslim. And so Roger assembled the bishops, priests, and knights, and they sentenced him to the stake. He was burnt in Ramaḍān (20 November – 19 December 1153). This was the beginning of the end for the Muslims of Sicily.[9]

The same account is given by Ibn Khaldūn, in almost identical words, except that he adds, after Philip's arrest: 'Then he was indicted for his religion'.[10] Both Arabic reports are derived from a common source which, in all probability, was composed by the Zīrid prince Ibn Shaddād, who visited Palermo in 1156–7, three or four years after Philip's execution.[11]

The Latin tale appears only as a modern marginal interpolation in the sole surviving 12th-century MS of the *Chronicon* (MS *Vatican Latin 3973*), and first occurs in two 14th-century MSS, which both derive from a common, missing, source. These 14th-century MSS contain about forty short passages not found in Vat. Lat. 3973, most of which concern events in Apulia and the Capitanata, and the deeds of Bohemond I and II in Apulia and Antioch, from 1062–32.[12] The Philip of al-Mahdīya story is set apart from these by content, length, and style. The editor of the *Chronicon*, Carlo Alberto Garufi, argued that the interpolation was added when the papacy was planning to grant the kingdom to Charles d'Anjou.[13] It seems improbable that a late 13th-century scribe should have been so passionately concerned with Roger's reputation, but, if so, he did not invent his material, and must have drawn upon a detailed contemporary account of Philip's trial and execution.

In his study of the *Chronicon*, Donald Matthew argued that Vat. Lat. 3973 is a late 12th-century copy of a text that had developed slowly, and over a long period. That text is in two parts: a historical review to the year 1126; and a contemporary chronicle of the years 1127–77, 'composed in the late 1170s to cover Norman papal

[9] Ibn al-Athīr 1851–76, vol.XI, p.123–4 (*BAS*^{2}, vol.I, p.338; *BAS*^{2}*(It.)*, vol.II, p.376): *Fī hādhihi l-sanati* [548/1153–4] *sāra usṭūlu rujāra maliki l-faranji bi-ṣiqillīyata ilā madīnati būnata wa-kāna l-muqaddamu ʿalay-him fatā-hu fīlibu l-mahdawīyu fa-ḥaṣara-hā wa-staʿāna bi-l-ʿarabi ʿalay-hā wa-akhada-hā fī rajabin. Wa-sabā ahla-hā wa-malaka mā fī-hā ghayra anna-hu aghḍā ʿan jamāʿatin mina l-ʿulamāʾi wa-l-ṣāliḥīna ḥattā kharajū bi-ahlī-him wa-amwāli-him ilā l-qurā fa-aqāma bi-hā ʿasharata ayyāmin wa-ʿāda ilā l-mahdīyati wa-baʿḍu l-asrā maʿa-hu wa-ʿāda ilā ṣiqillīyata fa-qabaḍa rujāru ʿalay-hi li-mā ʿtamada-hu mina l-rifqi bi-l-muslimīna fī būnata wa-kāna fīlibu yuqālu inna-hu wa-jamīʿa fityāni-hi muslimūna wa-yaktumūna-hu wa-shahidū ʿalay-hi anna-hu lā yaṣūmu maʿa l-maliki wa-anna-hu muslimun fa-jamaʿa rujāru l-asāqifata wa-l-qusūsa wa-l-fursāna fa-ḥakamū bi-an yuḥraqa fa-uḥriqa fī ramaḍāna wa-hādhā awwalu wahnin dakhala ʿalā l-muslimīna bi-ṣiqillīyata.*

[10] Ibn Khaldūn 1868, vol.V, p.204 (*BAS*^{2}, vol.II, p.553; *BAS*^{2}*(It.)*, vol.II, p.608): *thumma ttuhima fī dīni-hi.*

[11] Above, pp.87–8.

[12] Matthew 1981, *passim*, esp. pp.242–3, 267–74.

[13] Romuald of Salerno 1935, p.234, n.2.

history since the 1120s'. The latter is a coherent and carefully selective account of relations between the papacy and the rulers of Sicily, culminating in the Peace of Venice of 1177, but beginning with Roger's early difficulties, and covering the mid-12th century when the papacy was hostile to the kings of Sicily. According to Matthew, Romuald's account of Roger is thus 'an elaborate panegyric of a great Christian ruler whose bad relations with the pope disturb the chronicler'. In writing it, Romuald was forced to make 'some desperate moral reflections on God's reasons for punishing Roger' and, in the passage which immediately follows the Philip of al-Mahdīya story, 'to stress his efforts to convert Jews and Muslims to Christianity'.[14] This, of course, is exactly the sort of environment in which the Philip of al-Mahdīya tale belongs, but I have reluctantly come to the conclusion that it was neither written nor added by Romuald himself.

Léon-Robert Ménager observed that Philip's title, *ammiratus stolii*, is first attested here, and that it was not used, in Sicily, after the early decades of the 13th century. On this basis, he suggested that Romuald was his own interpolator, and that he composed the tale from his memory of events to which he had been a witness, and worked it into the text of the *Chronicon* between 1177 and his death on 1 April 1181.[15] There are two strong objections to this argument. First, the passage is clumsily inserted at a point where it breaks the flow of the text, in the middle of the account of the construction of the palace and park of La Favara.[16] Second, it is written in a style that is conspicuously not Romuald's own. Michele Amari addressed the latter difficulty (but not the former), by suggesting that what Romuald inserted was the original record of Philip's trial.[17] However, the tale is patently an elaborate and highly rhetorical piece of polemic, not an official record of court proceedings. What is more, it was apparently written after Roger's death (*fuit princeps christianissimus*).

In summary, the tale cannot have been added to the main text before Vat. Lat. 3973 was copied, which must have been after 1177. And yet, its close correspondence with the Arabic tradition demonstrates that it must be based upon a source written within a generation of the events that it describes. That source was more than a bald note of events, and clearly contained much of the circumstantial detail reproduced in the interpolation. What this source may have been, and when (before the 14th century) and by whom it was inserted into Romuald's *Chronicon*, remain unknown.[18] There is no reason to doubt, however, that it reflects an authentic, mid to late 12th-century, version of Philip's life and death.[19]

[14] Matthew 1981, p.268. [15] Ménager 1960, pp.66–7.

[16] The insertion comes at Romuald of Salerno 1935, p.232, line 21, after … *iusit adduci*.

[17] Amari 1933–9, vol.III, p.445–6, n.2.

[18] I have often wondered whether the author might not be the historian known as 'Hugo Falcandus'. The antithesis between good King Roger, who virtuously punished his eunuch Philip, and his tyrannical successors who used their eunuchs as instruments of oppression, would accord well with the theme of the *History*; which, moreover, discusses no less than seven trials, and displays an uncommon knowledge of, and interest in, the law. A detailed stylistic comparison of the two texts might resolve the question.

[19] In addition to the studies cited above, see Epifanio 1905–6, with a full bibliography of earlier works. The attempt by Jamison 1957, pp.41–3, to identify Philip of al-Mahdīya with Philip the son of the

Martin

On St Martin's Eve, 10 November 1160, the emir of emirs, Maio of Bari, was assassinated in the alleys of Palermo by Matthew Bonnellus. Bonnellus was the ambitious instrument of a group of barons from the mainland, who resented and feared the concentration of power in the hands of one, all-powerful minister. But, if 'Hugo Falcandus' is to be trusted, Maio was generally hated, and his murder released a pent-up flood of popular hostility against the late emir, his household, and his eunuch ministers. The *History* insists that the king himself participated in this persecution. Maio's brother and son, both named Stephen, both emirs, were arrested, as was the notary Matthew of Salerno, Maio's 'principal assistant'. Maio's house and his treasure were seized, and 'Andrew the eunuch, and several others, were tortured and forced to tell whatever they knew about Maio's possessions, whether hidden somewhere secretly or placed in the care of friends'. Even the houses of Maio's relatives were opened to the mob.[20] Maio's murderer, Matthew Bonnellus, was invited back to Palermo from Caccamo, whither he had fled after the crime, and was graciously received at court and acclaimed by the mob.

'Hugo Falcandus' reports that the palace eunuchs were so frightened by the new ascendancy of Bonnellus, because they had been so deeply involved in Maio's crimes and tyranny, that they strove to turn the king and queen against him, and eventually succeeded. They were supported by the palace chamberlain Atenulf, a minor Lombard noble, and one of the leading figures of the administration since the 1140s.[21] Bonnellus and his backers reacted by plotting to seize and depose the king, and to replace him with his eldest son, Roger, then a child of some nine years, whom they hoped to be able to control. The rebellion began with a contrived break-out from the prison beneath the Torre Greco in the royal palace, and the rebels, led by the king's illegitimate brother, Simon of Policastro, and by his nephew, Tancred of Lecce, soon succeeded in gaining control of the king. With William secure, the rebels proceeded to loot the royal palace. They initially concentrated upon the treasure and the women, but soon turned against the *dīwān*, its officers, and, by association, any Muslim.

> None of the eunuchs whom they could find escaped. Many of them had fled to the houses of their friends as soon as the operation began, and many of these were caught in the street, and killed by some knights who came out of the *Castellum Maris*, and by others who were beginning to roam through the city. Many of the Muslims who were involved in selling goods from their shops, or who were collecting fiscal dues in the *dīwān*, or unwisely going around outside their houses, were killed by the same knights.

logothete Leo is not successful. The former was a Muslim, Ifrīqiyan, eunuch slave; the latter, a Christian, Sicilian, free-man. That Ibn al-Athīr only knows the former as *Fīlib* does not prove that he was a Greek, but merely indicates that he was unaware of his Arabic *ism*.

[20] 'Hugo Falcandus' 1897, pp.44, 45 (trans. 'Hugo Falcandus' 1998, pp.98, 99). Throughout this chapter, I have relied heavily upon the extremely useful translation of the *History* by Graham Loud and Thomas Wiedemann: I have occasionally made minor, almost always cosmetic, changes to their translation.

[21] 'Hugo Falcandus' 1897, pp.48–9 (trans. 'Hugo Falcandus' 1998, pp.96–7, and n.68).

> Afterwards, when they realised the extent of the rioting, and they thought they were not strong enough to resist (since the previous year the admiral had forced them to hand in all their weapons to the court), the Muslims left the homes which most of them had in the centre of the city and withdrew to the suburb which lies across the River Papireto.[22] The Christians attacked them there, and for some time there was indecisive fighting. They could safely repulse our people from the entrances and narrow passageways.[23]

After their initial success, the tide of blood turned against the rebels. 'Hugo Falcandus' attributes this to a change of heart in the mob, which began to regret that 'the treasures, which had been gathered together with much labour for the defence of the realm by the efforts of a most excellent king, were being carried away and utterly wasted'.[24] The Palermitans rose against the rebels, besieged them in the royal palace, and forced them to release the king. The leaders fled to Caccamo and, after lengthy negotiations, Bonnellus was permitted to return to court, while others were exiled. Others still carried the revolt to the mainland, and to the centre and east of Sicily, where Tancred of Lecce and Simon of Policastro's bastard son, Roger Sclavus, led bands of Lombard rebels to massacre the Muslim inhabitants.[25] William prepared to march against them and, before leaving Palermo, he had Bonnellus maimed and blinded, and thrown into prison. Once rebellion on the island had been put down, early in 1162, William crossed to the mainland, leaving Palermo in the hands of the *qā'id* Martin.

Martin first appears a year earlier. In February 1161, the Jew Yaʿqūb ibn Faḍlūn ibn Ṣāliḥ purchased a piece of *dīwānī* land in Palermo from 'the lords of the *dīwān al-taḥqīq al-maʿmūr,* the elder, the *qā'id* Martin, and the elder, the *qā'id* Matthew (may God strengthen [all] the elders!)'. Martin and other officials of the *dīwān*, sign the deed at its foot with their 'well-known *ʿalāmāt*'.[26] Interestingly, Martin is here given precedence over Matthew, who is presumably the notary Matthew of Salerno, soon to be put in charge of the whole administration, and who can only recently have been released from prison, following his arrest in November 1160 for too close an association with Maio of Bari.[27]

22 The River Papireto lay north of the city centre, and separated it from the Sceralcadi (Arabic, *shāriʿ al-qāḍī*, 'the street of the cadi', or – possibly – *shirʿat al-qāḍī*, 'the law of the cadi'). See the reconstruction of the map of Palermo in Columba 1910, between pp.424–5, which revises and replaces the *Carta Topographica di Palermo* in Di Giovanni 1882–4, and all earlier attempts. See also De Simone 1968.

23 'Hugo Falcandus' 1897, pp.56–7 (trans. 'Hugo Falcandus' 1998, pp.109–10).

24 'Hugo Falcandus' 1897, p.59 (trans. 'Hugo Falcandus' 1998, p.111).

25 'Hugo Falcandus' 1897, p.70 (trans. 'Hugo Falcandus' 1998, pp.121–2).

26 *Aṣḥāb dīwān al-taḥqīq al-maʿmūr al-shaykh al-qā'id martīn wa-l-shaykh al-qā'id māthāw wa-l-shuyūkh aʿazza-hum Allāh*; Μαρτίνος καὶ Ματθαῖος καὶ οἱ λοιποὶ γέρωντες οἱ καὶ ἐπὶ τοῦ σεκρέτου (*Martinos kai Matthaios kai oi loipoi gerōntes oi kai epi tou sekretou*; 'Martin and Matthew and the other elders in charge of the *dīwān*'). This is the earliest and least competent version of Martin's *ʿalāma*, which reads *tawakkulī ʿalā ilāhī* or … *llāhi* ('My trust is in my God' or '… in God'): the other, later and more practised versions occur on ***Dīwānī* 37** (November 1166) and **Private 11** (March 1167). On this document (***Dīwānī* 35**), the *ʿalāma* to the right of Martin's could be an early, unpractised, and rather different version of Richard's mature *ʿalāma – lā yakhfā ʿalā llāhi shay'* ('Nothing is hidden from God'): below, p.232, note 81, but Richard is not named in the text. If this is his *ʿalāma*, then it is Richard's earliest appearance by some five years. After Martin's signature come the note concerning Ḥamza ibn Ḥamza, the *wakīl al-faḥṣ*, and the Greek signature of Iōannes.

27 'Hugo Falcandus' 1897, pp.45, 69 (trans. 'Hugo Falcandus' 1998, pp.99, 121).

The Martin of the *History* is a very different figure from the respected administrator of this document. 'Hugo Falcandus' claims that, like the eunuch Peter (see below), Martin had special judicial powers and his own court. On the pretext of hunting down and punishing the rebels of 1160–1, Martin is said to have taken a terrible revenge upon the Christians of Palermo, whom he held responsible for the murder of his brother during the attack on the palace. He used his judicial powers to foster all old feuds and quarrels, and exploited the institution of the *monomachia*, or judicial duel, to avenge his brother, by pretending to take seriously the accusations of any young blood who was willing to provoke a duel by falsely charging another citizen of having been amongst the rebels. According to 'Hugo Falcandus', many innocent Christians were ruined, imprisoned, beaten, tortured, and even 'hanged with the Muslims looking on and mocking them'.[28]

Soon after the king had returned to Palermo, another break-out of captives from the palace prison threatened him and his family. After being turned back at the upper entrance to the royal apartments, the fugitives made for the lower, with the intention of seizing the king or his young sons.

> It also happened that there were some men with *qāʾid* Martin, whose office was in the entrance just past the first door, and when they rushed in, one of these men opposed them and parried their first strokes. This slowed down their attack and destroyed their hopes; for in the meantime *qāʾid* Martin retreated into the palace and barred the doors.

The would-be rebels were slaughtered, and fed to the dogs. As a result, the royal prison was moved to the other end of the city, to the *Castellum Maris*, whence – as we shall see – Robert of Calatabiano and the eunuch Peter are said to have continued the terror, persecuting above all the citizens of the Lombard towns which had been centres of anti-Muslim pogroms in 1161.[29]

After the death of William I, and the succession of the young William II, under the regency of Margaret the queen-mother, Martin returned to less exciting duties as director of the royal *dīwān*, although he was also one of the royal familiars until at least May 1169.[30] In November 1166, he was responsible for handing over the archdeaconry of Messina to Archbishop Nicholas.[31] The following March, Martin witnessed an exchange of property between Ansaldus, the castellan of the royal palace, and Eutropius, a cantor in the palace chapel. Although he appears, under Matthew of Salerno, on the same line and with the same rank – *magister camerarius et familiaris* – as the *qāʾid* Richard, the latter's name is to the left of Martin's, a position which would suggest that Richard took precedence over him – if only, that is, we could be sure that the two rivals read this line from left to right and not, as

[28] 'Hugo Falcandus' 1897, pp.79–80 (trans. 'Hugo Falcandus' 1998, pp.129–31). For Frederick II's detailed legislation surrounding the *monomachia*, see Conrad, von der Lieck-Buyken and Wagner 1973, II.xxxii–xl, pp.218–32; von der Lieck-Buyken 1978, II.xxxii–xl, p.88–95; Powell 1971, II.xxxii(32)–xl(40), pp.90–8.

[29] 'Hugo Falcandus' 1897, p.85 (trans. 'Hugo Falcandus' 1998, pp.134–6).

[30] 'Hugo Falcandus' 1897, pp.108–9 (trans. 'Hugo Falcandus' 1998, p.158).

[31] ***Dīwānī* 37**: al-*shaykh al-qāʾid martīn ṣāḥib al-dīwān aʿazza-hu llāh*; Ὁ τοῦ μεγάλου παλατίου καΐτης Μαρτῆνος καὶ οἱ λοιποὶ γέροντες οἱ ἐπὶ τοῦ σεκρέτου. Martin signs with his *ʿalāma*: above, p.220, note 26.

Arabs, from right to left. They both sign with a cross, with their name and titles in Latin, and with an Arabic *ᶜalāma*.[32] Martin's name is missing from the list given by 'Hugo Falcandus' of the ten royal familiars appointed in the summer of 1168.[33] He is still master chamberlain in one document of February 1169,[34] but in another of the same month, and in one of May 1169, he is a mere chamberlain, beside the master chamberlain Richard: both were still royal familiars.[35] Perhaps Martin was already growing old, for he died a few years later, and in August 1176, Santa Maria di Monreale was granted a house in the Kemonia that had once belonged to 'the late *qāʾid* Martin, the royal chamberlain'.[36]

Barrūn, Peter, Aḥmad

In June 1141, King Roger ordered three officers of the *dīwān* to remake the boundary-description of the lands of San Giorgio di Triocala and Raḥl al-Baṣal (***Dīwānī* 15–17**). Two of them, John and Abū ᶜAlī, cannot be securely traced in any other source, but the third, under the name of ὁ καΐτης Περροῦν (*o kaitēs Perroun*), here makes the first appearance in what was to be a long and remarkable career.[37] There can be little doubt that this is the Greek version of the name of the *shaykh al-dīwān al-maᶜmūr al-qāʾid* Barrūn, who supervised the scribe ᶜUthmān in the issue of an official copy of a *dīwānī* decree to San Nicolò di Chùrchuro in December 1149 (***Dīwānī* 29**).[38] The *ᶜalāma* with which Barrūn signs this document, is apparently identical to the signature at the foot of the official record of a boundary inquest issued to San Giorgio di Triocala in May 1152 (***Dīwānī* 31**), and so this, too, seems to have been issued by Barrūn.[39]

Vera von Falkenhausen has suggested to me that Greek Perroun and Arabic Barrūn are derived from French Perron, the diminutive of Pierre.[40] This is confirmed

[32] **Private 11**: † *Matheus domini Regis magister notarius et familiaris* / † *Gaytus Ricardus domini Regis magister camerarius et familiaris* – *lā yakhfā ᶜalā llāhi shayʾ* ('Nothing is hidden from God') / † *tawakkulī ᶜalā ilāhī* or … *llāhi* ('My trust is in my God' or '… in God') – *Gaytus Martinus domini Regis magister camerarius et familiaris*.

[33] 'Hugo Falcandus' 1897, pp.161–2 (trans. 'Hugo Falcandus' 1998, p.214).

[34] Pratesi 1958, no.23, pp.60–2. [35] ed. Garufi 1899, nos 47–8, pp.109–12.

[36] Garufi 1902, no.15, pp.10–11; Pirri 1733, vol.I, pp.453–5.

[37] Above, p.103, p.106 and note 46. [38] Above, p.194.

[39] Johns and Metcalfe 1999, pp.231, 245 lines 19–20, and 247 lines 19–20, misread and misinterpret Barrūn's *ᶜalāma*. Read instead: *wa-awqaᶜa fī-hā shuyūkhu l-dīwāni l-maᶜmūri l-qāʾidu Barrūn wa-l-kātibu ᶜUthmānu ḥafiẓa-humā llāhu ᶜalāmata-humā tāʾkīdan la-hu wa-dalīlan ᶜalā ṣiḥḥati-hi … ṣāḥīḥun bi-l-taʾrīkhi* – *ᶜalā llāhi tawakkulī* or … *tawfīqī* ('And the elders of the *dīwān al-maᶜmūr*, the *qāʾid* Barrūn and the scribe ᶜUthmān, may God protect the two of them, set down their *ᶜalāmas* in confirmation of it and as proof of its authenticity … Correct on the date – My trust is in God' or 'My prosperity depends on God'). It has not yet been possible to inspect the original MS of ***Dīwānī* 31**, but it is hoped that Barrūn's signature there may decide between *tawakkulī* and *tawfīqī*. In ***Dīwānī* 29**, it is possible that *ṣaḥīḥun bi-l-taʾrīkhi* should be understood as ᶜUthmān's *ᶜalāma* (see Stern 1964a, pp.138–41), but I am more inclined to view this, and other similar notes on the *dīwānī* documents, as signs of authentication.

[40] See also Caracausi 1993, vol.II, p.1204; *pace* Johns and Metcalfe 1999, p.231, n.24.

by a trilingual inscription which seems to be the foundation inscription from a royal building, possibly a fountain, in Termini Imerese. The slab is broken but, crucially, all the surviving pieces fit together. The official charged with supervising the construction is named in the Arabic as 'the slave of the most royal presence, the eunuch Barrūn' (*ᶜabd al-ḥaḍra al-malakīya … al-fatā Barrūn*), and in the Latin as 'Peter, the servant of his [*i.e.* King Roger's] palace' (*Petrus servus palatii ejus*).[41] In short, the royal eunuch Barrūn and the royal servant Peter are identical.[42]

Peter is one of the leading figures at the court of William I in the dramatic account given by 'Hugo Falcandus' in *The History of the Tyrants of Sicily*. Maio of Bari is cast as the villain in the early chapters of the *History*, and is said to have allowed al-Mahdīya to fall to the Almohads by deliberately recalling the Norman fleet. 'At this time', he writes, 'it was commanded by *qāʾid* Peter, a eunuch. Like all the palace eunuchs, this man was a Christian only in name and appearance, but a Muslim by conviction.' Peter is said to have brought the fleet from Spain to al-Mahdīya, as if he meant to break the Almohad blockade. 'But that was not done. To everyone's amazement, just as many were already unfurling their sails, the *qāʾid* Peter (who was commanding the fleet and planned the whole thing) inexplicably turned to flee, exposing his sails to the winds. The other galleys followed their fleeing commander as best they could'. Romuald of Salerno gives a very different account, in which Peter's fleet engages with the Almohad navy and is badly defeated, losing many galleys, before escaping back to Sicily. This accords with the Arabic tradition, which is apparently based upon an eye-witness report.[43] The Almohad siege continued, and the Norman garrison began to suffer severely from hunger. Peter and the other eunuchs are said not only to have deliberately omitted to provision the garrison, but also to have informed the Almohad leader, ᶜAbd al-Muʾmin, of their treachery. Peter is even said to have spread the rumour that King William did not care if the city were to be lost, 'with the intention of showing that the king had gone mad'.[44]

According to the *History*, Maio paid for his treachery with his life,[45] while Peter was promoted. He seems to have accompanied King William to the mainland in his

[41] I have inspected the inscription in the Museo Civico, Termini Imerese – the surviving fragments undoubtedly all once belonged to a single inscription: ed. Amari 1875, no.8, pp.47–9 and pl.5, figs 2–3 (Amari 1971, pp.63–6): *mimmā amara bi-binā[ʾi] hādhihi … / ᶜabdu l-ḥaḍrati l-mal[akīyati] … / al-fatā barrūn sanata sabᶜ[in] … / raḥima llāhu man daᶜā la-[hu] …* ('The construction of this … was ordered … / the slave of the [most] ro[yal] presence … / the eunuch Barrūn in the year seven … / may God have mercy upon whomsoever prays for [him] …') Ἐν ἡμέραις Ῥογερίου □ / αὐτοῦ … ('In the days of Roger … / of this …') *Domino Rogerio … / Petrus servus palatii ejus regnantis feliciter* … ('By the Lord Roger … / Peter, servant of his palace, happily reigning …') The date is problematic: the calendar could be Julian (1137 or 1147), or Islamic (527/1132–3, 537/1142–3, or 547/1152–3), or Byzantine (6647/1139 or 6657/1149).

[42] This disproves the conclusion of Haskins 1911, p.441, that 'Kaid Brûn' was the Englishman Master Thomas Brown.

[43] Romuald of Salerno 1935, p.242: *Ueniens autem gaytus Petrus eunuchus regis, qui stolio preerat, ad Africam* [*i.e.* al-Mahdīya], *cum stolio Mesemutorum pugnauit, et pugnando in fugam conuersus est, et multis galeis suis amisit.* For the Arabic accounts, which do not mention Peter by name, see Idris 1962a, vol.I, pp.391–3.

[44] 'Hugo Falcandus' 1897, pp.24–8 (trans. 'Hugo Falcandus' 1998, pp.78–80).

[45] Above, p.219.

ruthless campaign against the baronial rebels of 1160–2. At that time, another eunuch, the *qā'id* Jawhar ('Jewel'), Latin Iohar, was master chamberlain of the palace (*magister camerarius palatii*). William is said to have beaten him so badly that he preferred to defect to the rebels who had so recently massacred his brother eunuchs, taking with him the royal seals. He was swiftly recaptured, and put to death by drowning.[46] Peter was appointed in his stead and, on the return of William to Palermo, was promoted to the triumvirate of royal familiars, beside Richard Palmer, bishop-elect of Syracuse, and Matthew of Salerno.[47]

According to the *History*, Peter's duties at this time were largely judicial, and included the prosecution of alleged rebels; a duty that, in effect, amounted to the arbitrary persecution of anyone who had fallen foul of the palace Saracens, or provoked 'the unquenchable cupidity of the eunuchs'. In Palermo, Robert of Calatabiano, the master of the *Castellum Maris*, which had recently been adopted as a royal prison, 'a man of extreme cruelty, particularly friendly to the eunuchs and dedicated to serving them', is said to have brought many innocent victims before Peter for judgement. On the mainland, the royal justiciar Bartholomew de Parisio and other justiciars are said to have led the witch-hunt, 'relying on the patronage of *qā'id* Peter'.[48] They were responsible for administering a notorious penal charge, the *redemptio*, upon the defeated rebels and their lands.

According to the *History*, when William I lay dying in May 1166, he named his young son William as his successor and Queen Margaret as regent until he should come of age. He confirmed Richard Palmer, Matthew of Salerno, and the *qā'id* Peter as *familiares curiae*, 'so that the queen should decide what ought to be done on the advice of these men'.[49] In his will, the king granted Peter his freedom, and this was subsequently confirmed by the new king and the queen-mother.[50] After William II was acclaimed king, in the summer of 1166, 'Hugo Falcandus' claims that Margaret curried favour by relaxing the harsh measures introduced after the rebellion. The *redemptio* was abolished, 'and she wrote to the Master Chamberlains that they should not demand redemption fees again from anyone on any grounds'. At the same time that she thus reduced the power of the eunuchs, the *History* has her promote the *qā'id* Peter to a position of supreme eminence, and instruct Richard Palmer and Matthew of Salerno 'that, as his assistants, they should indeed be present at council meetings and call themselves *familiares*, but that they should obey his orders in eveything'.[51]

46 'Hugo Falcandus' 1897, 77 (trans. 'Hugo Falcandus' 1998, p.128). The tentative identification of Iohar with the master chamberlain Theodore must be rejected (Jamison 1957, p.44, n.3). The *History*, our only source for Iohar, places his death during the campaign, before the capture of Taranto, in the early summer of 1162, while Theodore is said to have died in February 1163 (Garufi 1922, p.20).

47 'Hugo Falcandus' 1897, p.83 (trans. 'Hugo Falcandus' 1998, p.133).

48 'Hugo Falcandus' 1897, pp.85–6 (trans. 'Hugo Falcandus' 1998, pp.135–6). For Robert of Calatabiano, see below, p.229 (on p.135, Loud and Wiedemann misname Robert of Calatabiano as Robert of Calatabellota [*sic* for Caltabellotta]).

49 'Hugo Falcandus' 1897, p.88 (trans. 'Hugo Falcandus' 1998, p.137).

50 'Hugo Falcandus' 1897, p.100 (trans. 'Hugo Falcandus' 1998, p.148).

51 'Hugo Falcandus' 1897, p.88 (trans. 'Hugo Falcandus' 1998, p.139).

Having disapprovingly followed Peter's career to its zenith, 'Hugo Falcandus' gives the following, rather unexpected, sketch of his character:

> Although this man Peter was not a very shrewd man and tended to keep changing his mind, he was, however, gentle, pleasant and likeable, and his actions gave no grounds for criticism. He practised liberality above all the other virtues, and thought that giving gave more satisfaction than receiving. Because of this, his knights loved him dearly and followed his wishes and orders in every respect, and if the vice of his race had not cancelled out his innate peaceableness and prevented him from genuinely abandoning his hatred of Christianity, the kingdom of Sicily would have enjoyed much peace under his administration.[52]

As if to subvert the jibe about the innate vice of the Saracen, 'Hugo Falcandus' immediately follows with a long account of the depravity, greed, jealousy, and political manoeuvres of the leading Christian prelates of the kingdom, including the archbishops Romuald of Salerno and Roger of Reggio, and the bishops Tustan of Mazara and Gentile of Agrigento. He depicts the last as the rival of Richard Palmer for the see of Palermo, and as the champion of a Sicilian faction hostile to the growing influence at court of *transmontani* from north of the Alps, first generation immigrants, such as the Englishman Richard Palmer. Although Gentile is also said to have been opposed to 'the theft and extortion of the notaries and the ushers and the other court officials', by which the officers of the fiscal administration would seem to be meant, the *History* has him ally with their director, Matthew of Salerno. This faction set about recruiting Peter, and turned him so thoroughly against Richard Palmer that he determined to have him assassinated. Richard learnt of the plot, Peter withdrew; the bishops insisted, Peter reinstated the plan, then, 'having a gentle disposition', abandoned it again. As Peter vacillated, yet another leading churchman, Cardinal John of Naples, sought to persuade him to expel Richard Palmer, in hope of securing the see of Palermo for himself.[53]

Queen Margaret's blood-relation Gilbert, count of Gravina, whom William I had appointed governor of the mainland provinces excluding Calabria, now came to Sicily hoping

> to be appointed Master Captain of the whole realm, and to undertake the administration of the business of court in the top position after the queen. But the queen's inclination would not allow her to put the *qāʾid* Peter, of whom she was very fond, in second position to anyone, and the count had not come with the support of enough knights to be able to exclude the other familiars from the court against her wishes.[54]

And so Richard Palmer easily secured Gilbert's support, and turned him against the '*qāʾid* Peter and his associates'. Meanwhile, the ecclesiastical faction played a double game, flattering Gilbert to his face, but, behind his back, slandering him to the queen. Eventually, Gilbert obtained a semi-private audience with the queen and, with Peter in attendance, complained that

52 'Hugo Falcandus' 1897, pp.90–1; (trans. 'Hugo Falcandus' 1998, p.139).
53 'Hugo Falcandus' 1897, pp.91–3 (trans. 'Hugo Falcandus' 1998, pp.139–44).
54 'Hugo Falcandus' 1897, p.96 (trans. 'Hugo Falcandus' 1998, p.144).

> All the leading men were already angry that she had passed over the counts and other prudent men by whose judgement the court ought to be guided, and put an effeminate slave (*servum effeminatum*) in charge of the entire realm. For the king's judgement had not been sound, and his command on this matter should not be adhered to, when he thought that despicable persons, castrated men, in fact (*viros contemptibiles, immo deviratos homines*), sufficed to administer the realm. ... The queen, however, replied that the king's final wishes would be respected in every proper way, and should never be made void by any act of hers. If he thought the *qāʾid* Peter was not good enough to administer the realm, then he should remain at court as a familiar alongside him, so that his authority and wisdom might make up for that which the court lacked. Angered by this, the count said, 'How good of you to have granted the respect due to me as your blood-relative by deciding to assign me a wonderful position of honour in which you make me the equal of your slave'. ... He attacked her with these and other harsh phrases, and gradually broke into open abuse. When in the end he had made her cry, she nevertheless resisted his suggestion just as actively, so he left her, and went back to his residence in a huff.[55]

Peter, who had witnessed the whole scene, fully realised the danger of his position, and set about consolidating his support. According to 'Hugo Falcandus', Peter's champions were the master constable, Richard of Mandra, whom he had made count of Molise, and Hugh, son of Atton, another baron with lands in Molise and Samnium, whom Peter had made captain of his own knights. Thus, the salaried knights (*milites stipendiarii*), except for a few *transmontani*, followed their commanders and supported Peter, while those barons and nobles who held their lands in fief sided with Gilbert of Gravina. Peter 'started to ride about a lot with an enormous number of knights, preceded by sentries and archers' (*cum ingenti multitudine militum, hostiariis, sagitariisque*) and did his best to swear his allies to loyalty, and to buy further support. But rumours of a major plot against him persisted.

> So he was shaken by different and contradictory stories, and so frightened that he thought that he would only be able to escape from the count's hands by fleeing in the night. He had a fast boat made ready with the greatest possible speed and provided with sailors, weapons and whatever else was needed. After he had his treasure-chests carried there in the silence of night, on the next day, after sunset, he pretended that he wanted to go to a new palace which he had recently built in the part of the city called Kemonia, and he went down to the sea front with a few eunuchs whom he had decided to take with him. There he sent away the horses, went on board ship and sailed across to Africa to the King of the Almohads.[56]

'Hugo Falcandus' next gives an extraordinary account of the following day, when Peter's defection was discovered. Gilbert of Gravina accused Peter of having stolen the crown jewels, but this was vehemently denied by the queen herself. Next, he claimed that he had long been afraid of Peter's treachery, and that it was a

55 'Hugo Falcandus' 1897, pp.96–7 (trans. 'Hugo Falcandus' 1998, pp.145–6).

56 'Hugo Falcandus' 1897, pp.97–9 (trans. 'Hugo Falcandus' 1998, pp.146–7). See also Romuald of Salerno 1935, p.254: *Eodem tempore gaytus Petrus eunuchus et magister camerarius palatii cum quibusdam aliis fugam petit, et ad regem Morocho veniens multam secum pecuniam transportavit.*

miracle that this Saracen slave had not carried off not just the treasure but the king himself. Whereupon, Richard of Molise sprang to Peter's defence, and challenged Gilbert to single combat. The queen sided with Richard and his followers and, aided by Matthew, managed to persuade Gilbert to return to the mainland. In his place, Margaret appointed Richard, whom Peter had made count of Molise, 'since he had cherished great loyalty for the *qāʾid* Peter, and she granted him greater power than the other familiars'. The palace faction took the opportunity to blame Richard Palmer for Peter's defection and tried, unsuccessfully, to force him to leave for Rome.[57]

But this was not the end of Peter's career. Ibn Khaldūn writes of the manner in which the Almohads gained control of the coasts of both Spain and North Africa:

> When the Almohad dynasty became powerful in the 6th century [A.H., 12th century A.D.], and took over both coasts, they made the state of the fleet more perfect than had ever been known, and more important than had ever been seen. The admiral of their fleets was Aḥmad the Sicilian. He came originally from the Ṣadghiyān of Sadwīkish, inhabitants of the island of Gerba. The Christians captured him from its shores, and he was raised by them. The ruler of Sicily picked him out, and employed him, but then died. His son succeeded him, and was angered [with Aḥmad] through certain quarrels. [Aḥmad] was afraid for his life, and so came to Tunis and entered the service of its leader, one of the Banī ʿAbd al-Muʾmin [*i.e.* the Almohads]. Thence, he travelled to Morocco, where the caliph Yūsuf, son of ʿAbd al-Muʾmin, welcomed him charitably and with honour, and showered him with gifts. He entrusted him with the command of his fleets, and thus he distinguished himself in the *jihād* against the nations of Christendom. His exploits are commemorated in the chronicles of the Almohad dynasty. In his time, the fleets of the Muslims reached a size and fame which they attained neither before nor since.[58]

As Michele Amari observed, this account of Aḥmad's defection tallies so closely with that of Peter's that the protagonist of the two stories must be the same individual.[59] Barrūn, Peter, and Aḥmad are all the names of one man.

Elsewhere, Ibn Khaldūn reports that Aḥmad was still one of the commanders of the Almohad fleet which broke the blockade of Constantine in Ifrīquiya by the Almoravid ʿAlī ibn Ghāniya, and which recaptured Bougie from Yaḥyā ibn Ghāniya, in 1185.[60] Such a date would fit well, if Peter had been a youth when captured

57 'Hugo Falcandus' 1897, pp.100–2 (trans. 'Hugo Falcandus' 1998, pp.147–50).

58 Ibn Khaldūn 1858, vol.II, pp.37–8; *BAS*^{2}, vol.II, p.515; *BAS*^{2}*(It.)*, vol.II, p.568: *lammā stafḥalat dawlatu l-muwaḥḥidīna fī l-miʾati l-sādisati wa-malakū l-ʿudwatayni aqāmū khuṭṭata hādhā l-usṭūli ʿalā atammi mā ʿurifa wa-aʿẓami mā ʿuhida wa-kāna qāʾidu asāṭīli-him aḥmada l-ṣiqillīya aṣlu-hu min ṣadghiyāni l-muwaṭṭanīna bi-jazīrati jarbata min sadwīkish asara-hu l-naṣārā min sawāḥili-hā wa-rubbiya ʿinda-hum wa-stakhlaṣa-hu ṣāḥibu ṣiqillīyata wa-stakfā-hu thumma halaka wa-waliya bnu-hu fa-askhaṭa-hu bi-baʿḍi l-nizāʿāti wa-khashiya ʿalā nafsi-hi fa-laḥiqa bi-tūnisa wa-nazala ʿalā l-sayyidi bi-hā min banī ʿabdi l-muʾmini fa-ajāza ilā marrākusha fa-talaqqā-hu l-khalīfatu yūsufu bnu ʿabdi l-muʾmini bi-l-mabarrati wa-l-karāmati wa-ajzala la-hu l-ṣilata wa-qallada-hu amra asāṭīli-hi fa-jallā fī jihādi umami l-naṣranīyati wa-kānat la-hu āthārun wa-maqāmātun madhkūratun fī dawlati l-muwaḥḥidīna wa-ntahat asāṭīlu l-muslimīna ʿalā ʿahdi-hi fī l-kathrati wa-l-istijādati ilā mā lam tablugh-hu min qabli-hi wa-lā baʿdu.*

59 Amari 1933–9, vol.III, pp.505–6.

60 Ibn Khaldūn 1868, vol.VI, p.191; *BAS*^{2}, vol.II, p.559; *BAS*^{2}*(It.)*, vol.II, p.614. See Marçais 1965, p.1007.

during the Norman conquest of Gerba in 1135,[61] some five or six years before he first appears as an officer of the *dīwān*, with the name Perroun, in June 1141.

Intriguingly, Peter the eunuch may have had a 'son'. Amongst the signatories a record of a sale of land to the *duana baronum*, dated July 1176, there appears one 'Nicholas the secretary, son of the *qāʾid* Peter'.[62] There is no compelling reason to believe that Nicholas was the 'son' of the eunuch *qāʾid* Peter but, if he was, it need not mean that he was Peter's biological son, for the Greek could express the Arabic patronymic Ibn Fityān, literally 'Son of the Eunuchs', describing the close, almost paternal relationship between the eunuchs and their protégés.[63]

Richard

In the early summer of 1166, a year since the death of William I, after the *qāʾid* Peter's defection and the return of Gilbert of Gravina to the mainland, the court was still dominated by Peter's old champion, Richard, count of Molise, and by four other royal familiars: Richard Palmer, bishop-elect of Syracuse, who still hoped to be made archbishop of Palermo; the *magister notarius* Matthew of Salerno who, according to 'Hugo Falcandus', performed the duties of chancellor, and hoped to be appointed to that office, but only because the grander title of emir of emirs was now too widely hated for him to assume; the *qāʾid* Martin, 'who was in charge of the *dīwān*'; and the *qāʾid* Richard, 'who was master chamberlain of the palace'. The two eunuchs, according to the *History*, 'played just as much a part in policy-making and dealt with the affairs of the realm jointly with the above-mentioned familiars'.[64] Margaret, the queen-mother and regent, now invited a distant cousin to Palermo, Stephen, the younger son of Count Rotrou II of Perche, with the intention of making him archbishop, over the head of Richard Palmer. First, however, 'she appointed him chancellor, and ordered that thenceforth all court business should be brought to him in the first place'. Thereupon, the canons of Palermo elected him archbishop. By the winter of 1167–8, Stephen was the most powerful figure in the kingdom, and the hold of the old palace faction upon the administration seemed to have been broken.[65]

According to 'Hugo Falcandus', Stephen first attempted to root out corruption within the chancery, where the royal notaries used to charge immense sums for issuing documents. Peter the notary, a relative of Matthew of Salerno, had asked an outrageous bribe from some petitioners, who had complained to the new

[61] Idris 1962a, vol.I, pp.345–7.

[62] † Νικολάος ὁ σεκρετικός ὁ καῗτου Πετρου υἱός (*Nikolaos o sekretikos o kaitou Petrou uios*): Garufi 1902, pp.163–5.

[63] See Ibn Jubayr's reference to Yaḥyā *ibn Fityān* (literally '… son of the eunuchs', and his claim that 'there is not one of [the eunuchs] but … redeems prisoners, [and] brings up those of them who are children': above, p.213. See also Ayalon 1999, pp.290–2.

[64] 'Hugo Falcandus' 1897, pp.108–9 (trans. 'Hugo Falcandus' 1998, p.158).

[65] See also Romuald of Salerno 1935, p.255.

chancellor. Stephen ordered another notary to issue the writ, and the satisfied recipients set out for home. Peter the notary ambushed them, 'snatched the royal writ from them, broke the seal, and tore it up, insulting and beating the men themselves'. Stephen had Peter the notary imprisoned for the crime, increased the number of notaries in the chancery, and instituted a scale of fixed charges, despite the objections of Richard Palmer and the palace faction.

> When the people of Palermo saw that the chancellor could not be deflected from the path of justice either by bribes or by anyone's favour, they laid accusations before him against many people who had given up being Christians and become Muslims, and had long secretly been under the protection of the eunuchs. He let none of those who were guilty of this great crime off without punishment.[66]

In particular, Robert of Calatabiano, the royal jailer and keeper of the *Castellum Maris*, and an old ally of the *qā'id* Peter, was accused of a long list of crimes, including murder, the rape of a Christian girl, running a brothel in a wine-shop, and having restored an ancient Muslim shrine within the castle. When he found that bribes and threats could not secure his release, Robert 'threw himself upon the protection of the eunuchs. They fell at the feet of the king and queen, and with tears they begged them not to permit the condemnation of a man who was utterly essential to the realm, and had always tried to serve the court most faithfully'. The queen-mother ordered Stephen to discharge Robert: 'For the theft and the murders which he was said to have carried out were not to be ascribed to him but to *qā'id* Peter, at whose orders he had done them. It was obvious that, while Peter was in charge of the court, Robert himself had been unable to disobey his commands'. The courtiers (*familiares curie*) supported Robert, partly to gain favour with the queen-mother and the eunuchs, partly to attack the chancellor. Eventually, a compromise was reached, and Robert was found guilty, under canon law, of perjury, incest and adultery. He was flogged in public, and imprisoned in his own dungeon, where he soon died.[67]

That Stephen du Perche really did take seriously such hackneyed allegations against Muslims or crypto-Muslims is supported by a letter written in late 1167 for Pope Alexander III. Stephen, in his capacity as archbishop-elect, had asked 'what should be done about Saracens who seize Christian women and boys or even kill them, and whose excesses King William of Sicily has commissioned him and the other bishops to punish'. The pope replied that severe cases, where a fine or a light flogging would not suffice, should be handed over to the royal court, to suffer amputation of limbs or death.[68]

[66] 'Hugo Falcandus' 1897, pp.112–13 (trans. 'Hugo Falcandus' 1998, pp.163–5).
[67] 'Hugo Falcandus' 1897, pp.115–18 (trans. 'Hugo Falcandus' 1998, pp.166–8).
[68] Kehr, Holtzmann and Girgensohn 1906–75, vol.X, p.232, no.31, cited in 'Hugo Falcandus' 1998, p.166, n.184. It is worth quoting this little-known and somewhat inaccessible letter in full for the unusual light that it throws upon the attitude of the church to Muslims in Norman Sicily: *In archiepiscopatu tuo dicitur contigisse, quod quandoque Sarraceni mulieres Christianas rapiunt et pueros et eis abuti praesumunt, et quosdam etiam interdum occidunt. Cum autem excessus*

According to 'Hugo Falcandus', the prosecution of Robert of Calatabiano brought the palace eunuchs into direct conflict with Stephen du Perche. Their leader, the *qāʾid* Richard, master chamberlain of the royal palace, now became one of the chief conspirators against the chancellor. He began by winning the support of Abū l-Qāsim ibn Ḥammūd, and by transforming the initial enthusiasm of the Muslim population for Stephen into hostility.[69] By autumn 1167, the deepening rivalry between Stephen and Margaret's natural brother, Henry, count of Montescaglioso, seemed to offer Richard the opportunity for a palace coup, and he began to martial his forces. 'He was not content with his own knights, whom he paid himself, but had won the support of the majority of the king's knights and all the court archers (*militum regis et universos curie sagitarios*) through many gifts and favours, so that they would follow his wishes and commands in everything.'[70] But the chancellor, despite the late season and the atrocious weather, spirited the king and court off to Messina. There, he was able, first, to defeat and detain Henry of Montescaglioso, and to dispatch his supporters across the Straits to perish amongst the snows and wolves of the Sila; and, then, to master and imprison Richard of Molise, the old champion of the *qāʾid* Peter. Other leading opponents were imprisoned or excluded from court. On 20 March 1168, Stephen led the king back into Palermo, having apparently triumphed over his enemies.[71]

'Hugo Falcandus' reports that, in his absence, those practised conspirators, the *qāʾid* Richard, Matthew of Salerno, and Bishop Gentile of Agrigento, had hatched a plot to murder Stephen on Palm Sunday (24 March). He claims that what had won them support was the behaviour of one of Stephen's leading knights, the Tourainois noble John of Lavardin. At Stephen's insistence, he had been granted Matthew Bonnellus's estates around Caccamo and Prizzi. There, John had attempted to introduce what he claimed to be the custom of his native land, by demanding half of all the moveable property of the free-men of Latin race resident on his new

hujusmodi carissimus in Christo filius noster illustris rex Siciliae, tibi et aliis personis ecclesiasticis, quae pontificali supereminent dignitate, commisit puniendos: quid de Sarracenis agendum sit, qui fuerint in nefario scelere intercepti, nos duxit prudentia tua consulendos. Super quo utique tuae consultationi taliter respondemus, quod si tales in tua jurisdictione sint vel fuerint postmodum intercepti, pecuniaria poteris eos poena mulctare, et etiam flagellis afficere: ea tamen moderatione adhibita, quod flagella in vindictam sanguinis transire minime videantur. Si vero fuerint ita super hoc graves Sarracenorum excessus, quod mortem vel truncationem membrorum debeant sustinere, vindictam ipsam reserves regiae potestati. De illo autem qui se uxorem fratris sui, antequam ei matrimonio jungeretur, cognovisse proponit, hoc tuae prudentiae respondemus: quod nisi fuerit publicum et notorium, aut idoneis testibus approbatum, ipsum prius praedictum mulierem carnaliter cognovisse, praedictum matrimonium occasione illa dirimi non permittas. Super eo vero, quod afferis, Sarracenum quemdam de muliere quadam Christiana, quam quatuordecim annos tenuerat, filios suscepisse: discretioni tuae duximus respondendum, quod tam Sarracenus quam mulier pro tanto excessu gravi sunt animadversione plectendi (Mansi 1759–1927, vol.XXII, cols 445–6).

69 'Hugo Falcandus' 1897, p.119: *Gaytus quoque Richardus illi cum ceteris eunuchis infestissimus erat* (trans. 'Hugo Falcandus' 1998, p.170). This passage, and a note in the Dublin MS of the *dīwān* of Ibn Qalāqis (below, p.233, note 88), is the only explicit evidence that Richard was indeed a eunuch.

70 'Hugo Falcandus' 1897, pp.128–9 (trans. 'Hugo Falcandus' 1998, p.180). The court archers were commanded by Christian Arab captains: Abū l-Ṭayyib and Makhlūf, 'the *qāʾids* of the archers' (οἱ κάϊτες τῶν τοξότων and *quwwādu l-rumāti*) appear in October 1172 (***Dīwānī* 39**).

71 'Hugo Falcandus' 1897, pp.129–43 (trans. 'Hugo Falcandus' 1998, pp.170–96). For a much shorter and very different account of these same events, see Romuald of Salerno 1935, pp.256–7.

estates. They replied that they owed nothing to their lords, except what they chose to give of their own free will: 'it was only those Muslims and Greeks who were classified as villeins who had to pay tithes and an annual money rent'. The matter was put to the chancellor and, ignoring the advice of his Sicilian supporters, he sided with his French compatriots. This gave his enemies exactly the opening they needed, allowing them to claim that 'it was his intention that the entire population of Sicily should be forced to pay the annual renders and exactions, as was the custom in Gaul, where free citizens did not exist'. Stephen learnt of the plot against him in time, and had Matthew of Salerno, and some of the knights who had agreed to murder him, imprisoned.[72] 'But the Queen would in no way give her approval to the arrest of *qāʾid* Richard, who was the head and the origin of the conspiracy, and in the end the only thing the chancellor managed to obtain was that he was forbidden from leaving the palace and from talking to his knights'.[73] Bishop Gentile of Agrigento, however, was soon imprisoned, far from court, in the Valdemone.[74] Once again, the chancellor appeared to have triumphed. But, according to the *History*, his officer in Messina now managed to disaffect both the Latin and the Greek citizens and to provoke a popular uprising in the course of which he was murdered. The revolt spread rapidly. Reggio and Taormina fell to the rebels, and Count Henry of Montescaglioso and Count Richard of Molise were released from prison. Only the Lombard towns of the north-east of Sicily lay solidly behind the chancellor.[75]

Meanwhile, Matthew of Salerno, still a captive in the royal palace (not the *Castellum Maris*), took advantage of the convenient illness of the castellan to persuade his assistant, Constantine, 'to make all the palace servants (of whom there were about forty) take an oath that on a particular day, which he had announced to them, they should slay the chancellor as he arrived at court, between the first and second gate'. Although aware of some plot, the chancellor and his French supporters decided to stay in Palermo, not realising, says 'Hugo Falcandus', 'that traps can nowhere be laid more easily than in the palace itself'.[76] On the day set for his murder, with the palace servants waiting in ambush at the gate, Stephen was alerted and shut himself in the archiepiscopal residence which lay next to the cathedral, some two hundred metres from the royal palace. Seeing that the first attempt had failed, Constantine sent out the palace servants to raise the mob, and to besiege the chancellor's house. There, they were joined by the court archers. Meanwhile, supporters of the *qāʾid* Richard attacked some of Stephen's partisans, and were prevented from killing them only by the intervention of the king himself. As the assault upon his residence began in earnest, Stephen and his troops took refuge in the *campanile* of the cathedral.[77]

[72] Romuald of Salerno 1935, p.257, reports that Matthew's arrest was *sine causa*, and widely condemned because Matthew *homo erat sapiens et discretus, et in aula regia a puero enutritus, et in agendis regiis probate fidelitatis inuentus*.

[73] Note that Richard, at precisely this moment, was a director of the *duana baronum*: above, p.206.

[74] 'Hugo Falcandus' 1897, pp.143–7 (trans. 'Hugo Falcandus' 1998, pp.196–9).

[75] 'Hugo Falcandus' 1897, pp.147–55 (trans. 'Hugo Falcandus' 1998, pp.199–208).

[76] 'Hugo Falcandus' 1897, p.156 (trans. 'Hugo Falcandus' 1998, p.210).

[77] 'Hugo Falcandus' 1897, pp.156–8 (trans. 'Hugo Falcandus' 1998, pp.210–11).

Matthew of Salerno and the *qāʾid* Richard now let themselves out of prison, and, unopposed, reassumed their former offices and rank. They called out the Arab military band, and had them sound their trumpets and drums outside the chancellor's residence. The racket brought out the whole city – 'both the Muslims and the Christians', says 'Hugo Falcandus' – and the building was soon captured, leaving the chancellor and his exhausted knights trapped in the *campanile*. The leaders of the conspiracy had kept the king from intervening only with difficulty, and were now in danger of losing control of the mob, and so they offered terms to Stephen. Richard Palmer, Matthew of Salerno, the *qāʾid* Richard, Archbishop Romuald of Salerno, and Bishop John of Malta, all guaranteed Stephen and his knights safe-passage to a galley at Mondello (or Sferracavallo), and, with Bishop John to escort them, made sure that they safely left the island.[78] Stephen du Perche's stay in Sicily had come to an end. Of the thirty-seven companions who had accompanied him to Palermo, only two survived into 1170s, and he himself died soon after his arrival in Palestine.[79] The *qāʾid* Richard, an Arab eunuch, 'the head and origin of the conspiracy' against Stephen,[80] had seen off the French noble and would-be Crusader, the chancellor of Sicily, the archbishop-elect of Palermo, and the blood-relative of the queen-mother.

Like the *qāʾid* Martin after the suppression of the rebellions 1160–2, the *qāʾid* Richard now returned to his desk in the *dīwān*, and appears to have played no further role in high politics, although he remained a royal familiar until at least 1169. Richard may first appear in the *dīwān* as early as January 1161,[81] but it is only from 1166 that he appears as master chamberlain of the palace. Thereafter, he was one of the directors of the *dīwān al-taḥqīq* until at least March 1187, when he is heard of for the last time. In March 1168, at the climax of the struggle with Stephen du Perche, Richard had appeared as one of the directors of the *duana baronum* – the only time that he is seen in this office.[82]

78 'Hugo Falcandus' 1897, pp.158–62 (trans. 'Hugo Falcandus' 1998, pp.211–14). For a much shorter and very different account of these events, see again Romuald of Salerno 1935, p.257.

79 'Hugo Falcandus' 1897, p.165 (trans. 'Hugo Falcandus' 1998, p.218); William of Tyre 1986, book 20.3, vol.II, pp.914–15 (trans. William of Tyre 1943, vol.II, pp.346–7); Peter of Blois 1855, Epistle no.46, col.135.

80 'Hugo Falcandus' 1897, p.145: *Richardus gaytus, qui coniurationis caput erat et principium* (trans. 'Hugo Falcandus' 1998, p.198).

81 He may sign his *ʿalāma* next to Martin's at the foot of ***Dīwānī* 35**, but he is not named in the text: above, p.220, note 26.

82 March 1167: *Gaytus Ricardus domini Regis magister camerarius et familiaris* (see above, p.222, note 32). March 1168: τῶ πρωτοκαμπ[ερ]έρι καὶ φαμελλιαρίω ἡμῶν τῶ ἐπὶ τοῦ σεκρέτου τῶν ἀποκοπῶν καίτη Ῥιγκάρδη (ed. Kehr 1902, doc.19, pp.438–9). October 6677 A.M., Ind.12 (sic! = Ind.2, *i.e.* 1168 A.D.?): *thesaurius et familiaris noster qui est super omnes secretos Cait Riccardus* (Pirri 1733, vol.II, pp.1016–17 – the Latin is clearly an inaccurate translation of such a title as ὁ πρωτοκαμέραριος καὶ φαμιλιάρης ἐμός καὶ ὁ ἐπὶ τοῦ σεκρέτου ὁ καΐτης Ῥικκάρδος: see Takayama 1993, p.130). February 1169: *Gaytus Riccardus Regius magister camerarius* (Garufi 1899, no.47, pp.109–11). February 1169: *gaytus Riccardus regis magister camerarius* (Pratesi 1958, no.23, pp.60–2). May 1169: *Gaytus Riccardus regius magister Camerarius* (Garufi 1899, no.48, pp.111–12). October 1170: ὁ ἐνδωξότης κάϊτος Ῥικκάρδος καὶ [ὁ ἐπὶ?] τοῦ σεκρέτου (Haskins 1911, p.650 and n.160). January 1183: *magister palatinus Camerarius dominus Gaytus Riccardus magister regie duane de secretis* (Mattei-Cerasoli 1939, no.12, pp.292–4). April 1183: τῆς θεοφρούρήτου κούρτης καὶ ὁ ἐνδωξότης ἄρχων τοῦ σεκρέτου κυρίος κάϊτος Ῥικκάρδος

Adalgisa De Simone has recently identified the *qāʾid* Richard with a figure in the works of the Alexandrian poet, Ibn Qalāqis.[83] The author was in Sicily from 11 May 1168 until at least April 1169. In the summer of 1168, it seems that a temporary breakdown in relations between the poet and his patron, Abū l-Qāsim ibn Ḥammūd, persuaded Ibn Qalāqis to prepare to return to Egypt. He was ordered to be presented with a lavish viaticum of cheese, butter, oil, tuna,[84] cotton, walnuts, almonds, hazelnuts, wheat, flour, wine, and other gifts. Who gave the order is not absolutely clear, but, in light of what follows, it seems likely that the gift was a royal one, and that the order was issued through a royal official, possibly through Richard himself.[85] After the list of gifts, Ibn Qalāqis relates how a figure, identified only as Abū l-Sayyid,[86] presented him to William and Margaret. The poet had written two *qaṣīda*s for them, and these he introduced with a third, which is dedicated to 'Richard the vizier', as if this third *qaṣīda* were to introduce him into the royal presence, exactly as the vizier himself might do.[87] In the Dublin MS of the *dīwān* of Ibn Qalāqis, this poem is introduced as 'the *qaṣīda* in praise of *al-qāʾid* Richard the eunuch in Sicily'.[88] The *qaṣīda* itself dwells upon Richard's virtues and his

(Cusa 1868–82, no.142, pp.432–4). January 1186: *dominus Gaytus Riccardus domini Regis camerarius et magister regie duane de secretis* (White 1938, no.36, pp.278–9). March 1187: *dominus gaytus Riccardus domini regis camerarius et magister regie duane de secretis* and *al-qāʾid rijārdhī* (**Private 23**). March 1187: *Gaytus Riccardus domini Regis Camerarius et magister regie Dohane de Secretis* (Garufi 1899, no.88, pp.214–16).

83 De Simone 1991, pp.336–7; De Simone 1996, pp.22–4.

84 The editor of Ibn Qalāqis 1984a, p.22, reads *barāmīl bunn*, which, if 'barrels of coffee-beans' were intended, would be a gross anachronism – one which De Simone 1996, p.69 and n.104, elegantly avoids with *barili di grani grossi*. But, in the land of the *tonnara* and the *mattanza*, where *barrilia tunnine* frequently figure in contemporary Latin lists of provisions, I have little hesitation in reading *barāmīl tunn*, 'barrels of tuna'. Geert Jan van Gelder has drawn my attention to *bunn*, a sort of fish pickle (Dozy 1881, vol.I, p.116), also called *murrīy* (*ibid.*, vol.II, p.584) from the Latin *muria*. But the fact that tuna blood, trimmings and viscera were commonly used in the cheaper fish sauces, including *muria*, raises the possibility of yet another lexicographical pickle. Even if the reading *bunn*, meaning 'fish pickle', is accepted, in Sicily, the fish is likely to have been tuna and, in any case, could not have been Arabic *bunnī* or *binnī* (Lane 1984, vol.I, p.258), *Barbus bynni bynni* (*Cyprinus Bynni* Forsskål), a freshwater fish of the Nile and other African rivers.

85 De Simone 1996, pp.23–4, 69.

86 Could this be Richard's Arabic name? The name is a common one: in March 1169, Christodoulos son of Bū l-Sayyid (Χριστοδούλος υἱός Βουσσίτ) sold a house in Palermo to the groom of Richard Palmer, the bishop-elect of Syracuse (**Private 12**); in April 1202, Robert Faber granted all his possessions to the Magione, including property at Carini which he had bought from Gilbert, known as *Mahalufus* (Arabic Makhlūf), the nephew of *gayt[us] Bussit* (Mongitore 1721, pp.17–18). See also De Simone 1996, p.70, n.105.

87 'Abū l-Sayyid ... presented me to the two presences – the holy, dazzling, Williamian sovereign power, and the chaste, spotless, holy Lady – to whom I presented two *qaṣīda*s, which I dedicated to them in *Stringing necklaces [of verses] in praise of kings I have known*, and I added the following *qaṣīda* as an introduction' (*wa-tawallā ilā l-ḥadratayni: l-mamlakati l-muqaddasati l-ghulyalimīyati l-bāhirati wa-l-sayyidati l-qudsīyati l-munazzahati l-ṭāhirati fa-khadamtu-humā bi-qaṣīdatayni ʿallaqtu-humā fī naẓmi l-sulūki fī madāʾiḥi man laqītu mina l-mulūki wa-shafaʿtu-humā bi-qaṣīdatin wa-hiya ...*): Ibn Qalāqis 1984a, pp.22–3 (*qaṣīda*, pp.23–4). See De Simone 1996, pp.69–70 (*qaṣīda* translated, pp.71–2). The *Naẓm al-sulūk* is now lost (Ibn Qalāqis 1984a, pp.vi–viii) but a *qaṣīda* to William survives in Ibn Qalāqis 1988, no.36, pp.145–7 (dated 12 Shawwāl 563 / 21 July 1168).

88 *Wa-la-hu min qaṣīdatin yamdaḥu l-qāʾida y.z.j.r.da l-khaṣīya bi-ṣiqillīyata*: Ibn Qalāqis 1984a, p.80, n.189. Scribes and editors puzzled by Richard's outlandish name, which seems to have originally read *Yirjard* or similar, have variously read it as *Y.z.j.r.d* (close to the Persian Yazdgird), *Zajr.d*, *Jurdanā*, *etc.* (*ibid.*, p.80, n,189, and p.81, n.196).

pre-eminence within the royal administration, but in general terms, and without revealing new details about his life and work.

By January 1186, Richard seems to have provided for his retirement by acquiring a country estate from Bishop Stephen of Lipari-Patti. The priory of Santa Sofia di Vicari, and its *casale* of Manzil al-Khayr, lay far from Patti, and had become badly run down; its lands and woods had been occupied and usurped, and its villeins had fled. 'Therefore, because the *qā'id* Richard, the chamberlain of the lord king and the master of the *duana de secretis*, is a brother of our church, and because this church is especially eager for his patronage in our every need, it is our request, and the prayer of the whole convent of the church of Patti, that he should receive the aforesaid dependence of Santa Sofia, with the aforesaid *casale* of Myzalhar, and with Brother Gerard, the prior of that church, under his protection and patronage.' Richard was to enjoy all the revenue of its lands and villeins, in money and in kind, for the rest of his life, on the conditions that he did everything in his power to recover those lands that had been unlawfully occupied or usurped from its demesne, that he returned as many as possible of the fugitive villeins who belonged to the *casale* and to its *platea*, and that he improved the *casale* and the other possessions of Santa Sofia. On his death, everything was to revert to the church, including anything that Richard had built, planted, added, and improved. In return, Richard was to provide the bishop and his retinue with hay and with firewood for his kitchen, whenever he came to Palermo.[89] A year later, Richard was providing for his future in Palermo itself, by leasing from the archbishop and chapter of the cathedral a piece of abandoned land in the Kemonia. Perhaps, like Peter and Martin, Richard's own house lay in this district.[90] The land had been used as a rubbish tip, and threatened the citizens with disease. Richard undertook to enclose it and plant it, presumably with trees or vines. After seven years exemption, he was to pay a tithe of the crop to the cathedral. On his death, the estate was to revert to the church, with all the improvements he had made to it.[91]

Abū l-Qāsim ibn Ḥammūd

The *qā'id* Abū l-Qāsim appears twice as one of the directors of the royal *dīwān*. In June 1168, 'the archons of the court, the secretaries, Lord John and the *qā'id* Abū l-Qāsim' order the catepans of the royal demesne, and master foresters, Euphemius of Traina and William *de Mouritze* from Petralia, to grant an estate to San

[89] White 1938, Appendix no.36, pp.278–9, also pp.101–2.

[90] Kemonia, from Greek Χειμωνία, 'the Winter [River]' (Arabic *al-wādī l-shatawī*) the name of the seasonal water-course which ran to the south of the city centre, on the line of the modern via Albergheria. The district of Kemonia was enclosed by walls, and ran from the monastery of San Giovanni degli Eremiti, eastwards to the sea. The Kemonia was overlooked by the Torre Greco of the royal palace. For maps of 12th-century Palermo, see above, p.220, note 22.

[91] Garufi 1899, no.88, pp.214–16.

Salvatore di Capizzi, a dependence of the church of Cefalù, and to delimit its boundaries.[92] In November 1173, it was recorded how Geoffrey of Centuripe and the *qāʾid* Abū l-Qāsim, masters of the *duana de secretis*, had delimited the boundaries of an estate at Caccamo, granted to Santa Maria di Monte Maggiore.[93]

Abū l-Qāsim was a common name – it was the Prophet's *kunya* – but there is nonetheless good reason to identify this figure with Abū l-Qāsim ibn Ḥammūd, whom Ibn Jubayr calls the hereditary leader of the Muslims of Sicily. The poet Ibn Qalāqis, writing of his patron Abū l-Qāsim in the years 1168–9, compares him to the legendary Umayyad scribe ᶜAbd al-Ḥamīd ibn Yaḥyā, and to the great Būyid chancellors, Abū l-Faḍl Muḥammad ibn al-Ḥusayn, Abū l-Qāsim Ismāᶜīl ibn al-ᶜAbbās, and Abū Isḥāq Ibrāhīm ibn Hilāl. The poet puns that 'if the [administrative] *dīwān* were to be transformed into a *dīwān* of verse, and the court (*al-qurṭī*) into many-lobed earrings (*aqrāṭ*), then [Abū l-Qāsim] would be [both] the exalted subject of the eulogies of poets, and the most decorative of poetic jewels'. Two passages in verse similarly draw attention to Abū l-Qāsim's employment in the royal *dīwān*.[94] Ibn Jubayr reports that, as late as 1184–5, and after a temporary fall from favour, Abū l-Qāsim was still occasionally in royal service.[95] Thus, there can be no reasonable doubt that the *qāʾid* Abū l-Qāsim of the two royal documents is identical with Abū l-Qāsim ibn Ḥammūd.

Ibn Qalāqis's works allow us to trace the ancestry that he claimed for Abū l-Qāsim, and to reconstruct his immediate family tree (see Table 9.1). His father, the *qāʾid* Abū ᶜAbd Allāh Ḥammūd, may have been the Ibn Abī l-Qāsim who was patron to the poet Ibn Ẓafar, and to whom the latter dedicated his *Fürstenspiegel*, the *Sulwān al-muṭāᶜ fī ᶜudwān al-atbāᶜ* ('Consolation of the leader during the enmity of his followers'), in 554/1159–60.[96] Ibn Qalāqis described Abū l-Qāsim's brother, Abū ᶜAlī Ḥasan, as a scholar and a *faqīh*, and he composed a *qaṣīda* on the birth of his son, Abū l-Faḍl.[97] Abū l-Qāsim's own sons were named after the first

[92] Orig. PA, AdS, Cefalù, no.12: ed. Cusa 1868–82, no.108, pp.483–6: [ἡ πρόσταξις] τῶν ἀρχόντων τῆς κόρτης καὶ σεκρετικῶν κυροῦ Ἰωάννου καὶ κάϊτου Βουλκάσιμ.

[93] Bruel 1876–94, vol.V, pp.600–1: *Goffridus de Centurbio et Gaytus Bulcasseni, magistri duane nostre de secretis*.

[94] Ibn Qalāqis 1984a, p.5 (De Simone 1996, pp.40–1, and nn.15–18): *ḥattā lawi nqalaba l-dīwānu dīwāna shiᶜrin wa-l-qurṭī aqrāṭa shadhrin la-kāna huwa l-muqarraḍu l-muᶜallā wa-l-muqarraṭu l-muḥallā*. Compare the following passages : Ibn Qalāqis 1984a, p.15, line 8, and p.32, line 11 (De Simone 1996, p.57, line 29, and p.86, line 33. See also above, p.133 and note 64.

[95] Below, p.241.

[96] Ibn Qalāqis 1984a, p.45 (De Simone 1996, p.107). Michele Amari believed that the *Sulwān* was dedicated to our Abū l-Qāsim ibn Ḥammūd (*BAS*^{1}*(It.)*, vol.I, p.lxxiii; Amari 1933–9, vol.I, pp.100–1; vol.III, pp.175–6, 735–7). De Simone 1993, p.110 and n.8, has recently pointed out that the dedicatee was almost certainly his father. Ibn Ẓafar himself dedicated one of the editions of the *Sulwān* to *sāʾid al-sāda wa-qāʾid al-qāda* Abū ᶜAbd Allāh Muḥammad ibn Abī l-Qāsim ibn ᶜAlī ibn al-ᶜAlawī l-Qurashī (Ibn Ẓafar 1862, p.2; *BAS*^{2}, vol.II, p.836; *BAS*^{2}*(It.)*, vol.III, p.906). ᶜImād al-Dīn 1964–9, vol.I, p.422, reports that the work was written in Sicily in the year 554/1159–60 (*BAS*^{2}, vol.II, pp.729–30; *BAS*^{2}*(It.)*, vol.III, p.788). Later compilators concluded that it had been dedicated to a Sicilian *qāʾid*: *e.g.* Ibn Khallikān 1948, vol.4, p.29 (*BAS*^{2}, vol.II, p.761; *BAS*^{2}*(It.)*, vol.III, p.823).

[97] Ibn Qalāqis 1984a, pp.41–3, 45 (trans. De Simone 1996, pp.101–4, 107).

three Sunnī caliphs, a probable indication of his own Sunnism,[98] despite the resolutely Shīᶜī names borne by his ancestors and by his brother. This may be significant, because it seems to weaken the force of Ibn Qalāqis's claim that Abū l-Qāsim hailed from the Ḥammūdid family, by which he presumably intended the Ḥammūdid dynasty that ruled in Malaga and Algeciras (1010–57/58), and which claimed descent from the Shīᶜī Idrīsids of Morocco (see Table 9.1).[99] That Abū al-Qāsim's family, the Banū Ḥajjar, was descended from the Ḥammūdids of Malaga was accepted unquestioningly by Amari.[100] More recently, attention has been drawn to a report by the 14th-century Damascene author, al-Ṣafadī, that the geographer al-Idrīsī was the great-grandson of Idrīs II al-ᶜĀlī, the Ḥammūdid prince of Malaga (1043–6 and 1054–5). The latter's grandson, Muḥammad ibn ᶜAbd Allāh, is said to have fled to Sicily on the fall of his dynasty in 1057–8. There, after escaping assassination by Ibn al-Thumna, he was well-treated by Count Roger, just as his son, al-Idrīsī, was later to enjoy the patronage of King Roger and William I.[101] No source, however, is known to make an explicit link between al-Idrīsī and the Banū Ḥajjar.[102] Elsewhere, Ibn Qalāqis does not give much useful information concerning Abū l-Qāsim's more distant ancestry, beyond repeatedly emphasising that his patron belonged to al-Quraysh, the tribe of the Prophet, through Hāshim: despite a long genealogical excursus about al-Quraysh, Ibn Qalāqis makes no claims about the precise route through which his patron traced his descent, and one suspects that Abū l-Qāsim himself was unsure.[103] In 1175, he even told the Syrian pilgrim al-Harawī that his ancestor was ᶜUmar ibn ᶜAbd al-ᶜAzīz the Marwānid.[104]

Michele Amari, and others since, have sought to link Abū l-Qāsim ibn Ḥammud with Chamutus, the Arab defender of Enna against Roger I. According to Malaterra, Chamutus was defeated and converted to Christianity in 1087, and then resettled with his family on a 'sufficient' estate in Calabria.[105] Although the Latinised name

[98] Ibn Qalāqis 1984a, pp.12, 13, 15, 22 (De Simone 1996, pp.52, 54, 58, 68). Schimmel 1997, p.33.

[99] Ibn Qalāqis 1984a, p.3 (trans. De Simone 1996, p.37): *bi-l-usrati l-ḥammūdīyati l-mansabi.*

[100] Amari 1933–9, vol.III, p.175 and n.1.

[101] al-Ṣafadī 1931, vol.VIII, pp.324–6 (see also, vol.I, pp.163–4 and vol.XIV, pp.105–7; *BAS*², vol.III, p.797; *BAS²(It.)*, vol.III, p.859). Nothing in these reports justifies the surprising claim recently made by Amara and Nef 2001, pp.125–6, that al-Idrīsī was born in Sicily or in Calabria (!). Clearly, the hinterland of Mileto could not have been a centre for Muslim *ahl al-ᶜulūm al-falsafīya* in the mid-12th century (vol.XIV, p.105, l.18); and it follows that the *ᶜudwa* from which Roger summoned al-Idrīsī was patently not the *ᶜudwat al-Rūm*, but rather the Ifrīqiyan coast (vol.XIV, p.106, lines 1–2). Later in the same passage (vol.XIV, p.106, lines 10–12), al-Ṣafadī has King Roger persuade al-Idrīsī to remain in Sicily by stressing that, as a member of the *bayt al-khilāfa*, his life would be in danger were he to *return* to the Dār al-Islām.

[102] Could a dispute over the claims of the Banū Ḥajjar explain the crabby genealogical debate between Ibn Qalāqis and al-Sharīf al-Makīn, a figure who has been tentatively identified as al-Idrīsī (De Simone 1996, pp.17, 18, 21, 29)?

[103] Ibn Qalāqis 1984a, pp.3, 34, 41, 42, 49–52, 58 (trans. De Simone 1996, pp.38 – and n.3 – 90, 100, 102, 103, 113–18, 126.

[104] al-Harawī 1953, p.55 (trans. al-Harawī 1957, p.126 (*BAS*², vol.I, p.79; *BAS²(It.)*, vol.I, p.110–11).

[105] Malaterra, 1927–8, pp.87–8; Amari 1933–9, pp.175–9. See, most recently, Amara and Nef 2001, p.124.

Table 9.1 The descent claimed by Ibn Qalāqis for Abū l-Qāsim ibn Ḥammūd

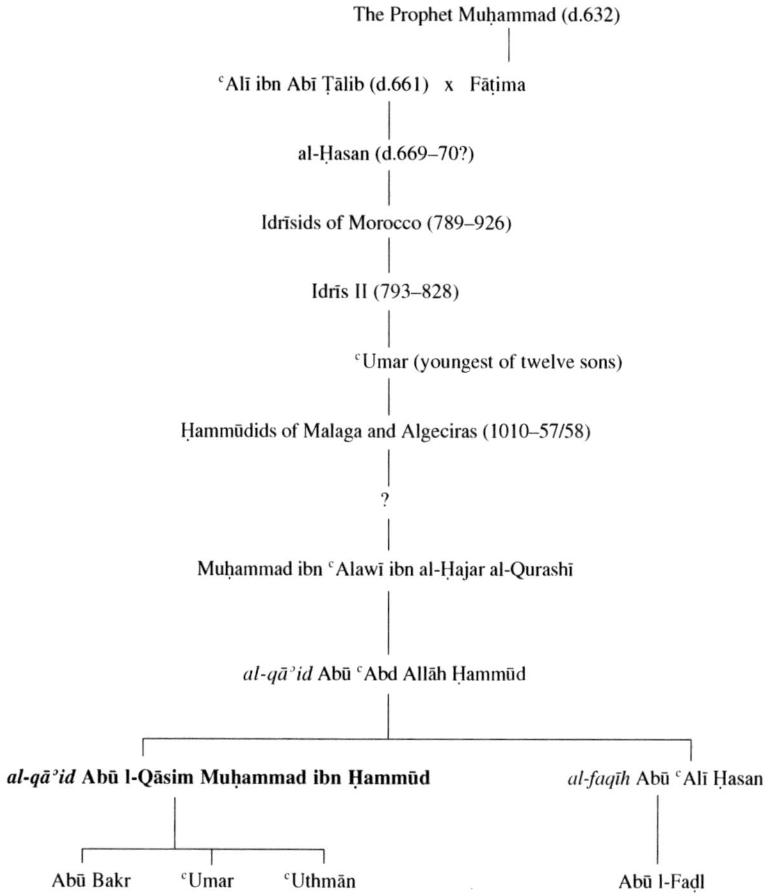
The Prophet Muḥammad (d.632)
ᶜAlī ibn Abī Ṭālib (d.661) x Fāṭima
al-Ḥasan (d.669–70?)
Idrīsids of Morocco (789–926)
Idrīs II (793–828)
ᶜUmar (youngest of twelve sons)
Ḥammūdids of Malaga and Algeciras (1010–57/58)
?
Muḥammad ibn ᶜAlawī ibn al-Ḥajar al-Qurashī
al-qāʾid Abū ᶜAbd Allāh Ḥammūd
***al-qāʾid* Abū l-Qāsim Muḥammad ibn Ḥammūd**
al-faqīh Abū ᶜAlī Ḥasan
Abū Bakr
ᶜUmar
ᶜUthmān
Abū l-Faḍl

Chamutus does almost certainly correspond to Arabic Ḥammūd, the temptation to refer to Chamutus as Ibn Ḥammūd should be firmly resisted. He is not mentioned by any Arab source, and his patronymic is unknown. Ḥammūd, moreover, is an extremely common *ism* – as are all names derived from the root *ḥmd*, whence come both Muḥammad and Aḥmad, for which Ḥammūd can be the hypocoristic form.[106] The *ism* Ḥammūd no more denotes descent from the Ḥammūdids of Malaga, than does the name ᶜAlī signify descent from ᶜAlī ibn Abī Ṭālib, and there is no reason whatsoever to conclude that Chamutus was the ancestor of our Abū l-Qāsim; still less that he was connected with Ḥammūdid dynasty.

There have been repeated attempts to link Malaterra's Chamutus with Abū l-Qāsim ibn Ḥammūd by means of two 12th-century intermediaries: Roger-Aḥmad

[106] Schimmel 1997, pp.31, 69.

and Roger Hamutus. In February 1141, at the royal court in Palermo, Roger, 'called Aḥmad, by the religion of the Hagarenes', granted Archbishop Roger Fesca of Palermo the three contiguous estates of Borginēsem, Rachaliōb, and Rasgaden, in the district of Naro and Licata. The lands had originally been granted him by his 'spiritual father', King Roger, who confirmed his gift to the church.[107] Roger's Arabic name was transliterated into Greek as Ἄχμετ (*Achmet*), which corresponds to Arabic Aḥmad not Ḥammūd, which is generally rendered Χαμμούτ (*Chammout*) in Greek. There is not the slightest reason, therefore, to link Roger-Aḥmad with Abū l-Qāsim.

Roger Hamutus first appears in March 1179 when Pope Alexander III confirmed the Sicilian holdings of the abbey of Our Lady of Mount Sion at Jerusalem. They included: 'In the fief of Geracello, the church of St Basil with the lands situated next to it and the waters above it, which Rogerius Chamuch gave to the aforesaid church'.[108] The same figure reappears in September 1216, when Frederick II confirmed Archbishop Berardus of Palermo in possession of the three estates of Perisium, Padhormum, and Giracellum, 'with all the land which Rogerius Hamutus held, both in the district of Castrogiovanni and elsewhere', which had been returned to the church by his widow.[109] Apparently, the lands that Roger had granted to Mount Sion in 1178 had not actually belonged to him; one raises an eyebrow to find that he was also a royal judge. In May 1189, Roggerius Hamutus, *regius Iusticiarius*, held yet another inquest to establish the boundary between Gàrcia and Ottumarrano, and in January 1193 he was on similar business near Castronuovo.[110] It seems probable, but is nowhere stated explicitly, that Roger Hamutus was a convert from Islam whose Arabic name was Ḥammūd. He is not identical with Roger-Aḥmad, as White suggests,[111] because the two men had different Arabic names, and, although each held three estates, Aḥmad's were near the south coast, while Ḥammūd's lay in the centre of the island. Apart from his name, which is extraordinarily common, and the fact that he was in royal service, there is nothing

[107] Orig. PA, Arch. Dioc., no.10: ed. Cusa 1868–82, no.59, pp.16–19: ἐγὼ Ῥογέριος ὁ ἐν τῇ τῶν Ἁγαρινῶν φρησκία ποτὲ καλοῦμενος Ἄχμετ. 'Spiritual-father': τοῦ ἐμοῦ πνευματικοῦ πατρὸς. The document once bore Roger-Aḥmad's own seal, which is now missing but is recorded in a MS of the 18th-century Palermitan scholar, Franceso Tardia (PA, Bibl. Com. MS Qq. F. 69 f. 117 v.): on the obverse, an image of the Virgin and Child and ΜΠ ΘΥ; on the reverse, ΡΟΓΕΡΙΟC and an Arabic inscription that Mortillaro translated *Dominus Christus servator eius* and read السيد المسيح الابقية which is improbable: perhaps the last word may be reconstructed الابقى reading *al-sayyid al-masīḥ al-abqā*, 'the Eternal…' or 'the Most Merciful Lord Messiah' (Mortillaro 1843, vol.I, p.173, n.1). The donation of 1141 was renewed in January 1144: Cusa 1868–82, no.74, pp.24–6. The three estates – Βουργινήσεμ and Βουργινίσσεμα (Ar. *Burj al-Nisām*, 'Tower of the Breezes'), mod. *Contrada Borginissimo* (Caracausi 1993, vol.I, p.180), Ῥαχαλιὼβ (Ar. *Raḥl Ayyūb*), and Ῥασγαδὲν (Ar. *Raʾs Ghaḍan*, 'wrinkled head'?) – lay between Naro and Licata, some 30km south-east of Agrigento.

[108] Jaffé and Loewenfeld 1885–8, vol.II, p.341, no.13333; Pirri 1733, vol.II, pp.753–4; see also White 1938, p.233.

[109] Huillard-Bréholles 1852–61, vol.I.2, pp.490–1. Of the three estates, Geracello lies 12km south of Enna (Caracausi 1993, vol.I, p.698).

[110] 1189: Orig. PA, AdS, Cefalù, no.27; ed. Garufi 1898, no.3, pp.153–4 (misreads *rogerius hamictus*). 1193: PA, AdS, Cefalù, no.47; ed. Garufi 1899, no.105, pp.253–5 (*Rogerius hamictus Regius Iusticiarius*).

[111] White 1938, p.233.

to connect Roger Hamutus with Abū l-Qāsim; as we shall see, the latter was based, not near Enna, but in Palermo and Trapani.[112]

After that unhelpful digression, we can return to Abū l-Qāsim himself. It is probable that he first appears in the cartulary of the Genoese notary Giovanni Scriba. On 18 September 1162, Simon, Bombarchet (Abū Bakr?), and Iusuph (Yūsuf), three agents of Caitus Bulcassemus received on loan from Solomon the Genoese, who described as the *fidelis* of William of Sicily, £55 Genoese, on the security of twelve bundles (*fardellis*) belonging to Caitus Bulcassemus, to be repaid to Solomon's agent in Sicily, on presentation of the Arabic original of the contract (*cartulam sarracenicam*). Another act, of the same date, implies that Solomon's agent also held a further ten bundles belonging to Caitus Bulcassemus.[113] Abū l-Qāsim was, indeed, a common name but the fact that Bulcassemus seems to have been based in Sicily, that he used the honorific *al-qā'id*, and that he was a man of substantial means, combine to make it likely that he is identical with Abū l-Qāsim ibn Ḥammūd.

During the summer or autumn of 1167, when the *qā'id* Richard launched his campaign against Stephen du Perche, he recruited the support of Abū l-Qāsim. In the words of 'Hugo Falcandus':

> The most noble and powerful of the Sicilian Muslims, Bulcassis, also stoked up a great deal of opposition against [Stephen] amongst the Muslims, although they liked him a great deal at first. For he was angry that the chancellor gave audience in too friendly a way to *qā'id* Sedictus, the richest of the Muslims, with whom he had a private feud, and seemed to make a great deal of his advice; consequently [Bulcassis] thought that he himself had fallen out of favour, although he had presented [Stephen] with many gifts, and that he would not be able to win his support again.[114]

The *qā'id* Sedictus had a house on one of the three main streets of the city centre, between the royal palace and George of Antioch's church.[115] He is perhaps to be identified with *al-shaykh* al-Sadīd Abū l-Makārim Hibat Allāh ibn al-Ḥuṣrī to whom Ibn Qalāqis addressed three *qaṣīda*s and a letter. Although al-Sadīd does not seem to have been a royal servant, he was clearly a courtier for Ibn Qalāqis claims that he guided the king.[116] Adalgisa De Simone has suggested that it may have been his acquaintance with al-Sadīd that caused the apparent rift between Ibn Qalāqis and his patron, Abū l-Qāsim.[117] The poet seems to have enjoyed a more relaxed relationship with al-Sadīd than with Abū l-Qāsim, and may even have known him before coming to Sicily, and have sought his patronage as early as 1161.[118]

[112] The possibility of a connection between Malaterra's Chamutus and Roger-Hamutus, however, seems strong, given that Castrogiovanni was the centre of both.
[113] Giovanni Scriba 1935, vol.II, p.80, docs 970 and 972; trans. and commentary in Abulafia 1977, 247–50. See also Johns 1999, p.56.
[114] 'Hugo Falcandus' 1897, p.119 (trans. 'Hugo Falcandus' 1998, p.170).
[115] 'Hugo Falcandus' 1897, p.182 (trans. 'Hugo Falcandus' 1998, p.260).
[116] Ibn Qalāqis 1988, no.266, pp.383–5: *fa-rabbu l-tāji taḥta qaḍā'i-hi bi-l-ʿadli.*
[117] De Simone 1996, p.19.
[118] Ibn Qalāqis 1988, no.266, pp.383–5 (rubric dates to 555/1160, from Alexandria), no.35, pp.143–5 (rubric dates to 563/1167–8, *i.e.* in Sicily), no.298, pp.420–1, and no.385, pp.498–500 (ʿĪd al-Fiṭr). Ibn Qalāqis 1984b, p.77 (trans. De Simone 1991, p.341).

In his *roman à lettres*, Ibn Qalāqis sends Abū l-Qāsim a *qaṣīda* from Alexandria in 561/1165–6, asking him to finance his pilgrimage to Mecca.[119] He does not seem to perform the *ḥajj*, but encounters unspecified difficulties in Egypt, and thus accepts Abū l-Qāsim's invitation to travel to Sicily, arriving at Messina on 11 May 1168.[120] Thence he travels to Palermo, arriving at the start of Ramaḍān 563 (9 June 1168). It may have been now that Ibn Qalāqis wrote an intimate and humorous letter to al-Sadīd al-Ḥuṣrī, wishing him well for the month of fasting.[121] He spends July enthusiastically recovering from the rigours of Ramaḍān in the gardens of the Conca d'Oro, and visiting the royal palaces.[122] Then, abruptly, he prepares to depart, and receives his viaticum as described above. Ibn Qalāqis here inserts into the narrative an exchange of letters with his friend and fellow poet, al-Umawī, that contains obscure hints that some rift with Abū l-Qāsim has prompted his sudden departure.[123] Via Termini, Cefalù, Caronia, Patti, Oliveri, Milazzo and Messina, he proceeds to Syracuse, whence he writes to Abū l-Qāsim on behalf of the Muslim citizens, asking that they be relieved from the *jizya*. This mends the rift, and the poet returns to his patron, cross-country, via Lentini, Caltavuturo and Termini. Back in Palermo, he composes a *qaṣīda* in celebration of the birth of a son to Abū l-Qāsim's brother, Abū ᶜAlī Ḥasan, on 2 January 1169.[124] The poet's farewell *qaṣīda* to Abū l-Qāsim is dated Rajab 564 (April 1169).[125]

Ibn Qalāqis does not contribute greatly to our knowledge of the events of Abū l-Qāsim's life, but he evokes vividly the atmosphere of the easy-going, intellectual circle surrounding his patron. This included poets and scholars, such as himself, al-Umawī,[126] *al-faqīh* Abū ᶜAlī Ḥasan ibn Ḥammūd,[127] perhaps the *qāḍī* Abū ᶜAbd Allāh Muḥammad ibn Rajāʾ, a member of the family to which Abū l-Ḍawʾ belonged,[128] and an obscure figure known as al-Sharīf al-Makīn with whom he and al-Umawī quarrel.[129] Also within the circle were officers of the royal *dīwān* and palace, such as Abū l-Qāsim himself, the *qāʾid* Richard,[130] Abū l-Sayyid,[131] the *ḥākim* Abū ᶜAmr ᶜUthmān ibn al-Muhadhdhib al-Judhāmī,[132] and the *qāʾid* Ghārāt ibn Jawshan, who seems to have been a military leader, and who is described as a

[119] Ibn Qalāqis 1984a, pp.8–10 (trans. De Simone 1996, pp.46–9).
[120] Ibn Qalāqis 1984a, p.7 (trans. De Simone 1996, p.45).
[121] Ibn Qalāqis 1984b, p.77 (trans. De Simone 1991, p.341).
[122] Ibn Qalāqis 1984a, pp.16–21 (trans. De Simone 1996, pp.58–66).
[123] Ibn Qalāqis 1984a, pp.24–9 (trans. De Simone 1996, pp.72–80). For Abū l-Ḥasan ᶜAlī ibn Abī l-Fatḥ ibn Khalaf al-Ṣiqillī al-Umawī, see De Simone 1996, pp.16, 22, 26–7, 72–3, 91, 104–9, 122.
[124] Ibn Qalāqis 1984a, pp.41–3 (trans. De Simone 1996, pp.101–4).
[125] Ibn Qalāqis 1984a, pp.41–3 (trans. De Simone 1996, pp.101–4).The poet may have completed the *ḥajj* in that year, for he next appears in the Yemen. He died at ᶜAydhab in 1172: see Rizzitano 1960.
[126] De Simone 1996, pp.8, 16, 72, 73, 79, 104; ᶜImād al-Dīn 1951, vol.I, pp.166.
[127] Ibn Qalāqis 1984a, pp.41–5; De Simone 1996, pp.30, 101–7.
[128] Ibn Qalāqis 1988, no.285, pp.411–13, is an elegy on his death in 562 A.H. (28 October 1166 – 16 October 1167).
[129] Ibn Qalāqis 1984a, pp.46–9; De Simone 1996, pp.10, 17–19, 28, 31, 108–12. De Simone (*ibid.*, pp.17–19) suggests that he may be the famous geographer al-Idrīsī.
[130] Ibn Qalāqis 1984a, pp.22–4; De Simone 1996, pp.22–4, 71.
[131] Ibn Qalāqis 1984a, pp.22–3, 31; De Simone 1996, pp.22, 24, 31, 70, 85.
[132] Ibn Qalāqis 1984a, p.38; De Simone 1996, pp.27, 31, 97.

'familiar' of King William.[133] What is particularly striking is the contrast between these light-hearted days of picnics and poetry, and the dark terrors that were to oppress Abū l-Qāsim sixteen years later.

The storm clouds had, perhaps, already begun to gather by 1175, when the Syrian pilgrim and ascetic, al-Harawī, was in Sicily visiting Muslim shrines. He fell sick, and sought a cure in the mosque of ᶜAyn al-Shifāʾ in Palermo. There, he was assisted by Abū l-Qāsim, who set him on the way for the East, after giving him 'letters for the sultan [Ṣalāḥ al-Dīn] urging him to capture this island'.[134] Ten years later, Abū l-Qāsim was to be accused of making similar overtures to the Almohads.

By the time that Ibn Jubayr met Abū l-Qāsim in Trapani, in the spring of 1185, he had lost his first enthusiasm for the Norman king, and had begun to appreciate the full weight of the burden borne by the Muslims of Sicily. He illustrates their plight with two contrasting examples: the *faqīh* Ibn Zurᶜa who had bowed to pressure from William's agents and converted to Christianity,[135] and the resolute paragon of Muslim virtue, Abū l-Qāsim.

> At this time, the leader and lord of the inhabitants of this island who are Muslims arrived in this town: the *qāʾid* Abū l-Qāsim ibn Ḥammūd, known as Ibn al-Ḥajar. This man belongs to a noble family of the island who have passed down the leadership from father to son through the generations. It was also told us that he is a man of virtuous conduct, who strives for good, who loves his people, and who is full of acts anticipating the life hereafter, including ransoming captives, distributing alms to strangers and stranded pilgrims, and many other excellent deeds, and glorious, noble feats.
>
> This city was convulsed by his arrival. At the time, he was out of favour with the tyrant, who had put him under house-arrest on charges brought against him by his enemies, which included false stories accusing him of communicating with the Almohads (may God support them!). Had it not been for his timely Protector, he would have been finished. He suffered a series of fines, compelling him to pay more than thirty-thousand *muʾminī* dinars, and he continued to part with houses and properties inherited from his ancestors, until he was left with nothing. Recently, it had come about that the tyrant favoured him, and entrusted him with the execution of an important matter concerning the affairs of his government, which he carried out with the resignation of a vanquished, impoverished slave.
>
> On his arrival in this town, he expressed a wish to receive us, and so we met him. He revealed to us some of his own secret business, and of the hidden circumstances of [the Muslims of] this island, in relation to their enemies, such as would make one's eyes weep blood, and one's heart break with suffering. For example, he said: 'I have wished myself and my family sold [into slavery], on the chance that the sale might deliver us from the state we are in, and lead to us reaching Muslim lands'. Consider the circumstances that would bring such a man, despite his eminent rank and his great dignity, to

133 Ibn Qalāqis 1988, no.465, p.596 (*ᶜaskarīy*); Ibn Qalāqis 1984b, p.53 (*ilā l-qāʾidi ghārāti bni jawshani khāṣṣati l-mamlakati al-ghulyalimīyati*); trans. De Simone 1991, p.340.

134 *Wa-kuntu akhadhtu kitāban ilā l-sulṭāni yaḥuththu-hu ᶜalā akhdhi hādhihi l-jazīrati*: al-Harawī 1953, p.55 (trans. al-Harawī 1957, p.126; *BAS*², vol.I, p.79; *BAS*²*(It.)*, vol.I, p.111).

135 Ibn Jubayr 1907, p.340 (Ibn Jubayr 1949–65, vol.III, pp.399–400; Ibn Jubayr 1952, pp.357–8; *BAS*², vol.I, p.101; *BAS*²*(It.)*, vol.I, p.141). Ibn Jubayr is prepared to allow that Ibn Zurᶜa may have practised *taqīya*, and concealed his true faith under compulsion. See below, pp.295–6.

express such a desire, and despite his heavy obligations to dependants, sons, and daughters. We prayed on his behalf, and on behalf of the rest of the Muslims amongst the inhabitants of this island, that Great and Mighty God might grant them happy escape from the state in which they are. It is the duty of every Muslim, to pray for them, wherever they stand before Great and Mighty God.

We left him weeping and arousing [our own] tears, but our spirits were enriched by the nobility of his manner, by his exceptional good qualities, by his calm forbearance, by the breadth of his charity and generosity, and by the goodness of his character and his nature. In Palermo, we had seen houses belonging to him, to his brothers, and to the members of his family, which were elegant, tall palaces. Their standing, in sum, is great, especially this man's. During his time here, he has done good deeds for pilgrims who are poor and destitute, putting their affairs in order, and helping them with their fares and provisions. May God help him for this, and repay him for it with the most just reward! ...

... This aforesaid Ḥammūdid has such a great reputation amongst the Christian people – may God destroy them! – that they say that, were he to convert to Christianity, there would not remain a single Muslim on the island, who would not do as he did, imitating him as his follower.[136]

Just four years later, on the death of William II, came the first of the series of Muslim revolts that eventually drove Frederick II to destroy the Muslim community of the island. Abū l-Qāsim and his family cannot be followed closely through these difficult years, but they seem to have chosen to collaborate, rather than to flee or to rebel. In 1200, Frederick II granted the Genoese a house in Trapani that had once belonged to Gaitus Abulcasim.[137] There is no indication here whether its owner was dead, disgraced, or had taken to the *macchia*, but his descendants reappear, with Christian names, until the late 13th century. A contract of 1289 refers to an earlier deed, now apparently lost, which recorded the purchase of land at Chinea by Enrico Abbate from 'the late John, son of the late *qāʾid* Philip of Ibn Ḥammūd'.[138] The *qāʾid* Philip is probably to be identified with Philip the notary, who was *qāʾid* of Palermo in 1240, in which case he was in Frederick's service, and was presumably still leader of at least those Muslims who remained in the capital.[139]

136 Ibn Jubayr 1907, pp.341–2 (*BAS*², vol.I, pp.101–2, 103; *BAS*²*(It.)*, vol.I, pp.141–3, 144; Ibn Jubayr 1949–65, vol.III, pp.400–1, 402; Ibn Jubayr 1952, pp.358–9, 360).

137 Huillard-Bréholles 1852–61, vol.I.1, pp.64–7.

138 Deed of sale made by *domino Henrico Abbati per quondam Iohannem filium quondam gayti Philippi de Ibn Hammud civem Panormi*: Sciascia 1989, p.1179 and doc.5, p.1218. Chinea lies 10km west of Calatafimi. Enrico Abbate, the founder of his family's fortunes, appears as a leading functionary of Frederick II in 1239–40. In February 1240, he was the leader of the embassy sent by Frederick to Abū Zakariyāʾ Yaḥyā I, the first Ḥafṣid sultan of Tunis. He was accompanied by Obert Fallamonaca (below, pp.245–6), and carried a letter written in Arabic by Master Theodore (for whom see Burnett 1995). Enrico was *secretus* of Sicily from *c*.1253–6. His son, Giliberto, was governor of Malta under Frederick II. Giliberto was dead by 1269, but his son, Palmerio, after having been governor of Pantelleria and Favignana, played an ambiguous role in the Vespers. See Sciascia 1989; Luttrell 1997.

139 Carcani 1992, p.250, col.a; p.280, col.a; p.369, col.a – 370, col.b; p.397, col.a (Huillard-Bréholles 1852–61, vol.V.1, pp.443–6, 548; vol.V.2, pp.819–22, 902). He is unlikely to be the same Philip the notary who wrote Latin documents for Constance and the young Frederick II: Huillard-Bréholles 1852–61, vol.I.1, pp.241–2, 253–5.

A miscellany of servants

In addition to those for whom detailed biographies can be written, many other Arab servants from the royal palace and *dīwān* are known only by one or two references. In 1174–6, the *qā'id* Mataracius, 'royal chamberlain and steward', was director of the *duana baronum*.[140] His Arabic name was presumably al-Muṭarriz, literally 'the embroider', which suggests that he was a worker in the royal *ṭirāz*, and links him to Ibn Jubayr's 'Yaḥyā ibn Fityān al-Ṭarrāz who embroiders in gold in the king's *ṭirāz*'.[141] In July 1191, Tancred ordered his *fidelis* Abdeserdus, presumably ᶜAbd al-Sayyid, 'palace chamberlain and master of the *duana baronum*', to grant the tithes of Oria in Apulia to Archbishop Peter of Brindisi.[142] In January–March 1187, the eunuch *qā'id* John, a royal chamberlain, rented from Sant'Andrea *de Bebbene*, two pieces of land in Palermo to make into a stable and hay-shed: he did so with the consent of 'his lord', the *qā'id* Richard, and in the presence of the eunuch ᶜAmmār.[143]

Other Arab servants who appear only once or twice include: the scribe ᶜUthmān who, under Barrūn's direction, wrote the copy to San Nicolò di Chùrchuro in 1149;[144] the anonymous eunuchs burnt with Philip of al-Mahdīya;[145] Ḥamza ibn Ḥamza, 'the controller of the *dīwānī* office of inquiry' in February 1161;[146] Maio of Bari's eunuch, Andrew;[147] Martin's unnamed brother, who was killed in November 1161;[148] the *qā'id* Jawhar, master chamberlain of the palace, whom William I had drowned for attempting to defect to the rebels in 1162;[149] the handful of eunuchs who fled with the *qā'id* Peter;[150] the Arab servants met by Ibn Qalāqis in 1168–9 – Abū l-Sayyid, the *ḥākim* al-Judhāmī, and the *qā'id* Ghārāt ibn Jawshān;[151] the Christians Abū l-Ṭayyib and Makhlūf, captains of the palace archers, and the Muslims *al-shaykh al-qā'id* Ḥamza, and the brothers Yaᶜqūb and Yūsuf, the sons of Yaᶜqūb, who all joined in a *dīwānī* staff-outing to Misilmeri in October 1172;[152] the secretary Nicholas, who is described as the 'son' of the *qā'id*

[140] 1174: Haskins 1911, p.653, n.186; Jamison 1957, Appendix 2, Cal.2, p.333; Takayama 1985, p.141, n.53: the proceeds of the sale of property in Salerno, authorised by *dominus Eugenius magister duane baronum*, are paid to Bartholomew, *regius ostiarius*, to reduce the debt of ten thousand *tarì* which Landulf Caputus, strategos of Salerno, had borrowed *a doana baronum cui preest Gaytus Materacius regius camerarius et senescalcus*. 1176: Garufi 1902, no.11, p.9, and Appendix no.2, pp.163–5: Count William of Marsico sells all his houses in Palermo *duane baronum in manibus uidelicet Gayti Mataracij Regij sacri palatii camerarij et magistri eiusdem duane*.

[141] Above, p.213.

[142] Zielinski 1982, no.17, pp.40–1: *Tancredus ... Abdeserdo palatino camerario et magistro duane baronum, fideli suo*.

[143] **Private 23**: a bilingual Latin-Arabic contract: the Latin is dated March 1187, Ind.V; the Arabic, mid January, 1184 (*sic!*), Ind.V.

[144] ***Dīwānī* 29**. [145] Above, p.216. [146] ***Dīwānī* 35**.

[147] 'Hugo Falcandus' 1897, p.45 (trans. 'Hugo Falcandus' 1998, p.99).

[148] 'Hugo Falcandus' 1897, p.79 (trans. 'Hugo Falcandus' 1998, p.129).

[149] 'Hugo Falcandus' 1897, pp.77, 83 ('Hugo Falcandus' 1998, p.128, 133).

[150] Above, p.226. [151] Above, p.240, respectively, notes 131, 132, and 133.

[152] ***Dīwānī* 38**.

Peter in July 1176;[153] Yūsuf, the Arab scribe of the Monreale *jarīdat al-ḥudūd* of 1182;[154] the *qāʾid* Thomas who was chamberlain of the *duana de secretis* shortly before 1183;[155] Yaḥya ibn Fityān, ʿAbd al-Masīḥ, and the other unnamed eunuchs met by Ibn Jubayr in Messina and Palermo during the winter of 1184–5;[156] the eunuch emir who commanded the Sicilian troops at the capture of Thessalonica on 24 August 1185, and who prevented the desecration of the shrine of St Demetrios;[157] and Niqūla Ashqar, the servant of the royal palace who helped to ransom the captive Zaynab in 1190.[158] Clearly, these are crowded on the tip of an iceberg. 'Hugo Falcandus' reports that the palace servants, upon whose loyalty Matthew of Salerno could count in the final struggle against Stephen du Perche, numbered about forty,[159] but we can rarely locate more than half a dozen at any one moment. The lives of many tens, perhaps even hundreds, of other Arab servants remain hidden beneath the surface:[160] the serving-girls and concubines; the black Muslim slaves; the kitchen staff; the archers, guards, and military band; the artisans in the royal *ṭirāz*, in the mint, and in the other royal workshops; the craftsmen employed in building and decorating the royal palaces; the falconers, and the keepers of the royal menagerie.

The late King Tancred's menagerie was eaten by the famished troops of Henry VI during the siege of Palermo in 1194, but Fate was kinder to the royal eunuchs and, as we shall see below, Peter of Eboli has a Palermitan Ping, Pang and Pong greet the victorious emperor on his entry into the palace. The detailed consideration of the Arab servants after 1194 lies beyond the scope of this study, but a few words must be said about Frederick's Palermitan servants, who rightly deserve a separate study. Nothing is known of the antecedents of Richard, Frederick's palace chamberlain from 1215 until at least September 1234, but he was born in Sicily and may well have been an Arab.[161] There is no doubt about his successor, John the Moor, 'a black slave of the Emperor's household', whom Conrad appointed first *magister camerarius* and then *arcadio*, or *al-qāʾid*, of the Saracens of Lucera.[162]

153 † Νικολάος ὁ σεκρετικός ὁ καῖτου Πετρου υἱός (*Nikolaos o sekretikos o kaitou Petrou uios*): Garufi 1902, pp.163–5. Above, p.228. 154 Above, p.187.

155 Mattei-Cerasoli 1939, no.12, pp.292–4 (not to be confused with Master Thomas Brown!).

156 Above, pp.212–14. 157 Eustathios of Tessaloniki 1988, pp.116–17. 158 **Private 26.**

159 'Hugo Falcandus' 1897, p.156 (trans. 'Hugo Falcandus' 1998, p.209).

160 See Bresc and Nef 1998, pp.152–5.

161 Huillard-Bréholles 1852–61, vol.I.1, pp.342; vol.I.2, pp.373, 374, 426, 430, 447, 448, 492, 498, 525, 530, 533, 572, 577, 590, 600, 605, 614, 618, 642, 668, 670, 717, 775, 782, 920; vol.II.1, pp.48, 66, 146, 209, 369, 372, 420, 493, 536, 552, 569; vol.II.2, pp.624, 659, 682, 940; vol.III, pp.285, 297; vol.IV.1, pp.272, 279, 288, 290, 296, 297, 308, 312, 314, 318, 323, 328, 334, 339, 341, 359, 360, 363, 375, 407, 414, 487; vol.IV.2, p.942; Carcani 1992, 337, cols a–b; p.340, col.b; p.363, col.b – p.364, col.a; (Huillard-Bréholles 1852–61, vol.V.2, pp.720, 730, 804).

162 Carcani 1992, p.261, col.b – p.262, col.a; p.263, col.a; p.299, col.b; p.300, col.a; p.311, col.a; p.350, cols a–b; p.363, col.a; p.387, col.b – p.388, col.a; p.389, col.a; p.391, col.a; p.393, col.b; p.398, col.a and col.b; p.407, col.a. Huillard-Bréholles 1852–61, Introduction, pp.CXLVII–CXLVIII; vol.V.1, pp.486, 492, 601–2, 602–3, 638; vol.V.2, pp.764, 800–1, 872, 877, 882–883, 891, 905, 907, 938; Nicolaos de Jamsilla 1726, cols 521D, 522B–C (*quidam servus niger de domo Imperatoris, qui pro eo quod a puerita sua visus fuit homo industriosus, et in omni obsequio sedulus, in Aula Imperatoris crevit, et in oculis suis satis acceptus fuit, adeo quod ipse Imperator, qui non tam conditionem originis in omnibus, quam virtutes moresque considerabat, cum illa sibi clarior videretur esse Nobilitas, quae ex moribus, quam illa, quae ex sanguine procedebat: praedictum Joannem, licet aspectu deformem et*

John of Palermo, a Latin scribe in the emperor's service from 1221, and a member of the embassy to Tunis in 1240, may also have been an Arab.[163] But Frederick does not seem to have had an office dedicated to the writing of Arabic, and he relied instead upon individuals to compose documents in Arabic as the need arose. On Christmas Eve 1239, for example, Frederick wrote from Pisa to John the Moor, 'We wish that *Abdolla* (ᶜAbd Allāh), a slave of the Chamber, who has been sent to learn to read and write Arabic, should be given his expenses, at the request of Master Joachim, from when he comes to him, for as long as he remains with him'.[164]

Nonetheless, from October 1239 until at least August 1245, one of Frederick's leading officials, the *secretus* first of Western Sicily and then of the whole island,[165] was an Arab, and it was he who issued the only Arabic document to survive from the imperial administration – the bilingual Latin-Arabic writ of January 1242, in which he appears in Arabic as 'lord Ubart Fallamūnaqa, lord of the royal *dīwān*s and of the revenues of all Sicily'.[166]

Obert first appears in October 1239. He had for some time been master portulan of Sicily west of the River Salso, and had recently been appointed the *secretus* of Palermo.[167] For the next seven months, his duties were a dotty mixture of the public and the domestic. At the same time that he received orders to establish new ports,[168] to allocate land to new settlers,[169] and to increase revenue from taxation,[170] he was also instructed to procure falcons,[171] to repair the palace colombarium and restock it with doves,[172] and to acquire five black slaves, aged between sixteen and twenty years, to have four of them taught to play the *tuba*, and one the *tubecta*.[173] In

ex Ancilla natum, Camerae suae Custodem et Secretorum Aulae participem et … suorum Praepositum fecerat), 527C–528A, 542A–E (Nicolas de Jamsilla 1868, pp.133, 134, 140, 155–6). See also: Amari 1933–9, vol.III, p.731; Egidi 1911, p.613; Collura 1951, p.15.

163 Carcani 1992, p.339, col.b – p.340, col.a; p.345, col.a; p.404, col.a. Huillard-Bréholles 1852–61, vol.II.1, p.185, vol.V.2, pp.726–7, 745, 928. See also: Amari 1933–9, vol.III, pp.711–12; Collura 1951, pp.15, 23–4.

164 Carcani 1992, p.300, col.a: *De mandato domini Iohannos Mauri scripsit Iohannes de Idronto. Alexandro filio Henrici. ut Abdolla servo Camere qui mictitur ad discendum legere & scribere licteras saracenicas det expensas ad requisitionem Magristri Iohachim. ex quo pervenerit ad eum. & cum eo morabitur*. Huillard-Bréholles 1852–61, Introduction, p.DXL, and vol.V.1, p.603. Unfortunately, we hear no more of ᶜAbd Allāh, nor of Master Joachim, who was presumably a Jew living in Palermo.

165 Kamp 1974, pp.88, 91. Kamp suggests that the family name of the *secretus Mateus Marclafaba de Salerno* indicates that he, too, was an Arab (pp.59–61, see also pp.77, 78, 85, 89), but the name – *Marchiafava* – is not obviously Arabic: see Caracausi 1993, vol.II, p.957.

166 ***Dīwānī* 46**.

167 Carcani 1992, p.416, col.a – 418, col.a; p.245, col.b – p.246, col.b; p.246, col.b – p.247, col.a; p.249, col.a – p.250, col.a = 13 October 1239: mandate to *Oberto Fallamonacho magistro portulano Sicilie ultra flumen Salsum et nunc secreto Panormi* (Huillard-Bréholles 1852–61, vol.V.1, pp.418–24, 435–7, 437–9, 443–6). Winkelmann 1880–5, vol.I, no.843, pp.650–1.

168 Carcani 1992, p.416, col.a – 418, col.a (Huillard-Bréholles 1852–61, vol.V.1, pp.418–24).

169 Carcani 1992, p.318, col.b (Huillard-Bréholles 1852–61, vol.V.2, pp.668–9).

170 Carcani 1992, p.298, col.b. – p.299, col.a (Huillard-Bréholles 1852–61, vol.V.1, pp.599–600).

171 Carcani 1992, p.381, col.b (Huillard-Bréholles 1852–61, vol.V.2, pp.857–8).

172 Carcani 1992, p.321, col.a (Huillard-Bréholles 1852–61, vol.V.2, pp.676–7).

173 Carcani 1992, p.279, col.b – p.280, col.a; p.321, col.a (Huillard-Bréholles 1852–61, vol.V.1, pp.535–6; vol.V.2, pp.676–7).

February 1240, Obert assisted in the preparations for Enrico Abbate's embassy to the Ḥafṣid sultan of Tunis, in which he took part.[174] And, on 3 May, he was rewarded for his 'prudence and loyalty' when Frederick appointed him *doanerius de secretis et questorum magister* for the whole island,[175] an office that he held until at least August 1245.[176] In September 1244, on his return from an embassy to the Almohad emir in Andalus, Obert regranted four workshops belonging to the imperial demesne to prior Thomas of Santa Maria di Ustica – although the *dīwānī* record was made 'only in Latin' (*hoc presens scriptum doane in latino tantum*), Obert signed with his Arabic *ᶜalāma* (*signo nostro Saracenico*).[177]

Henri Bresc has made the intriguing suggestion that Obert was a convert from Islam to Christianity, 'who took the Genoese name of Obberto Fallamonaca'.[178] He may be right, for the name Fallamonica is indeed attested in Genoa – but not before the 15th century. However, from Obert's Arabic signature to a Greek document of April 1238,[179] we learn that his father was *al-qāʾid* ᶜAbd al-Raḥmān, the son of *Fālaymūn*.[180] The names Fālaymūn and Fallamūnaqa are obviously connected, but the link may be merely assonantal.[181] The name of Obert's grandfather was presumably derived from Greek Φιλομένης (*Filomenēs*), and suggests that he was Christian.[182] ᶜAbd al-Raḥmān's name means, literally, 'Servant of the

[174] Carcani 1992, p.339, col.b (Huillard-Bréholles 1852–61, vol.V.2, pp.726–27). *Annales Siculi* 1928, p.118. Sciascia 1989, p.1176 and nn.9–10.

[175] Carcani 1992, p.411, col.b – p.412, col.a (Huillard-Bréholles 1852–61, vol.V.2, pp.951–2, 964–6).

[176] Orig. PA, AdS, San Filippo di Demenna, no. 29: ed. Cusa 1868–82, no.192, pp.452–6: [ἡ γραφή] τοῦ ἐνδοξοτάτου ἄρχοντος καὶ μεγάλου σεκρετικοῦ κυρίου Ῥομβέρτου Φαλλαμόνακα. For Obert's career after May 1240, see: Huillard-Bréholles 1852–61, vol.V.2, pp.964–7, 972, 975–7, 983–4, 993 (Carcani 1992 places the first four of these *sub anno* 1239, although they appear to be dated to Indiction XIII: p.236, col.a – p.237, col.b; p.240, col.a; p.243, col.b – p.244, col.a); and Winkelmann 1880–5, vol.I, pp.561–2, 661, 673, 681, 719.

[177] Winkelmann 1880–5, vol.I, no.707, pp.561–2. See also Collura 1951, pp.17–18.

[178] Bresc 1986, vol.I, p.416, n.176, where he adds that the Palermitan family of Calvelli descended from Obert Fallamonaca; also vol.II, p.757, 'Obberto Fallamonaca … whose family, rich in lands, linked itself in marriage with the Calvellis, of the middle aristocracy'. See also Bresc 1979, p.56, apparently claiming that a certain Fityān, at Enna in 1142, was the ancestor of the *shaykh* ᶜAbd al-Raḥmān 'who takes, on his conversion, the Genoese name of Fallamonaca, and leaves his mark on the great estates of Vicari and Partinico … the Calvelli of Palermo are descended from the Fallamonaca'. (All without references.)

[179] Beneath her husband's name, Obert's wife puts a cross to her Arabic signature, 'Suḥayliba, the wife of Ūbart'. Her name may come from the Arabic for 'orchid', but it is uncertain when *saḥlab*, 'orchid', *saḥlabīyāt*, 'orchidaceae', *etc*., was first coined. See Dozy 1881, vol.I, p.637, for the assertion that *saḥlab* is a 'modern' corruption of *khuṣā l-thaᶜlab*, 'fox's testicles'. The connection between ὄρχις and *khuṣā* requires no explanation; the 'corruption' envisaged is presumably from [*khu*]*ṣā* [*l-thaᶜ*]*lab* to *saḥlab*.

[180] **Private 31** Orig. PA, AdS, S. Maria della Grotta, no.13: ed. Cusa 1868–82, no.188, pp.676–78 (misreads فليمان).

[181] Caracausi 1993, vol.I, p.595. 'Fellamonaca' occurs as a medieval place-name to the south of Partinico (IGM S. Cipirello 258 IV NE 350040), but it should not be linked to the *Rabᶜ al-Janawī* or *Terra Ianuensis* adjoining the Monreale estate of Sūmminī, which lay far to the south-east (Cusa 1868–82, pp.184, 210; Nania 1995, pp.84–5, 218–32: the remarks of Abulafia 1977, p.281, and the map showing the Genoese *cultura* in Abulafia 1988 are mistaken (I have a faint but guilty memory that I may have contributed to the error). Another Fellamonica (*sic*) lies between Mezzoiuso and Vicari (IGM Ciminna 259 IV S.O. 700890).

[182] The *alifs* in Fālaymān presumably indicate *imāla*. Caracausi 1993, vol.I, p.615; see also Bresc 1989, p.336.

Merciful [God]', and was a common name amongst Arab Christians in Sicily.[183] In this deed, Obert, his wife, and sons, are clearly Christians, and grant a piece of arable land in Palermo to Abbot Athanasios of Santa Maria della Grotta. Moreover, Perrino Fallamonaca, who seems to have been Obert's son, was a canon of Palermo cathedral.[184] On balance, I am inclined to suspect that Obert came from a family of Arab Christians, rather than of Christianised Muslims, and that he was a native of Sicily, not Genoa.

Conclusion

In my introductory remarks to this chapter, I warned that the exceptional conspicuousness of the Arab servants of the royal palace and *dīwān* during the last fifty years of the Norman kingdom should put us on our guard. What makes them so visible is, very largely but by no means exclusively, their prominence in the two contemporary sources from which I have quoted extensively: *The History of the Tyrants of Sicily* by 'Hugo Falcandus', and the *Riḥla* of Ibn Jubayr.

The History of the Tyrants of Sicily was written, almost certainly before the death of William II in 1189, by an eyewitness to the events that it describes. The author was first called 'Hugo Falcandus' only in the *editio princeps* of the *History* published in Paris in 1550, and his real identity is unknown. He was a member of the court, and was steeped in Latin literature, especially in Sallust, whose *Catiline Conspiracy* and *Jugurthan War* served as models for the *History*. 'Hugo Falcandus' almost certainly also wrote, in spring 1190, the *Letter to Peter, treasurer of the church of Palermo, concerning the Sicilian tragedy.* Little more can be said of the author without excessive speculation. The *History* is in two parts: the first describes the reign of William I from his accession until the suppression of the rebellions of 1160–2; the second opens with the death of William I in May 1166, and tells the story of the struggle for power during the regency of Margaret, until the fall of Stephen du Perche, and the earthquake of February 1169. Nonetheless, the *History* forms a single, coherent whole, with a strong unifying theme – how the virtuous ruler brings glory, honour, justice, and tranquillity to his realm, while the tyrant infects his kingdom with corruption, misery, and war.[185]

It is therefore not surprising to find the Arab servants of the palace portrayed as the creatures of tyranny. William I abandons Palermo to the vicious and violent revenge of Martin and Peter, assisted by their evil henchman, Robert of Calatabiano.

[183] For example, Cusa 1868–82, pp.663, 664, 666; Mongitore 1721, pp.40–1.

[184] In September 1266, after the Angevin takeover, Obert witnessed (in Arabic) the lease of a house in Palermo, from the prebend of Perrino Fallamonaca, a canon of Palermo cathedral, to the judge Martin of Calatafimi: Trasselli 1965, pp.341–2, n.22 (= **Private 32**).

[185] I have relied heavily upon Loud and Wiedemann's introduction to 'Hugo Falcandus' 1998, pp.1–53, and Hoffmann 1967; see also Jamison 1957, and Garufi 1942, each of whom proposes a different (and unacceptable) identification of 'Hugo Falcandus'.

The two eunuchs pervert the rule of law, so that their court becomes not the seat of justice, but an arena in which, driven by bestial passions, they and their agents torture and destroy the innocent. Being servile themselves, they reverse the natural order of society, encouraging slaves and maidservants to accuse their masters. As Muslims, their violence is particularly directed at Christians. The figure of Robert of Calatabiano is drawn as a crude and ugly caricature in which all the features of contemporary anti-Muslim polemic are hideously exaggerated. All this is much as we might expect. But the passages in which 'Hugo Falcandus' rejects such crude archetypes, and treats the Arab servants with subtlety, even sympathy, are far more revealing.

The confrontation between the eunuch Peter and Gilbert of Gravina is a case in point. The issue at stake was central to the theme of the *History* – that the regent Margaret 'had passed over the counts and other prudent men by whose judgement the court ought to be guided, and put an effeminate slave in charge of the whole realm'. But, instead of staging a show-down between a paragon of knightly virtue and the creature of tyranny, 'Hugo Falcandus' introduces the eunuch Peter as the model of virtue (if only he had not been a Muslim), while the queen's kinsman, Gilbert of Gravina, is presented as a blustering buffoon, incapable of defeating a eunuch slave and a woman in tears. It is Peter who commands the loyalty of his knights, and is supported by the clever, valiant Hugh, son of Atton, and by Richard of Molise, the doughty but dim master constable; while Gilbert of Gravina attracts such feeble support that he can only rant, rave, and sulk. Later, after Peter has defected to the Almohads, the traitor who has fled for fear of his life still commands the loyalty of Richard, who challenges Gilbert to single combat, accusing him of cowardice and treachery.[186] Nor does 'Hugo Falcandus' withhold admiration when a eunuch acts virtuously. Had Peter not been a Muslim, 'the kingdom of Sicily would have enjoyed much peace under his administration'. Even Martin is given credit for thwarting the prison break-out of 1163. The treatment of Arab servants in the *History* is thus more rounded, and more subtle, than might at first appear.

Abū l-Ḥusayn Aḥmad ibn Jubayr was born in Valencia in 1145 and, following in the footsteps of his father, was trained as a *kātib*, rising to be one of the leading civil servants to the Almohad governor of Granada. After he was induced to drink wine, he was so overcome by remorse that he resolved to expiate his sin through pilgrimage to the holy places. He set out in February 1183 and, after visiting Medina, Mecca and Damascus began the return to Spain from Crusader Acre. His boat was shipwrecked at Messina, but the Muslim passengers were rescued at the order of King William, and he landed safely on 10 December 1184. After staying a week in Messina, he set out for Palermo by ship, calling at Cefalù and Termini. There, the wind turned against him, and he continued by land, arriving at the capital on 22 December. A week later he proceeded to Trapani, via Alcamo and Qal^{c}at al-Ḥamma. He remained in Trapani for three months, until 25 March 1185, when he set sail for Cartagena. The account he gives of Sicily is that of a pious Muslim who is

[186] Above, p.227, note 57.

horrified that his fellow believers should be living under Christian rule, and who repeatedly prays to God that they may be protected from the pressures and seductions of their surroundings, and that they may eventually come to a good end. Ibn Jubayr should have been no stranger to the phenomenon of Muslim subjects under Christian lords – not only must he have been familiar with the complexities of al-Andalus, but he had recently passed through the Crusader kingdom of Jerusalem. And yet, again and again, behind the screen of his pious rhetoric, Ibn Jubayr exhibits his astonishment at the topsy-turvy world of Norman Sicily – at Muslim slaves governing a Christian kingdom, and at a Christian king who behaved like a Muslim ruler. Only when he reaches Trapani, does he abandon this naïve, open-mouthed wonder, and develop a harder, uncompromisingly critical view of the Norman kingdom. This, he implies, was in part the result of his meeting with Abū l-Qāsim. His account of the eunuchs comes before he reaches Trapani, and is, at one and the same time, highly sympathetic to them in their plight, and grudgingly admiring of the attitude displayed by King William and his court to his Muslim servants, and to all things Arab.

Both 'Hugo Falcandus' and Ibn Jubayr thus offer, from opposite standpoints, refreshingly unhackneyed perspectives on the Arab servants of the Norman court, which unexpectedly converge at many points. At one level, this is an encouraging indication that their information may be authentic and reliable. At another, it raises the suspicion that the image that they reflect of the Arab servants may have been deliberately manipulated, and projected so effectively that both Latin and Arab observers, at their very different standpoints, received the same message. I shall return to this possibility after first discussing the points of convergence.

The narrative sources, both Arabic and Latin, pay most attention to the eunuch slaves.[187] Their terminology leaves no room for doubt that they were indeed castrated. Ibn Jubayr's phrase *al-fityān al-majābīb* indicates complete excision of the scrotum, testicles and penis, which was the standard practice; *al-khaṣīy*, which is the term used in the *Dīwān* and *Tarassul* of Ibn Qalāqis, need not suggest that only the testicles had been removed.[188] The Latin sources use *neuter*,[189] *eunuchus*, and such phrases as *servus effeminatus* and *devirati homines*.[190] Philip of al-Mahdīya and Peter both came from North Africa as children, and were raised in the palace. Philip may have come to Sicily in George of Antioch's household, but Peter was probably taken during the capture of Gerba, and may have been castrated in the palace. Nothing is known about the origins of the other eunuchs, but it seems probable that some, like Peter, were captured during military campaigns in North Africa, while others may have been purchased from Christian, or even Jewish,

[187] There is an extensive bibliography on eunuchs in Islam. See the various studies conveniently collected in Ayalon 1979, Ayalon 1988 and Ayalon 1994, which are not completely superseded by Ayalon 1999. See also Toru and Philips 2000. I shall make only occasional references to these works in the notes that follow, but I cannot stress too strongly how important they are for the understanding of the rôle of the eunuchs in Norman Sicily.

[188] Ayalon 1999, pp.304–15 and Hogendorn 2000.

[189] Below, p.254, note 203.

[190] 'Hugo Falcandus' 1897, p.97

merchants. Frederick II had his slaves bought in Palermo.[191] John the Moor, who may or may not have been a eunuch, was the son of a black household slave-girl of Frederick II's, and was raised in the imperial palace.[192] It seems improbable that any of the eunuchs were Sicilian Muslims. Islamic law forbade Muslims to be made slaves and, *a fortiori*, to be castrated, and Islamic courts generally acquired their slaves and eunuchs from beyond the frontiers of Islam. In the Roman and Byzantine empires, too, eunuchs were supposed to be foreign slaves. Had the Norman eunuchs been drawn from Sicily, they might have retained familial links which would have weakened their utter dependence upon the king.

It was their social isolation and their utter dependence upon the king, as much as the act of castration, that distinguished the eunuchs. They had been raised in the palace as the personal dependants of the king and his family, to whom they were bound by quasi-familial ties of affection, as well as by bonds of dependence and service. The omnicompetence of the eunuchs, as personal servants, as keepers of the harem and as custodians and perhaps even educators of the palace children, allowed them far closer intimacy with the king and his family than would have been granted to any Latin courtier. Philip 'on account of his honest service, became extremely dear and agreeable' to King Roger, whose love and affection for him increased with time. The king had raised him from boyhood, and thought of him almost as a son. Perhaps, like Roger-Aḥmad, Philip was in fact Roger's god-son. William I, on his death-bed, manumitted Peter and provided for him in his will. Queen Margaret would allow no one, not even her own blood-relative, to replace Peter, 'of whom she was very fond'. Margaret 'would in no way give her approval to the arrest of the *qāʾid* Richard', although she did allow the imprisonment of the other, Latin, conspirators against Stephen du Perche. Peter, Martin, and Richard were all royal familiars, and Peter and Richard seem to have had closer access to Margaret than any of her Latin barons. The intimate, quasi-familial relationship between the king and his eunuchs was reported, too, by Ibn Jubayr, who also seems to imply a sexual relationship when he writes that William II made 'great use of eunuchs and slave-girls', and that he kept 'slave-girls and concubines'. It is unlikely to be coincidence that the political influence of the eunuchs reached its peak during the years in which the regent was a woman.[193]

These close personal ties between the eunuchs and their masters brought them significant material rewards. As fiscal administrators and judges, they had ample opportunity to enrich themselves. 'Hugo Falcandus' enlarges on their greed, Ibn Jubayr upon their wealth and generosity. Peter, Martin, and Richard all had their own dwellings outside the palace, in the Kemonia, and maintained their own households with servants and knights. But the authority, position and wealth of the eunuchs was entirely dependent upon royal favour. Once that was withdrawn, as it was from Philip, Andrew, and Jawhar, they were utterly unprotected. When the

[191] For example, ed. Carcani 1992, p.279, col.b – p.280, col.a; p.308, col.b (Huillard-Bréholles 1852–61, vol.V.1, pp.535–6, 631–2).

[192] See above, p.244, note 162.

[193] See, in particular, Ayalon 1999, pp.195–9.

king's authority was suspended, as it was on the fall of Maio of Bari, and during the Palermo rebellion, the eunuchs were defenceless, and could be imprisoned, tortured or slaughtered by the mob.

The eunuchs attempted to weave networks of relationship to catch them if they fell from royal grace. In the close atmosphere of the palace, sharing exile, captivity, physical mutilation and a common, persecuted faith, the eunuchs came to think of themselves as a family, with siblings, and even sons – the Banū Fityān.[194] They also used their wealth and influence to buy the loyalty of the other servants, the Arab guard, the stipendiary knights and even minor nobles, such as Peter's champions, Hugh, son of Atton, and Richard of Molise. Beyond the palace, they cultivated relations with the Muslim élite, such as Abū l-Qāsim and his circle, and used their wealth to do good works for poor and vulnerable Muslims. Philip of al-Mahdīya was a patron of the mosques of Palermo, and Peter seems to have founded a public building, possibly a fountain, at Termini. Philip and ᶜAbd al-Masīḥ both recruited Muslim pilgrims so that they could participate in the *ḥajj* by proxy.[195] The leniency shown by Philip to the *ᶜulamāᵓ* of Bône may not have been entirely disinterested. Richard prepared for his retirement by exploiting his professional acquaintance with archbishops and bishops. But, without parents and without children, the authority and the status of the eunuchs was ephemeral and sterile, and they could do nothing which, in the last resort, would protect them from the whim of their master, or the fury of the mob.

Their one recourse was to heavenly authority, their one hope in the life to come.[196] Both Arabic and Latin sources emphasise that the eunuchs were Muslims at heart, beneath the cloak of *taqīya*. Lest this be dismissed as rhetoric, we have the eunuchs' own professions of faith, in their *ᶜalāmāt*. Significantly, none of the four religious formulae used by the eunuchs as signatures belongs to the standard repertoire of *ᶜalāmāt* – each appears to have been chosen or devised by the signatory for personal reasons. The *ᶜalāma*s used by Barrūn and by Martin – respectively, *ᶜalā llāhi tawakkulī* ('My trust is in God'), or just possibly *ᶜalā llāhi tawfīqī* ('My prosperity depends on God');[197] and *tawakkulī ᶜalā ilāhī* ('My trust is in my God') or *tawakkulī ᶜalā llāhi* ('My trust is in God')[198] – could have been read as referring to the Christian God, but only by a Christian, for a Muslim would instantly have heard their Qurᵓānic echoes – *wa-mā tawfīqī illā bi-llāhi ᶜalay-hi tawakkaltu* ('My prosperity is from God alone, in Him I trust': *Qurᵓān* 11.88). Richard's *ᶜalāma* – *lā yakhfā ᶜalā llāhi shayᵓ* ('Nothing is hidden from God')[199] – expresses precisely the principle upon which the practice of *taqīya* rests and, again, also resonates with Qurᵓānic language – *lā yakhfā ᶜalā llāhi min-hum shayᵓ* ('Nothing will be hidden from God concerning them' [*i.e.* the True Believers, on the Day of Judgement]: *Qurᵓān* 40.16). The *fatā* ᶜAmmār is the only one of the eunuchs to sign with his

[194] See Ayalon 1999, pp.290–2.
[195] See Ayalon 1999, p.338 and n.28.
[196] See Ayalon 1999, pp.337–8.
[197] ***Dīwānī* 29** and **31**: above, p.222, note 39.
[198] ***Dīwānī* 35** and **37**, and **Private 11**: above, p.220, note 26; p.222, note 32.
[199] ***Dīwānī* 35** (?), and **Private 11** and **23**: above, p.220, note 26; p.222, note 32; p.232, note 82; p.243, note 143.

Arabic *ism*, and not with a Christian name, and he alone employs an *ᶜalāma* which openly proclaims his faith – *ḥasbiya llāhu wa-l-muslimīn* ('God and the Muslims are sufficient for me').[200] It is extremely doubtful that anyone who was not a trained Arabic scribe could have read these intricate *ᶜalāmāt*, and I am inclined to interpret them primarily as secret professions of faith, shared amongst the Muslim eunuchs of the court. At the same time, ᶜAmmār's *ᶜalāma* reveals a further level of hidden meaning, one of rebellion and subversion. At this level, the Qurʾānic resonances evoked by these *ᶜalāmāt* carry a portentous, prophetic warning. The mottoes used by Barrūn and Martin echo the words of Shuᶜayb in the *Sūrat Hūd*, warning the Midyanites lest they suffer the fate of the people of Noah and Lot, of Hūd and Ṣāliḥ – words that fell on deaf ears 'because you (*i.e.* Shuᶜayb) have no rank amongst us', so that the Midyanites were overcome by a sudden evil (*Qurʾān* 11.88–95). Richard's *ᶜalāma* refers to the *Sūrat al-Muʾmin*, 'the Chapter of the Believer', which tells the story of a Believer at the court of Pharoah, 'who concealed his faith' (*yaktumu īmāna-hu*: *Qurʾān* 40.28), and warned of the catastrophes that would overwhelm the Egyptians if they did not turn to God. The verse to which Richard's motto refers continues with a question and an answer which are openly seditious in the mouth of a Muslim royal servant – 'On the Day [of Judgement] to whom will the kingdom belong? To God, the One, the Victorious' (*Qurʾān* 40.16). These eunuchs were politicians and survivors, and did not actively seek martyrdom, but their *ᶜalāmāt* allow us to glimpse behind the veil of their *taqīya*, and tend to confirm the claims of both the Arab and the Latin sources that they were members of a conspiracy that hoped to subvert and even to overthrow the Christian kings.

The position of the employees of the *dīwān* who were drawn from the Muslim élite, such as Abū l-Ḍawʾ and Abū l-Qāsim, was clearly very different from the precarious state of the eunuchs. Abū l-Ḍawʾ came from a cadet branch of the family who provided the *qāḍī* of Palermo for at least four successive generations under Norman rule. He was employed as a *kātib*, perhaps mostly for international correspondence, and appeared next to the *qāḍī* in the royal court in judgement of at least one inter-communal dispute. When given the opportunity to become vizier, he prudently declined, but he remained at court as a panegyricist to Roger. Both 'Hugo Falcandus' and Ibn Jubayr agree that Abū l-Qāsim was the leader of the Muslims of the island, but we do not know what form that leadership took, nor how it operated. The Muslims of Syracuse, who appealed to him through Ibn Qalāqis, clearly hoped that he had the power to relieve them of the *jizya*, although their confidence was probably misplaced. If the man whom 'Hugo Falcandus' calls the *qāʾid* Sedictus, the richest of the Muslims of Sicily and Abū l-Qāsim's enemy, was identical with al-Sadīd ibn al-Ḥuṣrī, then he too associated himself with the royal circle, but as a courtier, not an official. Another Muslim notable, the *ḥākim* Ibn al-Muhadhdhib al-Judhāmī, may have been employed in the *dīwān*. All these men were supported by a sturdy network of family, community, and property, which was wholly independent of the bonds of dependence and service that tied

200 **Private 23**: above, p.232, note 82; p.246, note 143.

them to the ruler. In Abū l-Qāsim's case, the safety-net was so strong that, even when he was accused of intriguing with the Almohads, fell from royal favour and lost much of his wealth, his rank outside the court was undiminished. It would be fascinating to know precisely what persuaded these men to go into royal service in the first place, but I see no reason to doubt that, once there, they acted as faithful advocates and representatives of the Muslim community of the island.

The extent to which the Arab servants maintained contacts with foreign Muslim powers is still more difficult to judge. Both the Arabic and the Latin sources report that such contacts did exist – Abū l-Ḍawʾ was certainly in touch with figures in the Zīrid court; Philip 'commended himself' to the 'priest' of Medina, which might indicate the Zanjid governor of the Ḥijāz; Peter was in touch with the Almohads; and Abū l-Qāsim with both the Almohads and Ṣalāḥ al-Dīn. It seems doubtful that any of these overtures could have posed a serious threat to the security of Sicily. Although the Arab servants must have passed information about the island to her enemies, they also collected news from the outside Muslim world – an Arab courtier is said to have told King Roger of the fall of Edessa, long before he had the news from a Christian source.[201] If Philip and Peter both led naval expeditions to North Africa, and if Obert Fallamonaca was Frederick's ambassador to Morocco and Spain, their masters can scarcely have been too concerned about their foreign contacts.[202]

The overseas excursions of Philip, Peter and Obert, underline the fact that the Arab servants were omnicompetent. Peter, for example, was an officer of the *dīwān*, a benefactor of the citizens of Termini, an admiral of the fleet, a judge during the suppression of the rebellions of 1160–2, and a royal familiar. Most of the eunuchs were chamberlains (*camerarii*) or master chamberlains (*magistri camerarii*), the officials who, after the murder of Maio of Bari and the disappearance of the office of emir of emirs, ran the administration in Palermo, under the direction of the royal familiars. In 1162, Jawhar, the master chamberlain of the palace (*magister camerarius palatii*) had the royal seals in his charge when he attempted to defect to the rebels. After the fall of Stephen du Perche, Arab chamberlains always directed the *dīwāns*, in addition to whatever unspecified duties they fulfilled within the household and the palace. The omnicompetent nature of their duties makes it highly unlikely their authority was primarily due to their being Arabic-speakers and -writers, still less to any putative mastery of arcane Arabic arithmetical and financial skills that were inaccessible to Greeks and Latins. The *duana baronum* was based in Salerno, kept its records in Latin, and, to judge from the *Catalogus baronum*, did its sums in clumsy Roman numerals, but was nonetheless directed by Arab chamberlains.

The Norman kings of Sicily, in their pursuit of autocratic and despotic kingship on the Mediterranean model, and in their rejection of a feudal monarchy in which the king was *primus inter pares*, and which tended to associate the leading lay and

[201] Ibn al-Athīr 1851–76, vol.XI, pp.66 (*BAS*^{2}, vol.I, pp.328–9; *BAS*^{2}*(It.)*, vol.II, p.366).
[202] On the use of eunuchs as military commanders, see Ayalon 1999, pp.339–44

ecclesiastical magnates of the realm with the king in his rule, sought to exploit fully the potential of government through officers of the palace whose authority and power was derived not from birth, strength, and wealth, but purely from their relationship with the monarch. The eunuchs were particularly suitable. Not only were they bound to the king and his family by close ties of affection, service and dependence, but also, as castrated slaves who had been removed from their native societies as children, and as Arabs and crypto-Muslims, they formed a group apart, and could be relied upon to protect their own interests, which coincided with the king's, against those who sought to weaken his autocratic rule. It is no paradox that, amongst their Arab servants, the Norman kings also employed a few members of the Muslim élite, such as Abū l-Ḍawʾ and Abū l-Qāsim, despite their status and wealth. Their interests, and those of the community which they served, lay always with the king and the eunuchs, never with the opponents of the autocratic regime which was the sole guarantor of their precarious position as *ahl al-dhimma*. This is confirmed not just by the pogroms and massacres of Muslims perpetrated by the rebels of 1160–2, but also by the high seriousness with which the chancellor and archbishop-elect, Stephen du Perche, took the hackneyed accusation that Muslims were sexual predators upon Christian boys and virgins, and by his persecution of crypto-Muslims.

For 'Hugo Falcandus', the eunuchs were manifestations of the tyranny of their masters. So too, for Peter of Eboli, the panegyricist of Henry VI, who thus describes the German emperor's triumphal entry into the royal palace on 20 November 1194:

> All the Potiphars bring the keys and record-chests, and hand over all the riches that the treasury has. They count out the treasures that the spider and the worm once guarded and the cobweb vainly sealed. The first eunuch unlocks all the chests; the second explains the receipts; the third, the revenues. All this – how much Calabria should render, how much Africa, how much Apulia and Sicily should render – was listed.[203]

In the Vulgate, Potiphar, whose wife failed to seduce Joseph, is called 'Potiphar the eunuch of Pharoah' (Genesis 39:1). If the eunuchs of the Norman king are Potiphars, Peter is implying, then their master was Pharoah, the archetypical tyrant. In this case, the jibe was aimed specifically at Tancred, but his predecessors were also called tyrants and compared unfavourably to the Greek tyrants of Sicily, to Nero, and to the Maccabees.[204] To their Latin critics, their Arab servants, especially the eunuchs, were manifestations of the tyranny of Norman kings.

Arab observers, on the other hand, may have hated the Norman kings for being Christian and for ruling over Muslims, but had only praise for their style of kingship, and for the use they made of Arab servants. Ibn al-Athīr says of Roger II that:

[203] Peter of Eboli 1994, pp.196–7, lines 1317–24 (Peter of Eboli 1906, pp.91–2; Peter of Eboli 1904, p.170;): *Putifares omnes claves et scrinia portant; / Adsignant quasquas fiscus habebat opes; / Thesauros numerant, quos vermis araneus ille / Auserat, et frustra retia nevit apris; / Primus neutrorum claves escriniat omnes, / Alter apodixas explicat; alter opes; / Hec quantum Calaber seu quantum debeat Afer, / Apulus aut Siculus debeat orbis habet.*

[204] Wieruszowski 1963.

> he followed the way of Muslim rulers with mounted companions,[205] chamberlains, arms-bearers, body-guards, and others of that kind. Thus, he broke with the custom of the Franks, who are not acquainted with such things. He founded a Court of Complaints, *dīwān al-maẓālim*,[206] to which those [Muslims] who had been unjustly treated brought their grievances, and [the king] would give them justice, even against his own son. He treated the Muslims with respect, took them as his companions, and kept the Franks off them, so that they loved him.[207]

Al-Maqrīzī, probably drawing upon the same source as Ibn al-Athīr, wrote that Roger dressed in the robes of a Muslim ruler and, on holidays, would ride out in cavalcade displaying himself in the manner of an Islamic monarch.[208] Ibn Jubayr, too, found that the court of William II imitated that of a Muslim ruler: 'He imitates the rulers of the Muslims in immersing himself in the luxury of his realm, in the provision of its laws, the invention of procedures, the allocation of degrees amongst his men, the elaboration of the ceremony of the realm, and the display of his finery'. As to his eunuch ministers and chamberlains: 'The magnificence of his kingship radiates through them'.[209] Thus, for Arab writers, the Arab servants of the Norman king are the manifestations not of his tyranny but of his glory, they are the essence of all that is good about his rule.

Al-Maqrīzī is quite clear that this had not come about by chance: it was George of Antioch who had deliberately 'organised the foundations of the kingdom', so that Roger came to resemble a Muslim ruler. I shall discuss this claim more fully in Chapter 10. Here, it only remains to stress that the Islamic facet of the Norman monarchy was a façade, a thin Islamic veneer that covered a solid Christian core. Where the veneer is cracked, we catch sight of Roger burning Philip for being a Muslim, of William I beating Jawhar so badly that he fled towards the very rebels who had slaughtered his brother eunuchs, of William II ordering Stephen du Perche to prosecute Muslims as sexual predators. Every action of a medieval king that is recorded was, of course, a public act, and these examples of anti-Muslim brutality are no less manipulations of the royal image than was the application of the Islamic veneer. The Norman kings and their ministers were perhaps the most innovative and effective manipulators of the royal image in contemporary Europe, and it would not have escaped them that the extravagant public display mounted by their Arab servants would send opposite messages to Arabs and to Latins. That their Arab subjects and foreign Muslim visitors should take a positive impression of their rule was clearly to the advantage of the Norman kings. But it need not follow that the hostility that their Arab servants aroused in Latin breasts necessarily redounded on the rulers. William I may have been content to leave the

[205] Dozy 1881, vol.I, p.221. [206] Below, pp.292–5.

[207] Ibn al-Athīr 1851–76, vol.X, p.133 (*BAS*², vol.I, p.320; *BAS*²*(It.)*, vol.I, p.367): *fa-salaka ṭarīqa mulūki l-muslimīna mina l-janāʾibi wa-l-ḥujjābi wa-l-silāḥīyati wa-l-jāndārīyati wa-ghayri dhālika wa-khālafa ʿādata l-faranji fa-inna-hum lā yaʿrifūna shayʾan min-hu wa-juʿila la-hu dīwānu l-maẓālimi yurfaʿu ilay-hi shakwā l-maẓlūmīna fa-yunṣifu-hum wa-law min waladi-hi wa-akrama l-muslimīna wa-qarraba-hum wa-manaʿa ʿan-humu l-faranja fa-aḥabbū-hu.*

[208] Above, p.82. [209] Above, p.213.

suppression of the Palermo rebellion to his eunuchs precisely because he could always claim that they had exceeded their orders. In the event, it was left to his widow, and to her relatives, Gilbert of Gravina and Stephen du Perche, to force Peter into flight, to stage the show trial of Robert of Calatabiano, and to enjoy popular acclaim for having restored the Golden Age.[210] That their Arab servants were hated by their Latin subjects, may have been no less useful to the Norman kings than was the good impression that they made upon Arab observers.

[210] Romuald of Salerno 1935, p.254; 'Hugo Falcandus' 1897, p.114.

CHAPTER 10

The Norman *dīwān* and Fāṭimid Egypt

In Chapters 1 and 2, it was argued that the origins of the Arabic administration of Norman Sicily are to be sought in the pre-conquest administration of the island, and in the adaptation of its practices and records to post-conquest needs. Chapter 3 showed that, after an initial burst of activity, Arabic all but disappeared as an administrative language from 1111 until after Roger's coronation. And yet, within a few years of 1130, as may be seen in Chapter 4, Roger was issuing Arabic and bilingual documents which had been produced by a professional and sophisticated Arabic *dīwān*. During the 1140s, and especially during the renewals of 1145, which were discussed in Chapter 5, the Arab scribes of the royal *dīwān* demonstrated themselves to be masters of the secretary's art as practised in contemporary Islamic chanceries. This dramatic renaissance of the Arabic administration was confined to the reign of King Roger. Thereafter, until the fall of the dynasty, the royal *dīwān* continued to develop along the lines then laid down, but did not undergo further revolutionary reconstruction comparable to that of the 1130s and '40s.

This chapter seeks to answer a series of questions which have, until now, remained obvious but unasked. What were the sources of the renaissance of the Arabic administration? Are they to be found in Sicily, or must they be sought in the wider Islamic world? And, if so, where precisely? And through what channels did they reach the island? Partial answers to some of these questions have already been given in order to support specific stages of the argument. In Chapter 8, for example, it was suggested that the introduction of the *dīwān al-taḥqīq* in *c.*1149 was inspired by the Fāṭimid office of the same name; in Chapter 5, attention was drawn to the close parallels between many of the titles and formulae employed in the renewals of 1145 and their equivalents in contemporary Egypt; in Chapter 3, al-Maqrīzī's life of George of Antioch identified him as the shaper of the Arabic facet of Roger's monarchy. It seems best, therefore, to anticipate the conclusion to this chapter, and to state plainly here that the principal source of the innovations of the 1130s and '40s was Fāṭimid Egypt, and that the chief architect of the reconstruction of the Norman *dīwān* was George of Antioch.

The nature of the evidence means that its weight will be cumulative, and that the argument will be largely circumstantial. The first points to establish are whether relations between Cairo and Palermo were such that the Fāṭimid *dīwān* could have influenced the Sicilian *dīwān* immediately before, and during, its transformation in the 1130s; and whether George of Antioch played such a rôle in relations between the two courts that he could have been the agent responsible for introducing elements from the Egyptian administration to Norman Sicily.

Norman Sicily and Fāṭimid Egypt

At first sight, the suggestion that the Christian kings of Sicily borrowed extensively from the Fāṭimid caliphs of Egypt may seem highly improbable. After all, the two dynasties should have been deadly enemies. The Norman conquest had not just ripped Sicily from the *Dār al-Islām*, but had also captured the island from its nominal overlord, the Fāṭimid caliph. There is no trace, however, of any Fāṭimid reaction to the loss of Sicily and, by the 1120s, friendly contact had been established between Cairo and Palermo.

It is difficult to know what part Fāṭimid-Zīrid relations may have had in shaping Cairo's attitude towards Sicily. The Zīrids' rejection of Fāṭimid authority, in favour of the ᶜAbbāsids of Baghdad, may have inclined Cairo to turn a blind eye to the Norman conquest; but this seems unlikely, given that the Zīrids had returned their allegiance to Cairo in 446/1054–5, five years before the Norman invasion.[1] The Normans rapidly reached an accommodation with their Zīrid neighbours, which lasted from the late 1080s until 1117.[2]

In the next decade, as the Normans sought to strengthen their hold upon Ifrīqiya, the Zīrīds appealed to the Fāṭimids for support. The Egyptian historian Ibn Muyassar reports that in Jumādā I 517 (June–July 1123) a Zīrid embassy arrived in Cairo. The ambassador re-pledged the allegiance of his master al-Ḥasan to the caliph al-Ḥāfiẓ, and begged him to intervene with Roger of Sicily to prevent him from attacking Ifrīqiya. The caliph dispatched an embassy to Palermo, led by one Musṭaniᶜ al-Dawla ᶜAlī ibn Aḥmad ibn Zayn al-Khadd, and, says Ibn Muyassar, peace was re-established between the Normans and the Zīrids. He makes no mention of the disastrous Sicilian attack upon al-Mahdīya, led by the emirs Christodoulos and George of Antioch, that was launched in the same month as the Zīrid ambassador arrived in Cairo – and perhaps he was unaware of it.[3]

Hady Roger Idris remarked that relations between Cairo and Palermo must have been friendly before July 1123 for al-Ḥasan to have asked al-Ḥāfiẓ to intervene with Roger.[4] South Italian merchants had been trading in Alexandria since the 10th century, and a letter concerning Italian merchants addressed to the caliph al-Āmir (1101–30) suggests that his administration took a direct interest in their activities.[5] It may be wrong, however, to conclude that the Norman conquest had

[1] Idris 1962a, vol.I, pp.172–203, 225–6. [2] Idris 1962a, vol.I, pp.286–91, 308, 319–24.
[3] Ibn Muyassar 1919, p.63; Idris 1962a, vol.I, pp.337–8. [4] Idris 1962a, vol.I, pp.337–8.
[5] Cahen 1953–4; Stern 1956, especially pp.533–4.

little impact upon trade between Egypt and Sicily. After the 1090s, no dated or securely datable correspondence regarding trade with Sicily has survived in the Cairo Geniza until a letter, written in or soon after 1122,[6] tells of Alexandrian Jews being attacked and robbed in Sicily by the Christian crew of the ship that they had chartered.[7] Although this interruption may be a mere chance of survival, the strong suspicion must be that it reflects a decline in trade between Egypt and Sicily over the same period.

At about the same time that the Geniza record recommences, George of Antioch was sent as ambassador to Cairo. George had been bailiff of Iato until at least 1114 and, according to al-Maqrīzī, he was sent to Cairo 'many times' by the emir Christodoulos, who himself disappears in 1126.[8] George's embassies therefore took place somewhere in the interval between these dates, which tends to support Idris's hypothesis that good relations had been established between Cairo and Palermo before July 1123. Indeed, the attention paid by Arab sources to the very fact of George's embassies implies that they were exceptional, and perhaps indicates that they were the beginning of contact between the two courts. The purpose of George's embassies is unknown. Al-Maqrīzī says nothing, and al-Tījānī merely reports that when 'Roger needed to send an ambassador to Egypt, ᶜAbd al-Raḥmān (*i.e.* Christodoulos) recommended this George, and [the king] dispatched him. He performed loyally, and returned with kingly treasures, for which he earned Roger's favour'.[9]

The next evidence for relations between Cairo and Palermo is the letter of al-Ḥāfiẓ to Roger. The letter does not survive in the original, but was preserved by al-Qalqashandī as a model of the sort of letter written by the Fāṭimid chancery to foreign rulers.[10] Marius Canard first studied aspects of the letter, and gave a partial translation of it, in two articles published in 1954.[11] He rightly deduced from the letter's concern with the Fāṭimid vizier, Bahrām, that it must date to 1137,[12] or immediately thereafter.

The greater part of the letter is written in *sajᶜ* or rhymed prose. In al-Qalqashandī's own day, the Mamlūk chancery used *sajᶜ* when corresponding with those great rulers of the Muslim world who took care that their own letters to the sultan were composed in the same elegant style; lesser rulers, with less refined chanceries, were addressed in ordinary epistolary style.[13] Elsewhere, he quotes the contradictory opinions of the late 12th-century authority Ibn Shīth al-Qurashī, and of an anonymous contemporary of the latter who held that *sajᶜ* should only be used for letters addressed by a superior to an inferior. Ibn Shīth insisted that the respective rank of the correspondent was immaterial, but that letters from the sultan

[6] The letter refers to the Almoravid raid against Nicotera in Calabria led by Abū ᶜAbd Allāh ibn Maymūn in early 516 A.H. (1122 A.D.): see Ibn ᶜIdhārī 1948–51, vol.I, p.307 (*BAS*², vol.I, p.425; *BAS*²*(It.)*, vol.II, p.478) and Ibn al-Athīr 1851–76, vol.X, p.431 (*BAS*², vol.I, p.324; *BAS*²*(It.)*, vol.II, p.365).

[7] Oxford, Bod. MS Heb. c.28.60: ed. Zeldes and Frankel 1997, no.1, pp.103–7; trans. Simonsohn 1997, no.171, pp.392–4.

[8] Above, p.74.

[9] Above, p.84.

[10] al-Qalqashandī 1913–72, vol.VI, pp.458–63.

[11] Canard 1955a; Canard 1954.

[12] Canard 1955a, p.136.

[13] al-Qalqashandī 1913–72, vol.VIII, p.24; Bosworth 1972, pp.215–16.

should always be composed in *saj*ᶜ.[14] Al-Ḥāfiẓ is scrupulously polite to Roger, but nonetheless treats him with majestic condescension which may indicate that, at least in this case, the use of *saj*ᶜ was intended to signal that a superior was addressing his inferior.

After the opening formulae (p.458, lines 1–8), the caliph begins by assuring Roger that he had received and carefully read his previous letter, and that he would reply to it point by point (p.458, lines 9–11). Roger's preamble had clearly enlarged upon the many blessings which he had received from God, but the caliph haughtily dismisses Roger's claims by stressing that he and his family have been so blessed that God has granted them not just this world, but also the next (p.458, line 12 – p.459, line 2).

The preliminaries over, the caliph turns to Roger's capture of Gerba in 1135 (p.459, lines 3–11). The island had long been a thorn in the flesh of the Zīrid emirs. It had been seized by Berber rebels against al-Muᶜizz and, after his death, had been used by Arabs and Berbers hostile to Zīrid authority as a base for raids upon shipping in the Gulf of Gabès, preying upon the trade between Egypt and Ifrīqiya. Soon after his succession, the emir ᶜAlī ibn Yaḥyā (1116–21) launched a major assault against the island which seems to have been successful for a time, for nothing more is heard of Gerban pirates nor of Zīrid efforts to subdue them.[15] Nonetheless, Roger had explained in his previous letter to al-Ḥāfiẓ that he had been forced to capture the island because of the aggression of its inhabitants. The Arabic sources tend to support this claim.[16] Ibn al-Athīr, who was probably basing himself upon the lost history of the Zīrid Ibn Shaddād, prefaces his report of the Norman conquest of Gerba with a note upon the irrepressible rebelliousness, evil-doing and piracy of its inhabitants.[17] In any case, al-Ḥāfiẓ's remarks suggest, in the most general terms, that the Gerbans had got only what they deserved.

Al-Ḥāfiẓ next makes a few polite observations, in agreement with what had clearly been a fulsome tribute to Roger's vizier, George of Antioch, to the effect that all George's qualities stem from Roger himself (p.459, lines 12–15). Presumably George had been largely responsible for the previous letter, and had taken the opportunity to enlarge upon his own merits and virtues.

The caliph goes on to thank Roger for the manner in which the ship *al-ᶜArūs* ('the Bride') had been treated (p.459, line 16 – p.460, line 2). This vessel had been 'under the protection of al-Ḥāfiẓ's private *dīwān*' (*jārin fī l-dīwāni l-khāṣṣi l-ḥāfiẓī*), a phrase which indicates that it was trading on the caliph's personal behalf. She had apparently been captured and her cargo seized before anyone was aware of her status. Once it was realised that she was the caliph's own vessel, the Sicilian admiral intervened, took her under his protection and restored her cargo. Al-Ḥāfiẓ interprets this as a sign that Roger's friendship for him is as strong as ever. As a consequence, the caliph has ordered his admirals to afford the same protection to Roger's ships,

[14] al-Qalqashandī 1913–72, vol.VI, p.307; Bosworth 1972, p.216.

[15] Idris 1962a, vol.I, pp.165–6, 298, 301, 314.

[16] *Pace* Idris 1962a, vol.I, p.346.

[17] Ibn al-Athīr 1851–76, vol.XI, p.20 (*BAS*², vol.I, p.327; *BAS*²*(It.)*, vol.II, p.364). See also Idris 1962a, vol.I, pp.345–7.

and he grants exemption from import and export taxes at Alexandria and Cairo to any ship of the king's, of George of Antioch, and of 'the two ambassadors who are yet to arrive' (p.460, lines 2–7). No further details are given of the latter but, as Canard suggests, they may have been connected with the city of Salerno, for, in November 1137, King Roger promised to secure for Salernitan merchants the same trading privileges in Egypt as were already enjoyed by their Sicilian counterparts.[18]

The caliph next acknowledges Roger's thanks for having released certain captives, and having sent them to Sicily. This is a mark of the special favour which Roger enjoys with al-Ḥāfiẓ – 'one of the indications that there is granted to you that which has not been granted to any of the kings of the Christians' (p.460, lines 8–11). The identity of the captives is not given, and in all probability they were Roger's subjects. But the manner in which this theme leads on to the next, leaves the possibility open that there was some connection between the captives and Bahrām.

The main subject of the letter, occupying little less than half of the whole, is the caliph's justification of his treatment of Bahrām, his Christian Armenian vizier (p.460, line 12 – p.463, line 3). The Saljūq invasion of Cappadocia had driven many Armenian refugees into the plains drained by the River Sajūr, a tributary of the Euphrates, to the north-east of Aleppo. Bahrām belonged to the noble Armenian family of Paḥlavuni. He was the grandson of Grigor Paḥlavuni Magistros (d.1058–9),[19] and the nephew of Grigor II Martyrophil (*Vkayasēr*), the Catholicos of All Armenians, who visited Egypt on at least one occasion in or around the 1070s, and ordained Bahrām's brother, another Grigor, as Catholicos of the Armenians in Egypt.[20] Bahrām's early career remains obscure. He was born at Tall Bāshir, and, at some point, he was driven out by Armenian opponents.[21] Like so many of his compatriots, Bahrām found his way to Egypt.[22] By early 1135, he was military governor of al-Gharbīya, the western province of the Delta.

[18] *Praeterea decatias, et alia jura mercatorum quae Salernitani in Alexandriam prius persolvere soliti erant ad morem, et modum Siciliae negotiatorum reduci faciemus, quatenus eamdem lex et similis consuetudo Siculis e Salernitanis permaneat*: Ughelli 1717–21, vol.VII, p.399; Canard 1955a, pp.133–4. [19] Dadoyan 1997, pp.62–7, 71–4.

[20] Canard 1955a, pp.145–51; Dadoyan 1997, pp.85–90. Seta Dadoyan has recently stressed that the intervention of the 'orthodox' Paḥlavunis in Egypt must be clearly distinguished from the long domination of the vizierate by Muslim Armenians from Badr al-Jamālī to Ruzzīk ibn Ṭalāʾiʿ (1074–1163). See also the important article by den Heijer 1999.

[21] Ibn Muyassar 1919, p.78; Canard 1954, pp.88–91; Canard 1955a, pp.151–4. Dadoyan 1997, pp.10–11, 91, 134, wrongly claims that Bahrām thereafter spent some time as the leader of an Armenian contingent fighting alongside the Crusaders against the Saljūqs. He was not, as she claims, at Acre in 1098. Her source is Wiet 1961, p.180, who pretends to cite William of Tyre *apud* Grousset, 1934–6, vol.I, p.161, for the following passage: 'Arrivée sous les murs de Jérusalem (*sic!*), elle [l'armée chrétienne] livra de grands combats. Dans ce moment, le seigneur Vahram, seigneur des Arméniens, se trouvait dans cette ville. Les infidèles voulurent le tuer, mais Dieu le sauva de leurs mains'. In fact, this passage, which is not actually quoted by Grousset, is taken from Matthew of Edessa 1869, p.45, where the Vahram concerned is identified as the Catholicos Vahram, *i.e.* Grigor II Martyrophil (*Vkayasēr*). He was Bahrām's uncle, after whom, states Dadoyan (*ibid.*, p.10), our Bahrām was named.

[22] Dadoyan 1997, pp.85–90, has recently suggested that Bahrām and his brother Bassak were sent to Egypt with an army of twenty thousand Armenians by their uncle, the Catholicos Grigor II, in order to support the Armenian community in Egypt. Dadoyan regards this as the 'first arrival' of Bahrām in Egypt, and implies that it occurred well before his 'second appearance' in *c.*1130 (*ibid.*, p.91). This version of events is explicitly contradicted by the letter of al-Ḥāfiẓ.

Meanwhile, al-Ḥāfiẓ had two Armenian viziers assassinated in rapid succession – Kutayfāt ibn al-Afḍal in 1131, and Yūnis in 1132 – and was now attempting to rule through his own sons. His firstborn, Sulaymān, was appointed vizier, but died young. He was replaced by Ḥaydara, who was promptly challenged by his brother, Ḥasan. Fierce fighting broke out between their supporters, and the army mutinied. Threatened with defeat, Ḥasan summoned Bahrām to his aid. Bahrām entered Cairo to find Ḥasan already dead, but soon re-established order, and was appointed vizier of both the army and the administration. Unlike his Armenian predecessors, Bahrām was openly a Christian, but al-Ḥāfiẓ voices no criticism of his faith, concentrating instead upon the manner in which he encouraged the mass immigration of Armenian supporters, until he came to command a private army numbering more than twenty thousand.

Early in 1137, Bahrām's successor as military governor of al-Gharbīya, Riḍwān ibn Walakhshī, a fervent Sunnī, led a military coup which assumed the character of an Islamist, anti-Armenian uprising, and forced Bahrām to flee Cairo. On 4 February 1137, as Riḍwān assumed the vizierate, and his troops massacred the Armenians of the capital, Bahrām hurried south to join his brother, Bassak, whom he had appointed governor of Qūṣ in Upper Egypt. Bahrām arrived to find him already murdered by the mob, and, after taking bloody revenge, he withdrew to al-Dayr al-Abyaḍ ('the White Monastery'), near Akhmīm. From there, Bahrām wrote to al-Ḥāfiẓ, offering to retire from public life into the monastery, and asking for his Armenian supporters be given safe-conduct to depart for their native land. The caliph replied giving him the choice between continuing in office as a provincial governor and withdrawing from the world, and subsequently wrote two further letters repeating assurances to Bahrām and his closest supporters. Meanwhile, Riḍwān laid siege to the monastery until an agreement was reached – Bahrām's supporters were given safe-conduct to Cairo, and thence to Syria, while he himself was confined to the monastery.

Clearly, al-Ḥāfiẓ much preferred Bahrām to Riḍwān as his vizier, and, after two years, when Riḍwān fell from power, Bahrām was recalled to Cairo and installed in the palace, but without his former rank. He died in 1140, mourned by al-Ḥāfiẓ who followed Bahrām's bier to his grave in the Dayr al-Khandaq.[23]

In his previous letter, Roger had interceded on Bahrām's behalf, and had asked the caliph to free him from captivity. This seems to be a reference to his confinement in the White Monastery (1137–9).[24] The caliph's reply is so critical of Bahrām,

[23] Ibn Muyassar 1919, pp.78–82; al-Qalqashandī 1913–72, vol.VI, pp.458–63 (the letter of al-Ḥāfiẓ to Roger), vol.VIII, pp.260–2, and vol.XIII, pp.325–6. I have followed the reconstruction of events proposed by Canard 1954, pp.101–10 and Canard 1955b, 138–41, rather than the reinterpretation recently advanced by Dadoyan 1997, pp.90–105. The latter, following what Canard plausibly takes to be a slip by al-Qalqashandī – could there perhaps be confusion between *Shām*, 'Syria', and *Shmin*, the Coptic name of Akhmīm? – has Bahrām flee first to Syria, whence he corresponds with al-Ḥāfiẓ (and Roger!), then return to Cairo, and finally flee for a second time to Upper Egypt. I fail to see why Riḍwān should have permitted his rival to return to Cairo, and how all this could have occurred in the three months between Riḍwān's appointment to al-Gharbīya in November 1136 and Bahrām's flight to Qūṣ on 4 February 1137.

[24] See Canard 1955b, pp.140–1.

and describes Riḍwān in such glowing terms, that the latter must have drafted the letter and have then been at the height of his power. Thus, allowing time for the exchange of correspondence between Egypt and Sicily, the surviving letter of al-Ḥāfiẓ to Roger must date to late 1137 or early 1138.

The caliph's (and Riḍwān's) anxiety to justify the fall of Bahrām are remarkable. Not only did al-Ḥāfiẓ write, in what are clearly Riḍwān's words, a long account of Bahrām's crimes and punishment, but he also dispatched the letter with 'one whose trustworthiness is guaranteed by the fame of his worth' – an ambassador who, it seems to be suggested, had been authorised to give a fuller and more frank version of events than his vizier would allow the caliph to commit to paper.

It is easier to account for Roger's concern with the fate of Bahrām. Bahrām had been vizier at the time of the capture of Gerba, and must have helped to formulate the policy of tacit approval expressed in the letter of al-Ḥāfiẓ. Roger, and George of Antioch, who led the subsequent assault upon the Zīrids, would have been concerned lest the fall of Bahrām and the rise of the fanatically anti-Christian Riḍwān might cause a change in Fāṭimid policy towards Norman expansion in the central Mediterranean. At the same time, Roger had his other eye upon the Latin East, and, as Marius Canard astutely proposed, he is likely to have sought the backing of Bahrām, the Paḥlavuni prince, in his scheme to unite the crown of Sicily with the Norman principality of Antioch, where the Armenian presence was considerable.[25] Bahrām's contacts with that community were still active and close in the 1130s, for he was able to attract large numbers of Armenian supporters to Egypt at a date which, to judge by their eagerness to return home on Bahrām's fall, cannot have been long before 1137.[26] Bohemond II, prince of Antioch, the grandson of Robert Guiscard, and Roger's cousin, had died in 1130, leaving no male heir, and only a young daughter, Constance. The king of Jerusalem stood in as regent of the principality while a husband was sought for her. William of Tyre relates how, in 1135, when Raymond of Poitiers was summoned to wed Constance, Roger did everything in his power to prevent him, so that Raymond only slipped through his clutches by assuming a disguise. When Raoul de Domfront, the patriarch of Antioch, and Raymond's principal supporter, subsequently landed in Sicily on his way to Rome, Roger had him detained. Raoul was soon released, and, on his return voyage, was escorted by a squadron of Sicilian ships. William of Tyre reports the rumour that he had made a secret accord with Roger to deliver him the principality.[27] It is not difficult to imagine how interested Roger, his Antiochene vizier, and Bahrām might all have been in such a scheme.[28] Moreover, the advent of a new, and

[25] Canard 1955b, pp.141–3.

[26] I owe this useful observation to Tim Greenwood of the Oriental Institute, Oxford, who kindly cast an expert eye over my most inexpert account of Bahrām's career.

[27] William of Tyre 1986, books 14.20 and 15.12–14, vol.II, pp.657, 691–5 (trans. William of Tyre 1943, vol.II, pp.77–8, 113–14, 116).

[28] It is intriguing that one MS of Ibn Abī Dīnār's *Kitāb al-mu'nis fī akhbār Ifrīqiya wa-Tūnis* (Ibn Abī Dīnār 1967, p.89; *BAS*^{2}, vol.II, pp.601–2; *BAS*^{2}*(It.)*, vol.III, p.658) should claim of Roger II that 'his expeditions extended to the East, and he took possession of Antioch (*wa-balaghat buʿūthu-hu ilā l-mashriqi wa-malaka anṭākiyata*)'.

friendly, player in the north of the Crusader states might even have served the interests of the Fāṭimids in the south, where the fall of Tyre in 1124 had heightened the strategic importance of Ascalon.[29]

Nor should the possibility of a direct connection between George of Antioch and Bahrām be discounted. Nothing is known of George's antecedents except that he came from Antioch, but the late Bruno Lavagnini drew attention to the widespread use by Armenian nobles, since the 7th century and with increasing frequency from the 10th century, of the Greek title employed by George, ἄρχων των ἀρχόντων, 'archon of archons', and thus raised the possibility that George himself may have been Armenian.[30] Be that as it may, there was a close connection between George's family and the Paḥlavuni. Al-Maqrīzī states that, before their flight to Ifrīqiya in 408/1087–8, George and his family had been in Byzantine service 'for some time'. Bassak Paḥlavuni, Bahrām's uncle, had been Byzantine duke of Antioch until his death in 1078, when the city was annexed by Philaretus,[31] and it is legitimate to conclude that George's family, perhaps even his father Michael, had served Duke Bassak. Although no other link between George and Bahrām can be demonstrated before 1135, it is certain that the two men were aware of each other, and highly possible that they were correspondents. In any case, their common origin adds another dimension to Roger's interest in Bahrām's fate.

After the lengthy section dedicated to Bahrām, which incorporates a tedious panegyric to Riḍwān, the letter of al-Ḥāfiẓ unexpectedly changes tack. In an earlier letter, Roger's scribe had committed a gaffe, for which he had been reproved in the caliph's reply. The scribe had made his excuses in Roger's last letter, and these are now graciously accepted by the caliph (p.463, lines 4–7).[32] This passage is doubly significant. First, it reveals that the correspondence between the two sovereigns had been continuing for some time, and that at least four letters were exchanged, of which only one survives. Second, it catches a Fāṭimid scribe in the very act of correcting his Sicilian counterpart in the proper use of a phrase or formula. Canard, commenting upon this passage, remarks, 'It seems, therefore, that Roger II's chancery did not use Arabic for correspondence with Egypt and the language to which allusion is made is undoubtedly Greek'.[33] Given that Roger already possessed a sophisticated Arabic *dīwān*, it is *a priori* most unlikely that he wrote to the caliph in Greek, and Canard's interpretation of this passage is almost certainly mistaken. Rather than apologising for an error committed in translating from Arabic to Greek, the scribe is surely excusing himself for an unhappy rendition of a foreign phrase or formula, whether Greek or Latin, into Arabic.[34] As Canard rightly remarks, the term in question seems to have been a title.

[29] Riley-Smith 1997, pp.58–9; see also Brett 1995, pp.48–9.
[30] Lavagnini 1994, p.220.
[31] Dadoyan 1997, pp.76, 78, 87.
[32] *wa-ammā ʿtidhāru l-kātibi ʿammā wujjiha ilay-hi bi-an mina l-kalāmi mā idhā nuqila min lughatin ilā lughatin ukhrā iḍṭaraba mabnā-hu fa-khtalla wa-lā sīyamā in ghurisa fī-hi lafẓun laysa fī iḥdā l-lughatayni sawāʾu-hu abāna fī-mā nusiba ilay-hi l-sahwu ʿan wuḍūḥi sababi-hi wa-qad qubila ʿudhru-hu.*
[33] Canard 1955b, p.144.
[34] Noth 1983, p.216.

The letter ends by reassuring Roger that his gifts had arrived safely, and had been checked against the inventory, and deposited in the treasury (p.463, lines 8–18). Roger's ambassador had been received with due ceremony, and the caliph had appointed one Abū Manṣūr Jaᶜfar al-Ḥāfiẓī to carry this letter and his gifts to Palermo. Finally, al-Ḥāfiẓ expresses the desire to have further news of Sicily, implying that the correspondence was set to continue (p.463, lines 18–19).

Although this letter alone survives from their correspondence, Ibn Muyassar reports a further embassy in 538/1143–4, the principal concern of which was, once again, George of Antioch's assault upon Zīrid Ifrīqiya.[35] Romuald of Salerno reports that a commercial treaty was concluded with Egypt at about the same time, which was greatly to the advantage of the king of Sicily.[36] It is remarkable that even after the Sicilian assault upon Zīrid Ifrīqiya had begun in earnest, and even after Sicilian fleets had twice intercepted ships passing between the Fāṭimid and Zīrid rulers,[37] Cairo and Palermo continued to remain on such friendly terms.

The letter of al-Ḥāfiẓ gives no details of the gifts exchanged between the two monarchs, and the inventories that accompanied them are lost. Other sources reveal that one of the gifts that al-Ḥāfiẓ sent to Roger, on this or another occasion, was the ceremonial parasol, or *miẓalla*. Al-Maqrīzī's life of George of Antioch reports that Roger used to process in cavalcade preceded by the *miẓalla*,[38] and the Berber historian Ibn Ḥammād, writing in *c.*1220, gives the following report:

> The parasol which [the Fāṭimids] possessed exclusively of other dynasties resembled a shield on top of a lance, strongly made, [and] shining to behold. No little craftsmanship was expended in fashioning it, and in setting it with prominent and precious stones, which astonished and delighted the sight of the beholder. One of the knights carried [the parasol], and was called after it 'the lord of the parasol' (*ṣāḥib al-miẓalla*). Those worthy of this office took turns at it amongst themselves. [The parasol] was placed between the king and whichever direction the sun came from in order to protect him by its shade from the heat ... No kings are known to have adopted this parasol other than the Banū ᶜUbayd (*i.e.* the Fāṭimids) and, then, the king of the Europeans in Sicily. I believe that [the Fāṭimids] presented it to him as one of their gifts; it seems to me that I have heard that.[39]

[35] Ibn Muyassar 1919, p.85.

[36] Romuald of Salerno 1935, p.227: (immediately after reporting the conquest of the Ifrīqiyan coast) *Cum rege Babylonie pacem ad honorem suum et comodum fecit.*

[37] Ibn al-Athīr 1851–76, vol.XI, p.60 (*BAS*^{2}, vol.I, p.327; *BAS*^{2}*(It.)*, vol.II, p.365; al-Tījānī 1958, p.340 (*BAS*^{2}, vol.II, p.456; *BAS*^{2}*(It.)*, vol.II, p.506). [38] Above, p.82.

[39] Ibn Hammād 1927, pp.14–15, 27–28 (*BAS*^{2}, vol.I, pp.355–6; *BAS*^{2}*(It.)*, vol.II, p.394): *wa-l-miẓallatu llatī khtaṣṣū bi-hā min dūni sāʾiri l-mulūki shibhu daraqatin fī raʾsi rumḥin muḥkamatu l-ṣanᶜati rāʾiqatu l-manẓarati ṣurifa ᶜalay-hā mina l-ṣināᶜati fī l-ṣiyāghati wa-naẓmi l-aḥjāri l-ᶜāliyati l-ghāliyati mā yarūqu marʾā-hu wa-yudhishu man raʾā-hu yamsuku-hā fārisun mina l-fursāni yuᶜrafu bi-hā fa-yuqālu la-hu ṣāḥiba l-miẓallati wa-kānat ᶜinda-hum khiṭṭatun yatadāwalu-hā man huwa ahlun la-hā fa-yuḥādhī bi-hā l-malika min ḥaythu kānati l-shamsu yaqī-hi ḥarra-hā bi-ẓilli-hā ... wa-lā yuᶜlamu aḥadun mina l-mulūki ttakhadha hādhihi l-miẓallata illā banū ᶜubaydin khāṣṣatan thumma maliku l-rūmi bi-ṣiqillīyata wa-aḥsibu anna-hum ahdaw-hā ilay-hi fī baᶜḍi hadāyā-hum wa-ka-annī samiᶜtu hādhā*. (The treatment of this passage by Halm 1996, p.352, is imprecise.) On the use of the ceremonial parasol see: al-Qalqashandī 1913–72, vol.III, p.473, and vol.II, p.133, vol.III, pp.469, 502, 506, 509, 512, 515, 517, vol.V, pp.28, 300–1, 334; the references to the court activity of the *ṣāḥib al-miẓalla* to al-Ẓāhir in al-Musabbiḥī 1978–84, pp.61, 66, 70, 86, 99; the bibliography cited by Canard 1955b, p.126, n.5; Espéronnier 1988, p.49; Sanders 1994, pp.25–6, and index.

King Roger also imported from Fāṭimid Egypt aspects of palace architecture and decoration. This is not the place for a full discussion of a subject which merits a book of its own. An extremely brief summary must suffice. The palaces built under Roger and his two successors, such as the Royal Palace, la Favara, l'Uscibene, la Zisa, and la Cuba, do not descend from any earlier structures yet discovered in Sicily.[40] But it has long been recognised that they do share many features of design, structure and decoration in common with the Ifrīqiyan palaces of the Fāṭimids, which were imitated by their Berber successors, the Zīrids and the Ḥammādids.[41] It is not possible to make a direct contrast between the palace architecture of Sicily and Cairo, because the sad surviving fragments of the Fāṭimid palaces there do not constitute a sufficient basis for comparison,[42] but the tradition followed by the Sicilian palaces was introduced to Ifrīqiya by the Fāṭimids, who rejected the archaic, early Islamic palace architecture of the Aghlabids in favour of a distinctive new style.[43]

Palace decoration is a more fruitful field for inquiry. Elsewhere, I have already remarked upon the parallels between the Arabic inscriptions which decorated the Royal Palace in Palermo, and which called upon Roger's courtiers to treat the building as an analogue of the Ka^{c}ba at Mecca, and Fāṭimid panegyric which figured the caliph's palace in precisely the same terms.[44] In the same article, I compared the painted depictions of a seated ruler from the ceiling of the Cappella Palatina, made for King Roger in *c.*1140–7,[45] with a relief carving of a seated ruler from the Fāṭimid palace at al-Mahdīya. Furthermore, I am convinced that a careful analysis of the iconography, style and technique of the painting of the ceiling, in its full historical context, leads inevitably to the conclusion that it was largely the work of an atelier of artists imported from Fāṭimid Egypt,[46] in much the same way that the contemporary mosaics in the sanctuary of the chapel were executed by a school of craftsmen imported from Constantinople.[47] In a similar vein, Avinoam Shalem has recently discussed how the carving of hard stone, such as porphyry and rock crystal, in Norman Palermo drew upon Fāṭimid traditions of rock crystal and ivory carving.[48] Again, the craftsmen who carved the panels for the wooden doors of

[40] The bibliography is extensive: see Di Stefano 1978; Ciotta 1993; Meier 1994; Bellafiore 1996; all with good bibliography.

[41] For example: Marçais 1955, 124–5; Golvin 1957, pp.194, 197, 203–4.

[42] Russell 1964; Hampikian and Cyran 1999; Sayyid 1999.

[43] For Aghlabid palace architecture, see al-Shābbī 1968.

[44] Johns 1993, pp.149–53; Johns 1995b, pp.31–40.

[45] In all probability the ceiling was completed by 29 June 1143: see Johns forthcoming c.

[46] I hope to publish, in the near future, a detailed argument to this effect. Meanwhile, for alternative views (and for illustrations of the ceiling) see: Ettinghausen 1942; Grabar 1957; Monneret de Villard 1950; Ettinghausen 1962, pp.44–50; Gabrieli and Scerrato 1979, pp.40–96, 359–98; Jones 1972; D'Erme 1997; and, especially, Grube forthcoming (with exhaustive bibliography).

[47] Kitzinger 1990, pp.243–4, compares the mosaics in the dome of the Cappella Palatina to a votive panel in the south gallery of Hagia Sophia which shows John II Comnenos and his family paying homage to the Virgin. He concludes: 'it is reasonable to suppose that the craftsmen who came to Palermo were schooled by those who had worked for the Emperor in the Great Church'.

[48] Vessels and other objects of carved rock crystal featured largely in the Fāṭimid treasury, and were frequently exchanged between rulers. The so-called Saint-Denis Ewer, now in the Louvre, is

George of Antioch's church, and the jambs from the adjacent Casa Martorana were trained in the Fāṭimid school.[49] All of these borrowings attest to the importation, not so much of ideas and objects, as of the craftsmen themselves.

To sum up this discussion of relations between Norman Sicily and Fāṭimid Egypt, there is ample evidence from a range of independent sources that, for at least twenty years (1123–43), the two courts maintained close, friendly, and regular contact with each other. Throughout this time, al-Ḥāfiẓ and Roger exchanged embassies, gifts, and letters. The caliph presented Roger with the ceremonial parasol, which a somewhat later, provincial, historian of the dynasty believed – wrongly – to be a *regalium* exclusive to the Fāṭimids. Each ruler engaged in trade on his own behalf in the country of the other, and protected the other's interests in his own land. Roger's intercession on behalf of Bahrām, the Christian Armenian vizier of al-Ḥāfiẓ, should probably be attributed to Bahrām's support for Roger's ambitions in Ifrīqiya and, perhaps, also in the principality of Antioch. Bahrām's uncle, Bassak Paḥlavuni, had been Byzantine duke of Antioch and, in all probability, had employed George of Antioch's family. George himself led several embassies to Cairo, and traded in Egypt on his own behalf, benefiting from the exemption from import and export taxes granted him by the caliph. George drafted Roger's correspondence with al-Ḥāfiẓ, and his master's interest in Bahrām may have been stimulated by the connection between the two viziers. On a different level, Egyptian craftsmen were attracted to Palermo, and were employed by Roger and his leading courtiers to build and decorate their palaces and churches. They included painters, carvers of wood and hard stone, and master builders and masons. Significantly, there is no evidence for the migration of craftsmen of the minor arts, such as potters – the attraction was Roger's court, not Sicily in general. All this amounts to an undeniable case that relations between Cairo and Palermo were such that elements of *dīwānī* practice and structure *could* have been imported from Egypt to Sicily, precisely in time to have influenced the renaissance of the Arabic administration. What is more, George of Antioch is shown to have been a key link in the chain between the two courts, so that he *could* have been the agent responsible for such imports.

The next stage in this argument is to establish that the renaissance of the Sicilian *dīwān* in the 1130s involved wholesale importation from a contemporary Islamic chancery. This is most readily seen in the Arabic titles of the Norman rulers, and I shall begin with these, before proceeding to discuss other elements of *dīwānī* practice and structure.

possibly the *lagena* given by Roger II to Count Theobald of Blois-Champagne, and by him to Abbot Suger. If so, then Roger almost certainly had it from al-Ḥāfiẓ (*Saint-Denis* 1991, no.27, pp.168–72; Montesquiou-Fezensac 1973–7, vol.I, no.33, p.153, vol.II, no.33, pp.124–6, vol.III, pp.44–5, pls 26–7; Gaborit-Chopin 1986, pp.284–5; Panofsky 1979, pp.78, 221–2). The Saint-Denis ewer is universally attributed to Fāṭimid Egypt (Lamm 1930, vol.I, pp.193–4, vol.II, pl.67/3). The ewer is enriched by gold-filigree mounts which have been identified as the work of the royal atelier of Palermo (Lipinsky 1973–4, pp.432–6). (For the identification of a Palermitan workshop dedicated to the carving of hard stone in the Fāṭimid tradition, see Shalem 1999.)

49 Gabrieli and Scerrato 1979, figs 114–16, 197–8, pp.522–4.

The Arabic titles of the Norman rulers of Sicily

In 1986, I was commissioned by the *Bollettino di Numismatica* to prepare a study of the Arabic titles of the Norman rulers of Sicily. I transcribed as many titles as I could find from coins, documents, inscriptions, and literary sources, and sorted them in chronological order. It was immediately apparent that the development of the Arabic titles had occurred in three stages, of which the third was dramatically distinct from its predecessors.[50] Until that moment I had not seriously doubted Michele Amari's conclusion that the Norman kings had followed the ways of the Kalbid emirs of Sicily, and had inherited from them all the Arab aspects of their rule.[51] This study of the development of the Arabic titles was to become the basis for a radically different interpretation of the Arab facet of the Sicilian monarchy.

In the first stage, Robert Guiscard, Roger Borsa, Roger I, and the young Count Roger II were content to do no more than to convert their Latin feudal titles into Arabic. Thus, *dux* and *comes* were transliterated, not translated, into Arabic as *al-dūqa* and *al-qūmis* – *Rogerius comes Siciliae* became *Rujār qūmis Ṣiqillīya*.[52] In the second stage, which chronologically partly overlaps the first, Robert Guiscard, Roger I, Adelaide and Count Roger II, all employed Arabic translations, not transliterations, of their Greek and Latin titles, including *malik* (fem. *malika*), *sulṭān*, *sayyida*, and *mawlā* (fem. *mawlāt*) – *Rogerius comes Siciliae* became *Rujār sulṭān Ṣiqillīya*.[53] The third stage in the development of the Arabic titles of the Norman rulers opens with the coronation of Roger II in 1130, and marks a sudden and dramatic break with the past. While Robert Guiscard and Roger I had merely transliterated their Latin feudal titles into Arabic, and Adelaide and the young Roger II had simply sought Arabic equivalents for their Greek and Latin styles, King Roger II imported an entire system of titulature from an Islamic chancery.

During the 1130s and '40s, the Arabic title of the Sicilian king rapidly reached its mature form, which was to remain constant until the fall of the dynasty. The *ism*, or personal name of the ruler – *Rujār, Ghulyālim, Tanqrīr* – or an impersonal substitute – for example, *al-ḥaḍra*, 'the presence' – was accompanied by the dynastic title of the de Hautevilles – *al-malik al-muʿaẓẓam*, 'the glorified king' – and by one or more royal *alqāb*, or epithets, chosen from a fairly wide repertoire. In addition, the territorial dominions of the king were listed: Italy, Langobardia, Calabria, Sicily and – for a short time under Roger II – Ifrīqiya. Finally, two specifically Christian titles were also employed: 'the defender of the Pope of Rome' and 'the protector of the Christian community'.

After the coronation of Roger II, the de Hautevilles consistently used the Arabic title *malik* as the equivalent of the Latin *rex* and Greek *rēx*. Although *malik* had been used by Robert Guiscard as early as 1072,[54] this element of the regnal formula later became so distinctive that, under Roger II, it was considered sufficient to

[50] Johns 1986. [51] Amari 1933–9, vol.III, p.875.
[52] For example, Travaini 1995, pp.109–13 (on p.113, read *naṣara-hu*?).
[53] Johns 1986, nos 1, 8–10 and 13–15. [54] Travaini 1995, pp.109–10.

distinguish the king from his father, and thus, after Roger's coronation, no further use was made of the ordinal number *al-thānī*, 'the second', which had been employed before 1130 – Roger II was simply *Rujār al-malik*. In addition, King Roger experimented with a wide variety of royal *alqāb*, only a few of which were incorporated into the 'official' royal protocol. The inscription from the so-called 'Coronation Robe', made in the royal *ṭirāz* in Palermo in 1133–4, lists approximately twenty such *alqāb*,[55] and the painted inscriptions on the ceiling of the Cappella Palatina amount to litany of royal power, in which some thirty kingly *alqāb* are repeated over and over again in various combinations.[56] None of these 'unofficial' *alqāb*, however, was included in the 'official' royal title, which was used principally in the products of the *dīwān* and the mint.

The dynastic title, *al-malik al-muᶜaẓẓam*, 'the glorified king', was the only *laqab* to be used by all the Norman kings (with the exception of the short-lived child, William III).[57] Following standard Islamic practice, each of the Sicilian kings was distinguished from the other members of his dynasty by means of a *laqab* exclusive to him alone; the pathetic figure of William III used the same *laqab* as Roger II during his brief reign, perhaps in a desperate bid for legitimacy.

- Roger II: *al-muᶜtazz bi-llāh,* 'the powerful through God'[58]
- William I: *al-hādī bi-amri llāh,* 'the guide according to the command of God'[59]
- William II: *al-mustaᶜizz bi-llāh,* 'the desirous of power through God'[60]
- Tancred: *al-manṣūr bi-llāh,* 'the assisted to victory by God'[61]
- William III: *al-muᶜtazz bi-llāh,* 'the powerful through God'[62]

These personal *alqāb* are all of the same form, a compound of two parts: the first is an active participle (*al-muᶜtazz,* 'the powerful'; *al-hādī*, lit. 'the guiding'; *al-mustaᶜizz,* lit. 'the desiring of power') or an adjectival passive (*al-manṣūr*, 'the victorious', lit. 'assisted to victory'), which emphasises that the sovereign's authority and power came from God; the second is the complement (*bi-llāh*, 'by' or 'through God'; *bi-amri llāh*, 'by the command of God'), which makes the theocratic principle explicit. Two pairs of supplementary *alqāb*, one used by Roger II (*al-muqtadiru bi-qudrati-hi l-manṣūr bi-qūwati-hi*, 'the potent through His omnipotence, the victorious through His strength')[63] and the other by William II (*al-muᶜtaḍidu bi-qudrati-hi l-mustanṣiru bi-qūwati-hi*, 'the aided by His omnipotence, the victorious through His strength'),[64] both have the same form.

[55] Bock 1864, vol.I, pp.27–31 and vol.II, tab.6, fig.8.

[56] Amari 1875, part1, no.6, pp.32–42, pl.3–4 (Amari 1971, pp.47–58); Monneret de Villard 1950, pp.31–3, 65–6 and plates cited. This is not the place to rehearse my many criticisms of Sinding-Larsen 1989. See also below, p.280. [57] Above, p.137.

[58] Travaini 1995, pp.119–23, 209; al-Idrīsī, 1970–6, p.4, lines 1–2; above, p.136, note 73 (1149 inscription). [59] Travaini 1995, pp.124–5.

[60] Travaini 1995, pp.125–9, 230–1; ***Dīwānī* 38, 43–5**; Amari 1875, part 1, nos 10–11, pp.58–76, pls 5, 7 (Amari 1971, pp.77–99); Bock 1864, vol.I, pp.32–5, vol.II, tab.VII, fig.9 (the alba of William II, 1181 A.D.); and vol.I, 56–8, vol.II, tab.XII, fig.XV (the leggings of William II);

[61] Travaini 1995, pp.129–32, 232–3. [62] Travaini 1995, pp.132–3.

[63] Above, p.136, note 73 (1149 inscription).

[64] ***Dīwānī* 38, 43–5**; Amari 1875, part 1, nos 10–11, pp.58–76, pls 5, 7 (Amari 1971, pp.77–99); Bock 1864, vol.I, pp.32–5, vol.II, tab.VII, fig.9 (the alba of William II, 1181 A.D.); and vol.I, 56–8, vol.II, tab.XII, fig.XV (the leggings of William II);

The Norman king was occasionally referred to by his personal *laqab* alone. William II, who was the only Norman always to incorporate his personal *laqab* into his Arabic title, was also known by it alone: for example, in the monumental inscriptions on William II's palaces, he is called *al-Musta^cizz* on La Cuba,[65] and on La Zisa it is proclaimed, 'This is *al-Musta^cizz* (William II) and this is *al-^cAzīz* (the palace of the Zisa)'.[66] A reference to La Favara (*al-Fawwāra*, 'the Fountain'), a suburban palace of Roger II, as *al-Mu^ctazzīya*, from Roger's personal *laqab*, *al-mu^ctazz*, indicates that this practice began as early as the 1130s.[67]

Armand Abel first pointed out the difference between the submissive titles of the early ^cAbbāsid caliphs, that were typically formed of adjectives or participles of a passive or reflexive character which stressed the bearer's reliance upon, and submission to, God, such as *al-Muṭī^c bi-llāh*, 'he who obeys God', and the more exuberant titles of their principal rivals to the caliphate, the Fāṭimids, that used active participles or adjectives to emphasise the rôle of the caliph as God's agent in this world, such as *al-Qā^ɔim bi-amri llāh*, 'he who takes charge of the execution of God's command'.[68] The personal *alqāb* of the Norman kings follow the ^cAbbāsid tradition.[69] The *alqāb*, al-Manṣūr (754–75), al-Hādī (785–6), al-Mu^ctazz (866–9), al-Mu^ctaḍid (892–902), and al-Muqtadir (908–32), all used by the Normans, had all been the titles of early ^cAbbāsid caliphs. I shall return to the significance of this below.

A little after the coronation of King Roger, the reverential Islamic usage was adopted whereby the ruler is not named directly but, rather, referred to obliquely, by means of an impersonal substitute for his name or title. Thus, for example, the *follis* of 1141–2 was issued not 'by order of the king', but 'by the ruling order', *bi-l-amr al-mālikīy*.[70] Similarly, as we saw in Chapter 5, the *dispositiones* of the *jarā^ɔid* renewed in 1145 all opened with the formula *kharaja l-amru … l-rujārīyu*, 'there went forth the … Rogerian order'.[71] Here, the personal name of the king has been transformed into a *nisba* (a relative adjective with a final *-īy*), 'the Rogerian'; a convention continued under William II – *al-ghulyālimīy*, 'the Williamian'.[72] In the *narrationes* of the 1145 renewals, Roger II is also referred to obliquely as *al-majlis al-sāmī*, 'the most exalted seat'. Again under Roger II, a third method of indirect reference to the sovereign is first employed – in two Palermitan inscriptions, Roger appears as *al-ḥaḍra al-malakīya*, 'the ruling presence'.[73] This use of *al-ḥaḍra* was continued under William II.[74]

The king's full Arabic title also included two distinctly Christian elements: *mu^cizz imām Rūmīya*, 'the defender of the pope of Rome', and *al-nāṣir li-l-milla*

[65] Amari 1875, part 1, no.11, p.72 (Amari 1971, p.95).
[66] Amari 1875, part 1, no.10, p.61 (Amari 1971, p.81).
[67] Rubric to verses on La Favara by ^cAbd al-Raḥmān of Trapani: ^cImād al-Dīn 1964–9, vol.I, p.26 (*BAS*², vo.2, p.708; *BAS*²*(It.)*, vol.III, pp.762–3).
[68] Abel 1957, pp.39–40.
[69] Contrary to my assertion in Johns 1986, p.23.
[70] Travaini 1995, pp.299–300.
[71] Above, p.136.
[72] For example, ***Dīwānī* 38, 43–5**.
[73] Above, p.136, note 73 (1149 inscription), and Amari 1879, part 2, no.17, pp.80–94, pl.9/2 (Amari 1971, pp.212–14).
[74] For example, ***Dīwānī* 38, 43–5**.

al-naṣrānīya, 'the protector of the Christian community'.[75] The latter formula is clearly related to the Greek style τῶν Χριστιανῶν βοηθός (*tōn Christianōn boēthos*, 'defender of the Christians') which was a standard element of the Greek title of Roger II and his successors. If the documents in which Roger I appears as τῶν Χριστιανῶν βοηθός are either forgeries or to be attributed to his son,[76] then the formula first appears in 1109, in Arabic, when Adelaide is styled *al-nāṣira li-dīn al-naṣrānīya*, 'the protectress of the Christian religion' (***Dīwānī* 7**).

I am inclined to suspect that both Christian formulae were awarded to the Norman ruler by an Islamic chancery. Amongst the titles given to the Doge of Venice by the Egyptian chancery are the almost identical formulae, *muᶜizz pāpā Rūmīya*, 'defender of the pope of Rome', and *majd al-milla al-naṣrānīya*, 'the glory of the Christian religion'.[77] This close parallel may indicate that such Christian formulae were selected by a foreign scribe from amongst what al-Qalqashandī calls *al-alqāb al-uṣūl*,[78] the repertoire of stock titles kept by an Islamic chancery, and applied to Christian rulers in diplomatic correspondence.

Alongside the *alqāb* of the Sicilian kings, must be considered the *adᶜiya*, or augural formulae, which typically followed the royal title and, in a sense, belonged to it. There follows the complete repertoire, in chronological order:

- Roger II (1142): *al-ḥaḍra ... abbada llāhu ayyāma-hā wa-ayyada aᶜlāma-hā*, 'the presence ... may God prolong its days and give strength to its banners!'[79]
- Roger II (1143): *al-malik ... khallada llāhu mulka-hu*, 'the king ... may God perpetuate his rule!' (***Dīwānī* 20**)
- Roger I (posthumously, 1145): *al-sulṭānu l-kabīru qaddasa llāhu rūḥa-hu wa-nawwara ḍarīḥa-hu*, 'the great sultan may God sanctify his spirit and illuminate his tomb!' (***Dīwānī* 21 and 25**)
- Roger II (1148): *al-ḥaḍra ... ṣammada llāhu mamlakata-hā*, 'the presence ... may God preserve its rule!'[80]
- Margaret and William II (1169): *al-malik ... wa ... l-malika ... khallada llāhu ayyāma-humā wa-naṣara aᶜlāma-humā*, 'the king ... and ... the queen ... may God perpetuate their days and assist their banners [against the enemy]!' (***Dīwānī* 38**)

[75] Above, p.136, note 73 (1149 inscription); al-Idrīsī, 1970–6, p.4, lines 1–2; ***Dīwānī* 38, 43–5**; Bock 1864, vol.I, pp.32–5, vol.II, tab.VII, fig.9 (the alba of William II). The *tarì* struck for King Roger and his successors in the mint of Salerno bore the title, on the obverse, *nāṣir al-naṣrānīya*, 'the protector of Christianity': Travaini 1995, pp.173–4, 179–80, 181–2.

[76] von Falkenhausen 1997, pp.281–2 and n.176 (citing *Messina* 1994, no.16, p.155), pp.293–4 and n.249.

[77] For the titles conferred upon Christian sovereigns by the Egyptian chancery, see al-Qalqashandī 1913–72, vol.VIII, pp.33–53; Amari, 1883–4; Lammens 1903; Lammens 1904; Bosworth 1972. The fact that, amongst the titles attributed to the pope was *mumallik mulūk al-naṣrānīya*, 'he who confers upon the kings of Christendom their authority to rule', raises the fascinating and pertinent question of the extent to which Christian rulers were able to influence the formulation of the Arabic titles awarded to them by Egyptian secretaries. Below, p.273–4.

[78] al-Qalqashandī 1913–72, vol.V, pp.493–8.

[79] Amari 1875, part 1, no.2, pp.17–25, pl.1/3 (Amari 1971, pp.29–39).

[80] Above, p.136, note 73 (1149 inscription).

- William II (1178, 1182): *al-ḥaḍra … khallada llāhu ayyāma-hā wa-naṣara aᶜlāma-hā wa-naffadha aḥkāma-hā*, 'the presence … may God perpetuate its days, and assist its standards, and fulfil its ordinances!' (***Dīwānī* 43–4**)
- William II (1183): *al-ḥaḍra … khallada llāhu mamlakata-hā wa-ayyāma-hā wa-abbada duhūra-hā wa-aᶜwāma-hā wa-naṣara juyūsha-hā wa-aᶜlāma-hā wa-ayyada suyūfa-hā wa-aqlāma-hā*, 'the presence … may God perpetuate its reign and its days, make eternal its ages and its years, assist its armies and its standards, and support its swords and its pens!' (***Dīwānī* 45**)
- Tancred (n.d.): *al-malik … khallada llāhu mulka-hu*, 'the king … may God perpetuate his rule!'[81]

It may be significant that the earliest known example of a *duᶜāʾ* referring to a Sicilian king comes in the letter of al-Ḥāfiẓ to King Roger: *waffaqa-hu llāhu fī maqāṣidi-hi wa-arshada-hu ilā al-ᶜamali bi-ṭāᶜati-hi fī maṣādiri-hi wa-mawāridi-hi*, 'may God grant him success in his plans, and guide him to act in obedience to Him from his every going out to every his coming in!'[82] This formula does not appear, however, on any known product of the royal *dīwān*.

I have dwelt at such length, here, upon the Arabic titles of the Sicilian kings, despite having already discussed King Roger's titles in Chapter 5, for three main reasons. First, to emphasise the revolution that occurred after 1130. No indigenous, insular process of evolution could have brought about the radical transformation of the Arabic title that occurred so rapidly in the 1130s and '40s, but only the importation of a complete system of titulature.

Second, as the continuing development of the Arabic title under King Roger and his successors clearly demonstrates, the system imported was not dead and fossilised in an unchanging form, but very much alive. No further revolutions occurred, comparable to that of *c.*1130, but the royal *alqāb* and *adᶜiya* continued to develop until the fall of the dynasty. What this suggests is that the new system of titulature was not imported to Sicily on paper, in a form already fixed, but that it was carried to Palermo as a living tradition by scribes who had been well trained in its use.

Third and finally, the relationship between the Norman king and the Fāṭimid caliph presented their scribes with a tricky problem of protocol: how could the conventions of Arabic diplomatics be employed to accommodate the conflicting claims of the two rulers? The Fāṭimid chancery, of course, could not accept the basis of the authority and legitimacy claimed by the Christian king. It is clear from the surviving letter that Roger had expanded upon the blessings and gifts he had received from God. In his reply, the caliph is gently but firmly dismissive: God favours each of His servants according to his deserts, and reserves His most perfect reward for His servant and representative, the Commander of the Faithful, the rightly-guided imam. The caliph's authority and legitimacy derives from 'his ancestor, Muḥammad, the Seal of the Prophets, the Lord of the Messengers', through 'his unblemished family, the rightly-guided imams', while Roger is merely *de facto* 'the ruler (*al-malik*) of the island of Sicily'.

[81] Travaini 1995, pp.231–2. [82] al-Qalqashandī 1913–72, vol.VI, p.458, line 5.

In Chapter 5, I showed that almost all the elements of the royal titles and *adᶜiya* employed in the renewals of 1145 are attested in the Fāṭimid chancery.[83] Here, I wish to stress only that the Arabic titles of the Norman kings were those that the Fāṭimid chancery would have considered most appropriate to a foreign potentate, to a vizier, or to a great lord, rather than to the caliph himself. Thus, the personal *alqāb* of the Norman kings stressed their dependence upon God, and not, like the titles of the Fāṭimids, their active rôle as the agents of God's will.[84] The Arabic style, *al-malik*, which the Norman kings adopted was generally reserved by the Fāṭimid chancery for foreign potentates and for viziers, and certainly carried none of the hierocratic and theocratic connotations of *imām* and *khalīfa*. After the fall of Bahrām in 1137, all the Fāṭimid viziers were styled *al-malik*.[85] Similarly, the strings of *alqāb* and *adᶜiya* used in the *dīwānī* documents from Sicily are inspired by the long lists of grandiose titles used from the last quarter of the 11th century onwards by Fāṭimid viziers, and not by the titles of the caliphs themselves.[86] Again, according to Ibn Shīth, some authorities held that the titles *al-ḥaḍra* and *al-majlis* were most appropriate to the leading men of the state below the rank of vizier.[87] All this seems to suggest that the Norman king was sent a package of titles which had been carefully selected for him by the Egyptian chancery. This was certainly done for Roger's vizier, George of Antioch, whose titles in the letter of al-Ḥāfiẓ to his master are extremely close to those given him in al-Maqrīzī's short biography.[88] The way in which, as we learn from the caliph's letter, a Fāṭimid scribe intervened on at least one occasion to correct the language of a Sicilian scribe – most probably, as Canard remarked, a title – further suggests that the Fāṭimid chancery continued to monitor the development of the Norman titles.[89]

But this is not the full story. The Egyptian chancery believed that the pope, the 'imam of Rome', occupied the same position amongst the Christians as the Fāṭimid imam claimed amongst the Muslims. Moreover, the pope was 'he who gives royal authority to the kings of Christendom' (*mumallikun mulūki l-naṣrānīyati*).[90] Of course, neither imamate could recognise the basis upon which its rival claimed authority: the caliph was an anti-pope; the pope an anti-caliph. The Sicilian royal title *muᶜizz imām Rūmīya*, 'the defender of the imam of Rome', thus implied that the king's royal authority was derived from the pope, from the anti-caliph.

This contraposition of an imamate and an anti-imamate offered multiple solutions to the tricky problem of protocol. The caliph could either interpret the king's Arabic titles as those appropriate to his inferior, or dismiss them as deriving from the illegitimate imamate of Rome.[91] The king could accept Arabic titles appropriate to

83 Above, pp.134–9. 84 Above, pp.269–70.

85 On the devaluation of the title *al-malik*, see al-Bāshā 1957, pp.496–502; Ayalon 1987, p.261.

86 Above, p.136, and note 72. 87 Above, p.137, note 79. 88 Above, p.82, note 136.

89 Above, p.264 and note 32.

90 al-Qalqashandī 1913–72, vol.V, p.472, and vol.VI, p.173; trans. Bosworth 1972, pp.67, 72. The distant influence of the papal chancery may also be discerned: *ibid.*, p.72, n.9.

91 Although there is no evidence that the Egyptian chancery ever used the title *muᶜizz imām Rūmīya* of the Sicilian king, it did address the Doge of Venice by an almost identical title – *muᶜizz pāpā Rūmīya*, 'defender of the pope of Rome': above, p.271, note 77.

a servant of the caliph and thus appear in the guise of great Islamic lord, because they proclaimed his allegiance to the Roman imamate, the assertion of which denied the legitimacy of the Fāṭimid imam. Such sophistry would not have appealed to the rulers themselves: neither Roger nor al-Ḥāfiẓ would have doubted that the basis of the other's claim to authority was illegitimate, and neither would have hesitated to say so. This diplomatic equivocation was rather devised by and for their ministers and scribes, perhaps first in Cairo, and then in Palermo, conceivably after consulting the papal chancery.

Al-dīwān al-maᶜmūr and the *dīwān al-taḥqīq al-maᶜmūr*

The titles and structure of the Sicilian *dīwān* also indicate Fāṭimid influence. Before 1130, only lone scribes, such as Abū l-Ḍawʾ, appear, and there is no trace of a *dīwān* in the sense of a specialised office dedicated to the issue of documents in Arabic, to the preservation of Arabic archives, and to administration on the basis of Arabic records. The early development of such a *dīwān* can be traced only from March 1132, little more than a year after Roger's coronation. The first of its products about which information survives, the *jarīda* of the villeins of Mutata (***Dīwānī* 10**), was compiled by George of Antioch. Twenty-two genuine Arabic and bilingual documents are known to have been issued by the royal *dīwān* under King Roger, an average of one a year; whereas only eight or so Arabic and bilingual documents are known from the previous forty years, all concentrated into the period 1093–1111. During the early to mid 1140s, at least six scribes were employed by the *dīwān* in writing documents that were issued to external recipients, and other staff were employed in an administrative and directorial capacity.[92] Thus, before the death of George of Antioch in 1151, a professional, sophisticated *dīwān*, with an articulated bureaucratic structure, and with its own specialised staff, archives, and established forms and practices, was firmly installed in the royal palace at Palermo.

The Arabic titles of the royal *dīwān* reflect Fāṭimid usage. *Al-maᶜmūr* was an epithet applied to the Fāṭimid *dīwān al-inshāʾ*,[93] and, before 1149, an office with the title of *dīwān al-taḥqīq* is known only in Fāṭimid Egypt. There, it was introduced by the Muslim Armenian vizier, al-Afḍal, in 501/1107–8, in order to supervise his reforms of the fiscal administration and of the system of *iqṭāᶜāt*. As was argued in Chapter 8, the circumstances surrounding both the creation of the *dīwān al-taḥqīq* by al-Afḍal, and the foundation of an office bearing the same name in Norman Sicily, are so similar that it is legitimate to conclude that the Sicilian office was introduced on the Egyptian model.[94] This might indicate the presence, in the Sicilian *dīwān*, of an Egyptian administrator or scribe who either had witnessed al-Afḍal's reforms, or had detailed knowledge of them.

[92] Below, p.276. [93] Stern 1964a, no.3, p.36, line 18. [94] Above, pp.195–8.

The Arabic scripts of the royal *dīwān*

Turning from administrative structure to practice, the most conspicuous of the external features exhibited by the products of the royal *dīwān* is the new, elegant, and highly professional *dīwānī* script which is employed in all but two royal documents.[95] Each of the four surviving Arabic documents from the comital period (***Dīwānī* 2, 4, 7 and 8**) is written by a different hand, and in a different script, none of which can be considered the ancestor of the royal *dīwānī* .[96] No administrative or legal documents survive in their original form from Muslim Sicily, nor from contemporary Ifrīqiya. Somewhat later Almohad and Ḥafṣid documents are written in Maghribī script, which has nothing in common with Sicilian *dīwānī*.[97] None of the rare surviving pre-Norman scripts from South Italy and Sicily bears comparison with the royal *dīwānī*.[98] In Norman Sicily, the royal script is not encountered outside the ambit of the royal palace and the court, and the private documents of the island display a variety of scripts none of which is closely related to that of the royal *dīwān*, while many of them exhibit strong Maghribī features.[99] The late Albrecht Noth gave an accurate preliminary account of the *dīwānī* script under Roger II, which must for the moment suffice until the planned edition and analysis of all of the Arabic documents from Norman Sicily is complete. Noth characterised Roger II's *dīwānī* (script RA1) as follows:

> an extremely elegant and fluid style, that presents all the characteristics of an administrative script ... There can be no doubt that we are confronted with a *ductus*, the mastery of which required a particular training, and not with an everyday or library hand that could be written once one had simply learned to write. More important to such a chancery – or *dīwānī* – script than easy legibility and the observance of basic rules, were decorative effects and effortless elegance. Thus RA1 is a script which is extremely beautiful from the aesthetic point of view, but is certainly not easy to read.[100]

The 11th-century Fāṭimid *kātib* ᶜAlī ibn Khalaf, author of a style-book for secretaries, distinguishes between two kinds of script: *muḥaqqaq*, 'exact', and *muṭlaq*,

[95] The exceptions are ***Dīwānī* 30**, written in the script termed RA2 by Noth 1983, p.204; a clear, careful, but rather laboured hand, which Noth termed 'una scrittura scolastica'('eine schulmäßige Schrift'). It seems to be RA2 that the forger of ***Dīwānī* †27** took as his model. ***Dīwānī* 46**, the sole surviving Arabic document of Frederick II, is not written in the Norman *dīwānī* script.

[96] ***Dīwānī* 2**: Johns 1983, vol.II, pl.1. ***Dīwānī* 4**: Johns 1983, vol.II, pl.2. ***Dīwānī* 7**: Noth 1983, pl.III. ***Dīwānī* 8**: Guillou 1963, pls II.a–b.

[97] See, for example: the letter of al-Murtaḍā to Pope Innocent IV (648/1250): Tisserant and Wiet, 1926, plates I–II; and the Ḥafṣid documents illustrated in Giménez Soler 1907, plates 1–5. See also Stern 1964a, pp.135–7 and notes.

[98] The unique Palermo *Qurʾān* of 372/982–3, fragments of which are in Istanbul (Nuruosmaniye Library, MS 23) and London (Khalili Collection, QUR261, QUR368), resembles nothing known from Norman Sicily: Déroche 1992, no.81, p.146, and plates. Nor does the bilingual St Luke of 1043 from Calabria or Sicily, now in Paris (Bibl. Nat., MS Suppl. Gr. no.911): Géhin 1997. In both, the scripts are 'kufic', *i.e.* Déroche's 'New Style'.

[99] See, for example, Cusa 1868–82, pl.IA: an act of sale from Palermo, 1161 (= **Private 9**).

[100] Noth 1983, p.204. It should be noted that RA1 is, in fact, far more easily read than some of the private scripts of Norman Sicily.

'unrestrained'. He claims that *muḥaqqaq* was used for all important documents, including appointments, registrations, grants of property, 'and letters addressed by kings to kings which must indicate the importance of the sender and the addressee'. '*Muṭlaq* is such that its letters run into each other and are joined together ... It appears more pleasing to the eye [than *muḥaqqaq*] as long as one looks at it as a whole, but as soon as the single letters are distinguished and are compared with the letters of *muḥaqqaq*, it becomes manifest how great the difference is'.[101] The surviving products of the Fāṭimid chancery are no less legible, no more 'unrestrained', than those of the Norman *dīwān*, but it is nonetheless intriguing that the Sicilian *dīwān* should have chosen to adopt such an elegant, but difficult, script: a point to which I shall return in Chapter 11.

Noth identified three different varieties of *dīwānī* in the documents of King Roger,[102] but this can now be extended. For example, each of the three copies of the *ḥudūd* for San Giorgio di Triocala (***Dīwānī* 15–17**) was written by a different hand, none of which corresponds to any of Noth's three varieties. Indeed, the scribe of ***Dīwānī* 17** was certainly no master of the *dīwānī* that he sought to reproduce: perhaps a trainee was allowed to write this copy. A preliminary estimate, therefore, indicates that, in the early to mid 1140s, King Roger's *dīwān* employed at least five or six professional scribes, and at least one trainee (or non-professional) scribe.[103]

As to the origins of the scribes and their scripts, it is my preliminary impression that some features which are traditionally held to be characteristically Maghribī – such as *fāʾ* with the point below the letter, *qāf* with a single point above – do occur in *dīwānī* products, but neither frequently, nor with significant regularity, while they tend to be more commonly attested in private documents from Norman Sicily. Other features which tend to be regarded as typically Maghribī – such as the prolongation of terminal *nūn* under the letters that follow it, or the similar profiles of the terminal loops of *qāf* and *nūn* – are indeed standard features of Sicilian *dīwānī*, but are also characteristic of the products of the Fāṭimid chancery and of other contemporary Levantine scripts: they should not, therefore, be regarded as indicating Maghribī provenance.[104]

Indeed, as John Wansbrough observed, the *dīwānī* scripts of contemporary Egypt and the Levant are broadly comparable to Sicilian *dīwānī*,[105] although it has not yet been possible to establish any more precise relationship between them.[106] The Archivio di Stato in Palermo preserves one of the two surviving Arabic

[101] Stern 1964a, pp.104–6.

[102] Noth 1983, p.205: RA1a: A = ***Dīwānī* 12**; RA1b: B, E, G, H = ***Dīwānī* 13, 22, 24, 25**; RA1c: F = ***Dīwānī* 21**. (I have minor reservations about this classification.)

[103] This large number of Arabic scribes, not counting other officers, helps to resolve the question of the existence of a distinct Arabic *dīwān*, first posed by Kehr 1902, pp.66–7, against Amari 1933–9, vol.III, pp.456–7, and now sensibly resolved by Noth 1983, pp.215–17.

[104] Traditional accounts of Maghribī script, such as Houdas 1886, are based primarily upon book-hands, and need to be revised for the medieval period in the light of recent discoveries of Fāṭimid, Levantine, Sicilian, and Andalusī documents.

[105] Wansbrough 1984, p.14, n.12. See, for example, the Fāṭimid documents illustrated by Stern 1956, Stern 1962, Stern 1964a, Richards 1973, Khan 1986, and Richards 1998.

[106] Noth 1983, p.204.

documents from the Latin East, a property lease, probably written by a public scribe of Antioch, in the year 1213.[107] So similar, at first glance, is the script of this Crusader document to the scripts of Norman Sicily that Salvatore Cusa and John Wansbrough both believed it to be Sicilian.[108] In all probability, therefore, the royal *dīwānī* script was imported into Sicily, in or shortly before 1132, from an East Mediterranean Islamic chancery, such as that of Fāṭimid Egypt. If so, then the few Maghribī features that occur sporadically in Sicilian *dīwānī* would indicate not the ancestry of the script itself, but, rather, the geographical origins (Ifrīqiya or Sicily) of some of the scribes who used it.[109] Even so, it is almost inconceivable that the *dīwānī* script was learnt by Sicilian scribes simply by copying the products of an Eastern chancery, and I believe that it can have arrived in Sicily only through the migration of one or more scribes trained in the chancery in which the parent script was employed. If so, such immigrant scribes are likely to have brought with them not only the script but also the diplomatic practices in which they had been trained.

The royal *ᶜalāma*

Amongst those practices, as we have already seen, was the system of Arabic titulature employed by the Norman kings. Another introduction was the tradition of the *ᶜalāma*, which Samuel Stern called 'the classical Islamic method of signature, namely the inscribing of a motto, rather than the name of the signatory'.[110] The use of the *ᶜalāma*, like the system of titulature, was imported as a living tradition, not a fossil, and continued under Roger's successors.

King Roger's *ᶜalāma* appears at the head of the Greek endowment charter for George of Antioch's church of Santa Maria dell'Ammiraglio (***Dīwānī* 20**).[111] The whole motto – *al-ḥamdu li-llāhi wa-shukrun li-anᶜumi-hi*, 'Praise be to God, and thanks for His blessings' – has been written in black ink, which contrasts with the light brown of the text, without once lifting the nib from the page, in fluid *dīwānī* script, with a final decorative flourish in the shape of a trefoil: the hand is that of a professional scribe, not the king's. At the foot of the Greek text come two lines of Arabic, already quoted in Chapter 4:

> When it was the month of May, in Indiction VI, we asked Our Majesty, the glorified and holy king – may God prolong his rule! – to place his noble signature (*ᶜalāma*) upon this document (*sijill*) to let it be known that he, may God maintain his power, has approved that [gift] and signed it. He graciously gave his consent, and sanctioned it, and placed his exalted *ᶜalāma* at the head of it. God is sufficient for us. How excellent a representative is He![112]

[107] PA, AdS, Santa Maria della Maddalena, no.81; ed. Cusa 1868–82, no.178, pp.645–9; see also Jamil and Johns forthcoming, a new edition and study, with a photograph of the original.

[108] Cusa 1868–82, p.740; Wansbrough 1984, p.13, no.178.

[109] Wansbrough 1984, p.14, n.12, makes this point. For the origins of the Arab servants and administrators of the Norman kings, see above, pp.249–50.

[110] Stern 1964a, pp.123–4.

[111] For the positioning of the *ᶜalāma*, see Stern 1964a, p.131.

[112] Above, pp.109–10.

This note, explaining the function of Roger's *ᶜalāma*, may indicate that it was not then a standard feature of *dīwānī* documents. Nor, it would appear, did it ever become so, for this is the only surviving occurrence of a royal *ᶜalāma* in Norman Sicily.[113] Nonetheless, Ibn Jubayr was told about the *ᶜalāmāt* of the Sicilian kings. He wrote of William II that 'amongst the extraordinary things told of him is that he reads and writes Arabic, and his *ᶜalāma*, according to what one of his qualified servants told us about him, is 'May God be praised, as it is right to praise Him' (*al-ḥamdu li-llāhi ḥaqqa ḥamdi-hi*), and his father's *ᶜalāma* was 'May God be praised in gratitude for his blessings (*al-ḥamdu li-llāhi shukran li-anᶜumi-hi*)'.[114] The latter is extremely close to that actually used by Roger II, but whether this really was precisely William I's motto, or whether Ibn Jubayr was misinformed, and, if so, whether William I really did continue to use his father's *ᶜalāma*, cannot now be determined. It is intriguing, in this context, to find that both Roger II and William I used the same motto on their coins struck in the mint of al-Mahdīya: 'May God be praised, as it is right to praise Him, and as He deserves and merits' (*al-ḥamdu li-llāhi ḥaqqa ḥamdi-hi wa-ka-mā huwa ahlu-hu wa-mustaḥiqqu-hu*).[115]

The *ḥamdala* had been a standard form for the *ᶜalāma* since at least the early 10th century, when it was used by the vizier of the ᶜAbbāsid chancery.[116] The Fāṭimids were perhaps the first to employ the *ḥamdala* as a royal signature, and all the Fāṭimid caliphs used the same *ᶜalāma: al-ḥamdu li-llāhi rabbi l-ᶜālamīna*, 'May God be praised, the Lord of the worlds'.[117] The Norman *ᶜalāma* was thus not modelled upon that of the caliph himself, but rather upon that of his leading officials and viziers. The 11th-century vizier, al-Jarjarāʾī, had an *ᶜalāma* which was extremely close, but not identical, to that of King Roger: *al-hamdu li-llāhi shukran li-niᶜmati-hi*, 'Praise be to God, in gratitude for His bounty'.[118] The *ḥamdala* used by Roger II and William I on coins minted at al-Mahdīya may be compared to two *ᶜalāma*s employed as registration marks on 11th-century Fāṭimid decrees : *al-ḥamdu li-llāhi ka-mā huwa ahlu-hu* ('Praise be to God according to what He deserves'), and *al-ḥamdu li-llāhi mustaḥaqqa l-ḥamdi* ('Praise be to God as He deserves').[119]

There is an intriguing footnote to the history of the Norman royal *ᶜalāma*. When the magistrates of Pisa wrote in Arabic to the Almohad caliph in 1181 A.D., they signed with *al-ḥamdu li-llāhi ḥaqqa ḥamdi-hi*, the very *ᶜalāma* attributed by Ibn Jubayr to William II of Sicily. But there is no telling whether the scribe from whom they learnt to do so was trained in an Islamic chancery or in the Norman *dīwān*.[120]

[113] The two copies issued to San Nicolò di Chùrchuro (***Dīwānī* 29 and 33**) both open with a *basmala* followed immediately by a *ḥamdala* – *bi-smi llāhi l-raḥmāni l-raḥīmi l-ḥamdu li-llāhi ḥaqqa ḥamdi-hi*. It was common practice in Islamic chanceries for the ruler's *ᶜalāma* to be placed immediately under the *basmala* (Stern 1964a, p.127 n.1, p.131). Because these two documents are copies, not originals, it remains just possible that the *ḥamdala* was the *ᶜalāma* of the king or one of his officials; but I doubt it.

[114] Ibn Jubayr 1907, p.325 (Ibn Jubayr 1949–65, vol.III, p.381; Ibn Jubayr 1952, p.341; *BAS*², vol.I, pp.86–87; *BAS*²*(It.)*, vol.I, p.120).

[115] Abdul-Wahhab 1930.

[116] Sourdel 1959–60, vol.II, pp.605–6.

[117] Stern 1964a, pp.127–30.

[118] Sourdel 1963; Stern 1964a, p.130.

[119] Stern 1964a, p.17, no.[3]; p.27.

[120] Amari 1863, nos 2–3, pp.7–13, and pp.LXVIII and 396.

The *basmala*

Islamic documents generally open with the *basmala*, and the absence of this pious invocation is a feature which characterises the products of the Sicilian *dīwān*. Nonetheless, four royal documents do open with the *basmala*: the copies of 1149 and 1154 to the monks of Chùrchuro (***Dīwānī* 29 and 33**); Martin's bilingual decree to the Archbishop of Messina (***Dīwānī* 37**); and William II's grant to the hospital in Khandaq al-Qirūz (***Dīwānī* 38**). The formula is not exclusively Islamic, and was used extensively in Christian Arabic. It seems unlikely, therefore, that it was omitted for religious reasons. In most bilingual documents, the Greek or Latin text precedes the Arabic, and opens with a pious *invocatio* that was possibly felt to fulfil the need for an Arabic *basmala*. The omission of the *basmala* from documents which open with Arabic text and have no Greek or Latin *invocatio*, such as the *jarāʾid* renewed in 1145 (***Dīwānī* 21, 24–5**), cannot be explained in this way.

The *ḥasbala*, and other authentication marks

At the foot of the customs exemption issued to Bishop John of Lipari-Patti in January 1134 (***Dīwānī* 13**), a formula known as the *ḥasbala* – *wa-ḥasbu-nā llāhu wa-niʿma l-wakīlu* ('God is sufficient for us. How excellent a representative is He!') – is employed for the first time in the place occupied by the *apprecatio* in Greek or Latin diplomatics.[121] This practice thereafter becomes standard on *dīwānī* documents.[122] Exactly the same formula was employed in precisely the same way by the Fāṭimid chancery from at least the 11th century.[123] Ibn Shīth, who wrote about the practices of the Fāṭimid chancery, makes much of the precise point in the line at which the *ḥasbala* should begin: 'the correct place [for the *ḥasbala*] to begin', he writes, 'is at the third part of the line from the right'.[124] In the surviving original documents from the Fāṭimid chancery, this rule is not rigidly applied, although the *ḥasbala* always appears on its own line, which is more or less sharply indented. In Sicily, the *ḥasbala* is frequently joined on to the preceding text, but in two early cases it does occur at approximately the position specified by Ibn Shīth (***Dīwānī* 13 and 31**).

There is an intriguing link between the *ḥasbala* and George of Antioch, which may suggest that he regarded the formula as his personal motto. In his church of Santa Maria dell'Ammiraglio, the two dedicatory mosaic panels, depicting Christ

121 Above, p.101.
122 ***Dīwānī* 13, 14, 16, 17, 20, 29, 31, 32, 36, 38, 41 and 44.**
123 Stern 1964a, no.1, p.17, line 38; no.2, p.26, line 51; no.3, p.36, line 34; no.5, p.54, line 34 (pl.16); no.6, p.60, line 37 (pl.25); no.7, p.66, line 20 (pl.32); no.8, p.72, line 45 (pl.43); no.9, p.78, line 47 (pl.48); and p.121.
124 Ibn Shīth al-Qurashī 1913, p.51; al-Qalqashandī 1913–72, vol.VI, pp.269–70.

crowning Roger II, and George of Antioch before the Virgin, probably decorated the east wall of the narthex, which was built for George's tomb, one on either side of the door leading into the church. They are not the only pair of symbols referring to the king and to his vizier; and two columns with Arabic inscriptions, now out of their original positions in the 16th-century new church, also allude, respectively, to Roger and to George. In all probability, the columns were originally employed in the porticoes of the forecourt,[125] flanking the western entrance. That which refers to the king is inscribed with four of the kingly attributes which are repeated in the litany of royal power in the painted inscriptions on the ceiling of the Cappella Palatina: 'victory, triumph, power, and good fortune' (*al-naṣr wa-l-ẓafar wa-l-ᶜizz wa-l-iqbāl*).[126] That which alludes to George, bears the *ḥasbala* – *ḥasbīya llāhu wa-niᶜma l-wakīl* – which, under his management of the administration, was first adopted on the documents of the royal *dīwān*.[127]

The other authentication marks that appear on the documents of the Sicilian *dīwān* were also amongst the practices introduced after 1130. These include the motto *ṣaḥḥa bi-l-taʾrīkhi* ('It was authenticated on the date') which 'seals' the seams on the *verso* of *jarāʾid* made up of two or more sheets of parchment, sewn together to form long rolls.[128] Similar mottoes also occur at the foot of documents, next to the *ḥasbala* and the signatures: *ṣaḥīḥ bi-l-taʾrīkhi*, 'Correct on the date' (***Dīwānī* 29**); *ṣaḥḥa dhālika [inta]h[ā]*, 'That was authenticated. It is complete' (***Dīwānī* 35**); and *ṣaḥīḥ dhālika*, 'That is authentic' (***Dīwānī* 37**). The use of such mottoes, using *ṣaḥḥa* or *ṣaḥīḥ*, is attested in the Fāṭimid chancery,[129] but became far more widespread in the late medieval Maghrib.[130]

Conclusion

A strong circumstantial case has been made that the renaissance of the royal *dīwān* in the 1130s and '40s was achieved largely by the importation of elements of structure and practice from the contemporary Fāṭimid chancery. However, the nature of the evidence is such that there can be no conclusive proof, and the alternatives must now be considered.

The first is the traditional argument that the royal *dīwān*, like all other aspects of the Arab facet of the Norman monarchy, was inherited from the Kalbid rulers of

125 The inscribed columns are now the second pair from the west in the new church. For their original position, see Kitzinger 1990, pp.49–51.

126 Amari 1875, no.18, p.79, pl.9/9 (Amari 1971, pp.103–4).

127 Collar below capital: *inna llāha maᶜa lladhīna ttaqā* (sic! corr. *ittaqaw*), 'Truly, God is with those who fear [Him]' (*Qurʾān* 16.128). Panel in middle of shaft: *bi-smi llāhi l-raḥmāni l-raḥīmi / ḥasbiya llāhu wa-niᶜma l-wakīl* ('In the name of God, the Merciful, the Compassionate. God is sufficient for me, and He is the best advocate': cf. *Qurʾān* 9.129 and 3.173). See photograph in Kitzinger 1990, figs A25–A26; Amari 1875, nos 16–17, pp.78–9 and pl.9, figs 7–8 (repr. Amari 1971, pp.102–3, without plates).

128 Above, p.129.

129 Stern 1964a, p.129; and Khan 1986, line 4 of doc.

130 Stern 1964a, pp.139–42.

Sicily who, in their turn, had imitated the Fāṭimid caliphs of Egypt.[131] As I have argued elsewhere, there are considerable difficulties with this initially attractive hypothesis.[132] An interval of ninety years, or three generations, separated the fall of the Kalbids, and the fragmentation of the government of Sicily in the mid 1040s, from the foundation of the Norman monarchy – too long for the traditions of the Kalbid *dīwān* to have been kept alive but dormant until they could be resurrected by the Norman kings. None of the most distinctive features of the royal *dīwān*, such as the *dīwānī* script or the royal *alqāb* and *adᶜiya*, can be traced before 1130. Those aspects of Arabic administration that the first Norman rulers did inherit directly from their Muslim predecessors, such as the fiscal records upon which the early *jarāʾid* issued in 1093–1111 (***Dīwānī* 1–6 and 8**) were based, do not display any of the characteristics of the royal *dīwān* that I am suggesting were imported from Fāṭimid Egypt after 1130. Moreover, a long interval of eighteen years separates the last comital document to use Arabic (***Dīwānī* 8**) from the renaissance of the royal *dīwān*. In other words, what was inherited from the Muslim period was apparently abandoned from 1112 until 1130, compelling Roger II and his ministers to import the labour and materials with which they rebuilt the royal *dīwān*. At least one of the most characteristic features of the royal *dīwān*, its direction by the executive and supervisory branch called the *dīwān al-taḥqīq*, could not have been inherited from the Kalbids, because this bureau was only created in 1107–8 in Fāṭimid Egypt. Thus, although the comital *dīwān* did inherit important aspects of fiscal administration from the Muslim rulers of the island, it seems highly improbable that the Kalbid *dīwān* could have been the model for the transformation of the Norman *dīwān* after 1130.

The second alternative is that the principal model for the royal *dīwān*, and the main source of the imports to Palermo after 1130, was the Zīrid administration of al-Mahdīya. Friendly contacts between the Normans and the Zīrids were rapidly established after the conquest of Sicily, and lasted until 1117 when Roger II began to meddle in Ifrīqiyan affairs. Thereafter, as Norman intervention increased, relations between the two courts grew ever more strained, until 1148 when George of Antioch captured al-Mahdīya and forced the last Zīrid emir to flee to the Almohads. George of Antioch and his family had been amongst the leading administrators of the Zīrid Tamīm before they defected to Sicily. At least two of the Arab eunuchs, Philip of al-Mahdīya and the *qāʾid* Peter, came from Ifrīqiya, and it seems highly probable that most, if not all, of the Arab and African slaves in Roger's palace came to Sicily from, or though, Zīrid Ifrīqiya. For fifteen years, 1146–60, the Normans governed the cities of the Ifrīqiyan coast. Arab sources attest to the migration of scholars and lawyers from Ifrīqiya to Sicily. In short, there exists an extremely strong *a priori* case that the Zīrid court strongly influenced the Arab facet of the Sicilian monarchy, and it seems highly probable that it is only because we are so poorly informed about the Zīrid *dīwān* and its products that its influence upon the Sicilian *dīwān* cannot be demonstrated.

[131] Amari 1933–9, vol.III, p.875. [132] Johns 1993, pp.134–5; Johns 1995b, pp.12–13.

Nonetheless, while acknowledging that the influence of the Zīrid *dīwān* was probably considerable, for two reasons, I am inclined to reject the proposal that it was the principal model for the renaissance of the Norman *dīwān*, and the principal source of imports to Palermo.

First, the renaissance of the Norman *dīwān* occurred in the 1130s and '40s, twenty years after George of Antioch and his family defected to Sicily, and at precisely that period when relations between Palermo and al-Mahdīya were at their worst. Had the Sicilian *dīwān* been transformed as early as the 1110s, immediately after the arrival of George, or as late as 1148, the year in which George captured al-Mahdīya, then the chronological coincidence would have strongly suggested that its transformation had been brought about by the immigration to Palermo of a cadre of Zīrid administrators. As it is, the renaissance of the Norman *dīwān* coincides precisely with the period of closest contact with Fāṭimid Egypt.

Second, as I shall argue further in Chapter 11, the renaissance of the royal *dīwān* must be seen as part of the creation of the Arab facet of Norman kingship; of the attempt to establish a multi-faceted Sicilian monarchy, which was intended to promote the Norman king as the equal, even as the superior, of his Mediterranean rivals. From this perspective, the Zīrid emir was a pathetic figure, the puppet of both Cairo and Palermo. Before the Almohad ᶜAbd al-Muʾmin had established his caliphate in Marrakesh in *c.*1150, before Nūr al-Dīn ibn Zanjī achieved the reunification of Muslim Syria in the 1150s, the Fāṭimid caliph was the only Islamic ruler around the shores of the Mediterranean of sufficient stature to serve as a model for the Norman king. Thus, it was not any Islamic chancery that the Normans took as their model, but the *dīwān* of the most magnificent Muslim ruler of the day – the Fāṭimid caliph.

Throughout this chapter, the figure of George of Antioch has been omnipresent. His family had been in the service of the uncle of the Fāṭimid vizier Bahrām. He had been a leading administrator in the court of Tamīm of al-Mahdīya. He was 'many times' Roger's ambassador to Cairo in *c.*1115–25. He drafted Roger's correspondence with al-Ḥāfiẓ. He led the Sicilian assault upon Ifrīqiya. He was Roger's vizier from 1126 until 1151, and he presided over the whole administration during the transformation of the royal *dīwān*. The earliest surviving products of the royal *dīwān* were compiled by him. Roger's *ᶜalāma* appears at the head of the endowment charter for George of Antioch's church. An inscribed column in that church bears the *ḥasbala* that was used to authenticate *dīwānī* documents. No other figure had the education, the experience, the international contacts and the opportunity necessary to transform the Arabic administration into a royal *dīwān* on the Islamic model. And, what is more, this is precisely what al-Maqrīzī's biography of George claims that he did:

> [George] amassed the revenues and organised the foundations of the kingdom. He veiled Roger from [his] subjects, and arranged for him to dress in clothes like [those of] Muslim [rulers] ... He acquainted Roger with the biographies of the [Muslim] kings, and

> ordered one of his secretaries ... to compile a biography of him. Roger's state grew under George's management.[133]

George was uniquely placed to compare the courts of Cairo and al-Mahdīya. As an ex-minister of the Zīrid court, he knew precisely the extent to which the Fāṭimid caliph was the overlord of the Zīrid emir. When he first went as Roger's ambassador to Cairo in 1115–25, George saw at first hand that the Fāṭimid caliph was the magnificent original of which the Zīrid emir was but a pale imitation. He was also intimately familiar with Byzantium and, to judge from his title *o panupersebastos ek tēs axias*, a palatine dignity which can only have been awarded him by the emperor himself, was at one point in his Sicilian career assiduously courted by Constantinople.[134] Thus, when George commissioned the mosaic panel of Roger II in Byzantine mode for the narthex of his church, he carefully selected the imperial model which most closely corresponded to the ambitions which he had for his king: not a lone imperial figure, but an emperor in the very act of receiving his crown from Christ, 'a visual counterpart to the phrase "a deo coronatus" ... [implying] the rejection of the terrestrial church as an indispensable intermediary in the bestowal of monarchic power'.[135] It is inconceivable that George would have taken any less care in selecting the Islamic model for Roger's Arab facet, and that he would have chosen the Zīrid imitation rather than the Fāṭimid original.

[133] Above, p.82.

[134] Longo 1981, pp.41–4, suggests that the only moment at which this dignity could have been conferred upon George was in c.1143–4 when, immediately after his accession, Manuel I Comnenus dispatched an ambassador to Palermo who negotiated a short-lived alliance. The coincidence with the foundation and endowment of Santa Maria dell'Ammiraglio is striking.

[135] Kitzinger 1990, pp.190–1, 195–6.

CHAPTER 11

Royal *dīwān* and royal image

The kings of Sicily governed a heterogeneous population which Peter of Eboli, referring to the citizens of Palermo and echoing an earlier Latin poet, famously called the *populus trilinguis*.[1] In the illustration on the folio facing this verse, the three language groups are all clearly depicted, united in mourning the dead King William.[2] Three folios later, a half-page illustration shows King Tancred's chancery at Palermo, with its three adjoining offices of scribes – Greek, Saracen, and Latin[3] – the illustration is reproduced as the frontispiece of this book. These two images both represent the three-tongued people and symbolise the Norman policy of *populus trilinguis* – that the cohesive rule of the king had united the three communities into a single Sicilian people. That policy of *populus trilinguis* – its introduction, evolution, partial and temporary successes, and its ultimate failure – lies beyond the scope of this study,[4] but it nonetheless underlies this final chapter – and, indeed, much of this book. Here it is sufficient to emphasise that, from the 1150s, if not earlier, until the 1190s, if not later, some Sicilians clearly understood that the peace and prosperity of the island depended upon the acquiescence of the Muslim majority to Christian rule, and upon the ability of the king to keep Christian rule within bounds that could be tolerated by the Muslims. As Ibn al-Athīr put it, on the authority of Ibn Shaddād who had visited Palermo in 1156–7, King Roger 'treated the Muslims with respect, took them as his companions, and kept the Franks off them, so that they loved him'. William I – William 'the Bad' – was believed to be an incompetent and wicked king by the Muslims of Sicily,[5] and

[1] *Hactenus urbs felix, populo dotata trilingui, / Corde ruit, fluitat pectore, mente cadit*: Peter of Eboli 1994, p.45, lines 56–7 (Peter of Eboli 1904, p.15; Peter of Eboli 1906, p.9). This passage probably contains a reference to Apuleius, *Metamorphoses*, XI.5 – *Siculi trilingues* (see Wilson 1990, pp.316–17).

[2] Peter of Eboli 1994, p.47 (f.98r.) (Peter of Eboli 1904, pl.4, p.14): Latins are shown in the *Cassarum* (*al-Qaṣr*); Greeks in the *Calza* (*al-Khāliṣa*); and Arabs (and Jews?) in the *Ideisini* (*al-Dayyāsīn*) and *Scerarchadium* (*Shāriʿ* or *Shirʿat al-qāḍī*): see map and bibliography cited above, p.220, note 22.

[3] Peter of Eboli 1994, p.59 (f.101r.) (Peter of Eboli 1904, pl.7, p.26).

[4] This is to be one of the themes of the forthcoming thesis of Annliese Nef, Université Paris X – Nanterre, under the supervision of Prof. Henri Bresc.

[5] 'He was [a ruler] of corrupt government [and] evil policy, and he made Maio the Christian his vizier' (*kāna fāsida l-tadbīri sayyiʾa l-taṣwīri wa-stawzara māyū l-haṣrānī* [sic?]: Ibn al-Athīr 1851–76, vol.XI, p.124 (*BAS*[2], vol.I, p.338; *BAS*[2]*(It.)*, vol.II, p.376).

they did suffer terrible pogroms during the rebellion that marred his reign, but they nonetheless mourned his passing as a king who had died before his heir was old enough to guarantee that the crown would continue to protect their community.[6] William II, too, was mourned by the Muslims of the island,[7] but with far greater cause, for violent persecution immediately broke out upon his death, driving the Muslims to flee the cities and the plains and to defend themselves in mountain refuges. A few years later, the author of the *Letter to Peter the Treasurer*, who may well be identical with 'Hugo Falcandus', expressed clearly how the fortunes of the Muslim community, and thus the unity of the whole island under threat of Henry VI's invasion, depended upon the speedy resumption of strong royal authority. With the advantage of hindsight, writing on the eve of the German assault, he urged that, in the power vacuum that followed William's death, if the Christians and Muslims were not immediately to agree and to choose 'a king of undoubted virtue',

> it would be difficult for the Christian population not to oppress the Muslims in a crisis as great as this, with fear of the king removed, so that the Muslims, worn down by many injuries at the hands of the Christians, would ... occupy forts along the coast and strongholds in the mountains.[8]

But that is exactly what they had already done, beginning the Muslim revolts which were to continue until the middle of the next century, and to prompt Frederick II to destroy the Muslim community of the island.

The rôle of the *dīwān* in the delicate political equilibrium upset by William's death was perhaps less that of administration, than what we would now call image manipulation, public relations, and spin. And the purpose of this final chapter is to isolate and to examine such non-administrative functions of the royal *dīwān*, and to assess their contribution to the formation and development of the royal image. But such a crude distinction between royal administration and royal image is anachronistic, and would have been incomprehensible to contemporaries. Al-Maqrīzī treats George of Antioch's king-making programme – fiscal administration, legislation, glorification of the monarch, ceremonial display, patronage of foreign intellectuals – as a seamless whole.[9] Ibn Jubayr wrote that William II 'imitates the rulers of the Muslims in immersing himself in the luxury of his realm, in the provision of its laws, the invention of procedures, the allocation of degrees amongst his men, the

[6] *Universi quoque cives, nigris induti vestibus, usque in diem tertium in eodem habitu permanserunt. Per totum autem hoc triduum mulieres nobilesque, maxime sarracene, quibus ex morte regis dolor non fictus obvenerat, saccis operte, passis crinibus et die noctuque turmatim incedentes, ancillarum preeunte multitudine, totam civitatem ululatu complebant ad pulsata tympana cantu flebili respondentes*: 'Hugo Falcandus' 1897, p.89 (trans. 'Hugo Falcandus' 1998, p.138).

[7] Peter of Eboli 1994, p.45, lines 56–83, and p.46 (f.98r.) (Peter of Eboli 1904, pp.15–16, pls 3–4; Peter of Eboli 1906, pp.9–10).

[8] *Certe si regem sibi non dubie virtutis elegerint nec a Christianis Sarraceni dissentiant, poterit rex creatus rebus licet quasi disperatis ... At vero quia difficile est Christianos in tanto rerum turbine, sublato regis timore, Sarracenos non opprimere, si Sarraceni multis illorum iniuriis fatigati ab eis ceperint dissidere et castella forte maritima vel montanas munitiones occupaverint*: 'Hugo Falcandus' 1897, pp.172, 173 (trans. 'Hugo Falcandus' 1998, p.255).

[9] Above, p.82.

elaboration of the ceremony of the realm, and the display of his finery'.[10] Ceremonial and display was no less a function of royal government than administration, legislation, and taxation. The same royal servants who administered the palace and the *dīwān*, also provided the most lavish public spectacle: through 'the inspectors of his government, and the people of his administration in his realm', there 'radiates the magnificence of [William II's] kingship, because they abound with sumptuous robes and lively horses'.[11]

Seclusion and display

After the mid-1140s, royal power had increasingly to be signalled symbolically, because the king himself was ever less visible. Contemporary observers were struck by the way in which the Norman kings withdrew from the public eye into their palaces. 'Hugo Falcandus' reports that, once Roger had brought peace to the kingdom and accumulated a vast treasure at Palermo, 'he devoted himself to peace and leisure', and handed over responsibility for government to his sons Alfonso, prince of Capua (d.1144), and Roger, duke of Apulia (d.1148): their early deaths date Roger's withdrawal to the mid-1140s.[12] Romuald of Salerno, too, dwells at length upon Roger's diversions and relaxations in his suburban retreats of La Favara and the hunting park at Altofonte.[13] A glance at Caspar's *regestum* confirms that, during the last decade of his life, Roger was indeed far less active than he had been in his youth, and spent most of his time *in palatio urbis Panormi*. As for William I, 'Hugo Falcandus' repeatedly describes how he 'shut himself off as if afraid of the sight of men', 'secreted himself from everyone in such a way that for a long period of time he appeared to no one at all', 'was unwilling to leave the palace', 'shut himself up in his palace', 'gave himself up to relaxation and rest [and] afraid of any event that would interrupt the enjoyment of his leisure ... [gave] his officials orders not to bring him any news that might cause him sadness or stress'.[14] William II, the most elusive of the Norman kings, followed his father's lead, and spent most of his life in retirement in his palaces in and around Palermo. Al-Maqrīzī's life of George of Antioch suggests that the seclusion of the king was an integral part of his creation of the Norman monarchy: George 'veiled Roger from [his] subjects, and arranged for him ... not to ride out, nor to show himself in public'.

Changes in the Arabic documents of the Norman rulers signal their retirement. Roger I, the regent Adelaide, and the young Roger II had appeared directly as

[10] Above, p.213. [11] Above, pp.212–13.

[12] *Is, ubi post multos labores ac pericula pacem regno quoad viveret peperit inconcussam, ingentes etiam thesauros ad regni tuitionem posteritati consulens preparavit ac Panormi reposuit. Exinde iam otio quietique deditus, faustaque se prole felicem existimans, filiis suis Rogerio duci Apulie Amphulsoque Capue principi ... regni sollicitiudinem participandam crediderat*: 'Hugo Falcandus' 1897, pp.6–7 (trans. 'Hugo Falcandus' 1998, pp.58–9).

[13] Romuald of Salerno 1935, pp.232–3 (trans. 'Hugo Falcandus' 1998, p.219).

[14] 'Hugo Falcandus' 1897, pp.11, 13, 18, 83, 87 (trans. 'Hugo Falcandus' 1998, pp.63, 65, 71, 133, 136).

themselves, but, after 1132, the royal *dīwān* used either a *nisba* ('the Rogerian', 'the Williamian') or an impersonal formula ('the Most Exalted Seat', 'the Most High Presence') to veil the royal person.[15] In much the same way, the earliest *dīwānī* documents had borne the ruler's signature which, although not an autograph, was intended to indicate his or her personal sanction. This practice was dropped from Arabic documents under Roger II and, after the donation to San Nicolò di Churchuro (***Dīwānī* 28–9**) of 1149, only one *dīwānī* document bore the royal signature (***Dīwānī* 30**), and one the royal *intitulatio* (***Dīwānī* 36**).

The veiling of the royal person in *dīwānī* documents corresponds to a change in the royal image. Alexander of Telese's idealised portrait of Roger II had shown the king using his every free moment to pore over the accounts of his kingdom.[16] Later observers agreed that Roger had been 'very concerned to gain money, [and] hardly prodigal in spending it',[17] but they abandoned the pretence that he personally had been responsible for taxation and expenditure:

> although the king himself was possessed of great wisdom, intelligence and judgement, he also gathered men of good sense of different classes from the various parts of the earth and made them partners in his decisions … he brought George, a man of mature wisdom, foresight and care, from Antioch, and made him great admiral'.[18]

William I, like his father, was known to have been 'very active in collecting money but not very generous in dispensing it',[19] but he had entrusted 'the care and government of the whole realm' to his great admiral, Maio of Bari.[20] After Maio's death and the lapse of that office, William had shut himself up in his palace, and the triumvirate of Richard Palmer, Matthew of Salerno, and the *qāʾid* Peter, had monopolised the king's counsel and the administration of the realm.[21] No contemporary observer pretends that William II was personally involved in the business of administration.

The seclusion of the king was also emphasised by the public display mounted by his ministers and administrators. From the mid-1140s until the death of William II, the 'lords' of the *dīwān* were always amongst the most prominent officers of the household and the court, and were numbered amongst the royal familiars until at least 1169. Surrounded by their guards and retainers, they rode out in cavalcade, displaying their finery and wealth to the citizens of Palermo.[22] On high days and holidays, when the royal veil was lifted and the king was displayed to citizens who had been deliberately starved of the sight of him, he was accompanied by his

[15] See above, pp.138, 270. Chapters 5 and 8. [16] See above, p.79.

[17] Romuald of Salerno 1935, pp.237 (trans. 'Hugo Falcandus' 1998, p.221).

[18] *Quamvis autem predictus rex, sapiencia ingenio et plurima discretione polleret, tamen sapientes viros diversorum ordinum et e diversis mundi partibus evocatos, suo faciebat consilio interesse. Nam Georgium virum utique maturum sapientem providum et discretum ab Antiochia adductum, magnum constituit ammiratum, cuius consilio et prudentia in mari et terra victorias multas optinuit*: Romuald of Salerno 1935, pp.233 (trans. 'Hugo Falcandus' 1998, p.219).

[19] Romuald of Salerno 1935, pp.253 (trans. 'Hugo Falcandus' 1998, p.238).

[20] 'Hugo Falcandus' 1897, pp.7–8 (trans. 'Hugo Falcandus' 1998, p.60).

[21] 'Hugo Falcandus' 1897, pp.83 (trans. 'Hugo Falcandus' 1998, p.135).

[22] Above, pp.212–13, 226, 230, 255.

administrators and officials.[23] Their leaders bore arms and, in times of need, they defended the king and his family, or led the palace servants in battle against their rivals.[24] Some were military and naval commanders, entrusted with important foreign expeditions.[25] They had their own courts, in which they crushed rebellion, and played to the mob.[26] They performed public acts of charity, and supervised the construction of public buildings dedicated in their names.[27] They had their own houses, lands, and business ventures outside the palace.[28] Even at their desks, the officers of the *dīwān* were on show. Their offices lay within the main royal palace, and visitors, such as Ibn Jubayr, passed them as they were led through its courts.[29] Martin's office, when he was one of the 'lords of the *dīwān al-taḥqīq*', lay between the inner and outer gates of the palace.[30] Petitioners seeking writs were permitted to enter the palace, and do their business face-to-face with royal officials.[31]

The exotic public spectacle presented by the palace Saracens enhanced the royal image of the king, their hidden master. Ibn Jubayr calls them the *ᶜuyūnu dawlati-hi*, a phrase which I have translated prosaically as 'the inspectors of his government', but which means literally that they were his 'eyes', the most precious organs of his rule, and, perhaps, also suggests that they were the 'springs' from which flowed his royal beneficence, just as 'the magnificence of his kingship radiates through them'.[32] At the same time, because their authority depended entirely upon the whim of the ruler, their exposed position afforded him valuable protection. They were perceived to be responsible for the most unpopular acts and failures of government, such as the loss of Ifrīqiya,[33] the suppression of rebellion in Palermo in 1161–2,[34] and the collection of the notorious *redemptio* or penal tax levied on the mainland.[35] The palace Saracens were believed to be personally responsible for all taxation levied by the crown, and when the palace was stormed in 1160, the rebels rushed straight to the *dīwān* and massacred its staff.[36] When political crisis threatened the crown, individual Muslim servants could be ruthlessly sacrificed to protect the image, and ultimately the person, of their royal master.[37]

The extent to which this rôle of the *dīwān* was the result of deliberate policy, rather than mere circumstance, is not easily determined. But the practice of appointing crypto-Muslim eunuch slaves to be the leading ministers and officers of the realm had not been inherited from the Kalbid emirs, still less carried by the Normans across the Straits, but was deliberately imported from the contemporary Fāṭimid world during the vizierate of George of Antioch who, in the Zīrid court, had experienced at first hand the precarious exposure suffered by a foreign servant. King Roger was known to have 'made every effort to find out the customs of other kings and peoples, in order to adopt any of them that seemed particularly

23 Above, p.82. 24 Above, pp.221, 226, 230, 231–2, 243, 246.
25 Above, pp.215, 217, 223, 226, 227, 243, 244, 245, 246.
26 Above, pp.221, 224. 27 Above, pp.213, 214, 215–16, 217, 223, 225, 241, 242.
28 Above, pp.222, 234, 243 (**Private 23**). 29 Above, p.214. 30 Above, p.221.
31 'Hugo Falcandus' 1897, pp.112–13 (trans. 'Hugo Falcandus' 1998, pp.163–5).
32 Above, pp.213, 254–5. 33 Above, p.223. 34 Above, pp.221. 35 Above, p.224.
36 Above, p.219–20. 37 Above, 215–17, 224.

admirable or useful',[38] and he was the first Sicilian ruler both to raise a Saracen eunuch to ministerial rank, and to sacrifice him to political expediency.[39]

Christian rule through Muslim leaders

The Sicilian king may have employed Muslim servants in part to veil him from his opponents, but Ibn al-Athīr claims that this also endeared him to his Muslim subjects:

> he followed the way of Muslim rulers with mounted companions, chamberlains, arms-bearers, body-guards, and others of that kind. Thus, he broke with the custom of the Franks, who are not acquainted with such things ... He treated the Muslims with respect, took them as his companions, and kept the Franks off them, so that they loved him.[40]

Elsewhere, Ibn al-Athīr went still further, and reported that Roger's use of Muslim counsellors had given rise to the rumour that the king himself was a Muslim:

> There was in Sicily a man who was one of the Muslim scholars and of the people of righteousness. The ruler of Sicily [Roger II] respected and revered him, and depended upon his counsel, and preferred him to the priests and monks about him, and so the inhabitants of his realm said that [Roger] was a Muslim.[41]

When, at the end of his reign, Roger arraigned and executed his leading Muslim minister, Philip of al-Mahdīya, alongside his fellow eunuchs, Ibn al-Athīr interpreted this as an ominous change of policy – 'This was the beginning of the end for the Muslims of Sicily'.[42]

Chapter 9 was largely devoted to the 'palace Saracens' as administrators and as officers and servants of the court and palace. We also saw how the *dīwān* enabled the Christian king to associate leaders of the Muslim community of the island in the business of administration and government. This began as early as the 1120s, with Abū l-Ḍawʾ, *kātib* and panegyricist to Roger II, who came from the leading Muslim family which provided the *qāḍī* of Sicily in three successive generations during the mid-12th century. In the 1160s–80s, again as we saw in Chapter 9, William II employed Abū l-Qāsim ibn Ḥammūd, the hereditary *sayyid* or 'lord' of the Muslims of Sicily. Abū l-Qāsim was one of the directors of the *dīwān* in the late 1160s and early 1170s. Shortly before the spring of 1185, he was put under house-arrest and heavily fined, allegedly for communicating with the Almohads.

[38] *Aliorum quoque regum ac gentium consuetudines diligentissime fecit inquiri, ut quod in eis pulcherimum aut utile videbatur sibi transumerat*: 'Hugo Falcandus' 1897, pp.6 (trans. 'Hugo Falcandus' 1998, p.58). [39] Philip of al-Mahdīya: above, pp.215–18. [40] Above, p.254–5.

[41] *Wa-kāna bi-ṣiqillīyata insānun mina l-ᶜulamāʾi l-muslimīna wa-huwa min ahli l-ṣalāḥi wa-kāna ṣāḥibu ṣiqillīyata yukarrimu-hu wa-yaḥtarimu-hu wa-yarjiᶜu ilā qawli-hi wa-yuqaddimu-hu ᶜalā man ᶜinda-hu min al-qusūsi wa-l-ruhbāni wa-kāna ahlu wilāyati-hi yaqūlūna inna-hu muslimun*: Ibn al-Athīr 1851–76, vol.XI, p.66 (*BAS*², vol.I, pp.328–329; *BAS*²*(It.)*, vol.II, p.366).

[42] *Wa-hādhā awwalu wahnin dakhala ᶜalā l-muslimīna bi-ṣiqillīyata*: above, p.217.

Either at that time, or earlier, he lost his post in the *dīwān*. Subsequently, William pardoned him, and 'entrusted him with the execution of an important matter concerning the affairs of the government', but did not, it would seem, restore him to the *dīwān*.[43]

There is no suggestion that Abū l-Qāsim's collaboration with the Christian king, not even his holding office within the *dīwān*, conflicted with his leadership of the Muslim community. The *shaykh* al-Sadīd, Abū l-Qāsim's great rival, could scarcely accuse him of treachery because he, too, was one of the king's counsellors, and was particularly close to the anti-Muslim chancellor Stephen du Perche.

Comparison with Ifrīqiya, where the *dīwān* enabled the Norman kings to rule not directly, as in Sicily itself, but by remote control, will help to clarify the position of the Muslim leaders of the island. By the 1140s, George of Antioch, on behalf of Roger, already claimed authority over all Ifrīqiya as overlord of the Zīrid emir,[44] although Palermo actually governed only the island of Gerba, where an *ᶜāmil* administered the *amān* that had reduced the population to the status of *khawal* or 'serfs'.[45] Roger's claims were made good when George of Antioch acquired the major cities of the coast, beginning with Tripoli in 1146. In 1148, after he had expelled al-Ḥasan and occupied al-Mahdīya itself, 'letters (*kutub*) arrived from Roger to the whole population of Ifrīqiya with [his] *amān* and fair promises (*al-mawāᶜīd al-ḥasana*)'.[46] Following Christian conquest, Muslim government and administration was restored to each urban centre individually, in the form of a Muslim governor and *qāḍī*. Only the capital, al-Mahdīya itself, seems to have had a Sicilian governor, and even there administrative offices were filled by local Muslim leaders, and a *qāḍī* appointed. The suburban city, Zawīla, which housed most of the population of the metropolitan region, had its own Muslim governor and officers.[47]

At Tripoli, the Sicilian army occupied the city for six months and then withdrew, appointing Abū Yaḥyā ibn Maṭrūḥ al-Tamīmī as *wālī*, and taking hostages from the Banī Maṭrūḥ. Abū Yaḥyā was sent a robe of office and a diploma from Palermo. The *qāḍī* was the eminent jurist Abū l-Ḥajjāj Yūsuf ibn Zīrī. Al-Tijānī reports that 'all the lawsuits of the Muslims were reserved to their *qāḍī* and their *wālī*, and the Christians could not oppose any of their judgements'. In order to repopulate Tripoli, it was announced in Sicily that any Muslim could resettle there.[48]

[43] *Wa-amara-hu bi-l-nufūdhi li-muhimmin min ashghāli-hi l-sulṭānīyati*: above, p.241.

[44] Ibn al-Athīr 1851–76, vol.XI, p.83 (*BAS*², vol.I, p.333; *BAS*²*(It.)*, vol.II, p.371); Ibn Abī Dīnār 1967, p.92 (*BAS*², vol.II, p.605; *BAS*²*(It.)*, vol.III, p.661). See also Brett 1999b, pp.8–9.

[45] Ibn Abī Dīnār 1967, p.93 (*BAS*², vol.II, p.605; *BAS*²*(It.)*, vol.III, p.661 and n.43).

[46] Ibn al-Athīr 1851–76, vol.XI, p.85, (*BAS*², vol.I, p.336; *BAS*²*(It.)*, vol.II, p.373).

[47] Ibn al-Athīr 1851–76, vol.XI, p.84–5 (*BAS*², vol.I, p.335–6; *BAS*²*(It.)*, vol.II, p.371–2); Ibn Abī Dīnār 1967, p.95 (*BAS*², vol.II, p.607; *BAS*²*(It.)*, vol.III, p.663). See also Idris 1962a, vol.I, pp.358, 382–3; Brett 1999b, p.12.

[48] Ibn al-Athīr 1851–76, vol.XI, p.71 (*BAS*², vol.I, p.329–30; *BAS*²*(It.)*, vol.II, p.367–8); Ibn Khaldūn 1868, vol.V, p.202–3 (*BAS*², vol.II, p.549–50; *BAS*²*(It.)*, vol.II, pp.604–5). al-Tījānī 1958, pp.239–42: *kānat aḥkāmu l-muslimīna kullu-hā maṣrūfatan ilā qāḍī-him wa-wālī-him wa-lam yakuni l-naṣrānīyu yataᶜarraḍu li-shayʾin min aḥkāmi-him* (*BAS*², vol.II, pp.443–45; *BAS*²*(It.)*, vol.II, pp.496–98). See also: Idris 1962a, vol.I, pp.351–52, 383–84; Brett, 1986.

At Gabès, on the death of its *ṣāḥib*, Rushayd ibn Kāmil ibn Jāmiᶜ in 1146–7, one of his *mawlā*s, named Yūsuf, seized power, ejected Rushayd's eldest son Muᶜammar, and installed his infant son, Muḥammad, as a puppet governor. Muᶜammar appealed to al-Ḥasan, who wrote to Yūsuf, but the latter only threatened: 'Unless al-Ḥasan leaves me alone, I shall submit (*sallamtu*) Gabès to the lord of Sicily'. When al-Ḥasan prepared an army against him, Yūsuf wrote to Roger

> and offered him his obedience (*ṭāᶜa*), saying 'I want from you a robe of office and a diploma of investiture to the governorship of Gabès so that I can be your representative (*urīdu … khilᶜatan wa-ahdan bi-wilāyati Qābisa li-akūna nāʾiban ᶜan-ka*), as you did with the Banī Maṭrūḥ in Tripoli'. Roger sent robes and diplomas to him, so he put one on, and read out the diplomas to an assembly of the people.

Whereupon, adds Ibn Abī Dīnār, Yūsuf 'collected the taxes (*amwāl*) of Gabès in obedience (*ṭāᶜa*) to [Roger]'. Yūsuf was killed within the year, and al-Ḥasan restored Muᶜammar as his governor. But Yūsuf's brother fled to Sicily with the young Muḥammad, whom George of Antioch eventually reinstated as *wālī* after the capture of al-Mahdīya.[49]

Sousse seems to have been entrusted to Jabbāra ibn Kāmil al-Fādighī, who had been closely allied to its Zīrid governor, and who may have governed with some sort of *shūrā* or council of leading citizens.[50] At Sfax, George originally sought to appoint the venerable Abū l-Ḥasan al-Furriyānī as his *ᶜāmil*, but was persuaded to accept his son, ᶜUmar, on condition that the *shaykh* became his hostage in Palermo.[51]

In every Ifrīqiyan city, except al-Mahdīya itself, Roger acted exactly as a Muslim ruler would have done in establishing a subordinate monarchy, according to established Islamic practice, by appointing or confirming a local leader as governor and sending him a robe of office and diploma of investiture, and by appointing a *qāḍī*. Thereafter, so long as he continued to acknowledge Sicilian overlordship, and to forward tax revenue to Palermo, each governor was left very much to himself. The royal *dīwān* thus governed by remote control: it composed and dispatched the *amān* and letters of appointment to the governor, and no doubt made sure that the *ṭirāz* sent him the right official robe; but thereafter it just received revenue, without interfering in the internal affairs of what were, in effect, independent city-states that acknowledged Norman overlordship. When the moment came, each governor led his citizens in revolt against Sicilian rule, and transferred his allegiance to the Almohads.

[49] Ibn al-Athīr 1851–76, vol.XI, p.79 (*BAS*², vol.I, p.330–31; *BAS*²*(It.)*, vol.II, p.368). Ibn Abī Dīnār 1967, p.94 (*BAS*², vol.II, p.606; *BAS*²*(It.)*, vol.III, p.662), tells substantially the same tale, but has Yūsuf offer to become Roger's *ᶜāmil*. Roger sends him a *sijill*, and 'one of the signs of honour of the Christians' (*mā yutasharrafu bi-hi min tashārīfi l-naṣārā*). See also: Idris 1962a, vol.I, pp.352–5; Brett 1999b, pp.8–9.

[50] Ibn al-Athīr 1851–76, vol.XI, pp.84–5 (*BAS*², vol.I, p.335; *BAS*²*(It.)*, vol.II, p.373); al-Tījānī 1958, p.30 (*BAS*², vol.II, pp.433; *BAS*²*(It.)*, vol.II, pp.487). See also: Idris 1962a, vol.I, pp.358–9, 394; Brett 1999b, pp.9, 11–12.

[51] Ibn al-Athīr 1851–76, vol.XI, pp.134 (*BAS*², vol.I, p.339; *BAS*²*(It.)*, vol.II, pp.377–8); al-Tījānī 1958, pp.74–6 (*BAS*², vol.II, pp.436–7; *BAS*²*(It.)*, vol.II, pp.489–91). See also Idris 1962a, vol.I, pp.359, 380–2, 394. Brett 1999b, p.9, 12–15.

The contrast with Sicily is striking. There, the local Muslim leader, Abū l-Qāsim, had never been officially delegated the powers of a subordinate ruler. His authority over the Muslim community of the island depended entirely upon his prestige and wealth, and the latter was subject to the whim of the Christian king. Although he might be asked to intervene with the *dīwān* on behalf of a Muslim community, his position as *sayyid* gave him no right to do so, and the *dīwān* governed the Muslims of Sicily directly, completely ignoring his *siyāda*. It is this that seems to explain Abū l-Qāsim's presence within the *dīwān* in an official position which gave him both the authority and the means to intervene between the Christian government and his Muslim subjects.

At the same time, such figures as Abū l-Qāsim, and his rival al-Sadīd, were so important to the Norman regime that their political blunders were promptly ignored or forgiven. Al-Sadīd had backed the loser in 1167, but he was still a royal counsellor in 1168. Abū l-Qāsim had been disgraced and punished for communicating with the Almohads, but he was left in place as the leader of the Muslim community, and entrusted with important government business. As Ibn al-Athīr, Ibn Qalāqis and Ibn Jubayr all attest, it enhanced the image of the king in Muslim eyes to have Muslim leaders as his companions and counsellors. But their association in government and administration also complicated and confused what would otherwise have seemed a more straightforward question of Christian oppression. When the Muslims of Syracuse sought relief from the Christian *jizya* and wrote to Abū l-Qāsim, and when he put their petition aside, pleading pressure of business, was he the Muslim *sayyid* or the servant of the Christian king? Unlike their Ifrīqiyan counterparts, who led the revolt against William I and retained power under the Almohads, the traditional leaders of the Muslim community in Sicily were ultimately disempowered by their ambiguous relationship with the Christian regime. The descendants of Abū l-Qāsim lost the *siyāda* and converted to Christianity, while a newly arrived immigrant, Muḥammad ibn ᶜAbbād, became the *amīr al-muslimīn bi-Ṣiqillīya*, 'the commander of the Muslims of Sicily', and united the Muslim rebels against Frederick II.[52]

Islamic justice and the royal *dīwān*

Ibn al-Athīr reported that King Roger 'founded a Court of Complaints, *dīwān al-maẓālim*, to which those [Muslims] who had been unjustly treated brought their grievances, and [the king] would give them justice, even against his own son'.[53]

[52] Muḥammad ibn ᶜAbbād is said to have been a native of al-Mahdīya who immigrated to Sicily as a young man and so endeared himself to an otherwise unknown Ibn Fākhir, the *ṣāḥib* of the Muslim rebels of Sicily, that the latter married him to one of his daughters and made him his successor: al-Ḥamāwī 1960 p.295, line 11 – p.298, line 10 (al-Ḥamāwī 1981, pp.99–101; *BAS*², vol.I, p.361; *BAS*²*(It.)*, vol.II, p.401). Ibn ᶜAbbād appears with the title quoted on an unpublished *fils*, photographs of which I have thanks to Sig. Giuseppe Di Martino of Palermo. For Ibn ᶜAbbād's other coins, see: D'Angelo 1975; De Luca 1998, p.391, nos 20–1. [53] Above, p.255.

This is a startling and apparently rhetorical claim, but should not be rejected or ignored on that count alone, and merits further consideration.

During the 2nd century of Islam, the early ᶜAbbāsid caliphs bound the office of *qāḍī* to the *sharīᶜa* or sacred law, and separated it from the general administration. Criminal justice, taxation, and administrative justice in general were retained by the caliph, or delegated to his governors, and came to be covered by the general term *siyāsa* or 'policy'. Although the *qāḍī* was theoretically independent of the temporal power, he was in fact appointed and dismissed by the ruler, he depended upon the temporal authorities to execute his judgements, and he was obliged in law to follow the instructions of the ruler insofar as they fell within the limits of the *sharīᶜa* – called *siyāsa sharᶜīya* or 'lawful policy-making'.

The early caliphs had assumed the prerogative of investigating complaints (*naẓar fī-l-maẓālim*) concerning miscarriages of justice and wrongs allegedly committed by *qāḍī*s, government officials, and other powerful individuals. In practice, the most important lawsuits concerning property, particularly the usurpation of property, or *ghaṣb*, although they theoretically fell under the *qāḍī*s' jurisdiction, tended to be treated as *maẓālim*, and in such cases Courts of Complaints tended to supersede the *qāḍī*s' tribunals.[54]

In Norman Sicily, both the king's law, and seigneurial interpretations of it, upheld the principle that each of the island's communities, Greek, Jewish, Latin, and Muslim, was to be judged by its own law.[55] Administrative justice, taxation, and the more serious criminal cases, belonged to the royal courts, or to those of Latin lords, as did intercommunal disputes.

Exactly what this meant in practice is difficult to judge on the evidence available, and is sure to have varied considerably from place to place and from time to time. In early 1230s, during a lull in the Muslim rebellions, Frederick II attempted to ensure that his law protected Jews and Muslims against Christians. He legislated against the deliberate concealment of such crimes as the felling of trees, the burning of dwellings, and other crimes committed under the cover of darkness, and remarked that 'We cannot in the least permit Jews and Saracens to be defrauded of the power of our protection and to be deprived of all other help, just because the difference of their religious practice (*sectae*) makes them hateful to Christians'.[56]

[54] Nielson 1990.

[55] From the Vatican Codex (MS Fond. lat. 8782) of the so-called 'Assizes of Ariano' (Roger II, 1140): *Leges a nostra maiestate noviter promulgatas, [pietatis intuitu asperitatem nimiam mitigantes, mollia quodam moderamine exacuentes, obscura dilucidantes,] generaliter ab omnibus precipimus observari: moribus, consuetudinibus, legibus non cassatis, [pro varietate populorum nostro regno subiectorum, sicut usque nunc apud eos optinuit,] nisi forte nostris his sanctionibus adversari quid in eis manifestissime videatur*: the passages enclosed by square brackets are omitted from the Monte Cassino Codex (MS 468/341/869): Brandilione 1884, pp.95–6, 119. On 22 December 1168 A.D., Bishop John of Catania decreed that *Latini, Graeci, Iudaei, et Sarraceni unusquisque, iuxta suam legem iudicetur* : De Grossis 1654, pp.88–9 (reproduced in the more accessible Lagumina 1884–1909, vol.I, p.12. no.15).

[56] Conrad, von der Lieck-Buyken and Wagner 1973, I.xxvii, p.40 *Nec minus Judaeos et etiam Saracenos, quos, quia sectae diversitas Christianis reddit infestos, omni auxilio alio destitutos protectionis Nostrae potentia pati non possumus defraudari*; von der Lieck-Buyken 1978, I.xxxi, p.32 Ναὶ μὴν καὶ τοὺς Ἰουδαίους καὶ [τοὺς] Σαρακηνούς, οὓς, ἐπειδὴ ἡ διαφορὰ τῆς

In cases where the identity of a murderer was deliberately concealed, the property-owners (*possessores*) of the community in which the crime had been committed were to be fined – one hundred *augustales* if the victim were Christian, fifty if he were a Jew or a Muslim – and the emperor took the opportunity to observe that he considered the persecution of Jews and Muslims by Christians to have grown excessive.[57] Elsewhere, he specifically included Jews and Muslims in a general right to initiate procedures (*defensae*) in the royal courts in order to protect their persons or property against attack by Christians whom they would otherwise have been powerless to resist. In doing so, he commented that he did not wish the innocent to be hindered from seeking his protection, just because they were Jews or Saracens.[58] These were exceptional times, of course, and one has the distinct impression that the emperor was seeking to halt a process of ethnic cleansing that he himself had favoured during the 1220s, but which had now grown beyond his control. Under the Norman kings, royal authority had apparently protected law-abiding Muslim subjects without the need for such extraordinary measures.

The Muslim community of the island had its own *qāḍī*. As would have been the case under a Muslim ruler, he was appointed and could be dismissed by the king, and he was obliged to recognise the king's law even when it clashed with the *sharīᶜa*. The legitimacy and authority of a *qāḍī*, and of other Islamic court officials, who had been appointed by a Christian king was a crucial and disputed matter. It hinged upon two questions: the legal propriety (*ᶜadāla*) of a *qāḍī* who dwelt under Christian rule, something that was not permissible by choice but only under necessity; and the validity of his appointment by a Christian ruler. The Ifrīqiyan jurist al-Māzarī (d.1141), who had been born in Sicily, argued that, even though the appointment of a *qāḍī* by the Sicilian king was not legally valid, because the Muslims of the island were isolated from the greater body of believers, and because the *qāḍī* must be allowed to have remained in Sicily out of the necessity of caring for them, there could be no objection to his rulings, nor to their execution, just as if he had been appointed by a Muslim ruler. Other authorities took the opposite view.[59]

πίστεως παρίστησι τοῖς χριστιανοῖς μισητούς, πάσης ἄλλης βοηθείας γεγυμνωμένους οὐ δυνάμεθα ὑποφέρειν ὑστερεῖσθαι τούτους τῆς δυνάμεως τῆς ἡμετέρας σκέπης καὶ βοηθείας; Powell 1971, I.xxvii(31), p.29.

[57] Conrad, von der Lieck-Buyken and Wagner 1973, I.xxviii, p.42 *Si vero Judaeus aut Saracenus sit, in quibus, prout certo perpendimus, Christianorum persecutio nimis abundat ad praesens, quinquaginta augustalibus praedictorum locorum incolas Nostro aerario applicandis damnandos esse censemus*; von der Lieck-Buyken 1978, I.xxxii, p.33 Εἰ δὲ Ἰουδαῖος ἢ Σαρακηνὸς [ἦν], ἐν οἷς, [καθὼς] ἀριδήλως ἐγνώκαμεν, ἡ τῶν χριστιανῶν δίωξις μᾶλλον ἐνδαψιλεύεται, πεντήκοντα αὐγουσταλίων ποινῇ τοὺς κατοίκους τῶν εἰρημένων τόπων τῷ ἡμετέρῳ ταμείῳ κατακρίτους εἶναι ὁρίζομεν; Powell 1971, I.xxviii(32), p.30.

[58] Conrad, von der Lieck-Buyken and Wagner 1973, I.xviii, p.28 *Judaeis autem et Saracenis et pro eis aliis, officialibus scilicet, in praedictis casibus imponendi defensas concedimus facultatem, quos non propterea, quia Judaei vel Saraceni sunt, arceri volumus innocentes*; von der Lieck-Buyken 1978, I.xxi, p.25 Τοῖς δὲ Ἰουδαίοις καὶ Σαρακηνοῖς, καὶ ὑπὲρ αὐτῶν τοῖς ὀφφικιαλίοις, ἐν τοῖς προειρημένοις θέμασι παρέχομεν ἄδειαν ἐπιτιθέναι ποινάς· ἐπειδὴ οὐ βουλόμεθα τούτους ἀδικεῖσθαι διὰ τὸ εἶναι αὐτοὺς Σαρακηνούς τε καὶ Ἰουδαίους; Powell 1971, I.xviii (21), p.22.

[59] al-Wansharīshī 1981, vol.X, pp.107–9; see also Turki 1984; Turki 1992; Udovitch 1995, pp.209–10; Brett 1999b, pp.4–6. For al-Māzarī, see ᶜAbd al-Wahhāb 1955, Idris 1962b, and Borruso 1978.

For much of the 12th century, from the 1120s until the 1160s, one family provided three successive *qāḍī*s of Sicily (see Table 3.1). They claimed as their ancestor, real or symbolic, one Rajāʾ, whose name, meaning 'Hope', was that of a legendary specialist in Islamic law of the late Umayyad period. In the private Arabic documents, the Banū Rajāʾ *qāḍī*s deal exclusively with property transactions in which all parties were Muslims, but this reflects the nature of the surviving documents, and does not indicate the full scope of their authority.[60]

Roger II's *kātib* and panegyricist, Abū l-Ḍawʾ Sirāj ibn Aḥmad ibn Rajāʾ, came from the same family. In January 1123, he and his uncle, *al-shaykh al-faqīh al-qāḍī* Abū l-Qāsim ᶜAbd al-Raḥmān ibn Rajāʾ, assisted the emir Christodoulos and the judge Nicholas of Reggio in a lawsuit brought before Roger's court. As we have seen repeatedly, the resolution of disputes arising out of allegations of usurpation of property was standard business for officers of the *dīwān*, who normally held a boundary-inquest to decide the issue. In this one case, however, in which both the ruler, through his delegates, and the *qāḍī* were involved, we see something which much more closely resembles the *dīwān al-maẓālim* of a Muslim ruler. A family of Muslims had accused Roger's cousin, Muriella of Petterrana, of having usurped property which had belonged to their parents – *i.e.* of *ghaṣb*. In her defence, Muriella's agents presented an Arabic deed of sale recording the purchase of the mill by her men. The *qāḍī* of Palermo was summoned to inspect the document, and found that it did indeed uphold Muriella's rights. But, significantly, the deed alone was considered insufficient proof, and witnesses from the neighbourhood were also called to testify that her accusers had no legal claim to the mill. This indicates the influence upon the judgement of Islamic law, in which legal proof was typically restricted to the evidence of witnesses, while the validity of written documents was denied. The presence of Abū l-Ḍawʾ may also indicate the influence of Islamic practice, for al-Maqrīzī calls him Roger's *kātib al-inshāʾ*, and, in Fāṭimid Egypt, it was the *dīwān al-inshāʾ* that played the central rôle in processing *maẓālim* petitions.[61]

The sale of Zaynab's house to the royal servant, Niqūla Ashqar, in September 1190, was another legal case that was completed through the close co-operation between the Islamic legal authorities and the royal *dīwān*. Here, King Tancred's delegate, who is called only 'the Lord Protector' (*al-mawlā al-nāṣir*), and the lords of the *dīwān al-fawāʾid* supervised the sale of Zaynab's house according to Islamic law, in order to raise the ransom demanded by her Christian captors.[62]

These two cases throw a rather different light upon the figure of Ibn Zurᶜa, as described by Ibn Jubayr:

> Sometimes exemplary punishments were inflicted [by William II] upon one of the sheikhs [of the Muslims] as the means of inducing him to give up his faith. Amongst these cases is a story which happened in recent years concerning one of the jurists in the

[60] Above, p.88 (**Private 6** and **9**).

[61] al-Qalqashandī 1913–72, vol.VI, pp.202–10; Nielson 1990, p.934. For the Fāṭimid *maẓālim*, see especially Stern 1962, pp.186–209.

[62] Above, pp.204–6 (**Private 26**).

> city which is the seat of their king the tyrant. He is called Ibn Zurʿa. [The royal officials[63]] oppressed him with [their] demand[s] until he made known [his] rejection of the faith of Islam and [his] immersion in the faith of Christianity. He became expert in the memorisation of the Gospels, in the study of the customs of the Europeans, and in the observance of the precepts of their sacred law, so that he came to belong to the body of priests who were asked to give legal opinions in Christian lawsuits. Sometimes a Muslim lawsuit arose, and he was asked to give his legal opinion upon it too, according to the experience that he had previously acquired in Islamic lawsuits. Thus his formal legal opinion was sought in both legal systems.[64]

Although Ibn Jubayr further claims that Ibn Zurʿa had converted his personal mosque into a church, and begs God to protect Muslims from such apostasy, he also reports the rumour that Ibn Zurʿa was a secret Muslim, and practised *taqīya*. What we may see here, through the uncomprehending eyes of a pious visitor, is not so much the apostasy of a *faqīh* as an attempt by the Christian authorities to develop a pragmatic approach to the perennial problem of inter-communal disputes.

Of course, the Christian king could never have persuaded his Muslim subjects that he was a legitimate source of legal authority, but, by allowing Muslims the *sharīʿa*, by appointing a *qāḍī* from one of their leading families, and by hearing disputes between Christians and Muslims in his own court – including complaints brought by Muslims against members of his own family – in the presence of the *qāḍī* and with reference to Islamic law, the Sicilian king sought – and, on Ibn al-Athīr's testimony, to some extent succeeded – to display himself in the robes of a Muslim ruler exercising the prerogative of lawful policy-making (*siyāsa sharʿīya*).

The Norman kings also used the officers of the *dīwān*, more widely than in the two cases discussed above, to impose and to execute aspects of administrative legislation, and to dispense elements of administrative justice. Notoriously, the *qāʾid* Martin used the judicial powers delegated to him by William I in his absence from Palermo to avenge himself upon the rebels of 1161. According to 'Hugo Falcandus', Martin presided over his own court (*pretorium*), encouraged Christians to settle their disputes through trial by combat, and even executed capital punishment, 'with the Muslims looking on and mocking [the victims]'.[65] A few months later, the *qāʾid* Peter was delegated unspecified judicial powers, apparently also to punish the rebels of 1161. 'Hugo Falcandus' again seems to imply that Peter, in league with his crypto-Muslim henchman Robert of Calatabiano, used his judicial

63 Supplied by Wright.

64 *Wa-rubbamā tasabbaba ilā baʿḍi ashyāki-him asbābun nakālīyatun tadʿū-hu ilā firāqi dīni-hi fa-min-hā qissatuni ttafaqat fī hādhihi l-sinīna l-qarībati li-baʿḍi fuqahāʾi madīnati-himi llatī hiya ḥaḍratu maliki-himi l-tāghiyati wa-yuʿrafu bi-bni zurʿata ḍaghaṭat-hu l-ʿummālu bi-l-muṭālabati ḥattā aẓhara firāqa dīni l-islāmi wa-l-inghimāsa fī dīni l-naṣrānīyati wa-mahara fī ḥifẓi l-injīli wa-muṭālaʿati siyari l-rūmi wa-ḥifẓi qawānīni sharīʿati-him fa-ʿāda fī jumlati l-qissīsīna lladhīna yustaftawna fī l-aḥkāmi l-naṣrānīyati wa-rubbamā ṭaraʾa ḥukmun islāmīyun fa-yustaftā ayḍan fī-hi li-mā sabaqa min maʿrifati-hi bi-l-aḥkāmi l-sharʿīyati wa-yaqaʿu l-wuqūfu ʿinda futyā-hu fī kilā l-ḥukmayni*: Ibn Jubayr 1907, p.340 (Ibn Jubayr 1949–65, vol.III, pp.399–400; Ibn Jubayr 1952, pp.357; *BAS*^{2}, vol.I, p.101; *BAS*^{2}*(It.)*, vol.I, p.141).

65 'Hugo Falcandus' 1897, pp.79–80 (trans. 'Hugo Falcandus' 1998, pp.129–131). See also above, p.221.

authority to the benefit of the Muslims of Palermo.[66] It is impossible to know the extent to which 'Hugo Falcandus' based such rhetorical claims upon real events.

The field of administrative legislation in which the *dīwān* was most active, of course, was taxation. By an inversion of Islamic practice, the Muslims of Sicily had been transformed into *dhimmīs* in their own land and required to pay the *jizya*. The Christian king, and his Muslim subjects, were both fully aware that he was treating them much as a Muslim ruler would have treated Christians.[67] This raises more questions than it answers. Did the familiarity of the *dhimma* and the *jizya* make them more acceptable to Sicilian Muslims? Did his use of the *dhimma* and the *jizya* enhance the image of the Norman king as a just ruler, or condemn him as an oppressor and tyrant? But such questions treat the Muslim community as a united whole, and take no account of variation in individual belief and material circumstances. Ibn Jubayr reports that the Muslims of Palermo were divided between those – the majority? – who accepted the Christian *dhimma*, and an Islamist group – the minority? – who rejected it, despite the cost. We may doubt that the former accepted the justice of their lot, but we know that the latter did not: 'In general, they are cut off from their brother Muslims [who live] under the *dhimma* of the unbelievers, and they have no security for their property, wives, and children'.[68]

'Sacred letters'

In conclusion, let us return to Peter of Eboli's use of the image of the trilingual chancery. Alone in the 12th-century Mediterranean, the Sicilian kings issued coins and documents, commissioned manuscripts, and set up monumental inscriptions in Arabic, Greek, and Latin. Under King Roger II, a remarkable series of trilingual inscriptions was composed within the palace, and with the collaboration of the royal *dīwān*. The Arabic text of the trilingual inscription from Roger II's clepsydra opens with a formula identical to that of *dīwānī* documents: 'There went forth the order of the most royal, the most glorified, the Rogerian, the most high presence, may God prolong its days and give strength to its banners'.[69] Similarly, Roger's Arabic protocol in the famous 'quadrilingual' inscription of 1148 was modelled upon that used in contemporary royal documents, and was composed within the *dīwān* for Grisantus, a priest of the Cappella Palatina.[70] When the *qāʾid* Peter, the royal chamberlain and elder of the *dīwān al-maʿmūr*, commemorated his patronage of a public building in Termini Imerese, he did so in an inscription composed in

[66] Above, p.224. [67] See, in particular, the case of Ifrīqiya: Brett 1999b.

[68] *Wa-bi-l-jumlati fa-hum ʿuzabāʾu ʿan ikhwāni-himi l-muslimīna taḥta dhimmati l-kuffāri wa-lā amna la-hum fī amwāli-him wa-lā fī ḥarīmi-him wa-lā abnāʾi-him*: Ibn Jubayr 1907, p.332 (Ibn Jubayr 1949–65, vol.III, pp.399–400; Ibn Jubayr 1952, pp.357; *BAS*², vol.I, p.93; *BAS*²*(It.)*, vol.I, p.130).

[69] *Kharaja amru l-ḥaḍrati l-malakīyati l-muʿaẓẓamīyati l-rujārīyati l-ʿalīyati abbada llāhu ayyāma-hā wa-ayyada aʿlāma-hā …*: see above, p.134. [70] Above, p.136, note 73.

Arabic, Greek, and Latin.[71] No trilingual documents are known to have been issued by the royal *dīwān*, but thirty of the thirty-six known *dīwānī* documents were bilingual. Roger II introduced bilingual coinage, and his godson, Roger-Aḥmad, had a bilingual seal. Trilingual and bilingual public texts were effectively a royal monopoly, broken by no institution or individual outside the narrow circle of the court and palace. They were symbols of royal power.

Horst Enzensberger has written perceptively of the way in which the royal documents of the Norman kings assumed a quasi-sacred character which transcended their function as mere administrative instruments.[72] Royal decrees were referred to as *sacrae litterae*,[73] and those who tampered with them were liable to the capital penalty.[74] Enzensberger was essentially concerned with documents written in Latin, and to a lesser extent in Greek, but the same is true, arguably *a fortiori*, of Arabic documents.

The Norman kings faced a particular problem in projecting the Arabic facet of their monarchy. The king was represented in the garb of a Muslim ruler in painted panels on the ceiling of the Cappella Palatina, but these images were not shown beyond the walls of the palace. It is impossible to know why this was so, but it may be significant that the conventions of Islamic art generally restricted figural representations of a ruler to the palace, and effectively forbade their dissemination throughout the kingdom or abroad. Not so with the Byzantine aspect of the royal persona. True, it was in the private foundation of his chief minister, George of Antioch, that King Roger was most splendidly portrayed in the robes of the Byzantine *basileus*,[75] but a similar image was widely disseminated throughout the realm, and abroad, on silver and copper coins,[76] and on seals.[77] Islamic documents were not validated with a seal that portrayed the ruler, but with his *ᶜalāma*. Islamic coins did not usually bear the portrait of the ruler, but only his written name. Nor did any Norman coin with an Arabic inscription carry a figural representation of the king. Those media other than representational art in which the Norman king could appear as a Muslim ruler – palace art and architecture, royal ceremonial, the patronage of Arab scholars and men of letters – were physically restricted to the palace and to a limited area around it. The only medium which allowed the image of the king as a Muslim ruler to be disseminated widely throughout Sicily, and the Muslim world beyond, was the written word.

In a classic article, Richard Ettinghausen suggested that Arabic inscriptions as a whole remained mostly unread.[78] By this he meant that, for any given religious inscription, 'a reading by the most learned *shaykh* or *mollā* is nearly always based

[71] Above, p.223, note 41. [72] Enzensberger 1981.

[73] Kehr 1902, p.129, n.4, and p.449; Enzensberger 1971, p.104.

[74] *Qui litteras regi[as] aut mutat aut ipsas ipse scribit aut eas notho sigillat sigillo, capitaliter puniatur*: Conrad, von der Lieck-Buyken and Wagner 1973, III.lxi, pp.328–9; von der Lieck-Buyken 1978, III.xxxix, p.139; Powell 1971, III.lxi(39), p.141.

[75] Kitzinger 1950; Kitzinger 1990, pp.313–16 and pls XXIII, XXV.

[76] Travaini 1995, nos 175–6, pp.279–82, no.241, pp.210–14, no.300, pp.220–2.

[77] Engel 1882, pp.85–7, nos 13 (pl.I.11), 15 (pl.I.12), 16 (pl.I.13), 17 (pl.I.14), 18 (pl.I.15), 20 (pl.I.16), 21 (pl.I.17). [78] Ettinghausen 1974, p.303.

on previous knowledge and not on direct visual word by word recognition. On the other hand, for the vast majority of the congregation and passers-by the inscription remains incomprehensible as a verbal communication in the modern sense'.[79] Nonetheless, Ettinghausen argued, such unread or incomprehensible inscriptions are 'a symbolic affirmation before God of the faith ... The lettering is the message, rather than its content'.[80] Ettinghausen was here concerned with but one of the two predominant ideas conveyed by Arabic inscriptions – with divine power, in the form of Qurʾānic quotations, pious invocations and phrases, confessions of faith, mystical allusions, and prayers for the dead. He points out, however, that his observations may be no less pertinent to the second predominant theme of Arabic epigraphy – absolute political authority, conveyed by the names of the sovereign, his titles, his exploits, and his perpetual praise.[81] Ettinghausen did not put forward a hard and fast rule – on the contrary, some texts were definitely meant to be read – but an inscription's readability and, in general, the non-communicative nature of inscriptions, should always be taken into account.

As to the use of Arabic by the kings of Sicily, the monumental and funerary inscriptions, the numismatic legends, and the *ṭirāz*-texts fit Ettinghausen's case well enough: here, it was the Arabic letters rather than their legible content which carried the message of royal power to the majority. One has only to think of the royal *alqāb* on the ceiling of the Cappella Palatina, too high to be read as words, just low enough to be recognised as letters. But the documents of the royal *dīwān* obviously constitute a very different case. Their content was – or should have been – of crucial importance to their recipients. And yet, as we have seen repeatedly, the vast majority of royal Arabic documents went to recipients who did not read Arabic, and did not use Arabic documents for the administrative or fiscal purposes for which they were ostensibly intended. In addition to their internal, textual meaning, the Arabic letters of *dīwānī* documents also carried a powerful external message – one which, at times, was of equal or even greater importance than the administrative value of the texts.

The Arabic administration grew out of memorials of Norman power over the conquered Arabs of the island. The *amān*s or treaties by which the Muslim communities of Sicily were incorporated under Norman rule, and the first *jarāʾid* or lists of Muslim *jizya*-payers, commemorated the act of conquest. They also subverted the practice by which vanquished Christians were incorporated into the *Dār al-Islām*. What is more, the subversion of what was believed to be a Qurʾānic prescription was effected in Arabic, in the language in which God had sent the Holy *Qurʾān*. Again in a subversion of Islamic practice, conquered Muslims were required to bind themselves as *dhimmī*s and as *rijāl al-jarāʾid* by swearing upon the *Qurʾān*.[82]

The *jarāʾid* were lists of the subjects over whom the king exercised power, either directly or through his feudatories. Those villeins who owed service upon

[79] Ettinghausen 1974, p.306.
[80] Ettinghausen 1974, p.307.
[81] Ettinghausen 1974, pp.311–17.
[82] Above, p.35 (**Private 16**).

their own persons did so specifically because their names were recorded in writing. They were known as the *rijāl al-jarāʾid*, 'the men of the registers', and οἱ ἐναπόγραφοι (*oi enapografoi*) and *adscriptitii*, 'the registered', and they were distinguished from those who – in theory, but not in practice – were 'the unregistered'.[83] Similarly, the *dafātir al-ḥudūd* recorded the boundaries of the lands over which the king ruled. And the power of written boundary-descriptions is apparent both in the formal procedure of the boundary inquest through which they were established, and in the weight that they carried in boundary disputes.[84]

The calligraphic scripts in which most *dīwānī* documents were written after 1132 distinguished them from the products of private scribes and, at a glance, identified them as royal documents. The elaborate care that was taken in the production of decrees and donations is not unexpected, but it is remarkable that King Roger's *jarāʾid*, lists of mere villeins, were prepared with the same scrupulous care, by the same master scribes, who made no attempt to restrain their pens to save costly parchment. The bilingual products of the *dīwān* were even more conspicuously royal than those in Arabic alone, for no comparable bilingual documents were composed outside the palace. Just as a coin could be instantly recognised as royal by the letters of its inscriptions, rather than by their legible content, so could a document be recognised as a product of the royal *dīwān* purely by the style of the Arabic letters, or by the combination of Arabic and Greek scripts.

The *jarāʾid* renewed in 1145 were of little or no practical use to their recipients, but they were potent memorials of royal authority. First had come the disconcerting edict *de resignandis privilegiis*, which had caused all the king's feudatories, from the bishop of distant Catania to a backwoods baron like Roger Forestal, to hunt out and dust off their half-forgotten, fifty-year-old *jarāʾid*. Then, there had been the great council of feudatories at Palermo in the winter of 1144–5, which had brought them into direct contact, often for the first time, with the new royal *dīwān*. At this meeting, most barons and churchmen had found themselves at a distinct disadvantage: uncertain that their privileges would be renewed; unfamiliar with the new customs and procedures; suspicious of the Arab eunuchs and Greek scribes; impatient at the long and unnerving delay, during which their old registers were scrutinised; uneasy lest their usurpations and evasions be discovered; resentful of the fees which they were bound to pay; and, at the end of it all, unable to make out the content of their new bilingual documents. As they returned to their estates and churches, they carried with them a vivid, but disturbing and perplexing, impression of the new regime, and a tangible statement of the authority of the royal *dīwān*, its central rôle in the administration of the kingdom and in the execution of royal policy, written in letters which they could understand only as symbols of royal power.

[83] Above, pp.145–51. [84] Above, pp.170–86.

APPENDIX 1

Catalogue of *dīwānī* documents

Count Roger I

1. [1093 A.D.] 6601 A.M., Indiction I [1 January to 31 August]. Mazara.

An unknown number of *plateiai* issued to Roger I and his barons. In the Greek conclusion to ***Dīwānī* 4**, Roger refers to 'the *plateiai* of my own lands and of my barons, which were written at Mazarra (*sic*) in the year 6601 [A.M. = 1093 A.D.], in Indiction I'. They are mentioned again in ***Dīwānī* 21–2** as 'the *jarā'id* which were written at Mazara two years earlier' [*i.e.* than ***Dīwānī* 3–4**]. All seem to be lost, but see ***Dīwānī* 5**.

Pp.54 note 111, 59–60, 144, 281.

2. [1095 A.D.] 12 February. Palermo.

A Greek donation and *plateia* in which Count Roger I grants to the cathedral church of Santa Maria di Palermo ninety-five households of 'Hagarenes', together with their lands, amounting to eleven 'ox-lands', in the districts of Iato, Corleone, and Limonos (*i.e.* near Maganoce, Arabic *Maghanūja*, 3km south of modern Piana degli Albanesi). The Hagarenes were to pay to the church a collective tribute of seven hundred and fifty *tarì* twice a year, in August and during the winter, and, again collectively, one hundred and fifty *modia* of wheat and the same amount of barley. The Greek privilege incorporates both an Arabic *jarīda* of seventy-five villeins, and a Greek *katonoma* of their twenty *neokamoi* (*sic* for *neogamoi*).

Original: PA, Arch. Dioc., no.5: ed. Mongitore 1734, pp.13–14 (Latin trans. of Greek only); Mortillaro 1843, no.5, pp.164–7; Cusa 1868–82, no.6, pp.1–3 (reg. pp.695–6).

Pp.46–51, 59–60, 107, 108, 140, 145, 146, 275 and note 96, 281.

3. [1095 A.D.]

An Arabic *jarīda* listing the population of Catania granted by Count Roger I to Ansgerius, bishop of Catania. A *deperditum* renewed on 1 January 1145 A.D. (= ***Dīwānī* 21**).

Pp.41, 52–8, 119–20, 131, 141, 281.

4. [1095 A.D.] 6603 A.M., Indiction III, 20 February. Messina.

An Arabic *jarīda*, called *plateia* in the short Greek introduction, of the 'Hagarenes' of Aci [Castello] (Γιάκην, *Liyāj*) granted by Count Roger to [Ansgerius], bishop of Catania. The *jarīda* lists 390 names, including 337 men and 53 'widows'. The *jarīda* is written in Arabic only. It is preceded by a short introduction and conclusion, both in Greek. It was renewed in [January?] 1145 = ***Dīwānī* 22**.

Original: CT, Arch. Dioc., arabo-greco no.1; ed. Cusa 1868–82, no.7, pp.541–9 (reg. p.696).

Pp.41, 51–8, 59, 107, 108, 120–1, 132, 139–40, 141, 275 and note 96, 281.

5. [1093–5? A.D.]

An Arabic *jarīda* of the population of Jāliṣū granted by Count Roger to Roger Forestal. A *deperditum* mentioned in the Arabic *narratio* of its renewal (***Dīwānī* 25**): 'a *jarīda* from the Great Sultan [i.e. Roger I] (may God sanctify his spirit and illuminate his tomb!) to Roger Forestal … in which was listed what he was granted of the men of the *jarīda* of Jāliṣū, but not those written in the *jarīda* of Corleone'.

Pp.58, 59, 125–6, 141, 281.

6. [1097–8 A.D.] 6606 A.M., Indiction VI.

A *deperditum*, in all probability a Greek *sigillion* containing an Arabic *jarīda*, listing the villeins granted by Count Roger I to San Giorgio di Triocala, mentioned in ***Dīwānī* 15–17** and renewed as ***Dīwānī* 18**. After having conquered Sicily from the Hagarenes, Count Roger I founded the monastery of San Giorgio in memory of the Christians who had died in the war, and issued various *sigillia* to the abbot. These included the Arabic *jarīda* renewed in November 1141 (***Dīwānī* 18**).

Pp.58–9, 107, 281.

Countess Adelaide and Count Roger II

7. [1109 A.D.], Indiction II, March 6. Messina.

A Greek-Arabic decree (*entalma, kitāb*), written on paper, in which the Countess Adelaide and the young Roger II order the officials of the district of Castrogiovanni (Enna) to protect the abbey of San Filippo di Fragalà at Demenna in the valley of San Marco d'Alunzio. The text may also have referred to the grant to San Filippo of the right to extract salt from the mines of Castrogiovanni.

Original: PA, AdS, San Filippo di Fragalà, no.9; Caspar 1904, reg.7, p.484; Collura 1955a, p.556, reg.6; von Falkenhausen 1998, p.108, reg.11; ed. Cusa 1868–82, no.23, pp.402–3 (reg. p.700); La Mantia 1908; Giuffrida and Rocco 1982; Prosperi 1996.

Pp.74–8, 270–1, 275 and note 96.

8. [1111 A.D.], Indiction IV, May. [Messina.]

An Arabic-Greek *jarīda* confirming the grant (by Roger I?) of 8 villeins and their lands, perhaps at the unidentified site of Labourzi near Messina, to the knight Julian.

Original: Paris, Bibl. Nat., MS. Gr. suppl. no.1315,1; Collura 1955a, pp.558–59, reg.9; von Falkenhausen 1998, p.111, reg.21; ed. Guillou 1963, no.3, pp.51–5, pl.II.a–b.

Pp.75–8, 107, 275 and note 96, 281.

Count Roger II

†9. [1124 A.D.] 6632 A.M., Indiction II, January. Mazara.

A Greek *sigillion* in which Roger, count of Italy, Calabria, and Sicily, endows the church of San Michele Arcangelo at Mazara, founded and built by the emir George of

Antioch, with ten families of Arabs from the *plateia* of Mazara, and with an eleventh household of Arabs 'to fish for the aforesaid church' (*bi-rasmi ṣaydi l-ḥūti li-l-kanīsati l-madhkūrati*); the names of all eleven are written in Arabic and Greek. With the villeins, Roger also grants the village of Manzil Bū l-Khayr, and two estates, one in the plain of Berzena, the other at Kouttaia: all lay in the region of Mazara, and modern Campobello di Mazara. The original of this *sigillion* is not known, and may never have existed: it now appears only in a what is probably a forged renewal, purportedly issued by King Roger in November 1145 (***Dīwānī* †27**), in which it is referred to as 'a chrysobul, almost entirely consumed by age, of our blessed father (*sic!*), the lord count Roger'.

For bibliography, see under ***Dīwānī* †27**.

King Roger

10. [1132, Indiction X, March. Palermo.]

A *jarīda* of the villeins of Mutata, approximately 17km south-west of Cefalù, granted by King Roger to San Salvatore di Cefalù. A *deperditum* mentioned in a Greek *sigillion* of the same date (PA, AdS, Cefalù, no.5; Caspar 1904, p.513, reg.74; ed. Spata 1862, 2nd ser., no.3, pp.423–8): 'the villeins given to the same church are in the *plateia* written in Greek and Saracen letters', *i.e.* the names were written in Arabic with Greek interlinear transliteration. The *sigillion* and *plateia* were both compiled by George of Antioch. This *jarīda* is probably that renewed in ***Dīwānī* 24**.

Pp.91–2, 93–4, 110–11, 123–7, 132, 208, 274.

11. [1132 A.D. 6640 A.M., Indiction X, March. Palermo.]

A Greek-Arabic decree issued by King Roger to San Salvatore di Cefalù. A *deperditum* renewed in a Latin-Greek writ of January 1180 (PA, AdS, Cefalù no.19: ed. Cusa 1868–82, no.136, pp.489–90, reg. p.730), from which it seems that the original was addressed to the king's customs-officers and port-officials, and instructed them to allow the monks of San Salvatore to import and export, throughout Sicily, Calabria and the principality of Salerno, in its own vessels, free of all charges and duty, such wheat, vegetables, and other necessities as were for the use of the monks and other servants of the church. In addition, San Salvatore was to be allowed to transport by land, free of all duty or tax, all necessities for the church, and to buy and sell in the interests of the church. What purports to be a more-or-less contemporary Latin translation of the original of 1132 (PA, AdS, Cefalù no.6: ed. Spata 1862, 2nd ser., no.4, pp.429–30; Caspar 1904, p.513, reg.73 wrongly dating translation to 1329 A.D.; White 1938, p.190, note 4.) refers to it as 'a Greek and Arabic privilege', but grants different and far more extensive exemptions, privileges, and rights. I doubt the authenticity of this 'translation'.

Pp.92–4, 112, 203, 208.

12. [1133 A.D.] 6641 A.M., Indiction XI, February. [Palermo.]

An official chancery copy of a Greek *sigillion*, incorporating a Greek *periorismos* and Arabic *ḥudūd*, confirming the boundaries of the estate of Mirto, 5km south-east of Partinico, to Bishop John of Lipari-Patti. Mirto had been granted to his church by the late Rainald Avenel, out of love for his wife Fresenda, and its boundaries determined by an inquest held by George of Antioch in 1114, 'when he had command of Iato, and was strategos of all the pertaining district'.

Original: Patti, Arch. Dioc., no.5; Caspar 1904, p.517, reg.82; Girgensohn and

Kamp 1965, p.16, reg.29; Noth 1983, letter 'A', pp.190–191; ed. Cusa 1868–82, no.45, pp.515–17 (reg. p.707); Ménager 1960, Appendix 2, no.24, pp.200–2.

Pp.94–9, 109, 111, 112, 208, 276 note 102.

13. [1134 A.D.] 6642 A.M., 528 A.H., Indiction XII, 21–31 January. [Palermo.]

A Greek-Arabic decree (*sigillion, sijill*) of King Roger, issued at the request and in favour of Bishop John of Lipari-Patti, and addressed to the royal customs-officers. The Greek instructed the 'marine officials' to permit the church to transport on its own ships, between Lipari and Patti, such wheat, butter, cheese as was for its own use, and any gifts made for the good of the church, free of all customs and duty; all merchandise was specifically excluded from this exemption. The Arabic was addressed to 'the strategoi, barons, district governors, and supervisors of the merchants', and granted essentially the same privileges.

Original: Patti, Arch. Dioc., no.6; Caspar 1904, p.521, reg.93; Girgensohn and Kamp 1965, p.16, reg.31; Noth 1983, letter 'B', p.191; ed. Cusa 1868–82, no.47, pp.517–19 (reg. pp.707–8).

Pp.77 note 106, 93, 99–101, 111, 112, 208, 276 note 102, 279.

14. [1136 A.D.] 6644 A.M., 530 A.H., Indiction XIV, April. Palermo.

A Greek-Arabic *sigillion*, incorporating a Greek *periorismos*, Arabic *ḥadd*, and Arabic *jarīda* with Greek interlinear transliteration of the names. King Roger grants to Adelina, the wet-nurse of his son Henry, an estate of five 'ox-lands' at Vicari, and five households of Arab villeins. The originals of both this privilege, and the renewal of it issued in January 1145 (= ***Dīwānī* 23**), are lost. They are known from: (1) an 18th-century copy and Italian translation of the Greek text, made by Pasquale Baffi, and once conserved in the Bibliotheca Maggiore, Naples, but destroyed in 1943 (Caspar 1904, p.529, reg.109; ed. Trinchera 1865, no.117, pp.155–7; Cusa 1868–82, no.50, pp.115–16, reg. p.708); (2) a Latin translation of the Greek and Arabic texts, made in February 1290 (PA, AdS, Magione, no.224; Garufi 1899, nos 12, 12bis and 21, pp.27–33; Brühl 1983, pp.20–1 for 13th-century introduction).

Pp.101–2, 109, 111, 121–3, 131, 132, 208, 279 note 122.

15. [1141 A.D.] 6649 A.M., 535 A.H., Indiction IV, June. Sciacca.

The working-draft (?) of a Greek *sigillion*, incorporating a Greek *periorismos* and Arabic *ḥudūd*. King Roger confirms to Luke, archimandrate of San Salvatore di Messina, the *sigillion* issued by Roger I in 6606 A.M. (1097–8 A.D.) in favour of the monastery of San Giorgio di Triocala near Sciacca. In the interim, certain barons had usurped some of the lands originally granted to San Giorgio, while the monastery had acquired others, not listed in the original privilege. Roger orders the protonotary Philip, the judge Stefanos Maleinos, and the officers of the *sekreton*, the *qā᾽id* Perroun (Barrūn), John, and Boualē (Abū ᶜAlī), to remake the boundary-description of the lands of San Giorgio di Triocala and Raḥl al-Baṣal, to be transcribed in Greek and Arabic into this document. The king also grants San Giorgio pasturage at Sciacca for one thousand sheep and two hundred cattle, and confirms the monastery's ownership of fifteen newly commended villeins, whose names were added to those in the old register. This is probably a working draft (it bears no signature and no seal), made in preparation for the issue of the final, official, and authenticated version of this privilege (***Dīwānī* 16**). The latter contains three substantial passages which are omitted from this version, all dealing with the settlement of a boundary dispute between San Giorgio and William, son of Richard, lord of Sciacca.

Original: Toledo, ADM, Messina, no.1104 (S 796) *recto*; unedited; *Messina* 1994, no.30, p.160.

Pp.58, 102–6, 1107, 181, 208, 222, 276.

16. [1141] 6649 A.M., 535 A.H., Indiction IV, June. Sciacca.

A Greek *sigillion*, incorporating a Greek *periorismos* and Arabic *ḥudūd*. The authentic, original, and official privilege, of which ***Dīwānī* 15** is a working draft (?), and ***Dīwānī* 17** an official chancery copy (?). This is an emended and expanded version of ***Dīwānī* 15**, and includes the three substantial passages missing from it, which deal with the settlement of a boundary dispute between San Giorgio and William, son of Richard, lord of Sciacca.

Original: Toledo, ADM, Messina, no.1120 (S 2002) *recto* (for *verso*, see ***Dīwānī* 31**); Noth 1983, letter 'M', p.199; *Messina* 1994, no.31, pp.160–1; partial edition in Latin translation, Pirri 1733, vol.II, p.1008.

Pp.58, 77 note 106, 102–6, 107, 109, 111, 181, 193, 208, 222, 276, 279 note 122.

17. [1141] 6649 A.M., 535 A.H., Indiction IV, June. Sciacca.

An official chancery copy (?) based upon ***Dīwānī* 15**, but adding a clause concerning the right of the monks to draw water wherever they wished.

Original: Toledo, ADM, Messina, no.1117 (S2003) *recto* (for *verso*, see ***Dīwānī* 32**); unedited; Noth 1983, letter 'N', p.199; *Messina* 1994, no.32, p.162.

Pp.58, 77 note 106, 102–6, 109, 181, 193, 208, 222, 276, 279 note 122.

18. [1141 A.D.] 536 A.H., Indiction V, November. [Palermo?]

An Arabic *jarīda* of the villeins held by San Giorgio di Triocala at Triocala and Raḥl al-Baṣal. In July 1141, at Agrigento, King Roger ordered that the old *plateia* of San Giorgio's villeins, which is referred to in ***Dīwānī* 15–17**, be renewed and updated. This was probably an Arabic *jarīda* (= ***Dīwānī* 6**). The renewed *jarīda* was written entirely in Arabic, except for Roger's Greek chancery-signature. Fifty names were registered at Triocala, and fifty at Raḥl al-Baṣal, and a further fifteen names of newly commended villeins were added.

Original: Toledo, ADM, Messina, no.1119 (S2001); Noth 1983, letter 'O', p.199; *Messina* 1994, no.33, pp.162–3; ed. Gálvez 1991; Gálvez 1995, pp.171–81 (both with many errors).

Pp.58–9, 77 note 106, 102, 107–8, 111, 130 note 47, 138, 147, 148, 208.

19. [1142 A.D.] 6650 A.M., Indiction V, March. Palermo.

A Greek privilege, incorporating a Greek *periorismos* and Arabic *ḥudūd*. At the request of the abbot of Santa Maria di Gala, 2km north-east of Castroreale, King Roger grants his monastery twenty *paricla* of land, for the sum of two hundred *tarì*. Santa Maria had previously illegally occupied [the same?] lands, belonging to the royal demesne, near Santa Maria's distant dependence of San Nicola approximately10km north of Mineo.

The bilingual original is lost. It was translated into Latin by Constantine Lascaris on 26 October 1495, and authenticated by the Messinese notary, Francesco de Silvestro, on 20 December 1516: this Latin version was inserted into Giovanni Luca Barberi's *Liber prelatarium regni Siciliae* (PA, AdS, ff.627v–8v), and was known to Pirri 1733, vol.II, p.1044 A second, much poorer, Latin translation (PA, Bibl. Com., MS Qq.F.69, f.138) was copied by Domenico Schiavo (PA, Bibl. Com., MS Qq.H.10, f.12), from which the edition of Garufi 1899, no.9, pp.19–20 (Caspar 1904, p.545, reg.144) is taken. Both Latin translations now edited by von Falkenhausen 2000, Appendix, no.1, pp.125–8.

Pp.79–80, 108–9, 111, 208.

20. [1143 A.D.] 6651 A.M., Indiction VI, May. [Palermo.]

The endowment charter issued by George of Antioch to Santa Maria dell'Ammiraglio, and authorised and confirmed by King Roger. It is in the form of a Greek *sigillion*, headed by Roger's Arabic *ᶜalāma*, incorporating an Arabic *jarīda* of ten names with Greek interlinear transliteration, and ending with an Arabic note in explanation of the *ᶜalāma*. The principal gift was the estate of Raḥl al-Shaᶜrānī, near Misilmeri 12km south-east of Palermo (see ***Dīwānī* 39**), and ten Arab villeins. Other gifts included: George's new *funduq* in Palermo near San Giacomo a Mare; another *funduq* in the Cassaro of Palermo that he had bought from Ḥasan b. Nāsikh; an oven near the house of his daughter Mary; a garden that he had bought from the *qāʾid* of Palermo; a vineyard that he had bought from [*lacuna*]; vases of bronze and silver; lamps, oil, and wax for the illumination of the church; books (which were listed in a separate catalogue); and an annuity of thirty *tarì*, to last for the lifetime of the Abbess Marina, for her keep and that of the nuns. The document ends with George's Greek autograph – 'the archon of archons, George the emir' – and was sealed with his own lead seal.

Original: PA, Cap. Pal., no.8; Caspar 1904, p.548, reg.153; Ménager 1960, Appendix 2, no.29, pp.208–9; Noth 1983, letter 'C', pp.191–2; ed. Garofalo 1835, no.5, pp.13–16; Morso 1842, no.2, pp.302–11; Cusa 1868–82, no.70, pp.68–70 (reg. 713–14). For the seal: Engel 1882, p.93, pl.3.8.

Pp.109–111, 112–13, 208, 271, 277–8, 279 note 122.

21. [1145 A.D.] 6653 A.M., 539 a.h., Indiction VIII, 1 January. Palermo.

An Arabic *jarīda*, with an Arabic introduction and conclusion; the names in the *jarīda* proper have interlinear Greek transliteration. This is the renewal of the *jarīda* of the population of Catania granted by Roger I to the church of Catania in 1095, a *deperditum* (***Dīwānī* 3**). It lists: the *ahl Qaṭāniya* ('People of Catania'), 525 names, all of the form *awlād Fulān*; the *asmāʾ al-arāmil* ('The names of the widows'), 94 names; the *ᶜabīd al-kanīsa* ('The slaves of the church'); *al-yahūd* ('The Jews'), 25 names, all of the form *awlād Fulān*; the *asmāʾ al-ᶜumy* ('The names of the blind'), 8 names. The church of Catania is confirmed in possession of those named on the condition that their names do not occur in the *jarāʾid* of the royal *dīwān* or of the barons, 'because the old *jarīda*, from which this *jarīda* was copied, was written after the *jarāʾid* which were written at Mazara two years earlier' [*i.e.* in 1093 = ***Dīwānī* 1**].

Original: CT, Arch. Dioc., arabo-greco no.6; Caspar 1904, p.559, reg.185; Noth 1983, letter 'F', p.193; ed. Cusa 1868–82, no.77, pp.563–85 (reg. 715–16).

Pp.77 note 106, 107, 116, 117 note 13, 119–21, 123, 127, 129, 130, 135, 141, 142, 148, 172, 194, 208, 271, 276 note 102, 279.

22. [1145 A.D., January? Palermo.]

A fragmentary Arabic *jarīda*, missing the beginning, and with an Arabic conclusion; the names in the *jarīda* proper have interlinear Greek transliteration. This is the renewal of the *jarīda* of the population of Aci Castello granted by Roger I to the church of Catania in 1095 (***Dīwānī* 4**). It lists the *ahl Liyāj* ('People of Aci'), 337 names, of which 213 survive, all of the form *awlād Fulān*; and the *asmāʾ al-arāmil* ('The names of the widows'), 53 names. The church of Catania is confirmed in possession of those named on the same condition as ***Dīwānī* 21**.

Original: CT, Arc. Cap., arabo-greco no.7; Caspar 1904, p.559, reg.186; Noth 1983, letter 'G', pp.193–5; ed. Cusa 1868–82, no.78, pp.586–95 (reg. p.716).

Pp.116, 117 note 13, 120–1, 128, 141, 142, 172, 194, 208.

23. [1145 A.D.] 6653 A.M., 539 A.H., Indiction VIII, 13 January.

A renewal of the Greek-Arabic *sigillion* issued by King Roger in April 1136 to Adelina, the wet-nurse of his son Henry, granting her an estate of five 'ox-lands' at Vicari, and five households of Arab villeins (= ***Dīwānī* 14**).

The original is lost (see above, ***Dīwānī* 14**); Caspar 1904, pp.559–60, reg.187; for editions, see above, ***Dīwānī* 14**).

Pp.101, 116, 117 note 13, 121–3, 129, 131, 132, 140, 194, 208.

24. [1145 A.D.] 6653 A.M., 539 A.H., Indiction VIII, 7 February. Palermo.

An Arabic-Greek *jarīda* which renews both a *jarīda* of the villeins of San Salvatore di Cefalù issued twelve years earlier (probably ***Dīwānī* 10**) 'on the condition set out in the aforementioned *jarīda*, namely: that, whenever one of these men is found in the *jarā*ʾ*id* of the barons or of others, you will send him back to his lord, and he will not compensate you for him with another one', and a Latin register of the villeins of San Cosma (on the outskirts of Cefalù) and San Giovanni di Rocella (12km west of the city) who were granted to Salvatore by Abbot David of Santissima Trinità di Mileto in January 1136. The text and name-lists are in Arabic, with interlinear Greek transliteration of the names.

Original: PA, AdS, Cefalù, no.2; Caspar 1904, p.559, reg.184; Noth 1983, letter 'E', p.192; ed. Cusa 1868–82, no.79, pp.472–80 (reg. p.716).

Pp.62 note 143, 77 note 106, 92, 107, 116, 117 note 13, 123–7, 129, 132, 135, 140, 141, 194, 208, 279.

25. [1145 A.D.] 6653 A.M., 539 a.h., Indiction VIII, 24 March. Palermo.

An Arabic *jarīda*, with an Arabic introduction and conclusion; the names in the *jarīda* proper have interlinear Greek transliteration. King Roger renews to Walter, son of Roger Forestal, the *jarīda* of the population of Jāliṣū granted by Count Roger to his father in 1093–5(?) (= ***Dīwānī* 5**). Thirty names are registered, plus a further five *mutazawwijūn*. The names are confirmed in Walter's possession 'on the condition[s] that you are legally entitled to them, and that the *mutazawwijūn* amongst the children are the children of those confirmed amongst the men in this *jarīda*, and [that], if any of them appears in the *jarā*ʾ*id* of the *dīwān al-ma*ʿ*mūr* or in the *jarā*ʾ*id* of the barons, you will strike him out'.

Original: PA, BCRS, Monreale, no.4; Caspar 1904, p.561, reg.193; Garufi 1902, no.4, pp.4–5; Noth 1983, letter 'H', p.195; ed. Cusa 1868–82, no.82, pp.127–9 (reg. p.717).

Pp.77 note 106, 107, 115 note 3, 116, 117 note 13, 127–8, 129, 132, 135, 140, 141, 194, 208, 271, 279.

26. [1145? A.D.] 6652 A.M., [January–April?] Palermo.

A fragmentary Greek-Arabic *jarīda* of villeins issued by King Roger to Roger Fesca (*i.e.* of Fécamp, in Normandy, see Haskins 1924, p.187, note 148.), archbishop-elect of Palermo, with a Greek introduction, and an Arabic name-list with Greek interlinear transliteration of the names. Only the year and the place of issue can be read but, assuming that it belongs to the series of renewals issued in 1144–5, it must belong to the period between January and April 1145, when business was done in Palermo.

Original: PA, AdS, Pergamene varie no.65; Caspar 1904, p.554, reg.169; Noth 1983, letter 'D', p.192; ed. Cusa 1868–82, no.73, pp.614–15 (reg. p.715).

Pp.116, 117 note 13, 208.

†27. [1145 A.D.] 6653 A.M., Indiction VIII, November. Mazara.

A Greek *sigillion* in which King Roger renews for the Lady Brienne, abbess of San Michele Arcangelo di Mazara, the *sigillion* issued by his father (*sic!*), Count Roger, in January 6632 A.M. (=1124 A.D.), Indiction II, granting her church eleven households of Arabs with the village of Manzil Bū l-Khayr, and two estates, one in the plain of Berzena, the other at Kouttaia, in the region of Mazara, and modern Campobello di Mazara (***Dīwānī* †9**). Four other features indicate that this document (and therefore also ***Dīwānī* †9**) is probably a forgery, although, in the absence of the document itself, final judgement must be suspended. First, the Arabic script is not the characteristic *dīwānī* used on all but one of King Roger II's bilingual and Arabic documents (although Ménager's claim that it was written with a goose quill from left to right is patently false): this script, in fact, seems to be carefully modelled upon Noth's RA2, which was used in ***Dīwānī* 30** (1151 A.D.). Second, the Greek script does not resemble any known from the royal chancery, and could well be 13th-century. Third, Roger's Greek signature is irregular (von Falkenhausen, 1997, p.285). Fourth, the document was given at Mazara, not at Messina or Palermo like all the other documents in this series. The original was once in the Bullaire de l'Abbaye de Maredsous, Denée, Belgium, but was apparently returned to the monks of San Michele, who seem to know nothing about it; Collura 1955a, p.590, reg.69; ed. Grégoire 1932a, pp.82–90 and fig.A. See also: Brühl 1983, pp.126–31 ('un capolavoro di falsificazione'); Ménager 1960, Appendix 2, no.30, pp.209–11, and nos.14, 16 and 19, pp.190, 191–2, 196–8 ('la plus grossière de toutes les imitations que nous possédons'); Dölger 1933 (false); Garufi 1933 (false); Grégoire 1933 (genuine); White 1933 ('A very strong assumption ... that [it] is authentic'); Grégoire, 1932a, pp.82–90 and fig.A; Grégoire 1932b, pp.54–9 (genuine).

Pp.116 note 10, 117 note 13, 209, 275 note 95.

28. [1149 A.D.] 543 A.H., 10 April, Indiction XIII. [Palermo.]

An Arabic *kitāb* in which King Roger granted four 'plough-lands', amounting to one hundred and twenty *salme*, at Raḥl al-Wazzān, and five households of villeins to the monks of San Nicolo di Chùrchuro. The original is lost, and exists only in the official *dīwānī* copy made in December 1149 (***Dīwānī* 29**).

For bibliography and references, see ***Dīwānī* 29** and ***Dīwānī* 33**.

Pp.175 note 25, 201, 208, 287.

29. [1149 A.D.] 544 A.H., Indiction XIII, December. [Palermo.]

An official *dīwānī* copy of ***Dīwānī* 28**. The copy was issued by the *qā'id* Barrūn, and written by the scribe ʿUthmān. ***Dīwānī* 33** purports to be an official *dīwānī* copy of this document.

Original: PA, Arch. Dioc., no.14; Mortillaro 1843, no.14, pp.180–1; Caspar 1904, p.571, reg.218; Noth 1983, letter 'K', pp.196–8; ed. Caruso 1834, pp.16–21; Cusa 1868–82, no.89, pp.28–30 (reg. pp.718–19); Johns and Metcalfe 1999, Appendix 1, pp.242–8.

Pp.77 note 106, 106, 135, 136 note 74, 147, 175–7, 178, 180, 194, 199, 200, 203 notes 49–50, 209, 222 and note 39, 243 note 144, 251 note 197, 278 note 113, 279 and note 122, 280, 287.

30. [1151 A.D.] 6659 A.M., Indiction XIV, May. Palermo.

At the request of Adelicia, abbess of Santa Maria Maddalena di Corleone, King Roger issues to her a Greek-Arabic *plateia*, incorporating two Arabic *katonoma*s of the men of Fuṭṭāsina (Φουττάσινη; 20 names) and Ṭurrus (Τούῤῥους; 30 names), and the *ḥadd* of Ṭurrus which is written only in Arabic.

Original: PA, Bibl. Reg, Monreale, no.5; Caspar 1904, pp.573–74, reg.227; Garufi 1902, no.5, pp.5–6 and pl.2; Noth 1983, letter 'I', pp.195–6; ed. Spata 1865, pp.59–70 (Greek only); Cusa 1868–82, no.91, pp.130–4 (reg. p.720).

Pp.201, 209, 275 note 95, 287; see also ***Dīwānī* †27** above.

31. [1152 A.D.] 547 A.H., Indiction XV[?], May. [Palermo?]

An Arabic *ḥadd*, or official record of a boundary-inquest. The *ᶜāmil*, or royal bailiff, of Sciacca was ordered by the chancellor, Maio of Bari, to settle the boundary-dispute between the monks of San Giorgio di Triocala and Hubert (or Herbert), lord of Calamonaci. The bailiff summoned a jury consisting of: at least twelve barons (*al-tarrārīya*) and elders knowledgeable about the boundary, William Milceri (*ghulyalim m.l.sīra)*; Geoffrey of Marturano (*jafarāy marturān)*; Bartholomew, son of ... *āmūn (barthulamāw ibn ... āmūn*); his brother, Matthew (*mathāw*); Tristan (*tristān*); William, the lord of Gurfa, a fief near Santa Margherita Belice (*ghulyalim ṣāḥib al-jurf*); Robert Manfrè, the governor(?) of Sciacca(?) (*r.b.rt m.n.frāy al-ḥākim*); William, the marshall(?) of the castle of Sciacca (*ghulyalim maniskhalqū ruqqati l-shāqqati*); Robert Alduina (*r.b.rt h.l.d.wīn*); his son-in-law Arnald (*arnald*); the sons of John Atria; (*awlādu j.wān aṭriya*); three burghers (*mina l-burjīsīna*), Nicola son of Lido(?) (*niqūla ibn līdū*[?]), Albert son-in-law of John Atria (*wa-alb.rt ṣihru j.wān aṭriya*), and ᶜAbd al-Raḥmān ibn Fityān; and at least three Muslims, Ṭāhir ibn ᶜUmar; the sons of al-Rūmīya, Abū l-Futūḥ ibn ᶜAmmār, 'and the rest of them'. The description of the boundary between Triocala and Calamonaci follows. At the foot of the text come: the notes of authentication Εκυρώθη (*Ekurōthē*, 'It has been authenticated') and, in Arabic, the *ḥasbala*, 'God is sufficient for us. How excellent a representative is He'; a Latin signature (perhaps reading †*Wual[t]er[ius]*); the *ᶜalāma* of Barrūn; and † *Maio d[omi]ni Regis Cancell[a]ri[us] s[ubscrip]s[i]*.

Original: Toledo, ADM, Fondo Messina, no.1120 *verso* (S2002 *verso*), for the *recto*, see ***Dīwānī* 16**; Noth 1983, letter 'P', pp.199–200; *Messina* 1994, no.31, pp.160–1; unedited.

Pp.77 note 105, 130 note 47, 135, 136 note 74, 187 note 56, 197, 198, 200, 201, 209, 222 and note 39, 251 note 197, 279 and note 122.

32. [1152 A.D.] 547 A.H., Indiction XV[?], May.

The official *dīwānī* copy of ***Dīwānī* 31**. The text is almost identical, except that it ends with the note 'this fair copy is the copy of the original *dīwānī* record, and this is a reproduction of the essence of it', followed by the *ḥasbala*, but with no signatures.

Original: Toledo, ADM, Messina, no.1117 (S2003) *verso* (for the *recto*, see ***Dīwānī* 17**); *Messina* 1994, no.32, p.162; unedited.

Pp.77 note 105, 130 note 47, 135, 136 note 74, 200, 201, 209, 279 note 122.

William I

33. [1154 A.D.] 549 A.H., Indiction II, June. Palermo.

A second official *dīwānī* copy of ***Dīwānī* 28**, in which King Roger granted four 'plough-lands', amounting to one hundred and twenty *salme*, and five households of Arab villeins, to the monks of San Nicolò di Chùrchuro. The first copy (***Dīwānī* 29**) had not borne the royal seal, and the monks therefore requested a second, sealed copy. This was duly issued, signed by † *Maio d[ei] & regia g[rati]a amir[atus] amirator[um] s[ubscrip]si*, and sealed. This copy, however, granted not the lands at Raḥl al-Wazzān described in ***Dīwānī* 29**, but the completely different estate of Raḥl Ibn Sahl.

Original: PA, Arch. Dioc., no.16; Mortillaro 1843, no.16, p.183; Caspar 1904, p.571, reg.218; Noth 1983, letter 'K', pp.196–8; ed. Caruso 1834, pp.7–16; Cusa 1868–82, no.93, pp.34–6 (reg. p.720); Johns and Metcalfe 1999, Appendix 2, pp.248–53; Johns 2001; Johns forthcoming a.

Pp.77 note 106, 136 note 74, 135, 147, 176–7, 179, 180, 194, 198, 199, 200 note 29, 201, 203 notes 49–50, 209, 278 note 113, 279.

34. [1154 A.D.] 6663 A.M., 549 A.H., Indiction III, December.
An Arabic privilege in which William I grants to San Giovanni dei Lebbrosi the estate of Margana with thirty-one villeins, and that of Ḥajar al-Zanātī with twenty-three villeins. The names of the villeins were written in Arabic with Greek interlinear transliteration, but the rest of the privilege – the introduction, and the boundary-descriptions of the two estates – was written in Arabic only.

The original privilege does not survive, and is known from a notarial translation into Latin of 11 February 1258 (PA, AdS, Magione, no.78), and from a transumpt of the latter dated 7 July 1286 (PA, AdS, Magione, no.173); Mortillaro 1858, p.1; Behring 1887, no.132, p.12; ed. Mongitore 1721, pp.161–63 (after 1258 translation); Enzensberger 1996, no. 4, pp.11–14. Enzensberger (1996, *Deperditum* 3, p.102) deduçes the existence of a missing Arabic document from the following phrase in the Latin version of this document: *exiit edictum a maiestate altissima Guillelmi, regis sancti … ad doanam regiam transmissum*. This phrase merely translates the standard Arabic formula which opens the *dispositio*, and may be reconstructed as follows: *kharaja amru l-ḥaḍrati l-ʿāliyati l-ʿalīyati l-mālikati l-malakīyati l-qiddīsīyati l-ghulyālimīyati … li-dīwāni l-taḥqīqi l-maʿmūri bi-katbi hādhihi l-jarīdati*. It certainly does not imply the issue of a separate document (see Johns forthcoming a).

Pp.180, 182–3, 200, 209.

35. [1161 A.D.] 556 A.H., Ṣafar [30 January – 27 February], January, Indiction IX. Palermo.
A Greek-Arabic deed (πρατικὸν, *kitāb*) recording the purchase by the Jew Yaʿqūb ibn Faḍlūn ibn Ṣāliḥ from the lords of the *dīwān al-taḥqīq al-maʿmūr*, the *qāʾid* Martin and Matthew of Salerno, for five hundred *tarì*, of a piece of *dīwānī* land 'in the plain to the west of the city of Palermo, near to the spring known as Ibn Abū Saʿīd' (*i.e.* north-west of the Royal Palace). The sale was recorded in the '*dīwānī* registers of receipt' (*dafātir al-īṣāl al-dīwānīya*) on 30 January, Indiction IX (1161 A.D.). At the foot of the text, on the right of the sheet, come two *ʿalāma*s, both in the form of complicated ligatures, one of which is just recognisable as an earlier and unpractised version of Martin's signature, while the other seems to be an earlier version of the *ʿalāma* of the *qāʾid* Richard (who is not mentioned in the document). Next, comes the signature of one Ḥamza ibn Ḥamza, immediately followed, in a different hand, by the phrase 'and he was at that time the controller of the *dīwānī* office of inquiry' (*wa-huwa ḥīnaʾidhin wakīlu l-faḥṣi l-dīwānīyi l-maʿmūr*). There follows an elaborate Greek signature, which also appears on ***Dīwānī* 37**, which reads Ἰω(άν)ν(ης) ἔγρα(ψεν) † although no one of that name appears in either document. The line ends with the note: 'That was authenticated. It is complete' (*ṣaḥḥa dhālika [inta]h[ā]*). Below the line of signatures, on the very edge of

the parchment are two Arabic notes, much damaged and in a minuscule hand: they have much deteriorated since 1979, when I was already unable to read them.

Original: PA, AdS, Santa Maria della Grotta, no.2; ed. Cusa 1868–82, no.101, pp.622–6 (reg. p.722); Simonsohn 1997, no.185, pp.418–21; Johns forthcoming a.

Pp.106 note 46, 173–4, 174 note 18, 177 note 34, 200, 201 note 39, 202, 209, 220 note 26, 232 note 81, 243 note 146, 251 note 198, 280.

36. [1164 A.D.] 6673 A.M., Indiction XIII, September. Palermo.

A Greek-Arabic privilege (*σιγίλλιον, al-sijill al-manshūr*) in which William I grants to John of Vitalba, prior of Santa Maria la Gadera near Polizzi, two plough-lands of arable land from the royal demesne near to the monastery. The monks were to select the land themselves on the condition that if, in future, it were to be discovered that they had taken more than they had been granted, then they would forfeit even the two plough-lands of the original donation. The privilege is authenticated with the *ḥasbala* and was sealed, but is not signed.

Original: PA, AdS, Santa Margherita di Polizzi, no.1; Behring 1887, p.15, reg.151; Di Giovanni 1880, pp.19–20 (18th-century translation of Greek only); Noth 1983, letter 'L', p.198; ed. Cusa 1868–82, no.49, pp.650–2 (reg. p.708); Enzensberger 1996, no.32, pp.85–7; Johns forthcoming a.

Pp.77 note 105, 130 note 47, 184, 200 note 29, 209, 279 note 122, 287.

William II and Margaret

37. [1166 A.D.] 6675 A.M., 562 A.H., Indiction XV, November. [Palermo].

An Arabic-Greek decree (*al-sijill al-jalīy*, σιγίλλιον) in which William II and Margaret order the *dīwān al-taḥqīq al-maʿmūr*, in the person of the *qāʾid* Martin, to hand over the archdeaconry of Messina to Nicholas, archbishop of Messina. At the foot of the text come: two Arabic *ʿalāma*s, one of which is Martin's, the other of an unknown officer of the *dīwān*; two Greek signatures, Ἰω(άν)ν(ης) ἔγρα(ψεν) † (see ***Dīwānī* 35**) and Ῥογέριος ἔγρα(φεν) † ; and the *dīwānī* note of authentication *ṣaḥīḥ dhālika*, 'that is authentic'.

Original: Toledo, ADM, Messina, no.1118 (S2004); Behring 1887, p.16, reg.163; *Messina* 1994, no.35, pp.164–5; ed. (Greek only, from a copy; Arabic unedited) Spata 1871, pp.58–9; Cusa 1868–82, no.120, p.321 (reg. p.726)

Pp.77 note 106, 106 note 46, 130 note 47, 131 note 53, 135, 136 note 74, 138 note 90, 200, 201 note 39, 202–3, 209, 220 note 26, 221 note 31, 251 note 198, 279, 280.

38. [1169 A.D.] 6677 A.M., Indiction II, July. [Palermo.]

An Arabic decree (*sijill*) in which William and Margaret grant to the hospital in Khandaq al-Qirūz, at Campograsso, near Altavilla Milicia, 14km south-west of Termini Imerese, the *raḥl* known as ʿAyn al-Liyān, and fourteen households of Arabs. Of these fourteen, six are adscripted villeins (*mina l-rijāli l-ḥurshi*), and eight are immigrants or newly commended villeins living on the estate (*mina l-rijāli l-ghurabāʾi wa-l-mulsi l-sākinīna bi-l-raḥli l-madhkūri*). The names of the villeins are written in Arabic with Greek interlinear transliteration. The grant was made on the condition that the men of Termini might continue to dwell on the estate, and to hold the lands which they, their fathers, or their grandfathers, had first occupied (*fataḥū-hā*), paying to the hospital what they used to pay to the royal bailiffs (*ʿummāl*) when ʿAyn al-Liyān was under the jurisdiction of (*fī ḥukmi*) the *dīwān al-maᶜmūr*. The other inhabitants of the estate, both sailors (reading *al-baḥrīyūn*) and others, were to deal as before in their dealings with the royal bailiffs. (Vera von Falkenhausen tells me that unedited documents in the ADM indicate that the royal demesne reserved certain rights over sailors resident on feudal lands.) The decree ends with the *ḥasbala*, and was sealed, but not signed.

Original: PA, Arch. Dioc., no.25; Mortillaro 1843, no.25, pp.189–90; Behring 1887, p.16, reg.170 (and pp.20–1, reg.214, *s.a.* 1179); ed. Cusa 1868–82, no.110, pp.37–9 (reg. p.724).

Pp.77 note 106, 130 note 47, 135, 147–8, 200, 209, 243 note 152, 269 notes 60 and 64, 270 notes 72 and 74, 271 and note 75, 279 and note 122.

William II

39. [1172 A.D.] 6681 A.M., Indiction VI, October. Palermo.

A Greek-Arabic writ (ἔγραφον, *sijill*) issued by Geoffrey of Centuripe, the *sekretikos*, the *ṣāḥib dīwān al-taḥqīq al-maᶜmūr*. He had been ordered by the three archons of the royal court, in Arabic 'the lord viziers', Walter, archbishop of Palermo, Matthew of Salerno, the vice-chancellor (in Arabic 'the lord chancellor'), and Bartholomew, bishop-elect of Agrigento, to establish the boundaries of the village of al-Shaᶜrānī which the late George of Antioch had granted to Santa Maria dell'Ammiraglio (see ***Dīwānī* 20**). Geoffrey led a party of nine courtiers to the spot, including: John, son of George of Antioch; Nicholas the logothete; Abū l-Ṭayyib and Makhlūf, captains of the royal archers; Nicholas the chamberlain; the notary Leo of Chousta; the *shaykh al-qāʾid* Ḥamza; and the brothers Yūsuf and Yaᶜqūb, sons of Yaᶜqūb. They were joined by six witnesses from Misilmeri: the Christians, Abū l-Ṭayyib, who had been bailiff; Philip, the bailiff; Nicholas son of John; Basil Bousa, the bailiff; and John son of al-Ḥājj; and the Muslim, Yūsuf ibn al-Saraqūsī. They established the boundary, here recorded in Greek and Arabic. This document was written in the church of Santa Maria dell'Ammiraglio, sealed by Geoffrey, and presented to John the Philosopher, the prior of Santa Maria.

Original: PA, Cap. Pal., no.16; ed. Garofalo 1835, no.13, pp.28–33, Buscemi 1839, p.17; Cusa 1868–82, no. 119, pp.80–3 (reg. p.726); Ménager 1960, Appendix 2, no.33, pp.214–24.

Pp.77 note 106, 130 note 47, 131 note 53, 137 note 87, 187 note 56, 202 note 42, 203 note 50, 209, 230 note 70.

40. [1173 A.D.] 6681 A.M., 568 A.H., Indiction VI, February. Palermo.

An Arabic privilege in which William II grants to the chancellor Matthew of Salerno the *casale* of Curbici (*i.e.* Qurūbnish, Corubnis Superioris), near Camporeale, with all its villeins and appurtenances, and confirms his grant of the same to the nunnery of Santa Maria *Latinorum* which he had founded in Palermo. The names of thirty villeins were listed, apparently in Arabic with Greek interlinear transliteration. The boundaries of Curbici were given in Arabic, according to the *dafātir al-ḥudūd* in the *dīwān al-taḥqīq al-maᶜmūr* (*secundum quod est notatum in quaternis finium seu divisarum in dohana constitit id est racitudinis abitabili*). The *casale* had once belonged to the barony of Calatrasi (see above, pp.181, 184). The document survives only in an 18th-century copy of a lost Latin transumpt of 24 April 1375: PA, AdS, MS Corporazioni Religiose

Soppresse, Fondo Monastero del Cancelliere, vol.367, ff.158r.–60r. (31–35); ed. Collura 1975.

Pp.181, 184, 203 notes 49–50, 209.

41. [1175 A.D.] 6683 A.M., Indiction VIII, 27 August. [Palermo.]

A Greek-Arabic record of the boundary-inquest held by the *sekretikos*, the lord of the *dīwān al-taḥqīq al-maʿmūr*, Eugenios tou Kalou / Abū l-Ṭayyib to determine the boundary between the royal estate of Ottumarrano and Gàrcia, an estate of S. Salvatore di Cefalù. The contents of this document are described in full above (pp.170–1).

The original is lost, and survives only as a Latin translation of 4 August 1286: PA, AdS, Cefalù, no.60; ed. Spata 1862, 2nd ser., no.11, pp.451–6.

Pp.170–1, 184, 203 notes 49 and 51, 209, 279 note 122.

42. [1177 A.D., March. Palermo.]

A *jarīda* of the villeins of the *casale* of Baida, 5km west of Palermo, which was granted by William II to Archbishop Walter of Palermo in return for the loss to Santa Maria di Monreale of all his rights over Corleone and the church of San Silvestro at Monreale.

A *deperditum*: referred to in donation of March 1177, granting *Casale quod Bayda dicitur, quod est prope Panormum a parte occidentis, cum omnibus justis divisis, et tenimentis ac villanis ipsius Casalis, nomina quorum villanorum continentur in platea facta inde a doana nostra de secretis que est plumbeo sigillo nostro sigillata* (PA, Arch. Dioc., no.24; Mortillaro 1843, no.24, p.189; Behring 1887, p.20, reg.204; ed. Pirri 1733, vol.1, cols 107–8; Mongitore 1721, pp.51–3).

Pp.202, 209.

43. [1178 A.D.] 6686 A.M., 573 A.H., Indiction XI, May. Palermo.

The Arabic-Greek *jarīda* of the villeins of the district of Corleone and the ex-barony of Calatrasi. This document is described in detail above (pp. 153–65).

Original: PA, BCRS, Monreale, no.22; Behring 1887, p.20, reg.210; Garufi 1902, no.22, pp.14–15; ed. Cusa 1868–82, no.132, pp.134–79 (reg. p.729).

Pp.107, 130 note 47, 135, 148, 150 note 22, 152, 153–65, 166, 167, 174 note 17, 184, 192, 200 note 29, 202 and note 44, 269 notes 60 and 64, 270 notes 72 and 74, 271 note 75, 272.

44. 1182 A.D., 6690 A.M., Indiction XV, May. Palermo.

The Latin-Arabic *jarīdat al-ḥudūd* listing the boundaries of the districts of Iato and Corleone, and of the estates within them, and of the ex-baronies of Battellaro and Calatrasi. This document is described in detail above (pp.186–92).

Original: PA, BCRS, Monreale, no.32; Behring 1887, p.21, reg.219; Garufi 1902, no.32, pp.18–20; ed. Cusa 1868–82, no.137, pp.179–244 (reg. pp.730–1).

Pp.130 note 47, 135, 152, 153 note 29, 162 note 35, 167, 175, 176, 178, 179, 180, 182–3, 184, 185, 186–92, 200 notes 31 and 34, 202 and note 44, 203 note 49, 209, 269 notes 60 and 64, 270 notes 72 and 74, 271 note 75, 272, 279 note 122.

45. [1183 A.D.] 6691 A.M., Indiction I, April. Palermo.

An Arabic-Greek *jarīda* listing the *rijāl al-maḥallāt*, or adscripted villeins, on the lands of Santa Maria di Monreale, who were not registered in ***Dīwānī* 42**, and the *rijāl al-muls*, or immigrants to the abbey's lands, who were exempted from a general recall to the royal demesne of all villeins belonging to the *dīwān*. This document is described in detail above (pp.165–9).

Original: PA, BCRS, no.45; Behring 1887, pp.21–2, reg.222; Garufi 1902, no.45, pp.25–6; ed. Cusa 1868–82, no.143, pp.245–86 (reg. pp.732–3).

Pp.77 note 105, 107, 130 note 47, 135, 148–9, 150, 152, 163 and note 37, 165–9, 192, 200 notes 30–1, 209, 269 notes 60 and 64, 270 notes 72 and 74, 271 note 75, 272.

FREDERICK II

46. [1242 A.D.] 6750 A.M., Indiction XV, 20 January. Palermo.

A Latin-Arabic writ (*scriptum, sijill*) recording the boundary-inquest ordered by Obertus Fallamonaca, *dominus Obertus Fallamonacha imperialis doane de secretis et questorum magister per totam Siciliam* ('lord Obert Fallamonaca master of the imperial *duana de secretis* and of the quaestors for all Sicily'), *al-mawlā ūbartu fallamūnaqa ṣāḥibu l-dawāwīni l-maᶜmūrati wa-l-fawāʾidi bi-jamīᶜi ṣiqillīyata* ('the lord Obert Fallamonaca, lord of the royal *dīwān*s and of the revenues of all Sicily'), at the request of Geoffrey, cleric of the Cappella Palatina and son of the notary Michael, a citizen of Palermo, to determine the boundaries of the Hospital of San Lorenzo in the territory of Cefalà [Diana], which Geoffrey held as a benefice from the church of Agrigento.

Original: AG, Arch. Dioc., no.21; ed. Cusa 1868–82, no.190, pp.602–5 (reg. pp.743–4; Collura 1961, no.63, pp.120–6, and pl.8.

Pp.77 note 105, 130 note 47, 184–5, 205, 246 note 166, 275 note 95.

APPENDIX 2

Provisional catalogue of private documents

1. Undated [12th-century?]

A contemporary copy (?) of an Arabic deed of sale, with Greek notes. *Al-Ghuman* ('the abbot'< Greek ἡγούμενος, *ēgoumenos*) ibn *al-qissīs* ('son of the priest') Abū Ghālib, lord of the monastery of Barḍālī (?) purchases from ᶜUmar ibn Ḥusayn al-Tamīmī, known as Ibn Ṣāfī, a piece of land known as Khandaq Iblaṭa (or Iblaṭuh), for the price of five *tarì* (*rubāᶜīya*). (The place-name has been identified implausibly with ἡ φαβάρα ... ἡβλάτου, *Fawwāra Iblāṭū*, near Partinico: Caracausi 1990, p.225). The witnesses: ᶜAbd al-Ghanī ibn Ibrāhīm al-Lawātī; *al-shaykh* Maymūn ibn Ḥasan al-Tamīmī; Yūsuf ibn Abū (*sic*!) Bakr al-Hawwārī; Abū l-Faraḥ (or al-Faraj?) ibn Ḥusayn al-Kutāmī; ᶜAlī ibn Ḥusayn al-Lawātī; Bū Jumᶜa ibn Yūsuf al-Rabīᶜī(?)

Original: PA, AdS, Cefalù, no.38. Ed. Cusa 1868–82, no.14, pp.505–6 (reg. p.698); trans. Trovato 1949, pp.76–7.

P.126 note 31.

2. 1–10 Rajab 506 A.H. (22–31 December 1112 A.D.) Palermo.

Arabic deed of sale. Zakarī al-Naṣrānī ('the Christian') ibn *al-shaykh* Sulaymān al-ᶜAṭṭār ('the Druggist'), at the commission of *al-qāʾid* Ghafūr ibn *al-shaykh* al-Arūṭū (?), purchases from *al-kātib* ('the scribe') Arghīsa (< Ἀργίσης) *al-muᶜallim* ('the master' – *i.e. magister notarius*?) [ibn?] ᶜAbd al-Raḥmān al-Qurashī, and from his mother, ᶜĀʾika (? possibly < Αἰκατερίνα), daughter of *al-kātib* Aḥmad ibn ... al-Tamīmī, a piece of land planted with canes, called al-Fawwāra, in the territory of the city of Palermo, near al-Dajjājīn ('the Chicken-sellers'), for the price of 90 *tarì* (*rubāᶜīyā dūqīya*). The witnesses: Mujāhid ibn Ḥusayn al-Kindī; Muḥammad ... ibn Muḥammad al-Qaysī; ᶜAlī ibn Abī l-Fatḥ ibn ... ; Muḥammad ibn Abī l-Fatḥ ibn ...

Original document not located. Ed. Cusa 1868–82, no.31, pp.610–13 (reg. p.702); trans. Trovato 1949, pp.37–9.

P.77 note 102.

3. Ṣafar 510 A.H. (15 June – 13 July 1116 A.D.) Palermo.

Latin transumpt (dated 15 May 1266) of Arabic deed of sale. Philip the Christian, son of Gaytus Phytien (*al-qāʾid Fityān*) the Christian, known as Ibn B..., sells to Charzalla, son of Abdelgani Ellahmi (*Ḥirz[?] Allāh ibn ᶜAbd al-Ghanī al-Lakhmī [or al-Laḥmī]*), a piece of arable land in the mountains south of Palermo at a place called Chifalie (Cefalà), in the territory of Cefalà, for the price of 350 *tarì*, each lacking one grain. (A series of Latin notes on the *verso* identify the place as Risalaimi near Marineo). The witnesses: Abdelgani filius Jusuph hegueri (*ᶜAbd al-Ghanī ibn Yūsuf al-Hawwārī[?]*);

Ahmed filius Abrahim Timimi (*Aḥmad ibn Ibrāhīm al-Tamīmī*); Habdeleauy filius Gebyr Elensari (*ʿAbd al-Ḥayy[?] ibn Jabr al-Anṣārī*); Bulcassim filius Habdelssamed Elkaysi (*Abū l-Qāsim ibn ʿAbd al-Ṣamad al-Qaysī*); Habdelkerim filius Bubiker Elinsari (*ʿAbd al-Karīm ibn Abī Bakr al-Anṣārī*); Abrahym filius Seuden Ettimimi (*Ibrāhīm ibn Sawdān al-Tamīmī*); Jusuph filius Abdelnur Ettennuchi (*Yūsuf ibn ʿAbd al-Nūr al-Tanūkhī*); Chamze filius Haly Ellegueri (*Ḥamza ibn ʿAlī al-Hawwārī*); Uthmen filius Habdalle Elkaysi (*ʿUthmān ibn ʿAbd Allāh al-Qaysī*); Senex Uthmen filius Haly Ettimimi (*al-shaykh ʿUthmān ibn ʿAlī al-Tamīmī*).

Transumpt: PA, AdS, Magione, no.110. Ed. Bresc 1995, pp.89–92.

4. Rajab 524 A.H. (10 June – 9 July 1130 A.D.) Palermo.

Latin transumpt (dated 24 July 1255) of Arabic deed of sale. Walter the Christian, known as *de Seyda*, of Palermo, son of the elder Matthew, purchases from Bulhasen son of Gayti Karram Essaly (*Abū l-Ḥasan ibn al-qāʾid Karrām[?] al-Ṣālī[?]*), the estate of Rahalkarram (*Raḥl Karrām*), between Montelepre and Partinico, for the price of 1,000 *tarì*, each lacking one grain. The witnesses: Abderahmen filius Ali Elcurasy (*ʿAbd al-Raḥmān ibn ʿAlī al-Qurashī*); Humur Buabdille (*ʿUmar Abū ʿAbd Allāh*); Hythie filius Abderrahmen Elhesin (*Yaḥyā[?] ibn ʿAbd al-Raḥmān al-Ḥasan*); Aly byn Ebielhasyn Sekilli (*ʿAlī ibn Abī l-Ḥusayn al-Ṣiqillī*); Aly filius Abdelmelek (*ʿAlī ibn ʿAbd al-Malik*); Ebusaad filius Hyse (*Abū Saʿd ibn ʿĪsā*); Aly filius Casi Ettimini (*ʿAlī ibn Qasīy [or Qusayy?] al-Tamīmī*).

Transumpt: PA, AdS, San Martino delle Scale, no.191. Ed. Bresc 1995, pp.92–5.

5. 1–10 Jumādā I 526 A.H. (20–29 March 1132 A.D.) Palermo.

Arabic record of exchange of irrigation-rights. *Al-ḥājj* ʿAbd al-Raḥmān ibn ʿUmar ibn Abī l-Samrāʾ al-Lawātī and Ḥasan ibn ʿAlī al-Kindī, known as Ibn al-Kh.n.d.rū(?), exchange *nawbas* (*i.e.* 'turns' of water for irrigation). ʿAbd al-Raḥmān's turn comes from the spring called al-Manānī at Burj al-Baṭṭāl and Faḥṣ Mārīya, to the west of Palermo. Ḥasan's turn comes from the springs called ʿAyn Faraj and ʿAyn al-Batīya, also to the west of Palermo. The witnesses: ʿAbd al-ʿAzīz *al-muʾaddib* ('the [Qurʾānic] teacher') ibn al-Sabʿ ibn Abī l-Qāsim al-Tamīmī; Ḥusayn ibn Yūsuf al-Lawātī; Aḥmad ibn Ḥusayn ibn Yūsuf al-Lawātī.

Original: PA, Arch. Dioc., no.9. Ed. Cusa 1868–82, no.43, pp.6–12 (reg. pp.706–7); trans. Trovato 1949, pp.40–5.

P.77 note 102.

6. 29 Dhū l-Qaʿda 531 A.H. (18 August 1137 A.D.): Ramaḍān 532 A.H. (13 May – 10 June 1138 A.D.) Palermo.

Arabic deed of sale. Ghartīl al-Naṣrānī ibn Ghartīl (Walter the Christian, son of Walter), acting on behalf of Henry, archbishop of Messina, buys a house in Palermo from ʿAlī ibn Abī l-Qāsim ibn ʿAbd Allāh al-ʿAṭṭār ('the Druggist'), known as Ibn al-Bārūqī, and from his mother, Sayyida bint Yūsuf al-Qaysī, who represents her son ʿAbd Allāh al-Murāhiq ('the Adolescent') and Bulbula al-Bikr ('the Virgin'), both the children of her (? late) husband, Abū l-Qāsim. Because [two of] the children are minors, the sale is overseen by *al-shaykh al-faqīh al-qāḍī* Abū l-Qāsim ʿAbd al-Raḥmān ibn Rajāʾ. The house lies in al-Qaṣr al-Qadīm (the Old City), amongst the houses of Zuqāq Ibn Khalfūn, which is to the south of the road leading from the Bāb al-Abnāʾ to the Bāb al-Sūdān, and to the north of the Simāṭ al-Balāṭ (modern Corso Vittorio Emanuele). The house was inherited by the three children from Abū l-Qāsim and from his uncle, ʿAbd al-Raḥmān al-ᶜAṭṭār ibn al-Barūqī, and was divided into five shares, two going to each of the sons, and one to the daughter. Subsequently, ᶜAlī made over to Bulbula one third of the entire house, as her dowry, on the occasion of her marriage, which third was added to her fifth. In this way, the shares became fifteen – six for each of the sons, and three for the daughter – so that, when ᶜAlī made over one third of the whole house, or five fifteenths, to Bulbula, she had eight shares, ᶜAbd Allāh had six, and ᶜAlī had one. Ghartīl purchased the house for the sum of 412 *tarì*, each lacking one grain of gold. The whole sum was deposited with the *qāḍī*, who then distributed the shares amongst the vendors. ᶜAlī's one share came to 27 *tarì* and $2^1/_3$ fifths of a *tarì*; Sayyida received $164^4/_5$ *tarì* on behalf of ᶜAbd Allāh, and 219 *tarì* and $3^1/_3$ fifths of a *tarì* on behalf of Bulbula. [A grand total of $411^{14}/_{15}$ *tarì*?]. The act is dated 29 Dhū l-Qaᶜda 531, and was witnessed by ᶜAlī ibn Naqīya(?) ibn ᶜAlī ibn Naqīya(?) al-Laḥmī (or al-Lakhmī), Mujāhid ibn Ḥusayn al-Kindī, and Yūsuf ibn Muḥammad ibn ᶜAbd al-Qāhir al-Lawātī. The transaction was officially registered (?) in Ramaḍān 532, and witnessed by ᶜAbd al-Raḥmān ibn Abī l-Qāsim al-Anṣārī, ᶜUmar ibn Muḥammad al-Qaysī, Muḥammad ibn Ḥusayn al-Qaysī, ᶜUdhr(?) ibn Muḥammad al-Tamīmī, ᶜUmar ibn ᶜĪsā al-Zanātī, Abū ᶜAbd Allāh ibn Abī l-Faḍl ibn ᶜAlī al-Qurashī, ᶜAbd Allāh ibn Abī Bakr al-Hawwārī, Ḥusayn ibn ᶜAtīq al-Tamīmī, Abū Bakr ibn ᶜUmar al-Qurashī, Muḥammad ibn ᶜUmar ibn Muḥammad al-Qaysī, ᶜAbd Allāh ibn Abī l-Qāsim al-Anṣārī, and Muḥammad ibn Muḥammad al-Lawātī.

Original: PA, Cap. Pal., no.4. Ed. Cusa 1868–82, no.54, pp.61–7 (reg. p.709); trans. Trovato 1949, pp.45–50.

Pp.77 note 102, 88 note 170, 131 note 53.

7. October, Indiction V [1141 A.D.?] Palermo.

Greek deed of sale of villeins, with a bilingual – Greek-Arabic – list of their names. Peter Markēsi sells to the lord Theodore the Antiochene (*i.e.* the son of George of Antioch), who had founded the monastery of San Nicolò (di Chùrchuro) outside Palermo, on the road to Corleone, four households of his villeins, to serve the monastery, for the sum of 200 *tarì* and one horse. The villeins: ᶜAwḍ ibn Bishr and his children; Ḥasan together with his brother and his children; ᶜAbd al-Ḥaqq ibn al-Rīḥ and his children; ᶜAlī ibn al-Bazāna, called Bū Qadīm, and his children. The witnesses: *Charbertos tou Sanemou* (Herbert of Sanemon); John, son of the emir Eugenios; *Chammettas* (Aḥmad or Ḥamid?); Robert *de Sēfregasta*; Roger *de Fales*; Philip, son of the aforesaid John.

Original: PA, Arch. Dioc., no.11. Ed. Cusa 1868–82, no.61, pp.22–3 (reg. p.711).

8. Undated [1130–c.1160] Cefalù?

Arabic *aide-memoire* containing the rough drafts of three contracts of sea-exchange, all made on the same occasion, setting out the terms upon which a Latin investor, Ser William (*Sar Ghulyalim*) lends various sums in silver pounds to Sicilian Muslims to be repaid in gold *tarì*.

Contract I. Ser William lends to the following Muslims from Cefalù: to Maymūn, his sister Ṣadaqa, and his son ᶜAlī, £35 to be repaid as 460 *tarì*; to Bū ᶜAbd Allāh, £14 to be repaid as 200 *tarì*; to Ḥasan, the son of the sister of Maymūn and Ṣadaqa, £15 10s to be repaid as 210 *tarì*; to Salām, £11 10s to be repaid as 260 *tarì*; to Bū l-Futūḥ, £12 15s to be repaid as 415 *tarì*; to the whole group, collectively, 13 new *muᵓminī* dinars, apparently for provisions, no repayment is stipulated. All assume collective responsibility for the sums borrowed. The loan is apparently made in Cefalù, and is to be repaid to Ser William himself, in Messina, within a term of 15 days. The witnesses are apparently those named on the *verso*: Ser William Arminio(?); Ser John Musso(?); Ser John Barbarossa; Ser Sardo(?); Ser Oliver; Ser Arnald from Messina; [ᶜAlī ibn ?] ᶜAbd al-Raḥmān [from Sciacca ?]; Muḥammad [ibn *al-ḥājj* ibn Khālid ?] from Sciacca (*sic*! *i.e.* from Corleone); Bū ᶜAbd Allāh from Termini Imerese; and *al-ḥājj* ᶜUthmān.

Contract II. Ser William lends to Muḥammad ibn *al-ḥājj* ibn Khālid from Corleone, £14 to be repaid to Ser William himself, at Messina, within a term of 20 days, as 240 *tarì*. Witnessed by Yaḥyā from Trapani; ᶜAlī ibn ᶜAbd al-Raḥmān from Sciacca; and Maymūn and his partners from Cefalù.

Contract III. Ser William lends to *al-ḥājj* ᶜUthmān an unspecified sum for which the repayment is to be 105 *tarì*, to be repaid to Ser William himself, at Messina, within a term of 20 days. Witnessed by Maymūn Ṣadaqa, Salām, and Bū ᶜAbd Allāh, all from Cefalù; by Muḥammad [ibn *al-ḥājj* ibn Khālid] from Corleone; and by Bū ᶜAbd Allāh from Termini Imerese.

Original: PA, AdS, Cefalù, no.37. Ed. and trans. Johns 1999.

9. Shawwāl 556 A.H. (23 September – 21 October 1161 A.D.) Palermo.

Arabic deed of sale. Rāw (*i.e.* Rao < Raoul), a priest of Palermo cathedral, purchases from Abū Bakr and Aḥmad, the tanners, sons of ᶜUmar al-Azdī(?), and from ᶜUmar ibn ᶜAtīq al-Qaysī, known as Ibn al-Muharīqa(?), who acts on behalf of his wife Manjūma, and on behalf of his sister-in-law, the spinster Amr al-Khayr, both daughters of ᶜUmar al-Azdī(?), a house in the Old City of Palermo, on the street leading from the Masjid al-Sabīyān to the Bāb al-Sūdān, for the price of 350 *tarì* (*al-rubāᶜīyāt al-dūqīya)*, each missing one grain. Abū Bakr and Aḥmad each receive $116^{2}/_{3}$ *tarì*, and ᶜUmar receives $58^{1}/_{3}$ *tarì* on behalf of each of the two sisters. The transaction is supervised by the *qāḍī* of Palermo, *al-shaykh al-faqīh al-qāḍī* Abū l-Faḍl Rajāᵓ ibn *al-shaykh al-faqīh al-qāḍī* Abī l-Ḥasan ᶜAlī ibn *al-shaykh al-faqīh al-qāḍī* Abī l-Qāsim ᶜAbd al-Raḥmān ibn Rajāᵓ. He was assisted two official witnesses: *al-shaykh al-faqīh* Abū l-Qāsim(?) ibn(?) ᶜAbd al-Raḥmān ibn Maḥmūd(?) ibn Jabr al-Tanūkhī(?); and *al-shaykh al-faqīh* Abū l-Ḥasan ᶜAlī ibn Qarqar(?) al-Tanūkhī(?). The witnesses: ᶜAbd al-Raḥmān ibn Maymūn ibn al-Lathīq; Ḥasan ibn Yūsuf ibn Muḥammad ibn ᶜĀdiyāᵓ(?) al-Lawātī(?); Muḥammad ibn ᶜAlī ibn ᶜAbd al-Raḥmān ibn Rajāᵓ al-L …; ᶜAlī ibn Muᶜāsh(?) ibn Abī l-Qāsim al-Tanūkhī; Hibat Allāh ibn Muḥammad ibn ᶜAlī al-Naṣrānī(?); ᶜAbd al-Rāḥmān ibn Muḥammad ibn ᶜAtīq al-Ḥarīrī(?); Ḥasan ibn Abī l-Qāsim al-Qurashī; Ḥusayn ibn ᶜAtīq al-Tamīmī.

Original: PA, AdS, Magione, no.2. 1161. Cusa 1868–82, no.102, pp.101–6 (reg. pp.722–3); trans. Trovato 1949, pp.51–6.

Pp.77 note 102, 88 note 171, 275 note 99.

10. March, 6673 A.M., Indiction XIII (1165 A.D.) Palermo.

Greek deed of sale with the Arabic superscription of the vendor. Liyūn ibn Abū (*sic*!) al-Faraḥ sells to Thomas, son of *Bagalabitar* (? – Cusa reads βαγαλα where now only … γα … is legible, plus βιτὰρ on the next line for which Caracausi 1990, p.88, proposes < Arabic *al-abtar*), his estate called *tou Uiou Atzēp* ('the Son of Atzēpas'), in the *Agros Marias* (*i.e.* Falsomiele) outside Palermo, for 135 *tarì*. The witnesses: Leo of Reggio; Christodoulos; Christodoulos son of *Boztēt*(?); Paganus; Zanthos the priest; Nikētas Panētērios; and Nikolaos.

Original: PA, AdS, Magione, no.3. Ed. Cusa 1868–82, no.105, pp.107–8 (reg. p.723).

11. March, 1167, Indiction XV. Palermo.
Latin record of exchange of houses, with two Arabic signatures. Eutropius, cantor of the Cappella Palatina, and Ansaldus, castellan of the royal palace, exchange houses in the Chalca of Palermo. The witnesses: Matthew [of Salerno] *domini Regis magister notarius et familiaris*; the *qāʾid* Richard – *Gaytus Riccardus domini Regis magister camerarius et familiaris lā yakhfā ͨalā llāhi shayʾ* ('Nothing is hidden from God'); the *qāʾid* Martin – *Gaytus martinus domini Regis magister camerarius et familiaris tawakkulī ͨalā llāhi* ('My trust is in God'); Eutropius, cantor of the royal chapel; Henry Martellus, canon of the royal chapel; Roboald, canon of the royal chapel; Walter, deacon of Agrigento and canon of the royal chapel; Girard, subcantor of the royal chapel; Falco, canon of the royal chapel; Baldwin, canon of the royal chapel.
Original: PA, Cap. Pal., no.13. Ed. Garofalo, 1835, no.10, pp.24–5; amended by Buscemi 1839, p.16.
Pp.220 note 26, 221, 222 note 32, 251 notes 198–9.

12. March, 6677 A.M., Indiction II (1169 A.D.) Palermo.
Greek deed of sale with one Arabic signature. Christodoulos or Abdesseit (Ar. *ͨAbd al-Sayyid*, lit. 'Servant of the Lord'), son of Boussit (Ar. *Abū l-Sayyid*), with his wife, Sētelchousoun (Ar. *Sitt al-Ḥusn*, lit. 'Mistress of Beauty'), daughter of Petros Kastronopou (Peter of Castronuovo), sells to Rompertos (Robert), the marshall of the bishop-elect of Syracuse, for 700 *tarì*, each lacking one grain, a house which he had as a marriage portion, in Palermo, in the *Rumē Uiou Kalfoun* (Ar. *Zuqāq Ibn Khalfūn*). The act is witnessed by: Filippos, son of Nikolaos Garzēfa; Magister Clarus; Fōtios son of Scholaros tou Kalou; Theodōros, son of Leo tou Chanzeri (Ar. *al-Khinzārī*, lit. 'the swineherd'); Basilios son of Theodōros; Petrus de Castronovo; Brachēmos, son of Iosēf (Ar. *Ibrāhīm ibn Yūsuf*); and Simiyūn ibn Andrayat al-R.ḥām(?) who signs in Arabic.
Original: PA, AdS, Cap. Pal., no.14. Ed. Cusa 1868–82, no.109, pp.76–7 (reg. p.724).
P.233 note 86.

13. April, 6678 A.M., Indiction III (1170 A.D.) Palermo.
Greek deed of sale, with five Arabic signatures. *Iohannes filius Medicis* (*i.e.* John, son of the Doctor?), with his wife, Maria, sells to Kērbuna, daughter of Kērbos Similias (*i.e.* Cervina, daughter of Cervus Similis?), for 250 *tarì*, each lacking one grain, a *choutzra* (Ar. *ḥujra*), or small house, within the big house belonging to him and to his mother, Iōannou, in Palermo, in the *Rumē Kes* (Arabic: *Zuqāq al-Kaʾs*[?], 'Alley of the Cup'). The act is witnessed by: Maimoun, son of Kalou; Georgius, son of Nicolaus; Filippos Pelekanos; and Eugenios, son of Leo; and by five witnesses who sign in Arabic: ͨĪsā ibn Sulaymān; Badr ibn al-Rūdinī(?); Dumīniq ibn ͨAbd al-Malik; Martīn al-Najjār; and ͨAbd al-Mawlā al-Naṣrānī.
Original: PA, Cap. Pal., no.15. Ed. Cusa 1868–82, no.111, pp.78–79 (reg. p.724).

14. August, 6680 A.M., Indiction V (1172 A.D.) Palermo.
Greek deed of sale, with Arabic notes on *recto* and *verso*. Christodoulēs, daughter of Abderrachmen Akpe (*i.e.* ͨAbd al-Raḥmān [ibn?] ͨUqba – in the Arabic note on the *recto*, she is *al-ͨajūz* bint ͨAbd al-Raḥmān al-Naṣrānī, 'the old woman, daughter of ͨAbd al-Raḥmān the Christian), with her sons Sumeōn and Boussit (*i.e.* Abū l-Sayyid), sells to the *kait Chamse* (*al-qāʾid* Ḥamza), their estate in the territory of the city of Palermo, in place called the *Sourtie* (Arabic *al-surtīya*), beneath the *Rabͨ al-Malf* (*i.e.* l'Amalfitano), for the price of 110 *tarì*. The witnesses: John, the master of the *charbatoi*

('spearmen' < Arabic *ḥarba* ?) and brother-in-law of the *qāʾid* Ranald; Kalokeros; Christodoulos son of Fōteinos; Peter, the ex-deacon (? ὁ ἐν διακόνοις ἐλάχιστος); Leo of Reggio; John the priest.

Original: PA, AdS, Santa Maria della Grotta, no.3. Ed. Cusa 1868–82, no.117, pp.663–4 (reg. p.726).

15. December, 6682 A.M., Indiction VII (1173 A.D.) Palermo.

Greek deed of sale, with one Arabic signature and Arabic note on *verso*. Nikolaos son of Christodoulos *Taneperi* (< Arabic *al-ṭanābīrī* – a name perhaps related to a profession involving either the mandolin-like *ṭunbūr* or the water-lifting device so-named because of its resemblance to the said musical instrument) sells the vineyard planted by him on the outskirts of Palermo, in the place called Lamis, to Ioustos for the price of 200 *tarì*. The witnesses: Christodoulos son of Solomon; Kōstantinos son of Solomon; Maimun (Latin); Yūḥannā ibn ʿAbd al-Raḥmān (Arabic); Agathonikos son of Leo; Christodoulos son of Asfordeuelēs; Noikolaos (*sic*!).

Original: PA, AdS, Santa Maria della Grotta, no.4. Ed. Cusa 1868–82, no.123, pp.665–66 (reg. p.727).

16. The first days of Rabīʿ I, August (1177–9 A.D.) Palermo.

Jabrūn, Ibrahīm and ʿAbd al-Raḥmān, the three sons of Mūsā, called *Sh.bʿāt*, acknowledge themselves and their ancestors to be 'men of the registers' of Manzil Yūsuf, modern Mezzoiuso, and agree to return to their lands, from which they had fled, and to obey their lord, Donatus, abbot of San Giovanni degli Eremiti in Palermo, paying a *jizya* of 30 *tarì* (*rubāʿīy*) and a *qānūn* or land-tax of 20 *mudd*s of wheat and 10 of barley. The witnesses: Abū l-Faraj ibn Salām al-Laḥmī, the maternal uncle of Jabrūn and his brothers; Aḥmad ibn Abī l-Qāsim al-Qaysī; Abū Jumʿa ibn Muḥammad al-Qurashī; ʿAlī ibn Yaʿlā al-Qurashī; Abū …

Original: PA, AdS, Magione, no.5. Ed. and trans. Johns forthcoming b.

Pp.35, 47, 61, 130 note 48, 145–6.

17. October, 6688 A.M., Indiction XIII (1179 A.D.).

Greek deed of sale, with one Arabic superscription. Abū l-Ṭayyib ibn Yānī – in Greek, 'the son of *Merakias*' – sells to the lord *qāʾid* John, son of Ananias, his estate to the south of Palermo, near to 'the tower of the daughter of *Serēp*', and a small piece of land to the north of it, for 50 *tarì*, each missing one grain. The witnesses: George, son of Peter, master of the archers(?); Ēlias son of Christodoulos.

Original: PA, AdS, Santa Maria della Grotta, no.5. Ed. Cusa 1868–82, no.134, pp.667–8 (reg. p.730).

18. 11–20 Jumādā II, 576 A.H. (3–12 October 1180 A.D.) Palermo.

Arabic deed of sale. *Al-shaykh al-muʿallim* Bāsīlī, at the order and on the behalf of Archbishop Walter II of Palermo, purchases from *al-shaykh* Abū l-ʿAbbās Aḥmad ibn ʿAbd al-Nūr al-Tamīmī and *al-shaykh al-muqriʾ* ('the Qurʾānic-reciter') *al-ḥājj* Abū l-Faḍl ibn Aḥmad al-Ḥ.dāmī(?) a *faddān* of Persian cane (*i.e. Arundo donax*) and the spring called ʿAyn al-Abrārī, situated to the south of Palermo and *al-Fawwāra al-Kabīra* ('the Great Spring' or 'Lake'), for the price of 300 *tarì* (*rubāʿī dhahaban dūqīya*). Abū l-ʿAbbās owned one-third, and Abū l-Faḍl two-thirds of the property. The witnesses: ʿAlī ibn Abī l-Fatḥ ibn Ḥ.l.fīsī(?); Abū l-Faḍl ibn ʿAbd al-Wāḥid al-Burjī(?); ʿAlī ibn ʿUmar ibn ʿAtīq al-R.y.ghī(?); ʿUthmān ibn ʿAbd al-Wāḥid al-Ḥaḍramī(?); Aḥmad ibn Khalīfa al-Azdī.

Original: PA, Arch. Dioc. No.20. Ed. Cusa 1868–82, no.135, pp.39–43 (reg. p.730); trans. Trovato 1949, pp.58–61.

P.137 note 87.

19. February, Indiction I; the first days of Shawwāl, 578 A.H. (1183 A.D.) Palermo.
Arabic deed of sale. Dame Margaret the Christian, the daughter of the nun from Agrigento (*Dāma Bargharīṭa al-naṣrānīya bint al-rāhiba al-Karkantīya*) purchases from Masʿūd ibn Tāmir al-Qurashī and from his son ʿAbd al-Salām their house in the southern suburb of the city of Palermo near to *al-Dayyāsīn al-Kibār* (see Caracausi 1983, pp.209–10), in the road once called Zuqāq Ibn al-Khāthira, for the price of 121 *tarì* (*rubāʿī ... al-dūqīya*). The father and the son each owned one-half share of the property. The witnesses: ʿAlī ibn Abī l-Faḍl al-Tamīmī; Abū l-Qāsim ibn ʿAbd al-Salām al-Azdī; Abū l-Qāsim ibn Abī ʿAbd Allāh al-Tamīmī; Aḥmad ibn Abī l-Qāsim al-Qaysī; ʿUthmān ibn ʿAlī al-Hawwārī; ʿAlī *al-ḥājj* ibn ʿUthmān al-Anṣārī; Aḥmad ibn ʿAbd Allāh *al-ḥājj* al-Hawwārī; ʿUmar ibn Abī l-Khayr al-Qurashī; Makhlūf ibn Makhlūf al-Qaysī; ʿAbd Allāh ibn ʿUthmān al-Ghāfir(?).

Original: PA, AdS, Cefalù, no.22. Ed. Cusa 1868–82, no.141, pp.491–3 (reg. p.732); trans. Trovato 1949, pp.62–4.

P.77 note 103.

20. May, 1183, Indiction I. Palermo.
Latin letter patent, with one 'Arabic' signature. On the marriage of Roger de Tarsia to Maria, daughter of the late Robert Malconvenant, King William II has granted the couple those lands lawfully held by the late Robert. In the presence of the Vice-chancellor Matthew of Salerno, the royal familiars, and others, the couple acknowledge that Bisacquino did not lawfully belong to the late Robert, and that they and their heirs have no right to it, and therefore restore it to the royal demesne. If they or their heirs make any claim to it in the future, they will be fined 100 ounces of gold. The signatories: Matthew of Salerno, vice-chancellor and familiar; Roger of Tarsia; Maria, his wife; Hugo Lupinus *domini Regis privatus*; Guillelmus Malconvenant *regie magne curie magister Justiciarius*, who also signs in 'Arabic', written from left to right, *Ghulyalim Malquwanant*; Richard, the son of the vice-chancellor; Iordanus Lupinus; Guillelmus Sorellus *regie private masnede solidarius*; Hugo de Sexto *regie private masnede solidarius*.

Original: Bibl. Reg., Monreale, no.46. Ed. Garufi 1899, no.77, pp.190–2.

21. June, 6691 A.M., Indiction I (1183 A.D.) Palermo.
Greek deed of sale, with one Arabic signature. Blasius, *clericus domini Regis*, sells his house in Palermo, in the street that runs to the church of Agios Kōnstantinos, to Bartholomew of Salerno, the king's doorkeeper (ὁ θυρορὸς), for the price of 468 *tarì*, each missing one grain. The witnesses: Philip, son of Michael of Mazara; Christodoulos, son of Gemma; Dēmētrios the priest; Nikolaos, son of the late Christodoulos; Christodoulos, son of Philip; Salmūn ibn ʿAbd Allāh al-Mahdawī (Arabic).

Original: PA, AdS, Magione, no.6. 1183. Ed. Cusa 1868–82, no.144, pp.109–10 (reg. p.733).

22. May, 6693 A.M., Indiction III (1185 a.d.) Palermo.
Greek letter patent, with one Arabic superscription and two Arabic signatures. ʿAbd al-ʿAzīz ibn Juwān – in Greek, the son of *Iōannēs Endoulsi* < Arabic *al-Andalusī* – and his wife Christodoulēs each give half of an uncultivated estate, known as *Kalamin*

('Cane'), on Monte Gallo (εἰς τὸ σάρφ [< Arabic *sharaf*, 'high place'] τοῦ γάλλεν), to George, son of the lord Nikolaos son of Megdie (? < Arabic *al-Mahdawī*), so that he may plant a vineyard. The witnesses: Simiyūn ibn Abī Layūn (Arabic); Philip, son of Joseph son of …; Stephen, son of John of Petralia; Juwān ibn ᶜAbd al-Malik (Arabic); the *tabularios* John the priest; Nikētas son of Theodore.

Original: PA, AdS, Santa Maria della Grotta, no.6. 1185. Ed. Cusa 1868–82, no.150, pp.669–70 (reg. p.735).

23. March, 1187, Indiction V (Latin); mid Yanār (January), 1184 (*sic!* Arabic), Indiction V. Palermo.

A Latin-Arabic letter patent (*instrumentum*; *kitāb*), in which the royal chamberlain, Gaytus Ioannes (Ar. *al-fatā Juwān*), rents from Frater Nife (Gr. *Nēfos*), monk of Sant'Andrea de Bebbene (*sic*?) – Ar. *bi-l-Kamūniya*), with the approval of Dominus Iacobus, precentor of the Royal Chapel and archdeacon of Catania, and of the whole chapter of the Chapel, two pieces of land belonging to Sant'Andrea: one, measuring five by three *canne*, in order to build a stable, at his own expense; the other, measuring five by two *canne*, as a straw-barn (*palearium*; *makhzan al-tibn*) for the stable. The lease is approved by John's *dominus*, Gaytus Riccardus (*al-qāʾid* Richard), the royal chamberlain and master of the royal *duana de secretis*. John is to hold the lands during his lifetime, after which they are to revert to Sant'Andrea. The rent is fixed at ten *raṭl*s of oil and two of wax to be paid each year on the Feast of St. Andrew. The Latin text was composed, at John's request, by Abraham, cleric of the Royal Chapel, and written by Ioannes, *campanarius* of the same chapel. The Arabic text summarises the Latin, and adds that the lands lay inside the city of Palermo, on the left entering by the Bāb al-Abnāʾ, and to the south of the *makhzan* of that gate, where there is the cemetery. The act is witnessed by the following, who all sign in Arabic: *al-fatā Juwān*; *al-qāʾid Rijardhī … lā yakhfā ᶜalā llāhi shayʾ* ('Nothing is hidden from God'); and *al-fatā ᶜAmmār … ḥasbiya llāhu wa-l-muslimīn* ('God and the Muslims are sufficient for me').

Original: PA, Cap. Pal., no.19. Ed. Cusa 1868–82, no.155, pp.83–5 (reg. pp.735–6). Pp.233 note 82, 243 note 143, 251 note 199.

24. Muḥarram 583 A.H. (13 March – 11 April 1187 A.D.) Palermo.

Latin transumpt (dated 19 June 1282) of Arabic deed of sale. The Christian *Ebu Suleyman* (Abū Sulaymān), son of *Scaleri*, purchases from Ebraym son of Sebeun (*Ibrāhīm ibn Sabᶜūn*), known as *Atrami*, an estate called *Rotundus* (*i.e. al-Mudawwara*?), in the territory of Vicari, on the road from Vicari to Petralia, for the price of 80 *tarì*, each missing one grain. The witnesses: Aly filius Abdalle Elhegueri (*ᶜAlī ibn ᶜAbd Allāh al-Hawwārī*); Ebubeker filius Abderrahmen Elheguerj (*Abū Bakr ibn ᶜAbd al-Raḥmān al-Hawwārī*); Aly ibin Abderrahmen Ettimimi (*ᶜAlī ibn ᶜAbd al-Raḥmān al-Tamīmī*); Ebrahym ibin Nasar Ellachmi (*Ibrāhīm ibn Naṣr al-Lakhmī*).

Latin transumpt: PA, AdS, Magione, no.152. Ed. Bresc 1995, pp.95–7.

25. Christmas, [4]948 Hebrew Era, Indiction VI (1187 A.D.)

Judaeo-Arabic letter patent. The Jewish community of Syracuse had asked Blasius (*Sīr Iblāṣ*), the prior of Santa Lucia of Syracuse, a priory of San Salvatore of Cefalù, to grant them a piece of land adjoining their cemetery. He mediated between them and the bishop of Cefalù, and obtained for them 4 *qiyam* (approx. 8 metres). He brought to them a letter patent (*sijill maftūḥ*) setting out the agreement: in return for the land, the Jews were to pay every year one *qafīz* (or 16 *raṭl*s) of olive oil to Santa Lucia. The witnesses:

Faḍlūn ibn Daʾūd; Yaʿqub bar Abraham; Yaḥyā bar Fraḥiah; Daʾūd bar Salmān; Yehūdah bar Abraham; Shlomo ibn Saʿīd; Shaul bar ʿAmram; Yaʿqub Ḥazn; Yaʿqub bar Balʿām; Saʿdiah bar Yitzḥaq; Moshe bar ʿAmram.

Original: PA, AdS, Cefalù, no.25. Ed. and trans. Wansbrough 1967; Golb 1973. See also: Wansbrough 1984, pp.19–20; Simonsohn 1997, no.190, pp.425–26.

Pp.77 note 104, 130 note 48.

26. Shaʿbān, 586 (3 September – 1 October 1190). Palermo.

Arabic deed of sale. Niqūla Ashqar, a servant (*khadīm*) of the royal palace, purchases from Zaynab bint ʿAbd Allāh al-Anṣārī, her house in the Old City of Palermo, near to the Bāb al-Sūdān, in the Darb al-Asquṭūnī, for the sum of 500 *tarì* (*rubāʿī dūqīya*). The sale was made on the order of the Lord Protector (*al-mawlā l-nāṣir*) and of the lords of the *dīwān al-fawāʾid*, because Zaynab was being held prisoner by foreign Rūm (*i.e.* the Byzantines, or Europeans from outside the kingdom of Sicily) in order to raise the sum demanded for her ransom. The sale was completed on 10 October (? reading *uttubra* or similar: Cusa reads *abrīra*, and translates 'April', but this not attested elsewhere), Indiction IX (1190 A.D.), after Zaynab's return from captivity, and was registered in the *dafātir al-dīwān al-maʿmūr.* The witnesses: Abū l-Qāsim ibn Muḥammad al-Tamīmī; Ḥasan ibn Abī l-Qāsim ibn Muḥammad al-Qurashī; al-Sabʿ ibn ʿĪsā ibn al-Sabʿ ibn ʿĪsā al-Lawātī; Muḥammad ibn al-Salām ibn ʿAbd Allāh al-Ḥ.mrī; Muḥammad ibn ʿUmar ibn Ḥasan al-Ṭāʾī(?).

Original: PA, Arch. Dioc., no.27. Ed. Cusa 1868–82, no.160, pp.44–6 (reg. p.737); trans. Trovato 1949, pp.65–8.

Pp.204 and note 54, 205, 244 note 158, 295.

27. 1–10 Rabīʿ I, 589 A.H. [7–16 March 1193]. Castrogiovanni?

Arabic deed of sale. Giles the Christian (*Jīlū al-Naṣrānī*) purchases from Ibrahīm ibn Muḥammad al-Qurashī his house in the Ḥarāt Asaqlāba in Castrogiovanni (Qaṣr Yānah) for the price of 44 'gold quarter-dinar coins (i.e. *tarì*) in perfect condition from the royal mint' (*rubāʿīyan ʿuyūnan dhahaban jiyādan sikkīyatan malakīyatan* – *i.e.* most definitely *not* Trovato's '*tarì* di forma ovale'!). The witnesses: Makhlūf ibn Abī l-Futūḥ al-Tamīmī; Aḥmad ibn ʿAbd al-Raḥmān al-Tamīmī; Abū Bakr ibn ʿAbd al-Mālik al-Hawwārī; ʿAbd al-Munʿim ibn ʿAbd al-Kāfī al-Zanātī; ʿUmar ibn ʿAbd al-Muḥsin al-Qurashī; Aḥmad ibn ʿAbd al-Karīm al-Hawwārī; Yaḥyā ibn ʿAbd al-Kāfī al-Zanātī.

Original: PA, AdS, Cefalù, no.29. 1193. Ed. Cusa 1868–82, no.169, pp.496–8 (reg. p.738); trans. Trovato 1949, pp.68–70.

28. April, 6704 A.M., Indiction [X]IV [1196 A.D.] Palermo.

Greek deed of sale, with one Arabic signature. The mother of Kōstantza, daughter of Boulfadl (*Qunṣtaṣa bint Abī l-Faḍl*), had sold to Iōannēs of Melfi (*Juwān min Malf*) her part of a *foundax* (*funduq*) in the Rachap (Ar. *al-Raḥaba*) of Palermo. In this act, Kōstantza confirms the sale – although she had sought to annul it because Iōannēs had failed to pay the purchase price of 60 *tarì* – and also sells her own part of the *funduq*, raising the price for the two shares to 75 *tarì*. She receives 15 *tarì* for her part of the sale. The witnesses: Omoddeos (< Latin *homo deus*, *homo dei*, 'Man of God'), the husband of Kōstantza; Bouttaib Afer (*Abū l-Ṭayyib al-Ifrīqī*); Dominēkos Pelekanos; Salmūn ibn ʿAbd Allāh al-Mahdawī, who signs in Arabic; Iōannēs the Taboularios; Nikolaos son of Tapechtēs (?); Kōnstantinos, son of the Notary Leo; and ??? son of the late Boolfoutouch (*Abū l-Futūḥ*).

Original now (*i.e.* both 1979 and 2000) missing from PA, Cap. Pal. Ed. Cusa 1868–82, no.171, pp.87–8 (reg. p.739).

29. 20–29 Jumādā I, 592 A.H. [21–30 April 1196]. Palermo

Arabic deed of sale. The priest Peter (*al-shaykh al-qissīs Bātrū*), priest of Ser Geoffrey D'Animato (reading *Jāfrāy dī Ānimātuh[?]* – Cusa reads *dī Armāna*, 'Goffredo Armanno'; Trovato, 'Goffredo di Armanno'), purchases from ᶜUthmān ibn Yūsuf al-Hawwārī his house (*ḥujra*) in the southern suburb of the city of Palermo, in the *Darb al-Simintārī* (lit. 'Street of the Cemetery'), near the Bāb al-Abnāʾ, for the price of 28 *tarì (rubāᶜīy [sic] ᶜuyūnan dhababan dūqīyatan)*, each missing one grain. The witnesses: ᶜAbd Allāh ibn Muḥammad al-Būnī; ᶜAlī ibn Abī Bakr al-Tamīmī(?); Abū l-Ṭāhir ibn ᶜUmar al-Tanūkhī; Ṭāhir ibn ᶜAbd al-Raḥmān al-Qurashī.

Original: PA, AdS, Cefalù, no.18. Ed. Cusa 1868–82, no.172, pp.499–501 (reg. p.739); trans. Trovato 1949, pp.71–3.

P.77 note 102.

30. May, 1198, Indiction I. Termini Imerese.

Latin letter patent, with one Arabic signature. William Malconvenant, Master Justiciar of the Imperial Court (*Guillelmus Malconvenant, Magne Imperialis Curie Magister Justiciarius*), and Roger Bussell, Imperial Justiciar of the Val di Noto (*Rogerius busellus Imperialis Justiciarius vallis Nothi*) were sent by the Empress Constance to determine the boundaries of the *casale* of Odesuer (*i.e. Wādī*), granted by her to San Salvatore di Cefalù. The two justiciars went to Termini Imerese and there held an inquest with a jury of the Christian and Saracen elders from Termini, Brucato, Burgitabis, Collesano, and Odesuer itself, to renew the boundaries which had been made in the days of King Roger and King William II. Signed by William Malconvenant in Latin and 'Arabic' – *Ghulyalim Malquwanant*; and by Roger Bussell.

Original: PA AdS, Cefalù no.35. Ed. Battaglia 1895, no.41, pp.123–4.

31. April, 6746 A.M., Indiction XI (1238 A.D.) Palermo.

Greek donation, with Arabic superscriptions of the two donors, and with seven Latin signatures. Obert Fallamonaca (*Ūbart Fallamūnaqa ibn al-qāʾid ᶜAbd al-Raḥmān ibn Fālaymūn*; in Greek, *Rombertos Fallamonaka*, son of the late elder, Lord *Abderrachmen*, the *qāʾid* of the city of Palermo), with the consent of his wife, Suḥayliba, and their sons, substitute a piece of arable land measuring $1^1/_4$ *salme* at San Drogo (*Agios Dourrounēs*) in Palermo, in place of two pieces of arable land at Santa Maria, which they had previously exchanged with Abbot Athanasios of Santa Maria della Grotta. The witnesses: the notary George of Palermo (Greek); Nicolaus de Ebdemonia, son of the late Lord Ha...(?), *secretus* of Palermo; the notary Michael, son of the late notary George; the notary James of Palermo; the notary John of Palermo; Philip son of Simon; Leo, son of the late notary John *Pezpouz* (Greek; < Arabic *bazbūz*, 'nozzle'?); Girardus Scavus; Marzucus (< Arabic *Marzūq*) de Plutino; Robert Pipotoni (Greek); the notary Basil (Greek).

Original: PA, AdS, Santa Maria della Grotta, no.13. Ed. Cusa 1868–82, no.188, pp.676–8 (reg. p.743).

P.246 and note 179.

32. 20 September, 1266. Palermo.

Latin deed, with one Arabic signature. This document has only recently come to my attention, and I have not yet had the opportunity to inspect the original. The following remarks are taken from Trasselli, 1965, p.341: '... il 20 settembre 1266 Perrino Fallamonaca, canonico palermitano, gli (*i.e.* the judge Martino di Calatafimi) concesse una casa della sua prebenda, pel censo annuo di 8 *tarì*, in ricompensa dei servizi resi'; and note 22: 'Tabulario della Martorana, perg.30. Censo annuo di *tarì* 8; la casa ruinosa, con stalla, è adiacente all'altra casa che Martino comprò dal Gallo [Guglielmo Gallo, in Ruga Marmorea, *cf.* p.338, and Martorana, perg. no.14]; si prevede che Martino dovrà spendervi 150 *tarì*. Fra le firme dei canonici è inserita una riga di scrittura araba che il Chiar.mo prof. Umberto Rizzitano, che qui ringrazio, ha letto: è l'approvazione all'atto di Oberto Fallamonaca, figlio di Abderrachmen, Gaito di Palermo, che pertanto si deve presumere padre di Perrino'.

P.247 note 184.

APPENDIX 3

Abū Tillīs –'Old Wheat-sack'

In his biography of George of Antioch (above, p.81), al-Maqrīzī employs the *kunya* or nickname Abū Tillīs for one of the protagonists. The meaning of this name rests upon two interdependent considerations: whether it belongs to ᶜAbd al-Raḥmān or to Roger; and the precise meaning of *tillīs*.

The Arabic reads *kataba ilā l-sulṭāni ᶜAbdi l-Raḥmāni wazīri l-maliki Rūjāra bni Rūjāra maliki l-faranji l-maᶜrūfi bi-Abī Tillīsin ṣāḥibi jazīrati Ṣiqillīyata* ('he wrote to the sultan ᶜAbd al-Raḥmān, the vizier of King Roger, son of Roger, king of the Franks, known as Abū Tillīs, lord of the island of Sicily').

The word-order of the Arabic, which is reproduced exactly in the English translation, is not decisive, but strongly suggests that Abū Tillīs is employed of Roger. Only if it were possible to show that the phrase *ṣāḥib jazīra Ṣiqillīya*, 'lord of the island of Sicily', belonged to ᶜAbd al-Raḥmān, rather than to Roger, could a strong syntactical case be made that Abū Tillīs also belonged to him. Indeed, Adalgisa De Simone assumes that both the *kunya* Abū Tillīs and the title *ṣāḥib jazīrati Ṣiqillīya* belonged to ᶜAbd al-Raḥmān.[1]

For two reasons, I find it exceedingly difficult to accept that *ṣāḥib jazīra Ṣiqillīya* could refer to anyone but Roger himself. First, although Roger was still a minor in 1108, the author nonetheless calls him *malik al-faranj* as if he had already attained his majority and become the ruler of his nation. There can be little doubt that the phrase which immediately follows – *ṣāḥib jazīra Ṣiqillīya* – is intended to mean that Roger was also 'lord of the island of Sicily'. Second, *ṣāḥib Ṣiqillīya* is one of the epithets most commonly used by Arab authors to describe the Norman king, and al-Maqrīzī himself elsewhere refers to Roger precisely as *ṣāḥib Ṣiqillīya*.[2] What is more, *ṣāḥib Ṣiqillīya* is used exclusively of the ruler of the island, and is never used of his ministers, not even of the great George of Antioch.[3]

As to the precise meaning of *tillīs*, Dozy plausibly traced the medieval Spanish words *telliz* ('caparison') and *telliza* ('counterpane') to Arabic *tillīs* and *tillīsa*. Dozy further derived *tillīs* from Latin *trilicium* (> *trilix*), whence also come English 'trellis', French *treillis*, Italian *traliccio*, and Spanish *terliz*, all originally meaning a triple-twilled fabric, one woven with three warp-threads. He is supported in this by the Spanish-Arabic dictionary of

[1] De Simone 1999a, p.277, n.73.

[2] See for example, *BAS*², vol.I, p.100 (Ibn Jubayr); pp.323, 326, 327, 329, 349 (Ibn al-Athīr); vol.II, p.474 (Abū l-Fidāʾ); pp.505, 506, 507 (al-Nuwayrī); pp.516, 538, 540, 541, 544, 545, 552, 553, 556 (Ibn Khaldūn); p.602 (Ibn Abī Dīnār); pp.706, 726, 736 (ᶜImād al-Dīn al-Iṣfahānī); p.775 (Ibn Khallikān); p.818 (al-Maqrīzī); p.863 (Ḥajjī Khalīfa).

[3] The passage in Ibn Khaldūn where George appears to be given the epithet is clearly lacunose, as the editors point out: *BAS*², vol.II, p.553.

Pedro de Alcala, who translates *terliç* (*texido a tres lizos*) as *tillīs*, pl. *talālīs*. Spanish *terliz* could also mean a rough multicoloured rug; and Moroccan Arabic *tillīs* or *tillīsa* had the same meaning.[4]

But the etymology of Arabic *tillīs* is more complicated, for the word seems to have different origins in the Mashriq. There, the Arab lexicographers do not know *tillīs*, but they give the primary meaning of *tillīsa*, plural *talālīs*, as a basket made from plaited palm-fronds – and (thence?) a bag woven from goat-hair or wool, and a measure of capacity.[5] They considered it to be an ancient loan-word into Arabic from Greek.[6] That Greek root seems to have been θαλλός, meaning a young shoot or branch, for the (probably) pre-Islamic text of the *Geoponika* gives θαλλοί as palm-leaves which were woven into baskets.[7] The Greek word may conceivably have come into Egyptian Arabic through the medium of Coptic θαλιc or ταλιc, 'a basket of palm-leaves'.[8]

Al-Balādhurī, uses *tillīsa* in the sense of a basket or sack for horse-fodder, presumably barley.[9] The word *tillīs*, also with plural *talālīs*, is first attested in the Egyptian papyri from the 8th century with the sense of both a sack and a measure of wheat.[10] In the 9th century, al-Muqaddasī knew *tillīs* as an Egyptian dry measure equivalent to 8 *wayba*s (96.4kg); he adds, 'it is out of use', but this was plainly not the case.[11] Under the Fāṭimid caliphs, the *tillīs* was a standard measure of capacity for wheat, barley, and flour. Ibn Mammātī reports that the *tallīs* (*sic*) of flour was equivalent to 150 Egyptian *raṭl*s (66.735kg.).[12] The word *tillīs* recurs monotonously as the standard measure for wheat throughout al-Musabbiḥī's account of the famine of 414–15/1023–4.[13] *Tillīs* also occurs in documents from the Cairo Geniza as both a sack of wheat and a measure of capacity.[14] The word continued to be used in Egypt throughout the centuries of Mamlūk and Ottoman rule, until at least the 1930s.[15] Despite Dozy's claim to the contrary, in Egypt *tillīs* always means a basket, sack or measure, and never, so far as I can ascertain, a rug.[16]

However, in Ifrīqiya, by the mid-12th century, *tillīs* could also mean a type of fabric, or a garment, which could signify religious asceticism,[17] and De Simone notes that it is still used in this sense today in Morocco, where it means a robe worn by *ṣūfī*s. De Simone therefore interprets *tillīs* in al-Maqrīzī's biography as 'una specie di mantello di stuffa ruvida', and translates Abū Tillīs as '"quel dal mantello" (o "quel del saio")'. Were the *kunya* Abū Tillīs to refer to ᶜAbd al-Raḥmān, and not to Roger, then De Simone's might be the correct interpretation. But I have already given my reasons for concluding that this *kunya*, whatever it means, must belong to Roger.

Why would Roger II have deserved the nick-name 'Father of a Wheat-sack' or 'Old Wheat-sack'? The answer is surely that both Roger II and his father were notoriously

[4] Dozy 1845, pp.369–70, n.3; Dozy and Engelmann 1869, pp.349–50.
[5] al-Fīrūzābādī, 1912, vol.II, p.203; Ibn Manẓūr 1984, vol.VI, p.33; al-Zabīdī 1889–90, vol.IV, p.116.
[6] Khafājī 1863, pp.60–1.
[7] *Geoponika* 1895, book 10, chap.6, p.270. For the date, see *Oxford Dictionary of Byzantium* 1991, vol.II, p.834a.
[8] Labīb 1896–1910, p.158; Crum 1939, pp.45a, 836a; Fleischer 1836, p.71.
[9] al-Balādhurī 1866, p.318 (Arabic text) and p.19 (glossary).
[10] Karabacek 1897, p.7; Khan 1992, no.17, lines 5 and 8; Grohmann 1955, pp.163–4.
[11] al-Muqaddasī 1906, p.204. [12] Ibn Mammātī 1943, pp.365–6.
[13] al-Musabbiḥī 1978–84, vol.I, pp.12, 32, 68, 69, 72, 74, 75, 86.
[14] Goitein 1967–93, vol.I, p.484 n.4, vol.II, p.478, vol.IV, p.240, p.438 n.112.
[15] Burckhardt 1984, p.80, no.254, p.115, no.367; Winkler 1934, p.143.
[16] See also: Ashtor 1986, p.19, col.a; Hinz 1955, pp.51–52; Sauvaire 1886, pp.153–4.
[17] ᶜIyāḍ 1965, vol.II, p.350.

jealous of the exceptionally lucrative export of Sicilian wheat to Ifrīqiya. Ibn al-Athīr even reports that it was in order to leave this profitable trade undisturbed that Roger I dismissed a request for assistance from the leader of the First Crusade with a resounding fart.[18]

This does not, of course, exclude the possibility that whoever originally gave Roger this nick-name – and it can scarcely have been al-Maqrīzī himself, who is unlikely to have known of the importance of the export of Sicilian wheat to Ifrīqiya some three centuries before his own day[19] – was also aware of another meaning of *tillīs* and, simultaneously, was punningly poking fun at Roger's ostentatious magnificence. Alex Metcalfe has drawn my attention to Khalaf ibn Saᶜīd Bū Tillīs amongst the *muls* of Raḥl al-Mitāwī (west of modern Prizzi).[20] If Abū Tillīs was indeed a common *fallāḥī* nick-name in Sicily, then the deflationary effect when used of King Roger would have been all the greater.

Finally, I should note that, in 19th-century Algeria and Morocco, Abū Tallīs (or Tillīs) meant either 'a nightmare' or 'a blindman', specifically one suffering from day-blindness.[21]

[18] Ibn al-Athīr 1851–76, vol.10, pp.185–6; *BAS²*, vol.I, pp.320–1; *BAS²(It.)*, vol.II, p.358. See also Idris 1962a, vol.I, p.290, vol.II, pp.663–7.

[19] However, it is worth noting that *tillīs*, to al-Maqrīzī, meant first and foremost a sack of wheat. In *al-Muqaffā*, he uses *tillīs* (exclusively?) to mean a measure of wheat: al-Maqrīzī 1991, pp.386, 387. Elsewhere, he reports that, in the mid-11th century, Cairo and Fusṭāṭ together consumed 1,000 *tillīs* of wheat each day, Fusṭāṭ 700 and Cairo 300: al-Maqrīzī 1967–73, vol.II, p.226; see also, for other references to *tillīs*, vol.II, pp.74, 135, 142, 161, 162, 164, 165, 166, 169, 226, 240, 296–7, 299, and vol.III, p.223.

[20] Cusa, 1868–82, p.265. On p.264, he reads *al-Mināwī*, but see Caracausi 1993, vol.II, p.1030.

[21] Dozy 1881, vol.I, p.3.

List of References

ʿAbd al-Wahhāb, Ḥasan Ḥusni 1955, *Al-Imām al-Māzari*, Tunis.

Abdul-Wahhab, Hasan 1930, 'Deux dinars normands de Mahdia', *Revue Tunisienne*, n.s., 1: 215–18.

Abel, Armand 1957, 'Le Khalife, presence sacrée', *Studia Islamica* 7: 29–45.

Abulafia, David 1977, *The two Italies. Economic relations between the Norman kingdom of Sicily and the northern communes*, Cambridge.

Abulafia, David 1985, 'The Norman kingdom of Africa and the Norman expedition to Majorca and the Muslim Mediterranean', in Brown, R. Allen (ed.), *Anglo-Norman Studies 7: Proceedings of the Battle Conference 1984*, Woodbridge, pp.26–49.

Abulafia, David 1988, *Frederick II: a medieval emperor*, London.

Alexander of Telese 1991, *Ystoria Rogerii regis Sicilie Calabriae atque Apulie*, ed. Ludovica De Nava, FSI, no.112, Rome.

Amara, Allaoua and Nef, Annliese 2001, 'Al-Idrīsī et les Ḥammūdides de Sicile: nouvelles données biographiques sur l'auteur du *Livre de Roger*', *Arabica* 48: 121–7.

Amari, Michele (ed.) 1863, *I diplomi arabi del Real Archivio fiorentino*, Florence.

Amari, Michele (ed.) 1875, *Le epigrafi arabiche di Sicilia, trascritte, tradotte e illustrate. Parte prima: Iscrizioni edili*, Palermo. (Reprinted in Amari 1971, but with very few plates.)

Amari, Michele 1878, 'Su la data degli sponsali di Arrigo VI con la Costanza erede al trono di Sicilia. Lettera dal dott. O. Hartwig e memoria del socio M. Amari', *Atti della Reale Accademia dei Lincei, Memorie della classe di scienze morali, storiche e filologiche*, 3rd ser., 2: 409–38. (Reprinted in Amari 1970, pp.55–96.)

Amari, Michele (ed.) 1879, *Le epigrafi arabiche di Sicilia, trascritte, tradotte e illustrate. Parte seconda: iscrizioni sepolcrali*, DPSASDS, 3rd ser., vol.1, Palermo. (Reprinted in Amari 1971, but with very few plates.)

Amari, Michele 1883–4, 'De'titoli che usava la cancelleria de'sultani di Egitto nel XIV secolo scrivendo a'reggitori di alcuni stati italiani', *Atti della Reale Accademia dei Lincei, Memorie della classe di scienze morali, storiche e filologiche*, 3rd ser., 12: 507–34. (Reprinted in Amari, Michele 1985, *Tardi studi di storia arabo-mediterranea*, ed. Francesco Giunta, Edizione nazionale delle opere di Michele Amari, Palermo, pp.199–226.)

Amari, Michele 1933–9, *Storia dei Musulmani di Sicilia*, 2nd rev. edn, ed. Carlo Alfonso Nallino, 3 vols, Catania.

Amari, Michele 1970, *Studi medievistici*, ed. Francesco Giunta, Edizione nazionale delle opere di Michele Amari, Palermo.

Amari, Michele (ed.) 1971, *Le epigrafi arabiche di Sicilia, trascritte, tradotte e illustrate*, ed. Francesco Gabrieli, Edizione nazionale delle opere di Michele Amari, Palermo.

Amatus of Monte Cassino 1935, *Storia de' Normanni di Amato di Montecassino volgarizzata in antico francese (Ystoire de li Normant laquelle compila un moine de Mont de Cassin et la manda à lo abbé Desidere de Mont de Cassyn)*, ed. Vincenzo De Bartholomaeis, FSI, no.76, Rome.

Annales Siculi 1928, in Malaterra 1927–8, pp.109–20.

Anonymous Vaticanus 1726, *Historia Sicula*, in Muratori, Ludovico Antonio (ed.), *Rerum Italicarum Scriptores*, 25 vols, ed. Filippo Argellati, Milan, 1723–51, vol.VIII, cols 741–80.

Antonucci, Giovanni 1935, 'Note critiche per la storia dei Normanni nel mezzogiorno d'Italia. IV: *Jus affidandi*', *ASCL* 5: 231–8.

Ashtor, Eliayahu 1986, '*Makāyil*: 1. In the Arabic, Persian and Turkish lands', in *E.I.*^{2} vol.VI, pp.117–21.

Atiya, Aziz Suriya 1955, *The Arabic manuscripts from Mount Sinai*, Baltimore.

Atiya, Aziz Suriya 1968, 'Ibn Mammātī', in *E.I.*^{2} vol.III, pp.862–3.

Ayalon, Ami 1987, 'Malik', in *E.I.*^{2} vol.VI, pp.261–2.

Ayalon, David 1979, *The Mamlūk military society*, London.

Ayalon, David 1988, *Outsiders in the lands of Islam: Mamlūks, Mongols and eunuchs*, London.

Ayalon, David 1994, *Islam and the abode of war: military slaves and Islamic adversaries*, 1994.

Ayalon, David 1999, *Eunuchs, caliphs and sultans. A study in power relationships*, Jerusalem.

Balog, Paul 1979, 'Dated Aghlabid lead and copper seals from Sicily', *Studi Magrebini* 11: 125–32.

al-Balādhurī, Aḥmad ibn Yaḥyā 1866, *Kitāb futūḥ al-buldān*, ed. Michael Jan de Goeje, BGA, Leiden.

Barrucand, Marianne (ed.) 1999, *L'Egypte Fatimide: son art et son histoire: Actes du colloque organisé à Paris les 28, 29 et 30 mai 1998*, Paris.

al-Bāshā, Ḥasan 1957, *Al-alqāb al-islāmīya fī l-taʾrīkh wa-l-wathāʾiq wa-l-āthār*, Cairo.

Bates, David 1982, *Normandy before 1066*, Harlow.

Battaglia, Giorgio (ed.) 1895, *I diplomi inediti relativi all'ordinamento della proprietà fondiaria in Sicilia sotto i Normanni e gli Svevi*, DPSASDS, 1st ser., vol.16, Palermo.

Behring, Wilhelm 1887, 'Sicilianische Studien II', *Königliches Gymnasium zu Elbing. (Zu der Jahresschußfeier und Abiturienten-Entlassung im Saale der Anstalt Sonnabend den 2 April Vormittags von 8 Uhr ab ladet ergebenst ein Dr Max Toeppen Director des Gymnasiums)* 30: 1–27.

Beit-Arié, Malachi, Entin Rokéah, Zefira and Banitt, Menahem 1985, *The only dated medieval Hebrew manuscript written in England (1189 CE) and the problem of pre-expulsion Anglo-Hebrew manuscripts*, London.

Bellafiore, Giuseppe 1996, *Parchi e giardini della Palermo normanna*, Palermo.

Ben-Sasson, Menahem (ed.) 1991, *The Jews of Sicily (825–1068). Documents and sources*, Oriens Judaicus, ser. 1, vol.1, Jerusalem. (Hebrew, with English title page and brief summary.)

Benvenisti, Meron 1970, *The Crusaders in the Holy Land*, Jerusalem.

Bercher, Henri, Courteaux, André and Mouton, Jean 1979, 'Une abbaye latine dans la société musulmane: Monreale au XIIe siècle', *Annales: économies, sociétés, civilisations* 34: 525–47.

Björkman, Walther 1928, *Beiträge zur Geschichte der Staatskanzlei in islamischen Ägypten*, Abhandlungen aus dem Gebiet der Auslandskunde, no.28, Hamburg.

Bock, Franz 1864, *Die Kleinodien des Heil-Römischen Reiches Deutscher Nation nebst den Kroninsignien Böhmens, Ungarns und der Lombardei*, 2 vols, Vienna.

Borruso, Andrea 1978, *Al-imàm al-Màzari. Mazarese del medioevo arabo-islamico*, Mazara del Vallo.

Borsari, Silvano 1954, 'L'amministrazione del tema di Sicilia', *Rivista storica italiana* 66: 133–58.

Bosworth, Clifford Edmund 1972, 'Christian and Jewish religious dignitaries in Mamlūk Egypt and Syria: Qalqashandī's information on their hierarchy, titulature and appointment', *International Journal of Middle East Studies* 3: 59–74, 199–216.

Bosworth, Clifford Edmund 1977, *The later Ghaznavids: splendour and decay, the dynasty in Afghanistan and northern India, 1040–1186*, Edinburgh.

Bover Fonts, Immaculada 1996, 'L'*iqlīm* di Corleone: studio del territorio e della sua popolazione durante l'epoca musulmana', *Annali Istituto universitario orientale di Napoli* 56: 255–64.

Bowman, Alan K. and Rogan, Eugene (eds) 1999, *Agriculture in Egypt from Pharaonic to modern times*, Proceedings of the British Academy, no.96, Oxford.

Brandilione, Francesco 1884, *Il diritto romano nelle leggi normanne e sveve del regno di Sicilia*, Rome, Turin and Florence.

Bresc, Henri 1979, 'Mudejars des pays da la Couronne d'Aragon et Sarrasins de la Sicile normand: le problème de l'acculturation', in *X Congreso de Historia de la Corona de Aragón: Jaime I y su época*, 3 vols, Zaragosa, vol.I (Comunicaciones 3, 4 y 5), pp.51–60.

Bresc, Henri 1986, *Un monde méditerranéen: économie et société en Sicile 1300–1450*, 2 vols, Accademia di scienze, lettere e arti di Palermo: Bibliothèque des Écoles françaises d'Athenes et de Rome, no.262, Palermo and Rome.

Bresc, Henri 1989, 'De l'Etat de minorité à l'Etat de résistance: le cas de la Sicile normande', in Bolard, Michel (ed.) *Etat et colonisation au Moyen Age et à la Renaissance*, Paris, pp.331–46.

Bresc, Henri 1995, 'La propriété foncière des Musulmans dans la Sicile du XIIe siècle: trois documents inédits', in Scarcia Amoretti 1995, pp.69–97.

Bresc, Henri and Nef, Annelise 1998, 'Les Mozarabes de Sicile (1100–1300)', in Cuozzo, Errico and Martin, Jean-Marie (eds) *Cavalieri alla Conquista del Sud. Studi sull'Italia normanna in memoria di Léon-Robert Ménager*, Rome, pp.134–56.

Brett, Michael 1969, '*Fitnat al-Qayrawān*', Ph.D. thesis, School of Oriental and African Studies, University of London.

Brett, Michael 1978, 'The Fāṭimid revolution (861–973) and its aftermath in North Africa', in Fage, John Donnelly (ed.) *The Cambridge history of Africa*, 8 vols, Cambridge, vol.II, pp.589–636.

Brett, Michael 1984, 'The way of the peasant', *BSOAS* 47: 44–56.

Brett, Michael 1986, 'The city-state in medieval Ifrīqiya: the case of Tripoli', *Cahiers de Tunisie* 34(137–8): 69–94. (Reprinted in Brett 1999a.)

Brett, Michael 1995, 'The origins of the Mamluk military system in Fatimid Egypt', in Vermeulen, Urbain and De Smet, Daniel (eds) *Egypt and Syria in the Fatimid, Ayyubid and Mamluk Eras [I]. Proceedings of the 1st, 2nd and 3rd International Colloquium organized at the Katholieke Universiteit Leuven in May 1992, 1993 and 1994*, Orientalia Lovaniensia Analecta, no.73, Leuven, pp.39–52.

Brett, Michael 1997, 'The armies of Ifriqiya', in *Guerre et paix dans l'histoire du Maghreb. VIe Congrès internationale d'histoire et de civilisation du Maghreb, Tunis, décembre 1993 = Cahiers de Tunisie*, 48: 107–25. (Reprinted in Brett 1999a.)

Brett, Michael 1999a, *Ibn Khaldun and the medieval Maghrib*, Variorum collected studies series, no.627, Aldershot.

Brett, Michael 1999b, 'The Normans in Ifriqiya', in Brett 1999a. (Revised and expanded version of Brett, Michael 1995, 'Muslim justice under infidel rule', *Cahiers de Tunisie* 43(155–6): 325–68.)

Brett, Michael 2001, *The rise of the Fatimids: the world of the Mediterranean and the Middle East in the fourth century of the Hijra, tenth century CE*, The medieval Mediterranean. Peoples, economies and cultures, 400–1453, no.30, Leiden.

Bruel, Louis Alexandre (ed.) 1876–1903, *Recueil des chartes de l'abbaye de Cluny*, 6 vols, Paris.

Brühl, Carlrichard 1978, *Urkunden und Kanzlei König Rogers II von Sizilien*, Studien zu den normannisch-staufischen Herrscherurkunden Siziliens, vol.1, Cologne and Vienna. (Brühl 1983, the revised Italian version of this work, is to be preferred.)

Brühl, Carlrichard 1983, *Diplomi e cancelleria di Ruggero II*, Palermo. (Revised Italian translation of Brühl 1978.)

Brühl, Carlrichard (ed.) 1987, *Rogerii II regis diplomata latina*, Codex diplomaticus Regni Siciliae: ser.1, Diplomata regum et principum e gente normannorum, vol.2, part 1, Cologne and Vienna.

Burckhardt, John L. (ed.) 1984, *Arabic proverbs; or the manners and customs of the modern Egyptians illustrated from their proverbial sayings current at Cairo*, London. (Reprint of 3rd edn, London, 1830.)

Burnett, Charles 1995, 'Master Theodore, Frederick II's philosopher', in *Federico II e le nuove culture*, Atti del XXXI Convegno storico internazionale del Centro italiano di studi sull'alto medioevo, Spoleto, pp.225–85.

Burns, Robert Ignatius 1973, *Islam under the crusaders. Colonial survival in the thirteenth-century kingdom of Valencia*, Princeton.

Burns, Robert Ignatius 1975, *Medieval colonialism: post-crusade exploitation of Islamic Valencia*, Princeton.

Burns, Robert Ignatius 1984, *Muslims, Christians and Jews in the crusader kingdom of Valencia: societies in symbiosis*, Cambridge.

Burns, Robert Ignatius (ed.) 1985, *Society and documentation in crusader Valencia, Diplomatarium of the crusader kingdom of Valencia: The registered charters of its conqueror, Jaume I, 1257–1276*. Volume I: Introduction, Princeton, New Jersey, and Guildford.

Burns, Robert Ignatius, Chevedden, Paul E. and De Epalza, Míkel (eds) 1999, *Negotiating Cultures. Bilingual surrender treaties in Muslim-Crusader Spain under James the Conqueror*, The medieval Mediterranean. Peoples, economies and cultures, 400–1453, no.22, Leiden.

Buscemi, Nicola 1839, *Appendix ad tabularium regiae ac imperialis capellae Divi Petri in regio palatio panhormitano*, Palermo.

Cahen, Claude 1937–8, 'Quelques chroniques anciennes relatives aux derniers Fāṭimides', *Bulletin de l'Institut français d'archéologie orientale* 37: 1–27.

Cahen, Claude 1953–4, 'Une texte peu connu relatif au commerce oriental d'Amalfi au Xe siècle', *ASPN*, n.s., 34: 61–6.

Cahen, Claude 1956, 'Le régime des impôts dans le Fayyūm ayyūbide', *Arabica* 3: 8–30. (Reprinted in Cahen 1977b, pp.184–216.)

Cahen, Claude 1957, 'La féodalité et les institutions politiques de l'Orient latin', in *Oriente ed occidente nel medioevo*, Accademia nazionale di Lincei: Atti del convegno di scienze morali, storiche e filologiche (27 maggio – 1 giugno, 1956), Rome, pp.167–91.

Cahen, Claude 1962a, 'Contribution à l'étude des impôts dans l'Égypte médiévale', *JESHO* 5: 244–78. (Reprinted in Cahen 1977b, pp.22–56.)

Cahen, Claude 1962b, 'Un traité financier inédit d'époque fāṭimide-ayyūbide', *JESHO* 5: 139–59. (Reprinted in Cahen 1977b, pp.1–21.)

Cahen, Claude 1963a, 'Dhimma', in *E.I.*² vol.II, pp.227–31.

Cahen, Claude 1963b, 'Djizya', in *E.I.*² vol.II, pp.559–62.

Cahen, Claude 1970, 'Iḳṭāʿ', in *E.I.*² vol.II, pp.1088–91.

Cahen, Claude 1972, 'Douanes et commerce dans les ports méditerranéens de l'Égypte médiévale d'après le *Minhādj* d'al-Makhzūmī', *JESHO* 15: 217–314. (Reprinted in Cahen 1977b, pp.57–154.)

Cahen, Claude 1977a, 'Kharādj', in *E.I.*² vol.IV, pp.1030–4.

Cahen, Claude 1977b, *Makhzūmiyyāt. Études sur l'histoire économique et financière de l'Égypte médiévale*, Leiden.

Cahen, Claude 1978, 'Un fait divers au temps des mamlūks', *Arabica* 25: 198–202.

Campbell, James 1975, 'Observations on English government from the tenth to the twelfth century', *Transactions of the Royal Historical Society*, 5th ser., 25: 39–54.

Canard, Marius 1954, 'Un vizir chrétien à l'époque fāṭimite, l'arménien Baḥrām', *Annales de l'Institut d'études orientales de la Faculté des lettres d'Alger* 12: 84–113. (Reprinted in Canard 1973.)

Canard, Marius 1955a, 'Notes sur les arméniens en Égypte à l'époque fāṭimite', *Annales de l'Institut d'études orientales de la Faculté des lettres d'Alger* 13: 143–57. (Reprinted in Canard 1973.)

Canard, Marius 1955b, 'Une lettre du calife Fāṭimite al-Ḥāfiẓ (524–544/1130–1149) à Roger II', in *Studi Ruggeriani*, vol.I, pp.125–46. (Reprinted in Canard 1973.)

Canard, Marius 1957a, 'Djawdhar', in *E.I.*² vol.II, p.491.

Canard, Marius 1957b, *Vie de l'ustadh Jaudhar (contenant sermons, lettres et rescrits des premiers califes fāṭimites) écrite par Manṣūr le secrétaire à l'époque du calife al-ʿAzīz billāh (365–386/975–996)*, Publications de l'Institut d'études orientales de la Faculté des lettres d'Alger, 2nd ser., no.20, Algiers.

Canard, Marius 1968, 'Ibn Killis', in *E.I.*² vol.III, pp.840–1.

Canard, Marius 1973, *Miscellanea Orientalia*, Variorum collected studies series, no.19, London.

Capialbi, Vito 1835, *Memorie per servire alla storia della santa chiesa miletese*, Naples.

Caracausi, Girolamo 1977, 'Ancora sul tipo "camminare riva riva"', *Bollettino del Centro di studi filologici e linguistici siciliani*, 13: 383–96.

Caracausi, Girolamo 1983, *Arabismi medievali di Sicilia*, Centro di studi filologici e linguistici siciliani: Supplementi al Bollettino del Centro di studi filologici e linguistici siciliani, no.5, Palermo.

Caracausi, Girolamo 1990, *Lessico greco della Sicilia e dell'Italia meridionale (secoli X–XIV)*, Centro di studi filologici e linguistici siciliani: Lessici siciliani, no.6, Palermo.

Caracausi, Girolamo 1993, *Dizionario onomastico della Sicilia. Repertorio storico-etimologico di nomi di famiglia e di luogo*, 2 vols, Centro di studi filologici e linguistici siciliani: Lessici siciliani, nos 7–8, Palermo.

Caravale, Mario 1966, *Il regno normanno di Sicilia*, *Ius Nostrum*. Studi e testi pubblicati dall'Istituto di storia del diritto italiano dell'Università di Roma, no.10.

Carcani, Gaetano (ed.) 1992, *Constitutiones regni Siciliae*, ed. Andrea Romano, Monumenta iuridica siciliensia, no.1, Messina. (Reprint of Naples edition of 1786.)

Caruso, Giuseppe 1834, 'Appendice all'opera del Mongitore *Bullae privilegia et instrumenta Eccl.[esiae] Pan.[ormitanae]*', *Biblioteca Sacra ossia Giornale letterario-scientifico-ecclesiastico per la Sicilia* 2: 40–60.

Caspar, Erich 1902, *Die Gründungsurkunden der sicilischen Bistümer und die Kirchenpolitik graf Rogers I (1082–1098)*, Innsbruck.

Caspar, Erich 1904, *Roger II (1101–1154) und die Gründung der normannisch-sicilischen Monarchie*, Innsbruck. (Now reprinted and translated as *Ruggero II e la fondazione della monarchia normanna di Sicilia*, Rome and Bari, 1999, with introduction by Ortensio Zecchino, and with references to some recent bibliography added to the register.)

Chalandon, Ferdinand 1907, *Histoire de la domination normande en Italie et en Sicile*, 2 vols, Paris. (Reprinted New York, 1960.)

The Cid 1975, *Cantar de Mio Cid*, ed. Ramón Menéndez Pidal and trans. William Stanley Merwin, New York.

Ciotta, Gianluigi 1993, *La cultura architettonica normanna in Sicilia*, Società messinese di storia patria: Biblioteca dell'Archivio storico messinese, no.18, Messina.

Clanchy, Michael T. 1993, *From memory to written record, England 1066–1307*, 2nd rev. edn, Oxford and Cambridge, Mass.

Clementi, Dione 1961, 'Notes on Norman Sicilian surveys', in Galbraith, Vivian Hunter (ed.) *The making of Domesday Book*, Oxford, pp.55–8.

Collura, Paolo 1951, *La produzione arabo-greca della cancelleria di Federico II*, Palermo.

Collura, Paolo 1955a, 'Appendice al regesto dei diplomi di re Ruggero compilato da Erich Caspar', in *Studi Ruggeriani*, vol.II, pp.545–625.

Collura, Paolo 1955b, 'Proposta di un Codice diplomatico normanno trilingue', *AASLAP*, 4th ser., 15(2): 307–19.

Collura, Paolo 1958–9, 'La polemica sui diplomi normanni dell'Archivio capitolare di Catania', *ASSO*, 4th ser., 11–12: 131–9.

Collura, Paolo 1961 *Le più antiche carte dell'Archivio Capitolare di Agrigento (1092–1282)*, DPSASDS, 1st ser., vol. 25, Palermo.

Collura, Paolo 1969–70, 'Frammenti di platee arabe dell'epoca normanna', *AASLAP*, 4th ser., 30(2): 255–60.

Collura, Paolo 1975, 'Un privilegio di Guglielmo II per il monastero di S. Maria *de Latinis* di Palermo', in Lavagnini, Bruno (ed.) *Bizantino-Sicula II: Miscellanea di scritti in memoria di Giuseppe Rossi-Taibbi*, Quaderni dell'Istituto siciliano di studi bizantini e neoellenici, Palermo, pp.165–9.

Columba, Gaetano M. 1910, 'Per la topografia antica di Palermo', in Besta, Enrico, Columba, Gaetano M., Nallino, Carlo A., Salinas, Antonino, Siragusa, Giambattista and Zuretti, Carlo O. (eds), *Centenario della nascita di Michele Amari: Scritti di filologia e storia araba*, 2 vols, Palermo, vol.II, pp.395–426.

Conrad, Hermann, von der Lieck-Buyken, Thea and Wagner, Wolfgang (eds) 1973, *Die Konstitutionen Friedrichs II von Hohenstaufen für sein Königreich Sizilien. Nach einer lateinischen Handschrifte des 13. Jahrhunderts (Ms. Vat. Lat. 6770) herausgegeben und übersetzt*, Studien und Quellen zur Welt Kaiser Friedrichs II, vol.2, Cologne and Vienna.

Cooper, Richard S. 1974, 'Land classification terminology and the assessment of the "kharādj" tax in medieval Egypt', *JESHO* 17: 91–102.

Cooper, Richard S. 1976, 'The assessment and collection of the "Kharāj" tax in medieval Egypt', *Journal of the American Oriental Society* 96: 365–82.

Cozza-Luzi, Giuseppe (ed.) 1890a, *La cronaca siculo-saracena di Cambridge con doppio testo greco*, DPSASDS, 4th ser., vol.2, Palermo. (The Greek text of the so-called 'Cambridge Chronicle', the Arabic *Taʾrīkh jazīra Ṣiqillīya*, edited in *BAS*², vol.I, pp.190–203.)

Cozza-Luzi, Giuseppe 1890b, 'Del testamento dell'abate fondatore di Demenna', *ASS* 15: 35–9.

Cracco Ruggini, Lellia 1995, *Economia e società nell' 'Italia annonaria'. Rapporti fra agricoltura e commercio dal IV al VI secolo d.C.*, 2nd rev. edn, Milan.

Crum, Walter Ewing 1939, *A Coptic dictionary*, Oxford.

Cusa, Salvatore 1868–82, *I diplomi greci ed arabi di Sicilia pubblicati nel testo originale, tradotti ed illustrati*, 2 vols: 1 only published in 2 parts, Palermo. (Reprinted Cologne and Vienna, 1982, with short introduction by Albrecht Noth.)

Dachraoui, Farhat 1981, *Le califat fāṭimide au Maghreb (296–365 H. – 909–975 J.-C.): histoire politique et institutions*, Tunis.

Dadoyan, Seta B. 1997, *The Fatimid Armenians. Cultural and political interaction in the Near East*, Islamic History and Civilisation, no.18, Leiden.

D'Angelo, Franco 1973, 'I casali di Santa Maria la Nuova di Monreale nei secoli XII–XV', *Bollettino del Centro di studi filologici e linguistici siciliani* 12: 333–9.

D'Angelo, Franco 1975, 'La monetazione di Muḥammad ibn ᶜAbbād emiro ribelle a Federico II di Sicilia', *Studi magrebini* 7: 149–53.

D'Angelo, Franco (forthcoming), 'Ulteriore rilettura dei documenti del territorio dell'Abbazia di Monreale', in *Studi in onore di Hans Peter Isler*, forthcoming.

Davis, Ralph Henry Carless 1976, *The Normans and their myth*, London.

al-Dāwudī, Abū Jaᶜfar Aḥmad ibn Naṣr 1962, '"*Kitāb al-Amwāl*": le régime foncier en Sicile au moyen age (IXe et Xe siècles), [Abdul-Wahhab, Hasan H. and Dachraoui, Farhat (eds and trans.)]', in *Études d'orientalisme dédiées à la mémoire de Evariste Levi-Provençal*, 2 vols, Paris, vol.II, pp.401–44.

De Grossis, Giovanni Battista 1654, *Catana sacra sive de episcopis catanensibus rebusque ab iis praeclare gestis a christiane religionis exordio ad nostram usque aetatem*, Catania.

Del Giudice, Giuseppe (ed.) 1863–9, *Codice diplomatico del regno di Carlo I e II d'Angiò*, 2 vols, Naples.

De Luca, Maria Amalia 1998, *Le monete con leggenda araba della Biblioteca Comunale di Palermo.*, Part 1, Città di Palermo, Biblioteca Comunale: *Aere Perennius*: Cataloghi no.1.

den Heijer, Johannes 1999, 'Considérations sur les communautés chrétiennes en Égypte fatimide: l'état et l'église sous le vizirat de Badr al-Jamālī (1074–1094)', in Barrucand 1999, pp.569–78.

D'Erme, Giovanni M. 1997, 'Contesto architettonico e aspetti culturali dei dipinti del soffitto della Cappella Palatina di Palermo', *Bollettino d'arte* 92: 1–32.

De Simone, Adalgisa 1968, 'Palermo nei geografi e viaggiatori arabi del medioevo', *Studi magrebini* 2: 129–89.

De Simone, Adalgisa 1984, 'Salvatore Cusa arabista siciliano del XIX secolo', in *La conoscenza dell'Asia e dell'Africa in Italia nei secoli XVIII e XIX*, Naples, pp.593–617.

De Simone, Adalgisa 1988, 'I diplomi arabi di Sicilia', in *Testimonianze degli Arabi in Italia (Roma, 10 dicembre 1987)*, Accademia Nazionale dei Lincei: Fondazione Leone Caetani, Giornata di Studio, no.22, Rome, pp.57–75.

De Simone, Adalgisa 1991, 'Ibn Qalāqis in Sicilia', in Scarcia Amoretti, Biancamaria and Rostagno, Lucia (eds) *Yād-Nāma in memoria di Alessandro Bausani*, 2 vols, Rome, vol.II, pp.323–44.

De Simone, Adalgisa 1993, 'Una ricostruzione del viaggio in Sicilia di Ibn Qalāqis sulla base dell'*az-Zahr al-bāsim*', in *Arabi e Normanni in Sicilia. Atti del Convegno internazionale euro-arabo (Agrigento, 22–25 febbraio 1992)*, Agrigento, pp.109–25.

De Simone, Adalgisa 1996, *Splendori e misteri di Sicilia in un'opera di Ibn Qalāqis*, Messina. (Study and Italian translation of Ibn Qalāqis 1984a.)

De Simone, Adalgisa 1999a, 'Il mezzogiorno normanno-svevo visto dall'Islam africano', in *Il mezzogiorno normanno-svevo visto dall'Europa e dal mondo mediterraneo (Bari, 21–24 ottobre 1997)*, ed. Giosuè Musca, Centro di studi normanno-svevi, Università degli Studi di Bari: Atti delle tredicesime giornate normanno-sveve, Bari, pp.261–93.

De Simone, Adalgisa 1999b, *Nella Sicilia 'araba' tra storia e filologia*, Palermo.

Déroche, François 1992, *The Abbasid tradition. Qur'āns of the 8th to the 10th centuries*, The Nasser D. Khalili Collection of Islamic Art, London.

Di Giovanni, Vincenzo 1880, 'Il monastero di Santa Maria la Gadera poi Santa Maria la Latina esistente nel secolo XII presso Polizzi', *ASS*, n.s., 5: 15–50.

Di Giovanni, Vincenzo 1882–4, *La topografia antica di Palermo dal secolo X al XV*, 2 vols, Palermo.

Di Giovanni, Vincenzo 1892, 'I casali esistenti nel secolo XII nel territorio della chiesa di Monreale', *ASS*, n.s., 17: 438–96.

Di Giovanni, Vincenzo 1896, 'Il transunto dei diplomi del monastero del presbitero Scholaro di Messina', *ASS*, n.s., 21: 325–42.

Di Stefano, Guido 1978, *Monumenti della Sicilia normanna*, ed. Wolfgang Krönig, Palermo. (Extensive revision of 1st edn, 1955.)

Dilcher, Hermann 1975, *Die sizilische Gesetzebung Kaiser Friedrichs II. Quellen der Constitutionen von Melfi und ihrer Novellen*, Studien und Quellen zur Welt Kaiser Friedrichs II, no.5, Cologne and Vienna.

Dölger, Franz 1927, *Beiträge zur Geschichte der byzantinischen Finanzverwaltung besonders des 10 und 11 Jahrhunderts*, Byzantinisches Archiv, vol.9, Leipzig and Berlin.

Dölger, Franz 1929, 'Der Kodikellos des Christodoulos in Palermo. Ein bisher unerkannter Typus der Byzantinischen Kaiserurkunde', *Archiv für Urkundenforschung*, 11: 1–65. (Reprinted in Dölger, Franz 1956, *Byzantinische Dipolomatik*, Munich, pp.1–74.)

Dölger, Franz 1933, 'Review of Henri Grégoire, "Diplômes de Mazara (Sicile)", *Annuaire de l'Institut de Philologie et d'Histoire orientales de l'Université de Bruxelles pour 1932–1933*, pp.79–107', *BZ* 33: 169–71.

Dölger, Franz 1956, *Byzantinische Diplomatik*, Munich.

Douglas, David C. 1969, *The Norman Achievement 1050–1100*, London.

Dozy, Reinhart Pieter A. 1845, *Dictionnaire détaillé des noms des vêtements chez les Arabes*, Amsterdam.

Dozy, Reinhart Pieter A. 1881, *Supplément aux dictionnaires arabes*, 2 vols, Leiden. (Reprinted Libraire du Liban, Beirut, 1991.)

Dozy, Reinhart Pieter A. and Engelmann, Willem Hermann 1869, *Glossaire des mots espagnoles et portugais dérivés de l'arabe*, 2nd edn, Leiden.

Duri, ᶜAbd al-ᶜAzīz, Gottschalk, Hans Ludwig and Colin, Georges Séraphim 1962, '*Dīwān*', in *E.I.*^{2} vol.II, pp.323–37.

Egidi, Pietro 1911, 'La colonia saracena di Lucera e la sua distruzione [part 1]', *ASPN* 36: 597–694. [Parts 2–4 in *ASPN* 37 (1912): 71–89, 664–96; 38 (1913): 115–44, 681–707; 39 (1914): 132–71, 697–766.]

Egidi, Pietro 1917, *Codice diplomatico dei Saraceni di Lucera dall'anno 1285 al 1343*, Naples. (Reprinted Rome, 1917.)

Engel, Arthur 1882, *Recherches sur la numismatique et la sigillographie des Normands de Sicile et d'Italie*, Paris. (Reprinted Bologna, 1972.)

Enzensberger, Horst 1971, *Beitrage zum Kanzlei- und Urkundenwesen der normannischen Herrscher Unteritaliens und Siziliens*, Münchener Universitäts-Schriften. Philosophische Fakultät. Münchener historische Studien. Abteilung geschichtliche Hilfswissenschaften, no.9, Kallmünz.

Enzensberger, Horst 1975, 'Bemerkungen zu Kanzlei und Diplomen Robert Guiskards', in *Roberto il Guiscardo*, pp.107–13.

Enzensberger, Horst 1977, 'Cancelleria e documentazione sotto Ruggero I di Sicilia', in *Ruggero il gran conte*, pp.15–23.

Enzensberger, Horst 1981, 'Il documento regio come strumento di potere', in *Potere, società e popolo nell'età dei due Guglielmi (Bari, 8–10 ottobre 1979)*, Centro di studi normanno-svevi, Università degli Studi di Bari: Relazioni e comunicazioni nelle quarte giornate normanno-sveve, pp.103–38.

Enzensberger, Horst 1981–2, '*Utilitas regia.* Note di storia amministrativa e giuridica e di propaganda politica nell'età dei due Guglielmi', in *Congresso Internazionale sulle Fonti documentarie e narrative per la storia della Sicilia normanna. Palermo, Dicembre 1980*, *AASLAP*, 5th ser., 1(2): 23–61.

Enzensberger, Horst 1995, 'Le cancellerie normanne: materiali per la storia della Siclia normanna', in Scarcia Amoretti 1995, pp.51–67.

Enzensberger, Horst (ed.) 1996, *Guillelmi I regis diplomata*, Codex diplomaticus Regni Siciliae: ser.1, Diplomata regum et principum e gente Normannorum, vol.3, Cologne, Weimar and Vienna.

Epifanio, Vincenzo 1905–6, 'Ruggero II e Filippo di Al Mahdiah', *ASS*, n.s., 30: 471–505.

Ernst, Hans 1960, *Die mamelukischen Sultanurkunden des Sinai-Klosters*, Wiesbaden.

Espéronnier, Martya 1988, 'Les fêtes civiles et les cérémonies d'origine antique sous les Fāṭimides d'Égypte. Extraits du tome III de "*Ṣubḥ al-Aʿshā*" d'al-Qalqashandī', *Der Islam* 65: 46–59.

Età normanna 1994, *L'età normanna e sveva in Sicilia. Mostra storico-documentaria e bibliografica. Palazzo dei Normanni, Palermo, 18 novembre – 15 dicembre 1994.*

Ettinghausen, Richard 1942 'Painting in the Fāṭimid period: a reconstruction', *Ars Islamica* 9: 112–24.

Ettinghausen, Richard 1962, *Arab painting*, Geneva.

Ettinghausen, Richard 1974, 'Arabic epigraphy: communication or symbolic affirmation', in Kouymjian, Dickran (ed.) *Near Eastern numismatics, iconography, epigraphy and history. Studies in honor of George C. Miles*, Beirut, pp.297–317.

Eustathios of Tessaloniki 1988, *The capture of Thessaloniki*, ed. John R. Melville Jones, Australian Association for Byzantine Studies: *Byzantina Australiensia*, no.8, Canberra.

Fabre, Paul and Duchesne, Louis 1901–10, *Le Liber censuum de l'Église romaine*, 2, Bibliothèque des Écoles françaises d'Athènes et de Rome, 2nd ser., no.6, Rome.

Fahmy, Aly Mohammed 1980, *Muslim naval organisation in the eastern Mediterranean from the seventh to the tenth century* A.D., Cairo.

Falco of Benevento 1868, *Chronicon*, in Del Re, Giuseppe (ed.) *Cronisti e scrittori sincroni napoletani*, 2 vols, Naples, 1845–68, vol.I, pp.161–252.

von Falkenhausen, Vera 1975, 'Aspetti storico-economici dell'età di Roberto il Guiscardo', in *Roberto il Guiscardo*, pp.115–34.

von Falkenhausen, Vera 1977, 'I ceti dirigenti prenormanni al tempo della costituzione degli stati normanni nell'Italia meridionale e in Sicilia', in Rossetti, Gabriella (ed.) *Forme di potere e struttura sociale in Italia nel medioevo*, Problemi e prospettive: Serie di storia. Istituzioni e società nella storia d'Italia, Bologna, pp.321–77.

von Falkenhausen, Vera 1978, *La dominazione bizantina nell' Italia meridionale dal IX all'XI secolo*, Bari.

von Falkenhausen, Vera 1979, 'I gruppi etnici nel regno di Ruggero II e la loro participazione al potere', in *Società, potere e popolo nell'età di Ruggero II (Bari, 23–25 maggio 1977)*, Centro di studi normanno-svevi, Università degli Studi di Bari: Atti delle terze giornate normanno-sveve, Bari, pp.133–57.

von Falkenhausen, Vera 1980a, 'L'incidenza della conquista normanna sulla terminologia giuridica e agraria nell'Italia meridionale e in Sicilia', in Fumagalli, Vito and Rossetti, Gabriella (eds) *Medioevo rurale: sulle tracce della civiltà contadina*, Problemi e prospettive: Serie di storia. Istituzioni e società nella storia d'Italia, Bologna, pp.219–45.

von Falkenhausen, Vera 1980b, 'Review of Carlrichard Brühl, *Urkunden und Kanzlei König Rogers II von Sizilien*, Cologne and Vienna, 1978', *Studi medievali* 21: 256–63.

von Falkenhausen, Vera 1984, 'Die Testamente des Abtes Gregor von S. Filippo di Fragalà', in ΟΚΕΑΝΟΣ. *Essays presented to Ihor Ševčenko on his sixtieth birthday by his colleagues and students*, Harvard Ukrainian Studies, no.7, Cambridge, Mass., pp.174–95.

von Falkenhausen, Vera 1985, 'Cristodulo', in *Dizionario biografico degli italiani*, Rome, vol.31, pp.49–51.

von Falkenhausen, Vera 1994, 'L'Archimandritato del S. Salvatore in lingua phari di Messina e il monachesimo italo-greco nel regno normanno-svevo (secoli XI–XIII)', in *Messina 1994*, pp.41–52.

von Falkenhausen, Vera 1996, 'L'Ebraismo dell'Italia meridionale nell'età bizantina (secoli VI–XI)', in Fonseca, Cosimo Damiano, Luzzati, Michele, Tamani, Giuliano and Colafemmina, Cesare (eds), *L'Ebraismo dell'Italia Meridionale Peninsulare dalle origini al 1541. Società, Economia, Cultura. IX Congresso internazionale dell'Associazione Italiana per lo studio del Giudaismo. Atti del Convegno internazionale di studio organizzato dall'Università degli Studi della Basilicata in occasione del Decennale della sua istituzione (Potenza-Venosa, 20–24 settembre 1992)*, Galatina, pp.25–46.

von Falkenhausen, Vera 1997, 'I diplomi dei re normanni in lingua greca', in De Gregorio, Giuseppe and Kresten, Otto (eds) *Documenti medievali greci e latini. Studi comparativi*, Centro Italiano di Studi sull'Alto Medioevo: Atti del seminario di Erice, 23–29 ottobre 1995, Spoleto, pp.253–308.

von Falkenhausen, Vera 1998, 'Zur Regentschaft der Grafin Adelasia del Vasto in Kalabrien und Sizilien (1101–1112)', in Ševčenko, Ihor and Hutter, Irmgard (eds) ΑΕΤΟΣ. *Studies in honour of Cyril Mango presented to him on April 14, 1998*, Stuttgart and Leipzig, pp.87–115.

von Falkenhausen, Vera 1999, 'S. Bartolomeo di Trigona: storia di un monastero greco nella Calabria normanno-sveva', *Rivista di studi bizantini e neoellenici* 36: 94–116.

von Falkenhausen, Vera 2000, 'Nuovi contributi documentari sul monstero greco di S. Maria di Gala (Sicilia orientale) in epoca normanna', in Rossetti, Gabriella and Vitolo, Giovanni (eds), *Medioevo Mezzogiorno Mediterraneo. Studi in onore di Mario Del Treppo*, Europea Mediterranea: Quaderni 12, 2 vols, Naples, vol.I, pp.111–31.

von Falkenhausen, Vera (forthcoming), 'La presenza dei Greci nella Sicilia normanna. L'apporto della documentazione archivistica in lingua greca'

Finocchiaro-Sartorio, Andrea 1908, 'Giziah e kharaj: note sulla condizione dei vinti in Sicilia durante la dominazione musulmana con speciale riguardo alla proprietà fondiaria', *Archivio giuridico 'Filippo Serafini'*, 3rd ser., 10(81): 177–268.

al-Fīrūzābādī, Muḥammad ibn Yaᶜqūb 1912, *Al-qāmūs al-muḥīt*, 4 vols, Cairo.

Fleischer, Heinrich Leberecht 1836, *De glossis Habichtianis in quatuor priores tomos MI Noctium dissertatio critica*, Leipzig.

Fonseca, Cosimo Damiano 1977, 'Le istituzioni ecclesiastiche dell'Italia meridionale e Ruggero il Gran Conte', in *Ruggero il gran conte*, pp.43–66.

Fonseca, Cosimo Damiano 1994, "Pontificali sede aptavit": la ricostituzione della Chiesa vescovile di Messina (secc. XI–XII)', in *Messina* 1994, pp.35–40.

Frantz-Murphy, Gladys 1986, *The agrarian administration of Egypt from the Arabs to the Ottomans*, Supplément aux *Annales Islamologiques*, Cahier no.9, Cairo.

Frantz-Murphy, Gladys 1999, 'Land-tenure in Egypt in the first five centuries of Islamic rule (seventh–twelfth centuries AD)', in Bowman and Rogan, pp.237–66.

Freytag, Georg Wilhelm 1830–7, *Lexicon Arabico-Latinum*, 4 vols in 2, Halle.

Gaborit-Chopin, Danielle 1986, 'Suger's liturgical vessels', in Gerson, Paula Lieber (ed.) *Abbot Suger and Saint-Denis: a symposium*, New York, pp.282–94.

Gabrieli, Francesco and Scerrato, Umberto 1979, *Gli Arabi in Italia*, Milan.

Gálvez, M. Eugenia 1991, 'Fragmento de yarida del Archivo Ducal de Medinaceli de Sevilla', *Historia, instituciones y documentos (Publicaciones de la Universidad de Sevilla)* 16: 1–14.

Gálvez, M. Eugenia 1995, 'Noticia sobre los documentos árabes de Sicilia del Archivo Ducal de Medinaceli', in Scarcia Amoretti 1995, pp.167–82.

Garofalo, Aloysio 1835, *Tabularium regiae ac imperialis capellae collegiatae Divi Petri in regio panormitano palatio Ferdinandi II regni utriusque Siciliae regis jussu editum ac notis illustratum*, Palermo.

Garufi, Carlo Alberto 1898, 'Monete e conii nella storia del diritto siculo degli Arabi ai Martini', *ASS* 23: 1–171.

Garufi, Carlo Alberto 1899, *I documenti inediti dell'epoca normanna in Sicilia*, DPSASDS, 1st ser., vol.18, Palermo.

Garufi, Carlo Alberto 1901, 'Sull'ordinamento amministrativo normanno in Sicilia. Exhiquier o diwan?', *Archivio storico italiano*, 5th ser., 27: 225–63.

Garufi, Carlo Alberto 1902, *Catalogo illustrato del tabulario di Santa Maria nuova in Monreale*, DPSASDS, 1st ser., vol.19, Palermo.

Garufi, Carlo Alberto 1905, 'Adelaide nipote di Bonifazio del Vasto e Goffredo figliolo del gran conte Ruggiero', *Rendiconti e memorie della Real Accademia di scienze, lettere ed arti dei zelanti di Acireale (Classe di lettere)*, 3rd ser., 4: 185–216.

Garufi, Carlo Alberto 1908, 'Un contratto agrario in Sicilia nel secolo XII per la fondazione del casale di Mesepe, presso Paternò', *ASSO* 5: 11–22 and plate.

Garufi, Carlo Alberto 1912, 'Per la storia dei sec. XI e XII. Miscellanea diplomatica (II) – i conti di Montescaglioso: (i) Goffredo di Lecce signor di Noto, Sclafani e Caltanisetta; (ii) Adelicia di Aderno', *ASSO* 9: 324–66.

Garufi, Carlo Alberto 1922, *Necrologio del 'Liber Confratrum' di S. Matteo di Salerno*, FSI, no.56, Rome.

Garufi, Carlo Alberto 1928, 'Censimento et catasto della popolazione servile. Nuovi studi e ricerche sull'ordinamento amministrativo dei Normanni in Sicilia nei secoli XI-XII', *ASS* 49: 1–101.

Garufi, Carlo Alberto 1933, 'Tre nuove pergamene greche del monastero di S. Michele di Mazara', *ASS*, n.s., vol.53: 219–24.

Garufi, Carlo Alberto 1940, 'Per la storia dei monasteri di Sicilia nel tempo normanno', *Archivio storico per la Sicilia* 6: 1–97.

Garufi, Carlo Alberto 1942, 'Roberto di San Giovanni, maestro notaio, e il "Liber de regno Sicilie"', *Archivio storico per la Sicilia* 8: 33–128.

Géhin, Paul 1997, 'Un manuscrit bilingue grec-arabe, BN Suppl. gr. 911 (année 1043)', in Déroche, François and Richard, Francis (eds) *Scribes et manuscrits du Moyen-Orient*, Paris, pp.161–75.

Genuardi, Luigi 1909, 'Documenti inediti di Frederico II', *QFIAB* 12: 236–43.

Genuardi, Luigi 1910, 'I defetari normanni', in Besta, Enrico, Columba, Gaetano M., Nallino, Carlo A., Salinas, Antonino, Siragusa, Giambattista and Zuretti, Carlo O. (eds), *Centenario della nascita di Michele Amari: Scritti di filologia e storia araba*, 2 vols, Palermo, 1: 159–64.

Geoponika 1895, *Geoponica sive Cassiani Bassi scholastici de re rustica eclogae*, ed. Heinrich Beckh, Leipzig.

Giardina, Camillo 1937, *Capitoli e privilegi di Messina*, Reale deputazione di storia patria per la Sicilia: Memorie e documenti di storia siciliana, 2nd ser., vol.1, Palermo.

Giarrizzo, Salvatore 1989, *Dizionario etimologico siciliano*, Palermo.

Gil, Moshe 1983, *Erets-Yisrael ba-tekufah ha-Muslemit ha-rishonah (634–1099)*, 3 vols, Pirsume ha-Makhon le-heker ha-tefutsot (Publications of the Diaspora Research Institute), nos 41, 57–8, Tel Aviv. (English translation and revised version of vol.I only: Gil, Moshe 1992, *A history of Palestine, 634–1099*, Cambridge.)

Gil, Moshe 1995, 'Sicily 827–1072 in light of the Geniza documents and parallel sources', in *Gli Ebrei in Sicilia sino all'espulsione del 1492. Atti del V Convegno internazionale Italia Judaica (Palermo 1992)*, Rome, pp.96–171.

Gil, Moshe 1997, *Be-malkhut Yishmael bi-tekufat ha-geonim* (Hebrew: 'In the kingdom of Ismael during the Gaonic period'), 4 vols, Pirsume ha-Makhon le-heker ha-tefutsot (Publications of the Diaspora Research Institute), nos 117–120, Jerusalem.

Giménez Soler, Andrés 1907, 'Episodios de la historia de las relaciones entre la Corona de Aragón y Túnez', *Annuari de l'Institut d'Estudis Catalans* 1: 195–224.

Giovanni Scriba 1935, *Il cartolare di Giovanni Scriba*, ed. Mario Chiaudano, 2 vols, Reale Istituto Storico Italiano per il Medio Evo: Regesta Chartarum Italiae, nos 19–20, Rome.

Girgensohn, Dieter and Kamp, Norbert 1965, 'Urkunden und Inquisitionen des 12 und 13 Jahrhunderts aus Patti', *QFIAB* 45: 1–240.

Giuffrida Romualdo and Rocco, Benedetto 1982, 'Il più antico documento in carta conservato nell'Archivio di Stato di Palermo', *Beni culturali e ambientali. Bollettino d'informazione trimestrale per la divulgazione dell'attività degli organi dell'Amministrazione per i Beni culturali e ambientali della Regione Siciliana*, 3(1–4): 251–4.

Goitein, Shlomo Dov 1942, 'The origin of the vizerate and its true character', *Islamic Culture* 16: 255–62, 380–92. (Reprinted in Goitein 1966, pp.168–93.)

Goitein, Shlomo Dov 1961, 'Appendix on the origin of the term vizier', *Journal of the American Oriental Society* 81: 425–6. (Reprinted in Goitein 1966, pp.194–6.)

Goitein, Shlomo Dov 1966, *Studies in Islamic history and institutions*, Leiden.

Goitein, Shlomo Dov 1967–93, *A Mediterranean society. The Jewish communities of the Arab world as portrayed in the documents of the Cairo Geniza*, 6 vols, Berkeley, Los Angeles and London.

Golb, Norman 1973, 'A Judaeo-Arabic court document of Syracuse, A.D. 1020', *Journal of Near Eastern Studies* 32: 105–23.

Golvin, Lucien 1957, *Le Magrib central à l'époque des Zirides*, Paris.

Grabar, André 1957, 'Image d'une église chrétienne parmi les peintures musulmanes de la Chapelle Palatine à Palerme', in Ettinghausen, Richard (ed.) *Aus der Welt der islamischen Kunst: Festschrift für Ernst Kühnel*, Berlin, pp.226–33.

Grégoire, Henri 1932a, 'Diplômes de Mazara (Sicile)', *Annuaire de l'Institut de Philologie et d'Histoire orientales de l'Université de Bruxelles pour 1932–1933*, pp.79–107.

Grégoire, Henri 1932b, 'Documents grecs de Mazzara', *Academie royale de Belgique: Bulletin de la classe de Lettres et des Sciences morales et politiques*, 5th ser., 18: 48–59.

Grégoire, Henri 1933, 'Review of Lynn Townsend White Jr, "The charters of St Michael's in Mazzara", *La Révue Bénédictine* 45: 234–41', *Byzantion* 8: 705–6.

Gregorio, Rosario 1972, *Considerazioni sopra la storia di Sicilia dai tempi dei Normanni sino ai presenti*, 4th edn, ed. Armando Saitta, 3 vols, Palermo. (Reprint of 3rd edn, Palermo, 1845.)

Grohmann, Adolf 1934, '*ᶜUshr*', in *E.I.*[1] vol.IV, pp.1050–2.

Grohmann, Adolf 1955, *Einführung und Chrestomathie zur arabischen Papyruskunde*, Studies, texts and translations published by the Czechoslovak Oriental Institute, no.13(1), Prague.

Grousset, René 1934–6, *Histoire des croisades et du royaume franc de Jérusalem*, 3 vols, Paris.

Grube, Ernst J. forthcoming, 'The painted ceiling of the Cappella Palatina in Palermo and its relation to the artistic traditions of the Muslim world and the art of the Middle Ages', *Islamic Art*, forthcoming.

Guillou, André (ed.) 1963, *Les actes grecs de S. Maria di Messina: enquête sur les populations grecques d'Italie du Sud et de Sicile (XIe–XIVe s.)*, Istituto siciliano di studi bizantine e neoellenici: Testi e monumenti, no.8, Palermo.

Guillou, André 1975–6, 'La Sicilia bizantina. Un bilancio delle ricerche attuali', *Archivio storico siracusano*, n.s., 4: 43–89.

Guillou, André 1977, 'La svolgimento della giustizia nell'Italia meridionale sotto il Gran Conte Ruggero e il suo significanto storico', in *Ruggero il gran conte*, pp.67–78.

Guillou, André and Holtzmann, Walther (eds) 1961, 'Zwei Katepansurkunden aus Tricarico', *QFIAB* 41: 1–28. (Reprinted in André Guillou, *Studies on Byzantine Italy*, London, 1970.)

Halm, Heinz 1979–82, *Ägypten nach den mamlukischen Lehensregistern*, 2 vols, Beihefte zum Tübinger Atlas der Vorderen Orients, Series B, no.38, Wiesbaden.

Halm, Heinz 1996, *The Empire of the Mahdi. The Rise of the Fatimids*, trans. Michael Bonner, Leiden, New York, and Cologne.

al-Ḥamāwī, Abū l-Faḍāʾil Muḥammad ibn ᶜAlī ibn ᶜAbd al-ᶜAzīz 1960, *Al-Taʾrīkh al-manṣūrī*, ed. P. A. Griaznevich and Viktor Ivanovich Beliaev as *Arabskii anonim XI veka*, Akademiia nauk SSSR. Institut vostokovedeniia, Pamiatniki literatury narodov

Vostoka. Teksty. Bol'shaia seriia, no.6, Moscow. (Photographic reproduction of the unique MS).

al-Ḥamāwī, Abū l-Faḍā'il Muḥammad ibn ᶜAlī ibn ᶜAbd al-ᶜAzīz 1981 (1982 on cover), *Al-Ta'rīkh al-manṣūrī*, ed. Abū l-ᶜId Dūdū and ᶜAdnān Darwīsh, Damascus.

Hampikian, Nairy and Cyran, Monica 1999, 'Recent discoveries concerning the Fatimid palaces uncovered during the conservation works on parts of the al-Ṣāliḥiyya complex', in Barrucand 1999, pp.649–64.

al-Harawī, ᶜAlī ibn Abī Bakr 1953, *Kitāb al-ishārāt fī maᶜrifat al-ziyārāt*, ed. Janine Sourdel-Thomine, Damascus.

al-Harawī, ᶜAlī ibn Abī Bakr 1957, *Guide aux lieux de Pèlerinage (Kitāb al-ishārāt fī maᶜrifat al-ziyārāt)*, trans. Janine Sourdel-Thomine, Damascus.

Haskins, Charles Homer 1911, 'England and Sicily in the twelfth century', *English Historical Review* 103: 433–665.

Haskins, Charles Homer 1915, *The Normans in European history*, Boston and New York.

Haskins, Charles Homer 1924, *Studies in the history of mediaeval science*, Cambridge, Mass.

Hinz, Walther 1955, *Islamische Masse und Gewichte*, Handbuch der Orientalistik: Ergänzungsband 1, no.1, Leiden.

Hoffmann, Hartmut 1967, 'Hugo Falcandus und Romauld von Salerno', *Deutsches Archiv für Erforschung des Mittelalters* 23: 116–70.

Hogendorn, Jan S. 2000, 'The location and "manufacture" of eunuchs', in Toru and Philips 2000, pp.41–68.

Holm, Adolf 1870–98, *Geschichte Siciliens im Alterthum*, 3 vols, Leipzig.

Hopkins, John Francis Price. 1958, *Medieval Muslim government in Barbary until the sixth centry of the Hijra*, London.

Hopkins, Simon A. 1984, *Studies in the grammar of early Arabic based upon papyri datable to before 300AH/912AD*, London oriental series, no.37, Oxford.

Houben, Hubert 1991, 'Adelaide "del Vasto" nella storia del regno di Sicilia', *Itinerari di ricerca storica* 4: 9–40.

Houben, Hubert 1992, 'Gli ebrei nell'Italia meridionale tra metà dell'XI e l'inizio del XIII secolo', *Itinerari di ricerca storica* 6: 9–28.

Houben, Hubert 1995, *Die Abtei Venosa und das Mönchtum im normannisch-staufischen Süditalien*, Bibliothek des Deutschen Historischen Instituts in Rom, no.80, Tübingen.

Houben, Hubert 1999, *Ruggero II di Sicilia. Un sovrano tra Orient e Occidente*, Rome and Bari.

Houdas, Octave 1886, 'Essai sur l'écriture maghrébine', in *Nouveaux mélanges orientaux. Mémoires textes et traductions publiés par les professeurs de l'École spéciale des langues orientales vivantes à l'occasion du septième congrès international des orientalistes réuni a Vienne (Septembre 1886)*, Publications de l'École des langues orientales vivantes, 2nd ser., no.19, Paris, pp.83–112 and plates.

'Hugo Falcandus' 1897, *Liber de regno Siciliae*, ed. Giovanni Battista Siragusa, FSI, no.22, Rome.

'Hugo Falcandus' 1998, *The history of the tyrants of Sicily by 'Hugo Falcandus' 1154–69*, trans. Graham A. Loud and Thomas Wiedemann, Manchester.

Huillard-Bréholles, Jean Louise Alphonse 1852–61, *Historia diplomatica Friderici Secundi, sive constitutiones, privilegia, mandata, instrumenta quae supersunt istius Imperatoris et filiorum ejus. Accedunt epistolae Paparum et documenta varia*, 7 vols in 12 parts, Paris.

Ibn Abī Dīnār, Muḥammad ibn ᶜUmar 1967, *Al-Muᵓnis fī akhbār Ifrīqīya wa-Tūnis*, Tunis.

Ibn al-Athīr, ᶜIzz al-Dīn Abū l-Ḥasan ᶜAlī ibn Muḥammad al-Jazarī 1851–76, *al-Kāmil fī l-taᵓrīkh*, ed. Carolus Johannes Tornberg, 13 vols, Leipzig. (Reprinted Beirut, 1979–82, with different pagination.)

Ibn Hammād, Muḥammad ibn ᶜAlī 1927, *Histoire des rois ᶜObaïdites*, ed. Madelaine Vonderheyden, Algiers and Paris.

Ibn Ḥawqal, Abū l-Qāsim Muḥammad 1938–9, *Opus geographicum (Ṣūrat al-arḍ)*, 2nd edn, ed. Johannes Hendric Kramers, 2 vols, BGA, no.2, Leiden.

Ibn Ḥawqal, Abū l-Qāsim Muḥammad 1964, *Configuration de la terre (Ṣūrat al-arḍ)*, trans. Johannes Hendrik Kramers and Gaston Wiet, 2 vols, Collection UNESCO d'œuvres représentatives. Série arabe, Beirut.

Ibn ᶜIdhārī al-Marrākushī 1901–04, *Al-bayān al-mughrib fī akhbar al-Maghrib*, trans. Edouard Fagnan, 1–2 of 3 vols, Leiden.

Ibn ᶜIdhārī al-Marrākushī 1948–51, *Al-bayān al-mughrib fī akhbar al-Maghrib*, ed. George Séraphim Colin and Evariste Lévi-Provençal, 2 vols (*i.e.* vol.1 and vol.2, part 1), Leiden.

Ibn Jubayr al-Kinānī, Abū l-Ḥusayn Muḥammad ibn Aḥmad 1907, *Riḥlat al-Kinānī*, 2nd edn, ed. Michael Jan de Goeje and William Wright, Gibb Memorial Series, no.5, Oxford.

Ibn Jubayr al-Kinānī, Abū l-Ḥusayn Muḥammad ibn Aḥmad 1949–65, *Les voyages d'Ibn Jobair (Riḥlat al-Kinānī)*, trans. Maurice Gaudefroy-Demombynes, 4 parts, L'Académie des inscriptions et belles-lettres: Documents relatifs à l'histoire des croisades, Paris.

Ibn Jubayr al-Kinānī, Abū l-Ḥusayn Muḥammad ibn Aḥmad 1952, *The Travels of Ibn Jubair*, trans. Ronald J.C. Broadhurst, 2nd edn, London.

Ibn Khaldūn, Abū Zayd ᶜAbd al-Raḥmān ibn Muḥammad 1858, *Muqaddima*, ed. M. Quatrèmere, 3 vols, Paris.

Ibn Khaldūn, Abū Zayd ᶜAbd al-Raḥmān ibn Muḥammad 1868, *Kitāb al-ᶜibar wa-dīwān al-mubtadaᵓ*, 7 vols, Būlāq.

Ibn Khallikān, Aḥmad ibn Muḥammad ibn Ibrahīm ibn Abī Bakr 1948, *Wafayāt al-aᶜyān*, ed. Muḥammad Muḥyī l-Dīn ᶜAbd al-Ḥamīd, 6 vols, Cairo.

Ibn Mammātī, Asᶜad ibn al-Muhadhdhab 1943, *Kitāb qawānīn al-dawāwīn*, ed. ᶜAzīz Sūrīya ᶜAṭiya, Cairo.

Ibn Mammātī, Asᶜad ibn al-Muhadhdhab 1986, *Cinq calendriers Égyptiens*, ed. Charles Pellat, Institut français d'archéologie orientale du Caire: Textes arabes et études islamiques, no.26, Cairo.

Ibn Manẓūr, Abū l-Faḍl Jimāl al-Dīn Muḥammad 1984, *Lisān al-ᶜarab*, 15 vols, Qumm.

Ibn Muyassar, Tāj al-Dīn 1919 *Akhbār Miṣr*, ed. Henri Massé, Institut français d'archéologie orientale: Textes arabes, no.2, Cairo.

Ibn Qalāqis, Abū l-Futūḥ Naṣr ibn ᶜAbd Allāh 1984a, *Al-Zahr al-bāsim wa-l-ᶜarf al-nāsim fī madīḥ al-ajall Abī l-Qāsim*, ed. ᶜAbd al-ᶜAzīz Ibn Nāṣir al-Māniᶜ, Riyāḍ.

Ibn Qalāqis, Abū l-Futūḥ Naṣr ibn ᶜAbd Allāh 1984b, *Tarassul Ibn Qalāqis al-Iskandarī*, ed. ᶜAbd al-ᶜAzīz Ibn Nāṣir al-Māniᶜ, Riyāḍ.

Ibn Qalāqis, Abū l-Futūḥ Naṣr ibn ᶜAbd Allāh 1988, *Dīwān Ibn Qalāqis*, ed. Sihām ᶜAbd al-Wahhab Furayḥ, Kuwayt.

Ibn al-Ṣayrafī, ᶜAlī ibn Munjib 1905, *Qānūn dīwān al-rasāᵓil*, Cairo.

Ibn al-Ṣayrafī, ᶜAlī ibn Munjib 1914, 'Qānūn dīwān al-rasāᵓil', *Bulletin de l'Institut français d'archéologie orientale* 11: 65–119.

Ibn al-Ṣayrafī, ᶜAlī ibn Munjib 1924, *Al-ishāra ilā man nāla al-wizāra* ('Guide to those who assumed the vizierate'), ed. ᶜAbd Allāh Mukhliṣ, Cairo.

Ibn Shīth al-Qurashī, ᶜAbd al-Raḥīm ibn ᶜAlī 1913, *Maᶜālim al-kitāba wa-maghānim al-iṣāba*, ed. Qusṭanṭīn al-Bāshā al-Mukhallisī, Beirut.

Ibn Ẓafar, Abū Hāshim Muḥammad ibn Abī Muḥammad 1862, *Sulwān al-muṭāᶜ fī ᶜudwān al-atbāᶜ*, Tunis.

Idris, Hady Roger 1962a, *La Berbérie orientale sous les Zīrīdes, Xe–XIIe siècles*, 2 vols, Faculté des lettres et sciences humaines d'Alger: Publications de l'Institut d'études orientales, no.21, Paris.

Idris, Hady Roger 1962b, 'L'école malikite de Mahdia: l'Imam al-Māzarī (m. 536H/1141)', in *Études d'orientalisme dédiées à la mémoire de Lévi-Provençal*, 2 vols, Paris, vol.I, pp.153–63.

al-Idrīsī, Abī ᶜAbd Allāh Muḥammad ibn Muḥammad ibn ᶜAbd Allāh ibn Idrīs 1883, *L'Italia descritta nel 'Libro del Re Ruggero' compilato da Edrisi. Testo arabo pubblicato con versione e note da M[ichele] Amari e C[armelo] Schiaparelli*, Atti della Reale Accademia dei Lincei, anno 274, 2nd ser., vol.8, Rome.

al-Idrīsī, Abī ᶜAbd Allāh Muḥammad ibn Muḥammad ibn ᶜAbd Allāh ibn Idrīs 1970–6, *Opus geographicum, sive 'Liber ad eorum delectationem qui terras peragrare studeant' (Kitab nuzhat al-mushtaq)*, ed. Alessio Bombaci, Umberto Rizzitano, Roberto Rubinacci and Laura Veccia Vaglieri, 9 parts, Naples and Rome.

ᶜImād al-Dīn, Abū ᶜAbd Allāh Muḥammad ibn Ḥammād al-Kātib al-Iṣfahānī 1951, *Kharīdat al-qaṣr wa-jarīdat al-ᶜaṣr: Qism shuᶜarāᵓ Miṣr*, 2 vols, Cairo.

ᶜImād al-Dīn, Abū ᶜAbd Allāh Muḥammad ibn Ḥammād al-Katib al-Iṣfahānī 1964–9, *Kharīdat al-qaṣr wa-jarīdat al-ᶜaṣr*, ed. ᶜUmar al-Dasūqī and ᶜAlī ᶜAbd al-ᶜAẓīm, 2 vols, Cairo.

ᶜImād al-Dīn, Abū ᶜAbd Allāh Muḥammad ibn Ḥammād al-Kātib al-Iṣfahānī 1966–72, *Kharīdat al-qaṣr wa-jarīdat al-ᶜaṣr*, ed. Muḥammad al-Marzūqī, Muḥammad al-ᶜArūsī al-Miṭwī and al-Jilānī ibn al-Ḥajj Yaḥyā, 3 vols, Tunis.

Irwin, Robert 1977, '*Iqṭāᶜ* and the end of the Crusader states', in Holt, Peter M. (ed.) *The Eastern Mediterranean lands in the period of the Crusades*, Warminster, pp.62–73.

ᶜIyāḍ ibn Mūsā al-Yaḥṣubī al-Sabtī 1965, *Tartīb al-madārik wa-taqrīb al-masālik bi-maᶜrifat aᶜlām madhhab Mālik*, ed. Aḥmad Bakr Maḥmūd, 4 parts in 2 vols, Beirut.

Jaffé, Philippe and Loewenfeld, Samuel 1885–8, *Regesta Pontificum Romanorum ab condita ecclesiae ad annum post Christum natum MCXCVIII*, 2nd edn, 2 vols, Leipzig.

Jamil, Nadia and Johns, Jeremy 2002 (forthcoming), 'An Arabic document from Crusader Antioch (1213 A.D.)', in Robinson, Chase (ed.), *Texts, documents and artefacts: Islamic studies in honour of D.S. Richards*, Leiden.

Jamison, Evelyn 1913, 'The Norman Administration of Apulia and Capua, more especially under Roger II and William I, 1127–1166', *Papers of the British School at Rome* 6: 211–481.

Jamison, Evelyn 1957, *Admiral Eugenius of Sicily: his life and work and the authorship of the* Epistola ad Petrum *and the* Historia Hugonis Falcandi Siculi, London.

Jamison, Evelyn, Cuozzo, Errico and Clementi, Dione (eds) 1972, *Catalogus baronum*, ed. Errico Cuozzo and Dione Clementi, FSI, no.101, Rome.

Johns, Jeremy 1983, 'The Muslims of Norman Sicily, *c.*1060–*c.*1194', D.Phil. thesis, Faculty of Modern History, University of Oxford.

Johns, Jeremy 1985, 'The Monreale Survey: indigenes and invaders in medieval west Sicily', in Malone, Caroline and Stoddart, Simon (eds) *Papers in Italian archaeology*

IV: the Cambridge conference, 4 vols, British archaeological reports: international series, no.246, Oxford, 4: 215–23.

Johns, Jeremy 1986, 'I titoli arabi dei sovrani normanni di Sicilia', *Bollettino di Numismatica* 6–7: 11–54.

Johns, Jeremy 1987, '*Malik Ifrīqiya*: the Norman kingdom of Africa and the Fāṭimids', *Libyan Studies* 18: 89–101.

Johns, Jeremy 1988, 'La Monreale Survey. Insediamento medievale in Sicilia occidentale: premesse, metodi, problemi e alcuni resultati preliminari', in Pesez, Jean-Marie (ed.), *Structures de l'habitat et occupation du sol dans les pays méditerranéens – Méthode et apport de l'archéologie extensive*, Rome and Madrid, pp.73–84.

Johns, Jeremy 1993, 'The Norman kings of Sicily and the Fatimid caliphate', in Chibnall, Marjorie (ed.) *Anglo-Norman Studies 15: Proceedings of the Battle Conference and of the XI Colloquio medievale of the Officina di Studi Medievali 1992*, Woodbridge, pp.133–59.

Johns, Jeremy 1995a, 'The Greek church and the conversion of Muslims in Norman Sicily?', *Byzantinische Forschungen* 21: 133–57.

Johns, Jeremy 1995b, 'I re normanni e il califfi fāṭimiti. Nuove prospettive su vecchi materiali', in Scarcia Amoretti 1995, pp.9–50.

Johns, Jeremy 1999, 'Arabic contracts of sea-exchange from Norman Sicily', in Xuereb, Paul (ed.) *Karissime Gotifride. Historical essays presented to Godfrey Wettinger on his seventieth birthday*, Malta, pp.55–78.

Johns, Jeremy 2001, 'Arabic 'June' (*bruṭuyūn*) and 'July' (*isṭiriyūn*) in Norman Sicily', *BSOAS* 64: 98–100.

Johns, Jeremy forthcoming a, 'The Arabic and bilingual documents issued by the *dīwān* of King William I of Sicily'.

Johns, Jeremy forthcoming b, 'The boys from Mezzoiuso. Muslim *jizya*-payers in Christian Sicily', in Hoyland, Robert and Kennedy, Phillip (eds) *Alan Jones Festschrift*, Gibb Memorial Series, Cambridge.

Johns, Jeremy forthcoming c, Jeremy Johns, 'The date of the ceiling of the Cappella Palatina in Palermo', *Islamic Art*, forthcoming.

Johns, Jeremy forthcoming d, 'Taxing the rough with the smooth: Muslim villeins in Norman Sicily'.

Johns, Jeremy forthcoming e, '1056 and all that. What was the (real) date of the Norman invasion of Sicily?'

Johns, Jeremy and Metcalfe, Alex 1999, 'The mystery at Chùrchuro: conspiracy or incompetence in twelfth-century Sicily', *BSOAS* 62: 226–59.

Johns, Jeremy and Metcalfe, Alex forthcoming, 'A Latin register of villeins (*platea*) from 12th-century Patti in Sicily'

Jones, Dalu 1972, 'The Cappella Palatina in Palermo: problems of attribution', *Art and Archaeology Research Papers* 2: 41–57.

Jones, Arnold Hugh Martin 1964, *The Later Roman Empire 284–602. A social, economic, and administrative survey*, 3 vols and atlas, Oxford.

Jordan, Edouard 1922, 'La politique ecclésiastique de Roger I et ses origines de la legation sicilienne [part 1]', *Le Moyen Age* 33: 237–73.

Jordan, Edouard 1923, 'La politique ecclésiastique de Roger I et ses origines de la legation sicilienne [part 2]', *Le Moyen Age* 34: 32–65.

Kamp, Nobert 1973–82, *Kirche und Monarchie im staufischen Königreich Sizilien*, 1 vol. in 4 parts, Munich.

Kamp, Norbert 1974, 'Von Kämmerer zum Sekreten: Wirtschaftsreformen und Finanzverwaltung im staufischen Königreich Sizilien', in Fleckstein, Josef (ed.) *Probleme um Friedrich II*, Konstanzer Arbeitskreis für mittelalterliche Geschichte: Vorträge und Forschungen, no.16 = Studien und Quellen zur Welt Kaiser Friedrichs II, no.4, Sigmaringen, pp.43–92.

Karabacek, Josef Ritter von 1897, 'Aegyptische Urkunden aus den königlichen Museen zu Berlin', *Vienna Oriental Journal (Wiener Zeitschrift für die Kunde des Morgenlandes)* 11(1): 1–21.

Keenan, James G. 1999, 'Fayyum agriculture at the end of the Ayyubid era: Nabulsi's *Survey*', in Bowman and Rogan 1999, pp.287–99.

Kehr, Karl Andreas 1902, *Die Urkunden der normannisch-sicilischen Könige. Eine diplomatische Untersuchung*, Innsbruck.

Kehr, Paulus Fridulinus, Holtzmann, Walther and Girgensohn, Dieter (eds) 1906–75, *Italia pontificia sive Repertorium privilegiorum et litterarum a Romanis pontificibus ante annum MCLXXXXVIII Italiae ecclesiis, monasteriis, civitatibus singulisque personis concessorum*, 10 vols, Berlin and Zurich.

Khafājī, Aḥmad ibn Muḥammad 1863, *Kitāb shifāʾ al-ghalīl*, Cairo.

Khan, Geoffrey 1986, 'A copy of a decree from the archives of the Fatimid chancery in Egypt', *BSOAS* 49: 439–53.

Khan, Geoffrey 1992, *Arabic papyri. Selected material from the Khalili Collection*, Studies in the Khalili Collection, no.1, Oxford.

Khan, Geoffrey 1993, *Arabic legal and administrative documents in the Cambridge Genizah collections*, Cambridge University Library Genizah Series, no.10, 1993.

Kitzinger, Ernst 1950, 'On the portrait of Roger II in the Martorana in Palermo', *Proporzioni* 3: 30–3. (Reprinted in Kitzinger 1976, pp.320–6, with *post scriptum* pp.394–5.)

Kitzinger, Ernst 1976, *The art of Byzantium and the medieval West*, ed. W. Eugene Kleinbauer, Bloomington and London.

Kitzinger, Ernst 1990, *The mosaics of St. Mary's of the Admiral in Palermo*, Dumbarton Oaks Studies no.27, Washington.

Kölzer, Theo (ed.) 1983, *Constantiae imperatricis et reginae Sicilae diplomata (1195–1198)*, Codex diplomaticus Regni Siciliae: ser. 2, Diplomata regum et gente Suevorum, vols 1–2, Cologne and Vienna.

Kramers, Johannes Hendric and Bosworth, Clifford Edmund 1997, 'Sulṭān', in *E.I.*^{2} vol.IX, pp.849–51.

Kriaras, Emmanuel 1968–, *Lexiko tēs mesaiōnikēs Ellēnikēs dēmōdous grammateias*, 14 vols to date, Thessalonica.

Krönig, Wolfgang 1989, 'Der viersprachige Grabstein von 1148', *Zeitschrift für Kunstgeschichte* 52: 550–8.

Labīb, Claudius Yuhanna 1896–1910. *Dictionnaire copte-arabe*, Cairo.

La Corte, Giorgio 1902, 'Appunti di toponomastica sul territorio della chiesa di Monreale nel secolo XII', *ASS* 27: 336–45.

Lagumina, Bartolomeo 1890, 'Nota sulla iscrizione quadrilingue esistente nel Museo Nazionale di Palermo', *ASS*, n.s., 15: 108–10.

Lagumina, Bartolomeo and Lagumina, Giuseppe 1884–1909, *Codice diplomatico dei giudei di Sicilia*, 3 vols, DPSASDS, 1st ser., vols 6, 12 and 17, Palermo.

La Mantia, Giuseppe 1908, *Il primo documento in carta (Contessa Adelaide, 1109) esistente in Sicilia e rimasto sinora sconosciuto*, Palermo.

Lamm, Carl Johan 1930, *Mittelalterliche Gläser und Steinschnittarbeiten aus dem Nahren Osten*, 2 vols, Berlin.

Lammens, Henri 1903, 'Relations officielles entre le cour romaine et les Sultans Mamlouks d'Égypte', *Revue de l'Orient Chrétien* 8: 101–10.

Lammens, Henri 1904, 'Correspondances diplomatiques entre les Sultans Mamlouks d'Égypte et les puissances chrétiennes', *Revue de l'Orient Chrétien* 9: 151–87, 359–92.

Lane, Edward William 1984, *An Arabic-English lexicon*, 8 parts in 2 vols, London. (Reprint of 1863–93 edn.)

Lavagnini, Bruno 1994 'Giorgio di Antiochia e il titolo di Ἄρχων τῶν Ἀρχόντων', in *ΣΥΝΔΕΣΜΟΣ. Studi in onore di Rosario Anastasi*, 2 vols, Catania, II: 215–20.

Lefort, Jacques and Martin, Jean-Marie 1986, 'Le sigillion du catépan d'Italie Eustathe Palatinos pour le juge Byzantios (décembre 1045)', *Mélanges de l'École française de Rome (Moyen Âges)* 98(2): 525–42.

Lewis, Bernard 1954, 'Daftar', in *E.I.*² vol.II, pp.77–81.

Liddell, Henry George and Scott, Robert 1940, *A Greek-English lexicon*, 9th edn, ed. Henry Stuart Jones and Roderick McKenzie, Oxford.

von der Lieck-Buyken, Thea (ed.) 1978. *Die Konstituten Friedrichs II. von Hohenstaufen für sein Königsreich sizilien. Ergänzungband 1. Teil: Der griechische Text (MS. Vat. Cod. Barb. Graec. 151 und Paris, Bibl. Nat., Cod. Graec. 1392)*, Studien und Quellen zur Welt Kaiser Friedrichs II, vol.5/1, Cologne and Vienna.

Lima, Antonietta Iolanda 1991, *Monreale (Palermo)*, Atlante storico delle città della Sicilia, no.1, Palermo.

Linant de Bellefonds, Yvon, Cahen, Claude, and İnalcik, Halil 1975, 'Ḳānūn', *E.I.*² vol.IV, pp.556–62.

Lipinsky, Angelo 1973–4, 'Ori e goielli della Sicilia Normanna', *AASLAP*, 4th ser., 33(2): 432–6.

Little, Donald Presgrave 1984, *A catalogue of the Islamic documents from al-Ḥaram aš-Šarīf in Jerusalem*, Beiruter Texte und Studien herausgegeben vom Orient-Institut der Deutschen Morgenländischen Gesellschaft, no.29, Beirut.

Løkkegaard, Frede 1950, *Islamic taxation in the classical period with special reference to circumstances in Iraq*, Copenhagen.

Løkkegaard, Frede 1964, 'Fayʾ', in *E.I.*² vol.II, pp.869–70.

Longo, Augusta Acconcia 1981, 'Gli epitaffi iambici per Giorgio di Antiochia, per la madre e per la moglie', *QFIAB* 61: 25–59.

Loyn, Henry R. 1983, *The Norman Conquest*, 3rd edn, London.

Luttrell, Anthony 1997 'Giliberto Abbate's report on Malta: circa 1241', in Sciberras, Keith (ed.), *Proceedings of History Week 1993*, Malta, 1997, pp.1–29. (Reprinted in Anthony Luttrell, *The making of Christian Malta: From the early Middle Ages to 1530*, London, 2002, no. IX.)

Mack Smith, Denis 1968 *A History of Sicily. Medieval Sicily 800–1713*, London.

Malaterra, Geoffrey 1927–8, *De rebus gestis Rogerii Calabriae et Siciliae Comitis et Roberti Guiscardi Ducis fratris eius*, ed. Ernesto Pontieri, RIS, 2nd ser., vol.2, Bologna.

Mansi, Giovanni Domenico 1759–1927, *Sacrorum conciliorum nova et amplissima collectio*, 53 vols, Florence.

al-Manṣūr al-Jawdharī al-ᶜAzīzī, Abū ᶜAlī 1954, *Sīrat al-ustādh Jawdhar*, ed. Muḥammad Kāmil Ḥusayn and Muḥammad ᶜAbd al-Hādī Shaᶜīra, Silsila makhṭūṭāt al-fāṭimiyyīn, no.11, Cairo.

al-Maqrīzī, Aḥmad ibn ᶜAlī 1853, *Al-Mawāᶜiẓ wa-l-iᶜtibār bi-dhikr al-khiṭaṭ wa-l-āthār*, ed. Muḥammad Qaṭṭah al-ᶜAdawī, 2 vols, Būlāq.

al-Maqrīzī, Aḥmad ibn ᶜAlī 1895–1920, *Al-Mawāᶜiẓ wa-l-iᶜtibār bi-dhikr al-khiṭaṭ wa-l-āthār*, trans. U. Bouriant and Paul Casanova, 3 vols, (vol.1 = *Mémoires ... de la Mission archéologique française du Caire*, vol.17, 1895; vols 2–3 = *Mémoires ... de l'Institut français d'archéologie orientale du Caire*, vols 3–4 incomplete, 1906 and 1920), Cairo.

al-Maqrīzī, Aḥmad ibn ᶜAlī 1911–27, *Al-Mawāᶜiẓ wa-l-iᶜtibār bi-dhikr al-khiṭaṭ wa-l-āthār*, ed. Gaston Wiet, *Mémoires publiés par l'Institut français d'archéologie orientale du Caire*, vols 30, 33, 46, 49, 53 (incomplete), Cairo.

al-Maqrīzī, Aḥmad ibn ᶜAlī 1967–73, *Ittiᶜāẓ al-ḥunafāʾ bi-akhbār al-aʾimmat al-fāṭimīyīn al-khulafāʾ*, ed. Jamal al-Dīn al-Shayyāl and Muḥammad H. M. Aḥmad, 3 vols, Cairo.

al-Maqrīzī, Aḥmad ibn ᶜAlī 1991, *Kitāb al-muqaffā al-kabīr*, ed. Muḥammad al-Yaᶜlāwī, 8 vols, Beirut.

Marçais, Georges 1955, *L'architecture musulmane d'Occident. Tunisie, Algérie, Maroc, Espagne et Sicile*, Paris.

Marçais, Georges 1965, 'G͟hāniya', in *E.I.*² vol.II, pp.1007–8.

Margoliouth, David Samuel 1933, *Catalogue of Arabic Papyri in the John Rylands Library Manchester*, Manchester.

al-Masᶜūdī, Abū l-Ḥasan ᶜAlī ibn al-Ḥusayn 1894, *Kitāb al-tanbīh wa-l-ishrāf* ('Book of advice and enquiry'), ed. Michael Jan de Goeje, BGA, no.8, Leiden.

Mattei-Cerasoli, Leone 1939, 'La Badia di Cava e i monasteri greci della Calabria Superiore [part 1]', *ASCL* 8: 167–82, 265–85.

Matthew of Edessa 1869, *Chronique*, in Dulaurier, Edouard (ed.) *Recueil des Historiens des Croisades. Documents Arméniens*, 2 vols, Paris, 1869, vol.I, pp.1–150.

Matthew, Donald 1981, 'The Chronicle of Romuald of Salerno', in Davis, R. H. C. and Wallace-Hadrill, J. Michael (eds) *The Writing of History in the Middle Ages: Essays Presented to Richard William Southern*, Oxford, pp.239–74.

Matthew, Donald 1992, *The Norman kingdom of Sicily*, Cambridge.

Maurici, Ferdinando 1998, *L'insediamento medievale nel territorio della Provincia di Palermo. Inventario preliminare degli abitati attestati dalle fonti d'archivio (secoli XI–XVI)*, Palermo.

al-Mawardī, Abū l-Ḥasan 1853, *Kitāb al-aḥkām al-sulṭānīya wa-l-wilāyāt al-dīnīya*, ed. Maximilian Enger, Bonn.

al-Mawardī, Abū l-Ḥasan 1996, *The ordinances of government. A translation of Al-Aḥkām al-Sulṭāniyya w'al-Wilāyāt al-Dīniyya*, trans. Wafaa H. Wahba, Reading.

al-Maydānī, Aḥmad ibn Muḥammad 1838–43, *Majmaᶜ al-amthāl (Arabum proverbia)*, ed. and trans. Georg Wilhelm Freytag, 3 vols, Bonn.

Mayer, Hans Eberhard 1988, *The Crusades*, 2nd revised edn, Oxford.

Mazzarese Fardella, Enrico 1966, *Aspetti dell'organizzazione amministrativa nello stato normanno e svevo*, Milan.

Meier, Hans-Rudolf 1994, *Die normannischen Königspaläste in Palermo: Studien zur hochmittelalterlichen Residenzbaukunst*, Manuskripte zur Kunstwissenschaft in der Wernerschen Verlagsgesellschaft, no.42, Worms.

Ménager, Léon-Robert 1956–57, 'Notes critiques sur quelques diplômes normandes de l'Archivio Capitolare di Catania', *Bullettino dell'Archivio Paleografico Italiano*, n.s., 2–3: 145–76.

Ménager, Léon-Robert 1957, 'Notes et documents sur quelques monastères de Calabre à l'époque normande', *BZ* 50: 7–30, 321–61.

Ménager, Léon-Robert 1958, 'La tradition en 'volgare italiano' des diplômes grecs du Patir de Rossano', *BZ* 51: 310–13.

Ménager, Léon-Robert 1958–9, 'L'abbaye bénédictine de la Trinité de Mileto, en Calabre, à l'époque normande', *Bullettino dell'Archivio Paleografico Italiano*, n.s., 4–5: 9–94 and plates 1–3.

Ménager, Léon-Robert 1959, 'L'institution monarchique dans les États normands d'Italie. Contribution à l'étude du pouvoir royal dans les principautés occidentales, aux XIe–XIIe siècles', *Cahiers de civilisation médiévale* 2: 303–31, 445–68.

Ménager, Léon-Robert 1960, *Amiratus – Ἀμερας. L'émirat et les origines de l'amirauté (XIe – XIIIe siècles)*, Bibliothèque générale de l'École pratique des hautes études, Paris.

Ménager, Léon-Robert 1975, 'Inventaire des familles normandes et franques émigrées en Italie méridionale et en Sicile (XIe–XIIe siècles)', in *Roberto il Guiscardo*, pp.259–390. (Reprinted in Ménager, Léon-Robert 1981, *Hommes et institutions dans l'Italie normande*, Variorum Collected Studies, no.136, London.)

Ménager, Léon-Robert 1981a, 'Additions à l'Inventaire des familles normandes et franques émigrées en Italie méridionale et en Sicile', in *Hommes et institutions dans l'Italie normande*, London, pp.IV.1–17.

Ménager, Léon-Robert (ed.) 1981b, *Recueil des actes des ducs normands d'Italie (1046–1127). Vol. I: Les premiers ducs (1046–1087)*, Società di storia patria per la Puglia: Documenti e monografie, no.45, Bari.

Mercati, Silvio Giuseppe 1939, 'Sulle reliquie del monastero di Santa Maria del Patire presso Rossano', *ASCL* 9: 1–14. (Reprinted his *Collecteana Byzantina*, ed. Longo, Augusta Acconcia, 2 vols, Bari, 1970, vol.2, pp.395–408.)

Messina 1994, *Messina: il ritorno della memoria. Messina, Palazzo Zanca, 1 marzo – 28 aprile 1994*, Palermo, 1994.

Metcalfe, Alex 1999, 'Arabic-speakers in Norman Sicily', D.Phil. thesis, Department of Arabic and Middle Eastern Studies, University of Leeds, 1999.

Metcalfe, Alex 2002 (forthcoming), *Muslims and Christians in 'Norman' Sicily: Arabic-speakers and the end of Islam*, Curzon.

Migliorini, Bruno 1968, 'Il tipo sintattico "camminare riva riva"', in Cesare Segre (ed.) *Linguistica e Filologia. Omaggio a Benvenuto Terracini*, Milan, pp.185–90. (Reprinted in Migliorini, Bruno 1973, *Lingua di oggi e di ieri*, Caltanisetta and Rome, pp.313–19.)

Monés, Hieras 1975, 'D̲jawhar al-Siḳillī', in *E.I.*[2] vol.II, pp.494–5.

Mongitore, Antonino 1721, *Monumenta historica sacrae domus mansioni SS. Trinitatis militaris ordinis theutonicorum urbis Panormi*, Palermo.

Mongitore, Antonino 1734, *Bullae, Privilegia, et Instrumenta Panormitanae Metropolitanae Ecclesiae, Regni Siciliae Primariae, Collecta, Notisque Illustrata*, Palermo.

Monneret de Villard, Ugo 1950, *Le pitture musulmane al soffitto della Cappella Palatina in Palermo*, Rome.

Montesquiou-Fezensac, Blaise comte de and Gaborit-Chopin, Danielle 1973–7, *Le Trésor de Saint-Denis*, 2 vols, Paris.

de Montfaucon, Bernard 1708, *Palaeographia Graeca*, Paris.

Morimoto, Kosei 1981, *The fiscal administration of Egypt in the early Islamic period*, Asian Historical Monographs, no.1, Kyoto.

Morony, Michael G. 1974, 'Religious communities in late Sassanian and early Muslim Iraq', *JESHO* 17: 113–35.

Morony, Michael G. 1984, *Iraq after the Muslim conquest*, Princeton, New Jersey.

Morso, Salvatore 1842, 'Memoria sulla chiesa di S. Maria l'Ammiraglio in Palermo', in Capozzo, Guglielmo (ed.) *Memorie su la Sicilia*, 5 vols, Palermo, 1842, 3: 335–49.

Mortillaro, Vincenzo 1843, 'Catalogo ragionato dei diplomi esistenti nel tabulario della metropolitana chiesa di Palermo', in *Opere*, 9 vols, Palermo, vol.I, pp.155–490.

Mortillaro, Vincenzo 1858, 'Elenco chronologico delle antiche pergamene pertinenti alla real chiesa della Magione', in *Opere*, 9 vols, Palermo, vol.VII, pp.i–xix, 1–305.

al-Muqaddasī, Abū ᶜAbd Allāh Muḥammad ibn Aḥmad 1906, *Kitāb aḥsan al-taqāsim*, 2nd edn, ed. Michael Jan de Goeje, BGA, Leiden.

Muratori, Ludovico Antonio (ed.) 1738–42, *Antiquitates Italicae Medii Aevi*, 6 vols, Milan.

al-Musabbiḥī, Muḥammad ibn ᶜUbayd Allāh ibn Aḥmad 1978–84, *Akhbār Miṣr. Tome quarantième de la Chronique d'Egypte de Musabbiḥī*, ed. Ayman Fuʾād Sayyid, Thierry Bianquis and Ḥusayn Naṣṣār, 2 vols, Institut français d'archéologie orientale du Caire: Textes arabes et études islamiques, vol.40, Cairo.

al-Nābulusī, Abū ᶜAmr ᶜUthmān ibn Ibrāhīm 1958–60, *Kitāb lumaᶜ al-qawānīn al-muḍīya fī dawāwīn al-diyār al-miṣrīya*, ed. Carl H. Becker and Claude Cahen, in *Bulletin d'études orientales de l'Institut française à Damas* 16: 119–34 and ١–٧٨.

Nagel, Tilman 1972, *Frühe Ismailiya und Fatimiden im Lichte der Risālat iftitāḥ al-daᶜwa. Eine religionsgeschichtliche Studie*, Bonner Orientalistische Studien, n.s, no.23, Bonn.

Nania, Gioacchino 1995, *Toponomastica e topografia storica nelle valli del Belice e dello Jato*, Palermo.

Nef, Annliese 2000, 'Conquêtes et reconquêtes médiévales: la Sicile normande est-elle une terre de réduction en servitude généralisée?', *Mélanges de l'École Française de Rome (Moyen Âge)* 112: 579–607.

Nicolas de Jamsilla 1726, *De rebus gestis Frederici II, Imperatoris ejusque filiorum Conradi et Manfredi Apuliae et Siciliae regum*, in Muratori, Ludovico Antonio (ed.), *Rerum Italicarum Scriptores*, 25 vols, ed. Filippo Argellati, Milan, 1723–51, vol.VIII, cols 489–616.

Nicolas de Jamsilla 1868, *De rebus gestis Frederici II, Imperatoris ejusque filiorum Conradi et Manfredi Apuliae et Siciliae regum*, in *Cronisti e scrittori sincroni napoletani*, ed. Giuseppe Del Re, 2 vols, Naples, 1845–68, vol.II, pp.101–200.

Nielson, Jørgen S. 1990, 'Maẓālim', in *E.I.*^{2} vol. VI, pp.933–5.

Niese, Hans 1910, *Die Gesetzgebung der normannischen Dynastie im Regnum Siciliae*, Halle.

Nitti Di Vito, Francesco 1900–6, *Le pergamene di S. Nicolo di Bari, 939–1266*, 3 vols, Commissione provinciale di archeologia e storia patria, Codice diplomatico barese, vols 4–6, Bari.

Noth, Albrecht 1977, 'Die arabischen Urkunden der Normannenherrscher Süditaliens und Siziliens. Ein vorläufiger Überblick', in *XIX Deutscher Orientalistentag 1975*, Zeitschrift der Deutschen Morgenländischen Gesellschaft, Supplement 3(1), pp.567–71.

Noth, Albrecht 1978 'Die arabischen Dokumente Roger II', in Brühl 1978, pp.217–61. (The revised Italian version, Noth 1983, is to be preferred.)

Noth, Albrecht 1981–82, 'Osservazioni sull'edizione dei documenti arabe dei re di Sicilia', in *Congresso Internazionale sulle Fonti documentarie e narrative per la storia della Sicilia normanna. Palermo, Dicembre 1980 = AASLAP*, 5th ser., 1(2): 121–9.

Noth, Albrecht 1983, 'I documenti arabi di Ruggero II', in Brühl 1983, pp.189–222.

al-Nuwayrī, Shihāb al-Dīn Aḥmad ibn ᶜAbd al-Wahhāb 1923–92, *Nihāyat al-arab fī funūn al-adab*, 31 vols, Cairo.

Oikonomides, Nicolas 1972, *Les listes des préséances byzantines des IXe et Xe siècles*, Paris.

Ordericus Vitalis 1969–80, *Historia ecclesiastica*, ed. and trans. Marjorie Chibnall, 6 vols, Oxford Medieval Texts, Oxford.

Ostrogorsky, George 1928, 'Die ländliche Steuergemeinde des byzantinischen Reiches im X Jahrhundert', *Vierteljahrschrift für Sozial- und Wirtschaftsgeschichte* 20: 1–108.

Ostrogorsky, George 1954, *Pour l'histoire de la féodalité byzantine*, Corpus Bruxellense Historiae Byzantinae, Subsidia 1, Brussels.

Ostrogorsky, George 1956, *Quelques problèmes d'histoire de la paysannerie byzantine*, Corpus Bruxellense Historiae Byzantinae, Subsidia 2, Brussels.

Oxford Dictionary of Byzantium 1991, ed. Alexander P. Khazhdan *et al.*, 3 vols, New York and Oxford.

Panofsky, Erwin 1979, *Abbot Suger on the abbey church of St Denis and its art treasures*, ed. Gerda Panofsky-Soergel, Princeton.

Pellitteri, Antonino 1994, 'The historical-ideological framework of Islamic Fāṭimid Sicily (fourth/tenth century) with reference to the works of the Qāḍī l-Nuᶜmān' *Al-Masāq* 7: 111–63.

Peter of Blois 1855, *Opera Omnia*, ed. Jean-Paul Migne, *Patrologia Latina*, vol.207, Paris.

Peter of Eboli 1904, *Petri Ansolini de Ebulo 'De Rebus Siculis Carmen'*, ed. Ettore Rota, RIS, 2nd ser., vol.31, Città del Castello.

Peter of Eboli 1906, *'Liber ad honorem Augusti' di Pietro da Eboli (sec. XII) secondo il cod. 120 della Biblioteca Civica di Berna*, ed. Gian-Battista Siragusa, 2 vols, FSI, vol.39, Rome.

Peter of Eboli 1994, *Liber ad honorem Augusti sive de rebus Siculis: Codex 120 II der Burgerbibliothek Bern; eine Bilderchronik der Stauferzeit*, ed. Theo Kölzer and Marlis Stähli, Sigmaringen.

Pétit, Louis and Korablev, B. (Vasily Nikolaevich) 1911, *Actes de Chilandar*. Actes de l'Athos, no.5 = *Buzantine Khronika* 17.

Pirri, Rocco 1733, *Sicilia sacra disquisitionibus et notitiis illustrata*, ed. Antonio Mongitore and Vito Maria Amico, 2 vols, Palermo.

Pontieri, Ernesto 1955, 'La madre di re Ruggero: Adelaide del Vasto, contessa di Sicilia, regina di gerusalemme (?–1118)', in *Studi Ruggeriani*, vol.II, pp.327–432.

Powell, James M. 1971, *The 'Liber Augustalis' or Constitutions of Melfi promulgated by the emperor Frederick II for the kingdom of Sicily in 1231*, Syracuse, New York.

Pratesi, Alessandro 1958, *Carte latine di abbazie calabresi provenienti dall'Archivio Aldobrandini*, Studi e Testi, vol.197, Vatican City.

Prawer, Joshua 1985, 'Social classes in the Crusader States: the "Minorities"', in Setton, Kenneth M., Zacour, Norman P., and Hazard, Harry W. (eds) *A History of the Crusades. Volume 5: The impact of the Crusades on the Near East*, Madison, Wisconsin, pp.59–115.

Prosperi, Cecilia 1996, 'Il restauro del Mandato di Adelasia', *Quaderni della Scuola di Archivistica Paleografia e Diplomatica (Archivio di Stato di Palermo) Studi e Strumenti* 1: 7–17.

Pryor, John H. 1982, 'Transportation of horses by sea during the era of the Crusades: eighth century to 1285 A.D.', *The Mariner's Mirror* 68: 9–27, 103–25.

al-Qāḍī l-Nuᶜmān ibn Muḥammad 1978, *Kitāb al-majālis wa-l-musāyarāt*, ed. al-Ḥabīb al-Faqī, Ibrāhīm Shabbūḥ and Muḥammad al-Yaᶜlāwī, Tunis.

al-Qalqashandī, Abū ᶜAbbās Aḥmad 1913–72, *Ṣubḥ al-aᶜshā fī ṣināᶜat al-inshāʾ*, 14 vols and Index, Cairo.

Rabie, Hassanein 1972, *The financial system of Egypt, A.H. 564–741 / A.D. 1169–1341*, London Oriental Series, no.25, London.

Regii Neapolitani Archivii Monumenta 1845–61, 6 vols in 2, Naples.

Richard, Jean 1985, 'Agricultural conditions in the Crusader States', in Setton, Kenneth M., Zacour, Norman P. and Hazard, Harry W. (eds) *A history of the Crusades. Volume 5: The impact of the Crusades on the Near East*, Madison, Wisconsin, pp.251–94.

Richards, Donald S. 1973, 'A Fāṭimid petition and a "small decree" from Sinai', *Israel Oriental Studies* 3: 140–58.

Richards, Donald S. 1977, 'A Mamlūk petition and a report from the *Dīwān al-Jaysh*', *BSOAS* 60: 1–14.

Richards, Donald S. 1978, 'A text of ᶜImād al-Dīn on 12th-century Frankish-Muslim relations', *Arabica* 25: 202–04.

Richards, Donald S. 1998, 'Some Muslim and Christian documents from Sinai concerning Christian property', in Vermeulen, U. and Van Reeth, J.M.F. (eds) *Law, Christianity and Modernism in Islamic Society. Proceedings of the Eighteenth Congress of the Union Européenne des Arabisants et Islamisants held at the Katholieke Universiteit Leuven (September 3 – September 9, 1996)*, Orientalia Lovaniensia Analecta 86, pp.161–70.

Richards, Donald S. 1999, 'A late Mamluk document concerning Frankish commercial practice at Tripoli', *BSOAS* 62: 21–35.

Richardson, Henry Gerald 1943, *The Memoranda roll for the Michaelmas term of the first year of the reign of king John (1199–1200)*, The Publications of the Pipe Roll Society, vol.59 (n.s., vol.21), London.

Richardson, Henry Gerald and Sayles, George Osborne 1963, *The Governance of medieval England from the Conquest to Magna Carta*, Edinburgh.

Riley-Smith, Jonathon 1977, 'The survival in Latin Palestine of Muslim administration', in Holt, Peter M. (ed.), *The Eastern Mediterranean Lands in the Period of the Crusades*, Warminster, pp.9–22.

Riley-Smith, Jonathon 1987, *The Crusades. A Short History*, London.

Riley-Smith, Jonathon 1997, 'King Fulk of Jerusalem and the "Sultan of Babylon"', in Kedar, Benjamin Z., Riley-Smith, Jonathon and Hiestand, Rudolf (eds) *Montjoie. Studies in Crusade history in honour of Hans Eberhard Mayer*, Aldershot, pp.55–66.

Rizzitano, Umberto 1960, 'Ibn Ḳalāḳis', in *E.I.*² vol.III, pp.814–15.

Rizzitano, Umberto 1968, 'Ibn al-Ḥawwās', in *E.I.*² vol.III, pp.788.

Rizzitano, Umberto 1969, 'Ibn al-Thumna', *E.I.*² vol.III, pp.956.

Roberto il Guiscardo e il suo tempo. (Bari, maggio 1973), Centro di studi normanno-svevi, Università degli Studi di Bari: Relazioni e comunicazioni nelle prime giornate normanno-sveve [and Fonti e studi del *Corpus membranarum italicarum*, no.11], Rome, 1975. (Reprinted Bari 1991.)

Rollus Rubeus 1972, *Rollus Rubeus: privilegia ecclesiae cephaleditane, a diversis regibus et imperatoribus concessa, recollecta et in hoc volumine scripta*, ed. Corrado Mirto, Società siciliana per la storia patria: Documenti per servire alla storia di Sicilia, ser.1, vol. 29, Palermo.

Romuald of Salerno 1935, *Chronicon*, ed. Carlo Alberto Garufi, RIS, 2nd ser., vol.8, Bologna.

Round, John Horace 1895, *Feudal England. Historical studies on the XIth and XIIth centuries*, London.

Rousseau, Alphonse 1852, 'Voyage du scheikh et-Tidjani dans la régence de Tunis, pendant les années 706, 707 et 708 de l'hégire (1306–1309) [part 1]', *JA*, 4th ser., 20: 57–208.

Rousseau, Alphonse 1853, 'Voyage du scheikh et-Tidjani dans la régence de Tunis, pendant les années 706, 707 et 708 de l'hégire (1306–1309) [part 2]', *JA*, 5th. ser., 1: 101–68, 354–425.

Ruggero il gran conte e l'inizio dello stato normanno (Bari, maggio 1975), Centro di studi normanno-svevi, Università degli Studi di Bari: Relazioni e comunicazioni nelle seconde giornate normanno-sveve [and Fonti e studi del *Corpus membranarum italicarum*, no.12], Rome, 1977. (Reprinted Bari, 1991.)

Russell, Dorothea 1964, 'Are there any remains of the Fāṭimid palaces of Cairo?', *Journal of the American Research Center in Egypt* 3: 115–21.

Rymer, Thomas 1816–69, *Foedera, conventiones, litterae, et cujuscunque generis acta publica, etc.*, 4 vols in 7 parts, London.

al-Ṣafadī, Khalīl ibn Aybak 1931–, *Kitāb al-wāfī bi-l-wafayāt. Das biographische Lexikon des Ṣalāḥaddīn Ḫalīl Aibak aṣ-Ṣafadī*, ed. Hellmut Ritter *et al.*, 29 vols to date, Bibliotheca Islamica, no.6, Leipzig, and Wiesbaden (since 1959).

Saint-Denis 1991, *Le Trésor de Saint-Denis. Musée du Louvre, Paris, 12 mars – 17 juin 1991*, Paris.

Sanders, Paula 1994, *Ritual, politics, and the city in Fatimid Cairo*, State University of New York Series in Medieval Middle East History, Albany, New York.

Sauvaire, Henri 1886, 'Matériaux pour servir à l'histoire de la numismatique et de la métrologie musulmanes: troisième partie – mesures de capacité', *JA*, 8th ser., 7: 124–77.

Sayyid, Ayman Fuʾād 'Le grand palais fatimide au Caire', in Barrucand 1999, pp.117–25.

Scaduto, Mario 1947, *Il monachismo basiliano nella Sicilia medievale. Rinascita e decadenza secc. XI–XIV*, Storia e letteratura, no.18, Rome.

Scalia, Giuseppe 1961, 'Nuove considerazioni storiche e paleografiche sui documenti dell'Archivio capitolare di Catania per il ristabilimento della sede vescovile nel 1091', *ASSO* 57: 5–53.

Scarcia Amoretti, Biancamaria (ed.) 1995, *Del nuovo sulla Sicilia musulmana (Roma, 3 maggio 1993)*, Accademia Nazionale dei Lincei: Fondazione Leone Caetani, Giornata di Studio, no.26, Rome.

Scaturro, Ignazio 1924–5, *Storia della città di Sciacca e dei comuni della contrada saccense fra il Belice e il Platani*, 2 vols, Naples.

Schacht, Josef 1956, 'Amān', in *E.I.²* vol.I, pp.429–30.

Schacht, Josef 1957, 'Droit byzantin et droit musulman', in *Atti del convegno di scienze morali, storiche e filologiche. Oriente ed occidente nel medioevo (Accademia nazionale dei Lincei, Rome, 27 maggio – 1 giugno, 1956)*, pp.197–218.

Schack, Dietlinde 1969, 'Die Araber im Reich Rogers II', 2 vols, Doctoral thesis, Berlin University.

Scheffer-Boichorst, Paul 1897, 'Die Vorbilder für Friedrichs II *Constitutio de resignandis privilegiis*', *Historische Studien*, 8: Zur Geschichte des XII und XIII Jahrhunderts. Diplomatische Forschungen, pp.244–9.

Scheffer-Boichorst, Paul 1900, 'Das Gesetz Kaiser Friedrichs II "De resignandis privilegiis"', *Sitzungsberichte der königlichen preußischen. Akademie der Wissenschaften zu Berlin Jahrg. 1900* 14: 132–52. (Reprinted in *Historische Studien* 43 (1905): Gesammelte Schriften von Paul Scheffer-Boichorst, vol.2, pp.248–73.)

Schiaparelli, Celestino 1871, *Vocabulista in arabico pubblicato per la prima volta sopra un codice della Biblioteca Riccardiana di Firenze*, Florence.

Schimmel, Annemarie 1997, *Islamic Names*, Edinburgh.

Schipa, Michelangelo 1883, 'Elenco delle pergamene già appartenenti alla famiglia Fusco [part 1]', *ASPN* 8: 153–61, 332–8, 775–87. (Part 2 in *ASPN* 12 (1887): 156–64, 436–48, 705–9, 822–35.)

Sciascia, Laura 1989, 'I cammelli e le rose. Gli Abbate di Trapani da Federico II a Martino il vecchio', in *Mediterraneo medievale: scritti in onore di Francesco Giunta*, 3 vols, Soveria Mannelli, vol.III, pp.1173–230.

al-Shābbī, Muḥammad Masᶜūd 1968, 'Taqrīru mukhtaṣaru ḥawla l-ḥafrīyāti l-jārīyati bi-Raqqāda', *Africa. Fouilles, monuments et collections archéologiques en Tunisie*, 2: 349–50, 392^5–88^9 (sic!) and plates. (Arabic: 'A short report about the current excavations at Raqqāda'. French summary.)

Shalem, Avinoam 1999, 'The rock-crystal lionhead in the Badisches Landesmuseum in Karlsruhe', in Barrucand (ed.), pp.359–66.

Simonsen, Jørgen Bæk 1988, *Studies in the genesis and early development of the caliphal taxation system*, Copenhagen.

Simonsohn, Shlomo 1997, *The Jews in Sicily. Volume 1: 383–1300*, Studia Post-Biblica, Leiden, New York and Cologne.

Sinding-Larsen, Staale 1989, 'Plura ordinantur ad unum. Some perspectives regarding the "Arab-Islamic" ceiling of the Cappella Palatina at Palermo (1132–1143)', *Institutum Romanum Norvegiae, Acta ad archaeologiam et artium historiam pertinentia* 7: 55–96.

Soudan, Frédérique 1990, 'Al-Mahdiyya et son histoire d'après le récit de voyage d'al-Tiğānī', *Revue des études islamiques* 58: 135–88.

Sourdel, Dominique 1959–60, *Le vizirat ᶜAbbāside de 749 à 936 (132 à 324 de l'Hégire)*, 2 vols, Damascus.

Sourdel, Dominique 1963, 'Al-Djardjarāʾī (4)', in *E.I.*[2] vol.II, p.462.

Spata, Giuseppe (ed.) 1862, *Le Pergamene greche esistenti nel Grande Archivio di Palermo*, Palermo.

Spata, Giuseppe 1871, 'Diplomi greci siciliani inediti (ultima serie) tradotti e pubblicati', *Miscellanea di Storia Italiana* 12: 5–112.

Spatafora, Francesca 1995, 'Resti di età medievale a Monte Maranfusa', in Di Stefano, Carmela Angela and Cadei, Antonio (eds) *Federico e la Sicilia dalla terra alla corona, archeologia e architettura*, ed. Palermo, pp.162–7.

Spatafora, Francesca, Denaro, Massimo and Brunazzi, Valeria 1997, 'Il Castello di Calatrasi', in Di Stefano, Carmela Angela, *Archeologia e Territorio*, Palermo, pp.391–410.

Spatafora, Francesca and Fresina, Adriana 1993, 'Monte Maranfusa', in *Di Terra in Terra. Nuove scoperte archeologiche nella provincia di Palermo. Museo Archeologico Regionale di Palermo, 18 aprile 1991*, Palermo, pp.3–26.

Starrabba, Raffaele 1876–90, *I diplomi della Cattedrale di Messina raccolti da Antonino Amico*, DPSASDS, 1st ser., vol.1, Palermo.

Starrabba, Raffaele 1893, 'Contributo allo studio della diplomatica siciliana dei tempi normanni: Diplomi di fondazione delle chiese episcopali di Sicilia (1082–1093)', *ASS*, n.s., 18: 30–135.

Stern, Samuel Miklos 1956, 'An original document of the Fāṭimid chancery concerning Italian merchants', in *Studi orientalistici in onore di Giorgio Levi Della Vida*, Rome, pp.529–38 and plates. (Reprinted in Stern 1986.)

Stern, Samuel Miklos 1962, 'Three Petitions of the Fatimid Period', *Oriens* 15: 172–209. (Reprinted in Stern 1986.)

Stern, Samuel Miklos 1964a, *Fatimid Decrees. Original Documents from the Fatimid Chancery*, All Souls Studies, no.3, London.

Stern, Samuel Miklos 1964b, 'Petitions from the Ayyūbid period', *BSOAS* 27: 1–32. (Reprinted Stern 1986.)

Stern, Samuel Miklos 1965, 'Two Ayyūbid decrees from Sinai', in *Documents from Islamic chanceries*, Oxford Oriental Studies 3, pp.9–38. (Reprinted in Stern 1986.)

Stern, Samuel Miklos 1966, 'Petitions from the Mamlūk period', *BSOAS* 29: 233–76. (Reprinted in Stern 1986.)

Stern, Samuel Miklos 1970, 'Tarì. The quarter dinar', *Studi Medievali*, 3rd ser., 11(1): 177–207.

Stern, Samuel Miklos 1986, *Coins and documents from the medieval Middle East*, Variorum Reprints, London.

Studi Ruggeriani 1955. *VIII Centenario della morte di Ruggero II. Atti del Convegno internazionale di studi ruggeriani (Palermo, 21–25 aprile 1954)*, 2 vols, Palermo.

Svoronos, Nicos G. 1959, 'Recherches sur le cadastre byzantin et la fiscalité aux XIe et XIIe siècles: le cadastre de Thèbes', *Bulletin de Correspondence Hellenique* 83: 1–166. (Reprinted in Svoronos, Nicos G. 1973, *Études sur l'organisation intérieure, la société et l'économie de l'empire byzantin*, London.)

Tabacco, Giovanni 1985, 'Il potere politico nel Mezzogiorno d'Italia dalla conquista normanna alla dominazione aragonese', in De Leo, Pietro (ed.) *Il Mezzogiorno medievale nella storiografia del secondo dopoguerra: risultati e prospettive. Atti del IV Convegno Nazionale dell'Associazione dei Medievalisti Italiani (Università di Calabria, 12–16 giugno 1982)*, Soveria Mannelli, pp.65–111.

Takayama, Hiroshi 1985, 'The financial and administrative organization of the Norman kingdom of Sicily', *Viator* 16: 129–57.

Takayama, Hiroshi 1993, *The administration of the Norman kingdom of Sicily*, Leiden.

Talbi, Mohamed 1960, 'Ibn Shaddād', in *E.I.*[2] vol.III, p.933.

Talbi, Mohamed 1966, *L'Émirat aghlabide, 184–296/800–909: histoire politique*, Paris.

al-Tījānī, Abū Muḥammad ᶜAbd Allāh ibn Aḥmad 1958, *Riḥlat al-Tījānī*, ed. Ḥasan Ḥ. ᶜAbd al-Wahhāb, Tunis.

Tisserant, Eugène and Wiet, Gaston 1926, 'Une lettre de l'almohade Murtaḍᶜâ au pape Innocent IV', *Hespéris* 6: 27–53.

Toru, Miura and Philips, John Edward (eds) 2000, *Slave elites in the Middle East and Africa*, London and New York.

Tramontana, Salvatore 1986, *La monarchia normanna e sveva*, Turin.

Trasselli, Carmelo 1965, 'Un giudice palermitano del duecento', *Economia e Storia* 12(3): 337–43.

Travaini, Lucia 1995, *La monetazione nell'Italia normanna*, Istituto storico italiano per il Medio Evo: Nuovi studi storici, no.28, Rome.

Tricoli, Giuseppe 1994, 'I privilegi di Messina nella storia della città e della Sicilia', in *Messina* 1994, pp.403–20.

Trinchera, Francesco 1865, *Syllabus graecarum membranarum*, Naples.

Trovato, Gaetano 1949, *Sopravvivenze arabe in Sicilia*, Monreale. (Reprinted in Arezzo, F. G. 1950, *Sicilia. Miscellanea di studi storici, giuridici ed economici sulla Sicilia, glossario di voci siciliane derivate dal greco, latino, arabo, spagnuolo, francese, tedesco, etc.*, Palermo.)

Turki, Abdel–Magid 1984, 'Consultation juridique d'al-Imān al-Māzari sur le cas des musulmans vivant en Sicile sous l'autorité des Normands', *Mélanges de l'Université Saint-Joseph* 50(2): 691–704.

Turki, Abdel–Magid 1992, 'Pour ou contre la légalité du séjour des musulmans au territoire reconquis par les chrétiens: justification doctrinale et réalité historique', in Lewis,

Bernard and Niewöhner, Friedrich (eds) *Religionsgespräche im Mittelalter*, Wolfenbütteler Mittelalter-Studien, vol.4, Mainz, pp.305–23.
Udovitch, Abraham L. 1981, *The Islamic Middle East 700–1900: studies in economic and social history*, Princeton, New Jersey.
Udovitch, Abraham L. 1995, 'New materials for the history of Islamic Sicily', in Scarcia Amoretti 1995, pp.183–210.
Ughelli, Fernando 1717–21, *Italia sacra*, revised and enlarged 2nd edn, ed. Nicola Coleti, 10 vols in 6, Venice.
Varvaro, Alberto 1981, *Lingua e storia in Sicilia (dalle guerre puniche alla conquista normanna)*, 1 vol. to date, Palermo.
Varvaro, Alberto 1986, *Vocabolario etimologico siciliano. Volume I (A–L)*, Centro di studi filologici e linguistici siciliani: Lessici siciliani, no.3, Palermo.
Varvaro, Pietro 1905, 'Giuseppe Vella e i suoi falsi codici arabi con un documento inedito', *ASS*, n.s., 30: 321–32
Wansbrough, John 1963, 'A Mamluk ambassador to Venice in 913/1507', *BSOAS* 26: 503–30.
Wansbrough, John 1965a, 'A Mamlūk commercial treaty concluded with the Republic of Florence 894/1489', in Stern, Samuel Miklos (ed.), *Documents from Islamic chanceries*, Oxford Oriental Studies 3, pp.39–79.
Wansbrough, John 1965b, 'Venice and Florence in the Mamluk commercial privileges', *BSOAS* 28: 483–523.
Wansbrough, John 1967, 'A Judaeo-Arabic document from Sicily', *BSOAS* 30: 305–13.
Wansbrough, John 1971, 'The Safe-conduct in Muslim chancery practice', *BSOAS* 34: 20–35.
Wansbrough, John 1984, 'Diplomatica siciliana', *BSOAS* 47: 10–21.
al-Wansharīshī,Aḥmad ibn Yaḥyā 1981–3, *al-Miʿyār al-muʿrib wa-l-jāmiʿ al-mughrib ʿan fatāwa ahl Ifrīqīya wa-l-Andalus wa-l-Maghrib*, 13 vols, Beirut.
Warren, Wilfred Lewis 1984, 'The myth of Norman administrative efficiency', *Transactions of the Royal Historical Society*, 5th ser., 34: 113–32.
White, Jr, Lynn Townsend 1933, 'The Charters of St. Michael's in Mazzara', *La Révue Bénédictine* 45: 234–41.
White Jr, Lynn Townsend 1938, *Latin monasticism in Norman Sicily*, The Medieval Academy of America: Monographs, no.13, Cambridge, Mass.
Wieruszowski, Helene 1963, 'Roger II of Sicily, "Rex-Tyrannus", in twelfth-century political thought', *Speculum* 38: 46–78. (Reprinted in Wieruszowski, Helene 1971, *Politics and culture in medieval Spain and Italy*, Storia e letteratura, Raccolta di studi e testi, no.121, Rome, pp.3–97).
Wiet, Gaston 1955, 'al-Afḍal b. Badr al-D̲j̲amālī', in *E.I.*^{2} vol.I, pp.215–16.
Wiet, Gaston 1961, *Le Grandeur de l'Islam*, Mayenne.
William of Apulia 1961, *La Geste de Robert Guiscard*, ed. and trans. M. Matthieu, Istituto siciliano di studi bizantini e neoellenici: Testi e Monumenti, no.4, Palermo.
William of Tyre 1943, *A History of deeds done beyond the sea*, ed. and trans. Krey, Emily Atwater and Babcock, August Charles, 2 vols, Columbia University Records of Civilisation, no.35, New York.
William of Tyre 1986, *Chronicon*, ed. Huygens, Robert B.C., Mayer, Hans E., and Rösch, Gerhard, 2 vols, Corpus Christianorum Continuatio Mediaevalis, nos. 63–63A, Turnholt.
Williams, Ann 1995, *The English and the Norman conquest*, Woodbridge.

Wilson, Roger J.A. 1990, *Sicily under the Roman Empire: the archaeology of a Roman province, 36BC–AD535*, Warminster.

Winkelmann, Eduard 1878, 'Reisefrüchte aus Italien und anderes zur deutsch-italienischen Geschichte', *Forschungen zur Deutschen Geschichte* 18: 469–92.

Winkelmann, Eduard 1880–85, *Acta imperii inedita seculi XIII et XIV. Urkunden und Briefe zur Geschichte des Kaiserreichs und Königsreichs Sizilien in den Jahren 1198 bis 1273*, 2 vols, Innsbruck.

Winkler, Hans Alexander 1934, *Bauern zwischen Wasser und Wüste*, Stuttgart.

Wüstenfeld, Ferdinand 1879, *Calcashandis Geographie und Verwaltung von Ägypten*, Abhandlungen der königlichen Gesellschaft der Wissenschaften zu Göttingen: Historisch-philologische Classe, vol.25, Göttingen.

Yāqūt al-Rūmī, Shahāb al-Dīn Abū ᶜAbd Allāh 1866–73, *Kitāb muᶜjam al-buldān*, ed. Ferdinand Wüstenfeld, 6 vols, Leipzig.

al-Zabīdī, Muḥammad al-Murtaḍa ibn Muḥammad 1889–90, *Tāj al-ᶜarūs*, 10 vols, Cairo.

Zaccagni, Gaia 1996, 'Il *Bios* di San Bartolomeo da Simeri (BHG 235)', *Rivista di studi bizantini e neoellenici*, n.s., 33: 193–274.

Zeitler, Barbara 1996, '"*Urbs felix dotata populo trilingui*": some thoughts about a twelfth-century funerary memorial from Palermo', *Medieval Encounters* 2: 114–39.

Zeldes, N. and Frankel, M. 1997, 'Trade with Sicily – Jewish Merchants in Mediterranean Trade in the 12th and 13th Centuries', *Michael* 14: 89–137 (Hebrew). (English version: 'The Sicilian trade – Jewish merchants in the Mediterranean in the twelfth and thirteenth centuries', in Bucaria, Nicolò (ed.) 1998, *Gli Ebrei in Sicilia dal tardoantico al medioevo. Studi in onore di mons. Benedetto Rocco*, Palermo, pp.243–56.)

Zielinski, Herbert (ed.) 1982, *Tancredi et Willelmi III regum diplomata*, Codex diplomaticus Regni Siciliae: ser.1, Diplomata regum et principum e gente normannorum, vol.5, Cologne and Vienna.

Index

As a rule, Arabic names have been entered under the name *ism* – *e.g.* Abū l-Qāsim Muḥammad ibn Ḥammūd is entered under 'Muḥammad' – but, because of the inevitable exceptions – *e.g.* names where the agnomen (*kunya* – *e.g.* Abū l-Sayyid) is preserved but not the *ism*; and names of individuals who are most familiar by their name of relation (*nisba* – *e.g.* al-Māzarī) or by their lineage name (*nasab* – e.g. Ibn al-Athīr etc.) – the reader should search the index for an unfamiliar name under more than one of its elements. Names common in the modern English repertoire have generally been entered under their standard English form, rather than their Arabic, Greek, or Latin version – *e.g.* Philip, not *Fīlib*, *Filippos*, or *Philippus* – but there are exceptions. The names of villeins from the *jarā'id* have not been indexed. Some common placenames have been Anglicised – *e.g.* Syracuse – but most are given in their modern Italian version – *e.g.* Palermo, not *Balārm*, *Panormos*, or *Panormus*. The names of estates, farms, and villages, however, have generally been left in the original, and not modernised (*e.g.* Jāliṣū, not Cangialeso), but again there are exceptions. All placenames in southern Italy and Sicily are followed by the standard abbreviation for the modern province in which they are located (*see List of Abbreviations*).

ʿAbbāsid caliphs of Baghdad, 14–15, 16, 258, 278, 293
Abbate
  Enrico, officer of Frederick II, 242 & n.138, 246
  Giliberto, son of Enrico, governor of Malta under Frederick II, 242 n.138
  Palmerio, governor of Pantelleria and Favignana, 242 n.138
ʿAbd Allāh ibn Abī Bakr al-Hawwārī, witness to **Private 6**, 317
ʿAbd Allāh ibn Abī l-Qāsim al-Anṣārī, witness to **Private 6**, 317
ʿAbd Allāh ibn Muḥammad al-Būnī, witness to **Private 29**, 324
ʿAbd Allāh ibn ʿUthmān al-Ghāfir(?), witness to **Private 19**, 321
ʿAbd Allāh al-Mahdī, first Fāṭimid caliph (909–34), 19, 20, 21
ʿAbd Allāh al-Murāhiq ibn Abī l-Qāsim ibn ʿAbd Allāh al-ʿAṭṭār, vendor in **Private 6**, 316–17
ʿAbd Allāh al-Naṣrānī, *see* Christodoulos
ʿAbd Allāh, slave of the chamber under Frederick II, 245 & n.164
ʿAbd al-ʿAzīz ibn Juwān, the son of Iōannēs Endoulsi (*i.e.* al-Andalusī), husband of Christodoulēs, vendor in **Private 22**, 321
ʿAbd al-ʿAzīz *al-mu'addib* ('the [Qur'ānic] teacher') ibn al-Sabʿ ibn Abī l-Qāsim al-Tamīmī, witness to **Private 5**, 316
ʿAbd al-Ghanī ibn Ibrāhīm al-Lawātī, witness in **Private 1**, 315

ʿAbd al-Ghanī ibn Yūsuf al-Hawwārī(?) (*Abdelgani filius Jusuph hegueri*), witness to **Private 3**, 315
ʿAbd al-Ḥayy(?) ibn Jabr al-Anṣārī (*Habdeleauy filius Gebyr Elensari*), witness to **Private 3**, 316
ʿAbd al-Karīm, agent of Muriella of Petterrana, 73
ʿAbd al-Karīm ibn Abī Bakr al-Anṣārī (*Habdelkerim filius Bubiker Elinsari*), witness to **Private 3**, 316
ʿAbd al-Masīḥ, eunuch of William II, 213–14, 244, 251
ʿAbd al-Mawlā, *dīwānī* scribe(?) under Roger II, 119 n.20
ʿAbd al-Mawlā al-Naṣrānī, witness to **Private 13**, 319
ʿAbd al-Muʾmin, first Almohad caliph (1130–63), 87, 282
ʿAbd al-Munʿim ibn ʿAbd al-Kāfī al-Zanātī, Muslim of Castrogiovanni, witness to **Private 27**, 323
ʿAbd al-Raḥmān al-ʿAṭṭār ibn [ʿAbd Allāh al-ʿAṭṭār, known as] Ibn al-Barūqī, brother of Abū l-Qāsim, uncle of vendors in **Private 6**, 316–17
ʿAbd al-Raḥmān ibn ʿAbd al-ʿAzīz, *see* Christodoulos
ʿAbd al-Raḥmān ibn Abī l-Qāsim al-Anṣārī, witness to **Private 6**, 317
ʿAbd al-Raḥmān ibn ʿAlī al-Qurashī (*Abderahmen filius Ali Elcurasy*), witness to **Private 4**, 316
ʿAbd al-Raḥmān ibn Fālaymūn, *al-qāʾid* of Palermo, father of Obert Fallamonaca, 246, 324 (**Private 31**)
ʿAbd al-Raḥmān ibn Fityān, Christian Arab burgher of Sciacca in ***Dīwānī* 31–2**, 309
ʿAbd al-Raḥmān ibn Maymūn ibn al-Lathīq, witness to **Private 9**, 318
ʿAbd al-Rāḥmān ibn Muḥammad ibn ʿAtīq al-Ḥarīrī(?), witness to **Private 9**, 318
ʿAbd al-Raḥmān ibn Mūsā Sh.bʿāt, brother of Ibrāhīm and Jabrūn, villein of S. Giovanni degli Eremiti in **Private 16**, 35, 47, 145–6, 320
ʿAbd al-Raḥmān ibn Rajāʾ, Abū l-Qāsim, *al-shaykh al-faqīh*, *qāḍī* of Norman Palermo, 74 & n.87, 88, 89, 295, 316 (**Private 6**)
ʿAbd al-Raḥmān ibn ʿUmar ibn Abī l-Samrāʾ al-Lawātī , *al-ḥājj*, one of the contracting parties in **Private 5**, 316
ʿAbd al-Raḥmān al-Naṣrānī, *see* Christodoulos
ʿAbd al-Salām ibn Masʿūd ibn Tāmir al-Qurashī, vendor in **Private 19**, 321
ʿAbd al-Sayyid (*Abdeserdus*), 'palace chamberlain and master of the *duana baronum*' under Tancred, 243 & n.142
Abdelgani filius Jusuph hegueri, *see* ʿAbd al-Ghanī ibn Yūsuf al-Hawwārī(?)
Abdelmule, *see* ʿAbd al-Mawlā
Abderahmen filius Ali Elcurasy, *see* ʿAbd al-Raḥmān ibn ʿAlī al-Qurashī
Abdeserdus, *see* ʿAbd al-Sayyid
Abdolla, *see* ʿAbd Allāh
Abraham, clerk of the Cappella Palatina, responsible for text of **Private 23**, 322
Abrahym filius Seuden Ettimimi, *see* Ibrāhīm ibn Sawdān al-Tamīmī
Abū ʿAbd Allāh ibn Maymūn, the Almoravid, 259 n.6
Abū ʿAbd Allāh ibn Abī l-Faḍl ibn ʿAlī al-Qurashī, witness to **Private 6**, 317
[A]bū ʿAbd Allāh, Muslim merchant from Termini Imerese, debtor in **Private 8**, 317–18
Abū ʿAlī, officer of royal *dīwān* under Roger II, 103 & n.40, 106, 222, 304 (***Dīwānī* 15**)
Abū Bakr ibn *al-qāʾid* Abū l-Qāsim Muḥammad ibn Ḥammūd, 234–6, 237
Abū Bakr ibn ʿAbd al-Mālik al-Hawwārī; Muslim of Castrogiovanni, witness to **Private 27**, 323
Abū Bakr ibn ʿAbd al-Raḥmān al-Hawwārī (*Ebubeker filius Abderrahmen Elhegueri*), witness to **Private 24**, 322
Abū Bakr ibn ʿUmar al-Azdī(?), brother of Aḥmad, Manjūma, and Amr al-Khayr, vendor in **Private 9,** 318
Abū Bakr ibn ʿUmar al-Qurashī, witness to **Private 6**, 317
Abū l-Ḍawʾ *see* Sirāj ibn Aḥmad ibn Rajāʾ
Abū l-Faḍl ibn ʿAbd al-Wāḥid al-Burjī(?), witness to **Private 18**, 320
Abū l-Faḍl ibn *al-faqīh* Abū ʿAlī Ḥasan ibn Ḥammūd, 235, 237, 240
Abū l-Faḍl ibn Aḥmad al-Ḥ.dāmī(?), *al-shaykh al-muqriʾ* ('the Qurʾānic-reciter') *al-ḥājj*, one of the vendors in **Private 18**, 320
Abū l-Faraj ibn Salām al-Laḥmī, maternal uncle of Jabrūn ibn Mūsā Sh.bʿāt and his brothers, witness to **Private 16**, 320
Abū l-Faraḥ (or l-Faraj) ibn Ḥusayn al-Kutāmī, witness in **Private 1**, 315
Abū l-Futūḥ ibn ʿAmmār, Muslim citizen of Sciacca in ***Dīwānī* 31–2**, 309
Abū l-Futūḥ ibn Ibrāhīm, witness to ***Dīwānī* 28**, **29** and **33**, 175 n.26
[A]bū l-Futūḥ, Muslim merchant from Cefalù, debtor in **Private 8**, 317–18
Abū Ghālib, *see* al-Ghumān

Abū l-Ḥasan al-Furriyānī, father of ᶜUmar, *ʿāmil* of Sfax under Norman rule, 291
Abū l-Ḥasan ibn *al-qāʾid* Karrām(?) al-Ṣālī(?) (*Bulhasen son of Gayti Karram Essaly*), vendor of **Private 4**, 316
Abū Jumᶜa ibn Muḥammad al-Qurashī, witness to **Private 16**, 320
[A]bū Jumᶜa ibn Yūsuf al-Rabīᶜī(?), witness in **Private 1**, 315
[A]bū Kināna (PA), Monreale estate, 155, 157, 162, 164, 168, 188
[A]bū Nifāṭ (TP), Monreale estate, 188, 191 n.66
Abū l-Qāsim, *see* Muḥammad ibn Ḥammūd
Abū l-Qāsim ibn ᶜAbd Allāh al-ᶜAṭṭār (known as Ibn al-Barūqī), father of the vendors in **Private 6**, 316–17
Abū l-Qāsim(?) ibn(?) ᶜAbd al-Raḥmān ibn Maḥmūd(?) ibn Jabr al-Tanūkhī(?), *al-shaykh al-faqīh*, official witness in **Private 9**, 318
Abū l-Qāsim ibn ᶜAbd al-Salām al-Azdī, witness to **Private 19**, 321
Abū l-Qāsim ibn ᶜAbd al-Ṣamad al-Qaysī (*Bulcassim filius Habdelssamed Elkaysi*), witness to **Private 3**, 316
Abū l-Qāsim ibn Abī ᶜAbd Allāh al-Tamīmī, witness to **Private 19**, 321
Abū l-Qāsim ibn Muḥammad al-Tamīmī, witness to **Private 26**, 323
Abū Saᶜd ibn ᶜĪsā (*Ebusaad filius Hyse*), witness to **Private 4**, 316
Abū l-Ṣalt Umayya ibn al-ᶜAzīz, Zīrid historian and polymath, 85, 86 & n.164, 87, 88, 90
Abū l-Sayyid, Muslim official and courtier of regent Margaret and William II, 233 & nn.86–7, 240, 243 & n.142
Abū l-Sayyid (*Boussit*), son of Christodoulēs, daughter of ᶜAbd al-Raḥmān [ibn?] ᶜUqba al-Naṣrānī, brother of Sumeōn, vendor in **Private 14**, 319
Abū Sayyīd, *al-qāʾid*, uncle of Gilbert, known as Mahalufus (*Makhlūf*), owner of property in Carini in 1202, 233 n.86
[A]bū Simāj, Monreale estate or landlord, 154, 162–3
Abū Sulaymān (*Ebu Suleyman*), son of Scaleri, purchaser in **Private 24**, 322
Abū l-Ṭāhir ibn ᶜUmar al-Tanūkhī, witness to **Private 29**, 324
Abū l-Ṭayyib, Arabic name of Eugenios tou Kalou, *see* Eugenios tou Kalou
Abū l-Ṭayyib, captain of the palace archers under William II, 230 n.70, 243, 312 (***Dīwānī* 39**)
Abū l-Ṭayyib ibn Yānī, the son of Merakias, vendor in **Private 17**, 320
Abū l-Ṭayyib al-Ifrīqī (*Bouttaib Afer*), witness to **Private 28**, 323
Abū l-Ṭayyib, son of *shaykh* Stephen, *ʿāmil* of Iato under Roger II, 175 & n.26, 176, 177
Abū l-Ṭayyib, once bailiff of Misilmeri in ***Dīwānī* 39**, 312
Abū Zakariyāʾ Yaḥyā I, first Ḥafṣid sultan of Tunis (1228–49), 242 n.138
Aci Castello (CT), 40, 51–8, 120–1, 141, 301–2 (***Dīwānī* 4**), 306 (***Dīwānī* 22**)
Acre (Palestine), 261 n.21
Adam Forestal, *see* Forestal, barons of Jāliṣū
Adelaide, wife of Roger I, 40–1
  regency of (1101–12), 64–5
    administration, 64–74
    Arabic and bilingual documents (***Dīwānī* 7–8**), 74–8, 302
    Arabic titles, 75, 77, 271
    signature, 75, 76
Adelicia, abbess of S. Maria Maddalena di Corleone under William I, 308 (***Dīwānī* 30**)
Adelina, wet nurse of Henry, son of Roger II, 101–2, 121–3, 140, 304 (***Dīwānī* 14**), 307 (***Dīwānī* 23**)
ᶜAdhr(?) ibn Muḥammad al-Tamīmī, witness to **Private 6**, 317
al-ᶜĀḍid li-dīn Allāh, fourteenth and last Fāṭimid caliph (1160–71), 133
Adragnum (AG), Monreale estate, 152
Adranone, Monte, *see* Adragnum
advenae, *see* villeins
al-Afḍal ibn Badr al-Jamālī, Fāṭimid vizier (*c*.1089–1121), 17, 195–7, 274
al-Afḍal Kutayfāt, Fāṭimid vizier (1130–1), 15
Agathonikos, son of Leo, witness to **Private 15**, 320
Aghlabid emirs of Ifrīqiya, *see* Ifrīqiya
Agrigento (AG), 24–5, 107, 108, 138, 238 n.107
al-Aḥāsī islands (Tunisia), 85
ahl al-dhimma, 13, 34: *see also dhimmī*
ahl [al-jarāʾid], *see* villeins
Aḥmad ibn ᶜAbd Allāh *al-ḥājj* al-Hawwārī, witness to **Private 19**, 321
Aḥmad ibn ᶜAbd al-Nūr al-Tamīmī, *al-shaykh* Abū l-ᶜAbbās, one of the vendors in **Private 18**, 320
Aḥmad ibn ᶜAbd al-Karīm al-Hawwārī, Muslim of Castrogiovanni, witness to **Private 27**, 323
Aḥmad ibn ᶜAbd al-Raḥmān al-Tamīmī; Muslim of Castrogiovanni, witness to **Private 27**, 323

Aḥmad ibn Abī l-Qāsim al-Qaysī, witness to **Private 16** and **Private 19**, 320, 321
Aḥmad ibn Ḥusayn ibn Yūsuf al-Lawātī, witness to **Private 5**, 316
Aḥmad ibn Ibrāhīm al-Tamīmī (*Ahmed filius Abrahim Timimi*), witness to **Private 3**, 316
Aḥmad ibn Khalīfa al-Azdī, witness to **Private 18,** 320
Aḥmad ibn ᶜUmar al-Azdī(?), brother of Abū Bakr, Manjūma, and Amr al-Khayr, vendor in **Private 9,** 318
Aḥmad al-Ṣiqillī, see Peter, *al-qā'id*
Ahmed filius Abrahim Timimi, *see* Aḥmad ibn Ibrāhīm al-Tamīmī
ᶜĀ'ika bint *al-kātib* Aḥmad ibn ... al-Tamīmī, mother of Arghīsa ibn ᶜAbd al-Raḥmān al-Qurashī, vendor in **Private 2**, 315
Akhmīm (Egypt), 262 & n.23
akrostikha ('registers'), 60
ᶜalāma , pl. *ᶜalāmāt*, standard form of signature in Islamic world, 277
  of Fāṭimid caliphs and viziers, 278
  of magistrates of Pisa, 278
  of Norman kings, 109–10, 111, 113, 114, 277–8, 298
  of palace Saracens, 187, 220 & n.26, 221–2 & nn.31–2, 232 n.81, 243 n.143, 251–2
Albert, son-in-law of John Atria (*Alb.rt ṣihr J.wān Aṭriya*), Latin burgher of Sciacca in ***Dīwānī* 31–2**, 309
Alcherius, first Norman archbishop of Palermo, 46
Aleppo (Syria), 261
Alexander III, pope, 229
Alexander, Latin scribe of William II, 187
Alexandria (Egypt), 258, 261 n.18
Alexius I Comnenus, Byzantine emperor (1081–1118), 66, 67, 71, 80 & n.124
Alfonso, son of Roger II (d.1144), 89, 286 & n.12
Ália (PA), 171 n.4
ᶜAlī ibn ᶜAbd Allāh al-Hawwārī (*Aly filius Abdalle Elhegueri*), witness to **Private 24**, 322
ᶜAlī ibn ᶜAbd al-Malik (*Aly filius Abdelmelek*), witness to **Private 4**, 316
ᶜAlī ibn ᶜAbd al-Raḥmān, Muslim merchant from Sciacca, witness to **Private 8**, 318
ᶜAlī ibn ᶜAbd al-Raḥmān, witness to ***Dīwānī* 28, 29** and **33**, 175 n.26
ᶜAlī ibn ᶜAbd al-Raḥmān al-Tamīmī (*Aly ibin Abderrahmen Ettimimi*), witness to **Private 24**, 322
ᶜAlī ibn Abī Bakr al-Tamīmī(?), witness to **Private 29**, 324
ᶜAlī ibn Abī Iṣḥāq al-Waddānī, Abū l-Ḥasan, *ṣāḥib al-dīwān bi-Ṣiqillīya*, 26
ᶜAlī ibn Abī l-Faḍl al-Tamīmī, witness to **Private 19**, 321
ᶜAlī ibn Abī l-Fatḥ ibn ..., witness to **Private 2**, brother of Muḥammad, 315
ᶜAlī ibn Abī l-Fatḥ ibn Ḥ.l.fīsī(?), witness to **Private 18**, 320
ᶜAlī ibn Abī l-Ḥusayn al-Ṣiqillī (*Aly byn Ebielhasyn Sekilli*), witness to **Private 4**, 316
ᶜAlī ibn Abī l-Qāsim ᶜAbd al-Raḥmān ibn Rajā', Abū l-Ḥasan, *al-shaykh al-faqīh*, *qāḍī* of Norman Palermo, 88
ᶜAlī ibn Abī l-Qāsim ibn ᶜAbd Allāh al-ᶜAṭṭār ('the Druggist'), known as Ibn al-Bārūqī, vendor in **Private 6**, 316–17
ᶜAlī ibn Aḥmad ibn Zayn al-Khadd, Muṣṭaniᶜ al-Dawla, ambassador of al-Ḥāfiẓ to Roger II, 258
ᶜAlī ibn Ḥusayn al-Lawātī, witness to **Private 1**, 315
ᶜAlī ibn Maymūn, debtor in **Private 8**, 317–18
ᶜAlī ibn Muᶜāsh(?) ibn Abī l-Qāsim al-Tanūkhī, witness to **Private 9**, 318
ᶜAlī ibn Naqīya(?) ibn ᶜAlī ibn Naqīya(?) al-Laḥmī (or al-Lakhmī), witness to **Private 6**, 317
ᶜAlī ibn Qarqar(?) al-Tanūkhī(?), Abū l-Ḥasan, *al-shaykh al-faqīh*, official witness in **Private 9**, 318
ᶜAlī ibn Qasīy (or Qusayy?) al-Tamīmī (*Aly filius Casi Ettimini*), witness to **Private 4**, 316
ᶜAlī ibn ᶜUmar ibn ᶜAtīq al-R.y.ghī(?), witness to **Private 18**, 320
ᶜAlī *al-ḥājj* ibn ᶜUthmān al-Anṣārī, witness to **Private 19**, 321
ᶜAlī ibn Yaḥyā, seventh Zīrid emir of Ifrīqiya (1116–21), 85
ᶜAlī ibn Yaᶜlā al-Qurashī, witness to **Private 16**, 320
ᶜAlī the *qā'id*, agent of Muriella of Petterrana, 73
Almohads (al-Muwaḥḥidūn), caliphs of North Africa and Spain, 19, 223, 226, 227, 241, 246, 248, 253, 275, 278, 281, 282, 289, 291, 292
Almoravids (al-Murābiṭūn), rulers of North Africa and Spain, 86, 259 n.6
Altavilla Milicia (PA), 147 n.10
Altofonte (PA), suburban palace and park built by Roger II, 286
Aly byn Ebielhasyn Sekilli, *see* ᶜAlī ibn Abī l-Ḥusayn al-Ṣiqillī

Aly filius Abdalle Elhegueri, *see* ᶜAlī ibn ᶜAbd Allāh al-Hawwārī
Aly filius Abdelmelek, *see* ᶜAlī ibn ᶜAbd al-Malik
Aly filius Casi Ettimini, *see* ᶜAlī ibn Qasīy [or Qusayy?] al-Tamīmī
Aly ibin Abderrahmen Ettimimi, *see* ᶜAlī ibn ᶜAbd al-Raḥmān al-Tamīmī
Amalfi (SA), 92
amān ('peace treaty')
  granted by Normans in Ifrīqiya, 34, 36, 39, 290–1
  granted by Normans to Muslims of Sicily, 33, 34, 37, 63, 299
Amari, Michele, 2, 6–7 & n.24, 35, 88, 206, 218, 227
Ambrose, first abbot of S. Bartolomeo di Lipari and S. Salvatore di Patti, 71
ᶜāmil, pl. *ᶜummāl* ('district administrative officer'), 17, 100 & n.25, 111, 311–12 (***Dīwānī* 38**)
amīn, pl. *ᶜumanāʾ* ('superintendent', administrative officer), 24–5, 29, 100 & n.25, 111
al-Āmir, tenth Fāṭimid caliph (1101–30), 195, 258
ᶜAmmār ibn Joshua al-Ḥalabī, Jew of Muslim Palermo, 29
ᶜAmmār, eunuch of William II, 243, 251–2, 322 (**Private 23**)
Amr al-Khayr bint ᶜUmar al-Azdī(?), sister of Abū Bakr, Aḥmad, and Manjūma, vendor in **Private 9,** 318
al-Andalusīn (PA), Monreale estate, 169, 188, 191 n.65
Andrew, eunuch of Maio of Bari, 219, 243
angariation, *see* labour services
Anglo-Norman administration, 1–7
Anglo-Norman language, 4–5
Anglo-Saxon administration, 1–4
Ansaldus, castellan of royal palace under Regent Margaret, contracting party in **Private 11**, 221, 319
Ansgerius, first abbot-bishop of Catania, 40, 301 (***Dīwānī* 4**)
Ansketill, *see* S.kīn
Antioch (Syria), 1, 80 n.124, 81 n.126, 82–3, 84, 263–4, 287
Apuleius, 284 n.1
al-Aqbāṭ (PA), Monreale estate, 189, 190
Arabic and bilingual documents of Norman Sicily, 8, 9–10
  dīwānī documents (for individual documents, *see* Appendix 1, 301–14)
    diplomatic form
      apprecatio
        Arabic, *see ḥasbala*
        Greek (symbol of the cross), 75
      arenga
        Greek, 94, 99–100, 101, 103, 117, 118
        Latin, 117 n.16, 118, 186
      basmala (*invocatio*), 75, 130, 279
      corroboratio
        Arabic, 100, 101, 166 & n.44
        Greek, 94, 100, 102, 104
      datatio
        Arabic (*taʾrīkh*), 75, 76–7, 100, 101, 102, 104, 109–10, 130, 153, 156 n.32, 166 & n.44, 187 & n.58
      Latin, 130
    dispositio
      Arabic, 75, 101, 119–20, 121, 123, 126, 127, 128, 129, 132, 134–8, 153, 156 & n.32, 166 & n.44, 187 & n.58, 201
      Greek, 75, 94, 99–100, 101, 103–4, 106
    eschatology
      Arabic, 75
      Greek, 75
    ḥasbala (*apprecatio*), 101, 102, 104, 106, 111, 114, 171, 187 & n.58, 279–80, 309 (***Dīwānī* 31**)
    ḥamdala (*ᶜalāma* and *dīwānī* motto), 109–10, 278
    intitulatio
      Arabic, 75, 101, 287
      Greek, 75, 101, 103, 117, 184 n.46
    invocatio
      Arabic, *see basmala*
      Latin, 130
    marks of authentication and registration, 279–80, 309 (***Dīwānī* 31**), 310–11 (***Dīwānī* 35**) : *see also* external features, seams 'sealed' on *verso*
    narratio
      Arabic, 119–20, 121–2, 123, 126 & nn.28, 31, 127–8, 129, 130–34, 153, 156 & n.32, 166 & n.44, 187 & n.58
      Greek, 94, 103, 104, 108
      Latin, 131–2
    sanctio
      Arabic (*taʾkīd*), 106
      Greek, 75, 104, 108
    seal, 52, 53, 54, 75, 92 n.3, 94 & n.9, 100, 101, 103, 104, 107, 119, 121, 123, 128, 129, 153, 165, 176, 186
    sharṭ, pl. *shurūṭ* ('stipulatory clause'), 107, 108, 119, 120, 121, 123, 126, 127–8, 139–40, 142, 144, 166–7 & n.44
    signature

Arabic, *see* ᶜ*alāma*
Greek, 53, 75, 94, 100, 101, 103, 104, 106 n.46, 107, 109, 110, 118, 119, 121, 123, 128, 129, 287
Latin, 153, 155, 186–7
superscriptio
Latin, 186
traditio
Greek, 94, 102, 104
external features
interlinear Greek transliteration of Arabic names and notes, 52, 53, 92, 93, 107, 110, 119, 120, 123, 124–5, 127, 129, 153, 165
script
Arabic
pre-Norman, 275
comital scripts, 52–3, 75, 275
Fāṭimid, 275, 277
Maghribī, 275, 277
royal *dīwāni* scripts, 53, 129, 275–7, 300, 308 (***Dīwānī*** **†27**)
Greek, 75, 76, 129, 308 (***Dīwānī*** **†27**)
seams 'sealed' on *verso*, 53, 119, 120, 123, 127, 129, 153, 186, 280
deperdita, see Appendix 1, ***Dīwānī*** **1, 3, 5–6, †9, 10–11, 42**
forgeries, *see* Appendix 1, ***Dīwānī*** **†9, †27**
translated in 13th century, 101, 121, 123
private documents, *see* Appendix 2
Arabic language
in Muslim Sicily, 4
in Norman Sicily, 4–5
as an administrative language, 4–5, 39, 140, 207–11
hiatus in use (1111–30), 63, 79, 80, 90, 91, 111–14, 257, 280–1
relationship between Arabic and Greek in bilingual documents, 94–101, 105–6, 109–10, 111–14, 124–5, 127, 143
relationship between Arabic and Latin in bilingual documents, 187, 190
return to Arabic (1130), 63, 80, 91, 93–4, 107–8, 111–14, 210–11, 257
use of Arabic in documents issued by the royal *dīwān*, 207–11, 297–300
'word-doubling', 180–1
Arabic titles of the Norman rulers of Sicily, 268–74
Duke Robert Guiscard, 77, 268
Roger I, 77, 120 & n.22, 128 & n.37, 138–9, 268, 271
Adelaide, 75, 77, 268, 271
Count Roger II, 75, 77, 268
royal titles, 120 & n.22, 122, 126 & n.28, 128 & n.37, 132–9, 153, 156 n.32, 166 & n.44, 187 & n.58, 201, 264, 268–74
*ad*ᶜ*iya*, sing. *du*ᶜ*ā*ʾ ('invocations'), 132, 138–9, 271–2, 273
alqāb, sing. *laqab* ('titles'), 269–70, 271, 272, 273
Christian styles, 75, 77, 137–8, 268, 270–1, 273–4
dynastic title (*al-malik al-mu*ᶜ*aẓẓam*), 111, 114, 137, 268, 269
al-ḥaḍra ('the [Royal] Presence'), 134, 135, 136, 137, 268, 270, 271–2, 273, 287
al-majlis al-sāmī ('the Most Exalted Seat'), 132–4, 139, 273, 287
malik, 268, 272, 273
*nisba*s, 134, 135, 138, 270, 287
Aramaic, 4
arāmil, see villeins
'archons of the court' (*oi archontes tēs kortēs*), 65, 67
Arghīsa [ibn?] ᶜAbd al-Raḥmān al-Qurashī, *al-kātib al-mu*ᶜ*allim* (*i.e. magister notarius*?), son of ᶜĀʾika bint *al-kātib* Aḥmad ibn ... al-Tamīmī, vendor in **Private 2**, 315
*aribbā*ʾ, *see* villeins
Aristippus, Henry, scholar, archdeacon of Catania, chancellor and royal familiar under William I, 177
Armenia, 261–4
Arnald (*Arnald*), son-in-law of Robert Alduina (*R.b.rt H.l.d.wīn*), baron of Roger II, 309 (***Dīwānī*** **31**)
Arnald of Messina, Ser, witness to **Private 8,** 318
Arnulf, canon of Palermo under Count Roger II, 94 n.12
Arsafia (RC), 65
Aschettinos, *see* S.kīn
Askettinos, *see* S.kīn
Atenulf, palace chamberlain under Roger II and William I, 219
Athanasios, abbot of S. Maria della Grotta, 247, 324 (**Private 31**)
Athos (Greece), 129 n.39
Avenel, Rainald, baron of Roger I, and his wife Fresenda, 94, 303 (***Dīwānī*** **12**)
ᶜAydhab (Egypt), 240 n.125
ᶜAyn al-Dāmūs (PA), Monreale estate, 168
ᶜAyn al-Liyān (PA), estate granted to S. Maria di Campograsso, 1147, 311–12 (***Dīwānī*** **38**)

Badr ibn al-Rūdinī(?), witness to **Private 13**, 319
Badr al-Jamālī, Armenian vizier of al-Mustanṣir (eighth Fāṭimid caliph, 1036–94), 196, 261 n.20

Bahrām, *see* Paḥlavuni, Bahrām
al-baḥrīyūn ('sailors'), 311–12 (***Dīwānī* 38**)
Baida (PA), estate granted to Palermo cathedral, 202, 313 (***Dīwānī* 42**)
Baldwin, canon of the Cappella Palatina, witness to **Private 11**, 319
al-Baluʾīn(?) (PA), Monreale estate, 188, 191 n.67
banalités, *see* labour services
Baqālṭa (Tunisia), 85 n.160
Barḍālī, monastery of (near Collesano PA), 315 (**Private 1**)
Bargharīṭa al-naṣrānīya bint al-rāhiba al-Karkantīya, Dāma, *see* Margaret the Christian
Barnard, canon of S. Salvatore di Cefalù under Roger II, 126
Barrūn, *see* Peter, al-qāʾid, the eunuch
Bartholomew, bishop-elect of Agrigento, 202, 312 (***Dīwānī* 39**)
Bartholomew de Parisio, royal justiciar under William I, 224
Bartholomew (*Barthulamāw ibn ...āmūn*), baron of Roger II, 309 (***Dīwānī* 31**)
Bartholomew of Salerno, William II's doorkeeper (*thuroros*), purchaser in **Private 21**, probably identical to Bartholomew *regius ostiarius* below, 321
Bartholomew, *regius ostiarius*, probably identical to Bartholomew of Salerno above, 243 n.140
Basento, Fiume (MT), 43 n.66
Basilios Boiōannēs, Byzantine catepan, 43
Basil Bousa, bailiff of Misilmeri(?) in ***Dīwānī* 39**, 312
Basil, son of Theodore, son of Leo *tou Chanzeri* (i.e. al-Khinzārī, 'the Swineherd'), witness to **Private 12,** 319
Basil the notary, witness to **Private 31**, 324
Basil the treasurer and chamberlain under Count Roger II, 72, 73
Bāsīlī, *al-shaykh al-muʿallim*, agent of Archbishop Walter II of Palermo, the purchaser in **Private 18**, 320
al-Baṭāʾiḥī, Abū ʿAbd Allāh Muḥammad ibn Fātik, Fāṭimid vizier (1121–5), 18
Bātrū, al-qissīs, *see* Peter the priest
Battellaro (PA), Monreale estate, 152, 168, 181, 185, 186, 189, 313 (***Dīwānī* 44**)
bayt al-māl ('treasury'), 14, 20, 21, 22
Belice destro, Fiume (PA), 46 n.81
Belisarius, general of Byzantine emperor Justinian I, 23
Benedict, son of Deodatus the Greek priest, 101
Berardus, archbishop of Palermo, 238
Berber language in Norman Sicily, 4
Berzena (TP), 303 (***Dīwānī* †9**), 308 (***Dīwānī* †27**)
besant, 37
Bijānū (PA), Monreale estate, 169, 189
Bingelir, *gaytus* (or *gaytus gaytorum*), royal officer under Count Roger II, 102 & n.34
Binkyramis, *see* Raḥl Ibn al-Karrām
Bisacquino (PA), 152 & n.26, 321 (**Private 20**)
Biththirrāna, *see* Petterrana
Blasius, *clericus domini Regis*, vendor in **Private 21**, 321
Blasius, prior of S. Lucia of Syracuse, party to **Private 25**, 322
blind-men of the church of Catania, 55, 56, 57, 119, 146
Boddaos the *qāʾid*, *see* Abū l-Ḍawʾ Sirāj
Bohemond II, prince of Antioch, 263
boidion, pl. *boidia* ('plough-land', area measure), xviii, 47
Bombarchet, agent of Abū l-Qāsim Muḥammad ibn Ḥammūd, 239
Bône (Algeria), 215, 217, 251
Bonnellus, Matthew, baron and rebel under William I, 219–20, 230
Bonos, notary and protonotary under Roger I, Adelaide, and Count Roger II, 65–6, 67, 71
Borginissimo, *see* Burj al-Nisām
Borrel, Robert, baron of Roger I, 64
boundary inquests, 41–2, 67, 80, 91, 94–9, 102, 103–5, 108, 111–12, 170–1, 172–3, 175–80, 184–5, 190
Bourginēsem, *see* Burj al-Nisām
Bourginisemma, *see* Burg al-Nisām
Bouttaib Afer, *see* Abū l-Ṭayyib al-Ifrīqī
Brachēmos uios Iosēf, *see* Ibrāhīm ibn Yūsuf
Brienne, Lady, abbess of S. Michele Arcangelo di Mazara, 308 (***Dīwānī* †27**)
Brucato (PA), 324 (**Private 30**)
Brown, master Thomas, 223 n.42, 244 n.155
Bulbula al-Bikr bint Abī l-Qāsim ibn ʿAbd Allāh al-ʿAṭṭār, vendor in **Private 6**, 316–17
Bū Kināna, *see* [A]bū Kināna
Bulcassim filius Habdelssamed Elkaysi, *see* Abū l-Qāsim ibn ʿAbd al-Ṣamad al-Qaysī
Bulhasen son of Gayti Karram Essaly, *see* Abū l-Ḥasan ibn al-qāʾid Karrām(?) al-Ṣalī(?)
Bundār, Jew in Muslim Palermo, 28
Bū Nifāṭ, *see* [A]bū Nifāṭ
Burj al-Nisām (AG), 238 n.107
Burgitabis (PA), 324 (**Private 30**)
Busambra, Rocca (PA), 180 n.35
Busenia (ME), 181 & n.40
Bū Simāj, *see* [A]bū Simāj
Butah, *see* Regalbuto
Buzantios, judge of Bari, 43–4

Caccamo (PA), 73 n.81, 219, 220, 230
Cairo Geniza, 12–13, 27–8, 30, 258–9
Caitus Bulcassemus, *see* Abū l-Qāsim ibn Ḥammūd
Calabria, 6
  Byzantine administration of, influence upon Norman administration, 43–5, 60
  Norman administration, 41, 43, 60, 203, 207 & n.67
  Muslim communities in, 31, 236 & n.101
Calamonaci (AG), 309 (***Dīwānī* 31**)
Calatafimi (TP), 242 n.138
Calatrasi (PA)
  barony of, 163, 185, 312 (***Dīwānī* 40**)
  Monreale estate, 152, 153, 155, 163, 164–5, 167, 168, 181, 186, 187, 189, 313 (***Dīwānī* 43–4**)
Caltabellotta (AG), 58 n.129, 152 n.27, 224 n.48
Calvelli family, of Palermo, 246 n.178
camera, 66
camerarius, *see* chamberlain
Cammarata (AG), 170 & n.4
Campobello di Mazara (TP), 303 (***Dīwānī* †9**), 308 (***Dīwānī* †27**)
Campofiorito (PA), 152 n.27
Campograsso (PA), 147 n.10
Camporeale (PA), 312 (***Dīwānī* 40**)
Cangialeso (PA), *see* Jāliṣū
canon, see *qānūn*, b. 'land-tax'
Cappadocia (Turkey), 261
Casaba (EN?), 170–1 & n.4
Cassaro (PA), 170–1 & n.4
Castrogiovanni (mod. Enna, EN), 75, 302 (***Dīwānī* 7**), 323 (**Private 27**)
Castroreale (ME), 108, 305 (***Dīwānī* 19**)
Castrum Sancti Adiutoris, 44
Catalogus Baronum, 174, 185, 192
Catania (CT), 40–1, 51–8, 119–20, 141–2, 301 (***Dīwānī* 3**), 306 (***Dīwānī* 21**): *see also* Churches and religious foundations
Cefalà [Diana] (PA), 184, 314 (***Dīwānī* 46**), 315 (**Private 3**)
Cefalù (PA), 62, 91–4: *see also* Churches and religious foundations
censiles, *see* villeins
censum, exacted by Normans from Muslims of Sicily, equivalent to Islamic *jizya*, 34, 37, 38
Cerami (ME), battle of, 33
chamberlain (*camerarius, o kapriliggas*), 65, 66, 67, 68, 69, 72, 106 n.46, 108, 203, 206, 213, 216, 219, 221, 222, 224 & n.46, 226 n.56, 228, 230, 231, 232, 234, 243 & n.140, 244, 253, 289, 291
Chammetta[s] (Aḥmad or Ḥamid?), member of court of Count Roger II, probably identical to witness to **Private 7**, 74 & n.87, 317
Chamse, *kait*, *see* Ḥamza, al-qāʾid
Chamutus, *see* Ḥammūd
Chamze filius Haly Ellegueri, *see* Ḥamza ibn ᶜAlī al-Hawwārī
Charbertos tou Sanemou, *see* Herbert of Sanemon
chartoularios, 23
Charzalla, son of Abdelgani Ellahmī, *see* Ḥirz(?) Allāh ibn ᶜAbd al-Ghanī al-Lakhmī (or al-Laḥmī)
Chinea (TP), 242 & n.138
Christodoulēs, *al-ᶜajūz* ('the old woman'), daughter of ᶜAbd al-Raḥmān [ibn?] ᶜUqba al-Naṣrānī, mother of Sumeōn and Abū l-Sayyid (Boussit), vendor in **Private 14**, 319–20
Christodoulēs, wife of ᶜAbd al-ᶜAzīz ibn Juwān al-Andalusī, vendor in **Private 22**, 321–2
Christodoulos, emir under Adelaide and Count Roger II
  origins and family, 70
  names, 69–70 & n.50, 81, 84, 85, 86
  career, duties and responsibilities, 71–4
    administrative activities (1107–25), 71–4
    elevation to rank of emir (1107 or earlier), 71
    arranges defection of and employs George of Antioch and his family (1108–9), 81, 83, 84
    sends George of Antioch as ambassador to Fāṭimid court, 81, 84, 259
    awarded rank of *protonobilissimos* by Alexius I Comnenus (April 1109), 66 n.19, 67, 71
    when Roger comes of age (1112), he 'shared absolute authority' with Christodoulos, 81
    sulṭān, *ṣāḥib al-ashghāl* and *wazīr* of Roger II, 81, 84, 90
    member of court hearing case against Muriella of Petterrana (January 1123), 73–4, 295
    military and naval commander (July 1123), 74, 85–6, 258
    fall and death engineered by George of Antioch (1126?), 70–1, 74, 81
  possessions, 70
Christodoulos, son of Asfordeuelēs, witness to **Private 15**, 320
Christodoulos, son of Boztēt(?), witness to **Private 10**, 318
Christodoulos, son of Fōteinos, witness to **Private 14**, 320

Christodoulos, son of Gemma, witness to **Private 21**, 321
Christodoulos, son of Philip, witness to **Private 21**, 321
Christodoulos, son of Solomon, brother of Kōstantinos, witness to **Private 15**, 320
Christodoulos, witness to **Private 10**, 318
Christoforous, *see* Christodoulos, emir
Christodoulos-Abdesseit (*ʿAbd al-Sayyid*), son of Boousit (*Abū l-Sayyid*), husband of Sitt al-Ḥusn, vendor in **Private 12**, 233 n.86, 319
Churches and religious foundations
  Mainland
    S. Agatha *de Gizofa* (VV), 65 n.13
    S. Angelo di Mileto (VV), 126
    S. Bartolomeo di Trigona (RC), 115
    S. Giovanni di Lama (FG), 44
    S. Leontios di Stilo (RC), 45
    S. Maria del Patire (CS), 70, 71
    S. Maria del Rifugio (MT), 43
    S. Maria di Bagnara (RC), 92
    S. Maria di Matina (CS), 44
    S. Maria di Mileto (VV), cathedral, 65
    S. Maria di Turri (CZ), 65, 115
    S. Nicola a Monte Pellaro (RC), 206
    S. Nicolò di Droso (RC), 60
    S. Sebastiano, near San Mauro (CS), 70
    SS. Trinità di Cava (SA), 44
    SS. Trinità di Mileto (VV), 126–7 & n.29, 140, 307 (***Dīwānī* 24**)
  Sicily
    Agios Dourrounēs ('S. Drogo'), Palermo (PA), 324 (**Private 31**)
    Agios Kōnstantinos, Palermo (PA), 321 (**Private 21**)
    Barḍālī, monastery of (near Collesano, PA), 315 (**Private 1**)
    Cappella Palatina, Palermo (PA), 109, 139 n.97, 184, 266 & n.47, 298, 299, 314 (***Dīwānī* 46**), 322 (**Private 23**)
    S. Agata, Catania (CT) cathedral, 12, 40–1, 51–8, 60, 119–21, 141, 142, 301–2 (***Dīwānī* 3–4**), 306 (***Dīwānī* 21–2**)
    S. Andrea de Bebbene, Palermo (PA), 243, 322 (**Private 23**)
    S. Angelo di Brolo (ME), 42
    S. Bartolomeo di Lipari-Patti (ME), 61 n.137, 71, 93, 94–101, 103 n.39, 111, 234, 303–4 (***Dīwānī* 12–13**)
    S. Basile di Geracello (EN), 238
    S. Cataldo, Agrigento (AG) cathedral, 58–9, 184, 202, 314 (***Dīwānī* 46**)
    S. Cosimano, Cefalù (PA), 123–7, 307 (***Dīwānī* 24**)
    S. Filippo d'Agira (ME), 103 n.38
    S. Filippo di Fragalà (ME), 67, 69, 75 & n.97, 115, 302 (***Dīwānī* 7**)
    S. Giacomo a Mare, Palermo (PA), 110, 306 (***Dīwānī* 20**)
    S. Giorgio di Triocala (AG), 58–9, 102–8, 111, 147, 181, 193–4, 222, 302 (***Dīwānī* 6**), 304–5 (***Dīwānī* 15–18**), 309 (***Dīwānī* 31–2**)
    S. Giovanni degli Eremiti, Palermo (PA), 35, 38, 93, 145–6, 234 n.90, 320 (**Private 16**)
    S. Giovanni dei Lebbrosi, Palermo (PA), 103 n.38, 180, 310 (***Dīwānī* 34**)
    S. Giovanni di Rocella (PA), 123–7, 307 (***Dīwānī* 24**)
    S. Lorenzo, hospital of, Cefalà [Diana] (PA), 184, 314 (***Dīwānī* 46**)
    S. Lucia, Syracuse (SR), 322–3 (**Private 25**)
    S. Maria dell'Ammiraglio ('La Martorana'), Palermo (PA), 109–11, 112, 266–7, 279, 306 (***Dīwānī* 20**), 312 (***Dīwānī* 39**)
    S. Maria della Grotta, Palermo (PA), 247, 324 (**Private 31**)
    S. Maria di Campograsso (PA), 147 n.10
    S. Maria di Gala (ME), 79–80, 108–9, 111, 305 (***Dīwānī* 19**)
    S. Maria di Marsala (TP), 70
    S. Maria di Messina (ME), 76 n.100
    S. Maria di Monreale (PA), 115 n.3, 145, 148, 150, 151–69, 175–92, 202, 222, 313–14 (***Dīwānī* 43–45**)
    S. Maria di Ustica (TP), 246
    S. Maria la Gadera, Polizzi (PA), 184, 311 (***Dīwānī* 36**)
    S. Maria *Latinorum* ('La Magione'), Palermo (PA), 312–13 (***Dīwānī* 40**)
    S. Maria la Vergine di Monte Gibello (CT), 181
    S. Maria Maddalena di Corleone (PA), 152 n.27, 201, 308–9 (***Dīwānī* 30**)
    S. Maria, Palermo (PA) cathedral, 45, 46–51, 60, 113, 116, 202, 238, 301 (***Dīwānī* 2**), 307 (***Dīwānī* 26**), 313 (***Dīwānī* 42**)
    SS. Maria, Matteo, Senatore, Viatore, e Cassiodoro, Palermo (PA), 70 & n.54
    S. Michele Arcangelo di Mazara (TP), 116 n.10, 302–3 (***Dīwānī* †9**), 308 (***Dīwānī* †27**)
    S. Michele di Troina (EN), 69
    S. Nicola, dependence of S. Maria di Gala, near Mineo (CT), 108, 305 (***Dīwānī* 19**)

S. Nicola, Messina (ME) cathedral, 11, 39–40, 65, 202–3, 221, 279, 311 (***Dīwānī* 37**)
S. Nicolò di Chùrchuro (PA), 106 n.46, 147, 175–80, 194, 201, 222, 243, 279, 287, 308 (***Dīwānī* 28–9**), 309–10 (***Dīwānī* 33**), 317 (**Private 7**)
S. Salvatore di Bordonaro (ME), 65
S. Salvatore, Cefalù (PA) cathedral, 62, 91–4, 112, 170–1, 203, 235, 303 (***Dīwānī* 10–11**), 307 (***Dīwānī* 24**), 313 (***Dīwānī* 41**), 322 (**Private 25**), 324 (**Private 30**)
S. Salvatore di Messina (ME), Greek archimandra, 58, 102, 103, 104, 115 & n.3, 304 (***Dīwānī* 15**)
S. Silvestro di Monreale (PA), 313 (***Dīwānī* 42**)
S. Sofia di Vicari (PA), 234
Ciminna (PA), 64, 74, 170
Clarus, *magister*, witness to **Private 12**, 319
Codex diplomaticus regni Siciliae, 8
Collesano (PA), 64, 324 (**Private 30**)
Comicchi (AG), estate granted to S. Maria di Monreale, 152
confoederati, term used for Muslims of Norman Sicily, equivalent to Islamic *ahl al-dhimma*, 34
Constance, daughter of Bohemond II, prince of Antioch, 263
Constance, daughter of Roger II and wife of Emperor Henry VI, empress and queen of Sicily (1195–98), 324 (**Private 30**)
Constantine, assistant castellan of royal palace under Regent Margaret, 231
Coppula, Robert, son of Nicholas, knight and citizen of Palermo, 101
Corleone (PA), 58, 180 n.35, 301 (***Dīwānī* 2**), 317–18 (**Private 8**)
Monreale estate, 152, 153–65, 168–9, 181, 182–3, 184, 185, 186–92, 313–14 (***Dīwānī* 43–5**)
curia regis, 133 & n.64, 193, 200
Cusa, Salvatore, 7–8
Cuscasino (PA), 170

dalīl, pl. *adillā*ʾ ('guide', tax-collector), 18
daftar, pl. *dafātir*, 16, 173: *see also* royal *dīwān*
dafātir al-ḥudūd, see royal *dīwān*
daftar al-majlis, 16
dār al-muḥāsabāt, 20
al-Darja (PA), Monreale estate, 168
Dasīsa (PA), Monreale estate, 168, 189
Daʾūd bar Salmān, Jew of Syracuse, witness to **Private 25**, 323
David, abbot of SS. Trinità di Mileto, 127, 307 (***Dīwānī* 24**)
David, Magister, Jew of Palermo and translator of Arabic, 101, 121, 131–2
al-Dāwudī, Abū Jaᶜfar Aḥmad ibn Naṣr, as a source for the administration of Muslim Sicily, 24–5, 26, 27, 42
al-Dayr al-Abyaḍ, Akhmīm (Egypt), 262
Dayr al-Khandaq (Egypt), 262
defetari, see daftar
demesne (*i.e.* comital or royal), 38, 60, 61, 65, 66, 71, 73, 101, 108, 118, 142, 144–5, 152, 162, 163, 164, 166, 167, 170, 171, 172, 174, 176, 177, 180, 184, 185, 192, 194, 198–203, 204, 210, 305 (***Dīwānī* 19**), 311 (***Dīwānī* 36**), 312 (***Dīwānī* 38**), 314 (***Dīwānī* 45**)
Dēmētrios the priest, witness to **Private 21**, 321
Deodatus, Greek priest, 101
deptarii, see daftar
dhimma ('protection' granted to subject communities), 13, 34, 36, 148, 297
dhimmī, pl. *dhimmīyūn* ('protected subject')
in early Islam, 13
in Fāṭimid Egypt, 16, 18
in Muslim Sicily, 23, 26–7
in Norman Sicily, 18, 34–8, 43, 47–8, 61, 145–51, 165, 297, 299
dīwān, pl. *dawāwīn* ('administrative bureau')
development under Umayyads and early ᶜAbbāsids, 14–15
etymology and meaning, 14
in Muslim Sicily, 24, 26, 29
Siculo-Norman, *see individual dīwāns listed under* royal *dīwān*
compared to English exchequer, 5
dīwān al-amwāl, 17, 196
dīwān al-ᶜaṭāʾ, 20
dīwān al-ḍiyāᶜ, 20
dīwān al-fawāʾid, see royal *dīwān*
dīwān al-inshāʾ, 16, 89, 195, 274, 295
dīwān al-inshāʾ wa-l-mukātabāt, 16, 89
dawāwīn al-jibāyāt, 20
dīwān al-juyūsh, 16
dīwān al-kharāj, 14, 20, 22, 29
dīwān al-majlis, 16, 195–6
al-dīwān al-maᶜmūr , *see* royal *dīwān*
dīwān al-Manṣūrīya, 20
dīwān al-maẓālim, 255, 292–5
dīwān al-mukātabāt, 16, 89
dīwān al-naẓar, 16, 89, 195, 196–7
dīwān al-rasāʾil, 16
dīwān al-taḥqīq
in Fāṭimid Egypt, 195–7, 274
in Norman Sicily, *see* royal dīwān

doana secreti, *see* royal dīwān
doma ('tax'), equivalent to Islamic *jizya*, 47, 146
Domesday Book, 3, 146 n.5
Donatus, abbot of S.Giovanni degli Eremiti, 35, 93, 145–6, 320 (**Private 16**)
Drogo, count of Apulia (1046–51), 32 n.7
duana baronum, *see* royal *dīwān*
duana de secretis, *see* royal *dīwān*
duana regia, *see* royal *dīwān*
Dumīniq ibn ᶜAbd al-Malik, witness to **Private 13**, 319
al-Duqqī (PA), Monreale estate, 169, 188

earthquake of 4 February 1169, 52, 53, 247
Eberardus, official in royal *dīwān* of William II, 153, 155, 187
Ebrahym ibin Nasar Ellachmi, *see* Ibrāhīm ibn Naṣr al-Lakhmī
Ebraym, son of Sebeun, known as Atrami, *see* Ibrāhīm ibn Sabᶜūn
Ebusaad filius Hyse, *see* Abū Saᶜd ibn ᶜĪsā
Ebu Suleyman, son of Scaleri, *see* Abū Sulaymān
Edessa (mod. Urfa, Turkey), 255
Egypt, *see* Fāṭimid Egypt
Ēlias, son of Christodoulos, witness to **Private 17**, 320
Eli ha-Kohen bar Yaḥyā or Yaᶜīsh-Ḥayyim, *see* Ibn Ḥayyīm
eleutheroi, *see* villeins
emir (*al-amīr*, *o amēras*, *ammiratus* and variants), honorific title in Norman court, 68–9
  emirs of Norman Palermo, 68–9
  see also undernames of individual emirs: Christodoulos, Eugenios the notary, George of Antioch, John the emir, Maio of Bari, Peter Bido, Stephen the emir
England, 1–5, 7
Enna, *see* Castrogiovanni
entalma ('decree'), 74
entopoi (also *entōpeoi*), *see* villeins
Eremburga, wife of Gosbert de Lucy, 73 n.82
Eugenios, son of Leo, witness to **Private 13,** 319
Eugenios the notary, posthumously called 'the emir', under Roger I, Adelaide, and Count Roger II, 69, 72, 317 (**Private 7**)
Eugenios tou Kalou Abū l-Ṭayyib, *ṣāḥib* of the *dīwān al-taḥqīq al-maᶜmūr* and *magister duane baronum* under William II, 170–1, 243 & n.140, 313 (***Dīwānī* 41**)
eunuchs, *see* palace Saracens
Eustathios, Byzantine catepan, 43–4
Eutropius, cantor of the Cappella Palatina, contracting party in **Private 11**, 221, 319
exchequer, Anglo-Norman, compared to Sicilian *dīwān*, 3, 6–7
exografoi, *see* villeins
ezeumenoi, *see* villeins

Faḍlūn ibn Daᵓūd, Jew of Syracuse, witness to **Private 25**, 323
Falco, canon of the Cappella Palatina, witness to **Private 11**, 319
Fallamonaca
  Obert, master of imperial *dīwāns* and of the finances of all Sicily under Frederick II
    origins and family, 246–7, 324
    ᶜalāma, 246
    Arabic and Latin titles, 184, 205, 246
    career and duties, 184–5, 245–7, 253, 314 (***Dīwānī* 46**)
    exchanges land in Palermo with Athanasios, abbot of S. Maria della Grotta, (**Private 31**) 324
  Perrino, son of Obert(?), canon of Palermo cathedral, 247, (**Private 32**) 324–5
  Suḥayliba, wife of Obert, *see* Suḥayliba
Fantasini, *see* Faṭṭāsina
Fāṭimid Egypt
  administration, 15–18, 195–7, 274
  as a source for Siculo-Norman administrative reforms, 7, 16, 17, 18, 118, 257–8, 264, 274, 275–83
  relations with Norman Sicily, 81, 84, 258–67, 282
Faṭṭāsina (PA), Monreale estate, 152 n.27, 168, 181, 189, 308–9 (***Dīwānī* 30**)
fayᵓ-land, 25
Fécamp (Normandy), 116 n.9, 307 (***Dīwānī* 26**)
Fellamonica (PA), 246 & n.181
Filadelfos, abbot of S. Bartolomeo di Trigona, 115
Fīlib al-Mahdawī, *see* Philip of al-Mahdīya
Focerò (ME), 60–1, 103 n.39
foedus, granted by Normans to Muslims of Sicily, equivalent to Islamic *amān*, 34, 37
Forestal, barons of Jāliṣū
  Adam, 127 n.34
  Roger, 58, 60, 115 n.3, 127–8, 141, 302 (***Dīwānī* 5**)
  Walter, son of Roger, 58, 127–8, 141, 142, 307 (***Dīwānī* 25**)
forgeries, 9, 12, 39–41, 44, 52–3, 70 n.54, 72 n.70, 92–3, 115 n.1, 116 n.10, 173 n.14, 302–5 (***Dīwānī* †9**), 308 (***Dīwānī* †27**)
Fōtios, son of Scholaros tou Kalou, witness to **Private 12**, 319

Frederick II, emperor, king of Sicily (1197–1250)
  Arabic document (***Dīwānī* 46**), 184–5, 314
  Arabic titles, 137
  boundary-registers, 184
  'Constitutions of Melfi', 149
  Muslim colony of Lucera, 36, 47, 244
  Muslims of Sicily, 242, 285, 292, 293–4
  palace Saracens under, 244–47
  protects Jews and Muslims in law, 293–4
Fuṭṭāsina, *see* Faṭṭāsina

Gabès (Tunisia), 34, 85, 147, 291
Gallo (PA), estate of Palermo cathedral, 45–6
Gàrcia (PA), 170–1, 313 (***Dīwānī* 41**)
Gaudius, Magister, son of Magister Moses, Jew of Palermo and translator of Arabic, 101, 121, 131
Geniza, *see* Cairo Geniza
Gentile, bishop of Agrigento, 225, 230, 231
Geoffrey D'Animato (*al-shaykh sar Jāfrāy dī Ānimātuh*), lord of purchaser in **Private 29**, 324
Geoffrey of Battellaro, lord of Battellaro, 152
Geoffrey of Centuripe, *sekretikos* and *ṣāḥib dīwān al-taḥqīq al-maᶜmūr*, 312 (***Dīwānī* 39**)
Geoffrey of Marturano, *magister justiciar* of William II, 80, 109
  perhaps identical to *Jafarāy Marturān*, a baron of Roger II in 1152, 309 (***Dīwānī* 31–2**)
Geoffrey of Modica, *palatinus camerarius et magister regie duane de secretis et duane baronum*, 203 n.48, 206
Geoffrey, son of John of Partinico, witness to ***Dīwānī* 28**, **29** and **33**, 175 n.26
Geoffrey, son of the notary Michael, cleric of the Cappella Palatina, 184, 314 (***Dīwānī* 46**)
Geoffrey, son of Roger I, 40
George of Antioch
  origins, birth, and early training in Antioch and Byzantine East, 74, 80, 83, 84, 264
  family, 80, 81, 83, 84, 110, 317 (**Private 7**)
  character , 81 & n.134
  possessions, 110
  moves to Zīrid Ifrīqiya (1087–1108), 74, 81, 83, 84
  fiscal officer (*ḥāsib*) under Tamīm ibn Bādīs the Zīrid, 81, 83, 84, 282, 283
  governor (*ᶜāmil*) of Sousse, 81
  brother, Simon, murdered by Yaḥyā ibn Tamīm, 81, 83
  defects to Sicily (1108–9), 74, 77, 81, 83, 84, 282
  district governor of Iato (1114), 74, 94, 96, 259, 303 (***Dīwānī* 12**)
  put in charge of the fiscal administration (*al-dawāwīn; al-jibāyāt*) of Sicily, 81, 84, 90
  ambassador to Fāṭimid court, 81, 83, 84, 91, 259, 282–3
  joint commander, with emir Christodoulos, of first Norman attack upon al-Mahdīya (1123), 74, 85–7, 258
  first appearance as emir (December 1125), 72
  engineers fall and death of emir Christodoulos (1126?), 74, 81
  appointed vizier to King Roger (1126?), 81
  holds boundary inquest at Mutata (February 1132), 91–2, 123, 274
  'presides over [Roger's] whole kingdom' (February 1132), 92, 94
  architect of the royal *dīwān*, 93–4, 257–8, 267, 282–3
  and letter of al-Ḥāfiẓ to Roger II, 260–1
  and Bahrām Paḥlavuni, 263–4, 267, 282
  founds and endows S. Maria dell'Ammiraglio, Palermo, 73 n.86, 109–10, 266–7, 306 (***Dīwānī* 20**), 312 (***Dīwānī* 39**)
    mosaic founder's panel in S. Maria dell'Ammiraglio, 109, 279–80, 283
  capture of al-Mahdīya and Ifrīqiyan coast (1148), 82, 87, 290–1
  commissions one of Roger's scribes, al-Ḥanash, to write master's biography, 82, 283
  fiscal management and reorganisation of the kingdom, 82, 84, 282–83
  manipulation of the royal image, 82, 282–3, 285, 286
  responsible for King Roger's Greek signature (1130–1151) and for his *ᶜalāma*, 110–11, 133–4
  seal, 110 & n.67, 306 (***Dīwānī* 20**)
  signature, 110 & n.67, 306 (***Dīwānī* 20**)
  titles
    Arabic, 82 & n.136, 83, 273
    Greek, 92, 94, 264
  death (summer 1151), 82, 197
  buried in Santa Maria dell'Ammiraglio, 109
  al-Maqrīzī's 'biography', 80–90
George of Palermo, notary, witness to **Private 31**, 324
George, son of Nicholas, witness to **Private 13,** 319
George, son of the lord Nikolaos, son of Megdie (*i.e.* al-Mahdawī?), purchaser in **Private 22**, 322
George, son of Peter, master of the archers(?), witness to **Private 17**, 320

Geracello (EN), 238 & n.109
Gerba (Tunisia), 227, 228, 249, 260, 263, 290
gesia, *see jizya*
Ghafūr ibn *al-shaykh* al-Arūṭū(?), *al-qā'id*, purchaser in **Private 2**, 315
al-Ghamma (PA), Monreale estate, 168
al-Ghār (PA), Monreale estate, 189
Ghār al-Ṣ.r.fī (PA), Monreale estate, 168
Ghār Shuᶜayb (PA), Monreale estate, 169, 189
Ghārāt ibn Jawshan, *al-qā'id*, military leader and familiar under Regent Margaret and William II, 240–1, 243
al-Gharbīya (Egypt), 307
Ghartīl al-Naṣrānī ibn Ghartīl, *see* Walter the Christian, son of Walter
Ghaznavid sultans of Khurasan, Afhhanistan and Northern India, 137
al-Ghumān ibn *al-qissīs* Abū Ghālib, abbot of the monastery of Barḍālī, purchaser in **Private 1**, 315
ghurabā', *see* villeins
Giakēn, *see* Aci Castello
Giarratana (RG), 70
Gilbert, count of Gravina, 225–7, 248, 256
Gilbert, known as Mahalufus (*Makhlūf*), nephew of *gaytus* Bussit (*al-qā'id Abū Sayyīd*), 233 n.86
Gildeibertus, *domini klericus*, 186–7
Giles the Christian (*Jīlū al-Naṣrānī*), purchaser in **Private 27**, 323
Giracello, *see* Geracello
Girald, subcantor of the Cappella Palatina, witness to **Private 11**, 319
Girardus Scavus, witness to **Private 31**, 324
Gisulf I, Lombard prince of Salerno, 44
Giuliana, *see* Juliana
Gosbert de Lucy, 73
Greek Christians in Norman Sicily
  employed as administrators 4–5, 63, 65–74
  employed as interpreters, negotiators, and spies during Norman conquest, 33, 63
Greek church
  archimandra of S. Salvatore di Messina, 58
  survival under Muslim rule, 42
  see also Churches and religioius foundations
Greek language
  in Muslim Sicily, 4
  in Norman Sicily, 4–5
    as an administrative language, 4–5, 39, 40, 91, 93–4, 116–18, 140, 207–10
    relationship between Arabic and Greek in bilingual documents, 94–101, 105–6, 110–11, 111–14, 124–5, 127, 143, 207–10
Gregory, abbot of S. Filippo di Fragalà, 67, 69
Grisantus, priest of the Cappella Palatina under Roger II, 136 n.73
Grotte di Gulfa, *see* Gurfa
Gurfa (PA), 170, 171 n.4

Habdeleauy filius Gebyr Elensari, *see* ᶜAbd al-Ḥayy[?] ibn Jabr al-Anṣārī
Habdelkerim filius Bubiker Elinsari, *see* ᶜAbd al-Karīm ibn Abī Bakr al-Anṣārī
ḥadd, pl. *ḥudūd*, 94, 99, 104, 106, 112, 170–92
al-Ḥāfiẓ li-dīn Allāh, eleventh Fāṭimid caliph, (1131–49), 134, 138, 267 n.48
  letter to Roger II, 82 n.136, 258, 259–65, 272
Ḥafṣid sultans of Ifrīqiya, 242 n.138, 246
Ḥajar al-Būqāl (PA), Monreale estate, 169, 188
Ḥajar al-Zanātī (PA)
  granted to San Giovanni dei Lebbrosi (1154), then Monreale estate, 180, 181, 182–3, 189, 310 (***Dīwānī* 34**)
al-Ḥākim bi-amri llāh, sixth Fāṭimid caliph (996–1021), 139
Ḥākim 'the villain', renegade Jew in Muslim Palermo, 29
Ḥammādid emirs of the western Maghrib, 86
al-Ḥammāmāt (Tunisia), 82
Ḥammūd (*Chamutus*), Muslim *qā'id* of Castrogiovanni, defeated by Roger I, 236–7
Ḥammūd ibn Muḥammad ibn ᶜAlawī ibn al-Ḥajar al-Qurashī, Abū ᶜAbd Allāh, *al-qā'id*, father of Abū l-Qāsim Muḥammad, 235 & n.96, 237
Ḥammūdid dynasty of Malaga and Algeciras, 236
Ḥamza ibn ᶜAlī al-Hawwārī (*Chamze filius Haly Ellegueri*), witness to **Private 3**, 316
Ḥamza, *al-qā'id* (*kait Chamse*), purchaser in **Private 14**, possibly identical to *al-shaykh al-qā'id* Ḥamza below, 319
Ḥamza, *al-shaykh al-qā'id*, Muslim courtier of William II, possibly identical to *al-qā'id* Ḥamza above, 243, 312 (***Dīwānī* 39**)
Ḥamza ibn Ḥamza, 'the controller of the *dīwānī* office of inquiry', 220 n.26, 243, 310–11 (***Dīwānī* 35**)
al-Ḥanash ('the Snake'), scribe and biographer of Roger II, 82
al-Harawī, ᶜAlī ibn Abī Bakr, visits Muslim shrines in Sicily in 1175, 241
Ḥasan ibn Abī l-Qāsim ibn Muḥammad al-Qurashī, witness to **Private 26**, 323
Ḥasan ibn Abī l-Qāsim al-Qurashī, witness to **Private 9**, 318
al-Ḥasan ibn ᶜAlī, eighth and last Zīrid emir of Ifrīqiya (1121–48), 86, 258, 290, 291

Ḥasan ibn ᶜAlī al-Kindī, known as Ibn al-Kh.n.d.rū(?), one of contracting parties in **Private 5**, 316
Ḥasan, son of al-Ḥāfiẓ (eleventh Fāṭimid caliph), 262
Ḥasan ibn Ḥammūd, Abū ᶜAlī, *al-faqīh*, brother of Abū l-Qāsim Muḥammad, 237, 240
al-Ḥasan ibn Muḥammad al-Bāghāʾī, *kātib* of Jaᶜfar ibn Yūsuf, 26
Ḥasan ibn Yūsuf ibn Muḥammad ibn ᶜĀdiyāʾ(?) al-Lawātī(?), witness to **Private 9**, 318
Ḥasan, nephew of Maymūn and Ṣadaqa, debtor in **Private 8**, 317–18
Ḥaydara, son of al-Ḥāfiẓ (eleventh Fāṭimid caliph), 262
ḥāshir, pl. *ḥushshār* ('gatherer', tax-collector), 18
Ḥayyīm, alias Khalaf ibn Yaᶜqūb the Spaniard, Jew of Muslim Palermo, 29
Ḥayyim ibn ᶜAmmār, representative of Jewish merchants in Palermo, 28 n.87
Hebrew language, 4
Henry I, king of England, 5
Henry II, king of England, 118 n.17
Henry, archbishop of Messina, purchaser in **Private 6**, 131 n.53, 316
Henry, count of Monte San Michele, 44
Henry Martellus, canon of the Cappella Palatina, witness to **Private 11**, 319
Henry of Montescaglioso, natural brother of Queen Margaret, 230, 231
Henry, son of Roger II (d. *c*.1145), 88, 101
Herbert, lord of Calamonaci, *see* Hubert, lord of Calamonaci
Herbert of Sanemon (*Charbertos tou Sanemou*), witness to **Private 7**, 317
Hibat Allāh ibn Muḥammad ibn ᶜAlī al-Naṣrānī(?), witness to **Private 9**, 318
Hilarion, abbot of S. Nicola a Monte Pellaro, 206
Ḥirz(?) Allāh ibn ᶜAbd al-Ghanī al-Lakhmī (or al-Laḥmī) (*Charzalla, son of Abdelgani Ellahmi*), purchaser in **Private 3**, 315
homines liberi, *see* villeins
hostiarius, 65, 68, 203 n.53
Hubert (or Herbert), lord of Calamonaci, 309 (***Dīwānī* 31–32**)
Hugh, son of Atton, supporter of the *qāʾid* Peter, 226, 248
Hugo de Sexto, *regie private masnede solidarius*, witness to **Private 20**, 321
'Hugo Falcandus', 212, 218 n.18, 230, 247–8, 249, 250, 252
Hugo Lupinus, brother of Hugo(?), *domini regis privatus* under William II, witness to **Private 20**, 321
Humphrey of Gravina, baron of Roger Borsa, 61 n.139
Humur Buabdille, *see ᶜUmar Abū ᶜAbd Allāh*
hundred, compared to Sicilian *iqlīm*, 3
ḥursh, *see* villeins
Ḥusayn ibn ᶜAtīq al-Tamīmī, witness to **Private 6** and **Private 9**, 317, 318
Ḥusayn ibn Yūsuf al-Lawātī, witness to **Private 5**, father of Aḥmad, 316
Hythie filius Abderrahmen Elhesin, *see* Yaḥyā(?) ibn ᶜAbd al-Raḥmān al-Ḥasan

Iato (S. Giuseppe Iato, PA), 64, 74, 94, 96, 97, 98, 259, 301 (***Dīwānī* 2**), 303 (***Dīwānī* 12**)
  Monreale estate, 152, 167, 168–9, 186–92, 313 (***Dīwānī* 44**)
Ibn Abī l-Futūḥ, anonymous son of the late Abū l-Futūḥ (*Boolfoutouch*), witness to **Private 28**, 323
Ibn Abī l-Layth, Yūḥannā, first director of Fāṭimid *dīwān al-taḥqīq*, 196, 198
Ibn Bashrūn al-Ṣiqillī, poet and anthologist in Norman Sicily, 88
Ibn al-Biththirrānī, Abū Maḍar, 73–4 & n.81, 89
Ibn Fākhir, leader of Muslim rebels against Frederick II, 292 n.52
Ibn Ḥawqal, Abū l-Qāsim Muḥammad, geographer, visits Muslim Sicily, 24
Ibn al-Ḥawwās, ᶜAlī ibn Niᶜma, Muslim *qāʾid* of central Sicily, 32
Ibn Ḥayyīm, *parnās* of Fusṭāṭ, 28
Ibn Jarīr, *see* Bingelir
Ibn Jubayr, Abū l-Ḥusayn Muḥammad ibn Aḥmad, al-Kinānī, Spanish pilgrim, visits Norman Sicily, 36, 47, 212–15, 235, 241–2, 243, 248–9, 249–50, 292, 295–6
Ibn Killis, Yaᶜqūb, Fāṭimid fiscal administrator and vizier, 21
Ibn Mammātī, Asᶜad ibn al-Muhadhdhab, as a source for the administration of Egypt, 15
Ibn Mankūd, Muslim *qāʾid* of Val di Mazara, 32
Ibn Maṭrūḥ al-Tamīmī, Abū Yaḥyā, wālī of Tripoli under Norman rule, 290
Ibn Nāsikh, Ḥasan, Muslim citizen of Norman Palermo, 73–4 & n.86, 110 & n.65, 306 (***Dīwānī* 20**)
Ibn al-Qadīm, Aghlabid fiscal administrator, 21
Ibn Qalāqis, Abū l-Futūḥ Naṣr ibn ᶜAbd Allāh, Alexandrian poet, 35, 133, 212, 233–4, 235–6, 237, 239–41
Ibn al-Qaṭṭāᶜ, Sicilian poet, 26
Ibn al-Ṣayrafī, ᶜAlī ibn Munjib, as a source for the administration of Egypt, 15 & n.14
Ibn Shaddād, ᶜAbd al-ᶜAzīz, Zīrid prince and historian, 85, 86, 87–8, 217, 284

Ibn Shīth al-Qurashī, ᶜAbd al-Raḥīm ibn ᶜAlī, as a source for the administration of Egypt, 15
Ibn Sūdān, Abū l-Dhikr, 'man of' Muriella of Petterrana, 73
Ibn al-Thumna, Muḥammad ibn Ibrāhīm, Muslim *qāʾid* of Syracuse, 32 & nn.7 & 9, 33
Ibn al-Ṭuwayr, Abū Muḥammad ᶜAbd al-Salām ibn al-Ḥasan, al-Qaysarānī, as a source for the Fāṭimid administration of Egypt, 15–16
Ibn al-Usquf, director of Fāṭimid *dīwān al-majlis*, 196, 198
Ibn Ẓafar, Abū Hāshim Muḥammad ibn Abī Muḥammad, author of the *Sulwān al-muṭāᶜ*, 235
Ibn Zurᶜa, *al-faqīh*, Muslim convert to Christianity under William II, 241, 295–6
Ibrahīm ibn Muḥammad al-Qurashī, Muslim of Castrogiovanni, vendor in **Private 27**, 323
Ibrāhīm ibn Mūsā Sh.bᶜāt, brother of Jabrūn and ᶜAbd al-Raḥmān, villein of S. Giovanni degli Eremiti in **Private 16**, 35, 145–6, 320
Ibrāhīm ibn Naṣr al-Lakhmī (*Ebrahym ibin Nasar Ellachmi*), witness to **Private 24**, 322
Ibrāhīm ibn Sabᶜūn (Ebraym, son of Sebeun), known as Atrami, vendor in **Private 24**, 322
Ibrāhīm ibn Sawdān al-Tamīmī (*Abrahym filius Seuden Ettimimi*), witness to **Private 3**, 316
Ibrāhīm ibn Yūsuf (*Brachēmos uios Iosēf*), witness to **Private 12**, 319
al-Idrīsī, Abī ᶜAbd Allāh Muḥammad ibn Muḥammad ibn ᶜAbd Allāh ibn Idrīs, geographer, 236 & n.101, 240 n.129
Ifrīqiya
  administration of
    Aghlabid, 19–20, 21
    Fāṭimid, 19, 20–22
    Zīrid, 22
  emigration from, to Norman Sicily, 82, 107, 147–8
  as a market for Sicilian wheat, 83, 326–8
  Norman conquest and rule of, 34, 74, 82, 84–8, 290–1
Ikhshīdid rulers of Egypt, 16, 19, 21
ᶜImrūn ibn Aḥmad, Aghlabid fiscal administrator, 21
Iōannēs Endoulsi, *see* John al-Andalusī
Iōannēs tēs Melfēs, *see* John of Melfi
Iōannou, mother of Iohannes filius Medicis, vendor in **Private 13**, 319
Iohannes filius Medicis, husband of Maria, son of Iōannou, vendor in **Private 13**, 319
Iohar, *see* Jawhar
Iordanus Lupinus, brother of Hugo(?), witness to **Private 20**, 321
Ioustos, purchaser in **Private 15**, 320
iqlīm, pl. *aqālim* ('administrative district'), 3, 184, 185
iqṭāᶜ, pl. *iqṭāᶜāt* ('portion', grant of land, etc.), 16 & n.21, 17–18, 196–7, 206, 274
ᶜĪsā ibn ᶜAbd al-Munᶜim al-Ṣiqillī, *al-faqīh*, recipient of verses by Abū l-Ḍawʾ Sirāj, 88
ᶜĪsā ibn Sulaymān, witness to **Private 13**, 319
itāwa ('tax'), 36, 47
Iusuph, agent of Abū l-Qāsim Muḥammad ibn Ḥammūd, *see* Yūsuf

Jabbāra ibn Kāmil al-Fādighī, governor of Sousse under Norman rule, 291
Jabrūn ibn Mūsā Sh.bᶜāt, villein of S. Giovanni degli Eremiti in **Private 16**, 35, 145–6, 320
Jacob, *dominus*, precentor of the Cappella Palatina and archdeacon of Catania in **Private 23**, 322
Jaʾfar al-Ḥāfiẓī, Abū Manṣūr, ambassador of al-Ḥāfiẓ to Roger II, 265
Jaᶜfar ibn Yūsuf, governor of Sicily, 26, 30
Jāfrāy dī Ānimātuh, *al-shaykh sar, see* Geoffrey D'Animato
Jāliṣū (PA), barony of the Forestal, 58, 128, 302 (***Dīwānī* 5**), 307 (***Dīwānī* 25**)
  Monreale estate, 154, 158, 162, 164, 189
James I of Aragon, 37, 38–9
James of Palermo, notary, witness to **Private 31**, 324
al-Jarjarāʾī, Abū l-Qāsim ᶜAlī ibn Aḥmad, Fāṭimid vizier (1027–45), 278
jarīda, pl. *jarāʾid* ('register')
  in Fāṭimid Egypt, 16, 18
  in Norman Sicily, *for individual jarāʾid, see* Appendix 1, ***Dīwānī* 1–6, 8, 10, 14, 18, 20–2, 24– 6, 30, 34, 38, 40, 42–5**
  compared to Domesday Book, 3
  earliest Norman *jarāʾid* (***Dīwānī* 1–6** & **8**)
    derived from pre-Islamic registers, 51, 56–8, 63
    functions of, 59–62, 299–300
    one of the roots of the Arabic administration, 63
  royal *jarāʾid* (Appendix 1, ***Dīwānī* 10, 14, 18, 20–2, 24– 6, 30, 34, 38, 40, 42–5**)
    jarāʾid renewed in 1145 (Appendix 1, ***Dīwānī* 21–†27**), 115–43
    Monreale *jarāʾid* (Appendix 1, ***Dīwānī* 43–5**), 152, 153–69, 186–92, 313–14
  updating procedures, *see mutazawwij*-system, *neogamos*-system
  see also: Arabic documents; *plateia*

Jaṭīna (PA), Monreale estate, 168, 189
Jawdhar, *safīr* to al-Mu^{c}izz (fourth Fāṭimid caliph), 20, 21
Jawhar, *al-qā'id*, eunuch master chamberlain of William I, 224, 243, 250
Jawhar al-Ṣiqlabī, *kātib* to al-Mu^{c}izz (fourth Fāṭimid caliph), 20–1
Jerusalem (Palestine), 261 n.21
Jews
 in Anglo-Norman England, 4
 in Islamic lands, 13, 16, 18
 in Muslim Sicily, 27–9
 in Norman Sicily, 18, 202, 293
  of the church of Catania, 55, 56, 57, 119
  of Syracuse, 77, 322–3 (**Private 25**)
  of Termini Imerese, 71
  protected in law by Frederick II, 293–4
  translators of Arabic documents in 13th-century Palermo, 101, 121–3, 131
jibāyāt al-māl, 21
Jimrīya (PA), Monreale estate, 168
Jinān Ibn Kināna, *see* Raḥl al-Mi'a
jizya (tax paid by *dhimmīyūn*)
 classes of *jizya*-payers, 18, 48, 51, 56, 57, 146–7, 165
 in early Islam, 13–14
 in Fāṭimid Egypt, 18, 48
 in Muslim Sicily, 26–7, 29, 30
 in Norman Sicily and Ifrīqiya, paid by Muslims (and Jews?), 18, 34–9, 43, 45, 47–8, 61, 71, 145–6, 150, 165, 297, 299, 320 (**Private 16**)
Joachim, master, palace officer of Frederick II, 245
Jocelm, bishop-elect of Cefalù, 126
John II Comnenos, Byzantine emperor, 266 n.47
John, abbot-bishop of Lipari-Patti, 61 n.137, 94, 303–4 (***Dīwānī* 12–13**)
John al-Andalusī, father of ^{c}Abd al-^{c}Azīz, vendor in **Private 22**, 321–2
John, archbishop of Naples, cardinal, 225
John Atria, the sons of (*awlād J.wān Aṭriya*), barons of Roger II, 309 (***Dīwānī* 31–2**)
John Barbarossa(?), Ser, witness to **Private 8**, 318
John, bishop of Malta, 93, 232
John, *campanarius*, of the Cappella Palatina, scribe of **Private 23**, 322
John, 'chamberlain of the great king' (*i.e.* Roger II), 106 n.46, 322 (**Private 23**)
John, *al-fatā*, *al-qā'id*, chamberlain and eunuch of William II, 220 n.26, 243
John, Greek officer of the royal *dīwān* under William I and II, 310, 311 (***Dīwānī* 35 & 37**)
John, lord *qā'id*, son of Ananias, purchaser in **Private 17**, 320
John, master of the *charbatoi* ('spearmen', from Arabic *ḥarba*?), brother-in-law of the *qā'id* Ranald, witness to **Private 14**, 319–20
John Musso(?), Ser, witness to **Private 8**, 318
John of Lavardin, follower of Stephen du Perche, 230–1
John of Melfi (*Juwān min Malf; Iōannēs tēs Melfēs*), purchaser in **Private 28**, 323
John of Naso, notary, 13th-century translator of Greek of ***Dīwānī* 14**, 101
John of Palermo, notary, witness to **Private 31**, 324
John of Palermo, Arab(?) scribe of Frederick II, 244–5
John of Romania, *imperialis dohane de secretis et questorum magister*, under Frederick II, 172 n.9
John of Troina, protonotary under Roger I, 53 & n.103, 54, 65, 67
John of Vitalba, prior of S. Maria la Gadera (PA), 311 (***Dīwānī* 36**)
John, officer of royal *dīwān* under Roger II, 103, 106 & n.46, 222, 304 (***Dīwānī* 15**)
John, son of ^{c}Abd al-Malik, *see* Juwān ibn ^{c}Abd al-Malik
John, son of ^{c}Abd al-Raḥmān, *see* Yūḥannā ibn ^{c}Abd al-Raḥmān
John, son of the Doctor, *see* Iohannes filius Medicis
John, son of George of Antioch, 312 (***Dīwānī* 39**)
John, son of al-Ḥājj, Christian(?) burgher of Misilmeri in ***Dīwānī* 39**, 312
John, son of *al-qā'id* Philip, son of Ibn Ḥammūd, 242 & n.138
John the emir, son of Eugenios the notary, 72, 317 (**Private 7**)
John the Moor, household slave and *magister camerarius* under Frederick II and Conrad, then *qa'id* of Saracens of Lucera, 244 & n.162, 250
John the Philosopher, prior of S. Maria dell'Ammiraglio, 312 (***Dīwānī* 39**)
John the priest, agent of Muriella of Petterrana, 73
John the priest, *taboularios* in **Private 22**, 322
John the priest, witness to **Private 14**, 320
John the *taboularios*, in **Private 28**, 323
John the Tuscan, Adelaide's chaplain, 71
John Zēkri, member of court of Count Roger II, 74
Jordan of Calatahaly, royal official under William II, 80

Jordan, son of Roger I, 40, 41, 46
Jordanus the chamberlain, under Count Roger II, 72
Judaeo-Arabic, 4, 77, 322–3 (**Private 25**)
Julian (*Juliyan, Giollen*), the knight (*al-fāris*), 76 & n.98
Juliana (PA), estate granted to S. Maria di Monreale, 152 & n.27
al-Jurf and al-Khurāsānī (PA), Monreale estate, 168
Jurf Bū Karīm (PA), Monreale estate, 189
jus affidandi, 60: *see also* villeins
Jusuph filius Abdelnur Ettennuchi, *see* Yūsuf ibn ᶜAbd al-Nūr al-Tanūkhī
Juwān al-Andalusī, *see* John al-Andalusī
Juwān ibn ᶜAbd al-Malik, witness to **Private 22**, 321–2
Juwān min Malf, *see* John of Melfi

Kaggio (PA), 46 n.81
Kaggiotto (PA), 46 n.81
Kalbid emirs of Sicily, 25–6, 29–30
  contribution to Norman monarchy, 5, 268, 280–1
Kalokeros, witness to **Private 14**, 320
kapriliggas, *see* chamberlain
katonoma ('name-list'), 45, 112
kātib ('scribe'), in early Islamic administrations, 15
kātib al-inshā', 81, 89–90, 295
Kērbuna, daughter of Kērbos Similias, purchaser in **Private 13**, 319
Khalīl ibn Isḥāq ibn al-Ward, Fāṭimid governor of Sicily, 24–5
Khandaq al-Qayrūz, hospital, *see* Churches and religious foundations, S. Maria di Campograsso
kharāj ('land-tax'), 13–14, 17, 20, 21, 22, 25, 29, 42, 61, 145 n.3
khāzin ('treasurer'), 16, 20
khāṣṣīyat bayt al-māl, 20
khums ('fifth', tax), 24, 25, 27
al-Khurasānī, *see* al-Jurf and al-Khurasānī
al-Kanisīya and Shantaghnī (PA), Monreale estate, 169
Kosmas, abbot of S. Maria del Rifugio, 43
Kōnstantinos, son of the Notary Leo, witness to **Private 28**, 323
Kōstantinos, son of Solomon, brother of Christodoulos, witness to **Private 15**, 320
Kōstantza, daughter of Boulfadl, *see* Qunṣṭaṣa bint Abī l-Faḍl
Kouttaia (TP), 303 (***Dīwānī*** **†9**), 308 (***Dīwānī*** **†27**)
Kutayfāt ibn al-Afḍal, vizier of al-Ḥāfiẓ, eleventh Fāṭimid caliph, 262

labour services, 61–62
Lachabuca (PA), Monreale estate, 152 & n.27
Landulf, Lombard prince of Benevento, 44
Landulf Caputus, strategot of Salerno, 243 n.140
language in Norman Sicily, 4–5: *see also* Arabic, Greek, Latin
Laqamūqa (PA), Monreale estate, 168, 188, 191 n.66
Latin, as an administrative language in Norman Sicily, 4–5, 40, 91, 92, 93, 96, 127, 140–2, 187, 190, 207–11
Laurence Maniscalco, witness to ***Dīwānī*** **28**, **29** and **33**, 175 n.26
Leo III, Byzantine emperor (717–41), 23
Leo of Chousta, notary under William II, 312 (***Dīwānī*** **39**)
Leo of Reggio, witness to **Private 10** and **Private 14**, 318, 320
Leo, son of the late notary John Pezpou, witness to **Private 31**, 324
Leo the logothete, under Roger I, Adelaide, and Count Roger II, 66, 67–8, 69
Licata (AG), 113, 238
Limonos (PA), 301 (***Dīwānī*** **2**)
Liyāj, *see* Aci Castello
Līyūn ibn Abū (*sic!*) al-Faraḥ, vendor in **Private 10**, 318
logothete, 23, 65, 66, 67, 68, 69
Lombards in rebellion of 1160–62, 220, 221
Lucera (FG), 13th-century Muslim colony of, 36, 47, 244
Luke, archimandrite of S. Salvatore di Messina, 104, 304 (***Dīwānī*** **15**)
al-Lūqa, Monreale estate, 169

al-Maḍīq (PA), Monreale estate, 169
Maganoce, *see* Maghanūja
al-Maghāghī, *see* Raḥl al-Maghāghī
Maghanūja (PA), 46 n.81, 301 (***Dīwānī*** **2**)
  Monreale estate, 162, 169, 188, 191 n.67
Magione, Contrada, 180 n.35
magister rationalis comitis, 65
Magunuche, Flumen de, *see* Belice destro
al-Mahdīya (Tunisia), 20, 25, 32 n.8, 34, 82, 84, 85, 86, 87, 215, 217, 223, 249, 290, 291
Maimoun, son of Kalou, witness to **Private 13**, 319
Maimun, witness to **Private 15**, 320
Maio of Bari,
  origins, family, and early career, 197–8, 219
  royal archivist (*scriniarius*) under Roger II, 197, 198
  made vice-chancellor (1149), 197
  succeeds Robert of Selby as chancellor, 197–8

appointed *magnus ammiratus* on succession of William I (1154), 198, 287
closely linked to renewals of 1144–45, creation of the *dīwān al-taḥqīq*, and institution of the *dafātir al-ḥudūd*, 197–8
first director of the *dīwān al-taḥqīq*, 201
'tyranny' of, 219, 223, 284 n.5
death (10 November 1160), 201, 202, 219, 287
Makhlūf, captain of the palace archers under William II, 230 n.70, 243, 312 (***Dīwānī* 39**)
Makhlūf, nephew of *gaytus* Bussit (*al-qā'id Abū Sayyīd*), *see* Gilbert, known as Mahalufus
Makhlūf ibn Abī l-Futūḥ al-Tamīmī; witness to **Private 27**, 323
Makhlūf ibn Makhlūf al-Qaysī, witness to **Private 19**, 321
al-Makhzūmī, 15
Malbīṭ (PA), Monreale estate, 169, 188, 190, 191 n.66
Malconvenant, lords of Calatrasi, 163
John, renounces Calatrasi in exchange for Turrus and Cellaro, 185
Robert, son of John, 152 n.26, 321 (**Private 20**)
William, *magister Justiciarius* under William II, Tancred and Constance, 321 (**Private 20**), 324 (**Private 30**)
Maleinos, Stefanos, judge under Roger II, 103 & n.39, 106, 304 (***Dīwānī* 15**)
Mālik ibn ᶜAlawī, *shaykh* of the Banū Ṣakhr in Ifrīqiya, 81 n.127
Malik ibn Hubāra, Christian *ra'īs* of Ṭūr in Sinai, 130
Malta, conquest by Roger I, 34, 37
Manjūma, wife of ᶜUmar ibn ᶜAtīq al-Qaysī, known as Ibn al-Muhāriqa(?), sister of Abū Bakr, Aḥmad, and Amr al-Khayr, vendors in **Private 9**, 318
al-Manṣūr bi-llāh, third Fāṭimid caliph (946–53), 20
al-Manṣūrīya (Tunisia), 20
Manzil ᶜAbd Allāh (PA), Monreale estate, 168, 189, 190
Manzil ᶜAbd al-Raḥmān and al-Qumayṭ (PA), Monreale estate, 168, 189
Manzil Bū l-Khayr (TP), 303 (***Dīwānī* †9**), 308 (***Dīwānī* †27**)
Manzil Handūn (PA), Monreale estate, 169
Manzil Kharrāz (PA), Monreale estate, 169
Manzil al-Khayr (PA), 234
Manzil Krishtī (PA), Monreale estate, 168, 189
Manzil Nikhīṭa (PA), Monreale estate, 169
Manzil Yūsuf, *see* Mezzoiuso
Manzil Zamūr (PA), Monreale estate, 168, 189
Manzil Zarqūn (PA), 168, 188, 191 n.65
al-Maqrīzī, 'biography' of George of Antioch, 80–90, 255, 282–3, 285
Maranfusa, monte (PA), *see* Calatrasi
al-marātib, *see* Procurator
Margana (PA), 180 & n.35, 310 (***Dīwānī* 34**)
Margaret of Navarre, wife of William I, mother of William II, regent, 221, 224, 225–7, 228, 230, 231, 232, 233, 247, 250, 311–12 (***Dīwānī* 37–8**)
Margaret the Christian, Lady, daughter of the nun from Agrigento (*Dāma Bargharīṭa al-naṣrānīya bint al-rāhiba al-Karkantīya*), purchaser in **Private 19**, 77, 321
Maria, wife of Iohannes filius Medicis, vendor in **Private 13**, 319
Maria, wife of Roger de Tarsia, daughter of Robert Malconvenant, party to **Private 20**, 152 n.26, 321
Marina, abbess of S. Maria dell'Ammiraglio, 110, 306 (***Dīwānī* 20**)
Marsala (TP), 70
marsūm, pl. *marāsīm* ('decree'), 101
Martin, witness to ***Dīwānī* 28**, **29** and **33**, 175 n.26
Martīn al-Najjār, witness to **Private 13**, 319
Martin of Calatafimi, judge, party to **Private 32**, 325
Martin, *al-qā'id*, leading eunuch and palace Saracen
brother, 219, 221, 243
punishes rebels of 1160–62, 221, 247–8
has his own court, 221, 247–8
magister camerarius et familiaris, 221, 228, 319 (**Private 11**)
ṣāḥib dīwān al-taḥqīq al-maᶜmūr, 201, 202, 203 n.47, 220, 279, 310 (***Dīwānī* 35**), 311 (***Dīwānī* 37**)
thwarts prison breakout of 1162, 221, 248
location of office, 221
signature (*ᶜalāma*), 220, 222, 251–2, 310 (***Dīwānī* 35**), 311 (***Dīwānī* 37**), 319 (**Private 11**)
property in Kemonia, 222, 234, 250
death (before August 1176), 222
Mārtū (PA), Monreale estate, 169, 188, 191–2
Mary, daughter of George of Antioch, 110
Marzucus (*i.e.* Marzūq?) de Plutino, witness to **Private 31**, 324
Masᶜūd ibn Tāmir al-Qurashī, father of ᶜAbd al-Salām, vendor in **Private 19**, 321
Mataracius, *see* al-Muṭarriz
Matthew (*Mathāw*), brother of Bartholomew (*Barthulamāw ibn ...āmūn*), baron of Roger II, 309 (***Dīwānī* 31–2**)

Matthew Marclafaba of Salerno, officer of Frederick II, 245 n.165
Matthew of Salerno, notary, then vice-chancellor, and chancellor, under William I, William II and Tancred
'principal assistant' to Maio of Bari, 219
imprisoned on death of Maio (10 November 1160), 219, 220
released by February 1161, 220
ṣāḥib dīwān al-taḥqīq al-maᶜmūr, 202 n.46, 220, 310 (***Dīwānī* 35**)
reconstitutes the *defetari*, 21 n.49, 177 & n.34, 180
domini Regis magister notarius et familiaris, 221, 319 (**Private 11**)
triumvir of royal familiars under William I and II, 224, 312 (***Dīwānī* 39**)
one of the leaders of the 'Sicilian' faction at court under regent Margaret, 225, 227, 228
leader of opposition to Stephen du Perche, 230–1
imprisoned by Stephen du Perche, 231
organizes coup against Stephen du Perche, 231–2, 244
granted Qurūbnish al-Suflī by William II, 181, 312 (***Dīwānī* 40**)
founds S. Maria *Latinorum*, 312 (***Dīwānī* 40**)
Matthew, son of Stephen of Carthage, 215
al-Mawlā l-Nāṣir, director(?) of the *dīwān al-fawāʾid*, 204, 205, 295, 323 (**Private 26**)
Maymūn ibn Ḥasan al-Tamīmī, witness in **Private 1**, 315
Maymūn, Muslim merchant from Cefalù, brother of Ṣadaqa, father of ᶜAlī, uncle of Ḥasan, debtor in **Private 8**, 317–18
Mazara del Vallo (TP), 32 n.9, 215, 302–3 (***Dīwānī* †9**), 308 (***Dīwānī* †27**)
Roger I's assembly of 1093, 54, 119, 120, 121, 144, 301 (***Dīwānī* 1**)
al-Māzarī, *al-imām*, Ifrīqiyan jurist, 294
Medinaceli, Archivo General de la Fundación Casa Ducal de (ADM), Messina city archive, x, 11–12, 40 nn.47, 49 & 52, 53 n.103, 65 n.14, 66 n.18, 67 n.32, 69 n.46, 71 n.70, 102, 103 n.38, 112 n.73, 115 & n.3, 117 n.13, 203 n.47, 204, 304–5 (***Dīwānī* 15–18**), 309 (***Dīwānī* 31–2**), 311 (***Dīwānī* 37**), 312 (***Dīwānī* 38**)
Melfi, council of (1059), 32 n.8
Meselimi (PA), 45–6
Messina (ME)
'capital' of Adelaide, 78
city archive,11–12: *see also* Medinaceli
Norman conquest, 33
court of King Roger at, 116, 117
rebels against Stephen du Perche, 231
palace and court of William II described by Ibn Jubayr, 212–13
rebellion of 1674, 11–12
see also Churches and religious foundations
Mezzoiuso (PA), 35, 38, 47, 145–6, 246 n.181, 320 (**Private 16**)
Michael, father of George of Antioch, 80
Michael, emir, son of George of Antioch, 82, 83
Michael the notary, son of the late notary George, witness to **Private 31**, 324
Michiken, *see* Villalba
Mileto (VV), 32 n.7, 78, 126, 127, 236 n.101
Mineo (CT), 108, 305 (***Dīwānī* 19**)
mint(s), 30 n.91, 77, 113, 268, 269, 278
Mirto (PA), 94–9, 112, 303 (***Dīwānī* 12**): *see also* Mārtū
Misilmeri (PA), 110, 112 n.73, 243, 306 (***Dīwānī* 20**), 312 (***Dīwānī* 39**)
al-miẓalla ('ceremonial parasol'), 82, 83, 265
modion (area and dry measure), xviii, 108
modius (area and dry measure), xviii, 146
Moli, Cozzo, *see* Faṭṭāsina
Monastīr (Tunisia), 85 n.160
Mondello (PA), 232
monomachia, 221
Montelepre (PA), 316 (**Private 4**)
Moses al-Ghudāmisī, 28
Moses ibn Yaḥyā the Perfumer, Jew of Muslim Palermo, 29
Moses, Magister, Jew of Palermo and translator of Arabic, 101, 121, 131
Moshe bar ᶜAmram, Jew of Syracuse, witness to **Private 25**, 323
Muᶜammar, eldest son of Rushayd ibn Kāmil ibn Jāmiᶜ, *ṣāḥib* of Gabès, 291
mudd (area and dry measure), xviii, 35, 190–2 nn.63–9 & 71
Muḥammad ibn ᶜAbbād, *amīr al-muslimīn bi-Ṣiqillīya*, rebel commander against Frederick II, 292
Muḥammad ibn Abī l-Fatḥ ibn ..., witness to **Private 2**, brother of ᶜAlī, 315
Muḥammad ibn Abī l-Ḥasan ᶜAlī ibn Abī l-Qāsim ᶜAbd al-Raḥmān ibn Rajāʾ, son and brother of *qāḍī* of Norman Palermo, 88, 89, 318 (**Private 9**)
Muḥammad ibn al-Ḥājj ibn Khālid, Muslim merchant from Corleone, debtor in **Private 8**, 317–18
Muḥammad ibn Ḥammūd, Abū l-Qāsim, 234–42, 251, 254
ancestry, 235–6, 237
assists al-Harawī, 241
assists pilgrims, 241, 242

base in Trapani, 212, 239, 241, 242
commercial activities, 239
employed in the royal *dīwān*, 234–5, 240, 241, 252–3, 289–90, 292
'the archon of the court, the secretary, *qāʾid* Abū l-Qāsim', 234–5
'the *qāʾid* Abū l-Qāsim, master of the *duana de secretis*', 234–5
asked to lift the *jizya* from the Muslims of Syracuse, 35, 38, 133, 240, 252, 292
hereditary leader of the Muslim community of Sicily, 239, 241, 252, 289, 292
opponent of Stephen du Perche, 230, 239
patron of Ibn Qalāqis, 35, 133, 235–6, 239–40
property
in Palermo, 242
in and around Trapani, 241, 242
host to Ibn Jubayr, 212
described by Ibn Jubayr, 241–2
redeems Muslim prisoners, 206, 241
seeks aid from Almohads, 241, 253, 289, 292
seeks aid from Ṣalāḥ al-Dīn, 241, 253
son, *see* Philip, son of Ibn Ḥammūd
Muḥammad ibn Ḥusayn al-Qaysī, witness to **Private 6**, 317
Muḥammad ibn Muḥammad al-Lawātī, witness to **Private 6**, 317
Muḥammad ... ibn Muḥammad al-Qaysī, witness to **Private 2**, 315
Muḥammad ibn Rajāʾ, Abū ᶜAbd Allāh, *al-qāḍī*, member of circle of Abū l-Qāsim Muḥammad ibn Ḥammūd, probably son of Rajā ibn Abī l-Ḥasan, 240
Muḥammad, infant son of Rushayd ibn Kāmil ibn Jāmiᶜ, *ṣāḥib* of Gabès, 291
Muḥammad ibn al-Salām ibn ᶜAbd Allāh al-Ḥ.mrī, witness to **Private 26**, 323
Muḥammad ibn ᶜUmar ibn Ḥasan al-Ṭāʾī(?), witness to **Private 26**, 323
Muḥammad ibn ᶜUmar ibn Muḥammad al-Qaysī, witness to **Private 6**, 317
Mujāhid ibn Ḥusayn al-Kindī, witness to **Private 2** and **Private 6**, 315, 317
muls, *see* villeins
al-Muᶜizz li-dīn Allāh, Maᶜadd ibn Ismāᶜīl, fourth Fāṭimid caliph (953–75), 20, 25, 260
Muriella of Petterrana, daughter of Gosbert de Lucy, cousin of Roger II, 73–4, 89, 295
mushārif ('district tax-officer'), 17
Muslims of Norman Sicily
Islamist group reject the Norman *dhimma*, 36, 297
leaders, compared to English earls and great thegns, 3–4
massacre of Muslims in Palermo (1161), 219–20, 254
massacres in 'Lombard' towns, 220, 254
massacres and pogroms on the death of William II, 285
permitted own law and *qāḍī*, 293, 294–5, 296
persecution of, 150, 229, 254
protected in law by Frederick II, 293–4
rebellions after conquest, 32, 64
rebellions of 1189–1246, 285, 293
reduced to status equivalent to *ahl al-dhimma* in Muslim lands, 33–9
rights dependant upon ability and will of crown to protect them, 150
Stephen du Perche's treatment of, 228–9
see also: palace Saracens; villeins
al-Mustaᶜlī bi-llāh, ninth Fāṭimid caliph (1094–1101), 195
al-Muṭarriz (*Mataracius*), *al-qāʾid*, royal chamberlain and steward under William II, 243 & n.140
Mutata (PA), 91, 123, 274, 303 (***Dīwānī* 10**)
mutazawwijūn, *see* villeins
mutazawwij-system, 47–8, 108, 127–8, 141, 158: *see also neogamos*-system
mystologue, 65, 68

al-Nābulusī, as a source for the administration of Egypt, 15
Naro (AG), 113, 238 & n.107
nashʾ ('new generation', new tax-payers), 18
nāsikh ('copyist'), 16
Nathan the cantor, Jew in Muslim Palermo, 29
nāẓir fī bayt al-māl, 20
Nēfos, monk of S. Andrea de Bebbene, lessor in **Private 23**, 322
neogamoi, *see* villeins
neogamos-system, 47–51, 57, 59: *see also mutazawwij*-system
neokamoi, *see neogamoi*
'newlyweds', *see* villeins, *ezeumenoi*, *neogamoi*, *mutazawwijūn*
Nicholas II, pope (1058–61), 32 n.8
Nicholas, archbishop of Messina, 131 n.53, 203, 221, 279, 311 (***Dīwānī* 37**)
Nicholas, archon of the great court, *protonobilissimus*, protonotary, judge of all Calabria, 67
Nicholas, brother of Urso the scribe, witness to ***Dīwānī* 28**, **29** and **33**, 175 n.26
Nicholas di Mesa, *protospatharios*, chamberlain and protonotary under Roger I, 65, 66–7, 69, 108
Nicholas of Reggio, judge under Count Roger II, 74, 295

Nicholas, son of the late Christodoulos, witness to **Private 21**, 321
Nicholas, son of Christodoulos *Taneperi* (*al-Ṭanābirī*?), vendor in **Private 15**, 320
Nicholas, son of John, burgher of Misilmeri in ***Dīwānī* 39**, 312
Nicholas, son of Scholarios, the Greek chaplain of Roger I, 66
Nicholas, son of Tapechtēs(?), witness to **Private 28**, 323
Nicholas the chamberlain, under William II, 312 (***Dīwānī* 39**)
Nicholas the logothete, under William II, 312 (***Dīwānī* 39**)
Nicholas the secretary, 'son' of *al-qā'id* Peter, 228, 243–4
Nicola Patrizio of Messina, notary, 115 n.3
Nicola, son of Lido(?), (*Niqūla ibn Līdū[?]*), Latin burgher of Sciacca in ***Dīwānī* 31–2**, 309
Nicolaus de Ebdemonia, son of the late Lord Ha...(?), *secretus* of Palermo, witness to **Private 31**, 324
Nicotera (VV), 259 n.6
Nife, Frater, *see* Nēfos
Nikētas Panētērios, witness to **Private 10**, 318
Nikētas son of Theodore, witness to **Private 22**, 322
Nikolaos, witness to **Private 10**, 318
Niqūla Ashqar, servant (*khadīm*) of the royal palace, purchaser in **Private 26**, 204, 244, 295, 323
Nissīm ibn Ḥayyīm alias Khalaf ibn Ya'qūb the Spaniard, Jew of Muslim Palermo, 29
Noikolaos (*sic*!), witness to **Private 15**, 320
Norman administrative efficiency, myth of, 1–3
Norman Sicily, a 'modern state', 3, 78
Normandy, administration of, 1–2, 66
Norse, 4, 126 n.27
Noth, Albrecht, and the study of the Arabic and bilingual documents of Norman Sicily, ix–x, 8
Noto (SR), surrender to Normans (1091), 31, **37**, 63
Nūr al-Dīn Maḥmūd ibn Zanjī, ruler of Damascus and Aleppo (1146–74), 282
Nuṣayr, Fāṭimid *khāzin*, 20, 21

Obert Fallamonica, *see* Fallamonica
Odesuer (PA), 324 (**Private 30**)
oikētōrai, *see* villeins
Oliver, Ser, witness to **Private 8**, 318
Oliveri (ME), 61
Omoddeos, husband of Qunṣṭaṣa bint Abī l-Faḍl, vendor in **Private 28**, 323
Orderic Vitalis (Anglo-Norman historian), 64–5
Ottumarrano (PA), 170–1, 313 (***Dīwānī* 41**)

Padhormum (EN), 238
Paenos, chamberlain and protochamberlain under Count Roger II, 72
Paganus, witness to **Private 10**, 318
Paḥlavuni family, 261 & n.20
  Bahrām, Christian Armenian vizier of al-Ḥāfiẓ the Fāṭimid caliph, 134, 259, 261–4, 267, 282
  Bassak, brother of Bahrām, governor of Qūṣ, 262
  Bassak, Byzantine duke of Antioch, uncle of Bahrām, 264, 267, 282
  Grigor, brother of Bahrām, Catholicos of Armenians in Egypt, 261
  Grigor II Martyrophil (Vkayasēr), Catholicos of all Armenians, 261
  Grigor Paḥlavuni Magristros, 261
'palace Saracens'
  activities, duties, and responsibilities, 212–13, 243–4, 287–8
  'alāmas, 251–2
  archers, 226, 230, 243, 244
  assist pilgrims, 213–14, 251
  blacks, 212, 244, 245
  concubines, 213, 244, 250
  craftsmen, 244
  display and ceremonial, 82, 213, 287–8
  eunuchs, 212–14, 243–4, 249–50
  falconers, 244, 245
  under Henry VI, 244, 254
  under Frederick II, 244–7, 250
  kitchen staff, 212, 244
  massacre of (1161), 219–20
  menagerie keepers, 244
  military band, 232, 244
  military commanders, 215, 217, 243, 244, 288
  mint, 244
  and Muslim community of Sicily, 251
  number, 244
  omnicompetence, 250, 253
  opposition to Matthew Bonnellus, 219
  opposition to Stephen du Perche, 230, 231, 232, 244
  personal ties with rulers, 250, 253–4
  redeem prisoners, 205–6, 213
  religion, 212, 213, 215–16, 217, 229, 251–2
  and the royal image, 253–6, 287–8
  royal familiars, 250
  scapegoats, 250–1, 254, 255–6, 288
  slave-girls, 213, 244, 250
  'sons' of the eunuchs (the Banū Fityān), 213, 228, 251

ṭirāz workers, 213, 243, 244
Palermo (PA)
Agios Kōnstantinos, street running to church of, 321 (**Private 21**)
Amalfitano, 319 (**Private 14**)
ᶜAyn al-Abrārī, 320 (**Private 18**)
ᶜAyn al-Batīya, 316 (**Private 5**)
ᶜAyn Faraj, 316 (**Private 5**)
ᶜAyn Ibn Abū Saᶜīd, 310 (***Dīwānī* 35**)
ᶜAyn al-Manānī, 316 (**Private 5**)
ᶜAyn al-Shifāᵓ mosque, 241
Bāb al-Abnāᵓ, 316 (**Private 6**), 322 (**Private 23**), 324 (**Private 29**)
Bāb al-Sūdān, 316 (**Private 6**), 318 (**Private 9**)
Burj al-Baṭṭāl, 316 (**Private 5**)
Calza, *see* al-Khāliṣa
'capital' of Adelaide and Count Roger II (1112), 78
Casa Martorana, 267
Cassarum (*al-Qaṣr*), 110, 284 n.2: *see also al-Qaṣr al-Qadīm*
Castellum Maris, 219, 221, 224, 229, 231
Chalca (al-Ḥalqa), 319 (**Private 11**)
cemetery, 322 (**Private 23**), 324 (**Private 29**)
La Cuba, palace of William II, 266, 270
al-Dajjājīn, 315 (**Private 2**)
Darb al-Asquṭūnī, 323 (**Private 26**)
Darb al-Siminṭārī (lit. 'Street of the Cemetery'), 324 (**Private 29**)
al-Dayyāsīn al-Kibār, 284 n.2, 321 (**Private 19**)
duᶜāᵓ, 138–9
emir of Norman Palermo, 68–9
Falsomiele, Arabic *Faḥṣ Mārīya*, Greek *Agros Marias*, 316 (**Private 5**), 318 (**Private 10**)
La Favara, palace of Roger II, 266, 270, 286
al-Fawwāra, 315 (**Private 2**)
al-Fawwāra al-Kabīra, 320 (**Private 18**)
*funduq*s, 110, 215, 306 (***Dīwānī* 20**), 323 (**Private 28**)
Gallo, Monte (*to sarf [i.e. al-sharaf] tou Gallen*), 321–2 (**Private 22**)
Ideisini (*al-Dayyāsīn*), 284 n.2
Kalamin, 321–2 (**Private 22**)
Kemonia, 222, 226, 234 & n.90, 250, 322 (**Private 23**)
al-Khāliṣa, 24, 33, 284 n.2
Lamis, 320 (**Private 15**)
Masjid al-Sabīyān, 318 (**Private 9**)
palace and court of William II, described by Ibn Jubayr, 214–15
Papireto (river), 220 & n.22
Purgos tēs Thugatros Serēp ('the Tower of the Daughter of Serep'), 320 (**Private 17**)
qāḍī of Norman Palermo, 74, 88, 110, 294–5
al-Qaṣr al-Qadīm (the Old City), 24, 33, 316 (**Private 6**), 323 (**Private 26**)
Rabᶜ al-Malf ('Amalfitano'), 319 (**Private 14**)
Rachap (*al-Raḥaba*), 323 (**Private 28**)
royal palace, 24, 82, 195, 214–15, 216, 221, 231, 232, 243, 244, 245, 250, 254, 286–7, 288, 319 (**Private 11**)
Ruga Marmorea, 325 (**Private 32**)
Rumē Kes (*Zuqāq al-Kaᵓs*?), 319 (**Private 13**)
Sceralcadi (*Shāriᶜ* or *Shirᶜat al-qāḍī*), 220 n.22, 284 n.2
Scerarchadium, *see* Sceralcadi
Simāṭ al-Balāṭ, 316 (**Private 6**)
surrender to Normans, 33–4, 37, 38
divided between Robert Guiscard and Roger I, 68–9
al-Surtīya, 319 (**Private 14**)
Torre Greco, 234 n.90
L'Uscibene, palace of Roger II, 266
La Zisa, palace of William II, 266, 270
Zuqāq Ibn Khalfūn, 316 (**Private 6**), 319 (**Private 12**)
Zuqāq Ibn al-Khāthira, 321 (**Private 19**)
Zuqāq al-Kaᵓs, *see* Rumē Kes
see also Churches and religious foundations
Pandulf, Lombard prince of Benevento, 44
Pantalica (SR), Muslim rebellion of 1079, 64
paper, use by Siculo-Norman chancery, 75 & n.97
papyrus, grown in Muslim Palermo and used for administrative documents, 24
parasol, ceremonial, *see miẓalla*
pariclum ('plough-land', area measure), xviii, 108, 191 n.70
paroikoi, *see* villeins
Partinico (PA), 94, 246 n.181
Patti (ME), 61, 64: *see also* Churches and religious foundations
Pelekanos, Dominēkos, witness to **Private 28,** 323
Pelekanos, Philip, witness to **Private 13,** 319
periorismos ('boundary-description'), 94, 96, 98, 99, 102, 103, 104, 105, 106, 109, 112, 113
Perisium (EN), 238
Perroun, *see* Peter, al-qāᵓid, the eunuch
Peter, archbishop of Brindisi, 243
Peter Bido (or Bidon), second Norman emir of Palermo, 68–9
Peter Markēsi, vendor in **Private 7**, 317
Peter of Alesna, baron of Duke Roger Borsa, 68
Peter of Castronuovo, father of Sitt al-Ḥusn, witness to **Private 12**, 319

Peter, *al-qā'id*, leading eunuch and palace Saracen (also known as Barrūn, Perroun, and Aḥmad al-Ṣiqillī)
origins, 227, 249
first appearance (1141) as *o kaitēs Perroun*, 103, 106, 222, 304 (***Dīwānī* 15**)
ʿabd al-ḥaḍrat al-malakīya ... al-fatā Barrūn and *Petrus servus palatii* founds public building at Termini Imerese, 222–3, 251, 288
shaykh al-dīwān al-maʿmūr al-qa'id Barrūn (1149 – ***Dīwānī* 29**), 194, 222, 308
commander of Norman fleet at loss of al-Mahdīya to the Almohads (30 July 1159), 223, 253
punishes rebels of 1160–62, 223–4, 229
has his own court, 221, 224, 296–7
triumvir of royal familiars under William I, 224
manumitted by William I (1166), 224, 250
promoted first minister by regent Margaret (1166), 224
plots to assassinate Richard Palmer, 225
attacked by Gilbert of Gravina, 225, 248
military escort and support, 226
defects to the Almohads, 226, 243, 248, 253
as Aḥmad al-Ṣiqillī, made admiral of the fleet of Yūsuf ibn ʿAbd al-Mu'min, 227
leads expeditions against the Almoravid Banū Ghāniya (1185), 227
character, 225, 248
property in Kemonia, 226, 234, 250
religion, 223, 225, 251–2
signature (*ʿalāma*), 222, 251–2, 308 (***Dīwānī* 29**), 309 (***Dīwānī* 31**)
his(?) 'son', Nicholas the secretary, 228
Peter the Deacon, Greek Christian spy for Robert Guiscard, 33
Peter, the ex-deacon(?), witness to **Private 14**, 320
Peter the notary, 228–9
Peter, the priest of Geoffrey D'Animato (*al-shaykh al-qissīs Bātrū qissīs al-shaykh sar Jāfrāy dī Ānimātuh*), purchaser in **Private 29**, 324
Petralia (PA), 32, 170, 184, 322 (**Private 24**)
Petterrana (PA), 73–74, 89, 295
Philagathos of Cerami, Greek cleric and theologian under Roger II, 139 n.97
Philip, bailiff of Misilmeri(?) in ***Dīwānī* 39**, 312
Philip *de Ecclesiastico*, notary, 101
Philip of al-Mahdīya, eunuch of Roger II, 198 n.25, 215–19, 249, 250, 251, 253, 255, 289
Philip, son of [Abū l-Qāsim Muḥammad?] ibn Ḥammūd, *al-qā'id*, 242
his son, John, son of *al-qā'id* Philip, son of Ibn Ḥammūd, 242
Philip, son of John, son of the emir Eugenios, witness to **Private 7**, 317
Philip son of Joseph son of ... , witness to **Private 22**, 322
Philip, son of Leo the logothete and 'great judge of all Calabria', 67, 218–19 n.19
Philip, son of Michael of Mazara, witness to **Private 21**, 321
Philip, son of Nikolaos Garzēfa, witness to **Private 12**, 319
Philip, son of the patrician Gregory, Greek Christian spy for Norman leaders, 33
Philip, son of Simon, witness to **Private 31**, 324
Philip the African, 215
Philip the Christian, son of Gaytus Phytien (*i.e. al-qā'id Fityān*) the Christian, known as Ibn B..., vendor in **Private 3**, 315
Philip the logothete, under Count Roger II, 72
Philip the notary, *al-qā'id* of Palermo under Frederick II, 242
Philip the protonotary, 103, 106, 304 (***Dīwānī* 15**)
Piana degli Albanesi (PA), 301 (***Dīwānī* 2**)
Pipitone, Pizzo, *see* Petterrana
plateia ('list', register of population), 53, 54, 58, 92, 102, 107, 121, 123, 144, 166, 172: *see also jarīda*
Polizzi (PA), 170
populus trilinguis, 284–5, 297
praktika ('tax-register'), 43
Prizzi (PA), 58 n.128
Procurator, the (*al-marātib*), in the palace of William II, 214
prosēlutoi, *see* villeins
protochamberlain, 72
protonobilissimus, 66, 67, 71, 72
protonotary, 23, 65, 66, 67, 68, 80, 103, 106, 304 (***Dīwānī* 15**)
protospatharios, 67: *see also* Nicholas di Mesa
ptōchoi, *see* villeins
Ptolemy of Capua, judge of city of Palermo, 101, 121

Q.n.sh (PA), Monreale estate, 169
Qabiyāna (PA), Monreale estate, 155, 162, 164, 168
qāḍī of Norman Palermo, 74, 88, 110, 294–5
al-Qāʾim bi-amr Allāh, second Fāṭimid caliph (934–46), 20
Qalānus (Tunisia), emigrant from in Norman Sicily, 147
Qalʿat al-Ṣirāt (PA), 64: *see also* Collesano

Qal^c^at al-Ṭ.razī, *see* Calatrasi
al-Qalqashandī, as a source for the administration of Egypt, 15
qānūn, pl. *qawānīn*
a. 'register', in Fāṭimid Egypt, 17, 42, 145 n.3
b. 'land-tax', in Norman Sicily, 35, 36, 47, 61, 145 & n.3, 320 (**Private 16**)
al-Qarīyānī (PA), Monreale estate, 169
Qaṣaba, *see* Casaba
Qaṣr al-Dīmās (Tunisia), 85–6
Qaṣr Yānah, *see* Castrogiovanni
Qaṣṭana (PA), Monreale estate, 155, 162, 164, 165, 168
al-Qayrawān (Tunisia), 82
qiṣṣa, pl. *qiṣaṣ* ('petition'), 101
quaterni, *quaterniones*, *quinterni*, *see daftar*
al-Qumayṭ (PA), 46 n.81
Monreale estate, 168, 189: *see also* Manzil ᶜAbd al-Raḥmān and al-Qumayṭ,
Qunṣṭaṣa bint Abī l-Faḍl (Kōstantza, daughter of Boulfadl), wife of Omoddeos, vendor in **Private 28**, 323
al-Qur'ān, used by Sicilian Muslims to pledge loyalty to Norman lords, 34, 35, 145, 146
Qurūbnish (PA), Monreale estate, 188, 191 n.65
Qurūbnish al-Suflī (PA)
granted by William II to Matthew of Salerno, 181, 184, 312–13 (***Dīwānī* 40**)
granted by Matthew of Salerno to S. Maria *Latinorum*, 184, 312–13 (***Dīwānī* 40**)
Monreale estate, 169, 181, 184, 188, 191 n.65
Qūṣ (Egypt), 262

Rabᶜ al-Janawī (PA), 246 n.181
Rabanūsha (PA), Monreale estate, 169
Rachaliōb, *see* Raḥl Ayyūb
Rachal Exames, *see* Raḥl Ibn al-Karrām
Rachaltzouchar, *see* Raḥl Jawhar
Rāfiᶜ ibn Makkan, Arab lord of Gabès, 85, 90
Rahal Binkyramis, *see* Raḥl Ibn al-Karrām
Rahalkarram, *see* Raḥl Karrām
Rahal Kerains, *see* Raḥl Ibn al-Karrām
Rahal Senec, Lentini (SR), 181
Raḥl ᶜAbbūd, *see* Regalbuto
Raḥl ᶜAbd al-Aᶜlā (PA), Monreale estate, 168
Raḥl [A]bū Furīra (PA), Monreale estate, 188, 191 & n.64
Raḥl [A]bū l-Luqum (PA), Monreale estate, 169
Raḥl ᶜAlīy, *see* Regaleali
Raḥl ᶜAmmār (PA), Monreale estate, 169
Raḥl ᶜAmrūn (PA), Monreale estate, 188, 191 n.70
Raḥl Ayyūb (AG), 238 n.107
Raḥl al-Balāṭ (PA), Monreale estate, 168, 188, 191 n.65
Raḥl al-Baṣal (AG), 59, 103 & n.41, 107, 147, 222, 304–5 (***Dīwānī* 15–18**)
Raḥl Bijānū, *see* Bijānū
Raḥl al-Būqāl, *see* Ḥajar al-Būqāl
Raḥl al-Ghalīẓ (PA), Monreale estate, 168, 188
Raḥl Ibn Barka (PA), Monreale estate, 188, 191 n.68
Raḥl Ibn Ghurk (PA), Monreale estate, 169
Raḥl Ibn al-Karrām (PA), 101 n.32
Raḥl Ibn Sahl (PA), Monreale estate, 176–80, 181, 189, 309–10 (***Dīwānī* 33**)
Raḥl al-Jadīd (PA), Monreale estate, 188, 191 n.69
Raḥl Jawhar, 112 n.72
Raḥl al-Jawz (PA), Monreale estate, 189
Raḥl Karrām (PA), 316 (**Private 4**)
Raḥl al-Kilāᶜī (PA), Monreale estate, 188, 191 n.66
Raḥl Laqamūqa, *see* Laqamūqa
Raḥl al-Maghāghī (PA), Monreale estate, 169, 188, 191 n.66
Raḥl Marā'us (PA), Monreale estate, 188
Raḥl al-Mi'a (also called Jinān Ibn Kināna) (PA), Monreale estate, 188, 191
Raḥl al-Mitāwī (PA), Monreale estate, 168
Raḥl al-Mudd (PA), Monreale estate, 189, 191 n.65
Raḥl al-Shāmis, *see* Raḥl Ibn al-Karrām
Raḥl al-Shaᶜrānī (PA), granted by George of Antioch to S. Maria dell'Ammiraglio, 110, 306 (***Dīwānī* 20**), 312 (***Dīwānī* 39**)
Raḥl al-Sikkāk (PA), Monreale estate, 189, 191 n.65
Raḥl al-Wazzān (PA), estate granted to S. Nicolò di Chùrchuro and then to Monreale, 175–80, 181, 189, 191 n.65, 194, 308 (***Dīwānī* 28–9**), 309–10 (***Dīwānī* 33**)
Raḥl al-Wuṭā' (PA), Monreale estate, 188, 191 n.65
Rajā' ibn Abī l-Ḥasan ᶜAlī ibn Abī l-Qāsim ᶜAbd al-Raḥmān ibn Rajā', Abū l-Faḍl, *al-shaykh al-faqīh al-qāḍī*, *qāḍī* of Norman Palermo, 88, 295, 318 (**Private 9**)
Ranald, *qā'id*, brother-in-law of John, master of the *charbatoi*, witness to **Private 14**, 319–20
al-Randa (PA), Monreale estate, 169, 189
Raoul de Domfront, patriarch of Antioch, 263
Raqla (PA), Monreale estate, 168
Raqqāda (Tunisia), 20
Rasgaden, *see* Ra's Ghaḍan
Ra's Ghaḍan(?) (AG), 238 n.107
rātib ('established' tax-payer), 18
Rāw, priest of Palermo cathedral, purchaser of **Private 9**, 318

rawk ('cadastral survey'), 16 n.21, 17, 26, 196–7
Ray, son of John N.ẓ.r.d, witness to ***Dīwānī* 28**, **29** and **33**, 175 n.26
Rāya (PA), Monreale estate, 169: *see also* Jāliṣū
Raymond of Poitiers, husband of Constance, daughter of Bohemond II, prince of Antioch, 263
redemptio (penal tax), 224, 288
Regalbuto (EN), 39–40 & n.47, 103 n.38, 112 n.73
Regaleali (PA), 170
Reggio di Calabria (RC), 31, 32 n.5, 231
registers of boundaries, estates, or lands
  in Muslim Sicily, 24–5, 30, 41–2
  in Norman Sicily: *see* records of the royal *dīwān*, *dafātir al-ḥudūd*
registers of people
  in Byzantine Calabria, 42–4
  in Muslim Sicily, 29, 51, 57–8
  in Norman Calabria, 44–5, 60
  in Norman Sicily: see *jarīda, akrostikha, katonoma, plateia*
Rendicella (PA/AG?), Monreale estate, 152
Riccardus, signatory of 1182 Monreale *jarīda* (***Dīwānī* 44**), 187
Richard I, king of England, 118
Richard II, duke of Normandy, 66
Richard Palmer, bishop-elect of Syracuse and royal familiar, 35 n.26, 177, 186, 224, 225, 227, 228, 232
Richard of Mandra, count of Molise, 226, 227, 228, 230, 231, 248, 251
Richard, *al-qā'id*, leading eunuch and palace Saracen
  magister camerarius et familiaris, 221–2, 232 & n.82, 319 (**Private 11**)
  magister camerarius palatium, 228, 232
  ṣāḥib dīwān al-taḥqīq al-maʿmūr, 201, 203, 232
  director of the *duana baronum*, 206, 232
  leader of opposition to Stephen du Perche, 230–2, 239
  military escort and support,
  protected from imprisonment by regent Margaret, 231, 250
  releases himself from confinement, 232
  as 'Richard the vizier', dedicatee of a *qaṣīda* by Ibn Qalāqis, 233–4
  acquires priory of S. Sofia di Vicari, 234
  leases land in Kemonia, 234, 250
  signature (*ʿalāma*), 187, 221–2, 232 n.81, 82, 251–2, 310 (***Dīwānī* 35**), 322 (**Private 23**)
Richard, 'the men who once belonged to Richard' listed in 1178 Monreale *jarīda* (***Dīwānī* 43**), 154, 162–3
Richard of Iato, witness to ***Dīwānī* 28**, **29** and **33**, 175 n.26
Richard, palace chamberlain of Frederick II, 244
Richard, son of Matthew of Salerno, witness to **Private 20**, 321
Riḍwān ibn Walakhshī, vizier of al-Ḥāfiẓ (eleventh Fāṭimid caliph), 262–3
rijāl al-jarā'id, see villeins
rijāl al-maḥallāt, see villeins
Risalaimi, near Marineo (PA), 315
Robert Alduina (*R.b.rt H.l.d.wīn*), baron of Roger II, 309 (***Dīwānī* 31–2**)
Robert Borrel, a leading baron under Roger I, 64
Robert *de Sēfregasta*, witness to **Private 7**, 317
Robert Faber, donor to the Magione, 233 n.86
Robert Fesca, archbishop-elect of Palermo, 116, 307 (***Dīwānī* 26**)
Robert Guiscard, duke of Apulia (1057–85)
  Arabic titles, 77, 268
  conquest of Palermo, 33–4, 68
  conquest of Sicily, 31–4
Robert, first bishop of Messina, 39
Robert Manfrè (*R.b.rt M.nfrāy al-ḥākim*), governor(?) of Sciacca(?) in ***Dīwānī* 31–2**, 309
Robert of Calatabiano, master of *Castellum Maris* under William I and regent Margaret, 221, 224, 229, 247–8, 296–7
Robert of Selby, chancellor of Roger II, 197–8
Robert Pipotoni, witness to **Private 31**, 324
Robert, 'son of the duke of Burgundy', 64
Robert, marshall of [Richard Palmer], bishop-elect of Syracuse, purchaser in **Private 12**, 319
Roboald, canon of the Cappella Palatina, witness to **Private 11**, 319
rock-crystal, 266
Roger I, count of Sicily (1057–1101)
  administration, 63, 65–71
  Arabic and bilingual documents, 46–59: *see also* Appendix 1, ***Dīwānī* 1–6**
  Arabic titles, 77, 120, 128, 138–9, 268, 271
  arrival in Italy, 32 n.7
  'capital' Mileto (VV), 78
  comitatus of, 4, 64
  conquest of Sicily, 31–4, 58–9, 103
  death (22 June 1101), 46, 64
  division of the land, 39–42, 63
  division of the population, 42–62
  foundation and endowment of episcopal sees, 39–41
  Mazara assembly of 1093, 54, 119, 120, 121, 144, 301 (***Dīwānī* 1**)
  rebellion of barons of Calabria, 46
  rebellions of Sicilian Muslims, 63–4

sons: *see also* Roger II
Geoffrey, 40
Jordan, 40, 41, 46
Simon, 64
succession problems, 64
Troina assembly of 1094, 60–1
Roger II
minor with Adelaide as regent (1105–1112), 64
Arabic administration under, 68–74, 80
Arabic and bilingual documents, 74–8: *see* Appendix 1, ***Dīwānī* 7–8**
Greek administration under, 63, 65–74
Greek education, 78–9
rebellions against, 63–4, 73
embassy to Yaḥyā ibn Tamīm, sixth Zīrid emir of Ifrīqiya (1108–9), 81
count of Sicily (1112–30)
activities concentrated in east Sicily and Calabria, 78
administration under, 63, 65–74, 78–80, 90
Arabic titles, 76, 77, 268
no Arabic documents known to survive, 63, 79, 91, 257
problem of continuity, 63, 78–80, 91, 257
'shared absolute authority' with emir Christodoulos (ᶜAbd al-Raḥmān), 81
contacts and correspondence with Zīrids, 81, 90, 326–8
embassies to Fāṭimid Cairo, 81, 83, 84, 90, 259
imprisons and executes emir Christodoulos (1126?), 74, 81, 83
offers vizierate to Abū l-Ḍawʾ Sirāj, 81, 90
appoints George of Antioch vizier (1126?), 81
king of Sicily (1130–54)
administrative reforms, 5–6
De resignandis privilegiis (1144–45), 115–18, *see also* 42, 108
Arabic administration: *see also* royal *dīwān*
Arabic titles, 120, 122, 126, 128, 132–9, 257, 268–74
dīwān al-maẓālim, 255, 292–3, 295
earliest products of royal *dīwān*, 91–114: *see also* Appendix 1, ***Dīwānī* 10–20**
renewed *jarāʾid* of 1145, 115–43: *see also* Appendix 1, ***Dīwānī* 21–27**
Arabic facet of his monarchy, 82, 253–56, 282–83, 289
biography by al-Ḥanash, 82
ceremonial and display, 82, 287–8, 289
death (26 February 1154), 82, 198 n.25
'good' treatment of the Muslims of Sicily, 284, 289
and the Latin East, 263–4
letter from al-Ḥāfiẓ, 82 n.136, 259–65, 272
mosaic 'portrait' in S. Maria dell'Ammiraglio, 109, 279–80, 283
nickname (Abū Tillīs, 'Old Wheat-sack'?), 81, 83, 326–8
patronage of Arab scholars and men of letters, 82
royal image, 82, 253–6, 285–6
seclusion, 286–7
signature
Arabic (*ᶜalāma*), 109–10, 111, 113, 277–8, 306 (***Dīwānī* 20**)
Greek, 53, 94, 100, 101, 104, 107, 109, 201, 308 (***Dīwānī* 27**)
sons, 88–9: *see also* William I
Roger, abbot of S. Giovanni degli Eremiti, 93
Roger, archbishop of Reggio, 225
Roger-Aḥmad, convert from Islam and godson of Roger II, 113, 237–8, 250
Roger Borsa, duke of Apulia (1085–1111), 44, 45, 67, 68–9, 268
Roger Busellus, Imperial Justiciar of the Val di Noto under Empress Constance, 324 (**Private 30**)
Roger de Barneville, baron of Duke Roger Borsa, 68
Roger *de Fales*, witness to **Private 7**, 317
Roger de Tarsia, husband of Maria, daughter of Robert Malconvenant, baron of William II, party to **Private 20**, 152 n.26, 321
Roger, duke of Apulia, son of Roger II (d.1148), 286
Roger Forestal, *see* Forestal, barons of Jāliṣū
Roger Hamutus, royal justiciar under William II, 238–9
Roger, officer of the royal *dīwān* under William II, 311 (***Dīwānī* 37**)
Roger Sclavus, illegitimate son of Simon of Policastro, 220
Roger, son of Bonos the protonotary, 66
Roger, son of Roger II (d.1149), 88
Roger, son of William I, 219
Roger, 'the men of Roger' (*rijāl Rujayr*) listed in the 1178 Monreale *jarīda* (***Dīwānī* 43**), 154, 162, 164
Romance vernaculars in Norman Sicily, 4
Rometta (ME), surrender to Normans (1061), 33
Romuald, archbishop of Salerno and chronicler, 212, 215, 217–18, 225, 232
royal *dīwān*
foundation and earliest products of the royal *dīwān*, 91–114, 257, 274: *see also* Appendix 1, ***Dīwānī* 10–20**

dīwān al-fawāʾid ('the *dīwān* of the revenues'), 200, 204–6, 295
dīwān al-maᶜmūr ('the royal *dīwān*'), 52, 53, 104, 120, 121, 126, 128, 153, 193–204
first appearance (1141), 106, 114, 193–4
significance of title, 195
imprecise term for whole Arabic administration, 199–200, 201
range of activities, 198–201
reaches maturity with renewals of 1145, 142–3
dīwān al-maẓālim, 255, 292–3, 295
dīwān al-taḥqīq al-maᶜmūr ('the royal *dīwān* of verification), 15, 108, 153, 156 n.32, 163, 175, 176–7, 187 & n.58, 193–204, 257, 274
first appearance (1149), 193–4, 257, 274
significance of title, 195
based upon Fāṭimid model, 195–8, 257, 274, 281
circumstances surrounding foundation in Sicily, 197–8
executive department of the royal *dīwān*, 194, 199–203
first director Maio of Bari, 201
thereafter directed by group of 'lords' (*aṣḥāb*) or 'elders' (*gerontes*), including leading palace Saracens, 201
range of activities, 199–203
authority restricted to Sicily and Calabria, 203
duana baronum
first appearance (1167–68), 201–2, 203, 206–7
titles and their significance, 201–2, 206
range of activities, 206–7
authority restricted to mainland provinces except Calabria(?), 206–7 & n.67
duana de secretis, Latin translation of *dīwān al-taḥqīq*, 199, 202, 203
duana regia, Latin translation of *dīwān al-maᶜmūr*, 107, 163, 193
to sekreton (Latin *secretum*), 106, 193, 199
before foundation of *dīwān al-taḥqīq*, Greek title of *al-dīwān al-maᶜmūr*, 199
after 1149, used also as Greek title of *dīwān al-taḥqīq*, 199, 201–2
to sekreton tōn apokopōn, Greek title of *duana baronum*, 201–2, 206
after foundation of *duana baronum*, *to mega sekreton* (*magnum secretum*) used as Greek title for royal *dīwān*, 201–2
records of the royal *dīwān*
accuracy and completeness, 144–5, 164–5, 167, 192
dafātir al-dīwān al-maᶜmūr, 175, 200–1, 204, 323 (**Private 26**)
dafātir al-ḥudūd, 17, 144, 164, 172–86, 187 & n.58, 300, 312 (***Dīwānī* 40**)
first appearance, 175
subsequent development, 175–86
organization and internal structure, 185, 190–2
possibly linked to registers of feudal holdings, analogous to the *Catalogus Baronum*, 185, 192
maintained and supervised by *dīwān al-taḥqīq*, 203
dafātir al-īṣāl al-dīwānīya, 144, 174, 310 (***Dīwānī* 35**)
jarāʾid and *dafātir al-rijāl*, 144–5, 153, 156 & n.32, 163–4, 167
switch from *jarāʾid al-rijāl* to *dafātir al-ḥudūd*, 144–5, 172
and administrative justice and legislation, 296–7
rôle in manipulation of the royal image, 284–300
al-Rūmīya, the sons of, Muslim citizens of Sciacca in ***Dīwānī* 31–2**, 309
Rushayd ibn Kāmil ibn Jāmiᶜ, *ṣaḥib* of Gabès, 291
rustici, *see* villeins
Ruzzīk ibn Ṭalāʾī, Fāṭimid vizier (1161–63), 133, 261 n.20

S.kīn, canon of S. Salvatore di Cefalù under Roger II, 126 & n.27
al-Sabᶜ ibn ᶜĪsā ibn al-Sabᶜ ibn ᶜĪsā al-Lawātī, witness to **Private 26**, 323
Ṣadaqa, sister of Maymūn, debtor in **Private 8**, 317–18
Saᶜdiah bar Yitzḥaq, Jew of Syracuse in **Private 25**, 323
al-Sadīd Abū l-Makārim Hibat Allāh ibn al-Ḥuṣrī, Muslim leader and courtier of regent Margaret and William II, and patron of Ibn Qalāqis, 239, 240, 252, 290, 292: *see also* Sedictus
safīr ('intermediary' between caliph and administration), 20, 22
ṣaḥāba dīwān al-inshā wa-l-mukātabāt, 16, 89
ṣāḥib al-dīwān bi-Ṣiqillīya, 26
ṣāḥib dīwān al-inshāʾ, 16
ṣāḥib dīwān al-majlis, 16
ṣāḥib al-khums, in Muslim Sicily, 24, 25, 27
Ṣalāḥ al-Dīn, al-Malik al-Nāṣir, Ayyūbid sultan (Saladin), (1169–73), 241, 253
Salām, Muslim merchant from Cefalù, debtor in **Private 8**, 317–18

Salerno (SA), 261
Saljūqs, 80 n.124, 137, 261 & n.21
salma (area and dry measure), xviii, 75 n.93, 190–2 & nn.63–9, n.71
Salmūn ibn ᶜAbd Allāh al-Mahdawī, witness to **Private 21** and **28**, 321, 323
Samānids, 137
Sambuca di Sicilia (AG), 152 n.27
Sambuchi (PA), 73 n.81
San Calogero, Monte (PA), 91 n.1
San Marco d'Alunzio (ME), 61
Sanson, royal bailiff of Ottumarrano, 170–1
Sant'Agnese, *see* Shantaghnī
Sant'Anna (AG), 58 n.129
Sardo, Ser, witness to **Private 8**, 318
Sayyida bint Yūsuf al-Qaysī, wife of Abū l-Qāsim ibn ᶜAbd Allāh al-ᶜAṭṭār, vendor in **Private 6**, 316–17
Scholarios, Greek chaplain of Roger I, 65
Scribla (CS), 32 n.7
Sciacca (AG), 58, 103, 104–5, 201, 304–5 (***Dīwānī* 15–17**), 309 (***Dīwānī* 31–2**)
Sedictus, *al-qāʾid*, wealthy Muslim of Palermo under the regent Margaret, 239, 252: *see also* al-Sadīd Abū l-Makārim Hibat Allāh ibn al-Ḥuṣrī
sekreton, *see* royal *dīwān*
sekreton tōn apokopōn, *see* royal *dīwān*
Senore, *see* Senure
Senure (AG), Monreale estate, 152
Sētelchousoun, *see* Sitt al-Ḥusn
Sfax (Tunisia), 34, 147, 291
Sferracavallo (PA), 232
Shantaghnī, Usbiṭāl (Hospital of Sant'Agnese), Monreale estate, 162, 181, 189: *see also* al-Kanisīya and Shantaghnī
al-Sharīf al-Makīn, Muslim scholar and genealogist under regent Margaret, 240
Shaul bar ᶜAmram, Jew of Syracuse, witness to **Private 25**, 323
Shlomo ibn Saᶜīd; witness to **Private 25**, 323
Sichelgaita, wife of Robert Guiscard, 45
Sichinolf, *see* S.kīn
Sicily
  administration of
    Byzantine, 23
    Muslim, 23–30: *see also*, Kalbid emirs
    Norman, *passim*
  Arab conquest of, 23, 24, 26–7
  Norman conquest of, 30, 31–4, 59, 63–4, 103
  period of rival *qāʾids*, 30, 32
Sighinus, *see* S.kīn
sigillion ('document'), 58, 94, 103, 106, 109, 113: *see also* ***Dīwānī* 6, †9–10, 12–16, 20, 23, †27, 36–37, 39**
sijill ('document'), 94, 100: *see also* ***Dīwānī* 13, 36–39**
al-Sikkāk, Monreale estate, 169
Simeon, bishop of Mount Sinai under Ayyūbid rule, 137 n.87
Simiyūn ibn Abī Layūn, witness to **Private 22**, 322
Simiyūn ibn Andrayat al-R.ḥām(?), witness to **Private 12**, 319
Simon, count of Sicily (1101–5), 64
Simon, agent of Abū l-Qāsim Muḥammad ibn Ḥammūd, 239
Simon (*Simᶜān*), brother of George of Antioch, 81, 83
Simon of Policastro, illegitimate son of Roger II, 219, 220
Simon, son of George of Antioch, 83
Simon, son of Scholarios, the Greek chaplain of Roger I, 66
Sinai (Egypt)
  St Catherine's, 130–1, 133, 138
  Ṭūr district, 130
Sirāj ibn Aḥmad ibn Rajāʾ, Abū l-Ḍawʾ, *al-qāʾid*, *kātib* and panegyricist to Roger II, 74 n.87, 81, 83, 86, 88–90, 212, 215, 252, 253, 274, 289, 295
Sitt al-Ḥusn, wife of Christodoulos-Abdesseit, daughter of Peter of Castronuovo, vendor in **Private 12**, 319
slaves, of the church of Catania, 55, 56, 57, 119
Soldanus de Gualdo, lord of Buchalie, 172 n.9
Solomon the Genoese, commercial associate of Abū l-Qāsim Muḥammad ibn Ḥammūd, 239
Le Sorelle islands (Tunisia), 85
Sousse (Tunisia), 81, 291
Squillace (CZ), bishop of, 116
Stephen du Perche, archbishop of Palermo and chancellor under Regent Margaret, 228–32, 254, 256
Stephen, emir, brother of Maio of Bari, 219
Stephen, emir, son of Maio of Bari, 219
Stephen of Carthage, 215
Stephen, son of John of Petralia, witness to **Private 22**, 322
Suḥayliba, wife of Obert Fallamonaca, 246 nn.179–80, 324 (**Private 31**)
Sulaymān, son of al-Ḥāfiẓ, 262
ṣulḥ-lands, 13
Sumeōn, son of Christodoulēs, daughter of ᶜAbd al-Raḥmān [ibn?] ᶜUqba al-Naṣrānī, brother of Abū l-Sayyid (*Boussit*), vendor in **Private 14**, 319
Sūmminī, Monreale estate, 188, 191 n.66, 246 n.181

Sūq al-Mir'āh (PA), Monreale estate, 155, 162, 164, 165
Sylvester, count of Marsico, 177
Syracuse (SR)
Ibn al-Thumna *qā'id* of Syracuse, 32 & nn. 7 & 9, 33
Jews of Norman Syracuse, 77, 322–3 (**Private 25**)
Muslims of Norman Syracuse request relief from the *jizya*, 35, 38, 133, 240, 252, 292

tadhākir, sing. *tadhkār* ('memorandum'), 16
Ṭāhir ibn ᶜAbd al-Raḥmān al-Qurashī, witness to **Private 29**, 324
Ṭāhir ibn ᶜUmar, Muslim citizen of Sciacca in ***Dīwānī* 31–2**, 309
Tall Bāshir (Turkey), 261
Tamīm ibn Bādīs, fifth Zīrid emir of Ifrīqiya (1062–1108), 22, 81, 83, 84, 85, 87
al-Ṭanābirī, 'the men of al-Ṭanābirī' listed in 1178 Monreale *jarīda* (***Dīwānī* 43**), 154, 163
Tancred
count of Lecce
in rebellion of 1160–62, 219, 220
king of Sicily (1190–94), 138, 295
Arabic titles, 205 n.60, 268, 269, 272
Tancred, son of Roger II (d.1138–42), 89
Taormina (ME), 231
taqsīṭ ('payment in instalments'), 21
tarì, gold quarter-dinar, 28 n.88
ṭarīy
a. 'new' *jizya*-payer, 18, 148
b. newly minted coin, *see tarì*
taxation, *see census*, *doma*, *itāwa*, *jizya*, *kharāj*, *khums*, *qānūn*, *redemptio*, *tributum*, *ᶜushr*
Termini Imerese (PA), 147 & n.10, 223 & n.41, 311 (***Dīwānī* 38**), 324 (**Private 30**)
Jews of, 71
Terra Ianuensis (PA), *see* Rabᶜ al-Janawī
Terrosa, Contrada, *see* Ṭurrus
Terrusium, *see* Ṭurrus
tetradion, *see daftar*
Thapsus (Tunisia), 85 n.160
Theodore from Desisa, witness to ***Dīwānī* 28**, **29** and **33**, 175 n.26
Theodore, master, courtier of Frederick II, 242 n.138
Theodore, master chamberlain, 224 n.46
Theodore, son of George of Antioch, purchaser in **Private 7**, 317
Theodore, son of Leo *tou Chanzeri* (i.e. al-Khinzārī, 'the Swineherd'), father of Basil, witness to **Private 12,** 319
Theodosius, abbot of S. Angelo di Brolo, 42
Thessalonica (Greece), captured by Sicilians (1185), 244
Thomas, prior of S. Maria di Ustica, 246
Thomas, *al-qā'id*, *camerarius duane de secretis*, 203, 244
Thomas, son of Bagalbitar(?), purchaser in **Private 10**, 318
al-Tījānī, account of George of Antioch, 83–8
ṭirāz, in Norman Palermo, 213, 243, 244, 269
Tommaso da Butera, bishop of Cefalù, 62
Torto, Fiume (PA), 91 n.1
Trapani (TP), 212, 239, 241
Tranchina, Vallone della (AG), 103 n.41
treasurer (*thesaurarius*), 72
tributarii, used of Christian *jizya*-payers (*i.e. dhimmīyūn*) in Muslim Sicily, 37
tributum, exacted by Normans from Muslims of Sicily, equivalent to Islamic *jizya*, 34, 37, 38
Tricarico (MT), 43 n.66
Triocala (AG): *see* Churches and religious foundations, S. Giorgio di Triocala
Tripoli (Libya), 34, 82, 147, 290
Troina (EN), 32, 40, 69
Ṭūlūnid governors of Egypt, 16
Tumarrano, Vallone (PA), 170 n.1
Tunis (Tunisia), 82, 147
Ṭurrus (PA), Monreale estate, 152 n.27, 169, 309 (***Dīwānī* 30**)
Tustan, bishop of Mazara, 225

ᶜUmar Abū ᶜAbd Allāh (*Humur Buabdille*), witness to **Private 4**, 316
ᶜUmar ibn ᶜAbd al-Muḥsin al-Qurashī; Muslim of Castrogiovanni, witness to **Private 27**, 323
ᶜUmar ibn Abī l-Ḥasan al-Furriyānī, *ᶜāmil* of Sfax under Norman rule, 291
ᶜUmar ibn ᶜAbd al-Jabbār, witness to ***Dīwānī* 28**, **29** and **33**, 175 n.26
ᶜUmar ibn Abī l-Khayr al-Qurashī, witness to **Private 19**, 321
ᶜUmar ibn *al-qā'id* Abī l-Qāsim Muḥammad ibn Ḥammūd, 236, 237
ᶜUmar ibn ᶜAtīq al-Qaysī, known as Ibn al-Muhāriqa(?), husband of Manjūma, and representative of her and her sister, Amr al-Khayr, vendors in **Private 9**, 318
ᶜUmar ibn Ḥusayn al-Tamīmī, Ibn Ṣāfī, vendor in **Private 1**, 315
ᶜUmar ibn ᶜĪsā al-Zanātī, witness to **Private 6**, 316–17
ᶜUmar ibn Muḥammad al-Qaysī, witness to **Private 6**, 316–17
ᶜUmar ibn al-Muᶜizz the Zīrid, 81 n.128

al-Umāwī, Abū l-Ḥasan ᶜAlī ibn Abī l-Fatḥ ibn Khalaf al-Ṣiqillī, Sicilian poet under William II, friend and correspondent of Ibn Qalāqis, 133, 240
Umayyads, 14
Urban II, pope (1088–99), 40
Urso, the scribe, witness to ***Dīwānī* 28**, **29** and **33**, 175 n.26
ᶜushr ('tithe'), 13, 21, 27
ᶜUthmān al-Ḥājj, debtor in **Private 8**, 317–18
ᶜUthmān ibn ᶜAbd Allāh al-Qaysī (*Uthmen filius Habdalle Elkaysi*), witness to **Private 3**, 315–16
ᶜUthmān ibn ᶜAbd al-Wāḥid al-Ḥaḍramī(?), witness to **Private 18**, 320
ᶜUthmān ibn *al-qā'id* Abī l-Qāsim Muḥammad ibn Ḥammūd, 237
ᶜUthmān ibn ᶜAlī al-Hawwārī, witness to **Private 19**, 321
ᶜUthmān ibn ᶜAlī al-Tamīmī, *al-shaykh* (*Senex Uthmen filius Haly Ettimimi*), witness to **Private 3**, 316
ᶜUthmān ibn al-Muhadhdhib al-Judhāmī, Abū ᶜAmr, *al-ḥākim*, Muslim official and courtier of regent Margaret and William II, 240, 243, 252
ᶜUthmān ibn Yūsuf al-Hawwārī, vendor in **Private 29**, 324
ᶜUthmān, *kātib* of the *dīwān al-maᶜmūr*, 194, 222, 243
Uthmen filius Habdalle Elkaysi, *see* ᶜUthmān ibn ᶜAbd Allāh al-Qaysī
Uthmen filius Haly Ettimimi, Senex, *see* al-shaykh ᶜUthmān ibn ᶜAlī al-Tamīmī

Valencia, Aragonese conquest of, 37, 38–9
Valledolmo (PA), 170–1 n.4
Verdura, Vallone della (AG), 103 n.41
Vicari (PA), 80, 101, 102, 170, 180 n.35, 184, 246 n.181, 304 (***Dīwānī* 14**), 307 (***Dīwānī* 23**), 322 (**Private 24**)
Villalba (CL), 170 & n.1&4
villani civitatenses, *see* villeins
villani exteri, *see* villeins
villeins, 146 n.5.
  in Calabria, 43–5
    advenae, 45, 151
    eleutheroi, 43
    jus affidandi, 60, 61
    nativi, 146 n.5, 151
    oikētōrai, 44
    paroikoi, 43, 146 n.5
    prosēlutoi, 43
    ptōchoi, 43
    xenoi, 43, 45, 151
  in Lombard lands, 44
    censiles, 44
    homines liberi, 44
  in Norman Sicily
    Arab Christian villeins, 124–5, 154, 157, 165
    bellanoi, 146 n.5
    commendation of 'unregistered' villeins, 61
    French and Sicilian systems 'compared', 230–1
    fugitives, 35, 61, 142, 146, 234
    labour service, 61–62
    Muslim villeins, 45–62, 75–6, 91–2, 104, 107–8, 110–11, 111–12, 119–28, 139–40, 140–2, 144–69, 194, 198, 200, 201, 202, 203: *see also* Appendix 1, ***Dīwānī* 2–6, 8–10, 14–15, 18–30, 33–4, 38, 40, 42–3, 45**
      ahl [al-jarā'id], 53, 55, 119, 120, 151, 164
      arāmil, 50–51, 54, 55, 56–7, 119,121, 146, 162, 165
      aribbā', 159–62
      enapografoi, 149 n.21, 151, 300
      entopoi (also *entōpeoi*), 146 n.51, 148, 149, 151
      exografoi, 62, 149, 150, 151
      ezeumenoi, 48 & n.89
      ghurabā', 60–1 n.136, 62, 119 n.20, 147–8, 149, 150, 151
      glabri, 150, 151
      ḥursh, 147, 150, 151, 311 (***Dīwānī* 38**)
      muls, 60–1 n.136, 107, 147, 148, 149, 150, 151, 166, 168–9, 311 (***Dīwānī* 38**), 313–14 (***Dīwānī* 45**)
      mutazawwijūn, 48, 108, 127–8, 140, 141, 147, 148, 154–5, 157–8, 161, 162, 163, 164, 165, 307 (***Dīwānī* 25**)
      neogamoi, 47–51, 57, 59, 146–7
      rijāl al-dīwān al-maᶜmūr, 166 & n.44, 200
      rijāl al-jarā'id, 35, 61, 145–7, 148, 149, 150, 151, 166, 300, 320 (**Private 16**)
      rijāl al-maḥallāt, 62, 119 n.20, 148–9, 150, 151, 166, 167, 168–9
      rustici, 45, 150, 151
      villani civitatenses, 62
      villani exteri, 62
    Roman law categories
      adscriptitii, 149, 151, 300
      coloni adscriptitii, 149
      coloni originales, 149
      inscriptitii, 151
      qui personaliter ... servire tenentur, 149 & n.21, 151

qui ... respectu tenimenti ... servire tenentur, 149 & n.21, 151
servi glebae, 146 n.5, 151
status in law and in fact, 150
'unregistered' villeins, 60–1, 148–9, 150, 151
vizier (*wazīr*), 14–15, 16, 278: *see also* George of Antioch, Richard *al-qā'id*, and the Fāṭimid viziers al-Afḍal ibn Badr, al-Afḍal Kutayfāt, Badr al-Jamālī, Bahrām, al-Baṭā'iḥī, Ibn Killīs, al-Jarjarā'ī, Kutayfāt, Riḍwan, Ruzzīk

wakīl al-faḥṣ al-dīwānī al-ma'mūr, 200, 310 (***Dīwānī* 35**)
Walter II, archbishop of Palermo, and royal familiar, 131 n.53, 137 n.87, 186, 202, 312 (***Dīwānī* 39**), 313 (***Dīwānī* 42**)
Walter *de Seyda*, the Christian, of Palermo, son of the elder Matthew, purchaser of **Private 4**, 316
Walter the Christian, son of Walter (*Ghartīl al-Naṣrānī ibn Ghartīl*), agent for purchaser in **Private 6**, 316–17
Walter, deacon of Agrigento and canon of the Cappella Palatina, witness to **Private 11**, 319
Walter Forestal, *see* Forestal, barons of Jāliṣū
wazīr, *see* vizier
'widows', *see* villeins, *arāmil*
William I, king of Sicily (1154–66)
'alāma, 278
Arabic titles, 269
'bad' treatment of the Muslims of Sicily, 284–5
coronation, 198 n.25
death, 221, 224, 228, 247, 250
eldest son (Roger), 219
rebellion of 1160–62, 21 n.49, 150, 164, 177, 219–20, 224, 254, 288
royal image, 284–5, 287
seclusion, 255–6, 286
William II, king of Sicily (1166–89)
'alāma, 278
Arabic titles, 138, 153, 156 & n.32, 166 & n.44, 187 & n.58, 269–70, 271–2
Arabic facet of his monarchy, 255, 285–6, 287–8
ceremonial and display, 285–6
death, 285
foundation and endowment of S. Maria di Monreale, 151–2, 153, 156, 166, 187
minority and regency of Margaret, 221, 224–5
orders Stephen du Perche to prosecute Muslims, 229 & n.68, 255–6
palaces and court described by Ibn Jubayr, 212–15, 228 n.63, 250
seclusion, 286, 287–8
William III, king of Sicily (d.1194), 137, 269
William, duke of Apulia, son of Roger Borsa (1111–27), 68–9
William II, duke of Normandy, 66
William, lord of Gurfa (*Ghulyalim ṣāḥib al-Jurf*), 309 (***Dīwānī* 31–2**)
William (*Ghulyalim maniskhalqū ruqqati l-Shāqqati*), the marshall(?) of the castle of Sciacca in ***Dīwānī* 31–2**, 309
William Arminio(?), Ser, witness to **Private 8**, 318
William Gallo, vendor in **Private 32**, 324–5
William Milceri (*Ghulyalim M.l.sīra*), baron of Roger II, 309 (***Dīwānī* 31–2**)
William, son of Richard of Sciacca, baron of Roger II, 104–5, 194, 304–5 (***Dīwānī* 15–17**)
William Sorellus, *regie private masnede solidarius*, witness to **Private 20**, 321
William, Ser (*Sar Ghulyalim*), Genoese(?) merchant, creditor in **Private 8**, 317–18
Wualterius (?), Latin official of the royal *dīwān* under Roger II, 309 (***Dīwānī* 31**)

xenoi, *see* villeins

Yaḥyā bar Fraḥiah; witness to **Private 25**, 323
Yaḥyā ibn 'Abd al-Kāfī al-Zanātī, Muslim of Castrogiovanni, witness to **Private 27**, 323
Yaḥyā[?] ibn 'Abd al-Raḥmān al-Ḥasan (*Hythie filius Abderrahmen Elhesin*), witness to **Private 4**, 316
Yaḥyā ibn Fityān al-Ṭarrāz ('the Embroiderer'), eunuch of William II, 213, 243, 244
Yaḥyā ibn Tamīm, sixth Zīrid emir of Ifrīqiya (1108–16), 81, 83, 84
Yaḥyā, Muslim merchant from Trapani, witness to **Private 8**, 318
Ya'qub bar Abraham; witness to **Private 25**, 323
Ya'qub bar Bal'ām, Jew of Syracuse, witness to **Private 25**, 323
Ya'qub Ḥazn, Jew of Syracuse, witness to **Private 25**, 323
Ya'qūb ibn Faḍlūn ibn Ṣāliḥ, Jew of Norman Palermo, 202, 310–11 (***Dīwānī* 35**)
Ya'qūb ibn Ya'qūb, 'palace Saracen' under William II, 243, 312 (***Dīwānī* 39**)
Yehūdah bar Abraham; witness to **Private 25**, 323
Yemen, 240 n.125

Yhale, Casale, *see* Regaleali
Yūḥannā ibn ᶜAbd al-Raḥmān, witness to **Private 15**, 320
Yūnis, vizier of al-Ḥāfiẓ (eleventh Fāṭimid caliph), 262
Yūsuf ibn ᶜAbd al-Nūr al-Tanūkhī (*Jusuph filius Abdelnur Ettennuchi*), witness to **Private 3**, 316
Yūsuf ibn Abū (*sic!*) Bakr al-Hawwārī, witness in **Private 1**, 315
Yūsuf ibn Jabr, *al-qāʾid*, 'the four men who belong to the *qāʾid* Y. ibn J.' referred to in the 1178 Monreale *jarīda* (***Dīwānī* 43**), 150 n.22, 154, 164
Yūsuf ibn Muḥammad ibn ᶜAbd al-Qāhir al-Lawātī, witness to **Private 6**, 317
Yūsuf ibn al-Saraqūsī, Muslim of Misilmeri in ***Dīwānī* 39**, 312
Yūsuf ibn Yaᶜqūb, 'palace Saracen' under William II, 243, 312 (***Dīwānī* 39**)
Yūsuf ibn Zīrī, Abū l-Ḥajjāj, *qāḍī* of Tripoli under Norman rule, 290
Yūsuf (*Iusuph*), agent of Abū l-Qāsim Muḥammad ibn Ḥammūd, 239
Yūsuf, *kātib* of the *dīwān al-taḥqīq* responsible for 1182 Monreale *jarīda* (***Dīwānī* 44**), 187, 202 n.44, 244
Yūsuf, *mawlā* of Rushayd ibn Kāmil ibn Jāmiᶜ, *ṣāḥib* of Gabès, 291

al-Ẓāhir, seventh Fāṭimid caliph (1021–36), 265 n.39
Zakarī al-Naṣrānī ('the Christian') ibn *al-shaykh* Sulaymān al-ᶜAṭṭār ('the Druggist'), citizen of Palermo under Count Roger II, agent of purchaser in **Private 2**, 315
Zanthos the priest, witness to **Private 10**, 318
zawj, pl. *azwāj* ('plough-land', area measure), xviii, 191 n.70
Zaynab bint ᶜAbd Allāh al-Anṣārī, vendor in **Private 26**, 204 & n.54, 205, 244 & n.158, 295, 323
zeugarion ('plough-land', area measure), xviii, 191 n.70
zimām al-azimma, 15
Zīrid emirs of Ifrīqiya, 22, 63, 74, 77, 81, 83, 84, 85, 86, 87, 88, 90, 258, 281–3, 290–1
Zuwāwa, Berber tribe, 147

Other titles in the series

Popular Culture in Medieval Cairo
BOAZ SHOSHAN 0 521 43209 X

Early Philosophical Shiism
The Ismaili Neoplatonism of Abū Ya'qūb al-Sijistāni
PAUL E. WALKER 0 521 44129 3

Indian Merchants and Eurasian Trade, 1600–1750
STEPHEN FREDERIC DALE
0 521 45460 3

Palestinian Peasants and Ottoman Officials
Rural Administration around Sixteenth-century Jerusalem
AMY SINGER 0 521 45238 4 hardback
0 521 47679 8 paperback

Arabic Historical Thought in the Classical Period
TARIF KHALIDI 0 521 46554 0
hardback 0 521 58938 X paperback

Mongols and Mamluks
The Mamluk-Īlkhānid War, 1260–1281
REUVEN AMITAI-PREISS
0 521 46226 6

Hierarchy and Egalitarianism in Islamic Thought
LOUISE MARLOW 0 521 56430 1

The Politics of Households in Ottoman Egypt
The Rise of the Qazdağlis
JANE HATHAWAY 0 521 57110 3

Commodity and Exchange in the Mongol Empire
A Cultural History of Islamic Textiles
THOMAS T. ALLSEN 0 521 58301 2

State and Provincial Society in the Early Modern Ottoman Empire
Mosul, 1540–1834
DINA RIZK KHOURY 0 521 59060 4

The Mamluks in Egyptian Politics and Society
THOMAS PHILIPP AND ULRICH HAARMANN (eds) 0 521 59115 5

The Delhi Sultanate
A Political and Military History
PETER JACKSON 0 521 40477 0

European and Islamic Trade in the Early Ottoman State
The Merchants of Genoa and Turkey
KATE FLEET 0 521 64221 3

Reinterpreting Islamic Historiography
Harun al-Rashid and the Narrative of the 'Abbāsid Caliphate
TAYEB EL-HIBRI 0 521 65023 2

The Ottoman City between East and West
Aleppo, Izmir, and Istanbul
EDHEM ELDEM, DANIEL GOFFMAN AND BRUCE MASTERS
0 521 64304 X

A Monetary History of the Ottoman Empire
SEVKET PAMUK 0 521 44197 8

The Politics of Trade in Safavid Iran:
Silk for Silver, 1600–1730
RUDOLPH P. MATTHEE
0 521 64131 4

The Idea of Idolatry and the Emergence of Islam: *From Polemic to History*
G.R. HAWTING 0 521 65165 4

Classical Arabic Biography: *The Heirs of the Prophets in the Age of al-Ma'mūn*
MICHAEL COOPERSON 0 521 66199 4

Empire and Elites after the Muslim Conquest:
The Transformation of Northern Mesopotamia
CHASE F. ROBINSON 0 521 78115 9

Poverty and Charity in Medieval Islam:
Mamluk Egypt, 1250–1517
ADAM SABRA 0 521 77291 5

Christians and Jews in the Ottoman Arab World
The Roots of Sectarianism
BRUCE MASTERS 0 521 80333 0

Culture and Conquest in Mongol Eurasia
THOMAS T. ALLSEN
0 521 80335 7

Printed in the United Kingdom by
Lightning Source UK Ltd., Milton Keynes
139831UK00001BA/42/A

9 780521 037020